MASS COMMUNICATION THEORIES

EXPLAINING ORIGINS, PROCESSES, AND EFFECTS

MASS COMMUNICATION THEORIES

EXPLAINING ORIGINS, PROCESSES, AND EFFECTS

Melvin L. DeFleur

Distinguished Professor

The Manship School of Mass Communication

Lousiana State University

Routledge
Taylor & Francis Group

LONDON AND NEW YORK

First published 2010 by Pearson Education, Inc.

Published 2016 by Routledge

2 Park Square, Milton Park, Abingdon, Oxon OX14 4RN

711 Third Avenue, New York, NY 10017, USA

Routledge is an imprint of the Taylor & Francis Group, an informa business

ISBN: 9780205331727 (pbk)

Designer Cover: KML

Library of Congress Cataloging-in-Publication Data
Defleur, Melvin L. (Melvin Lawrence),
  Mass communication theories: explaining origins, processes and effects / Melvin L. Defleur.
    p. cm.
  ISBN 978-0-205-33172-7
  1. Mass media.   I. Title.
  P90.D44185 2010
  302.2301—dc22

                                                                    2009035425

BRIEF CONTENTS

DETAILED CONTENTS

FOREWORD

TO STUDENTS USING THIS BOOK

This book has four objectives: (1) It will set forth the background of each theory, explaining where it came from; (2) It will discuss and clarify the basic ideas of each of the theories presented; (3) It will describe and explain four new theories that have been developed specifically for this book; And (4) it will provide a "formalization" of each of the theories presented as a set of simplified statements of their basic assumptions and predictions.

Thus, the first objective is to *explain for you the origins* of each of the various theories discussed in the included chapters. As will be made clear in the text, some theories emerged from specific research studies that encouraged their authors to develop a new explanation of the processes or the effects of the mass media that were available at the time. The nature of those founding studies will be explained in detail in each such case.

Other theories included in the book were based on conceptions and beliefs about *the nature of the American society*—the way in which it is organized and the manner in which people relate to and communicate with each other. These conceptions have changed over time with the continuing development of the social sciences. At earlier times such conceptions included the belief that people in modern societies were made up of a mix of unlike people—that is, people who had few ties to each other. Thus, it was thought that they lacked interpersonal channels of communication and were essentially a "lonely crowd" of unlike individuals. This conception implied that each individual could be influenced in similar and powerful ways by the existing mass media. Later, as the social and behavioral sciences developed, research in those fields showed that this conception was naive. It became clear that people in modern societies communicated regularly and interpersonally with friends, neighbors, and relatives. That process limited the influence of the media. In other words, these different interpretations of society at various points in history influenced thinking about the process and effects of mass communication. These issues will made clear in the chapters that follow.

Previous scholarly understanding about the *nature of human psychological organization and cognitive functioning* also influenced the development of several mass communication theories discussed in the text. Such psychological issues as the nature of perception, as well as the processes of individual learning and remembering played a part in the ways in which scholars viewed the nature and influences of mass communications. These issues will also be clarified.

In more recent times, a (relatively) new academic discipline has emerged. The field of media communication is composed of scholars who specialize in the study of the mass media that exist today—print, broadcasting, film, and digital systems. These scholars have made profound contributions to our current understanding of mass communication. Every year, they continue to provide a substantial flow of research findings concerning how the media function, the nature of their audiences and the influences that mass communications have on individuals, their societies, and their cultures. The background understandings about human nature have influenced the theories that contemporary media scholars have produced and that are discussed in the chapters that follow.

The second objective of the book is to clarify for you in detail *the basic ideas of each of the theories discussed*. These are complex issues, and the aim of the book is to make each theory understandable without making use of elaborate or technical jargon. The author hopes that the ways in which they have been set forth will enable each student to grasp where the theory came from, what issues it addresses, and how it explains some process or effect of the various media to which it applies.

The third objective is to describe and explain *the basic ideas of each of the theories discussed*. Obviously, since they are new, these have yet to be tested by media scholars. They are offered, however, in an effort to advance knowledge about the processes and effects of mass communication. Presumably, they will be studied in relevant future research efforts to determine if they have validity. These theories are discussed in the following chapters: Chapter 15, "Media Information Utility Theory", which discusses the ways in which the media offer practical information to their audiences—such as where to locate an apartment to rent, where to buy a car, where needed products are on sale, and so on. Chapter 17, "Social Expectations Theory," explains how audiences can learn and understand what they or other participants will be expected to do in many situations. For example, here they can learn the roles and procedures followed in a criminal court trial, even though they have never personally been involved in such an event. Chapter 20, "The Creeping Cycle of Desensitization Theory," explains how the mass media, constantly under pressure to increase the size of their audiences so as to be profitable, press forward the boundaries of social acceptability of violence and sexual depictions, which at first may arouse audience criticism but which eventually come to be accepted. Then they press the boundaries even further, and the cycle goes on.

A fourth objective is to set forth *a set of interrelated propositions*. These simplified statements of the basic assumptions and predictions of each of the theories will be found at the end of each corresponding chapter. Not only does the presentation of theories in this manner help clarify them, but it also aims to "formalize" them in a manner similar to how theories are presented in other scientific disciplines. As research continues to accumulate in mass communication studies, aimed at testing these various theories, some of these formalized versions will undoubtedly need to be revised.

In some cases, a limited number of the studies aimed at testing or verifying a particular theory in the book will be discussed. New studies related to the assessment of specific mass communication theories are published regularly by media researchers and scholars—and they accumulate rapidly month by month. If an attempt were made in this type of book to present a full and up-to-date summary of what these studies have shown, it would be outdated and incomplete within a very short time thus a limited selection is provided for student use and application.

The best source for understanding what contemporary media scholars have found when assessing these theories by conducting mass communication research are the various refereed journals in which mass communication scholars regularly publish their results. Your instructor or your librarian can provide guidance concerning the nature and focus of these journals and how to access them in your local library.

As a final note, it will be evident that the author chose not to discuss the Internet or the World Wide Web as "mass media." These technologies are obviously large-scale and complex systems by which large numbers of people communicate. The same can be said of the U.S. mail, large audiences to cultural events, the telephone, or other forms of communication by which large numbers of people communicate. However, such systems do not meet the criteria by which "mass communication" is defined. Essentially, the mass media in the U.S. are private enterprises that are operated for profit. Their content is developed and transmitted by professional communicators using print, broadcasting, and film while other forms of communication, such as email, telephone conversations, and the exchange of letters, are used mainly by individuals communicating with other persons. In that sense they are clearly different from the traditional media. In other words, sheer numbers is not the essential feature that defines mass communication. A formal definition of "mass communication" is provided in Chapter 2.

Finally, I truly enjoyed writing this book. It was such a pleasure to prepare what I think will provide useful knowledge for students who take a course in mass communication theory. I would like to thank the reviewers who helped with the development of this project including, Eric A. Abbott, Idaho State University; Michael W. Barberich, University at Albany, SUNY; Frederick W. Busselle, Washington State University; Glenn Cummins, Texas Tech University; Barna W. Donovan, St. Peter's College; George A. Gladney, University of Wyoming; Beverly Kelley, California Lutheran University; Kevin C. Lee, Western Carolina University; Mark A. Nordstrom, Lincoln University; Elizabeth M. Perse, University of Deleware; Patricia Prijatel, Drake University; Robert Scott, Monmouth University; Tracy R. Worrell, Emerson College. I hope that the book serves you well.

Melvin L. DeFleur,
Distinguished Professor

The Manship School of Mass
Communication
Lousiana State University

MASS COMMUNICATION THEORIES

Explaining Origins, Processes, and Effects

CHAPTER 1

Shaping the American Mass Media: A Brief Overview

To understand the origins of both our contemporary mass media as well as the theories that explain their processes and their influences on their audiences, it is necessary to look back at *where they came from and how they developed.* It does not take any great flight of imagination to realize that the mass communication system we have today is quite different from what we have had in the past. Similarly, it is obvious that our system will continue to develop, and what we have in the future will not be the same as what we now have. For that reason, we begin with a historical overview of how our mass communication system developed within an ever-changing society to produce what we have today.

The American society essentially began in September of 1620, when 101 passengers, along with 48 crew members and a number of chickens and pigs, left Plymouth, England, on the *Mayflower.* Nearly two months later, they landed on Cape Cod, where they spent another eight weeks before moving to the mainland. There they quickly laid out a road up from the shore and began constructing shelters. Within two years they had a small village of simple homes that they named New Plymouth. The houses they built were small and compactly arranged close together on each side of the road, each with its own garden plot.

The people in the new community worked hard all day, tending gardens and animals, but had very little to do after sunset, other than talk with their families and friends. There were religious services on the Sabbath and daily family prayers, but the strict codes of the Pilgrims did not permit frivolous activities. Aside from the family Bible, there was nothing to read in most of the houses. Even if there had been, the majority could neither read nor write. Even for the few who could, it was difficult. After dark, tallow candles, crude lamps, and the fireplace provided barely enough light to move around inside. Thus, by comparison with today, the citizens of New Plymouth led a life almost free of any form of communication other than talking.[1]

The contrast between the availability of mass communications to the people of New Plymouth in the early 1600s and their counterparts in any community in the United States in the 2000s is startling, to say the least. Today, any of us can select from an almost bewildering set of choices among media. Information and news, entertainment, and other content can be delivered instantly to homes via copper wire, optic cable, microwaves, and even satellite transmissions from space. A typical citizen has available, twenty-four hours a day, virtually any form of communication content from gangsta rap and spectator sports to classical music and serious political analysis. He or she can read a book or a magazine, peruse the newspaper, listen to the radio, go to the movies, view a rented film on the home DVD player, check out a sitcom or game show on television, view TV on a cell phone, play games on a computer, log on to the Internet, or exchange text messages with strangers from all parts of the world. Thus, an almost incredible spectrum of mass communication content is instantly available from intensely competing media.

THE RELATIONSHIP BETWEEN MASS MEDIA AND SOCIETY

The American system of mass communication today—its media, those who pay its costs, and the audiences it serves—are embedded in a larger context. They are part of the American society as a whole. That society, as is perfectly obvious, has constantly *undergone change*. Nowhere is this change more obvious and visible than in the case of our means of communicating. As our opening section indicated, the earliest English colonists in our New World society had virtually nothing we would classify as mass communication. In contrast, today we live in a sea of mediated messages.

This incredible change from *what we were* to *what we are* raises a critical question for anyone wanting to understand our contemporary system of mass communications in the United States: *How did we get here from there?* That is, why do we have the kind of mass communication systems that we do—the most complex in the world? What social and cultural factors within the society shaped their nature? How did they come to be based on such market concepts as *free enterprise, competition*, the *profit motive*, and *private ownership*? Moreover, why is it that our government has such *limited control* over the content of the media? Other societies do not have identical mass communication systems. Some are similar, but many are very different indeed.

The answer, of course, is that each society's mass communication system is a *product of its history* and has been *shaped by the culture* developed by its people over many generations. To be sure, each system at any point in time has been influenced in important ways by existing *technologies*. However, these technologies are essentially the *same* from one society to the next. For example, printing presses or television sets operating in, say, China, Cuba, Iceland, Iran, or the United States all use the similar physical principles. The *differences* between those mass media systems and the one in the United States have come about because each nation has developed uses and controls over the process of mass communication in different ways—within its own set of values, political system, economic institution, and other cultural factors. Therefore, to gain a clear understanding of a specific society's media system, just knowing the technology is not enough. It is essential to understand the social, political, economic, and cultural context within which each nation's media developed and now functions.

Essentially, the critical factors that have most influenced the media in the United States have been the country's *basic cultural values*. It is these values that have shaped its *political* and *economic* systems along with its *moral norms* and *laws*. These values are products of our past, and they continue to define our contemporary way of life—including the nature of our mass communication system. In the future these values will continue to determine the characteristics of the system's content, controls, operations, patterns of use, and influences on audiences. For that reason it is essential to understand them, including where they came from. Our system of mass communication will influence your work, your leisure, your ideas, and even your children in the decades ahead.

The basic values of a society are, in turn, a product of its collective historical experience. Clearly, the events of our past, such as the founding of the original colonies, the American Revolution, expansion of the frontier, the Industrial Revolution, population growth, complex patterns of immigration, various wars, legislation, and the development of technology have all had significant influences on each new medium as it was introduced and widely adopted. In a very real sense, then, the development of mass communication in the U.S. has been profoundly influenced by what took place in the American society in years past.

But there is another side to the coin. While the mass media in the United States have been shaped by social and cultural factors, they have, in turn, had a powerful influence on all of us, both individually and socially. There is little doubt that the numbers of people who receive, and are influenced in some way by, mass-communicated information on a daily basis are simply staggering. In fact, the recipients and users of media-provided information include virtually every American, excluding only those too young, too old, or too ill to attend. Their purchasing decisions are shaped in significant ways by a vast advertising industry that supports the media financially. Those decisions, in turn, shape what the manufacturing and service industries can successfully produce and market. In a very real sense, then, the work that Americans perform and the health of their economy are intimately linked to mass communications. Moreover, most forms of recreation enjoyed by citizens are linked to print, film, broadcasting, or computer media in some way. The same is true of political participation. Patterns of voting are shaped to a considerable degree by mass-communicated news and mediated political campaigns. Therefore, the relationship between media and society is a very complex and reciprocal one.

The bottom line is that understanding our contemporary mass media, and how they came to be shaped into their present form, is no idle academic enterprise. It is a key to understanding life in our time and how it will undoubtedly be shaped in the future. Against the background provided by the present chapter, additional ones will provide summaries of various theories that have been advanced to explain their *origins, as well as the processes and effects of mass communications as they influence both individuals and society.* Without first understanding this background, however, there is no way in which their nature can truly be appreciated.

The purpose of the remainder of the present chapter, then, is to summarize very briefly, and in a general way, the circumstances that shaped our mass communication system into its present form during a span of nearly four hundred years. The chapter not only provides an answer to the question of *how we got here from there*, but also it provides a foundation for understanding basic aspects of the structure and functioning of our contemporary mass media today and how they are likely to develop in the future. Thus, the overview that follows focuses less on specific media than on features of the American experience that have had consequences for our entire media system. The more detailed events and circumstances that shaped each specific medium will be addressed in subsequent chapters.

THE LEGACY OF THE EARLY PERIOD: THE 1600S

Few media scholars write about the influence of the earliest settlements in North America on our mass communication systems today. In many ways that connection may seem remote. Nevertheless, there is a relationship between the shared values and beliefs that developed in the earliest American colonies and the nature of our contemporary mass communication system. The unique lifestyle that quickly came to characterize those early communities provided the beginnings of the *general American culture* that we know now. It was within the limits of that culture, as it was developed over succeeding generations, that our present mass media came into existence. Therefore, it is important to understand the origins of the central features of American shared beliefs and values that are relevant to understanding how our modern mass communications systems developed.

The first task in looking briefly at the American colonial experience is to understand the underlying values of our *economic system*. The second will be to examine the *political values* that came to characterize Americans as they moved toward a separation from England. A third is to understand the very early role played by newspapers and other forms of print in the *process of achieving independence*.

Mercantilism: The Importance of Private Enterprise

The early 1600s were an age of *mercantilism*—a concept that is still with us. It is based on the idea of *trade*—the ancient idea of buying and selling goods and products to make a profit. A related idea is *industrialization*—using machines to *produce* goods to sell. That would come later, beginning about the end of the 1700s. More recently, providing *services for fees* has also become increasingly important. Together they are the basis of modern *capitalism*. Thus, capitalism refers to an economic system designed to make profits for those who invest in the means by which goods and services are produced and distributed—or by which some resource is "exploited" (used to produce products to sell).

While traders have been a part of human life for many centuries, the era of mercantilism began to expand and mature about the time of Columbus. European merchants had begun routinely to send ships to foreign lands (mainly India and China) to buy goods that they could sell for a profit when they returned. They bought products that were in high demand, such as spices and silk, that they could easily sell to European markets. Thus, exploration of routes to places where such goods could be bought was critical. Thus, the profit motive was a major factor that motivated Columbus and other early explorers to set sail for the New World.

During the 1600s, after sea routes to the New World were better understood, came an *era of colonization* of the Americas by a number of European nations. The initial purpose of these settlements was (again) to make profits for those who bankrolled each project. A secondary purpose was to establish global political claims by the monarchies of the time. In North America these were mainly the English, the French, and the Dutch.

At first, the English, like the Spanish farther South, sought *gold*. They paid lip service to converting the Indians to Christianity. However, the English were about a century late in getting established in the Americas. The only area left that was open to them for settlement was along the Atlantic seaboard north of St. Augustine (in Florida) and to the south of what is now Newfoundland. It soon became apparent that there was little gold to be had in that part of the New World, so investors had to try to make their profits in other ways.

The first successful English settlement in the New World was in Bermuda. It was followed in 1607 by a colony at Jamestown, in what is now Virginia. A third was the one established in 1620 at New Plymouth, in what later became Massachusetts. Within a decade, a number of others were authorized and settled in both Massachusetts and Maryland. By the middle of the 1600s, English settlements were in place all up and down the Atlantic seaboard. Thus, by the end of the seventeenth century, with substantial immigration from England, these became the thirteen original colonies.

As noted, each of the thirteen English colonies started as a commercial undertaking. Groups of "merchant adventurers" sold shares in the enterprise and recruited people to establish a new "plantation." They obtained a charter from a supervising government agency to locate a community in a particular area approved by the Crown. The goal of such a settlement ("plantation") was to exploit some sort of local resource in order to ship products back to England to be sold at a profit. These commodities could be crops, such as tobacco or grain, or whatever was available. In more northern areas, dried and salted fish were particularly profitable. Thus, the practice of risking capital in private enterprises for potential gain was very much a part of our cultural inheritance from England.

Today, we live in a society characterized by *controlled capitalism*. It is not the totally unfettered, sink-or-swim capitalism first described in 1776 by Adam Smith in his famous book, *An Inquiry into the Nature and Causes of the Wealth of Nations*. It has long been one in which both local and national governments—whether British or American—have played parts in regulating economic activities. An important lesson is that, from the very beginning, economic considerations have been a primary factor in the movement of populations from the old world to the new. Another important lesson is that the main values underlying our contemporary American economic system began to be set into place with the very first settlements in our part of the New World.

A Commitment to Local and Autonomous Government

Shifting from economic considerations to political factors, it is important to note that a critical early development that would influence our media was the establishment of *local systems of laws* to provide stable government within each new plantation. It is not difficult to see this situation as laying the foundation for resentment of outside controls. That would develop at a later date—resentment of the faraway government of England. For example, the *Mayflower* colonists designed their own system of local self-government even before they sighted land. They were supposed to have landed much farther south and be bound by the prior agreements of the Virginia colony. However, during their voyage, ocean currents swept them north to Cape Cod. To avoid anarchy, they decided to design their own rules for living together, and they drafted the *Mayflower Compact* while still at sea. It set forth rules for orderly collective living.

As early as 1639, three small communities in Massachusetts banded together and prepared a document of *Fundamental Orders,* which served as a constitution for a *Public State or Commonwealth.*[2] It made no reference to England whatsoever, and it incorporated almost all of the provisions that would eventually become part of the U.S. Constitution. Thus, the idea of local autonomy, and freedom from big government that was far away, became a part of the colonial culture very early. Later, that idea would play a critical role in shaping our nation's press.

Separating Church and State

While the plantations were funded and organized for a return on investment, those that were initially established in the Massachusetts area had a second important purpose for their members. Those who came to New Plymouth on the *Mayflower* called themselves "Pilgrims"—which even today means "people who journey to alien lands in search of truth." They saw themselves as seeking *religious truth*. From the standpoint of the Crown, however, they were little more than troublesome religious radicals. The Crown saw them as "separatists" who had split from the official (Anglican) Church of England. Like many religious sects today, the Pilgrims had rejected the established Church in favor of their own sectarian beliefs. Indeed, because of religious persecution in England, they had fled to Holland earlier and then on to the New World. Many in England said "good riddance."

Others, who were also religious dissidents, but still living in England, soon followed to establish a second settlement—the Massachusetts Bay Colony (now Boston). These settlers believed themselves to be "Puritans" because they were intent upon "purifying" the beliefs of the Anglican Church. A main point is that these early New England colonists were determined to be free from religious interference by the state. This concept—the separation of church and state—of course prevailed through subsequent generations and became a critical part of the political culture of the new nation that would emerge.

Individualism: The Frontier Mentality

Other factors shaped the emerging fundamental cultural values of the colonists. For one thing, they were by no means environmentalists! In front of them was a sea rich with resources and at their backs was a vast continent with unlimited land, forests, minerals, and wild animals. Almost immediately they set about to exploit those assets. They set up fishing and whaling industries. Acre by acre they hacked their way into the forests. They killed the deer and sent the skins to England, along with the furs of other animals that they could trap or obtain in trade from Native Americans. They mined small deposits of iron for export. They burned down the trees to clear fields on which to grow crops. When these lands were exhausted, they simply moved farther inland. It was an economy of exploitation.

More and more people arrived from England. Indeed, the population doubled every generation right up until the time of the American Revolution. As this happened, the pace of destructive activities increased. By the time the United States was established as a new nation with its own Constitution (1787), the deer, furs, and fish from the rivers and streams were greatly diminished in most of the areas east of the Mississippi. As the population had moved westward, the land was denuded. By the mid-1800s, just before the Civil War, there was little virgin forest left from the Atlantic clear to the Missouri River.

This economic system, based on exploitable resources, land exhaustion, and relocation, produced a set of shared cultural beliefs that has often been called a *frontier mentality*. It was a set of shared beliefs that saw "rugged individuals" pitted against nature—with a justifiable right to subjugate the environment for their own uses. Such individuals not only saw no need for controls by a powerful government, but also they resented attempts by rulers far away to regulate any aspect of their lives. In other societies, the activities of the individual remained under collective control. But in the emerging America, an emphasis on *individuality, personal responsibility,* and *freedom from government interference* became an important part of the national culture from the beginning. Such values continue to shape the thinking of many Americans, and they clearly played a part in shaping our contemporary mass communication system as it developed.

Another feature of life in the American colonies was that it lacked the aristocratic system that prevailed in Europe. That was particularly true in the North. In the southern colonies, large land holdings, along with abundant cheap labor, were needed by plantation owners to grow such crops as rice, cotton, and tobacco. Slaves provided the agricultural labor in such settings and a kind of unofficial aristocracy developed based on ownership of both land and slaves. Even so, the majority of the population in southern colonies were poor subsistence farmers who worked the land themselves. In New England, and later elsewhere, most people established small farms or ranches and worked them as a family team.

Generally, then, in the New World, there was more democracy and fewer social distinctions between haves and have nots. There were social class levels, of course, but the rigid and inherited class structure that characterized England never took root in the colonies. This yielded the shared belief that each citizen was just as good as the next—except for black people—and each should have the same rights as the next. These beliefs provided a strong foundation for a sense of *equality* that would shape the nation's political values during the centuries ahead.

Overview of the Influences of the Early Period

From the above, the influences from the 1600s that would eventually shape our contemporary mass media can be summarized briefly: The conditions of life that the colonists established in the New World were not the same as those that prevailed in the mother country. They brought with them an economic structure that emphasized private ownership, profits, and an almost complete dependence on extracting natural resources. Eventually, this would produce a kind of frontier mentality emphasizing rugged individualism and a distaste for government interference. Life in the new settlements was much less bound by class and social distinctions than was the case in England, leading to greater feelings of political equality. Moreover, there were far more opportunities for poor people to move up the social ladder—mainly by acquiring land. The early settlers placed great importance on autonomous local government, as opposed to rule by powerful people far away. These were important foundations for a change from *monarchy* to *democracy*. Those in the New England area, in particular, insisted on a total separation between church and state, because religion, and the right to worship in their own way, was an important part of their lives.

In many ways, these emphases from the period of early settlement still define some of the most basic values of Americans. We continue to believe in the importance of individual responsibility, political equality, limited government, and local autonomy. Americans still approve of private ownership, the legitimacy of a pursuit of profits, and a separation between government and religion. It was on this cultural foundation that the mass communication system of the nation would eventually develop, and it continues to shape its contemporary nature in important ways.

INFLUENCES OF THE LATER COLONIAL ERA: THE 1700S

Between the end of the 1600s and the late 1700s, the settlements and inhabited areas along the eastern seaboard developed rapidly into thirteen prosperous and successful English colonies with specific geographical boundaries. While there were many similarities among the colonies in their separate governments, there was no overall federation—no central assembly or national legislature that brought the separate colonies together into a single political system. That concept would develop during the 1700s.

Basically, during the 1700s, each colony was politically controlled by the English king and Parliament through a governor. This administrator was sometimes locally elected but always had to be confirmed by the king. Each colony had a local legislative body whose members were chosen by the "freemen." Local towns (townships) elected "selectmen"—which they still do today in many communities in New England. Those allowed to vote were white male property owners. In some cases, they also had to be of the right religion. Those who were elected sometimes appointed other officials, such as assistants to the governor as well as judges. Thus, the basic three-part form of government, *executive, legislative,* and *judicial,* was in some respects already a familiar idea by the time that a refined version would be built into the U. S. Constitution of 1787.

By the mid-1700s, the American colonies had become of critical economic importance to England. The British Empire was being established all over the world, and the pattern was much the same in each colonial area. Each was required to send back to England whatever products they could produce for their merchants to sell. In return, English craftsmen and merchants supplied the colonies with processed goods, such as cloth, shoes, tools, or whatever was being produced in the home country. For many years it was a system within which each party prospered. The abundant resources of the American colonies yielded wealth for many locals, while the processed goods from England sold into the colonial market created wealth for the English entrepreneurs. In addition, the colonies benefitted because the powerful English navy and armed forces kept out potential invaders.

Deep Distrust of Big Government

As the 1700s wore on, however, many dissatisfactions with the system developed. Great Britain continued rigidly to control the pattern of commerce between its colonies and the homeland. By the 1760s, a number of serious problems became evident. For one thing, there was a substantial *negative balance of trade* between England and the colonies. In some ways it was just like our current relationship with countries like Japan and China. The colonists bought goods from England, costing far more in total value than what was earned from the products they sold to the mother country. This created a lopsided flow of money from the colonies to England. This began to produce economic difficulties and great resentment in the colonies. However, England would not change the rules. It came to be widely believed among the colonists that the far-distant government in London was not sensitive to their needs, was exploiting them economically, and was ruling them with a heavy hand. A particularly sensitive issue was "representation." There were no elected representatives from the colonies in the English Parliament.

Growing Dissatisfaction with England's Controls

As dissatisfaction grew, a number of men joined political groups with names like the Sons of Liberty, or quasi-military militia such as the Minute Men (who pledged to be ready to fight with a minute's notice). These militias thought of themselves as patriots and felt that some day it might be necessary to resist the English government by force of arms. They stockpiled arms and ammunition—which was against the law. Their members met regularly in taverns and other places to discuss ways to resist the government, and they developed networks of spies and messengers to keep themselves informed about the activities of the British armed forces.

The single most galling issue was *taxes*. England had been almost constantly at war with other European countries—especially with France. These protracted conflicts drained the English treasury, and great debts piled up. Ways had to be found to pay them off. King George and the English Parliament decided that money should be raised by taxing the people in the American colonies. After all, they had protected the colonies for many decades. Thus, a Stamp Act was passed in 1765, requiring a small fee (about a nickel in current terms) for a little imprinted stamp on every official document produced in the colonies. The colonials were outraged, not so much by the size of the fee, but by the principle. It was "taxation without representation." Because of the outcry, the Stamp Act was repealed by the British a year later.

Meanwhile, in 1765 the first step was taken that would lead to a *federation of colonies*. Nine colonies sent representatives to the American Union—a group that met in New York. There the participants drew up resolutions concerning such issues as *inalienable rights, personal liberties,* and *freedom from taxation* (by Britain) without having elected representatives in Parliament. The Parliament back in England, however, insisted that *it* was in total control and then went on to impose a new series of *import taxes* on the colonies. One such tax was levied on *tea*. Hotheads in the colonies—especially in Boston—saw these impositions as a total outrage (again, taxation without representation). Dressed like Native Americans, a small band boarded and burned several ships and threw 26,000 pounds of tea packaged in lead boxes into the bay.

By 1774, a group of self-appointed colonial leaders would form the Continental Congress. That group would unite and guide the colonies through the eight years of war that would soon start. On July 4, 1776, that Congress formally and publically announced political separation from England with the Declaration of Independence. It was a critical step, and the newspapers of the time played a key role in making the document known to the public.

The Role of Newspapers in the Independence Movement

The importance of these various developments for shaping our current media system was that *distrust of powerful government* became an important element in shaping the role of the press in the American society. It laid the foundation for the role of contemporary journalists as the "watchdogs" of society—calling attention to the transgressions of those in positions of power. Many of the early newspapers publishers risked going to jail by speaking out against the Crown. As England tightened its grip to make sure that the colonies remained under its control, a number of very able writers prepared public statements advocating separation from England, and they did go to jail! It is important to understand that the colonial press became the medium that carried those messages to an increasingly enthusiastic audience. Using not only newspapers but also other printed tracts and pamphlets, those who spoke out strongly made a convincing case for *total independence* from England. Their essays and other appeals were widely read. These media played an important part in shaping the thinking of those who saw English rule as repressive. The print media of the time, then, *were an important factor* in shaping the popular support for political separation from the mother country.

Overview of Influences of the Colonial Era

In summary, the colonial period, before the time of the Revolution, saw the beginnings of the American press. A number of important traditions and features that are retained today, not only by newspapers but also by later media, were established during the period. Clearly, newspapers helped shape and clarify opinion during the time when the colonies were moving toward separation from England. Many provided the means by which important views on various sides of the issue were made available to the population.

Another important tradition was defining the role of the press as the "watchdog" of society. Those who published newspapers saw themselves as totally independent of, and even antagonistic to, government. They saw their mission as keeping an eye on politicians and officials, and their policies, to make sure that power was not being misused. When such abuses were detected, it was the duty of the newspaper, according to this conception, to call public attention to what was going on. Through such disclosures, it was believed, government excesses could be held in check. Today, *investigative journalism*—which is now an important feature not only of newspapers but also of other media—remains a strong tradition in the American media system.

Newspapers also provided a great deal of useful information of a nonpolitical nature. They published notices of ship arrivals, accounts of events that had occurred in their area, and even some foreign news. This was the beginning of the critical *information function* that the press (all news media) serves today. During the 1700s, newspapers even provided a certain amount of lighter fare. Often, they contained poems, essays on manners, and other material that was neither news nor political commentary. While these efforts were limited, they foreshadowed the *entertainment function* of the media that has also become a central feature today.

Overall, then, the 1700s saw not only the remarkable American Revolution and the establishment of the United States as a new and independent nation but also the beginnings of a mass communication system that was a product of the emerging American culture. These features of the mass media of the time were added on to the accepted concept of private ownership and the emphasis on the profit motive that were brought forward from the previous century.

MASS MEDIA IN AN EXPANDING NATION: THE 1800S

By any measure the 1600s and the 1700s were periods of slow but steady change, punctuated with dramatic events, such as American struggle for independence. In contrast, the 1800s saw constant and often rapid change. The term "Industrial Revolution" is used to characterize the transformations of society that began early in the 1800s. However, the people of the time did not realize how rapidly their way of life was being altered. We think of the last half of the 1900s and the early years of the 2000s as a period of social and technological change. Indeed, that is the case, but in many ways the first half of the 1800s was even more dramatic.[3]

As the 1800s began, travel was still a matter of either walking, riding a horse, or bumping along in a wagon or carriage pulled by horses or mules. Sending a message to a loved one, or for business purposes, took weeks or even months—depending on the distance the letter had to be carried. Just five decades later, by mid-century, people were riding on trains that could get up to the astonishing speed of 45 miles an hour. Messages sent by telegraph, along copper wires that connected many distant towns and cities, traveled at a mind-boggling 186,000 miles per second!

Early in the nineteenth century, the boundaries of what is now the United States (mainland) were greatly expanded by acquisition of vast territories from the French as well as from Mexico. Other areas were acquired as well by various means to establish the boundaries of what is now the continental United States. For the most part, those areas were occupied by a few Europeans and by scattered tribes of native people. These Native Americans, in particular, were seen mainly as troublesome barriers to the advance of civilization. Consequently, they were systematically killed off, rounded up, or moved to be confined to reservations.

American leaders of the time developed policies favoring *immigration*, especially from Europe. The new country needed people—and they came in great waves. To protect against potential foreign incursion, the huge middle and the far western reaches of the country had to have people. It was a land of great natural resources—minerals, forests, and farmland. Continuing the frontier mentality of the first two centuries, the shared belief was that the wilderness had to be tamed and its resources brought under control for economic gain.

The Industrial Revolution and Its Consequences

It was a combination of a new source of brute power, the inventive genius of vigorous people, and the prospect of great economic rewards that drove the ever-increasing pace of the Industrial Revolution. It had begun when the steam engine became a reality.

STEAM AS A NEW SOURCE OF POWER.   It is difficult today to understand fully what took place after the steam engine arrived. Until that happened, power was something obtained from wind, water, or muscles—human or animal. Steam engines came into the picture early in the 1800s. By the 1830s, steam was driving early railroads, ships, river boats, and machinery in factories. Some parts of the country made the change more quickly than others. In New England, with poor and rocky soil, a steam-based factory economy came as a blessing. In the South and in the West, where much of the land had yet to be settled, the industrial society developed much more slowly.

Coupling a steam engine to a printing press was only one of many such applications, but it revolutionized the business of publication. It had a profound effect on the nature of newspapers. By 1830, a cylinder-type press became available. It had two big rotors about three feet long and a foot and a half in diameter (rather like a giant version of an old-fashioned washing machine ringer). The rotors were turned by the steam engine. A cast lead "stereotype" was placed over the roller. It contained all the letters and characters for the passages that were to be printed on single big sheets of paper. Such sheets were fed into the rollers. Several pages of a book or magazine could be printed at one time, to be folded and cut after printing.

The power press was a godsend for book publishing, but it was also quickly adapted for newspapers. By 1834, a new kind of newspaper—the "penny" press—would come into existence in New York City. It was the forerunner of the modern mass newspaper. It would never have been possible without the advertising brought by the Industrial Revolution, the power of the steam engine, and the efficiency of the rotary press. As will be made clear, the financial format and content of the penny press was quickly and widely adopted in communities throughout the United States. Within a very short time, the "daily newspaper" became a very different type of publication than those of the colonial press that had preceded it.

LITERACY.   Another factor that would make it possible for newspapers to serve much larger audiences was a historic change in *public education* that began during the early 1800s. Horace Mann, an educator and politician in Massachusetts, persuaded the Commonwealth's legislature to establish an innovative system of compulsory (and tax-based) education to ensure that children would be able to read, write, and do basic arithmetic. These skills were seen as important in a democracy and in a part of the nation in which industrial work was becoming more and more important. As public schools became common, increasing levels of literacy greatly expanded the potential market for newspapers.

ADVERTISING.   In addition, as industrialization continued, the flow of goods produced in factories produced a growing need for *advertising*. Newspapers were able to take advantage of steadily increasing revenues from both advertising and subscriptions, which increased their profitability. All of these factors worked together, and the result was a surge of growth in both the number of daily papers being published and the proportion of the population that was able to subscribe to and read them. In fact, as the nation continued to expand, both in terms of territory and population, both the number of newspapers and the size of their audiences increased rapidly.

REVOLUTIONS IN TRANSPORTATION.   Railroads would not be widely established until the 1840s, and it would be 1874 before the two coasts were linked by rail. Meanwhile, another form of transportation played a key role in the developing nation, and it had a very clear effect on the mass communication industries that would come in the future. At a time before steam, *canals* were a relatively efficient way to move goods and even people. Because no roads linked regions, boats on rivers and other waterways were the most efficient and most comfortable way to travel. However, rivers and lakes were not conveniently located in places where they were needed, so canals linking them had to be dug to serve as an alternative.

One of the most remarkable construction projects ever undertaken in the early 1800s was the Erie Canal. It was a 363-mile system of ditches and locks, connecting several lakes and rivers, between Albany on the Hudson River on the eastern border of New York and Buffalo and Lake Erie at the western end. Long barges pulled slowly by horses or mules walking on a path beside the waterways could float heavy cargoes and passengers across the entire state. Its importance was that it connected much of what is now the Midwest with New York City and the Atlantic Ocean.

This great new waterway opened the entire Great Lakes area to commerce and settlement. Agricultural products came across the state by canal and then down the Hudson to be shipped from the docks of New York City to foreign markets. Many kinds of finished goods were taken back up the waterways to supply the new communities in the new states surrounding the Great Lakes. Because of the canal, the entire Northwest Territory (Ohio, Indiana, Illinois, Michigan, and Minnesota) became a kind of vast "inland empire," producing products that were sold world wide. New York City became the economic beneficiary of this bounty, and New York State came to call itself the "empire state." (Later, the Empire State Building would be constructed in New York City.) Because of its economic dominance and its large population, New York City became the center of America's emerging media industries.

NEW COMMUNICATION TECHNOLOGIES.   In 1844, Samuel F. B. Morse sent a telegraph message from Washington, D.C, to Baltimore (a distance of about thirty-five miles). The message moved at the speed of lightening— an astounding 186,000 miles per second. Actually, Morse did not "invent" the telegraph. Other working systems were already in use in Great Britain. However, they were cumbersome and rather unreliable. Morse's system was simple, reliable, and quite easy to use. He also developed a code that remains in use even today. The telegraph was so practical and effective that by the time of the Civil War, an underseas cable was being laid across the Atlantic Ocean. Regular telegraph service with England began in 1866. It was the first step toward a high-speed global communication system.

The telegraph and the transatlantic cable truly opened a new era in communication. Within a few years, newspapers and press associations would establish *wire services* that would bring reports of important events in both Europe and the United States to many of the nation's newspapers within a much shorter time than had ever before been possible. Other cables soon linked additional continents and countries. By 1874 the telephone would follow, increasing once again the speed at which people could communicate over distance.

In 1839, five years before Morse demonstrated his telegraph, Louis Daguerre and Joseph Niepce showed the world the first *photograph*. The science of chemistry had advanced to a point where it was possible to make photographs on shining plates of metal with a process that came to be called the "daguerreotype." Although photography did not find its way into newspapers and magazines for several decades, the daguerreotype provided the initial foundation upon which both photojournalism and eventually a great movie industry would be built.

Territorial Expansion

The nation had begun to expand even before the Revolution. Daniel Boone had explored the Kentucky and Tennessee areas as early as 1769, leading a group of settlers from Virginia through the Cumberland Gap (a pass between mountains). He lived to see a million people pour into the new territory. After the nation was founded, other migrants went still farther and took up lands in the Northwest Territory (around the Great Lakes), and new states in the region quickly came into the union.

The nation's new boundaries were growing at an astonishing rate. In 1803, Napoleon Bonaparte was having trouble financing his wars in Europe. Short of cash, he decided to sell off "Le Louisiannne"—vast territories in North America (about a third of the territory in the middle of current U.S. boundaries). This land was claimed and loosely controlled by France. He felt that the land was a drag on his budget and had no future in any case. Little was known about what was there. Some even claimed that prehistoric animals roamed the area. The Americans had proposed to buy only an area around New Orleans (as a means of controlling access to the Mississippi River). But Napoleon said "Take the whole territory or nothing." The result was one of the most spectacular real estate deals in history. The United States paid $ 15 million for Louisiana—a huge triangular area that stretched west of the Mississippi clear to the Rocky Mountains and north from the Gulf of Mexico to Canada. It cost just under three cents per acre.

A short time later, disputes between Mexico and the United States brought about a war (in 1846). At the time, Mexico was a formidable foe, with an army twice as big as that of the Americans. Nevertheless, the leaders in Washington wanted to take over much of the northern tier of Mexican territories and add them to what is now the continental United States. As a result, President James Polk sent American troops under General Zachary Taylor into Mexico and a force under General Winfield Scott to California. Scott had two young officers with him— Captain Robert E. Lee and Lieutenant Ulysses S. Grant.

The war did not last long. In 1847, U.S. Marines entered Mexico City (The "Halls of Montezuma"), and negotiations were commenced. The conflict was formally concluded in 1848 with the signing of the Treaty of Guadalupe Hidalgo and a payment of $ 15 million to Mexico. The United States then took over what is now California, New Mexico, and Utah; parts of Arizona, Texas, and Colorado; plus smaller sections of other states. Again, vast territories came under the American flag for about three cents per acre. The continental United States was now an enormous land mass that stretched from the Atlantic to the Pacific and from the Rio Grande on the south to the long border with Canada to the north.

The Mexican war had a strong influence on American newspapers for two reasons. One was that a huge new area eventually came to be settled, and many newspapers were established to serve their growing populations. Another was in the way news was gathered at the scene of an event and a report sent back to editors. Understandably, the American public was deeply concerned about the battles in Mexico. Many papers had sent correspondents (reporters) into the area to write about the engagements and their outcomes. These reports were taken as quickly as possible to New Orleans, where the copper "lightening lines" were used to transmit the stories by telegraph directly to newsrooms in most of the major cities in the northeast. It was from this arrangement that the *Associated Press*, the first national wire service, was developed.

Influence of the Civil War

The Civil War began on April 12, 1861, when Confederate cannons bombarded and all but destroyed Fort Sumpter—which was located on a small island in the harbor of Charleston, South Carolina. Although there was only one death (due to an accident), it was a momentous act, touching off a great conflict. The war raged on for four years, until April 9, 1865, when Robert E. Lee surrendered to Ulysses S. Grant at Appomattox Courthouse. More than 2.3 million men fought, and more than 600,000 (one out of every four) were killed or died of their wounds or diseases. It remains the greatest number of war deaths ever experienced by the nation in any conflict.

The Civil War understandably created a great demand for news. The papers of the time were able to supply it. The great technological advances in steam-powered printing, electric communication, and swift distribution brought about by the Industrial Revolution had made it possible for virtually every major city to have one or more daily papers. Newspaper readership had increased greatly. During the war years, about four families out of every ten in the nation subscribed to a daily paper. Almost all of the larger papers had one or more reporters observing each battle. News from the conflict was sent via telegraph wire to editors back home, and reports of the victories and losses were provided to the public on a timely basis. Of special interest were the casualty lists for families waiting anxiously at home to hear whether their loved ones had been killed or wounded.

Increased Pace of Urbanization

An important change in the society was the growth of towns and cities. As the 1800s began, the United States was a nation mainly of farmers and ranchers. Only a small proportion of the population lived in cities and towns. However, factories and their related jobs began to draw more and more people to urban communities. That process increased sharply in the upper Midwest as great deposits of iron ore and coal were discovered and exploited to establish iron and steel industries. As the century wore on, the nation was slowly transforming itself into a great industrial power. Large parts of the country remained rural, and agriculture was their major industry. However, more and more people were moving to towns and cities to find employment in the developing manufacturing industries.

The movement of people from farms to cities is called *urbanization*. This was a constant and accelerating process all during the last half of the 1800s. Rural families moved to the city, and many of the foreigners who arrived from abroad also settled there. Urbanization was important for the development of mass communications because it was far easier for a newspaper or magazine to serve a population concentrated in a city than one thinly scattered on farms.

Consequences of Population Increases and Migrations

Of major significance for the development of newspapers and magazines were massive population movements into and within the United States. As noted, immigration from abroad was encouraged in order to settle the huge land masses acquired from France and Mexico. The pace of immigration increased beginning in the late 1840s, when waves of migrants arrived from Ireland to escape the great potato famine. A factor that greatly encouraged additional immigration was the first Homestead Act. President Lincoln signed the legislation in 1862. It providing for 180 acres of *free land* for any American citizen—or even a person who declared his or her *intention* of becoming a citizen—who would agree to establish a farm. This was a remarkable opportunity for many Europeans. No country had ever given away free land! Large numbers of Northern Europeans came to take up farming in the Midwest and on the great plains. Later, millions would arrive from southern and eastern Europe to labor in the new industries. They hoped to escape political turmoil, religious persecution, or grinding poverty in their mother lands.

In all of these areas, communities were established. Some were economic centers for agriculture. Others served mining or industrial economies. Some that were located at points where transportation brought rapidly increasing commerce grew and became cities. In each of these communities, *daily and weekly newspapers were needed*. The American population was growing rapidly. Free and mandatory public education had been widely adopted, and an increasing number of people could read and write. Conditions were very favorable, in other words, for a considerable growth in newspaper and magazine readership. In 1870, five years after the end of the Civil War, three out of every ten households in the United States subscribed to a *daily* newspaper. By the end of the nineteenth century, the U.S. Census reported that (on average) there was one newspaper subscription *for every household*. Saturation had been achieved.

Immigration from abroad was not the only factor promoting growth in newspapers. There was a great movement of population from *east to west* all during the last half of the 1800s. Even during the 1840s, wagon trains streamed across the prairie, bound for the Oregon Territory. Many families stopped along the way and established farms and communities in the Dakotas or in other parts of what are now the mountain states. When gold was discovered in California in 1848, more than 250,000 people (mainly men) descended on Northern California within a few months.

Meanwhile, as the century was coming to an end, the pace of immigration picked up. Millions of people passed through the great immigration station at Ellis Island. Many stayed in the cities along the eastern seaboard, but others traveled on to join relatives or earlier migrants in the Midwest and elsewhere. At about the same time, in a real sense, the frontier came to an end. Most of our states had already been admitted to the union. However, additional territories and populations came under American control just as the century was ending. In a war with Spain that lasted only ten weeks, Puerto Rico and the Philippines became American overseas possessions. Hawaii and Alaska were taken over at about the same time.

Overview of the Influences of the Nineteenth Century

As the foregoing indicates, the changes that took place during the Nineteenth century are truly remarkable. As the period began, the United States was an insignificant country with a population of just over five million people in fifteen states located mainly east of the Mississippi and south of the Ohio. By the end of the century it was a vast country of forty-eight states and other territories, with a population of seventy-six million, many of whom were immigrants from other countries. Its population had begun shifting from farming to urban life. It had impressive industries concentrated in the Northeast, a huge agricultural base in the South, and millions of fertile acres under production in the Midwest. Great advances in technology directly and indirectly related to communication had been achieved at an ever-increasing pace.

As the 1900s were about to begin, people could travel relatively swiftly from the Atlantic to the Pacific by rail or take a swift steam-driven vessel from San Francisco to New York. They could send messages along thousands of miles of telegraph lines and even across the oceans to other countries. They could call on the telephone for business and social reasons, and they could use a small "Kodak" to record family scenes and other activities in still photos. In addition, scientific discoveries had been made, and practical inventions developed, that within two decades would bring totally new and remarkable mass media—home radio and the motion picture. These media, like magazines and newspapers before them, would also be shaped by the economic, political, and cultural factors that had been brought forward from earlier times.

NEW MEDIA IN AN URBAN-INDUSTRIAL SOCIETY: THE 1900S

The 1900s saw the rise of new media that could not possibly have been imagined by people in the 1600s. All were products of the continuing Industrial Revolution and its scientific counterpart. Black-and-white silent movies, along with home radio, came early in the century. Just after mid-century, television was available in virtually every American home. It was soon followed by the VCR, the DVD, cable systems, direct broadcast satellites, cellular phones, fax, and the computer-based Internet.

As the twentieth century came to a close, the pace of change in new mass communication technologies became almost frantic. Some media were shrinking; others were expanding. Still others were converging. The pace was so fast that it became difficult to predict in a detailed way what people would have available in the early decades of the twenty-first century or, in some cases, even the next month. In spite of this pace, however, the new mass media to come, like what came earlier, will be shaped by the same factors that have operated in the past.

The United States Becomes a Mass Communication Society

One of the first major mass media developments of the 1900s was the rise of a new kind of journalism within the magazine industry. Starting in 1900, an almost endless number of articles were prepared to expose political, economic, and social problems in American life. President Theodore Roosevelt called these writers "muckrakers." He did so because they concentrated on corruption in American politics, ruthlessness in business, and the plight of the poor—rather than championing the remarkable achievements of the American society. However, by the time of World War I, the public was tired of such exposures, and the muckraker era came to an end. Nevertheless, its lasting influence was to ensure the place of investigative journalism in the American press.

THE GOLDEN AGE OF THE PRINT MEDIA.   The first World War was of great significance to the ninety-two million people in the United States when it broke out in 1914. However, America did not enter the war actively until 1917. Before it ended, in November of 1918, more than two million young men and a few hundred women went to France. Of the young men who served in the trenches, or in ships in the Atlantic, 130,000 lost their lives. Understandably, the public was horrified—but eager to follow the war news from France. During the period, subscriptions to daily newspapers rose to a historic high. Newspapers were literally in a "golden age"—one that they would never see again. On average, American families subscribed to more than 1.3 daily newspapers. Many families had both a morning and evening paper delivered to their doors, or they bought them from street vendors. The newspaper had a total monopoly on the news because it had no rivals.

Magazines also came into a kind of golden age during the first several decades of the 1900s and especially between 1920 and 1950. Beautifully printed general magazines with slick paper and huge circulations rose to great prominence. They prospered because they were an ideal vehicle for delivering advertising of nationally mass-marketed products. For that purpose, they too had no serious rivals. Millions of subscribers in all parts of the country received their magazines by mail.

Such magazines as the *Saturday Evening Post, Colliers,* or *Cosmopolitan* also served the entertainment function by providing collections of short stories, serialized novels, simple analyses of public affairs, recipes, and humor.

AMERICAN MOVIES COME TO DOMINATE THE WORLD MARKET. One of the major consequences of World War I for our contemporary media system had to do with global markets for American entertainment products. With France, Germany, and Britain locked in the Great War, motion picture production facilities in Europe were essentially shut down after 1914. American film makers rushed to supply the world market. The silent black-and-white movies of the time used subtitles to tell the ongoing story. Almost any language could be used. Thus, the movies were a flexible product that sold well in every country that had even primitive movie theaters. People in those countries, especially the young, adored them. American films established a world dominance by this means, and they retain that dominance even to this day. Those global distribution systems have now been greatly expanded, and American movies, TV programs, music, video cassettes, and other entertainment products are both loved and hated all over the world. (The consequences of this global exportation will be explained in Chapter 24.)

The motion picture industry matured greatly between the two World Wars. Going to the movies became the recreation of choice for millions of American families as well as for audiences in almost all other countries. The experience was cheap, wholesome, available, and fun. The movies were ideal for dating couples. American kids of the time loved the Saturday matinees with cowboys, comics, and serialized adventures. Many movies attracted the whole family. Mom, pop, and the kids all went together. Attendance in the U.S. rose to record heights between 1930 and 1950, when more than two tickets were sold per family every week. However, that golden age would soon go into serious decline as television became the dominant medium.

RADIO AS A NEW MASS COMMUNICATION TECHNOLOGY. By the beginnings of the 1920s, radio was transformed from a wireless dot-dash telegraph used for commercial, navigational, and governmental purposes into a home medium. Regularly scheduled broadcasts of music, drama, and comedians began early in the 1920s, and in the U.S. the medium quickly turned to advertising as a means of financial support. That had been the solution taken by the popular newspapers nearly a century earlier and by magazines as they developed during the last half of the 1800s. It was the American way—*private ownership, profit-oriented,* and *minimal governmental interference* in terms of content. Radio did require certain technical regulation to avoid signal interference, but (except for dirty words) the system essentially retained the freedom of speech that was a deep-seated cultural value.

TELEVISION CHALLENGES OTHER MASS MEDIA. Television was about to become a mass medium in the United States when the Japanese attacked Pearl Harbor. Little was done to develop the medium during the war years. However, when the conflict was over, a number of stations quickly went on the air, and wherever there was a signal to receive, television sets were snapped up by a waiting public. The Federal Communications Commission restrained growth of the medium for four years while developing a plan to avoid signal overlap. Even so, the public could not get enough of television broadcasts.

Television created significant displacements among the other media. It quickly attracted advertising dollars from print and radio, and it took audiences away from the movies. TV inherited radio's financial structure, its relationship with the Federal Communication Commission, much of its programming, and most of its audience. In addition, its advantages as an advertising medium drew dollars away from the general magazines, many of which went out of business. Television's advertising and its news services made inroads into the financial health of newspapers.

New Technologies and Changing Mass Media Systems

After the middle of the twentieth century, the American mass communication system was deeply established in essentially its present form (but without the Internet, which came later). There have been recent changes and additions, but by the late 1950s, television had already become the medium to which most Americans paid close attention. Books retained their niche as a specialized medium for information, education, and entertainment. Movies remained popular, but the numbers paying at the box office were clearly declining. Newspapers were losing readers steadily, and many papers were either going bankrupt or being absorbed into chains to reduce costs. Magazines were hard hit at first but rebounded by becoming increasingly specialized. Few of the older, general, large-circulation magazines survived, and niche publishing had become the predominant mode. Radio rebounded by turning to music, news, and talk-show programming after being nearly put out of business by TV. However, still further changes were coming. They would be based on both satellites and the digital technology of the computer.

THE INCREASING IMPORTANCE OF COMPUTERS.   No one quite foresaw the truly remarkable role that computers would play in the media industries. At first, the huge electronic computers, like the ENIAC (more than one hundred feet long) developed for the military during and just after World War II, were seen by the public as scientific curiosities. They were seen as little more than "electronic brains," used by the military and operated by geeky scientists with thick glasses and nerd packs in the pockets of their white coats.

By comparison with today's computers, the early machines were not only huge but very slow. Moreover, they seemed to have little or no significance for ordinary citizens. However, by the mid-1950s it became clear to businesses and government agencies that computers could be used for a great many practical purposes. The card-programmed, mainframe computers of the time were soon in use in every large corporation, educational institution, and government agency. Because of their efficiency, they soon helped to move the United States into the *information age.*[4] What that means is that, after the middle of the century, more people were manipulating numbers and words than were producing objects with hands and machines. By 1960, the age of the digital, electronic computer had truly arrived, and it would soon change the lives of almost everyone.

THE CONSTANT INVENTION AND REPLACEMENT OF MEDIA.   During the 1960s and '70s, using a large mainframe computer was accomplished only by highly trained specialists using arcane commands and programming "languages." Early in the 1980s, however, the small "desktop" machines came onto the market. They were quickly adopted and pressed into use for thousands of different applications. Within a decade, the computer had literally transformed the ways in which business was conducted in almost every walk of life. By 2000, a computer could be found in about four out of every ten American homes, and the rate of adoption was rising rapidly. Currently, millions of people are subscribers to such online services as America Online. The numbers continue to increase every month.

Overview of Factors Influencing Mass Media Development in the 1900s

The above review indicates that, as the twentieth century began, people could subscribe to a sophisticated morning and afternoon daily newspaper or receive many kinds of magazines in the mail. The more affluent could call friends on the telephone (but long-distance was not well developed). People could also send a telegram. However, there were no movie theaters to attend, no radio to hear, and no television to view. Computer networks could not even be imagined. The population of the United States continued to expand rapidly in the early decades (slowing in more recent times) and educational levels increased greatly. These trends provided a larger and more literate market for print media. As a result, the early part of the century was the "golden age" of print.

The change from agriculture to industry gave people more expendable income on average and more scheduled free time. The result was a corresponding interest and need for diversion and amusement. Entertainment-oriented media developed to meet these needs—the movies, radio, television, and its related systems—and more recently the Internet. By the mid nineteenth century, and in more recent times, the newer media were growing while the older traditional print media began a slow decline in audience share. Among them, only books resisted the trend.

The pace of scientific and technological development was spurred by the increase in the standard of living, brought by the advance of the industrial revolution. The 1900s brought not only dramatic increases in the accomplishments of science but also growth in average family income. People could afford the new gadgets and amusements that were being produced. In addition, two World Wars spurred technology of many kinds. In particular, World War II and the following Cold War stimulated the development of computers. Digital technology, now at the heart of the almost daily media modifications and advances we read about, will bring great changes in our media systems in the twenty-first century.

WHAT LIES AHEAD?

Digital technology, the foundation of computer operations, will continue to bring us new forms of information, advertising, and entertainment. We now enjoy new systems for delivering clearer television signals to our home sets. While all are not technically mass media, constant innovations are bringing Americans and others many kinds of information, services, and entertainment on the Internet and its World Wide Web as well as on hand-held devices, such as cell phones and iPods.

The basic principle that will prevail is that, in a technological society, there is a constant invention, obsolescence, and replacement of media. In an economic system based on capitalism, new products capable of earning profits are constantly being invented, tried, and developed. Many displace older systems that lose profitability. It is a pattern as old as the Industrial Revolution. To illustrate, in the early 1900s a strong ice industry thrived in New England. Big blocks of ice were sawn from frozen lakes to be shipped in the insulated holds of vessels all over the world. When ice-making machines were invented, that industry collapsed, and factories in the area began making and shipping the new machines. Then, the home refrigerator came on the market. Few commercial ice-making machines were needed, and the "iceman" who delivered to homes lost his job.

The same invention/replacement pattern can be seen in media technology. An example is the VCR, which began life as a machine the size of a small piano. At first, it was used by television broadcasters to record and replay their shows. After refinement and standardization, the video-cassette tape came into use in the majority of American households for watching movies. It is now almost fully replaced by movies on small discs, which use digital technology and are much more durable and easier to store. At some point, it is likely that our now familiar DVDs will also become obsolete. And so it goes. New technologies come, are widely adopted, and then fall into obsolescence as more effective ones are developed.

It is difficult to specify the exact form of new mass communication systems that will exist in the years ahead. The pace of invention is very fast. Also, the plans and ownership patterns among the major corporations developing such systems undergo change and modification every day. Generally, however, the following seem likely:

1. More and more homes will have large, flat-panel, very clear television screens. high-definition television (HDTV), based on digital technology, has now become the standard. As the 1900s came to an end, it was forecast to quickly replace conventional-format TV, but adaptations to this new technology slowed somewhat as conventional TV pictures got better. Now, however it is clear that digital HDTV broadcasts have arrived. By mid-2009, TV signals received in homes were all in this format, and older TV sets required special "boxes" to transform the signals.

2. Far more channels will be available on our home TV receivers, including the World Wide Web. New ways of delivering digital signals to small satellite dishes and home receivers have rapidly been developed and adopted. Older systems for delivering information by wires and cables may decline. Television and computer reception will converge, allowing Internet communication to use the TV screen.

3. Interactive menus on our TV screens have become the norm, where we click with a pointer and get information similar to the manner in which we can now "jump" from a "button" on a computer screen to another screen. That will continue. The remote control has changed advertising from "in your face" (whether you want it or not) to more voluntary exposure selected by the viewer.

4. There will be a continuing slow decline in the proportion of families who subscribe to traditional print media (newspapers and magazines). However, these will not disappear because they will combine with online delivery of news and other information.

5. The current slow decline in the proportion of people who pay at the box office to go to the movies will continue. The availability of motion pictures on television and computer screens will correspondingly increase. However, financial health and vigor of the movie production (as opposed to the exhibition) industry will increase because of a growing demand for entertainment products, both in the U.S. and abroad, for existing and new media.

6. There will be a continued production and use of traditional printed books. This venerable medium remains vital in the fields of entertainment, education, and many other uses. Contrary to predictions that they would be replaced by computer-based readers that receive text online, this does not appear to be taking place in any real sense. However, electronic forms of books may become more common as the new technologies become cheaper and easier to use.

Notes and References

1. See John E. Ponfret, *Founding the American Colonies: 1583–1660* (New York: Harper and Row, 1970).

2. Vincent Wilson, Jr., ed., *The Book of Great American Documents* (Brookeville, MD: American History Research Associates, 1993).

3. J. C. Furnas, *The Americans: A Social History of the United States, 1587–1914* (New York: G.P. Putnam and Sons, 1969).

4. Wilson Dizard, *The Coming Information Society* (New York: Longman, 1990).

CHAPTER 2

Introduction to the Origins, Nature, and Uses of Theories

hy should scholars specializing in the study of mass communication and their influences bother to develop theories about their origins, processes, and effects? Similarly, why should students studying such fields as journalism, advertising, marketing, television broadcasting, the use of the Internet, or other media-based fields bother with the study of those issues? After all, aren't theories just guesses and speculations dreamed up by a bunch of pointy-headed professors sitting in their armchairs? What do they have to do with the "real world" as its practical affairs are conducted in the hard-headed community of profit and loss? Similarly, how can the origins and nature of theories have any importance for success and failures for people pursuing media-related careers?

These are important questions, and they demand answers. This chapter focuses on those issues. It discusses the nature of theories and where they come from. It also provides reasons why they are important in the day-to-day activities of professional communicators and others. It explains how scholars, both in the past and more recently, have gone about developing a number of explanations for the processes and effects of mass communication. Finally, it summarizes briefly what theories are included in this book.

WHAT IS A THEORY?

In a very basic sense, a theory can be regarded as *a description of how something works*. That "something" can be anything people are trying to study and understand. It may be a physical phenomenon—like why substances burn. It man be a biological "something," like what causes a particular disease. Or it can be a psychological issue, like how people store experience in memory. In the same sense, it may be a question about mass communication—like what influences mass media depictions of some behavior have on the way people think about it. In other words, theories are an important kind of knowledge that is developed in *any* field where some description is needed of how something works. Another way of saying that is that theories provide *explanations of what conditions or factors seem to bring about some sort of consequence.*

Concepts as Beginning Points for Theory Development

It is not possible to develop or even describe a theory without stating and defining its *concepts.* In other words, concepts are the basic building blocks of a theory. In an analogous way, they can be thought of as the bricks with which a wall will be made. Each brick is an important part. If it were missing, or seriously flawed, the resulting wall would be defective.

The basic nature of a concept is not particularly difficult to understand. It is just a named condition, factor, or situation that exists in reality that plays some necessary part in the process that the theory describes and explains. The phrase "exists in reality" is an important one. Theories can get into trouble if they incorporate concepts that actually do not have such real existence. A classic example is an early theory of *burning* proposed by Richard Kirwan in a book published in 1787; he maintained that things burn because of the release of a mysterious substance called "phlogiston." Needless to say, that explanation did not survive. Kirwan's theory was replaced later by one developed by Joseph Priestly—the discoverer of oxygen. Priestly was able to demonstrate that oxygen did actually exist in reality and was essential to the burning process.

Examples of simple concepts founded in reality that are often involved in the study of mass communication are *age, income, and socioeconomic status* (of the members of an audience) or *hours per day spent viewing* (by persons attending to that medium). As subsequent chapters will indicate, there are many other concepts involved in theories of mass communication. Some are complex, but they all must share the requirement of real existence, meaning that *their concepts can be observed* in some way by researchers and theory-builders.

Concepts can *vary*. That is, they can take different, numerical values. For example, *age* obviously can be expressed quite conventionally as a particular number of years since the person was born. Thus, age is a *variable* concept. Similarly, a family's *income* can be expressed as some (variable) amount of dollars earned per year. In quite the same way, a person's television behavior can be expressed as the numbers of *hours per day spent watching TV.*

As these examples suggest, concepts can often be expressed in terms of some *quantity* because they can take different numerical values. For that reason, procedures for their *measurement* become very important in theory-building or testing research. And, because such concepts can take varying numerical values, they are sometimes referred to simply as *variables.* (But that really means "variable concepts.")

Even concepts that do not seem to vary actually do so—in a limited sort of way. Take, for example, the concept of "married" (which can be an important concept in some kinds of research and theory development). Now, one cannot be "just a tiny bit" married, "somewhat married," or "a lot married." Technically (and legally) one is either *married* or *not.* But is this a variable concept? Yes, it is. One can assign a value of unity (1) to the condition of being married and a value of zero (0) to those who are not married. In that limited sense, then, the factor (concept, variable) of "married" can be measured and quantified. There are many variables like this— *employed* vs. *unemployed, computer owner* vs. *non-owner, magazine subscriber* vs. *non-subscriber,* and so forth. This may seem like an obscure technical point, but it can be important in assessing the ways that research observations are made for the development of theories.

Some of the concepts in a theory are said to be "independent." What this means is that they are *not thought to be a consequence of something else.* For example, suppose that a person smokes three packs of cigarettes every day. As a consequence, there is an increased likelihood that he or she will eventually suffer from lung cancer. If that does indeed happen, the cigarette smoking is an *independent* condition (variable). That is, smoking is not caused by the lung cancer—it's the other way around. The lung problem, then, is a *dependent* condition (variable) because it is influenced, brought about, or caused by the *independent* action of smoking.

In developing theories in any science, careful distinctions are made between the independent and the dependent concepts that are included. In developing a mass communication theory, the logic is similar. If a child spends many hours every night playing video games while avoiding homework, and if as a consequence his or her grades go down, there is an obvious "independent" concept here (*hours spent playing video games*) and another obvious "dependent" variable (*grades*). It would not be immediately logical to interpret the causal sequence in the reverse direction—that the low grades are brought about the excessive game playing. The propositions that make up a theory, then, are formulated in such a way that these independent and dependent relationships are made clear.

Theories as Sets of Related Propositions

A theory is made up of a set of *related statements of relationships between its concepts*. While some theories in advanced sciences may be "stated" in mathematical formulae, like $e = mc^2$, others are set forth in ordinary language explaining what factors or conditions bring about what consequences. For example, Charles Darwin stated his theory of evolution, explaining how distinct species developed through a process of *natural selection*. He set forth his theory in a lengthy book using only descriptive prose.[1] Another example of a theory set forth in this way is that of Sigmund Freud, who described relationships between various concepts of the human psyche (*ego, superego and id*) and their consequences for behavior.[2] In the field of mass communication, many of the contemporary theories that have been developed, indeed most, are set forth in books that way—often in lengthy works that describe the factors and conditions that are thought to bring about certain kinds of consequences.

An alternative to such lengthy discussions of the nature of a theory is to summarize it in a more formal manner *as a limited set of related statements from which certain logical inferences can be drawn*. People who develop theories in this more formal manner sometimes call the theory's statements *propositions*. The propositions of a given "formal" theory are designed in such a way that they set forth in brief statements the *assumed relationships* that are thought to exist between two or more variables (concepts) that are used to describe and explain how things work. A number of examples of such formal theories are presented in this book.

The advantage of a formal statement of propositions is this: if its assumed propositions can be regarded as correct descriptions of the relationships between the concepts, the theory provides a basis for a logical derivation of some sort of consequence or implication. In other words, an important question is *what does the theory (logically) imply*—if all of its assumptions can be thought of as true? This idea—of being able to obtain some sort of logical implication about whatever is under study—is a truly valuable feature of formal theories. The reason is that such logical implications provide *guidelines as to what researchers should look for* as evidence in order to assess the merits of the theory (more will be said about this feature later).

In the chapters of this book, in which specific theories of processes and effects of mass communication will be discussed, an attempt is made to summarize them in this formal way—as sets of related propositions stating the theory's assumptions. This can be a difficult task, given the complexity of the mass communication process, the audiences that receive media messages, and the many kinds of influences that result. For that reason, the formalized theories set forth in each chapter are to be regarded as very tentative.

Generally, then, a theory is a set of statements or propositions that set forth assumed relationships between independent and dependent concepts (variables) that are important in trying to understand how (whatever is under study) "works" or comes about. Formalization of such theories is intended to make them easier to understand and also to indicate what logical implications that they reveal—implications that can be assessed through observational research.

Theories as Explanations

As noted above, a theory is an attempt to *explain* something.[3] The statements or propositions of a theory are just sentences that describe both the *assumptions* that are made about how its concepts are related and some logical *prediction* of what can be expected (in reality) if those assumptions are regarded as true. This may sound complicated, but it is really a very common procedure that people use all the time to predict some consequence of a set of prior conditions. To illustrate, consider the commonly observed fact that the American mass media (e.g., movies and television) overwhelmingly produce and disseminate to their audiences entertainment content that is of shallow and limited artistic merit. Categories of content that could be characterized in this way are soap operas, spectator sports, situational comedies, survivor formats, music videos, quiz shows, and so forth. Few people would describe this type of content as truly serious, intellectually challenging, or as having high artistic merit. A similar situation exists in the daily news that is printed or broadcast. Some truly serious stories are delivered, of course, but the majority deal with crime, human interest events, bizarre happenings, accidents, fires, and other topics or information that have a certain "entertainment" value. Indeed, the term "infotainment" has recently come into use to describe the news stories that predominate in the nation's press and newscasts.

How can this be explained? A theory that both describes and explains these practices can be stated in a series of formal propositions. It is essentially an *economic theory* that recognizes the *competitive business environment* within which the media in the U.S. operate. For example, its formal propositions can be stated in the following terms:

An Economic Theory of the Factors that Shape the Content of American News and Entertainment Media

1. The economic (social) institution of the United States is one of *political capitalism.**

2. The most fundamental requirement of that institution is that products or services that are produced and marketed must *make a profit* for their owners and stockholders so as to avoid financial failure.

3. Making a profit requires *maximizing the difference* between the costs of production and the earnings obtained from the product or service.

4. News and entertainment media in the United States are *privately owned enterprises* that operate on those economic principles (with some minor exceptions).

5. Those who manage and produce content for privately owned media *must make a profit* in order to conduct their operations, and without profits they could not continue their activities.

6. The major source of income from which profits are derived is fees and revenues *paid by advertisers* for placing their messages in the print and broadcast media delivering news and entertainment (plus box office receipts in the case of movies).

7. For a medium to earn profits from these sources, it must attract *the largest possible numbers* of paid admissions, subscribers, listeners, or viewers to the content in which the advertisers' announcements are embedded.

8. The types of content that have the greatest appeal to the largest audiences are those that contain entertaining themes of *violence, crime, and sex.*

9. *Therefore*, given the factors and requirements above, producing media news, movies, TV, or other entertainment content that fails to include these themes—so as to appeal to the largest possible audiences—will not attract maximum revenues and is very likely to lead to *financial difficulties* due to limited profits.

*****Definitions of concepts:** A social institution is that complex of norms, laws, customs, and other accepted regularities in a society that are deeply established by social tradition and serve to make the behavior of its population stable and predictable in a broad sphere of behavior. Examples are the society's family pattern, prevailing religion, means of education, political system, and (as discussed) economic activities. Political capitalism is an economic institution in which privately owned enterprises produce marketable products and services by keeping costs of production at a minimum and the price of that which is produced at a maximum in order to maximize profits—but within a system of legal requirements and limits imposed by the political institution. (See Adam Smith, *An Inquiry into the Nature and Causes of the Wealth of Nations* [Chicago: The University of Chicago Press, 1976]. This work in various forms has been published by a number of editors, authors, and interpreters since 1776.)

This theory contains independent concepts—capitalism, profits, income, and so on. It also contains the dependent variable "large audiences." Its propositions describe assumed relationships between them. When a theory is stated formally in this way, the list of the assumptions comes first. They summarize the *independent* conditions, factors, or situations (concepts) that need to be present before some consequence can be expected. Note that the *dependent* consequence (concept or variable) follows in the "therefore" statement. That is, if the assumptions stated can be regarded as true, that concept—"financial difficulties"—should be present as an observable consequence. If a research project were conducted, it would not be difficult to check up to see if the prediction was accurate—to see if news or entertainment media that failed to proceed in these ways, and produced only dull fare, actually did have difficulties in earning profits.

While this theory may seem obvious, it serves to illustrate an important set of rules about theory-building: (1) A "formal" theory is one set forth *as a limited set of related propositions* (as opposed to lengthy descriptive prose). (2) That set of propositions expresses the *relationships that are assumed to exist* between the independent and the dependent concepts incorporated into the theory. (3) The concepts used must refer to situations, events, or conditions that have *observable counterparts* in the realities that are under consideration. Finally, (4) the set of stated assumptions lead to a *predicted consequence* that can be empirically observed. This set of four rules provides a valuable framework for evaluating the merits of any existing or proposed theory of mass communication. As was noted earlier, to "explain" how something works is to set forth what "causes" it.[4] In the economic theory above, the news or entertainment medium would be expected to suffer financially if the conditions described in the stated assumptions were not met.

Theories as Guides to Research

As indicted, a well-formulated theory leads to *the logical conclusion* that certain consequences will be observable—provided one looks in the right place. It is in this way that theories offer *guidelines to researchers* by predicting what they should find if they conduct studies of what has been predicted and can make the appropriate observations.[5]

To illustrate, suppose that a researcher sets out to test the prediction made by the above economic theory about the financial survival of the medium. The researcher is confident that the theory provides an accurate prediction and that the majority of media that fit the assumptions will indeed remain profitable. In designing a research project to test this prediction, the researcher is able to find a large number of media that behave in *exactly the manner described in the theory.* They are all making solid profits. So far, so good! There is a reality that is described by the concepts. Now the researcher looks at the profit reports of others that do not seem to follow the same pattern. To his or her dismay, *a number of those observed actually do show profits, even though they present less entertaining and more serious news.*

Now what? The theory cannot be accepted as valid if it does not predict with reasonable accuracy what happens in reality when the assumptions are met. What to do? The answer is that *it is time for revision and further research.* What might have been overlooked? It finally dawns on the researcher that the medium's actual ownership (a concept) was not considered in the original version of the theory. Some media are operated by organizations that support their financial costs without depending on large circulations or audiences. A corporation or a religious group may support a broadcast station or a printed newspaper to serve its members—thus ensuring the medium's survival without making a profit. If the research project is revised by eliminating such media from the set to be studied, then the theory would make an accurate prediction. If further research establishes that the theory consistently does this, with appropriately selected media for observation, then it has received strong support.

Some theories may seem to be obviously correct—at least at first glance. However, it is not difficult to illustrate how troublesome facts can wreak havoc with a wonderful-looking theory that seems intuitively unassailable. For example, consider a real case. Here is what happened: The Internet is often proclaimed to be yielding significant psychological benefits to its users. A main feature of the Internet that is assumed to lead to these personal benefits is that it is "interactive" for those who use it—as opposed to being "passive," like radio or television. Actively being in contact with others, this Internet theory predicts, leads to greater enjoyment, fulfillment, and *personal satisfaction* on the part of the individual user—in contrast with passive alternatives such as couch potatoes watching television, which leads away from contact with others. Actually, this theory has never been developed formally as a set of assumed propositions. However, it is easy to see its assumptions and the prediction that they provides. In summary, its propositions would be something like this:

1. Activities that provide expanded contacts with other people lead to enjoyment, personal satisfaction, and a reduction in loneliness and depression.
2. Through the use of the Internet, people can expand their contacts with others and increase their level of social participation.
3. Such Internet users can get acquainted and stay in touch with people by email that they would never meet in other ways.

4. Internet users can exchange ideas with others, even strangers, on topics that interest them through bulletin boards and by participating in chat rooms.

5. Therefore: Those who use the Internet extensively in this interactive way will be more socially engaged and less depressed than those more passive unfortunates who are not online.

Obviously, the research question is whether or not this logical prediction is true. In 1998 researchers at Carnegie Mellon University's Human Computer Interaction Institute conducted empirical observations on this issue and were surprised to learn that *exactly the opposite was the case.* Those who regularly used the Internet in the ways described in the theory were more lonely and depressed than non-users.

Was this some trivial study of a few people? No! These were the findings of a large-scale study with a budget of $1.5 million.[5] It was a careful investigation designed by experienced social science researchers. The people involved were studied for two years. These subjects were not extreme "computer geeks." They were normal adults and families who used their computers for at least a few hours a day for communicating with other people by email. What happened was that the subjects reported that they had *less interaction with members of their families* than they had earlier—before using the Internet. They also reported that they *lost friends* (whom they neglected) during the period. In other words, the time spent in electronic communication *reduced their amount of interaction on a face-to-face basis,* and this seemed to bring a consequence of greater depression and loneliness—exactly the opposite of what the researchers had anticipated. On the basis of what was found, would you say that this theory needs further work?

Theories as Practical Tools

The answer to whether theories have practical importance in the "real world" is that in almost any field they are essential to developing *applications* that work to solve many kinds of problems. For example, routinely, in everyday life and probably without realizing that we are doing so, we make daily use of valid theories from many fields that have provided profound benefits. Every time you turn on a light, drive a car, take a pill, enjoy air conditioning, buy a new CD, or drink water without serious health consequences, you are engaging in activities that would not be possible without the existence of valid theories that led to these applications. They may be from physics, medicine, music, public health, or some other specialized field. But the bottom line is that modern life would not be possible if no one had developed the theories that have provided the explanations and guides to research leading to the products and procedures on which we are so dependent.

But what about mass communication? That has little to do with such obvious products of scientific theories, such as sending space vehicles to Mars, curing dread diseases, or predicting tomorrow's weather. The answer is that all of the theories developed in the physical and biological sciences were developed by bright human beings who painstakingly observed factual evidence over long periods of time—sometimes centuries—sorting out what set of antecedent (independent) conditions seemed to be causing which observable (dependent) consequences. That is exactly what people in the much newer field of mass communication are attempting to do. Moreover, as subsequent chapters in the present book will indicate, they are having some success.

In each physical, biological, and social science, someone eventually put together a systematic explanation (a theory) of how things worked in whatever they were investigating. Sometimes they got it wrong, and their explanation could not be verified by further observations. In that case, the theory had to be abandoned. In other cases, they got it partially right, and others had to improve the explanation through further observation and correction of the original theory. Eventually, however, theories were tested and validated in many fields to yield the technological wonders of our time, the remarkable advances that have extended human life for decades, led to an understanding of many forms of human behavior, and even predicted devastating hurricanes in a way that allowed the saving of many human lives. In short, such theories were *enormously practical.* There is really no alternative to using that same approach in mass communication if we want to understand the way in which our mass media and their content influence our lives, individually, socially, and culturally.

The question was raised as to whether the development of theories of mass communication is important. The answer is that, if we are to understand the problems and processes of modern society, it is critical. For example, taken together, more people in the United States work in businesses and industries dependent on mass communication than in any other segment of the economy. During the 1800s, the majority of people made their livings in activities associated with *agriculture.* By the mid-1900s, that had changed to *manufacturing*. People used machines to make "things." Today the information industries dominate. People work with *words and other symbols*. Vast numbers of people work in jobs that are either directly or indirectly dependent on the existence of newspapers, magazines, books, radio, television, VCRs, CDs, DVDs, the movies, and the Internet. All of these ever-changing media present information and entertainment that come to the attention of each of hundreds of millions of people for several hours every day. That is true not only in the United States but in virtually all parts of the industrialized world. The only exceptions are those who are desperately poor and live in the most remote regions. The influence of these media and what they present is under constant review, analysis, comment, discussion, and criticism. For the most part, however, all of this attention is dominated by guesses, speculation, and opinion, rather than by solid understanding of how things actually work.

It is essential, then, that media scholars continue to develop valid understandings and explanations of the nature of those influences and the processes by which they are brought about. In other words, theories of mass communication are badly needed to help us all sort out the benefits, costs, and other consequences of the media that we all use and support. Because of its importance, then, the study of mass communication theory has become a lively area in which researchers and scholars continuously try out new ideas in order to push forward the cutting edge of understanding.

As will be clear in the present book, some of the theories presented in subsequent chapters have been extensively studied for decades and have stood the test of research. However, not all theories of mass communication that will be discussed have as yet been tested thoroughly. For some, initial research has been done—and the results seem promising. Others are in an even more tentative stage. That is, they are new and have yet to be extensively investigated and verified by research. But those that are as yet only partially tested, or even those that are newly formulated, do have value. They offer at least *candidate* explanations and predictions about media processes of effects for researchers to probe.

At least some of the theories that have withstood the test of research are being used for practical purposes in the mass media–related professions. To illustrate, imagine that you are now employed in the advertising and marketing department of a company making household products. Your boss has just asked you to design a communication strategy to help market one of the company's new products. Assume that it is a much improved liquid for removing stains from clothing. The first thing is to try and understand the way in which any new product will be adopted by the public. Are such adoptions made on a random basis among a population, or do they follow some predictable pattern? Say, for example, you recall hearing about a communication theory called the Diffusion of Innovation Theory (which you will read about in Chapter 18). You check out what the theory says about the conditions under which such a new product will be taken up over time by those members of the public that use this type of thing. You discover a crucial role is played by the media in *providing information* about an innovation like your product—leading to a so-called "S-shaped curve of adoption." You also discover the importance of "personal influence" on buying decisions as a part played by *opinion leaders*. This is discussed in the "Two-Step Flow of Communication Theory" (Chapter 13), which explains what happens when people turn to others that they think are knowledgeable for advice about new products. These theories prove to be useful in designing a promotional campaign. You develop strategies for identifying and designing messages in specific media, aimed at opinion leaders who are likely to influence the purchasing decisions of those they advise. That will probably have a higher probability of success than just randomly placing advertising messages in various media.

Or, take a rather different example. Your boss comes in a few weeks later and asks you to figure out how a new laundry detergent should be advertised. You recall mass communication theories that predict how people of various social and personal characteristics *selectively attend to different types of media content* as they seek information consistent with their needs. So who needs laundry detergent? Obviously it is not kids or most adult males! Common sense tells you that it is largely housewives who use such products. But what type of media content do such women select? What is most likely to gain their attention? That is the key. Is it sports programs? Professional wrestling? Unlikely. The answer, revealed by much media research guided by the "Selective and Limited Influences Theory" (Chapter 10), indicates that the best bet for such consumers are *daytime serials and romance movies*. Bingo! You advise the client to advertise the new product on daytime serials and romance movies on television. You develop ad copy showing the wonderful things that the product does. Sales are brisk.

Generally, then, mass communication theories can, at least in some cases, have significant practical as well as academic research value. Indeed, professional communicators have been using some of them in one way or another for many years—often without knowing their origins. Others have been only recently formulated and have not yet been fully evaluated. These may offer less in the way of immediate practical applications. However, they do offer guidelines for further systematic research to see if they really are good explanations. In time they will either be validated or rejected.

In this book the background and research origins of each of the theories presented is discussed briefly in its chapter. It is then summarized in a basically formal propositional form. Where relevant research has been done to try to assess the theory, those findings are summarized. Admittedly, each chapter is only a summary of the major points and ideas. This may provide an oversimplification. However, these summaries have been prepared for the convenience of those who want an *overview* of the foundations for development of mass communication theory. A full mastery of each theory's origins, background, research support, and other details requires turning to the *original documents* where it was first presented and, in some cases, the subsequent technical literature that discusses its testing and validity. At least some of those sources are listed in the references provided for each chapter. No attempt has been made to provide a full report of all studies ever done.

Generally, then, theories are not mysterious, highly abstract, or difficult to understand. They are practical descriptions of how something works. They are explanations and logical predictions that can be checked out with relevant research. Some are already tested; others are partially so. Still others are new and remain to be confirmed. These new theories add to the cutting edge of our knowledge and will come under study by scholars. But all discussed in the present book provide systematic descriptions of some feature of the process or effects of mass communication. In that sense, they can lead to a better understanding of what they address rather than depending on popular lore or speculation.

WHERE DO THEORIES COME FROM?

It was noted above that theories can guide research by providing logical predictions of what facts should be there for investigators to look for if the theory is valid. But research plays another very critical role. Often, research *generates* theories. That is, in many cases, theories are formulated after some sort of scholarly investigation shows that an explanation of the facts uncovered is needed—or could be formulated in a certain way. Thus, theories are not just "hunches" that people come up with out of thin air. Ordinary citizens often use hunches, guesses, and speculations based on personal opinion when they are seeking to explain something and refer to them as "theories." None of these kinds of "explanations" represents theories as this concept is used in virtually every form of science.

Theories Derived from Research

A theory may begin in the mind of a researcher as a tentative explanation about whatever he or she has been studying. But no one would call it a theory at this initial stage. It has to be put together in a systematic form—as a written set of descriptive and explanatory statements—before it can be called a theory. In other words, theories are usually developed after some researcher has studied a particular kind of behavior (or other type of phenomenon in his or her specialty) and has started to gain some insight as to what might be causing whatever he or she has observed. In many cases, this early research process is not based on experiments, surveys, or other forms of "quantitative" analysis. Ideas for theories are often generated by those engaging in "qualitative" studies, where researchers conduct extended observations on an informal basis. These can initially identify what concepts may be important and give clues as to how they might be related. Then, when these issues have been identified, an initial version of the theory can be put together so that more systematic research can be undertaken. This is often called a process of *induction*, and it has been an important part of the scientific method for centuries.

An example of how a theory can have its inductive beginning in some sort of systematic investigation is the case of an early theory—the two-step flow of communication (Chapter 13). The theory—which abundant subsequent research has shown is valid—was an unexpected outgrowth of a large-scale research project on the informational and persuasive roles of the mass media in the 1940 national presidential campaign (Franklin D. Roosevelt vs. Wendell Wilkie). Researchers repeatedly asked several hundred people in Erie County, Ohio, to indicate from which medium they received most of their information about the political issues and personalities in the forthcoming presidential election. They were convinced that people learned about the candidates and issues from radio, newspapers, and magazines (TV was not available at the time).

As it turned out, many people mentioned a *very different source* of information—one that the researchers had not anticipated. That source was "other people." Those under study were getting a lot of information about the election by *word-of-mouth* from friends, family, fellow workers, neighbors, and so on. In fact, some voters got far more information about the candidates and issues from such interpersonal communication than from the mass media.

The investigators immediately recognized the importance of this unanticipated channel of information and went on to study such person-to-person communication in depth. In an informal way, they formulated a tentative theory (inductively) that predicted a "two-step" flow of information—from the mass media *to certain kinds of individuals* who paid close attention to mass communications—and from them on *to a less attentive larger audience*, via word-of-mouth transmission. Guided by this induced theory, this type of communication came under intense study by quantitative researchers. Various testable hypotheses were *deduced* (logically derived) from its basic propositions. As more and more research evidence on the two-step flow was uncovered, the theory received a great deal of support. Today it is recognized as an important and valid explanation of how certain kinds of information spreads through a society after first being presented by the mass media (see Chapter 13).

Another example of a theory more recently induced from empirical research is that presented in Chapter 23 ("A Theory of Collateral Media Instruction, Audience Incidental Learning and Flawed Constructions of Reality"). In this case, the developers of the research had completed a large-scale study of more than 1,300 teenage high school youths in twelve countries. They found that (1) most of the youths studied had negative beliefs and attitudes toward ordinary Americans and (2) that they were heavily exposed to U.S.-produced movies, TV programming, and other entertainment products in which the lifestyles of people who lived in the United States were depicted. As Chapter 23 explains, the authors inductively developed the explanation that this exposure to movies and TV dramas—with their emphasis on violence, crime, and sex—provided *unrealistic but unintended lessons* about Americans that were quite negative. Thus, the youths studied had few or no actual contacts with ordinary Americans, but they unwittingly learned about them while being entertained. It is quite possible that news stories from the U.S. with similar sensational emphases may also be bringing about similar results. Further research will have to be conducted to test this theory over time.

The lesson here is that the relationship between research (qualitative and quantitative), as it is commonly conducted within the rules of science, and theory is a *reciprocal* one. That is a fancy way of saying that it is a "two-way street." The need for a new theory becomes apparent as a result of one or more (qualitative or quantitative) research studies, and the investigators begin to put together a possible explanation of what has been found in the form of clear statements, concepts, and descriptions. Then more research is done using quantitative procedures to see if the tentative theory can reliably and accurately predict the relationship between independent conditions and dependent consequences (to see if it predicts and explains what is being studied). If so, the theory is increasingly seen as a valid explanation and as a tool for guiding still more research to make doubly sure that it is correctly formulated. If all works out, then, the theory consistently describes, explains, and predicts what seems to cause specific kinds of events and consequences in the real world. If that is the case, the theory has potential practical application for the people who deal with those kinds of events.

Theories Derived from Ideologies

It is important for the student of mass communications to understand that there is another very different (and controversial) category of theories that do not fit what has been said thus far. These are theories that are not derived from, or tested by, conducting research within a scientific framework *but are obtained from some sort of ideology*. An ideology is a set of coordinated beliefs about the nature of human life, culture, or the world. The term "ideology" comes from the word "idea" (a concept or representation) and "logos" (a body of wisdom or knowledge).

The unique thing about ideologies is that, for their believers, *they require no "proof"* in the sense of scientifically gathered empirical evidence. An ideology is unquestionably accepted by its advocates *a priori* ("from what comes before"). This is a logical process in which consequences are deduced from principles that are *assumed to be true, ahead of time* (before research) as the "true explanation" or situation.

The use of an ideology to derive an explanation that needs no empirical verification can be illustrated easily. Most people are familiar with the Book of Genesis, which offers an explanation of the origins of the earth and all that is on the planet. It includes an account of the creation of human beings. Accepting that explanation is an *a priori* act of religious faith. If the principle of an omnipotent God is accepted, then it logically follows that He was the Creator and "intelligent designer" of the heavens and the earth and all the creatures thereon. That form of reasoning has been the guiding perspective for billions of people for centuries, who have regarded it as a flawless explanation of the origins of the earth, its animals, and humankind.

Accepting this creationist account makes it *unnecessary* to examine empirical evidence gathered by geologists, paleontologists, or other scientific researchers. Conclusions can be reached directly from the ideology alone, without all of that scientific evidence. Indeed, the empirical evidence gathered by large numbers of such scientists poses a problem because often it offers *alternative* interpretations and support for very different explanations. People must decide on their own whether they accept the creationist accounts or the theories of origins offered by science. If they do accept the former, they do so because they have already subscribed to (accepted as true) the ideology provided by sacred writings.

One need have no quarrel with those who prefer creationist explanations, or those of other ideologies, over those of science. Such ideologies offer alternatives to theories developed from the methods and requirements of science, and for many people the explanations that they provide are intellectually and emotionally satisfying. For others, the opposite is true, and their preference is for the theories developed from scientific research. This situation has generated fierce debates over a long period of time, and they promise to continue into the foreseeable future.

The point here is that some theories of mass communication *have their origins in ideologies.* To illustrate the nature of this type of explanation, examples of such theories have been included in this book. One example is the critical cultural theory (Chapter 21). It offers an interesting perspective on the owners and managers who control the mass media, the ways in which they exercise that control, and the consequences for people in the audience and for society as a whole. The intellectual foundations for this theory come *a priori* from the political and economic interpretations (ideologies) originally set forth by Karl Marx.

To illustrate the use of ideology as a source for the critical cultural theory more fully, a brief review of certain assumptions made by Karl Marx will be helpful: Beginning in the 1840s, when the Industrial Revolution was well under way, Marx put together an elaborate interpretation of history. He portrayed it as a constant struggle between "haves" and "have nots." He described how (early) factory owners regularly *exploited* (made use of) workers in order to increase their own power and profits—while deliberately keeping the employees in a state of dependency and deprivation. He described how those in power manipulated laws, religion, art, and other features of the society and culture to keep workers in a state of subjugation while (at the same time) convincing them that their society was just and fair.[7]

Critical cultural theory, derived from such interpretations, is based on similar *a priori* assumptions. The theory maintains that those in control of the mass media today are exploiting (making use of) their audiences by exercising *hegemony* (powerful control) over their ideas and beliefs by using mass communications. They do this by making sure that the content of the news and entertainment media keeps people believing that *capitalism and democracy are the best of all possible conditions.*

That may not seem consistent with Marx's attack on capitalism, but those who advance the theory show how it is. Those who are in power want, say the supporters of the theory, to keep their control over their industries to maximize their profits. Therefore, they make sure that the political system that protects their enterprises, profits, and advantages (capitalism and democracy) stays in place. Praise of democracy and support of capitalism by those who control the media, say advocates of critical cultural theory, are accomplished by shaping the content of soap operas, the news, movies, magazines, and so on. This is done in such as way as to convince the public that what they have now is the ideal political and economic system—and that even thinking about alternatives would be unpatriotic. Thus, by controlling media content and shaping people's beliefs in this way, power and profits are protected.

The champions of critical cultural theory go on to maintain that capitalism and democracy are essentially *unfair* because only a few have power and because wealth is not evenly distributed. Thus, guidelines for designing a fair society (essentially derived from basic Marxian ideology) are given a contemporary interpretation. The conclusion, logically drawn, that media controllers are *exploiting* audiences is used to explain why the mass media offer much of their content in support of democracy and capitalism. It is clear that systematic research based on empirical observation, with careful attention to measurement of variables, has played no real part in either developing or testing this theory.

While such ideological theories come from a different source than those derived from a basis of scientific research, they do offer interesting perspectives and bases for lively debates. It is difficult at best to see how they offer guides to research, because the conclusions are accepted as true *a priori*, that is, *without checking any empirical evidence*. Moreover, new evidence is not likely to change such theories. Like the creationist accounts, their validity is in the mind of the believer, rather than open to reassessment on the basis of new research findings.

How, then, does one decide which theories to accept? Is it better to accept those derived from research or those from ideology? The best answer that can be provided is that it is a matter of *personal preference*. There must be room for all ideas in the intellectual debate about the process and effects of mass communication. Most media scholars subscribe to the view that, in the long run, those theories that will prevail will be those that provide (1) the *most accurate descriptions of reality*, (2) the *best explanations of why situations occur*, and (3) those that make logical predictions that *can be verified by systematic and unbiased observation*. Others that cannot survive these criteria will in time be discarded. Essentially, this is a statement of the "marketplace of ideas" that John Milton described very well in his *Aeropagitica*—a paper he wrote in 1644—defending the right to publish one's ideas freely:

> Give me the liberty to know, to utter and to argue freely according to conscience. . . . Though all the winds of doctrine were let loose to play upon the earth, so Truth be in the field. . . . Let her and falsehood grapple; whoever knew Truth put to the worse in a free and open encounter?[8]

HOW DO SCHOLARS DEVELOP NEW THEORIES OF MASS COMMUNICATION?

How do scholars proceed when they set out to develop a theory explaining some feature or consequence of mass communication? As the foregoing discussions explain, the first step is *conceptualization*. This means identifying and defining the major concepts that will be a part of the explanations that will be developed and tested. Some that are already available can be identified from existing theories, but others may have to be developed for the new theory. An appropriate place to start, however, is to begin with a careful explanation of the *process* of mass communication. That means, in part, identifying the channels of communication that are, or are not, mass media. The section that follows focuses on that issue.

Before World War II, there were no academic programs offering degrees in mass communication as a specialty. Some social scientists had turned their attention to the influences of the media, both on individuals and on the society and culture as a whole. But, for the most part, their efforts were seen as contributing to knowledge in psychology, sociology, and political science—rather than as efforts undertaken to develop a distinct body of knowledge specifically focused on the processes and effects of mass communication. There were also well-established schools of journalism, but those degree programs were focused on training people for work as reporters, editors, and related roles in the vocational field of gathering and reporting the news. However, after the war there grew an increasing recognition that mass communications were playing an important part in providing influences on beliefs, attitudes, and behavior on the part of ordinary people in the society as a whole.

It was at that point, with that understanding, beginning in the late 1940s and early 1950s—and especially with the development and adoption of television—that interest grew in developing mass communication as an academic specialty in its own right. During the 1950s, a number of universities added programs that over the years became Colleges, Schools, and Departments of Mass Communication, with a clear focus on the study of the media and their influences on individual and social life.

Conceptualizing Mass Communication

Scholars from the social sciences, such as Paul Lazarsfeld, Robert Merton, Harold Lasswell, and Carl Hovland, led this movement. Immediately, they faced the task of *conceptualizing* what mass communication was actually all about. One of the pioneers developing the new field was Wilbur Schramm, who put together one of the first textbooks specifically devoted to the new discipline.[9] In that book of readings, he brought together a number of important research reports that helped in defining of what the study of mass communication was to consist. One of those reports described in very simple terms the major concepts that would provide the foundation of the new field. In 1948, Harold Lasswell, who had put the definition together, maintained the following:

A convenient way to describe an act of communication is to answer the following questions:

Who

Says What

In What Channel

To Whom

With What Effect[10]

Even today, that ultra simple statement sets forth the basic concepts that are at the heart of the study of the processes and effects of mass communication. Thus, the main areas of major concern are still the *source*, the message *content*, the *channel* or medium, the *audience*, and, of course, the influences or *effects* that take place as a result.

During that formative period, another way to look at communication was described by two physicists who were working on communication problems from a mechanical or physical perspective. During the late 1940s, Dr. Claude E. Shannon was a physicist working in Bell Telephone Laboratories. Drawing on the 1894 work of Boltzman in statistical physics, papers by Szilard published in 1925, as well as more contemporary scientists, Shannon developed a formulation to describe *physical events* in the accuracy of transmission of information in a mechanical system such as the electrical impulses that move through a telephone line. Its basic concept was the idea of "entropy." The term *entropy* originally was developed as a concept in thermodynamics. It referred to a measure of the amount of energy in a system that is not available for doing work. That is, entropy in this sense referred to *inefficiency* in a thermodynamic system. Entropy had the implication of *random* rather than structured energy. The greater the entropy, the lesser the efficiency of the system. Entropy defined in this way can be expressed in mathematical terms.

In 1949, in collaboration with Warren Weaver, Shannon published *The Mathematical Theory of Communication*.[11] At first, this theory focused on the technical problem of transmitting information (not to be confused with meaning) along a telephone wire. Later it was expanded to a more general theory of communication describing the accuracy of transmitting any pattern of signals used to interpret language symbols. The general idea of entropy as "randomness" became a central concept in this new formulation. The greater the entropy in such a system—that is, the more the randomness in a message—the more difficult it would be for a receiving person to "make sense" out of it when trying to understand the patterned signals being transmitted.

In an analogous sense to the usage in thermodynamics, then, entropy could be conceptualized as a measure of the *efficiency* of a system (as in a code or language) in transmitting messages effectively. The higher the entropy factor, the more difficult it is to achieve accuracy between the sender and the receiver of a message. Entropy, therefore, refers in this context to "uncertainty" in meanings that can be resolved in the decoding phase of reception of a message. The lower the randomness in the signals received, the more likely it is that the receiving party can interpret accurately the meanings intentionally placed into the system.

To portray the problem in simple terms, these theorists described the act of communication as a movement of information by a medium from a "source" to a "destination." The source selects a desired "message" (a set of written or spoken words with related meanings), which a "transmitter" "encodes" into patterned "signals" that can be sent over a communication channel (like a telephone wire, radio waves, or even just over air as in interpersonal communication) from the transmitter to a receiver. The receiver reverses the process of the transmitter and decodes the patterned signals back into a message that can be understood (as meanings) by the "destination."

Shannon and Weaver recognized that, in both a mechanical and semantic sense, things could always go wrong. Indeed, they could go wrong at virtually any point in the communication process. To describe problems between source and destination, they used the term "noise." Noise referred to any category of events, whether physical or behavioral, that increased rather than decreased entropy (thereby reducing the accuracy of the message as understood by the destination).

They developed a simple graphic model of a communication system that explained their system of concepts in linear terms. In this communication system, information moved in a straight line from a starting point at the source through the transmitter and the channel to the receiver and then to the final destination. Expressed as a graphic representation, the Shannon and Weaver model incorporated their central concepts, as shown in Figure 1.[12]

Beginning during the 1950s, Shannon and Weaver's central concepts—source, encoding, transmitter, signal, receiver, decoding, destination, and noise—found an enthusiastic audience among mass communication scholars who were trying to develop the field. These communication theorists were less interested in Shannon and Weaver's mathematics referring to such concepts as *entropy*, or in the physical difficulties involved in mechanical communication systems. However, their linear model did seem to describe the communication process as used with mass media. Many variations of Shannon and Weaver's basic, graphic, linear model were developed over the years in attempts to conceptualize the process of mass communication.

Essentially, this early graphic description and explanation of the communication process can be summarized in a verbally expressed set of propositions, as indicated in the following terms:

Shannon and Weaver's Information Theory

1. Human communication [including mass communication] can be conceptualized as beginning with a "source" or sender who selects a desired message that he or she wants to send to one or more other people.
2. The source makes use of a transmitter to change (encode) this message into patterned signals—corresponding to words and other symbols that the sender believes will arouse the intended meanings of the original message on the part of a destination person or persons.
3. The patterned signals—making up the encoded message—are transmitted by sending them over a channel capable of moving the signals across the intervening space to a receiver.
4. The receiver decodes the patterned signals back into a message of words or other symbols that can be interpreted and understood by the destination (person or persons).
5. Various kinds of "noise," of either a mechanical or semantic type, can limit accuracy by distorting the reception and interpretation of the message. Thus, "noise" in a process of human communication is the semantic counterpart of excessive "entropy" in a physical system.

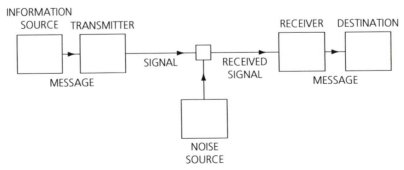

FIGURE 1 Shannon and Weaver's Conceptualization of the Communication Process

1. The information *SOURCE* selects a desired *MESSAGE*.

2. The *TRANSMITTER* changes (encodes) this message into the *SIGNAL*.

3. The *SIGNAL* is sent over the channel to the *RECEIVER*.

4. The *RECEIVER* changes (decodes) the transmitted *SIGNAL* back into a *MESSAGE*.

5. Various distortions and errors (*NOISE*) enter the process to reduce accuracy.

The concepts of these pioneers, then, became important as "building blocks" in attempts to develop theories of the mass communication process and ways in which media content has influences on audiences. In many ways, these early ideas are still valuable today.

A Formal Definition of Mass Communication

It was the work of the early scholars that made it possible to formulate a precise definition of mass communication. At first glance, a formal definition of this familiar part of our daily world may seem unnecessary. After all, we are already intimately familiar with movies, newspapers, television sets, and so on. But when people use film, print, broadcasting, or computers to communicate with large audiences, what is actually happening? Do all the media operate according to the same underlying principles of communication—or is each medium unique in some way? And are the principles underlying mass communication different from those for a face-to-face conversation between two people? These questions are critical to understanding the nature of mass communication.

We cannot define mass communication in a quick and simple way because each medium includes its own special kinds of communicators, technologies, groups, kinds of content, types of audiences, and effects. To develop a good definition of mass communication, we must take all these aspects into account and proceed one step at a time, describing each of the major features before pulling them together. In the sections that follow, that is exactly our strategy. We shall look at each "stage" in the mass communication process before combining them into an overall basic definition. The first step is to explain how and why mass communication is a *linear process.*

A LINEAR PROCESS Mass communication, with traditional print, broadcast, and film media, can be conceptualized within what theorists call a basic "linear model." We noted earlier that this was the way that Shannon and Weaver defined communication. What the term "linear" implies is that the message originates at one point and is received at another different point (or simultaneously at many different points) in a basic *one-way process*—without ongoing interaction between the parties during the transmission and reception. For example, when people in a large audience read their paper, or view their favorite national TV news anchor or film star in a movie, the transmitted message is going only one way, and nothing is going back—at least in an immediate sense. In other words, there is no "simultaneous interaction" between the parties, such as that which takes place when two people talk face to face, on the telephone, or (in some situations) on the Internet.[13]

AN ABSENCE OF DIRECT ROLE-TAKING AND FEEDBACK More specifically, in linear communication, the anchorperson or actor who is serving as a source simply has no way of looking directly at any specific receiving individual in the audience, assessing what that person might or might not react to or understand. Consequently, that source cannot modify what is being said in an ongoing manner in order to increase understanding on the part of the receiver. Technically, this condition is described by saying that in mass communication there is no opportunity for "role-taking," which is an important part of the interpersonal communication process.

Similarly, in this form of communication, nothing is immediately *sent back* by the receiver to the source during the process. A receiver may react with facial expressions, bodily movements, or verbal comments. However, in mass communication these are all invisible to the source. Thus, there is no ongoing and immediate "feedback" as is the case in interpersonal communication. Thus, *mass communication is a linear process that flows one way from the source initiating the message to a multitude of receivers who are anonymous to the source.*

It is true that after the communication has taken place there may be *delayed feedback* in the form of later phone calls to the station, letters to the editor, assessments of ratings or other research results. Or, even before the broadcast or printing of the daily newspaper, there may be research assessments of the nature and interests of the audience. But these are outside the actual communication process as it takes place between the professional communicator and an individual member of his or her audience receiving the message.

For the reasons stated above, then, a linear model can be used to describe the basics of the mass communication process. That formulation is in many ways an elaborate version of the one developed in the 1940s by Harold Lasswell and the graphic model used by Claude Shannon and Warren Weaver. Each stage is far more complex than either of the earlier versions, but essentially they include the same steps and consist of the following linear stages or steps that provide a formal definition:

Stages in the Mass Communication Process: A Formal Definition

1. Mass communication begins with senders who are "professional communicators" whose principal objective is to *realize a profit*. They *decide on the meanings and goals of a message* to be presented to an audience via their particular medium. (That message may be a news report, an advertising campaign, a movie, or some other media presentation that can be expected to aid in achieving profits.)*

2. The intended *meanings are encoded* by production specialists (a news team, film company, a magazine staff, etc.). The encoding process includes not only the selection of verbal and nonverbal symbols but also the special effects that are possible with a particular medium (sound, graphics, color, etc.).

3. The *message is transmitted* through the use of specialized media technologies characteristic of print, film, broadcasting, or digital systems to disseminate it as widely as possible.

4. Large and diverse (mass) audiences of individual receivers *attend to* the media and *perceive* the incoming messages in very selective ways.

5. Individual receivers *decode*—that is, construct *interpretations* of the message—in such a way that they experience subjective meanings, which are, to at least some degree, parallel to those intended by the professional communicators.

6. As a result of experiencing media messages, receivers are *influenced* in some way. That is, the messages have some effect on their feelings, thoughts, or actions.

*It can be noted that in non-capitalistic societies, where the media may be owned and controlled by government, the profit motive may be replaced by the objective of achieving or consolidating political power. Thus, the definition above is one that applies mainly to Western and similar societies where private enterprises seek profits from their mass communication activities.

The last stage (number 6) in the definition above indicates that, as a result of interpreting the meaning of the message, receivers in the audience may be *changed* in some way, in terms of their feelings, thoughts, or actions. The changes may or may not be immediately visible, and they can range from trivial to profound. Most are minor. For example, a person may learn some relatively inconsequential new facts by hearing a weather report on the radio or be amused by reading a comic strip. However, exposure to the content of mass communications can also change individuals in far more significant ways. Under some circumstances, it can influence their beliefs, opinions, and attitudes—altering their thinking about their lifestyle, a public issue, or a political party preference. Moreover, meanings aroused by media messages can alter people's *actions*—influencing them to buy, donate, dress differently, give up or start smoking, vote, go on a diet, or bring about many other forms of behavior.

Each of the six stages we have described must be part of a succinct definition of mass communication. They can be brought together to form a concise formal definition in this way:

Mass communication is a linear process in which professional communicators use media to design and disseminate messages widely, rapidly, and continually to arouse intended meanings in large, diverse, and selectively attending and interpreting audiences in attempts to influence them in a variety of ways.

With this rather complex definition in mind, we must ask which media really are (or are not) mass media. This is not an idle question because it sets *boundaries* on what needs to be studied in a course devoted to understanding mass communication and mass media.

Which Media Are Mass Media?

Is the telephone a mass medium? How about a fax machine or personal computers linked in a local area network? What about a large museum? Should we include rock concerts, theatrical performances, church services, or even parades in our study of mass communication? After all, each of these human activities is a form of communication. For our purposes, whether they are *mass media* depends on whether they can carry out the process of mass communication we have just defined.

To be true to our definition, we would have to conclude that talking on the telephone is *not* really "mass" communication, because the audience is not large and diverse; usually there is only one person at each end of the line. Furthermore, telephone users usually are not "professional communicators." The same is true of a fax machine with phone lines or even a set of personal computers linked within a given company on which individuals exchange email messages. A museum does not participate in mass communication because it does not provide "rapid dissemination" with "media." Neither does a rock concert qualify, because it does not disseminate messages "over distance"; it is a form of direct communication to physically present audiences. Similarly, no situation in which live performers and an audience can see each other directly—in a theater or church, at a sports event, or parade—is an example of mediated communication. Large-scale advertising by direct mail might qualify—except that it is not really "continual."

Thus, our definition turns out to be relatively rigorous. It enables us to set definite boundaries on what can be included and studied as a medium and process of mass communication. By definition, none of the activities listed above qualifies, although all of them can potentially arouse meanings and influence people.

By exercising the criteria set forth in our definition, then, we can identify precisely what we consider to be mass media in the present book. The major mass media are *print* (including books, magazines, and newspapers), *film* (principally commercial motion pictures), and *broadcasting* (mainly radio and television but also several associated forms such as cable, VCRs and DVDs, and in some cases certain *computer systems*, such as the Internet—but only when used in a point-to-multipoint manner by professional communicators to communicate linearly to large audiences, which does not happen often). Although other kinds of media are important and worthy of study, the focus of our attention will be on those that closely fit our definition of mass communication.

WHAT THEORIES ARE INCLUDED IN THIS BOOK?

Six distinct sets or categories of theories important in the study of mass communication are explained in the chapters that follow. Overall, these six parts include a total of some two dozen theories related to mass communication. Some are historical; most are contemporary. Classifying them into categories is difficult. Each theory was developed at a different time for a different purpose by people in different disciplines who did not coordinate their work with that of others. The result is a hodgepodge of well-tested, partially tested, and new relatively untested tentative explanations of various (and often unrelated) aspects of the communication process—or of different kinds of influences that mass communication can have on individuals and society. Some of the theories presented are broad; others are narrowly focused. Some are widely accepted; others are controversial. But in each case, the origins and at least some relevant related research for each theory is summarized in this book in a simple way. In each case, a set of formal assumptions and a predictive statement are set forth, where possible, that summarize what the theory is about—what it attempts to explain. As noted, such summaries are by necessity *simplifications*. For each, references are provided where the theory can be studied in greater depth.

Backgrounds and Origins from Philosophy and Social Science

Part One discusses four theories drawn from philosophy and the social sciences that need to be understood as *intellectual foundations* for developing an understanding of the process and effects of mass communication. These theories were originally developed in scholarly disciplines that were not specifically focused on the study of mass communication. These disciplines are *philosophy, psychology, sociology, and political science*. While these foundation theories do not deal solely or even directly with the mass media, they do they provide important explanations of individual or collective forms of human behavior that play a critical part in the way we contact and experience the content of the media. For that reason, they need to be understood by anyone seriously interested in how the media select and process their content, and how people attend to media presentations, apprehend their meaning in some way, and are influenced by that exposure.

More specifically, the first of these intellectual foundations are contributions from philosophy, which have been twofold. Chapter 3 ("The Contributions of Philosophy") explains how one of these, *the scientific method*, is now used with appropriate modifications in a broad spectrum of sciences—including mass communication—to develop and test all kinds of theories. The chapter also discusses how human beings come to "know reality" not only from their personal sensory contacts with the physical and social world but also as social constructions of reality obtained *through communication with other people*—which now includes that which they obtain from the mass media. This has profound consequences for peoples' experiences with mass communication.

The contribution of political science is discussed in Chapter 4. This discipline is devoted to the study of the origins, functioning, and consequences of governments. There are many kinds of governmental structures, but many political scientists believe that the *relationship between rulers and the ruled* is the pivotal situation that influences behavior within any of them. That relationship depends on what the founders of the field initially referred to as the "general will." The term "*vox populi*" (the voice of the people) expresses a similar idea. If rulers lose the support of those governed, those who try to lead will have problems. Essentially, people do not see them as legitimate.

In modern terms, *public opinion* is used to describe this critical factor. According to classical political theorists, rulers and governments stand or fall, depending on whether they are supported by public opinion or not. Thus, political science has long studied the role of public opinion, including its formation and structure in shaping the relationship between rulers and the ruled. With the arrival of newspapers, and later more contemporary media—and then public opinion polling—this aspect of government assumed greater and greater importance. The study of public opinion and (especially) the role played by media, then, has been much enriched by the scholarly contributions and research of political science. Today, the mass media play a truly significant role in its formation, change, and influences. For that reason, *public opinion theory* (as discussed in Chapter 4) provides an important part of the intellectual background of media studies.

Another intellectual foundation is discussed in Chapter 5 ("The Contributions of Psychology"). This is also a twofold contribution. During the twentieth century, psychologists developed deep insights explaining *the processes of perception and learning*—fundamental for gaining ideas from the media. In addition, psychology has developed theories of what is called *cognitive processing*. The term "cognitive" refers to what laypersons would call "activities of the mind." Thus, *cognitive processing theory* (discussed in Chapter 5) provides an explanation of the way each person "makes sense" out of the messages he or she encounters from others—including those obtained from the media. Each does so by filtering the information through such factors as selective attention patterns, tastes, interests, attitudes, prior beliefs, and many other personal factors—and then formulating its meanings.

The contributions of still another related discipline are set forth in Chapter 6 (the contributions of sociology). In fact, the systematic and scientific study of the nature and influences of mass communication actually started early in this field. In a broader sense, sociology has contributed theories of the way in which society is structured. This is important to the audiences of the mass media. *Mass society theory* (discussed in Chapter 6) indicates that each of us is located within a web of social relationships that either facilitate close contacts with other people or tend to isolate us from them. Thus, the conditions of mass society pose conditions that lead us to be more dependent on information gained from media sources than from close personal associates or family members. These factors have important consequences for the way that media content can influence us.

Early Theories of the Effects of Mass Communication

The second category or set of theories included in this book consists of four theories that focus more directly on mass communication. That is, each was developed many years ago in the search for understanding of either the process or the influences of mass communication. Chapters 7 and 8 discuss the theories of James Bryce and of Walter Lippman. Both were scholars who sought to understand the functioning and consequences of the mass media of their time (newspapers) on both the society broadly and on individuals. In Chapter 9, what is undoubtedly the earliest conceptualization of the process and effects of mass communication (the *magic bullet theory*) is set forth. It was in a certain sense developed by sociologists in the late 1800s, when the era of the newly arrived mass newspaper was at its height. (It was never formalized as it is presented in this book.) It was not long, however, before this theory of powerful and uniform effects came to be discredited. It was replaced with a much more modern one (*the selective and limited influences theory*) more solidly supported by research, indicating that the influences of the media were much more modest (presented in Chapter 10).

Still another major question that needed to be addressed was why people turned so avidly to mass communications. Within a short time, an explanation was developed. Research seemed to reveal that people turned to the media to obtain "satisfactions"—that is, to fulfill deep-seated needs—by attending to their content (Chapter 14, "Uses for Gratifications Theory").

These early theories represented the first attempts to use systematic observation to assess explanations of the process and effects of mass communication. Even though the Magic Bullet Theory has been completely abandoned (because it was inconsistent with research findings), it has historical significance. It initially led researchers and scholars down a false path, which they came to recognize when research failed to support the theory. This brought scholars to rethink their attempts to explain the nature and influences of mass communication, and, as the scientific strategy came to be increasingly used, alternative theories were proposed.

Early Theories of the Process of Mass Communication

Building on the foundations of the pioneers, an early set of milestone theories consisted of five distinct formulations that were developed to deal with some aspect of the *process* of mass communication—that is, what takes place as media content is decided upon, designed and formed, or processed by a sender and then disseminated via a media channel to members of audiences. Each of these early theories is still regarded as a valid and useful explanation of some feature of the mass communication process.

First, in the case of news content, how does a particular report *come to be chosen* from all the potential stories available to those who put together newspapers, news broadcasts, and so forth? This is explained in Chapter 11, "Gatekeeping Theory." Second, how are decisions made, and by whom, as to *what stories to emphasize* by their positioning in space and time within a news medium and with what consequences? This issue is addressed in Chapter 12, "Agenda-Setting Theory." Third, how does news or some other kind of message move through an audience *by word-of-mouth*—from people who attend closely to the media and then on to others who do not? Also, when such interpersonal transmission does take place, does this make those who play an active role in disseminating information "opinion leaders," people who influence the ideas and interpretations of others as they pass on information? Chapter 13, "The Two-Step Flow of Communication Theory," discusses these issues.

In each case, these "process" theories aid in understanding how various features of the system—producers, disseminators, audience, and regulators—have an influence on what content is ultimately offered to the public. They remain, therefore, essential for understanding the development of mass communication theories.

Early Theories of the Influences on Individuals

Other theories are less concerned with the "process" of mass communication than with how the messages disseminated have some *influence or effect on those who receive them*. A number of theories have been developed to try to explain how these effects take place—how individuals are influenced by what they read, hear, or view when they make use of the media. Some address dramatic concerns, such as whether children become violent when they see violence portrayed in television or the movies. Other are less dramatic and focus on ways that media messages can influence people's beliefs, opinions, and attitudes.

Do the media actually have influences on individuals? If the theories developed to provide answers to that question are correct, the answer is "yes, they do"—but often in ways that are not obvious to the public. For example, people obtain a great amount of *practical information* from the media that they use in day-to-day behavior. They watch weather reports on TV and take a raincoat if a storm is forecast. They read the ads in newspapers to see where bargains in tomatoes can be obtained at the supermarket. They turn to magazines for lessons about everything from cooking and bodybuilding to the latest hints on the effective use of makeup. These are utilitarian matters—not related to deep-seated satisfactions and needs. For that reason, Chapter 15 presents a theory of media information utility.

An important question is whether audience members imitate what they see people doing in the media. Research evidence seems to make it clear that the answer is yes—at least sometimes. Behavior performed on TV, or depicted in other media, can serve as a "model" that people can emulate when confronted with a situation where the depicted behavior solves a problem for them. It does not always happen, or happen to everyone, but sometimes such imitation does take place. Chapter 16 presents Modeling Theory as an explanation of such patterns.

A subtle, but nevertheless real, influence on individuals is that depictions on television, in the movies, or in other media teach people *how to behave in groups*. Thus, ordinary citizens gain conceptions of what would be expected of them if they were a member of an airline crew, how they would have to behave if they joined the Marines—or even what behavior is expected of a convict in prison—even if they will actually never become members of such groups. Thus, Chapter 17 sets forth (the new) Social Expectations Theory, which explains how such knowledge is acquired from the media.

Theories of Media Influences on Society and Culture

All contemporary societies constantly change. Some do so swiftly, others do so more slowly. One of the major mechanisms of such change is the *adoption of new forms of culture*. These can be material things, such as new technology. They can also be nonmaterial, like a dance form, new words in the language, or new foods like pizza (unheard of by most Americans before World War II). The media play a major role in bringing new cultural items to the attention of people in a variety of ways. For that reason, Chapter 18 presents Diffusion of Innovation Theory, linking portrayals of cultural items from other societies and new inventions to their patterns of acceptance by the population.

Theories of Why Certain Forms of Media Content Dominate

Explanations are needed to account for the nature of what the media provide to their audiences in their content. Many critics deplore the low intellectual level of television and the depictions of violence, sexuality, and vulgar language of the movies. Such critics note that there seems to be a continuing and constant erosion of moral and ethical standards in the behavior depicted in such content. For that reason, Chapter 19 presents a theory of Media Dependence on Popular Culture. (The term refers to such content as sports, soap operas, reality TV, rock and other popular music, and print content of limited significance). Critics would prefer more sophisticated content.

To try and explain why depictions and reports of sex, violence, and crime seem increasingly to dominate the media—and why older standards of proper human conduct are constantly eroded—Chapter 20 presents the (new) Creeping Cycle of Desensitization Theory, which explains that, because the public enjoys these themes in media content (enhancing profits), standards are constantly lowered. At some point, however, the media go too far, and the public begins to object. The process stops at that point, only to begin again when criticism dies down. Thus, there is a constant cycle that takes place, moving the society constantly toward less ethical and moral standards in what is depicted in the media.

Chapter 21 presents Critical Cultural Theory–which, as noted earlier, is a formulation drawn from an ideological (Marxian) base. In this case, those who own and manage the media are portrayed as doing everything they can to *protect their power and to increase their profits*. They do so by depicting both our democratic system (which allows them power) and the capitalistic economy (which allows them profits) as the best of all possible worlds. This interesting theory, which is very critical of our present media system, assumes that both democracy and capitalism are in fact repressive systems that result in great gaps in wealth and power among the population.

Another account of societal change is provided by Chapter 22, which presents Cultural Imperialism Theory. This is an interesting example of another theory derived not from empirical research but from an ideology—from *a priori* assumptions about the nature of American business and government. Essentially, it proposes that there is a complex conspiracy among advanced societies (particularly the U.S.) to change the cultures and habits of those that are less developed. The presumed goal is political and economic domination. This is achieved by vigorously imposing our entertainment products on those less developed societies to get them to want both our goods and our way of life.

A recently formulated theory focuses on social constructions of reality that audiences can develop by viewing depictions of ordinary Americans as these are contained in entertainment products and news. Such products, developed in the U.S. and marketed worldwide, offer in many cases and countries the only information available to audiences as to the nature, values, and conduct of the people who live in the United States. From this they construct beliefs and attitudes concerning the realities of people who live in the United States, which are often seriously flawed. These issues are discussed in Chapter 23, "Collateral Media Instruction Theory."

There are a number of additional tentative or controversial concepts, ideas, and theories that need to be considered. Some are so broadly focused that they provide little in the way of guides to research. Others deal with minor or very narrow issues. Still others have yet to be explored by researchers. All, however, are important in that they can potentially offer insights—even though tentative—into the process and effects of mass communication. (Several of these are addressed in Chapter 24, Other Perspectives.)

Finally, it is important to understand that, overall, no claim can be made that the new or old theories set forth in the chapters of this book are the final ones that will be developed by media scholars and researchers. As investigations into the nature of the processes and effects of mass communication continue, new explanations will be added, ones that now are seen as valid may be discredited, and others will undoubtedly have to undergo modification.

Notes and References

1. Charles Darwin, *On the Origin of Species Through a Process of Natural Selection* (Cambridge, MA: Harvard University Press, 1964). This is a "facsimile" edition for modern use. The original was published in 1859.

2. See *Sigmund Freud: Collected Papers* (London: Hogarth Press, 1909).

3. Em Griffin, *A First Look at Communication Theory* (New York: McGraw-Hill, Inc., 1991), pp. 4–6.

4. Unfortunately, the word "cause" can be a slippery one because it has many meanings. In this book, it will be used to mean that the antecedent conditions, when present, increase the likelihood that the predicted outcome will occur.

5. Hubert M. Blalock, *Theory Construction: From Verbal to Mathematical Formulations* (Englewood Cliffs, NJ: Prentice-Hall, Inc., 1969), pp. 1–9.

6. Amy Harmon, "A Sad, Lonely World Is Discovered in Cyberspace, Surprising Researchers," *The New York Times*, August 30, 1998.

7. Karl Marx and Frederick Engels, *The Communist Manifesto* (Chicago: Charles H. Kerr and Co., 1947). First published in German in 1848. See also Isaiah Berlin, *Karl Marx*, 2nd ed. (New York: Home University Library, 1948).

8. John Milton, *Aeropagitica: A Speech of Mr. John Milton/For the Liberty of Unlicensed Printing/to the Parliament of England.* (This was a document sent to the parliament and not published independently.)

See Frederick Seaton Siebert, *Freedom of the Press in England, 1476–1776: The Rise and Decline of Government Control* (Urbana, IL: University of Illinois Press, 1965), p. 195.

9. Wilbur Schramm, established the Institute for Communication Research at the University of Illinois in 1950. He published a book of readings that brought together important works from diverse disciplines, but they all focused in one way or another on the process or effects of mass communication. See *Mass Communications* (Urbana, IL: University of Illinois Press, 1950). This book served as the first major text for the fledgling field in its early years.

10. Harold S. Lasswell, "The Structure and Function of Communication in Society," in Lymon Bryson, ed., *The Communication of Ideas* (New York: The Institute for Religious and Social Studies, 1948). pp. 111–118.

11. Claude E. Shannon and Warren Weaver, *The Mathematical Theory of Communication* (Urbana, IL.: The University of Illinois Press, 1949).

12. See Shannon and Weaver, p. 98.

13. For a detailed discussion of the linear and simultaneous transactions models for analyses of interpersonal communication, see Melvin L. DeFleur, Patricia Kearney, and Timothy Plax, *Fundamentals of Human Communication* (Mountain View, CA: Mayfield Publishing Company, 1993), pp. 12–25.

CHAPTER 3

The Scientific Method and the Social Construction of Reality: The Contributions of Philosophy to Media Theory

Sir Isaac Newton, one of the most famous physicists and mathematicians of all time, said it very well in a letter to a friend: "*If I have seen farther [than others] it is by standing on the shoulders of giants.*"[1] That comment helps to explain how we today—in a world that Newton could not even remotely have imagined—are able to use the logic and methods of science to conduct research on an almost unlimited number of topics—and then to develop theories, test them through systematic observation, and apply them for practical purposes. It also helps to explain how we as human beings came to understand the processes by which we each learn about the nature of the world we live in and the rules for relating to each other in acceptable ways. That is, because of the contributions to philosophy of intellectual giants in the past, scholars and scientists today can explain an almost incredible number of phenomena—including the origins, processes, and effects of mass communication.

From the huge and mind-boggling body of philosophical writing that has accumulated over more than two thousand years, two developments stand out as critically important to the study of mass communication today. One is the development of the *logic and methods of science*. That development had its roots in the writings of Plato and Aristotle but accelerated greatly during the 1500s. The methodology of science is now so universally useful that it can be used to study virtually any subject matter that can be observed by the senses—whether revealed by microscopes probing objects so small that they defy the imagination, by powerful telescopes probing the far-off reaches of the universe, or with systematic procedures that record the mass communication behavior of human beings.

The second significant contribution of philosophy to the study of the mass media is our current understanding of the role and importance of *all forms of communication* in human life, whether verbal, nonverbal, print, by wire, broadcast, or via computer. The significance of human communication for human beings did not become well understood for many centuries. Today, however, we recognize that communicating with others—in person, or with the use of media—is the means by which each of us acquires "pictures in our heads of the world outside."[2]

Understanding that process is a major contribution of philosophy to developing theories of mass communication. In ancient times, Plato explained how this takes place through processes of communication as we develop our personal *social constructions of reality*. Although he did not use those words, he did have that goal. Many others since his time have described the same basic idea in their theories of media effects. That is, people do not inherit at birth their personal and shared understandings of the realities of the physical and social worlds in which they live. They *learn them in association with others through processes of communication*—from their families, their friends, their schools, and, in more modern times, also from mass communications. As various chapters in this book will show, this is a consequence of profound importance for understanding the influences of mass communication. Communication with language and visual images, then, is a *uniquely human activity* that enables us to think, remember, cope routinely with events that confront us, and participate in the complexities of our shared culture. At the same time, the images, depictions, and interpretations of reality provided to us by others—including the mass media—can at times be seriously flawed, leading to distorted "pictures in our heads."

THE INITIAL SEARCH FOR UNDERSTANDING

When researchers and scholars today use the intellectual tools of scientific investigation, they depend upon an accumulation of philosophical thought that began thousands of years ago. Long before the birth of Christ, intelligent individuals began to think about, debate, and reach conclusions concerning *the nature of reality*. It seems likely that debate about the features of nature—the earth, the sky, plants, and animals—began around campfires in caves when human beings first became able to speak, to develop language, and to use it to talk to each other.

Language and Writing

From what we know now, the change from the use of simple gestures and nonverbal grunts and noises (as signs with which to communicate) to speaking—that is, making use of complex vocabularies and rules of grammar—seems to have taken place somewhere between 35,000 and 45,000 years ago. It had profound consequences. The Age of Speech and Language, as that transition has been called, began when the Cro Magnon people appeared and spread across Europe.[3] They displaced the existing Neanderthal people, who, paleontologists believe (because of their physical anatomy), could not effectively use speech and language as we know it.[4]

Because they could communicate using language very effectively, the Cro Magnon—the direct ancestors of contemporary Europeans—developed a culture that was far more complex than that of any previous form of human beings.[5] By 10,000 B.C. they had solved problem after problem, including the domestication of plants and animals; living in fixed villages; using pottery, metals, and weaving cloth; and many other contributions from which we still benefit today.

Eventually, about 5,000 years ago, people in what is now the area surrounding and near the Mediterranean invented ways of *recording ideas in graphic form*. The Age of Writing had begun.[6] At first, writing was cumbersome, and the only medium used was stone. At the time, only those who studied the complexities of written forms for years could master the writing process or read what others had written. Eventually, however, writing was enormously simplified. Alphabets with letters corresponding to *sounds* came into use. That was a truly important advance. It greatly increased access to written words. Later, *portable media*—papyrus and parchment at first—were developed. This innovation simplified both the act of writing and the transfer of information over distance. That change permitted expanded commerce, more efficient military coordination, and the effective administration of empires.[7] By about the time of Columbus (in the fifteenth century), *paper* and then *printing* had been developed to greatly expand communication technology. Eventually the media we know today were developed. In each case, the implications for society were profound.

The Emergence of Philosophy

As noted, these advances came from the thoughts, ideas, and accomplishments of philosophers. The term "philosophy" is a combination of the classic Greek words for "love" (*philos*) and for seeking "wisdom" (*sophos*). It was not until writing was simplified that philosophers were able to record their ideas in ways that made them available to later generations. As noted, the major key was the development of a simple alphabet. While there were many earlier attempts, it was not until about 500 B.C. that the Ionian Greeks agreed upon an efficient and standardized set of symbols *representing sounds*. It was a huge advance. Their alphabet (from *alpha* and *beta*, the first letters) was passed on to the Romans, who adapted it to their needs. The words on this page are formatted in the Roman alphabet—little changed from the one in use at the time of Julius Caesar.

It is not surprising, then, that the foundations of philosophy are almost universally attributed to the classic Greek scholars. By the sixth century B.C., they began the systematic investigation of both the physical and political worlds. That is, the earliest steps toward what was eventually to become scientific investigation were initiated during that time. A number of early philosophers changed their strategies for explaining things from stories, myths, and legends to rational and written accounts that tried to explain reality.[8]

THE BASIC ISSUES

As philosophers undertook to understand human existence more fully, they focused their attention on three very basic issues. These were questions about (1) *being*, about (2) *knowing*, and about (3) *doing*. Essentially, these three issues refer to (1) the nature of the physical world that independently exists around us, (2) the knowledge of that world that we somehow acquire in our human minds, and (3) the ways in which we use that knowledge to respond both to the physical world and to each other. As philosophy advanced, these issues came to be at the center of discussion and debate.

Being: The Existence of Reality

The idea of "being" turned out to be very difficult to address. Essentially, this idea refers to how things actually exist and how they got there in the first place. One view advanced was that common objects around us are really just "fictions in our heads"—that we only think they are there because we are able to see, feel, taste, and smell what we *assume* are realities. An opposing view was that the trees, rivers, mountains, and all the rest are *actually there*, whether we are present or not. That is, reality has an existence that is *independent* of human experience. That may seem like a pretty abstract issue, but the early (and even later) philosophers worried about it a lot. In other words, they were concerned with the nature of "being"—how it is that all of the physical things in the world came to have an existence that may or may not be independent of our ability to know them.

It was an extension of this basic question that brought into existence what we know today as the major *physical sciences* that eventually split off from the mainstream of philosophy. The process started early as thinkers began to notice, contemplate, and study systematically the movements of the heavenly bodies. Astronomy and its handmaiden, mathematics, were well established long before any of the other physical sciences amounted to much. Later, physics, chemistry, and eventually biology became pathways to knowledge about the existence and functions of the various physical and biological phenomena that are now routinely studied. Nevertheless, these physical sciences were born in philosophy, where their basic questions got their start.

Today, we see that the question of how things came to exist has alternative answers. Some religious authorities tell us that an omnipotent God created the earth and all that is upon it—some say a little over 4,000 years ago. That would include all the animals, humankind, and every aspect of the physical environment as well. Other authorities, such as geologists and paleontologists, have different answers. They conclude that the earth in its present state came slowly into being over billions of years as a result of complex geological transformations—and that human beings came into being as a result of a very long process of biological evolution from simple to complex organisms. For present purposes, however, we need not choose between these competing explanations of being. We can accept pragmatically the philosophical premises that (1) there is a physical world out there and (2) that its existence is independent of us as human beings. We can safely leave further developments and debates about "being" to scientists, religious authorities, and advocates of "intelligent design" explanations.

Knowing: Human Understanding of Reality

The question of how we come to *know* reality is a different matter. It also has a long history of debate and development. Today we understand the importance of human communication in the process. But, in retrospect, only in relatively recent times have learning and knowing about reality been linked solidly and extensively to human communication. Throughout most of history, philosophers paid scant attention to human communication. They believed that each individual constructs his or her own interpretations of reality from *direct personal experience with the real world*. In other words, they concluded, people gain their knowledge about the physical and social world not by communicating with other people but by *contacting it directly through sensory impressions*. In that way, said those subscribing to this view, our knowledge—our personal interpretations of reality—are supposedly constructed by each of us, independently and without influences from other people. Thus, in this view, they are solely a consequence of personal experiences and perceptions. That focus on the individual survived through the ages and, as subsequent chapters will show, in some ways led to a failure to appreciate the powerful role of communication in human existence.

The issue of *how we know* began to change somewhat during the seventeenth and eighteenth centuries. The writings of Thomas Hobbes in the mid-1600s included at least some attention to the part played by speech in acquiring new knowledge and in remembering ideas.[9] Toward the end of that same century, John Locke described the relationship between words, the meanings we acquire for them, and how these shape our thoughts and our conduct.[10] Yet, for the most part, philosophy remained concerned with the sensory basis of individual knowledge, as well as with human relationships with the supernatural. In other words, until more recent times, little attention was given to the process of human communication and its consequences.

Doing: Responding to Reality

The third question, as to how knowledge of the things and social aspects of our world *influences our conduct*, also was addressed through the ages by philosophers. Many answers were put forth. In this case, their concerns were with both the *ethical behavior of individuals* and with *systems of government* that would provide fair social conditions. Several branches of philosophy were developed to address a number of different issues. Some were devoted to religious questions and what conduct was required to meet the demands of sacred teachings. Others set forth the ways in which rulers and the ruled should be related and how leaders should be legitimately selected. Still others sought answers to the nature of ethical codes and just laws.

In more recent times, philosophers sought understandings of the basis of human behavior—that is, whether it was a product of what one *inherited* or what one *experienced* in the environment. It was with these questions that the field of *psychology* emerged during the early 1800s. Psychologists began to study *conduct* using methods that were different from, but based on, those of the scientific concerns of philosophy. That is, the field was developed by adapting the *empirical (observational) methods of physical science*, as opposed to depending on solely rational argumentation and logic. Other fields made similar changes. For example, modern economics got a powerful advance as an independent field with the work of Adam Smith in the late 1700s.[11] Other branches of social and behavioral science also split from traditional philosophy to study various categories and aspects of human behavior. Sociology got its start early in the 1840s. Political science, arguably the oldest of the social sciences (and long closely linked with philosophy), also became an independent discipline. Anthropology developed during the 1880s. The study of *doing*, then—long central to philosophy—became the subject matters of a number of very complex and highly specialized fields. In some respects, however, they can all still be regarded as *extensions of philosophy* in that they are devoted to the "love of knowledge" in their focuses on their specialized subject matters.

THE SEARCH FOR A STRATEGY FOR OBTAINING VALID KNOWLEDGE

Within a short time after the development of an efficient alphabet, Plato (427–347 B.C.) would write his *Republic*. It remains the first and best-known complete book of philosophy that has survived. It was both a treatise on what he defined as a just social order and a commentary on human nature. In other works, such as his *Theaetetus*, he tried to explain how human beings come to know the physical world.

A second intellectual giant from classical Greece was Aristotle (384–322 B.C.). He was a student of Plato, and he was a prolific writer. In many ways, the beginnings of systematic science were advanced greatly by Aristotle. But, in other ways, he held back the development of science for centuries. His writings included extensive analyses of the nature of animals, the earth, the heavenly bodies, and other aspects of reality. However, Aristotle's works on *logic*, on how reality should be studied, on the nature of society, on the world of nature, and on many other topics seemed to provide all the knowledge about such topics that would ever be needed. He came to be called the great *Authority*, to whom philosophers turned for valid knowledge. This strategy served for centuries. Aristotle was referred to by scholars for over a thousand years as "The Philosopher" or "The Master" (of secular knowledge).

After Aristotle, the big questions that needed answers were not of this world. With the rise of Christianity, European philosophers turned to determining the nature and characteristics of *God* and the ways in which humankind should behave in order to reach *salvation*. Thus, during the Middle Ages, scholars of the Church devoted their intellectual energies to questions of theology. A return to secular philosophy would not come until the beginnings of the Renaissance (which took place in Europe starting roughly from the fourteenth to the sixteenth centuries).

Sensory Experience as a Strategy

While Plato's and Aristotle's theories of reality are now of little more than historical interest, it is important to note that they, and the religious philosophers who followed them, *distrusted sensory experience* as a strategy for acquiring valid knowledge. For example, Plato claimed that sensory experience was *untrustworthy* as a strategy for obtaining valid knowledge because it could provide false illusions. Instead, he maintained, it was necessary to rely on *pure reason* as a source for obtaining valid knowledge. Gaining knowledge of reality through logic alone is a process we now call *metaphysical reasoning*. The term "meta" combined with "physics" means *beyond the physical world* (which human beings apprehend through sensory experience).

Plato illustrated the dangers of depending on unreliable sensory experience with his famous Allegory of the Cave. It is important to note, however, that today this same allegory provides a vivid explanation of the process we now call the "social construction of reality."

In *The Republic* Plato asks us to visualize in our imagination a situation in which a small number of men participated in a curious kind of (what we would now call) an experiment:

> Imagine the condition of men," he asks us, "who had always lived deep within a sort of cavernous chamber underground, with an entrance open only to the light and a long passage all down the cave.[12]

Plato goes on further to ask us to imagine that these men had since early childhood been chained on a bench, in such a way that they could see only the wall of the cave straight ahead. (Needless to say, he could not get away with using men in this way as subjects today, but the ethics of his time were different.) Furthermore, and obviously, he really never actually conducted the experiment.

In any case, just behind the men chained to the bench in this imaginary situation is a high wall running down the middle of the cave. On the side opposite the men (where they can't see it) is a kind of walkway built along the wall several feet below the top. This walkway provides a sort of narrow track along which people can walk carrying various objects. The men chained on the bench below cannot see the people or the track because they are facing the other way. Behind the wall, still farther, Plato wants us to imagine, is a very bright fire whose light will be reflected on the opposite side of the cave, where the men can see it.

Now imagine people walking along the track, holding up figures and shapes of various kinds—like silhouettes of animals and men, or other shapes. They are holding them up on poles just above the top of the wall. Remember that there is a fire burning very brightly and its light can be seen glowing strongly against the opposite wall of the cave where the chained men are unable to see it. These conditions will result in *shadows* (of the objects held up by the people) being cast on the wall as the people move along. The chained and seated men can clearly see these shadows (but nothing else).

Under these conditions, the men in chains will observe a kind of *phantasmagoria*— a moving-shadow show. They will not see the people holding up the silhouettes because they are below the top of the wall on the other side. It is important to note that the seated men must use their *sensory experience* to observe the shadows. The question that Plato asked is this: How, then, do they *interpret* the shadows that confront them?

Plato added sound to the show. Suppose, he said, that the people behind the wall, carrying the objects, talk freely. These sounds come to the men as echoes off the wall that they can observe, so that it appears that the shadows are making the sounds. The chained men can also talk freely among themselves as they exchange ideas and try to understand and interpret the reality of what they are seeing and hearing. Thus, two senses are involved—seeing and hearing.

What is the purpose of this imaginary experiment? Plato maintained that the chained men would *use their sensory experience to try to interpret the shadows*—to construct personal knowledge—that is, *meanings* for the only realities that they were able to experience with their senses. He maintained that such prisoners would believe that *the shadows were reality*. Plato also believed that the men would develop, *by communicating among themselves*, shared rules for understanding them. There is little doubt, Plato maintained, that they would invent names for the different kinds of shadows. (These are, after all, the actions we all perform today in understanding our perceived realities.)

In the cave, Plato suggested, the seated men would congratulate the one with the keenest eye for identifying the passing shapes and the one who had the best memory for the order in which they passed. In fact, said Plato, they might give prizes for the one who could best predict what shadows would appear next in what patterns. Thus, the knowledge that they developed would be based solidly on their sensory experience. However, he noted, this would lead to a *very false view of reality*. Obviously, the fact that they worked out shared rules of interpretation indicates that, in addition to sensory experience, there was a critical communication basis for their interpretations—*a social construction of reality*, on which they agreed and which they shared.

But now, said Plato, let us introduce a dramatic condition. Suppose that one of the chained men were suddenly set free. First, he would be allowed to see the wall, the walkway, the people carrying the silhouettes, the fire, and the whole system by which the shadows had been produced. It would be explained to him that what he had been seeing (the shadows) was *only an illusion* and what he was now experiencing was their true nature. He would then be taken out of the cave altogether and be shown a totally different reality—the world of everyday life and reality in Greece at the time. He would see animals, forests, rivers, buildings, and all the rest. In all likelihood, and given time, said Plato, he would come to recognize and understand that the new world that he was now experiencing was indeed the true and objective nature of reality. Thus, he would understand that his earlier sensory experience provided a completely unreliable and flawed view of the world.

For the final phase of the experiment, Plato went on to introduce still another dramatic condition. Try to predict, he said, what would take place if the man were taken back into the cave to be chained again in his former place. Try also, Plato asked, to anticipate what would happen when he tried to explain to his former companions that what they were all seeing was not reality at all but merely an illusionary world of no substance. He would explain that he had a true understanding of reality.

How would the others react? Plato was convinced that they would laugh at him and reject his explanations as the ravings of a madman. Their response would be like ours if a person claimed he had been abducted by alien beings and transported to another world where he was shown a totally new reality. We might merely call for authorities with a straightjacket and have him placed in a rubber room. But Plato said that if the man made such claims, and then attempted to set his companions free to experience the new reality he had found, they might kill him.

Metaphysical Reasoning as a Strategy

Rejecting sensory experience as the sole basis of knowing reality and *relying on reasoning alone* turned out to be a fundamental mistake on the part of Plato. That mistake would long haunt and mislead those seeking valid knowledge who came after him. Indeed, that mistake would not be corrected for nearly two thousand years. Specifically, it would delay the recognition of sensory experience *as the basis of scientific observation* until the mid-1500s.

While Plato showed that sensory experiences can create illusions, it is not difficult to illustrate how a total dependence on pure logic, devoid of checks against the facts through empirical observation—based on sensory experience—can lead also to totally false conclusions. In fact, Xeno, a fifth-century B.C. Greek philosopher who preceded Plato, was skeptical of pure logic. He provided a wonderful example of how misleading it can be solely on logic to rely:

Imagine, Xeno proposed, a race between a human being and an animal.[13] To represent the human being, he chose the mythical Achilles, a swift runner. To illustrate the animal, he selected a tortoise. To be fair, said Xeno, the tortoise moves slowly, so in a race it should have a considerable head start. Therefore, let the tortoise begin at a point well down on the race track. Then, with all parties ready, the race was to begin when an arrow was shot into the air.

Now the issue at stake here is not who will win. It is obvious that Achilles can run much faster, so he would cross the finish line long before the tortoise. The real issue to be settled by pure logic is *at what point will Achilles overtake the tortoise*? How can that be determined? Let us try, said Xeno, to answer that question through the use of pure logic. He posed his argument in the following way.

To begin with, once the race has begun, it is perfectly obvious that Achilles will quickly run up to the point where the tortoise started. Again, obviously, the tortoise will have already moved down the race track a short distance by the time Achilles gets to that point. Achilles will then run on. But, while he is doing this, the tortoise (logically) will have already moved ahead a bit. Achilles will again close that gap—only to find that the tortoise has moved on a bit more.

Achilles tries again and again, said Xeno, with the same result. Every time that Achilles closes the gap between his position and where the tortoise *was*, he still has a bit farther to go because the tortoise has forged on ahead. The distances get smaller and smaller, to be sure, but the logical principle does not change. With this reasoning, Achilles will *never overtake the tortoise*. Every time he tries, the tortoise will always have gone a bit more. The logic is flawless! No one of Xeno's time (or even now) can fault it.

Xeno's "paradox"—as such examples came to be called—illustrates dramatically a serious limitation of relying solely on logic to seek the truth. He illustrated how it can lead to absurd conclusions. Today, of course, we have a clear understanding of the mathematical relationships between time, rate, and distance. Such relationships were worked out long ago through processes of empirical observation. That led to the development of the necessary algebra, and the exact point and time at which Achilles would overtake the tortoise could be accurately calculated. Indeed, school children perform similar calculations every time they take a math class.

In spite of such difficulties, metaphysical reasoning remained the way in which philosophers sought valid knowledge for many centuries. It was Aristotle, the Master, who perfected a system of logical reasoning that seemed unassailable. His use of the *syllogism* seemed so perfectly designed as a way to seek truth that it was not challenged until the sixteenth century.

A syllogism is a structure of formal logic—a series of related statements that yield a formal "therefore" conclusion. In its most basic form it consists of two (or sometimes more) statements that are "premises" (these are truths that are "given"—that is, taken as true) and then a conclusion that can be logically drawn from them, which establishes a new "truth." For example, suppose one wanted to decide whether whales are fish or animals. A very simple example of a syllogism using logic to provide a valid answer would be this:

> All creatures that breathe air are animals. (true premise 1)
> Whales are creatures that breathe air. (true premise 2)
> *Therefore*, whales are animals, not fish. (the new truth)

While this example is an elementary one, it shows the basic structure of such reasoning. If the two premises are correct, or assumed to be correct, the "therefore" conclusion, deduced logically, can also be regarded as correct. The syllogism was expanded over the centuries into many complex forms that seemed at the time to provide totally valid answers to questions, logically derived—particularly about the supernatural but also about nature. Clearly, it seemed, there was no need to go out and depend on sensory impressions to make empirical observations to obtain valid knowledge. Plato had shown how that could lead to illusions and false knowledge. Moreover, Aristotle, The Master, had already provided all that was needed to be known about natural phenomena.

The use of metaphysical logic and systematic reasoning, in place of empirical observation as a route for gaining knowledge, prevailed for centuries as philosophers analyzed religious questions. For example, six hundred years after Plato wrote his *Republic*, St. Augustine (354–430 A.D.), a major religious philosopher, brought together many teachings of Plato and Christian thought. Augustine was a rather remarkable figure. In his youth he was almost a "rebel without a cause," behaving very unlike a Christian saint. For example, he associated with a group of students who, like street gangs of today, amused themselves by attacking innocent bystanders at night. He thought little of stealing fruit from a neighbor's tree just for the fun of doing it. He had many lovers during his youth, even taking a mistress just as he was about to be married to the daughter of a prominent family.[14] Later, he settled down and became a bishop of the Church.

In his writings Augustine used reason to study such questions as to whether God had created the world *out of nothing* (an idea that philosophers call *ex nihilo*). He began his analysis with the conclusion that this question should not even be asked, because God was *timeless*. Thus, he reasoned, time began when God created the earth and the heavens. This led him further to ask *what is time*? He finally reasoned that, since the past cannot exist and the future has as yet no actual reality, time has no existence. It is just a product of the human mind—a completely subjective phenomenon existing only in our heads.

Hundreds of years later, formal logic was still the only recognized strategy for reaching truth. For example, St. Thomas Aquinas (1226–1274), the great religious philosopher, used both metaphysical reasoning based on complex syllogisms and revelations of the Christian faith to reach conclusions. His reasoning, he believed, not only proved the existence of God—a task often undertaken by religious philosophers—but also provided proof that many angels could occupy the same space at the same time.[15] This issue has in modern times been described, with tongue in cheek, as a search for an answer to the burning question of *how many angels can dance on the head of a pin?*

While such a question may seem odd today, during the thirteenth century such religious issues were at the forefront of philosophy. No attention was given to science or the search for further understandings of nature. There was no scientific investigation as we think of it today because the logic and methods of that approach to knowledge had not yet been developed. The Philosopher (Aristotle) had supplied all of the answers about nature that were needed. Thus, for nearly two thousand years, strategies for reaching truth had changed little. During that time, the major questions facing truth-seekers were about God, the soul, and how to conduct oneself in this world in order to achieve salvation in the next. Those were the central issues confronting humankind. It should not be surprising, therefore, that philosophers devoted themselves almost exclusively to the study of theological issues through the use of formal logic.

THE MODERN PHILOSOPHY OF SCIENCE DEVELOPS

It was during the Renaissance that philosophy finally began to look beyond its preoccupation with religious questions. In particular, during the 1600s new modes of developing knowledge about nature were being advanced. In many ways, the scientific revolution, based on theories derived from empirical observation, began a bit earlier—in astronomy. Copernicus (1473–1543) advanced the revolutionary idea that *the earth rotated about the sun*, rather than the reverse. A century later, Galileo got himself into big trouble with the authorities of the Church for teaching his students, at the University of Padua, that his observations (made through a telescope that he had built) seemed to verify the Copernican theory. Moreover, his empirical (sensory) observations had led to his discovery of more than seven planets—an idea not accepted by religious authorities at the time. He also saw satellites circling Jupiter. The conclusion that there were more than seven planets was easily knocked down by his contemporary Francesco Sizi, who used *superior logic* to show that Galileo was mistaken. Here was his proof:

> There are seven windows in the head, two nostrils, two ears, two eyes and a mouth; so in the heavens there are two favorable stars, two unpropitious, two luminaries and Mercury alone undecided and indifferent. Since [many other phenomena of nature come in sevens] we gather that the number of planets is seven.[16]

Galileo was tried for heresy by the Church for making his claims, and he almost lost his life. He was forced to renounce his theories and live under house arrest for the remainder of his days.

Francis Bacon and the Inductive Strategy

Early in the 1600s, a drastic change took place: Francis Bacon (1561–1626), one of the most dramatic figures in philosophy of all time, proposed a radically different approach to the discovery of new knowledge. Imagine this: If a serious scholar today announced that *all knowledge about nature that had been accumulated in the preceding two thousand years is unreliable and worthless*, how would his peers react? Furthermore, imagine the reaction of those peers if that same individual claimed that *only through using a different method of study* (developed by himself) would it be possible to obtain valid knowledge in the future. There is little doubt that he would be pursued with a net and straightjacket, and brought in for a "vacation" behind bars in a mental institution.

Remarkably, however, that was what Francis Bacon announced to the world in 1620. He set forth a new approach to scientific investigation *making use of exhaustive inductive reasoning based solidly on extensive empirical observations* (obtained through the senses). That idea boldly challenged metaphysical logic as a route to valid knowledge—and the accumulated works of virtually every philosopher since Plato. Many of his contemporaries were aghast.

Although Bacon's archaic sentence structure is not easy to understand today, the following passage from his *Great Instauration* (his new plan for conducting scientific investigation) reveals what he had in mind.[17] Essentially, he is saying that hasty and casual observation leads to flawed understandings of whatever is being studied. That is, reaching conclusions from a quick examination of an event, object, or situation, or by examining only a few cases, is likely to produce knowledge that is not valid:

> But as the mind hastily and without choice, imbibes and treasures up the first notices of things, from whence all the rest proceed, errors must forever prevail, and remain uncorrected, either by the natural powers of the understanding or the assistance of logic; for the original notions being visited, confused and inconsiderately taken from things, and the secondary ones formed no less rashly, the thing employed in all our researches is not well put together nor justly formed, but resembles a magnificent structure that has no foundation.

Going on, Bacon rejected the idea of accepting the views of authorities of the past—such as the knowledge about nature that had been developed by Aristotle—and that later generations had accepted without checking for accuracy. Putting it bluntly, he categorically dismissed as worthless all previous knowledge in the sciences that "proceeds from the assurances of only a few and the sloth and ignorance of many."[18]

Instead, he advocated that scientific knowledge be developed through a process of *patient, extensive, and exhaustive empirical observation*. The way to go, he maintained, was to observe every identifiable aspect of one's subject matter thoroughly and painstakingly, so that all of its characteristics are well understood. Then, and only then, would it be possible to develop more general ideas and statements describing the characteristics or behavior of each aspect. Every feature and detail should be studied in the same careful and complete way through painstaking observation—repeating the process until all aspects of the phenomenon had been fully observed. Only that, he maintained, would permit the investigator to develop statements of how those aspects were related to one another.

Today we would say that Bacon's procedure of *exhaustive induction*, based on extensive empirical observation, would enable *concepts* to be formed to label the separate identifiable characteristics of whatever is under study. This is the first stage in an inductive process—working from observed facts to form clear definitions of concepts. Once these concepts have been identified, named, and clarified, then they can be brought together into generalized relationships.

To give a simple example from today's mass communication research, imagine certain members of an audience are continuously observed to view a particular type of television programming—say *news* (a concept). As the first stage in an inductive strategy, they could be said to have *preference* for that type of content (another concept). If, furthermore, those who consistently selected that type of content were all more or less older citizens, then *senior citizen* status (still another concept) could also be identified as a characteristic of one segment of that viewing audience. After intensive observation of these characteristics, a generalization could be inductively formed, bringing these several concepts together. It would be something like this: *senior citizens have a clear preference for news programming*. Forming such a generalization is the second stage in the induction process.

Following that, other age categories could be observed carefully to see what type of programming they preferred. Undoubtedly, extensive observation would reveal that *males* prefer sports, *children* prefer cartoons, *teenagers* like MTV, *middle-aged housewives* enjoy soap operas and romance movies, and so on through a number of conceptualized audience characteristics and programming types.

Eventually, with a number of such generalizations linking specific audience characteristics with particular viewing preferences, a third stage in the induction process could be undertaken. The goal here would be to develop even more general statements that seem to bring together even more abstract concepts and relationships. For example, one could induce a statement to the effect that *audience members of different personal and social characteristics tend to select distinctive patterns of media content as their viewing preferences.*

What we have here is one of the basic propositions of a mass communication theory. The Selective and Limited Influences Theory will be explained in Chapter 10. The actual theory is more complex than just this one proposition, but the example illustrates the kind of inductive process that Bacon was advocating—moving from observed facts to increasingly general and abstract statements of concepts and their relationships that describe what is going on. Clearly this inductive procedure for generating knowledge was totally different from forming a conclusion solely through the exercise of formal metaphysical logic or by accepting a conclusion because it had been pronounced by some earlier authority.

Bacon's contribution, then—viewed within the context of the development of a universally applicable methodology for scientific investigation—was that induction is used to *develop* formal theories. As was noted in Chapter 2, initial research is undertaken to gain a clear idea of the main factors (concepts) that are present in some set of events, objects, or situations that are selected for study. Such research is often largely descriptive. That is, no particular hypotheses are at stake, and a theory is yet to be developed. After extensive observation, generalizations can be formed inductively to describe the relationships between concepts that have been developed through empirical observation.

When these concepts and relationships have been thoroughly investigated, and their relationships brought together into a set of formal statements, a theory has become available. Presumably, that theory provides a *description* and an (as yet unverified) *explanation* of the events, objects, or situations that have been observed in reality. It lays out propositions relating the concepts in such a way that, taken as a whole, they appear to explain why the phenomena behave as they do. (See Chapter 23, "Collateral Media Instruction Theory," a new theory developed by the author for the present book.)

But in Chapter 2 the discussion of the nature and uses of theory went on to maintain that it was necessary to see if the predictions and explanations of the inductively derived theory were consistent with the facts. That was said to require a different strategy—research conducted not for *theory development* but for *theory assessment*. In fact, today we regard that second process as essential. Francis Bacon, however, did not provide answers as to how that could be accomplished. He developed the inductive logic of science but stopped there. It would be the task of others who followed to lay out the *deductive* steps that are necessary for testing a theory—deriving statements of relationship (hypotheses) that provide guidelines as to what one should observe in the real world—if the theory is correct.

In spite of Bacon's focus only on inductive theory development, his was a monumental accomplishment. He almost single-handedly discredited two thousand years of procedures for generating valid knowledge through the use of metaphysical reasoning alone. He also called into question the entire body of scientific knowledge that had been handed down and followed since Aristotle. He is truly one of those giants on whose shoulders we stand today when we undertake research and theory development on the processes and effects of mass communication.

Rene Descartes and the Deductive Strategy

Living during the same general period as Bacon, Rene Descartes (1596–1650) is another towering intellectual figure whose contributions to the development of the scientific method cannot be overstated. His writings in philosophy, mathematics, and science were numerous, but, for present purposes, it was his *criterion for truth*, which was based on a *deductive method*, that provided a second foundation for the logic of modern science. It should be noted that Descartes was concerned with the world of nature—specifically with physics. He was not a student of human behavior, and the specific theories he developed have no direct application to such subject matter. The use of the scientific method in social science, much modified from these original sources, would not come for another three hundred years. Nevertheless, his focus on the *deductive strategy* of theory building and testing proved to be essential to all branches of science, whether they deal with physical, biological, or behavioral subject matters.

Essentially, Descartes' idea was that in seeking verified knowledge one begins with very basic definitions and assumptions—called *axioms* or *postulates*. These are "propositions" (statements) that are *assumed to be true* (at least temporarily). His most famous axiom, with which he began much of his deductive reasoning, was the legendary *cogito, ergo sum*. This was a fundamental assumption in his philosophy from which much of his thinking proceeded. How is it, he asked, that I can know anything? How do I determine if I am only experiencing the world through dreams? His answer was the assumption that, even though he could doubt everything else, *he could not doubt his own existence*. That is, he assumed *cogito, ergo sum*: I am able to think; therefore, I exist (in the real world and not just in dreams).

He went on (deductively) to make conclusions about the existence of God and an external world of reality that was there beyond his own subjective experience. But it was when he turned to analyses of that world of physical reality that his criterion of proof based on a deductive strategy became important to the development of the scientific method.

Descartes believed that physical reality could be studied through the precision of deductive mathematics—using a system of reasoning developed originally by Euclid. Starting with axioms (assumed to be true), consequences were systematically derived, bringing each step closer to what could be observed. Thus, even though he accepted the idea (as had Plato and many others) that the senses could deceive, it was through *deductive logic* that one arrived at and defined what could properly become the object of empirical investigation.

Consistent with his concerns with knowing physical reality, Descartes developed his deductive approach to knowledge by focusing on such concepts as motion, quantity, substance, and what physicists could observe in the "visible world." It was in that context, therefore, that his deductive method as a means of achieving truth was set forth:

> I openly state that the only matter that I recognize in corporeal things is that which is subject to every sort of division, shape and movement—what geometers call quantity and take as the object of their demonstrations. Moreover, I consider nothing in quantity apart from these divisions, shapes and movements; and I admit that nothing is true of them that is not deduced, with the clarity of mathematical demonstration, from common notions whose truth we cannot doubt. Because all the phenomena of nature can be explained in this way, I think that no other principles of physics need be admitted, nor are to be desired.[19]

Note that the major ideas that show up in the above quotation are *axioms* ("common notions whose truth we cannot doubt"): *quantity* (stressing the importance of measurement), *deduction* (in this case, using the logic of mathematics) and *explanation* (by proceeding deductively from the general to the specific). These are all important features of the scientific method today.

The Development of the Sciences

From the time of Bacon and Descartes and on to the present, virtually all branches of science accelerated in their development at an ever-increasing pace. In the 1700s, great discoveries were made in astronomy, chemistry, physics, and the study of the human body. The 1800s saw an increasing pace of further developments, including the birth of the social sciences—anthropology, economics, psychology, sociology, and many other fields of inquiry. In the twentieth century, science soared to new heights—even to the moon and beyond. By the twenty-first century, science was a complex structure of fields and specialties using inductive/deductive theory building to accumulate knowledge on almost every conceivable subject. In other words, underlying all these endeavors was the increasing ability of scholars, researchers and other investigators to conduct *empirical research*, to develop *explanatory theories*, and to test them through *observation*.

The process of explanation in some of the sciences came to be very different from the models advanced by Bacon and Descartes. Not all forms of explanation today are based on the inductive-deductive-empirical observation approach as this was expressed in the ideas of Bacon and Descartes. However, the use of induction to form theories and deduction, from basic propositions assumed to be true, to test their validity has survived as an important model for scientific explanation. Ernest Nagle, a respected contemporary philosopher of science, put it this way:

[The basic model], a type of explanation commonly encountered in the physical sciences, though not exclusively in those disciplines, has the formal structure of a deductive argument, in which [that to be explained] is a logically necessary consequence of the explanatory premises.... This type has been extensively studied since ancient times. It is widely regarded as the paradigm for any "genuine" explanation, and has often been adopted as the ideal form to which all efforts at explanation should strive.[20]

Nagel goes on to note that three other types of explanations are widely found in the sciences today. One is *probabilistic explanations*, which often have the same propositional structure as the inductive/deductive type, with basic assumptions derived from research and deduced hypotheses used to assess their validity. However, the statements or propositions in a probabilistic theory are expressed as *tendencies* rather than as immutable laws. This is the strategy that is used widely in the social sciences—and in the study of mass communication. Another type is *"functional" (teleological) explanations*, which accounts for the behavior of some phenomenon in terms of its contribution to a larger system. Finally, *genetic explanation* has long been popular. For example, this has been widely used by those who seek to explain various forms of human conduct as inevitable (or at least highly probable) because of what one has inherited as part one's genes. This type is not particularly applicable to the study of mass communication.

The Probabilistic Strategy

The most widely used strategy for theory assessment today is undoubtedly what came to be termed *probabilistic explanations*. As noted, this procedure, based on statistical premises and deductions, is common in fields where the phenomena under study behave in less than rigidly predictable and precise ways (such as is often the case in physics). The inductive and deductive strategies brought into science by Bacon and Descartes play a clear role in this strategy. Immutable relationships between concepts are not essential if they are characterized by clear and discoverable "regularities"—that is, when they are *reasonably predictable* in their action.

Thus, the postulates, or basic assumptions in a probabilistic theory, express relationships between concepts as *regularities that have some exceptions*, rather than as unvarying correspondences. This is an adaptation of the inductive/deductive strategies. For example, a statement in such a probabilistic explanation might read: "most people over age 65 tend to follow the news closely." Or consider another example: "the majority of those who go to the movies in theaters today are under the age of 35." Statements of this type express regularities, but they allow for exceptions for those cases that violate the rule. In other words, the relationship is still there, even if some exceptions exist.

This approach to explanation based on tendency statements depends on the field of *statistics*, which developed separately from philosophy but came to be a central part of the scientific method during the nineteenth and the twentieth centuries. Most of the theories of mass communication that are developed in this book are of this type. That is, they state basic probabilistic assumptions induced from a body of empirical research or other systematic observation. Their formal statements provide both a summary description of what factors have what consequences, and they offer a guide as to what aspects of the process or effects of mass communication need to be observed to verify the explanation. Other types of theories—derived from *ideologies*, such as the teachings of Karl Marx, are also discussed in this book. These are not based on empirical observation leading to inductive theory building or verified by deductive theory testing through empirical studies. Their "basic truths" are accepted *a priori*—as valid, with no need for a body of inductive investigations from which to derive them and no need to be verified by research.

In overview, then, an incalculable debt is owed to philosophy by all fields of study that make use of the scientific method. That is also true of the study of the process and effects of mass communication. The tools for advancing knowledge in the field of mass communication today—the methodology of scientific research and the philosophy of scientific explanation—have been derived from the intellectual contributions made by a long list of remarkable writers over more than two thousand years. As today's media scholars conduct research and attempt to formulate theories that explain the process and effects of mass communication, they truly are standing on the shoulders of, not just a few, but a virtual army of intellectual giants.

HOW PEOPLE COME TO KNOW REALITY

A second major contribution made by philosophy concerns not how we should best go about studying the phenomena of nature but from what sources we as individuals develop the body of understandings, beliefs, and convictions that provide us with guides to our personal conduct. That is, *from what sources* do we come to know our world—to develop what Walter Lippmann, a philosopher and journalist of the early twentieth century, called the "pictures in our heads of the world outside"?[21]

This issue is, of course, the ancient problem of *knowing* that was so dramatically addressed by Plato. It focuses on the process of how we grasp, subjectively in our minds, the objective world of reality in which we live. It is a critical question, because it has been understood for centuries that *doing*—our actual conduct in the world toward physical reality and toward other people—is based solidly on those subjective understandings. People do not shape their actions on the basis of reality. They do so on the basis of what they *believe reality to be*. Those beliefs, the philosophers understood, could be accurate representations of reality, or only illusions. For two thousand years, philosophers sought to understand this issue by examining the nature and reliability of peoples' *perceptions* and their *sense impressions* as the link between being, knowing, and doing. Recall that Plato, in his allegory of the cave, made a forceful argument against depending on the sense impressions as a means of knowing reality because that could lead to false illusions.

One thing that held back the philosophers in coming to grips with this issue before modern times was their *individualistic focus*. They analyzed the relationship between being and knowing within a framework of the individual—who developed knowledge only by personally seeing, hearing, touching, smelling, and so on. They did not fully consider as a source of knowledge the beliefs shared and communicated to the person by others in the groups and society in which that individual lived. Today, we understand fully that people develop a great part of their knowledge of the world of reality not by personally experiencing it with their senses but *by communicating about it with other people*.

The Part Played by Other People

It is commonplace knowledge now that many of the lessons we learn are not products of individual sensory impressions of things in reality. They are lessons derived from *what other people tell us*. For example, as children most of us learned to fear snakes and spiders. Others—parents, peers, and others—taught us how awful and dangerous such creatures are and how they should be avoided at all costs. The fact is that, among the thousands of species of snakes and spiders that live among us, only a handful pose any danger—and these are almost never encountered in ordinary life. The rest are just harmless little creatures trying to get along. Nevertheless, many peoples' reactions on seeing one is close to panic. What this means is that our knowledge of such creatures was *socially constructed* in a process of language exchanges with other people.[22]

This is a very important principle, and the social process of communication is now recognized as a fundamental way in which we construct our personal understandings of the physical and social world. In particular, in terms of the objectives of this book, recognizing that most of our knowledge is socially constructed, and is not solely a product of sensory experience, has truly important implications for the study of the process and effects of mass communication.

But when did this social construction principle become a part of the accumulated knowledge about the nature of human nature? It was not until the end of the nineteenth century. By that time, the social sciences had split off from the main body of philosophy and were attempting to understand the psychological, sociological, and cultural nature of humankind. An individual who provided an important foundation for understanding the role of communication in the development of our knowledge about the social world was Charles Horton Cooley (1864–1929).

Cooley developed an interpretation of the nature of social relationships that came to be called "symbolic interaction."[23] His idea was that each person in communication with others develops an internal "image" (picture in his or her head) about each other individual with whom he or she associates. Relating to others in society is done through these "images," rather than on the basis of detailed actual knowledge about the true characteristics of those individuals—which we can never fully grasp. Furthermore, each person constructs his or her own "self image"—a subjective understanding of his or her own personal attributes and qualities. This can only be done by assessing the reactions of other people to one's conduct. The individual sees approval or disapproval, acceptance or rejection, admiration or disdain in the responses of others. Thus, the behavior of others toward the individual serves as a kind of *mirror* from which he or she can see his or her own qualities reflected. From this, each of us constructs a "looking glass self" by interpreting how other people see us. Cooley also discussed at length the role of "modern communication" (with media) in these processes.

When this image-construction process is looked at within the perspective of traditional philosophy, Cooley's interpretations provide interesting answers to the ancient questions of being, knowing, and doing. They do so within a context of interpersonal interaction and society. But the important point is that "reality" (the nature of other people and of ourselves) is constructed through a process of symbolic interaction (language and mediated exchanges with others).

More broadly, a number of scholars in the twentieth century have probed the role of society and its forms of communication as sources from which people developed their personal structures of beliefs. Complex ideologies, such as Marxism, Freudian psychoanalytic interpretations, or even Fascism, have been seen as constructions derived from the language and general cultures of the societies in which they developed. The study of the relationship between society and beliefs came to be called the *sociology of knowledge*. One of the pioneers in this new field was Alfred Schutz, who saw in the exchanges between individuals and society the source by which each person constructed an internal body of knowledge enabling him or her to cope with the demands of the physical and social worlds. As was true of many scholars, philosophers, and theorists before him, his major theme was that the foundations of knowledge can be found in the communicative exchanges a person has with others in everyday life.[24]

In 1966, sociologists Peter L. Berger and Thomas Luckman published a treatise on the sociology of knowledge that has now become a well-known work in this field.[25] Their focus, however, is on the role of language in everyday life and not on how the mass media play a part in developing the views, beliefs, and convictions that constitute an individual's grasp of the realities in which he or she lives and acts. Nevertheless, such analyses provide an important part of the intellectual foundation for understanding that issue.

What is relevant in tracing this contribution of philosophy (and its extensions, such as symbolic interaction and the sociology of knowledge) to understanding the social sources of knowledge is that in the modern world *the mass media are critically important as a part of people's communication activities in everyday life*. Print, film, broadcasting, and computer systems have developed an overwhelming presence that plays a central role in urban-industrial societies, such as the United States. They are a central part of our economy, our political process, recreational patterns, and the manner in which we instruct our young. On average, Americans spend as much time with their media as they do any other single activity—including sleeping! It may be no exaggeration to say that the mass media now command more of our time than such traditional institutions as the church or even the school. With religious participation usually confined to one day a week, the time it absorbs does not remotely compete with that spent attending to mass communications. Indeed, on average, children spend more time watching television than they spend in their classrooms. The majority of people read books, magazines, and newspapers. They listen to the radio, watch TV, and go to the movies, and millions log on to the Internet.

Given this level of usage, then, it is very important to develop explanations of ways in which these media have an influence on our lives, both as individuals and as a society. As has been suggested, they have grown in importance all during the twentieth century, and it appears that in the twenty-first century their scope and influence will be even greater. For that reason, the development of systematic explanations of various aspects of the process and effects of mass communication is an essential task.

Mass Communication and Depictions of Reality

Human communication—the source of many of our constructions of reality—has become a global mediated exchange of massive amounts of information that makes use of incredible technologies that instantly conquer space and time. Millions, even billions, of individuals share in these exchanges to a greater or lesser degree every day. The media bring to each of us a daily tidal wave of *depictions of reality*, explanations of the physical and social world, and models, good or bad, of how people behave or are expected to behave. These provide what can be called "collateral instruction"—unintended lessons in the content of media-presented news and entertainment that shape audiences' social construction of reality. (This concept is more fully developed in Chapter 23.) Collateral instruction in media content, then, shapes not only the ideas, thoughts, beliefs, and convictions of individuals but also the shared interpretations that make up the normative beliefs of the society.

There is little control over these collateral lessons. They may depict physical reality accurately or in totally unrealistic terms; they may provide knowledge that is critically important, or it may be totally flawed and trivially absurd. They may present the rules of conduct in an ethical manner or in despicable ways. But the fact is that the media are *teachers providing unintended instruction on being, knowing, and doing* as they seek to entertain and to present news.

The Media as Teachers of Incidental Lessons

When our modern mass media provide us with information and guidance about the world in which we live, their audiences experience "incidental" learning. That is, the producers of the content of mass communication are not deliberately attempting to educate us. Their purpose is to make money. On the other hand, as we seek out and attend to the kinds of news and media content we like, we do not do so to receive guidance about cultural uplift or moral conduct. We probably just want to be entertained or get some information that we think we need. Nevertheless, the lessons are there, and we attend to them and *unwittingly learn* perhaps more enthusiastically than we do to our mothers' advice or to lectures we may receive in a classroom.

Thus, the mass media today have become truly significant, if unwitting, *instructors*. They offer at least as much information about the nature of things and act as models of how people should behave in social relationships, as do churches, schools, family, and peers. That is not to say that what they teach us is planned, deliberate, correct, ethical, or particularly useful. Nevertheless, as we watch television, go to the movies, read newspapers and magazines, or surf the Internet, lessons are thrust at us, and we absorb them, even without realizing that a teacher-student relationship exists.

A classic example of the ways in which mass communication can serve as a source for the social construction of reality is the part played by radio in October 1938, when Orson Welles—a well-known radio personality and film star of the time—broadcasted a play depicting an "invasion from Mars." It was intended as a Halloween spoof, and it was clearly identified as a play in newspapers and at the end of the broadcast. However, he produced the play in a "you are there" news format. Many people who tuned in late became convinced that the Earth was indeed being invaded by sinister and ruthless Martians, and they began to take what they thought was appropriate action. They could have checked with a simple telephone call or even by changing to another station. About six million Americans failed to do so and engaged in what was essentially panic behavior.

Such a situation is by no means rare. Both radio and television have for decades served as sources for the social construction of reality for many people in their audiences. Producers of soap operas, both earlier when they were on radio and currently on television, have reported audience behavior revealing that many listeners or viewers have a difficult time separating fantasy from reality. For example, when a character in such a show dies, large numbers of sympathy cards are received by the network or even by the local station. When a character in the show is depicted as pregnant, baby gifts arrive. When birthdays are in the story, cards are sent, and so on.

Similarly, a movie designed as fictional entertainment can be interpreted by many as a true depiction of reality to be used as a guide to behavior. For example, in 1999, a movie called *The Blair Witch Project* was released and shown in theaters around the country. Costing only $60,000 to produce, the film soon earned millions of dollars.[26] It was a story about three film students who were producing a documentary about an eighteenth-century witch. The witch never existed, and the entire film was fiction. However, in the story, the three students disappear and are never found. Soon, the small town in which the story was filmed (Burkittsville, Maryland, population 197) began to be plagued by hordes of visitors interested in the witch. The local authorities began to receive hundreds of phone calls from people around the country who had seen the movie and believed that the story was true. Many wanted to know if the missing students had been found. Again, many people in the audience were unable to separate mediated fantasy from fact.

It is clear, then, that the mass media play an important part in the process of "knowing" by which people in modern societies create personal or shared meanings (pictures in their heads) for events, objects, and situations through communication that they encounter in their environment. Those understanding may be correct or deeply flawed. The social construction of reality, therefore, is a process based not only on the interpersonal exchanges people have with each other but also on their exposure to print, broadcasting, film, and Internet content.

In summary, philosophy has provided us with a set of remarkable intellectual tools for developing understanding and explanation—the scientific method. The field also has provided us with insights (derived from that method) about how communication, including mass communication, may serve as a source for developing beliefs and interpretations (right or wrong) of reality, which can have profound influences on our behavior.

Perhaps the most essential idea that has emerged from centuries of attention by scientists to the issue of how we can explain things is this: Among the various strategies for obtaining valid knowledge about how things work, *science seems to be the best bet*. Those who practice its requirements do not wear impressive robes; hold meetings in magnificent buildings; burn incense; obtain instructions from supernatural sources; conduct group singing; exculpate people from their sins; preside over births, marriages, or deaths; or generally offer prescriptions on how we should conduct our lives. Scientists are just ordinary people. They look like our neighbors or anyone we might encounter in the street. It is *what they do* that counts and *the way they do it*. They constantly push ahead the frontiers of knowledge, testing and retesting conclusions already reached, in order to make more accurate and potentially useful the knowledge we need of the way things are—whether they are studying physical, biological, or social processes, including the process and effects of mass communication.

THE SOCIAL CONSTRUCTION OF REALITY THEORY: A FORMAL SUMMARY

Using the scientific approach outlined above, insights about the influence of communication on "the meanings in our heads" can be stated in a relatively simple and tentative theory. It can be expressed in the form of a probabilistic explanation that incorporates both an inductive and deductive strategy. It explains how the personal convictions that people have about the physical world, their society, and themselves, or about what is false or realistic, important or unimportant, unethical or proper, valuable or inconsequential, are derived through their participation in language—much of which takes place today via mass media.

Knowing reality, in this sense, then, for the individual, and by extension for a society, *is socially constructed through a process of interpersonal and mass communication*. Stated as a set of systematic and related propositions, the theory can be summarized in the following form:

Social Construction of Reality Theory

1. All human beings require *understanding* of the world in which they live and to which they must adapt in order to survive on a daily basis.
2. To provide food, shelter, and protection, and to perpetuate the species, human beings have always been *communicating* creatures—at first using only nonverbal signs and signals to coordinate activities in families and in small communities.
3. *Language* became a part of human existence when evolutionary changes to the human body made possible the control of sound with the vocal chords and the storing of complex meanings in a larger brain.
4. With words available, features of the environment with which people had to deal could be given names, with associated conventions of internally aroused meanings, permitting *standardization of interpretations* of phenomena, stabilizing the meanings attached to all the aspects of reality with which people had to deal.
5. In modern times, *media*, including mass media, play a part in developing the meanings individuals acquire for events, situations and objects in the human environment through their depictions and representations in entertainment and other content.
6. **Therefore**, the meanings—either personal and private, or the culturally shared interpretations—of any aspect of reality to which people must adjust are developed in a process of communication, indicating that reality, in the sense of individual interpretations or a consensus of shared meanings people attach to objects, actions, events, and situations, are *socially constructed*.

In many respects, this fundamental theory, obtained from a combination of ancient and modern philosophies, and from contemporary behavioral science, provides an important foundation on which at least some explanations of the process and influences of mass communication can be developed. People acquire conceptions of their physical and social world from others through a process of social interaction. They use language to access ideas obtained from various sources in their society to develop pictures in their heads—meanings that serve as their guides as to how they should behave. Earlier, we obtained such information solely through parents or others in the small bands or villages in which we lived. Today, however, the social construction of reality is a process that also takes place when print, broadcast, or other media offer information from which people can develop conceptions, beliefs, expectations, and attitudes about what their physical and social world is like and how they should behave toward it.

As additional theories—including contributions from more modern branches of philosophy (i.e., the social sciences)—are discussed, they too will offer fundamental explanations that will provide additional bricks for the foundation on which theories of mass communication must be built. But as new mass communication theories are developed, let us be aware of the difficulties ahead. It is very clear that the study of the process and effects of mass communication is a very new field. The earliest attempts to explain such phenomena extend back only about a century and a half. This is because the media as we know them now are of recent origin. Moreover, during that time they have continued to change, often rapidly. These facts pose clear difficulties for those who seek to develop valid theories of how the media function and how they influence us both individually and collectively.

Thus, the accomplishments of those now trying to develop theories of mass communication should not be compared unfavorably with scientists in other fields who have had centuries to pursue their knowledge. Similarly, it would be shortsighted indeed to declare that pursuing knowledge about the media with the use of the powerful intellectual tools that have been so successful in the physical, biological, and social sciences is a fruitless or unworthy exercise. There is no doubt whatsoever that it will be a long time before media theories now under investigation will take their place alongside of verified and sophisticated explanations from other fields. However, the pathway to developing valid and reliable knowledge is to continue to make use of the scientific method and the theory-building strategies that have so greatly benefitted those older disciplines. Thus, while media researchers may now be standing on the shoulders of giants, they have just recently arrived there! Only the future will reveal whether that will permit them to see farther than others who make use of different routes to obtain valid knowledge.

Notes and References

1. Sir Isaac Newton (1642–1727) was responsible not only for his laws of universal gravitation but also for major developments in other fields of physics as well as a system of calculus. His theories of gravity became the world's standard until Albert Einstein developed his theories of relativity early in the twentieth century. See Isaac Newton, *Mathematical Principles of Natural Philosophy*, Florian Cajori, ed. (Berkeley, CA: Scholium, 1947). First published in 1687.

2. This phrase is the title of a chapter in a classic work on the role of the press in society. See Walter Lippmann, *Public Opinion* (Harcourt, Brace and Company, 1922).

3. See Philip Lieberman, "The Evolution of Human Speech: The Fossil Record," in *The Biology and Evolution of Language* (Cambridge, MA: Harvard University Press, 1984), pp. 287–329.

4. E. Trinkhaus and W. W. Howells, "The Neanderthals," *Scientific American* 241, 1979, pp. 118–133.

5. Charles F. Hockett, "The Origins of Speech," *Scientific American*, 203, 1960, pp. 89–96.

6. For a readable summary of the development of writing, see John McCrone, *The Ape That Spoke* (New York: William Morrow and Company, Inc., 1991), pp. 204–209.

7. For a discussion of the role of writing and portable media for the process of expansion and administration of empires, such as that of the Romans, see Harold A. Innis, *Empire and Communications* (New York: Oxford University Press, 1950).

8. Errol E. Harris, *Fundamentals of Philosophy: A Study of Classical Texts* (New York: Holt, Rinehart and Winston, Inc., 1969), pp. 13–27. For a review of that beginning, see also John Burnett, *Greek Philosophy from Thales to Plato* (New York: MacMillan, 1960).

9. Thomas Hobbes, *Leviathan* (New York: E. P. Dutton and Company, 1950), p. 21–22. First published in 1651.

10. John Locke, *An Essay Concerning Human Understanding* (Oxford: Clarendon Press, 1975), p. 402. First published in 1690.

11. Adam Smith, *An Inquiry into the Nature and Causes of the Wealth of Nations* (Chicago: The University of Chicago Press, 1976). First published in London in 1776.

12. *The Republic of Plato*, trans. Francis MacDonald Cornfield (New York: Oxford University Press, 1958). See pp. 227–235. Plato's work was written in 387 B.C.

13. For a review of philosophical thought prior to Plato, including that of Xeno, see John Burnet, *Greek Philosophy from Thales to Plato* (New York: Macmillan, 1960).

14. Augustine, *Confessions*, John K. Ryan, trans. (Garden City, NY: Image Books, 1962).

15. See Vol. I, Question 52, Article 2, St. Thomas Aquinas, *Summa Theologica*, ed. Anton Pegis (New York: Random House, 1944), p. 488. First published circa 1245.

16. Quoted in Carl Hempel, *Philosophy of Natural Science* (Englewood Cliffs, NJ: Prentice Hall, Inc., 1966), p. 48.

17. From p. 1 of "The Great Instauration." See Joseph Devey, ed., *The Physical and Metaphysical Works of Lord Bacon, Including the Advancement of Learning and Novum Organum* (London: George Bell and Sons, 1901).

18. *Ibid*, p. 4.

19. From Rene Descartes, *Principles of Philosophy*, II, p. 64. See Elizabeth S. Haldane and G. R. T. Ross, trans., *The Philosophical Works of Descartes*, Vols. I and II. (Cambridge: Cambridge University Press, 1911–1912).

20. Ernst Nagel, *The Structure of Science: Problems in the Logic of Scientific Explanation* (New York: Harcourt, Brace and World, 1961), p. 1921.

21. Walter Lippmann developed a theory that explains how the news gets distorted when the press gathers information, packages it into an understandable form, and presents it to the audience. His theory is addressed in this book in Chapter 8. The quotation is the title of Chapter One of Walter Lippmann, *Public Opinion* (New York: Harcourt Brace and Company, 1922).

22. Contemporary writers who have contributed significantly to this tradition are Peter L. Berger and Thomas Luckman, *The Social Construction of Reality: A Treatise in the Sociology of Knowledge* (New York: Anchor Books, 1967); Burkart Holzner, *Reality Construction in Society*, rev. ed. (Cambridge, MA: Schenkman Publishing Company, 1972); Ladislav Holy, ed., *Knowledge and Behavior* (Belfast: Mayne, Boyd and Son, Ltd., 1976); John R. Searle, *The Construction of Social Reality* (New York: The Free Press, 1995); and Jonathan Potter, *Representing Reality* (Thousand Oaks, CA: Sage Publications, 1996).

23. In 1937, this name was applied by sociologist Herbert Blumer to the specialty of studying the ways in which communicating through language between human beings has profound consequences for their beliefs about other people and themselves, as well as for their social conduct. Herbert Blumer, *Symbolic Interactionism: Perspective and Method* (Englewood Cliffs, NJ: Prentice Hall, 1969), p. 1.

24. Alfred Schutz, *Der Sinnhafte Aufbau der sozialen Welt* (Vienna: Springer, 1960).

25. Peter L. Berger and Thomas Luckmann, *op. cit.*

26. Richard Lezin Jones, "Blair Witch" Town Bothered, *The Boston Globe*, August 9, 1999, p. A4.

CHAPTER 4

Public Opinion as Shaped by the Press: The Contribution of Political Science

The study of political affairs is, arguably, one of the oldest intellectual concerns among the many fields of specialized knowledge that are pursued today by scholars and researchers. Political theorists began teaching the principles of good government from very early times—centuries before the birth of Christ. Almost as soon as efficient writing was developed, they started recording their ideas about politics. Not long after a standard alphabet came into wide use in Greece (about 500 B.C.), philosophers such as Plato (427–347 B.C.) had developed relatively elaborate ideas about the nature of government. As was noted in Chapter 3, his *Republic,* which sets forth his views about the nature of justice and how rulers should be selected, is the oldest book on political philosophy to survive.

As was also explained earlier, the Greek alphabet was passed on to the Romans, who refined it into virtually the same letters we used today. Thus, even in ancient times, philosophers had prepared elaborate analyses of government systems and the relationship between rulers and the ruled. These remarkable thinkers gave us many of the political terms and concepts that we continue to use today—such as *politics, republic, citizen, democracy, senate, tyranny,* and dozens more.

FROM POLITICAL PHILOSOPHY TO POLITICAL SCIENCE

The study and analysis of systems of government continued for more than two thousand years. Dozens of philosophers made contributions to human understanding of political systems and their consequences for individual and social life. Meanwhile, as was discussed in Chapter 3, other philosophers had developed the logic and procedures of science that became so important in the study of the physical world. As was also discussed in Chapter 3, these developments were an extension of the ancient quests to understand the three basic questions with which philosophy began: 1) *What is the nature of the world of reality, out there beyond our bodies* (the study of "being")? 2) *How do we come to comprehend that world within our minds* (the study of "knowing")? 3) *How should we act toward that world—and especially toward each other—to ensure a just human existence* (the study of "doing")?

The early thinkers tried diligently to provide answers to the first question, but lacking a scientific method as an epistemology (route to valid knowledge), their answers were often flawed. That improved greatly after the scientific method as we know it now was developed. In the previous chapter, it was explained how understanding the physical world began to improve when Francis Bacon, early in the 1600s, began the establishment of science based on observations as the best route to valid knowledge. It continued with the work of Descartes and Newton and right on to the present day. Over the past three centuries, reliable bodies of knowledge have been developed concerning the nature of the earth, the larger universe, biological processes, and other workings of physical nature. To say that these accomplishments are impressive is to understate the situation drastically.

Using Scientific Strategies to Study Political Behavior

As the remarkable successes of the physical and biological sciences became apparent, the methods of inquiry that had yielded such valid knowledge came under review for possible use in the study of many forms of *human behavior*. However, it was not the instruments and tools of observation used by the physical and biological sciences—telescopes, microscopes, etc.—that were eventually adopted by those interested in human conduct. It was the *underlying logic of their observational procedures* and their means for assessing and interpreting their recorded data. During the 1800s, it became clear to those attempting to study human behavior that, above all, science was based on using the *senses* to detect phenomena—that is, making *empirical observations* of whatever was under study. Moreover, those observations had to be recorded in some way—presumably in quantitative form. Various techniques, procedures, and instruments were developed to accomplish those objectives.

For the developing "behavioral" sciences, it was *human conduct*— the actions people took and the stable patterns that their activities formed—that needed to be observed. If suitable tools could be devised for making and recording such empirical observations, then central tendencies (averages), trends, and differences could be detected in the behavior of various kinds of human beings. From this descriptive information, probabilistic hypotheses could be generated and then tested, using the newly developed procedures of *statistics* (which became virtually universal in science by the early 1900s). With sufficient descriptive information at hand, inductively developed theories could be stated—and their logical predictions deduced and studied by making suitable empirical observations to decide whether their explanations made sense. In other words, as they became increasingly sophisticated, the new behavioral sciences made use of the same general logic and epistemology in their inquires that had been successful in the other fields of scientific knowledge.

Each of the fields in these new and emerging branches of science developed a variety of specialized procedures, tools, and strategies that permitted them to make and record empirical observations of different types of human conduct. The new fields shared the same tools for research, such as statistical logic, opinion surveys based on samples, attitude scales, experimental protocols, procedures for analyzing the content of messages, and many others. Although these tools were sometimes developed and used in different ways in each field, they used the same underlying concepts of analysis and explanation—that is, hypotheses, theory-development, and an epistemology based on probability. By the last years of the 1800s, virtually all of what are now the social and behavioral sciences studying human conduct had begun to turn to the logic of scientific inquiry as a means of investigating their problems and domains. Those who focused on political behavior and issues in this way came to identify themselves as *political scientists*.

Traditionalists vs. Empiricists

As this change of strategies took place, it created something of a division in the study of politics. Even today, some of the field's scholars continue in the classical tradition to assemble knowledge about the formal arrangements of governments and the details of their rules and practices. Such *traditionalists* find it useful to compare different governmental processes and structures, such as the features of different constitutions or systems for selecting leaders. Traditional scholars have little interest in making empirical observations of political behavior of the rank and file, such as conducting interviews with voters to try to understand how they make up their minds, or how conflicts are resolved among legislators.

Another set of scholars, the *empiricists*, prefer to make use of the logic and tools of science for observing people's political behavior. These investigators are interested in observable and measurable conduct of both rulers and the ruled—actions that can be observed, in some way, and recorded in quantifiable form. They develop ways of measuring political attitudes, of using statistics to analyze reports on beliefs and actions obtained in interviews with voters, legislators, or others, analyzing census data or other information obtained from government agencies. They are concerned with testing the validity of their findings, assessing their statistical reliability, and determining the degree to which their observations may represent only chance. In short, political scholars of this category are *social scientists* who use quantitative methods to study behavior related to politics.

Today, both the traditionalists and the empiricists make important contributions to what we now call "political science." While the traditionalists may prefer to call their field the study of "government," their work remains central to the field. There is a continuing need to describe and assess formal structures and arrangements that are used in various parts of the world to bring stability to social life through systems of law and orderly selection of leaders. In like manner, empiricists make an important contribution to their field by systematically measuring people's political behavior, developing and testing hypotheses concerning its patterns and regularities through the use of statistical reasoning, and developing theories that help explain the relationship between rulers and the ruled.

DISTINCT PERIODS OF POLITICAL THOUGHT

To appreciate the how political scholars have assessed the contemporary role of public opinion in the functioning of government and the relationship that it has with the "press" (broadly defined as the news industry), it is appropriate to look first at a time when the beliefs and opinions of the people who were governed were thought to be of limited consequence. The earliest analyses of the nature and functioning of government paid little attention to what we refer today as "public opinion." And, of course, there were no mass media available to help form or modify that opinion. The classical theorists focused mainly on the process by which rulers came into power and their claims about the sources of their legitimacy.

Obviously, then, the traditional study of governments began centuries earlier than the analysis of political behavior using an empirical approach. The earliest political philosophers set forth a number of classical explanations of government that were thought to provide answers as to how rulers and the ruled should relate to each other. However, political philosophy changed drastically over the centuries as new ideas regarding the nature and sources of authority and power were proposed. Roughly speaking, contemporary political scientists divide the timeline between (as they say) "Plato and NATO" into at least four general periods—the *ancient, medieval, early modern,* and *contemporary* eras—each characterized by different concerns with political thought and governing systems.

The ancient period started about four hundred years before the birth of Christ, with the political writings of Plato and his pupil Aristotle. Writers of the period gave very little attention to what we now think of as public opinion or its role in the relationship between citizens and government. Indeed, the concept and the term were not known at the time. These early writers focused in large part on what government *ought to be like* rather than what it was in reality. The ancient era continued until the final collapse of Rome around 500 A.D.

The second or medieval period began with the beginnings of Christian domination of Europe. By the end of the first millennium, the Catholic (that is "universal") Church was centered in Rome, and the pope was the leading interpreter of Christianity's sacred scriptures. The philosophers of the time were preoccupied with a long search for the ways in which human beings could best relate to the requirements of God. Kings and princes were believed to have their authority directly from Him as a *divine right.*

An early modern period began more or less about the time that Columbus made his famous voyage. It was a time when the divine right of kings was coming under critical analysis—not in the sense that it challenged ecclesiastic authority but because of a new idea—that the authority of a monarch was not of divine origin, but the startling idea that it was actually dependent upon the *consent of the people* themselves. It was this emerging interpretation ultimately that laid the foundation for an increasing concern with public opinion.

A more contemporary era emerged during the late decades of the nineteenth century. Political theorists of the early part of this period increasingly concluded that public opinion was a vital force that rulers ignored at their peril. Later, during the early years of the twentieth century, procedures were developed for actually *measuring* public opinion. This was truly a significant innovation.

By the mid-1800s, modern newspapers had developed, and by the late nineteenth century they had come to be seen as playing an essential part in the *process by which public opinion was formed and changed.* Later, as other news media arrived, they were also linked to public opinion and were said to be very powerful influences on what citizens felt and thought about government and about other types of issues that came to public attention. Thus, in more recent times, concern about the news media, public opinion, and public opinion measurement with polls became major factors in shaping elections and in the formation and enforcement of public policy.

In summary, then, during the long period from "Plato to NATO," the attention of political philosophers shifted from a concern with formal structures of government, and rulers' claims of a right to exercise power awarded by God, to another form of power that had its source in the beliefs and desires of ordinary citizens. Slowly, public opinion—the convictions and preferences of ordinary citizens—came to be recognized as the most fundamental factor deciding which of those who led would be retained or dismissed. The ability to measure such opinion, which came in the early decades of the twentieth century, added to its significance.

The Ancient Period: The Search for the Just Society

The idea of "public opinion" (but not the term) as an important part of the political process began to emerge in philosophy late in the 1700s. However, as Glaser and Simon note, there were a few minor concerns with the basic idea as far back as the time of Plato (427–347 B.C.). At that time, concerns of ordinary people were generally dismissed as untrustworthy and unimportant compared with more valid knowledge:

> The relevant intellectual history of opinion starts with Plato's contrast of *doxa* (opinion) with *episteme* (knowledge). Against the [arguments of the] sophists, who claimed that *doxa* was all that was available to human cognition, Plato made a fundamental contrast between the transient and the eternal: *doxa* was popular belief, unshaped by the rigors of philosophy, and was fickle and fleeting; *episteme* was sure knowledge of the unchanging "Ideas" underlying the visible world. *Doxa* was the stuff of the untutored many; *episteme* of the few.[1]

Plato developed one of the first of the classical theories of government. He described the "ideal" state in his *Republic.*[2] Because opinion (*doxa*) was fickle, transient, and ill-informed, he believed that it provided no foundation for governing. Only unchanging knowledge (*episteme*)—developed by philosophers—provided both the basis for designing the governing system of a state and for selecting its leaders.

Above all, Plato was concerned with the nature of *justice* and how it could be achieved within a well-designed political structure. In his description of the arrangements needed in such a political system, he did recognize that a trusting relationship between the ruler and the ruled was a feature of paramount importance. No ruler, he said, should act selfishly for his own benefit. He must be ever conscious of the needs of those who are ruled—a limited but important recognition of the role of those ruled. In some ways this was a rather limited recognition of what we would call public opinion today. Plato put it this way:

> And so with government of any kind, no ruler, in so far as he is acting as a ruler, will study or enjoin what is for his own interest. All that he says and does will be said and done with a view to what is good and proper for the subjects for whom he practices his art.[3]

While there were no regular news media in his day remotely comparable to those that came later, Plato fully understood the role of communication in creating people's beliefs about their world. For example, he warned that communications to children stressing hostile or negative relationships between human beings could be dangerous. They would be influenced, he maintained, by entertaining tales and stories transmitted to them by mothers and nurses. Character and behavior, he believed, were derived (as communicated social constructions of reality) from stories passed on to children as they were being reared. If Plato were alive today to see what children can obtain from our contemporary media, he would undoubtedly be deeply distressed.

Plato was greatly concerned with the basis of *legitimacy* in the relationship between a ruler and those over whom he held domain. In particular, he wrote extensively about how rulers should be selected. Plato's answer was that it was the *philosophers who must be kings*. It was their wisdom, their desire to do good, and their freedom from avarice that made them the best choice. He set forth an elaborate description about how such philosopher-kings should be chosen, the best way to educate them, and how they should be judged on the basis of their deeds in office. Thus, a positive relationship between rulers and their subjects—which might be defined as an early concern with public opinion—was thought to be a *key to a just society*.

Democracy was the closest system to the model of a truly just government that Plato envisioned. However, his conception of democracy—based in a small city-state—was unwieldy and unworkable. The reason is that every citizen was to have an equal voice in all decisions that were to be made. Wisely, he rejected such a system as inefficient and impractical. What developed later, of course, was *representative* democracy—systems in which members of parliaments, congresses, or similar bodies are freely chosen by large populations of citizens to make laws and policies on their behalf—laws that are interpreted and enforced fairly by agencies of the state.

The Medieval Period: The Struggle Between Secular and Ecclesiastical Power

After the decline of Greece, and later of the Roman Empire, philosophers turned away from analyzing politics solely in terms of the relationship between *secular* rulers and their subjects. Christianity had become deeply established in virtually all parts of Europe and its set of beliefs increasingly came to be the dominant cultural foundation for interpreting individual human nature. Furthermore, Christianity provided the intellectual and spiritual culture that defined the requirements of the social order.

It took many years before the Church became the center of power. However, by 500 A.D., paganism, based on the gods of Rome, was in disarray. Moreover, a clear separation of *secular* things and *sacred* things had been defined in the teachings of Jesus: ("Render unto Caesar the things that are Caesar's, and to God the thing's that are God's." Mark 12:17). For some centuries, this distinction led political power to shift between secular rulers, such as Charlemagne (ninth century) and various popes. As the centuries went on, however, the popes led an increasingly universal Church. As their authority increased during the medieval period, Christian doctrines, thought, and values—largely disseminated from Rome—began to permeate every aspect of European life.

Given the overwhelming concern with religion during the period, there was no attention given by political philosophers (or anyone else) to the concept of public opinion, or the idea that common people had any political role to play. Princes and monarchs inherited their lands, along with undisputed sovereignty over their domains. The lives and activities of ordinary citizens were completely controlled by their "station" in life. The vast majority of Europeans were agricultural serfs. The children of serfs became serfs themselves, as did their children. Few rose above that station. Indeed, the entire structure of society was seen as a fulfillment of God's plan, and to suggest that it should be changed was a violation of the interpretations and wisdom of the Church. Obviously, few in such a population had any voice in determining who would lead them or any influence on the decisions of their leaders.

There were, from time to time, conflicts—sometimes very bitter ones—between secular and religious leaders. However, by the twelfth century, papal power clearly dominated across Europe. Increasingly, the universal Church tolerated no deviation from its interpretations of God's requirements, including those of local princes and monarchs. Understandably, within this environment, philosophers had little interest in the thoughts, satisfactions, judgements, or political opinions of common people. They turned their attention to understanding the relationship between human beings and God. That relationship included the nature of government. Essentially, they came to believe that there was no distinction between *ecclesiastical* power (based on the authority of the Church) and *secular* power (exercised by governments to regulate society). They were one and the same.

At the very beginning of this period, a philosopher of note was St. Augustine (354–430). His work *The City of God*, written in the early 400s, is a strong affirmation of Christian idealism and an attack on paganism (Christianity was not yet universal in his time, and many people subscribed to the Roman gods). *The City of God* was less a treatise on government arrangements than a description of a basic conflict between good and evil, in a "heavenly" vs. "earthly" city.

Later, as the medieval period progressed, John of Salisbury (1120–1180) wrote his notable work *The Statesman's Book*. It was a time when there was still occasional conflict concerning the supremacy of spiritual vs. secular power. Salisbury championed ecclesiastical authority over the temporal. He stated firmly that the Church had every right to depose a prince who violated the laws of God. The authority of Rome was becoming indisputable.

Perhaps the most notable of the writers of the medieval period was Thomas Aquinas (1224–1274), who took up and elaborated the theme of Salisbury. Essentially, Aquinas was a theologian and the most dominant figure of a group that came to be called the *Scholastics*. Writing on such topics as sin, angels, the nature of the soul, and the importance of moral virtue, his writings are still regarded as one of the important intellectual foundations of Catholic philosophy. Indeed, because of his contributions, he was elevated to sainthood. His thesis on "The Divine Government" in his *Summa Theologica* (written during the 1200s) sets forth the logical basis for concluding that religion, reason, and monarchy, in both church and empire, stemmed from *a universal* principle—namely, God's total rule of the universe. As he put it:

> For the same reason that God is the ruler of things as He is their cause, because the same cause that gives being gives perfection; and this belongs to government. Now God is the cause, not of some particular kind of being, but of the whole universal being. Therefore, as there can be nothing which is not created by God, so that there can be nothing which is not subject to His government.[4]

It is not difficult to understand, from the foundation of philosophical thought provided by philosophers of the medieval period, that God provided the justification for the power of kings. Indeed, virtually all of the monarchs of the late Middle Ages proclaimed that they ruled on the basis of His mandates. The "divine right of kings," in other words, was the foundation for their secular authority. Few challenged their claim that they had been placed in power by the hand of God. To question their authority was tantamount to *an act of sacrilege*.

The Early Modern Period: The Emergence of Democracy

During the medieval period, the claim by rulers that their authority was derived directly from God was a difficult position against which to argue. Doing so could have very nasty consequences (like being burned at the stake). Nevertheless, just such challenges developed during the *early modern* period—which can be identified roughly as between about 1500 to 1800. What makes this time so noteworthy is that philosophers of the period openly and directly challenged the concept of the divine right of kings.

The ideas about government expressed during the early modern period were in part a result of the Protestant Reformation, which was in some ways a part of the more general Renaissance, which began in Italy in the fourteenth century. As the Age of Reason slowly developed. A a period of transition took place between the medieval and the early modern period. By the 1500s, the overwhelming power of the Catholic Church began to be challenged. Various religious reformers were protesting what they saw as abuses of power by the pope and by religious authorities more generally. These protests ultimately led to a rejection, or at least major modifications, of Church doctrines and the formation of various Protestant ("protesting") groups. During the 1600s, and especially the 1700s, philosophers turned away from religious interpretations. Specifically, they openly challenged the claims of monarchs that they received their power directly from God.

One of the most significant writers of this transitional period was Thomas Hobbes (1588–1679). His work *The Leviathan*, published in the mid-1600s, argued that *sovereignty* (the right to govern over a specified territory and people) was obtained by *assent of the governed* (and did not come from God). It was a remarkable and truly radical position at the time. Hobbes played a key role in developing what is arguably one of the most significant ideas ever developed by political theorists—the concept of the *social contract*. Essentially, he envisioned an implicit contract-like agreement between ruler and the ruled. That agreement required those who held power to act on behalf of, and with the approval of, those under their domain. This was a direct challenge to the idea that monarchs received their authority from a divine mandate and were responsible only to God.

Hobbes maintained, essentially, that all men (we would say human beings today) are *naturally equal*. That is, he noted, even the weak can kill the strong, although they might have to use guile or forge an alliance with others who were stronger. Hobbes stated that this was a source of great problems when humankind lived in what he called a "state of nature" (a time before there were organized governments). Hobbes posed this idea as a theoretical concept. (He made no claim that such a time actually existed historically.) His purpose was to explain why the "social contract" emerged and was a valid interpretation of the nature of government.

More specifically, Hobbes said, life before government was truly miserable. People had no laws or anyone to enforce order or even to provide basic protection. It was, he claimed, a time of *war of all against all*. There were, he said,

> no Arts; no Letters; no Society; and worst of all, continual feare, and danger of violent death: And the life of man, solitary, poore, nasty, brutish, and short.[5]

Thus, the origin of government, Hobbes maintained, was based in the need of human beings to have some authority "to declare among the diversity of men's opinions, what is right and what is wrong, and what is not in accord with the law of nature." That need, Hobbes stated, could be met by selecting one person—one who could be trusted to act honorably—and form a *covenant*—a contract in which that person would be allowed to have and use the power of a sovereign to make just laws and enforce them fairly. The result would be, Hobbes wrote, a *Christian Commonwealth*—a multitude united in one person. This, then, is "the Generation of the great Leviathan."[6] Thus, his vision was that all the people would unite and then award the power to rule to a carefully selected person, but in return they would demand that peace be maintained with justice for all.

The concept of a "social contract" between a leader and the led represents a remarkable turning point in political philosophy. For one thing, it openly and directly disputed the claims of monarchs that they had a mandate directly from God to impose their rule. The true source of power, according to Hobbes, was in *the consent of the governed*. If this was indeed the case, and a contractual agreement between leader and led gave the sovereign the right to exercise power, it followed that, if the contract were to be broken by the ruler, *the people had a right to replace the sovereign*. It is in this conclusion that the importance of public satisfaction with government (the foundation of public opinion) increasingly came to be fully and dramatically recognized.

Also important among the early modern writers was John Locke (1632–1704). He advocated the creation of a social order outside the control of either church or state.[7] His contributions during the late part of the seventeenth century included not only a rejection of the divine right of kings—as set forth in his *Two Treatises on Government*—but also the importance of a *legislature* to which both the monarch and the people would be responsible. While there had always been many kinds of groups who served as councils and advisors to kings, the idea of an elected legislature—serving as an intermediary between the sovereign and the people, and to whom each was responsible—was very important. As an elected body of representatives, it had to represent the will of the people. If that relationship of trust and confidence was violated, that legislature, as well as the ruler, could be replaced.

Other influential writers, following Hobbes and Locke, refined the idea of the covenant between leader and the led. Among them was John Jacques Rousseau (1712–1778). His work, titled *The Social Contract*, was published in 1762. It was a time when dissatisfaction with British rule was growing in the American colonies and discontent with the monarchy was becoming increasingly common in France.

In his *Social Contract*, Rousseau maintained that the sovereignty of the people is both *inalienable* and *indivisible*. That was a truly powerful statement. It could not have been more opposite to the earlier idea that the sovereignty of monarchs was God-given. While Hobbes, Locke, and Rousseau each had very different concepts of the condition of human beings in the so-called "state of nature," each argued forcibly that it was the people of a nation who had the ultimate political power and that those who ruled did so by the people's consent.

More than a century would go by after Hobbes published his *Leviathan* before the theories that the citizens of a government were the ultimate source of power came to be represented in reality. Those theories formed the basis for potential action against unpopular monarchs. By the end of the 1700s, however, just such events did take place. The rule of kings was replaced by the rule of citizens in both the French and the American revolutions. Independence from England was declared by the colonists in 1776, and a short time later, in 1789, the French deposed their king. Thus, dissatisfactions with rulers seen as tyrannical led to their overthrow, and their systems of government were replaced by others designed to be more sensitive to the wishes, beliefs, and feelings of those governed.

Obviously, the classical theorists of the early modern period had become very much aware of the importance of what we today refer to as public opinion. However, it was not yet conceptualized in quite the way it is now. At the time, the opinions that were seen as important were not those of the illiterate and ignorant hordes of common citizens. The ones of importance were the views of the educated and affluent elite—those who owned property or who conducted businesses. For example, Jeremy Bentham, writing in 1791, was not impressed with the opinions of the common people. He maintained that the majority did not have either the intellectual skills or the time to read and preoccupy themselves with public affairs.[8]

Even so, the views, assessments, and levels of satisfaction on the part of ordinary citizens with government was becoming increasingly recognized. For example, in Rousseau's *The Social Contract*, he posed the concept of the *general will*, which in many ways was an important conceptual forerunner to what would come to be commonly called "public opinion." In an ideal state, he maintained, the laws that are enacted must express a moral standpoint that supports the common good. Rousseau assumed that all people are capable of holding views consistent with high moral standards and that they can agree on the nature of laws that express them. Thus, the beliefs and opinions of the rank and file concerning the policies and laws put in place by leaders provided for Rousseau a foundation for acceptance of their authority.

The Contemporary Period: Public Opinion Becomes Dominant

As the Age of Reason came to a close, these concepts and ideas about consent of the governed developed into what we now call "public opinion." The term itself began to be used widely in the 1800s, and its significant relationship to government was increasingly recognized by both politicians and the general population. Indeed, public opinion came to be seen as a powerful force that leaders ignored at their peril—either in democracies where rulers are designated or replaced at the ballot box or in authoritarian systems where revolutions can replace leaders in more drastic ways.

At the time, however, public opinion remained a slippery concept. It was difficult to define and impossible to assess with any degree of accuracy. Moreover, it was still being conceptualized as the views of the educated elite. For example, William A. MacKinnon was a British writer who wrote the first book in the 1820s that focused exclusively on the nature, formation, and functions of public opinion. He defined it in terms of the sentiments held by those who were *intelligent and well-informed*:

> Public Opinion may be said to be, that sentiment on any given subject which is entertained by the best-informed, most intelligent, and most moral persons in the community, which is gradually spread and adopted by nearly all persons of any education or proper feeling in a civilized state.[9]

Nevertheless, as the nineteenth century moved on, it was becoming increasingly clear that, if the views, assessments, and levels of satisfaction of the rank and file do not support the people in power and their policies, change is likely. In a representative democracy such change is not all that difficult. Elections are held periodically, and it is not difficult to "throw the rascals out." In a monarchy, however, or in a modern dictatorship, it is not all that easy. Those in charge can enforce their power through various means—secret police, harsh use of the military, strict control of the press, and in many other ways. For public opinion to be an effective force in a social contract, therefore, the system must include a means by which citizens can make the ultimate decision about who should be in charge. That condition exists most visibly in governmental systems where top leaders and bodies of representatives are periodically elected.

During the mid- and late 1800s, two writers played key roles in identifying the significance of public opinion in the functioning of government. One was the French political writer Alexis de Tocqueville, whose two-volume work *Democracy in America* was published shortly before mid-century.[10] De Tocqueville spent a number of years in the United States, observing its people and especially the functioning of the American government. It was, after all, still a relatively new experiment. But giving so much power to the rank and file seemed dangerous to many in Europe. Indeed, it also did in many ways to de Tocqueville, who feared that such a system had the potential for what he termed a *tyranny of the majority*. He concluded that having a system where even the uncultured and illiterate are allowed to select their leaders was a dangerous feature of the American democracy:

> If it be admitted that a man, possessing absolute power, may misuse that power by wronging his adversaries, why should a majority not be liable to the same reproach? Men are not apt to change their characters by agglomeration; nor does their patience in the presence of obstacles increase with the consciousness of their strength. And for these reasons I can never willingly invest any number of my fellow creatures with that unlimited authority which I should refuse in any one of them.[11]

Another writer of special significance during the nineteenth century was James Bryce, a British political philosopher who visited the United States for several extended periods. He set forth in the 1880s an insightful theory of the formation and functioning of public opinion in all forms of government (see Chapter 7). He portrayed it as a powerful political force that leaders could not ignore—indeed an almost overwhelming consideration in determining their actions and policies. Equally important for the objectives of the present text, *he linked its formation directly to the mass media*—the (new) daily newspapers of his time.

While Bryce developed a particularly insightful analysis of the influence on public opinion on political leaders, he also recognized that it was a very difficult matter to *assess* it in any degree of precision. He noted that some indications were available to those who could attend town meetings, listen to the opinions expressed by representatives of groups, or even observe torchlight parades that protested or supported a specific issue or cause. But the only sure measure of how people felt, he maintained, was by counting the votes at election time.

Statisticians had not yet provided probability theory permitting the design of samples, on which polls would be based, and psychologists had not yet developed techniques for systematic assessment and recording of opinions, beliefs, and attitudes. Thus, Bryce could not anticipate the development of public opinion polls, which would not come until early in the 1900s. As he put it:

> The machinery for weighing or measuring the popular will from week-to-week or month-to-month has not been, and is not likely to be, invented.[12]

In summary, this brief tour through four periods in the history of political philosophy shows that a belief in the *source of power in government* underwent truly remarkable shifts over the centuries. In the ancient period, only scattered and indirect references were made by political philosophers to what we might recognize as public opinion. During the medieval period, it was not an issue. There was little dispute that the right to rule rested in a monarch—who received his or her authority directly from God. If his or her subjects did not like the monarch's laws and policies, that was just too bad.

During the early modern period, however, beliefs in the "divine right of kings" began to erode—indeed drastically in many ways. The ultimate source of power to make and enforce laws increasingly came to be seen as possessed by those who were governed. That was a truly remarkable idea. What it meant was that, in one way or another, those who were governed entered into an agreement—an implicit contract—with their rulers. The terms of the compact were that the people would allocate to their ruler the authority to make and enforce laws but only insofar as he or she did so in a just and humane way. If that agreement was not kept, if the contract were violated, it was understood that the people had the right to take the ruler's power away. This was the underlying principle on which both the French and the American revolutions were based. It remains today the most fundamental assumption underlying democratic government—although elections rather than revolutions have been accepted as the legitimate means by which change can be accomplished.

A major consequence of this change was that it thrust into glaring importance the way in which people thought about their rulers and their actions. If they were satisfied with the laws and policies devised by those in charge, there was little dissent and unrest. If the people became unhappy or believed that they were being unjustly ruled, there was always the danger that they would conclude that the contract had been broken. In this general sense, then, the feelings, assessments, and shared beliefs of the people who were being governed came to play a central and critical role in assuring the stability of governments.

While there was now wide agreement among the public, among politicians, and among philosophers that public opinion was a factor of paramount importance, two major problems remained. One was that *it was not clear how the majority formed or modified their opinions*. The second was that it seemed impossible to *assess or measure public opinion* once it had formed.

PUBLIC OPINION AND THE PRESS

It was, of course, during the early modern period that the printing press became a reality. It was to become a major factor in the process by which public opinion was formed and changed. The period began when Gutenberg produced his famous forty-line Bible (1455). Very quickly, the technology spread to all major populations' centers in Europe and then on to other areas, such as the colonies in the New World. As a consequence, books became increasingly available to those with the means to acquire them and the skills to read them. Also as a consequence, writers such as Hobbes, Locke, and Rousseau were able to reach audiences who would play key roles in shaping ideas about government. For some, this was a disturbing trend. By those in power, books were often seen as tools used by those who wanted unwelcome change. In 1559, for example, only a century after Gutenberg printed his famous Bible, Pope Paul IV drew up an *Index of Prohibited Books*. But, in reality, the works of such philosophers were read by only a small number of well-educated people.

Like the evil forces released from Pandora's box, however, the printing press soon produced another kind of product for those who did not welcome political change. Even during the 1500s, *pamphlets* of various kinds expressing political views were circulated. These often provided subject matter for speeches, sermons, and face-to-face discussions. In this way their ideas reached beyond the well-educated and the financial elite. Through this "two-step flow" of ideas (see Chapter 14), common people came into contact with dissenting views, and these broadsides and pamphlets were seldom welcomed by those in power.

Another product of the printing press was *news*. Many kinds of specialized private news sheets had long been prepared by scribes and sent to those who paid for their services. Clearly, there was a demand for such news. By the early 1600s, the first regularly printed news sheets appeared. They were primitive affairs—small, limited in content, often inaccurate, and badly out of date by the time they reached their readers. Nevertheless, they were an important step toward the eventual development of modern newspapers.

The Arrival of Newspapers

Ultimately, it would be *newspapers* that would increasingly reach beyond the well-to-do and the well educated to inform the much larger body of the politically interested. They had become increasingly available to the literate during the 1700s. These early newspapers often conveyed truly important ideas, and they began to print complaints about government to politically active people.

At first, the simple *newspapers* of the eighteenth century were read mainly by those who could afford their rather costly subscriptions. Thus, their audience was still an educated and affluent elite. But in many ways these were the very kinds of people who were in a position to insist on new directions in government. However, the newspaper situation changed dramatically when *steam-driven presses* came into existence by the early 1800s. Cities were expanding, and the Industrial Revolution was off to a good start. Cheap popular newspapers, supported by advertising of the new goods produced by steam-powered factories, were being developed for the common people. Moreover, now many more people could read. Even before mid-century, literacy had increased in the United States as tax-supported schools were established and attendance became mandatory. Thus, as the circulations of newspapers continued to grow, they became increasingly capable of influencing the political ideas of larger and larger numbers.

By the late 1800s, the important relationship between public opinion and the press came to be fully recognized. It was the political scientists who most closely focused attention on that relationship. They pointed out that it is precisely in representative democracies where the relationship between rulers and the ruled can most rapidly and effectively be influenced by a press that is free of official control and censorship. Those who have been elected usually want to be kept in office. This makes them sensitive to the shared opinions of the electorate—which in a democracy can determine whether they will be retained or replaced at election time. Those officials know that a free press can influence what people think about both them and their policies during the time they are in office.

In systems that are not democratic—as in monarchies, dictatorships, and other systems ruled strongly without a basis in popular consent, a free press is a truly dangerous entity. Very quickly after the printing press became a reality—even before newspapers became common—European monarchs recognized that printed material could easily be used by their opponents to create dissent. Strong controls over print were quickly established. For example, in England, when the first newspapers began to be published, systems of *prior restraint* were exercised over stories that might be potentially harmful to the Crown. The term "prior restraint" means that an official representative of the ruler must examine all news stories before allowing them to be printed. It was a common practice, especially in the American colonies, where stirring up feelings against the Crown was seen as a significant threat. England, after all, was far away, and the colonies were a great economic asset. A representative of the governor in each colony reviewed every news story before the editor was allowed to publish it "by permission." It was a practice that came to be deeply resented, and the ultimate consequence was that, when the Constitution of the United States was finally adopted, the new nation had a First Amendment that specifically provided for a press free from such prior censorship.

By the end of the nineteenth century, then, the term "public opinion" was in wide use among political scientists, and its importance was well-understood by almost everyone—politicians, journalists, and indeed the educated public at large. There was, however, no accepted and clear definition of its exact nature. Furthermore, no one had the vaguest idea about how it might be accurately assessed or measured. Also well understood was the fact that newspapers (the only news medium of the time) played a central role in its formation and change. Thus, in democracies, and even in other systems, the press came to be seen as the critical link between ordinary citizens and those whom they had elected to office, but it was still not seen as trustworthy.

Recognizing That "News Is Not Truth"

Early in the twentieth century, one of the most insightful scholars who addressed the nature of public opinion, the part that it plays in government and the ways in which newspapers influence its formation and change, was Walter Lippmann. (His ideas are discussed in detail in Chapter 8). Even before World War I, he became a very successful and respected journalist—one who had acquired a background in philosophy and political science. This led him to focus on the relationships among public opinion, government, and the press.

What came to be regarded as a classic book by Lippmann was titled *Public Opinion*. It was published in 1922, shortly after World War I, and it remains profoundly important. In that book, he stated that the function of the press is to "*create pictures in our heads of the world outside.*"[13] (Actually, that phrase was the title of his first chapter.) The central idea was that citizens learned about what was going on through the newspapers. After all, they really had no other way to gain information about the political events that were taking place. The problem that Lippmann saw was that news stories have features that limit their relationship to what actually takes place in the events and situations about which they report. As we see it today, Lippmann was recognizing the role of mass communications in the "*social construction of reality.*"

Lippmann pointed out ways in which those "pictures" were often distorted and incorrect. He based his conclusion that "news is not truth" on his understanding of the way in which the news media of his time (newspapers then, but all news media today) gathered, processed, and disseminated accounts of what was happening in the world. He knew that news reports were at best misleading and at worst deeply flawed. Thus, the "pictures in our heads," he maintained, create a "pseudo reality" and do not accurately represent "the world outside."

The problem was, he explained, that even though reporters, editors, and others who assembled the news agenda on a daily basis tried very hard to be accurate and complete in what was reported to the public, they could not do so. Clearly, the ethics of journalism required them to do their best. Nevertheless, the accounts that reached the public were distorted. This came about, Lippmann explained, because those who provided the flow of news were always limited by time, budget, and the preferences of their audiences. There was simply no way that they could provide full details on any story that they covered. That might take weeks for a single story, but they had to meet their 5:00 p.m. deadline every day to get the next morning's paper out on time. Moreover, to keep the profits coming, editors often had to select and report those stories that their customers wanted to read about, whether they were actually important or not. Much of what happened of importance on a given day, therefore, never reached public attention.

Thus, Lippmann developed an explanation of the nature and functions of news that is labeled in this book as the theory of the unintentional distortion of the news. (see Chapter 8.) The bottom line is that, because news reports on issues and candidates are often unintentionally distorted, citizens have to *form their opinions on the basis of flawed information*. Thus, in deciding on their political behavior—votes, allegiances, and support—Lippmann maintained, citizens wind up making their choices on the basis of a "pseudo environment" existing in their heads—a flawed version of reality based on the distorted representations that they encounter in the press.

That idea, that the press can never provide full, flawless, unbiased, and totally accurate information to citizens about the events that occur in their environment, received further support later in the second half of the 1900s from two additional theorists. One was David Manning White, who developed the basic ideas of what in this book is called Gatekeeping Theory (see Chapter 11). In an insightful article published in 1950, he outlined the process by which editors select (or reject) stories to include in their daily newspaper, on the basis of various criteria—thereby distorting the information that audiences receive.[14]

The point White made was that a huge number of accounts and reports came to the editor over the "news wires"—as well as from other sources. The number of such stories vastly exceeds the space available (or time in broadcast news). It is the editor's responsibility to *select*, from that abundance, the list of stories that will actually be included in the daily presentation to the audience. A variety of criteria are used, but the essential point is that much of what happened in the world on any given day never reaches the attention of the public, simply because the "gatekeeper" does not select them. Thus, the public develops "pictures in their heads of the world outside" (social constructions of reality) on the basis of selected and limited information.

Another contribution to the general idea of the "pseudo-environment" was developed in the early 1970s by communication scholars Maxwell McCombs and Donald Shaw.[15] They contributed what is called the Agenda-Setting Theory of the Press (see Chapter 12). They pointed out that editors have the responsibility to *design* the daily news report—regardless of what medium is used. They must select some stories to put on page one vs. those on page two or buried on the back pages (or at the beginning or middle of a broadcast rather than at its end). They do this on the assumption that some reports are of significant interest—or that audiences will find them interesting. Thus, because of the very factors emphasized by Lippmann (limitations on time, space, budget, etc.), some stories receive *greater or lesser prominence* in the daily news report. This influences the interpretations of the audience. Research shows clearly that a story appearing on the back pages of the newspaper, or late in the broadcast, does not seem as important to the members of the audience as one with a prominent headline and located "above the fold" on page one (or as the lead story in the broadcast). Thus, Lippmann's theory of the unintentional distortion of the news (which journalists cannot control) is further supported by both gatekeeping and agenda-setting theories.

THE DEVELOPMENT OF PUBLIC OPINION POLLS

By the 1920s, the field of statistical theory had been well developed. Originally, it came from agricultural research related to beer production and from studies of gaming tables in European casinos. By the 1920s, however, statistical analysis had become truly important in scientific research. The use of *probability* as an epistemological criterion for deciding whether an outcome of a research project represented *mere chance*—or was an indication of a possible cause-effect relationship—had been adopted in many fields. In particular, the concept of *representative sampling* had become particularly useful. It provided the means by which a limited number of units—in some large population of such units—selected in such a way that each unit had an equal chance of being included, could be studied closely to reveal general tendencies, patterns, regularities, and conclusions that characterized the large population.

Thus, *random* sampling came into use to study everything from shrimp populations in marine biology to the qualities of grain in fields. Variations of this idea (e.g., systematic sampling, quota sampling, stratified sampling, etc.) were invented to be used in situations where it might not be possible to select units by purely random means from a list of those in an entire population.

These statistical techniques also caught on quickly in the social and behavioral sciences, where investigators were faced with the daunting task of developing generalizations about entire populations of unlike people. Thus, psychologists, sociologists, political scientists, economists, and various kinds of market researchers were using statistical techniques, and especially sampling procedures, by the beginning of the 1930s. In addition, techniques for the systematic assessment and quantification of opinions and attitudes as well as other psychological factors through the use of specially designed questionnaires had been developed by social psychologists even earlier.

The Measurement of Public Opinion Becomes a Reality

These scientific procedures were quickly put to use by those interested in assessing public opinion—a goal that had eluded political theorists for centuries. Building on the techniques and procedures for sampling and those for measurement that were being used successfully in several of the sciences. Pioneer pollsters such as George Gallup, Elmo Roper, and Archibald Crossley (acting independently but employing similar techniques) undertook to study how Americans felt about political candidates. Their first success was the prediction that Franklin Delano Roosevelt would win the 1936 election over his rival Alfred M. Landon. Their predictions were remarkably accurate.

Americans were impressed with public opinion polling. It quickly caught the imagination of the population. No one in earlier times had ever been able to accomplish the results it provided. In fact, it was seen as such a valuable tool that private agencies were quickly formed to provide polls for paying clients. One of the most successful was that of George Gallup, who had established the American Institute of Public Opinion in 1935. His organization soon had branches in other countries. The term "Gallup Poll" quickly became a household word.

Gallup and others were not always successful in their assessments. Their prediction that Harry S. Truman would lose to John Dewey in the very close presidential election of 1948 was faulty. Nevertheless, as the years progressed, the measurement of public opinion became increasingly refined and precise. The basic procedures have become standard in marketing research of all kinds and in many other fields where generalizations about the feelings and preferences of large numbers of people can be ascertained with some precision by careful study of a well-selected sample.

The Preoccupation with Public Opinion by Contemporary Leaders

Today, no election campaign is planned or conducted without input from pollsters. Added to the arsenal are procedures for conducting *focus groups*—which in some ways are miniature polls but from which much greater depths of feelings and concerns can be uncovered. The bottom line today is that the relationship between the political process and public opinion is so well understood that any political candidate in a democracy—or indeed any elected public official—would be foolhardy if he or she did not take into account the nature of public opinion concerning policies developed or supported by him or her as a person. A contemporary politician's worst nightmare is to see public opinion turn against him or her. That can be a clear predictor of disaster at the ballot box.

In addition, the relationship between the press and public opinion is well understood. Every incumbent in the Congress, or in other major political offices, has a "press secretary." That person's major function is to develop and release a flow of news stories to the folks back home, or the electorate at large, showing how concerned the legislator is with the problems about which constituents are worried and how he or she "feels their pain."

It is important to identify clearly the role of the press in the complex relationships among politics, public opinion, and the news media. Without the news media, the public would have little knowledge of what is taking place in the halls of legislatures or in the offices of public officials. The press, therefore, is the "window on the world" used by citizens to understand the social environment and political realities beyond their own homes, neighborhoods, jobs, and communities. Without the press, in most cases, there can be no political issues around which citizens need to form opinions. Conditions in society that need to be addressed politically are revealed in news reports and analyses by journalists—or at least by fellow citizens who have attended to the media, learned about the issues, and passed on information and interpretations to others. That process has been widely studied by communication theorists, and the formulation that explains it is commonly called the theory of the Two-Step Flow of Communication. (See Chapter 13.)

A THEORY OF PUBLIC OPINION AS SHAPED BY THE PRESS: A FORMAL SUMMARY

Understanding the relationships among politics, public opinion, and the role of the press, then, was slowly developed over centuries by political scientists (with input from other fields as well). That basic theory is related in important ways to other media theories that are set forth in this book (gatekeeping, agenda-setting, and the two-step flow).

The theory of public opinion as shaped by the press can be summed up in terms of the following set of relatively simple propositions:

1. The press monitors the social and political environment through its surveillance function and *selects* those issues and events that its managers deem worthy of reporting to the public.
2. The public attends (selectively) to those reports and *assesses* the significance of a given issue or event for themselves or for others about whom they are concerned.
3. On the basis of this information and assessment of the issue or event, members of the public form *individual opinions* as to what personal political actions may or may not be appropriate as a response.
4. Their individual opinions are shared with others, and possibly modified, as discussion among interested parties takes place. In this way, personal political orientations become common *as consensus is reached* among the segment of the public that is participating.
5. **Therefore**, as the shared opinions of such segments of the public become known to their members, they become the *public opinion* of that part of the population. That shared opinion may represent the majority or a minority. In any case, those shared opinions can be ascertained by systematic polling.

In summary, then, the power and role of public opinion in the political process has become widely understood by political leaders, by the press, and by the public. The ways in which the "press" (news industry using several media) plays a central role in its formation and change, even though its information is often flawed, have also become clear. The manner in which public opinion is assessed by polls is also well understood by both leaders and followers.

Insight into these relationships was developed over centuries by ancient and modern political philosophers, traditional and empiricist political scientists, statistical theorists, other social scientists, and modern polling experts. Above all, however, it was the contributions of political scholars over a period of many centuries who brought it all together.

Notes and References

1. Theodore L. Glaser and Charles T. Salmon, *Public Opinion and the Communication of Consent* (New York: The Guilford Press, 1995), p. 4.
2. See *The Republic of Plato*, trans. by Francis MacDonald Cornford (London: Oxford University Press, 1945).
3. *Ibid.* p. 24.
4. *The Basic Writings of Saint Thomas Aquinas*, edited and annotated by Anton C. Pegis (New York: Random House, 1945), p. 956.
5. Thomas Hobbes, *The Leviathan* (New York: E. P. Dutton and Company, 1950), p. 104. First published in England in 1651.
6. *Ibid.* p. 143.
7. John Locke, *As Essay Concerning Human Understanding*, P. H. Nidditch, ed. (Oxford: Clarendon Press, 1975). First published in 1690.
8. See Slavko Splichal, *Public Opinion* (Lanham, MD: Rowman and Littlefield, Inc., 1999), p. 59.
9. William A. MacKinnon, *On the Rise, Progress and Present State of Public Opinion, in Great Britain and Other Parts of the World* (Shannon: Irish University Press, 1971), p. 15. First published in 1828.
10. Alexis de Tocqueville, *Democracy in America*, trans. by J. P. Mayer (Garden City: Anchor Books, 1969). First published in 1835 and 1840).
11. *Ibid.* 131.
12. Bryce, James, "Government by Public Opinion," *The American Commonwealth* (London: Macmillan, 1888), pp. 14–23.
13. Walter Lippmann, *Public Opinion* (New York: Harcourt Brace and Company, 1922).
14. David Manning White, "The 'Gatekeeper'; A Case Study in the Selection of News," *Journalism Quarterly*, Vol. 27, 1950, pp. 383–390.
15. Maxwell E. McCombs and Donald Shaw, "The Agenda-Setting Function of the Mass Media," *Public Opinion Quarterly*, 1972, pp. 176–187.

CHAPTER 5

Cognitive Processing: The Contributions of Psychology to Mass Communication Theory

After the contributions of Bacon and Descartes in the 1500s and 1600s, the use of the scientific method became increasingly common for studying the world of natural phenomena. As explained in Chapter 3, the founders of modern physical sciences no longer relied on logic and reason alone in their efforts to understand nature. As the strategies of modern science became available, the fields of physics, chemistry, and biology began to develop independently from philosophy. By the end of the 1700s, they had become distinct branches of science. By the 1800s, this transition also began for the social sciences, including the field of psychology.

The unique feature of the new social sciences was that their conclusions and explanations were also founded on *empirical observation*— Bacon's system for the use of the senses to observe relevant facts. Inductive and deductive reasoning were also an important part of their investigative strategies, especially for developing theory—but reaching conclusions solely through the use of formal logic alone was no longer accepted. During the 1700s, important discoveries had been made that would provide the foundation, not only for what were then called the "exact" sciences (physics, chemistry, and biology) but also for emerging specialized fields, such as physiology, medicine, botany, zoology, oceanography, meteorology, geology, and the many others that exist today. It was *the scientific method, based on empirical observation, that made these advances in human knowledge possible*. It would be psychology, however, that would develop the most thorough understanding of the ways in which individual human beings come to know and deal with the world of reality.

For the contemporary study of the process and effects of mass communication, psychology occupies a special place. Many contemporary psychologists are active researchers who study the media and their influences. But more fundamental for understanding the field's contribution to mass communication research and theory development was psychology's scientific studies of the fundamental factors and influences—both biological and learned—that shape individual human behavior from "within people's heads."

During the 1800s, great advances were made by the founders of psychology through the use of the scientific method applied to the age-old philosophical question of *knowing*. During the 1800s, they began to unravel how human beings *observe things with their senses* that are taking place in the world around them; how they *organize personal meanings and interpretations* in memory for those objects, situations, and events; and how they *respond to them* by engaging in distinctive patterns of behavior. (Those processes are obviously central to what audiences obtain from media content.)

Thus, by the end of the 1800s, the essential domains for developing a science of psychology were said to be (1) *stimuli*— that is, situations, states, and events in reality of which individuals become aware via their senses, (2) *cognitive processes*— certain conditions and processes in people's heads (conscious or not) that play a part in how they understand, interpret, and remember those external events, and (3) habits of *response*— the forms or patterns of behavior that people exhibit as they cope with those features of reality. Stated in a very simple acronym, these fundamental domains are S–O–R, *stimulus, organism,* and *response.*

As will be explained in more detail, there were significant disagreements within the field as to whether the factors in the organism that shaped responses to stimuli were mainly biological, and acquired as part of one's *inherited physical endowment*, or whether they were primarily conditions and states acquired by *learning through experience*. Great debates took place between those who held that it was *nature* (inherited biological factors) that were paramount in shaping behavior and those who said it was *nurture* (learning in a social environment) that was the primary shaper of the conduct of the human individual. These debates continue today.

Up until the late 1920s, the (nature) concept of *instinct* was popular among psychologists. Instincts (such as guide behavior in many animals) were said to be *both inherited* and *universal* in a particular species, and were the motivators or shapers of *complex patterns of human behavior*. However, this idea came to be rejected by the field during the 1920s. It was realized that, while many animal species do indeed have such universal instincts as part of their inherited genetic makeup, human beings apparently do not. (Many people in our population still believe that this popular idea applies to human beings.)

As instincts and other biological explanations of behavior lost favor, psychologists turned with enthusiasm to how human beings *learn*; how they remember, or forget, their experiences of the external world; and how this learning has an influence on their conduct. A variety of theories were developed to address these issues, and a large body of experimental evidence was assembled to assess those theories. The basic consensus, as the field advanced, was that stimuli and responses were linked through *habit*—which was defined as an increased probability that a particular stimulus would arouse a specific kind of response in the individual.

Increasingly, during the 1900s, psychology became a sophisticated discipline studying both animals and human beings. The field focused on both normal and abnormal behavior. Of special interest to mass communication researchers and theorists are the ways in which people *perceive* complex communication content, how they *organize and store* what they receive in memory, and how they use what they obtain from the media as *guides for their behavior*.

Thus, psychology emerged as a discipline, distinct from philosophy, over a period of less than a century. It became a specialized field that combined the ancient search for understanding the process of "knowing"—which had been debated by philosophers since ancient times—and the *scientific method* as a new way of seeking valid knowledge. Essentially psychology became, in one way or another, the study of the human mind, how it processes information received by the senses, and how the result influences behavior. It relied on experiments and other forms of systematic observation to develop its theories. The new field initially focused on *sensation, perception, learning,* and *memory* and how these influenced *conduct*. Later it explored a number of other aspects of human cognition, all of which are a part of an individual's ways of contacting, understanding, and responding to the world outside.

SENSATION AND PERCEPTION: KNOWING THE WORLD OF REALITY

The earliest concepts addressed by psychologists as they began to develop their field in the 1800s were *sensation* and *perception*. These aspects of human behavior continue to play an important part in the study of the process and effects of mass communication. It is for that reason that modern media researchers owe a great debt to those psychological pioneers who established their field, as well as those who continue its development today.

Sensation

It was no accident that one of the first psychological issues that the founders of the field took up was the nature of *sensory impressions*. The choice of this topic can be seen as an extension of the ancient struggle by philosophers to understand how human beings come to know the external reality in which they live. As has been discussed, for centuries they had debated the question of whether the senses provided a reliable or a faulty picture in our minds of the "world outside." While Plato rejected sensory impressions as valid sources of knowledge—demonstrating his reasoning with the allegory of the cave—Aristotle relied extensively on personal observation for his explanations of the natural world.

In 1834, German physiologist Ernst Weber published a book titled *De Tactu*, describing experiments that he had conducted on *touch*. He had subjects compare a series of different weights, two at a time. What he found was that a person could not tell if a second one was heavier than the first unless its physical weight was a certain *constant percent* heavier. This was the case even if the two weights being compared were very light, somewhat heavier, or very heavy. This gave rise to a remarkable formula, which showed that human behavior did, at least in the case of sensations, reliably follow predictable regularities.[1] The idea that "sensations" could be observed and precisely quantified was a revolutionary idea at the time. Following Weber's lead, Gustav Fechner, who some consider a father of modern psychology, studied sensations very extensively during the 1850s. He conducted a series of very carefully controlled experiments that confirmed and expanded Weber's findings to other sensory modalities. This work established the field of *psychophysics*—a specialty that studies quantitative relationships among sensory impressions, including vision, hearing, taste, and smell.[2]

Another well-regarded pioneer in psychology was Wilhelm Wundt. In 1859, he actually developed the first course in what can be considered psychology at the University of Heidelberg. It was actually a sort of combination of anthropology and physiology, and he developed a textbook for his course.[3] Some consider Wundt as the actual father of psychology, not only because he taught the course and developed a text, but also because he went on to establish the first experimental psychological laboratory at the University of Leipzig in 1879.[4] At first, it was a modest affair. Essentially, his experiments focused on sensation. He used a number of ingenious devices and contraptions (which came to be called his "brass instruments") to measure how long it took for a person receiving a *stimulus*, such as a sound, to *respond* in a specific way, such as by pressing on a telegraph-type key.

Wundt was also interested in what went on in the minds of his subjects as they participated in his experiments. To assess this, he used a method that came to be called "introspection." This was a process whereby a person *reflected inward* on his or her own thoughts and feelings that took place while the experiment was conducted. The method of introspection became a major form of observation by which early psychologists tried to study the inner workings of human consciousness. Introspection, as a mode of observation, became very controversial in later years. A number of psychologists denounced the idea, claiming that it was impossible to engage in objective empirical observation of what was hidden in people's minds.

During the twentieth century, psychologists continued to study the sensory processes. The human senses are not only important in terms of their relationship to the ancient debates about the scientific method but also in understanding the more general problem of how people are in contact with and come to know the realities of the world around them. Today, the ways in which we see, hear, touch, smell, taste, and retain experience have been exhaustively investigated. Their anatomical foundations are well understood. The importance of this knowledge for the study of mass communication theory is that sensation is the *first stage in the process of perception*— that is, deciding on the meaning of what our senses detect when seeing, hearing, or viewing media content.

Perception

The experimental work on sensation of the 1800s was clearly defined by conducting it within a *stimulus–response* (S–R) conceptualization. As was noted above, this S–R conceptual framework became central to psychology early in its development, and it remains a fundamental perspective today. That is, the world outside a person's consciousness is seen as a source of many kinds and patterns of "stimuli" that are detected by the individual's sensory functions. Then, after this information is processed internally and meanings are assigned to it, a response can be made.

The early psychologists understood that there was much more to human behavior than merely detecting stimuli with the senses and then acting in some way. It was for that reason that Wundt wanted to explore people's consciousness through introspection. The implications of the stimuli for the individual had to be sorted out through a process of *perception*—interpreting sensory input by constructing *meanings* for what one sees, feels, touches, or hears, based on one's personal background of experience. This had to be done by the individual before an appropriate response could be made. Thus, it was seen very early that the S–R concept had to be revised to S–O–R, meaning that the psychological (and possibly biological) characteristics of the "organism" (human being) played a key role in determining what kind of response would be made.

In simpler terms, an individual detecting a pattern of stimuli has to determine its meaning for him or her personally in order to relate to it. This is done by classifying it in ways that have been learned from prior experience. That is, "if it looks like a duck, walks like a duck, and quacks like a duck," the person can reasonably interpret (perceive) that it is a duck. Thus, depending on the stimulus, the individual decides whether what he or she sees is edible or not, a man or a woman, a river or a road, a tiger or a cow, a harmless situation or a dangerous one, and so on. Intervening between the stimulus and the response, then, are all of the functions of a complex and conscious organism with a background of experience—with learned meanings and understandings, attitudes and beliefs, likes and dislikes, preferences and aversions, and so on. It was recognized early that these factors played a key role in determining *what meanings would be assigned* to a pattern of stimuli, and that, in turn, shaped the response that the individual made to that pattern.

One of the great pioneers in the study of the perception of physical stimuli was physiologist Hermann von Helmholz.[5] He did not think of himself as a psychologist, but his studies of vision in the 1860s established the ways in which the human being sees such matters as color, brightness, depth, and other physical features of stimuli. The human being puts these together in a process of *inference*, based on learned prior experience, and decides what the object is in a meaningful sense (e.g., whether it is a duck, pig, or dog).

Later, during the early 1920s, a group of German psychologists developed a set of insights into the process of perception that came to be known as the *Gestalt principles*.[6] Their basic concerns were how we interpret sensory impressions of physical objects and relationships in terms of *patterns*. There were a number of principles that revealed the way we see and interpret such patterns, including "optical illusions." The Gestalt psychologists did not study people's perceptions of social situations, such as are depicted in the mass media, but their principles appear to apply to this type of stimulus as well. As will be discussed in a later section, this "patterning" idea also became important in the study of memory.

Such "mental" factors and their influence on selective perception have not always been accepted by psychologists. In the early part of the twentieth century, some psychologists (such as John Watson and later B. F. Skinner) rejected the idea that the field should consider any "mental" processes. The only legitimate data that could be used to develop the science, they maintained, was *overt behavior* that could be observed directly by a recording scientist. Trying to observe what was going on in people's heads, they claimed, went beyond the acceptable rules of a science based on empirical observation.[7] Others, however, felt that legitimate *inferences* could be made about "cognitive" processes by observing people's *verbal reports* of their beliefs, feelings, and preferences. Today, few strict "behaviorists" remain who reject the study of cognitive processes. This was an important issue for students of mass communication who came later. The study of such factors as selective perception, influenced by opinions, attitudes, and beliefs, has been widely accepted by psychologists as legitimate in scientific research, offering important clues to patterns of individual behavior.

LEARNING AND MEMORY

During the late 1800s and early 1900s, a natural question for psychologists was this: If the human individual has all of these "mental" factors, where do they come from? One early answer was that they were *inherited* as part of the genetic characteristics of human beings. Another, equally old answer was that human knowledge and superior mental capacities were acquired through experience—that is, through *learning*. These two very different views provided the foundation for a great controversy as to the origins of human nature. Do human beings have their superior mental capacities due to some *natural* (that is, inherited) process, or do they acquire them in some way through *nurturing* experiences (that is, learning) in their environment.

The Nature-Nurture Debate

The idea that human beings come into this world already equipped with a superior intellect was a very old one. For centuries, the superiority of human beings over animals was attributed to their creation by God in His own image. This meant that new generations *inherited* their superior mental properties. The creationist accounts were almost universally accepted—until Charles Darwin advanced a very different interpretation of human origins in 1854. He offered scientific evidence (and a theory) that there had been a long process of biological evolution through "natural selection," during which the condition of human beings improved as they adapted more and more successfully to their environments. At the time, many people were unwilling to accept that idea (and some feel the same today).

Darwin's ideas not only set off a fierce debate between creationists and evolutionists, but it also led to increased psychological attention to the role of the brain and the nervous system in determining human conduct.[8] During the early and mid-1800s, great discoveries had been made concerning the nature and functioning of the human body, including various areas of the brain.[9] This led many psychologists to believe that the behavior of the human individual was highly controlled by his or her biological inheritance—whatever the origin of the human species. One important theory that was derived from this principle was that, like other animals, each human being inherited a set of complex and more-or-less identical *instincts*.

Instincts, it was believed, were not learned but inherited—and they provided automatic guides that shaped much of our behavior. Indeed, this was a very respected and widely held view as the 1900s began. A major spokesman for this view was John Watson, a renowned psychologist at the time. He maintained that inherited human instincts determined how people behave with respect to such activities as hunting, fighting, maternal care, gregariousness, imitation, and play.[10] Other experts had more extensive lists. Students in psychology courses at the time of World War I typically had to memorize long lists of human instincts in preparation for their exams.

Another ancient answer (going back to Plato) concerning the origin of superior human mental processes was that each individual started out at birth as a *tabula rasa*—a blank slate—in terms of mental factors. This meant that the source of the human mind, the superior mental condition of human beings (as compared to animals), was a product of their *experience* as they came to know the physical and social world in which they lived. A later idea, advanced by Descartes, was *mind-body dualism*. The body was a mere mechanical system, while the mind existed in separate spheres of existence.[11]

Learning

These confusing and often conflicting ideas about the human mind and how it came to be developed began to be sorted out as the 1800s came to a close. It became increasingly clear that the responses people made to patterns of stimuli that they perceived were indeed a product of *learning*. The study of learning, through experiments with both animals and human subjects, began in earnest during the last decade of the 1800s. As the new century began, it quickly came to be, by some accounts, the central concept studied by psychologists during the twentieth century. Today, there are a large number of theories about different types of learning that continue to be studied in experiments and other settings.[12]

Some of the first experiments on learning were conducted on animals. Perhaps the best know were those of Ivan Pavlov. In 1905 he started by having a dog strapped into a kind of harness. He then repeatedly sounded a bell to see what happened. Actually, nothing happened. There was no reason it should. The bell had no significance for the dog, and Pavlov knew that this would be the case. He wanted to establish that as a baseline fact. Then he shifted his strategy. He would sound the bell and then inject meat powder into the dog's mouth. The dog would salivate. That was a "natural response" to the meat powder stimulus. Pavlov then began repeatedly to sound the bell and follow it shortly afterward with the meat powder. After a few trials, the dog would salivate at the sound of the bell alone—without the meat powder. That was a very *unnatural* situation. A natural reflex had been called out by a very unnatural stimulus. Pavlov called this "conditioning." It was a form of learning that no one had ever demonstrated before. He went on to many other complex experiments, but the basic idea was always the same. The animals learned to respond to stimuli that had never before triggered a natural response.

Pavlov's work set off great debates about the role and nature of learning—particularly in human behavior. The great *nature vs. nurture debate* took a new turn. Other experiments conducted before and after Pavlov published his findings raised the possibility that the cognitive processes that seemed so important to many in determining human conduct were *learned* in various ways. One outcome of the intense focus on learning was that it increasingly called into question the whole concept of instinct-determined behavior in human beings. In fact, by the late 1920s, the nurture (learning) side of the debate became predominant, and the idea that human behavior was governed by an elaborate list of inborn instincts was virtually abandoned.

Learning implies that human beings acquire *habits*— meaning that particular stimuli are very likely to call out specific forms of response regularly in the individual. This is a bit different from the ordinary person's use of the term "habit," but the idea is that learning *stabilizes behavior around relatively predictable forms of conduct*. A number of learning theories addressed this issue, exploring how this consequence takes place. By about 1950, at least a dozen different theories of learning were under systematic study.[13]

Social Learning

Today, the process of learning remains under vigorous examination. Of particular interest to students of the influences of mass communications is the general theory of *social learning*. Introduced in 1950 by psychologists Dollard and Miller, the basic idea is that people actively learn from observing the behavior of others in their society. They acquire certain ways of thinking and acting that are "reinforced" by others around them. These become a part of their habit structure.[14] A version called *observational learning* was described by psychologist Albert Bandura in the 1970s.[15] Earlier, in experiments done during the 1960s, he was able to show that children can acquire very complicated new behaviors—including acting aggressively—by directly observing the activities of others who demonstrate or "model" those patterns.[16] This research and social learning theory in general will be discussed more fully in Chapter 16, devoted to Modeling Theory.

Incidental Learning

Another important form of social learning takes place almost accidentally from observing what people do and say as they are depicted in mass communications. What is called *incidental learning* has long been central to efforts to assess the effects of the visual media—especially television and motion pictures—that present depictions of people acting out social roles and other forms of behavior. Such learning is *subtle* and *unwitting*. It takes place when a person goes to media content for purposes of entertainment—for fun and diversion—or even to the news for information. That individual has no intention of learning about whatever is in the content and indeed has no realization that such process is taking place. Nevertheless, while being entertained or informed, the person unwittingly acquires understandings, knowledge, and beliefs about the topics, people, or situations being presented (see Chapter 23).

As noted, incidental learning theory is derived from the more general social learning theory developed by psychologist Albert Bandura in the 1960s.[17] The formal version of incidental learning theory is also drawn from the 1970s application of Bandura's theory by Donald Roberts and Wilbur Schramm to social learning from television.[18] The other closely related theory of the effects of human communication was discussed in Chapter 3—the much older "social construction of reality" theory originally set forth in 387 B.C. by Plato in his *Republic* and specifically in the allegory of the cave.[19] It can also be noted that the theory of Uses for Gratification (Chapter 14) is implied. That theory explains the reasons for which audiences seek out and attend to many forms of media content in the first place. The concept of "collateral instruction" (derived from military meanings, where unintended damage accidentally results from bombing or shelling a target) is a new one—introduced in this text and discussed in detail in Chapter 23.

It is important to understand the basics of all of these related psychological theories. They can provide explanations of the process by which audiences seek media content for information or gratification, and then, from their exposure, unwittingly develop beliefs, ideas, and attitudes toward significant features of their social environment.

Socialization and Enculturation

Gaining an understanding of the nature of the norms, roles, ranking systems, and behavioral controls that are present in the social organization patterns of various kinds of human groups—such as from one's family and circle of friends, large associations, and even society itself—is also a product of learning. Sociologists refer to the process as *socialization*. Simply put, it is by that process that individuals acquire understandings of how one is "expected" to behave in the groups to which they belong. For example, a recruit entering the military has to undergo a process of acquiring and adopting the norms, the roles, the ranking system, and the nature of social controls used in that setting in order to fit in and act effectively as a group member. Thus, "socialization" is a process that begins early and continues through life as one enters many kinds of groups—to become a member of a family, a student in various schools, a worker on the job, a father or mother, a member of a community or a society, and so on.

A related concept used by anthropologists is *enculturation*. This refers to the process by which a person acquires and internalizes knowledge about the entire culture of a society. An example would be an immigrant coming from a society in which the Chinese way of life is standard and then learning the different ways of life and behavioral expectations of the culture of the United States.

As has been indicated, the mass media can play a part in the socialization process by presenting depictions of social groups. Again, incidental and social learning can play a part in the social construction of reality. For example, a person may never have been arrested or brought to trial for a crime. However, by viewing many TV dramas or movies where such events take place, that individual can readily learn—either deliberately or unwittingly—what each player (judge, prosecutor, witnesses, defendant, etc.) does in such a social setting. Thus, through a process of observational and incidental learning from media depictions, one can develop social constructions of reality of the nature of many kinds of groups and acquire understandings of the patterns of social expectations that the actors have of each other in such a context.

Memory

Along with learning, the process of *forgetting* came under study during the last part of the 1800s. It has an obvious relationship to learning. That is, how long and how accurately does something that is learned remain in memory? The most famous early experiments on memory and forgetting were those of Hermann Ebbinghaus, done during the 1880s.[20] What happened was that he, like other early psychologists of the time, rejected the analysis of memory through the use of logic and debate alone and decided to conduct a systematic observational study. However, there was a problem. An observer cannot see into the memory of another person. How, then, can the necessary empirical observations be made? Ebbinghaus's solution was to study *himself* through a process of introspection—looking inward at his own psychological processes.

To test and study his own memory, he first created 2,000 so-called "nonsense" syllables. Each consisted of two consonants separated by a noun—but in such a way that each had no meaning (in his German language). Examples would be yat, toc, cip, bik, rin, and so on. He then set about to learn various lists by rote memory. Then he would allow certain periods of time to elapse and test himself to see how many he could remember. The result was a famous "curve of forgetting," which fell rapidly during the first few days and then leveled off at a low level of recall.

Today, the study of memory has become very elaborate and complex. A number of different types of memory have been identified, and it is well understood that information apprehended by the senses is processed and stored in different ways. Understanding how well, and under what circumstances, people can remember complex patterns of stimuli is an important consideration when trying to sort out the influences of particular types of mass communication content.

In overview, all of these pioneering efforts of the earlier psychologists provided a set of concepts, principles, and theories that aid greatly in trying to understand and explain how people *attend* to the media, how they *select* specific forms of information from their content, how they commit some of it to *memory*—and how they use what they have learned to guide their *actions* and behavioral choices. Today, psychology has become a broad field, based solidly on the scientific method, relying heavily (but not exclusively) on the experiment as a research strategy. Of greatest interest in the many topics that psychologists have studied is the concept of *cognitive processing* of information. For example, when a person encounters configurations of stimuli while reading a newspaper; listening to the radio; or watching TV, a movie, or the computer screen, how is the information and its meanings *selected, interpreted, stored, and acted upon*? Cognitive processing theories, developed on a basis of nearly two centuries of psychological investigation, help explain how this takes place among audiences in the mass communication process.

THE BASICS OF CONTEMPORARY COGNITIVE PROCESSING THEORY

As suggested, cognitive processing refers to the way people handle information "mentally" when they consciously encounter some object, event, or situation with their senses. When individuals have such an experience—as we all do constantly during our waking hours—they normally identify what it is, what it means to them, and how they may need to act or not act toward it. Usually, some record of the experience is stored in their memory, and in some cases they may need to recount it to someone else.

Stated simply in everyday terms, cognition refers to *how people think and how that influences their actions*. Today psychologists realize that thinking is influenced by a host of factors. Included are beliefs, attitudes, values, opinions, tastes, interests, stored memory structures, habits of attention and perception, imagery, and even intelligence. Just what should and should not be included in a final definition has not yet been set. But it is clear that each of the factors mentioned in the foregoing list, and possibly many more, play a part in the ways that individuals think about and decide to act during their daily experiences—including when they attend to the mass media.

Selective Attention to Media Presentations

Consider the example of two people watching a newscast together. Each will have different patterns of attention. One, a young businesswoman, may be very aware of the clothing worn by the female news anchor. She may identify her suit as "sage," a color term with which her male companion will probably not be familiar when applied to clothing. If he noticed it at all, he would probably call it "sort of pale green." The woman may also take notice of the anchor's jewelry and even her hairstyle. Her male friend would be less likely to notice these features and would probably take more note of the anchor's possible bosom size. On the other hand, if a news story came on about a record-breaking baseball player, the male's attention might be riveted on the details. The young woman, on the other hand, might at that point check out her fingernails and notice that she needed a manicure.

The basic idea being illustrated is that attention to a complex stimulus field, such as a news program, is *highly selective*. Moreover, that selectivity is consistent with the interests of each individual that have been established by prior learning and experience. The examples above are somewhat stereotyped—portraying a female as interested in dress, colors, hairstyles, and jewelry and a male who has an interest in baseball. Such gender-linked interests are not universal. Nevertheless, the example gets the point across. A person's past experiences build up *interests* in particular topics and issues, and these play a significant part in what media content he or she will attend to and with what pattern of intensity.

Selective Perception of Media Content

Perception on the part of a member of a media audience is a second important factor in cognitive processing. It is one thing to pay attention to an event, such as a news story. It is quite another to "make sense" out of the information that is being taken in as one views it. As was explained earlier, perception is a cognitive process in which whatever is being apprehended by the person's senses—that is, what is being seen, heard, smelled, felt, and so on—is interpreted within a framework of meanings that the individual has already learned.

As a simple example, consider again the young couple watching TV. Imagine that the male sees a commercial for exercise equipment. He would have little difficulty identifying what the device was and what it was used for. He had a prior set of meanings and a set of labels (words) for the TV sights and sounds that were being presented in the commercial. These enabled him to assign appropriate meanings instantly. He did not have to ponder what the contraption was, how it might be used, and then sort out whether it might be relevant for him. The woman, we will assume, was not familiar with such an apparatus and might simply ignore the commercial without understanding in detail what was being advertised.

Perception takes place virtually instantaneously. All of us see things, hear sounds, taste or smell things, and immediately select a *label* for them by assigning a word that names them. We know immediately that it's a truck, a motorcycle, a candy bar, a duck, or some other familiar object. Then, at almost the same moment, we experience the meaning for the label we have assigned. We have a host of possible meanings stored in memory in association with the words we also store there. Thus, perception is a process that depends on selecting labels from the language that we share with others and meanings for those labels that we have individually learned from prior experience. By this means, we can interpret—that is, *perceive*—what our senses are taking in. It is an "automated" process in that we seldom have to wonder what we are experiencing, or try to assess it as a possible representative of many possible meanings. Thus, perception takes place so quickly that few of us are aware of its steps or stages.

An important feature of the process of perception is that, like attention, it is *highly selective*. This idea was illustrated in a simple way in the example of the football game between Dartmouth and Princeton. The general principle is that meanings we assign come from our prior experience, from our interests, needs, and motivations. We do not assign and experience meanings randomly. Stated simply, what this means is that the experiences we have had in the past play a key role in what we attend to and the meanings we assign to what we see, hear, and so on. As a female participating in the gender subculture of her society, the young businesswoman in our illustration would have had a far greater depth of experience with women's clothing; she would have an extensive color vocabulary and far greater experience with jewelry and hairstyles than her male companion. It was this that would lead her to focus immediately on the appearance of the anchorwoman. This would clearly result in *selective perception*—focusing on an event and assigning meanings consistent with her prior experience. The same can be said of the man's immediate recognition of the baseball player's record and his in-depth interest and interpretation of that news story.

Perception tends to be *patterned*. One of the findings of the Gestalt psychologists early in the twentieth century was that individuals "see" (or hear, etc.) an *overall pattern* when they apprehend something with their senses and determine its meaning. For example, when the young woman in our example saw and recognized the anchorwoman, she did not just see a lot of individual elements—a face, a sage-colored suit, a pendant, a set of earrings, and a hairstyle. She instantly saw a whole pattern—a complete well-groomed person in an attractive ensemble. It was the Gestalt psychologists who developed the principles of "patterning" in perceptions. Today, when a person perceives a scene, situation, or event as a pattern or configuration, it is referred to as a "Gestalt" (the name given to such patterns).

In general, then, the student of mass communication must assume that both attention to media presentations and perception of content are highly selective. Some of the content of a TV program, a movie, or a presentation in print will receive the full and immediate attention of an individual member of the audience. Other parts of that content will be ignored or have little meaning for such a person. It simply *cannot be assumed* that among the audience for a newscast, a play, or a drama—or any other media presentation—that such content will be experienced in the same uniform way by everyone.

Limitations on Human Memory for Media Content

It has been well established by dozens of studies that people do not remember news stories very well.[21] Much the same can be said for content presented in movies or any other information transmitted by any other medium. A large body of research has shown that clear differences in recall are found from one medium to the next—with recall from print being somewhat better than from broadcast or film.[22] However, overall, people just do not recall media content accurately or fully, even immediately after it has been presented. To illustrate, in a survey study, adult viewers of TV news could recall the topic of slightly more than a single story from an average of twenty presented in a broadcast. In another study, more than half of the viewers interviewed could not recall the content of even a single story from a newscast that presented nineteen items.[23] Even when people are phoned ahead of time, and they agree to pay close attention, they still could recall very little.[24] Thus, a number of research reports indicate that recall of media content of any type is very limited, regardless of demographics or production variables.

It is difficult to say why memory for such media content is so poor. Memory is an important aspect of cognitive processing, but it is not fully understood. There are literally dozens and dozens of theories and concepts that have been developed to try to explain how human memory functions. To provide an idea of the scope of current psychological studies of memory, investigations have recently been conducted into the following (which represent only a partial list): autobiographical memory, conceptual memory, contextual memory, dual-process influences on memory, episodic memory, eidetic memory, emotional memory, everyday memory, false memories, flashbulb memory, generic recollective memory, hierarchically organized memory, imagery in memory, linguistic memory, long-term vs. short-term memory, nonverbal memory, narrative recall, permanent memory, procedural memory, recollective memory, repressed memories, retrospective memory, schemas in memory, scripts in memory, sensory memory, sensory-motor memory (as in driving), spatial memory, temporal memory, visual memory, and working memory. It is a mind-boggling list, implying that there remains a great deal to be learned about memory and how it works in various settings.

Perhaps most relevant for recalling information from media presentations is the concept of *working memory*. In simple terms, we retain experience in our consciousness for at least a limited period, like we do when we look up from the phone book and then dial a number. When we experience a more complex event, such as a newscast, a movie, or a TV play, we are able to describe in words much of what we have stored our working memory, at least for a short time. Included are both visual and spatial elements. Those features of memory do appear relevant and applicable in understanding how people recall such media content.

Schemata and Memory for Media Content

The term *schema* is important in understanding how we store experience in memory (plural is *schemata*). It refers to the way individuals organize and encode into memory something like a movie, a TV play, or a news story to which the person has attended. The term came originally from the work of Bartlett, a psychologist who studied memory for folk tales in the 1930s.[25] A schema is a kind of "mental organization" that a person uses to remember ideas and events. Defined very simply, a schema is a personally organized structure of perceived and remembered experiences. Schemata provide the mental patterns in which we send what we perceive to memory. This is what takes place when we encode almost any kind of complex experience, including media content.

As has been suggested, then, each person has a unique cognitive organization. That organization has been developed from a lifetime of his or her prior experience. Therefore, it is not surprising that each individual will encode and store in working memory a personally unique pattern of the details and relationships perceived in a complex experience, such as attending to a media presentation.[26] What this means is that one person's schema for a particular news story, or some other form of media information, may be quite different from that of another. As psychologist R. J. Harris put it:

> The way we comprehend a program we watch on TV is through a constant interaction of the content of the program and the knowledge already in our minds. The mind thinks in response to what we see and those thoughts become an important part of the constructive process of comprehension.[27]

Narration Schemata

Another related concept that helps understand how we remember media content is *narration schema*.[28] This type of memory organization is very important for understanding the recall of media content because it concerns storytelling. Narration schemata for stories include identification of one or some set of *actors*, a number of *events* that the actors have experienced, and some set of *consequences* that are brought about by those events. This type of mental organization provides convenient categories that any member of an audience can use in encoding and storing the details of the Gestalt of meanings developed during the process of perception. It is this type of patterning of memory that enables us to read a book or watch a movie while remembering the identities of the actors and the details of the unfolding plot that have gone before. Without the ability to do this, we would not be able to experience the story as a coherent pattern of events.

Differences in Cognitive Functioning by Medium

A substantial body of research has indicated that features of cognitive functioning, such as memory, take place in different ways, depending on what medium, or what content, to which the audience member is attending. In general, then, nearly two hundred years of psychological investigation and theory building have shown that each human being develops a cognitive organization over a long period of time as a result of his or her life experiences. That organization includes their knowledge, beliefs, and attitudes about the physical and social world. Broader sets of very general beliefs about what is important, positive or negative, in life make up a person's values. Cognitive organization also includes the person's interests in various kinds of things and his or her tastes and preferences that developed as a product of past experience. In short, the person's entire psychological makeup plays a part in shaping the way he or she processes information into patterns of attention, perception, memory, and recall.

It must be remembered, however, that psychologists have not abandoned their early commitment to the concepts of *stimulus, organism*, and *response*. As they have turned their attention to the mass media and tried to unravel how their content plays a role in shaping the behavior of those who attend, the S–O–R framework still guides psychological thinking. This basic conceptualization of the field, applied to the study of mass communication, was posed succinctly by Spiegalman, Terilliger, and Fearing as far back as 1950:

> It is important to establish...the theoretical frame of reference as a basis for hypotheses [concerning media influences]...communication content is conceived to be a stimulus field subject to the perceptual dynamics of the person or persons reacting in it. More specifically, there is conceived to be an interdependent relationship between the individual's need-value system and the structural pattern presented by the content.[29]

Putting it all together into a single set of propositions can scarcely do justice to the complexities involved in what this chapter has discussed. However, stating the relevant factors as a set of interrelated propositions can summarize in a single formal theory the concepts and relationships of central importance that psychology has provided for the study of the process and influences of mass communication. It is clear that the fundamental S–O–R framework for interpreting the relationships between events in the world outside, what takes place internally, and the behavior that results has been retained. Obviously, psychologists have also developed over a long period of time a great many other perspectives, concepts, theories, and considerations that are important in understanding a range of human behaviors and conditions. But focusing on the basics, the following will provide an important foundation for understanding both the process and effects of mass communication as these are addressed in a number of theories discussed later in this book:

COGNITIVE PROCESSING THEORY: A FORMAL SUMMARY

1. A person attends to, and comes into contact via, the senses, with some aspect of reality as an *empirical experience*. That is, a person apprehends and is aware of something, event, situation, or other phenomenon that has stimulated a sense of sight, hearing, touch, or smell.
2. Drawing on learned meanings stored in memory from both prior individual experience and socialization within the culture of his or her language community, the individual *perceives*, that is, assigns initial interpretations, labels, and meanings to what he or she is experiencing.
3. The individual *evaluates* the significance of the meanings of the perceived phenomenon for his or her current and future situation. That is, the individual sorts out its implications, deciding whether it is dangerous, amusing, neutral, or something unimportant.
4. After interpreting and assessing the phenomenon, the individual commits to *memory* the meanings and implications of what has been perceived, fitting it into schemata of previously remembered experience.
5. The individual reaches a decision as to what form of *response or action* is needed or appropriate, if any, in the face of the interpretation and assessment of what has been experienced.
6. Finally, the individual *performs* whatever action or other response has been selected. This can range from dismissing the phenomenon as trivial to complex activities and behavioral adjustments.

In summary, then, because of the S–O–R nature of cognitive processing, and the way that each person does it somewhat uniquely, each member of an audience will have a different experience in reading a newspaper, attending to a movie, listening to a radio program, viewing a televised newscast, or surfing the Internet. Their prior interests and experiences will lead each to pay attention to different topics and details. Each will construct what he or she sees and hears into different patterns of meaning, using his or her interests, understandings, and prior experiences. Each will organize his or her schemata of experience in a different way for storage into his or her individual working memory. Finally, when called upon by another person to recall and retell what he or she saw or heard, each will come up with a somewhat different account. It is by describing and explaining these complex processes that psychology has made a truly significant contribution to the study of mass communication.

Notes and References

1. Ernst H. Weber, *De Pulsa, Resorpitione, Auditu et Tactu: Annotationes Anatomicae et Physiologicae* (Leipzig: Koehlor, 1834).

2. Gustav T. Fechner, *Element der Psychophysik* (Leipzig: Breitkopf and Harteri, 1860).

3. Wilhem Wundt, *Principles of Physiological Psychology*, 5th ed. (New York: Macmillan, 1904). Trans. by E. Tishner and first published in 1874.

4. David Hothersall, "Wilhelm Wundt and the Founding of Psychology," Chapter 4 in *History of Psychology* (Philadelphia: Temple University Press, 1984), pp. 83–99.

5. See R. M. Warren and R. P. Warren, eds. and trans., *Helmholz on Perception: Its Physiology and Development* (New York: Wiley, 1968). Helmholz's original work was published in 1866.

6. Kurt Koffka, "Perception: An Introduction to the Gestalt Theories," *Psychological Bulletin*, 19, 1922, pp. 531–585. See also Wolfgang Kohler, "An Aspect of Gestalt Psychology," in C. Murchison, *Psychologies of 1925* (Worcester, MA: Clark University Press, 1925), pp. 163–195.

7. Edwin G. Boring, *A History of Experimental Psychology*, 2nd ed. (New York: Appleton-Century-Crofts, Inc., 1950), pp. 641–651.

8. Charles Darwin, *The Origin of Species*, 6th ed. (New York: Hurst, 1899). First published in 1859. See also *The Expression of Emotion in Man and Animals* (London: John Murray, 1872).

9. David Hothersall, op. cit. See Chapter 3, "Nineteenth Century Studies of the Central Nervous System," pp. 57–80.

10. John B. Watson, *Psychology from the Standpoint of a Behaviorist* (Philadelphia: Lippincott, 1919).

11. Rene Descartes, *Treatise on Man* (Cambridge, MA: Harvard University Press, 1972). T. S. Hall, trans. First published in 1637.

12. James D. Laird and Nicholas S. Thompson, *Psychology* (Boston: Houghton Mifflin Company, 1992). See Chapter 6, "Learning," pp. 150–177.

13. Ernest R. Hilgard, *Theories of Learning* (New York: Appleton-Century-Crofts, Inc., 1948).

14. J. Dollard and N. E. Miller, *Personality and Psychotherapy: An Analysis in Terms of Learning, Thinking and Culture* (New York: McGraw Hill, 1950).

15. Albert Bandura, *Social Learning Theory* (Englewood Cliffs, NJ: Prentice-Hall, 1977).

16. Albert Bandura, "Transmission of Aggression Through Imitation of Aggressive Models," *Journal of Abnormal and Social Psychology*, 63, 1961, pp. 575–582.

17. See Albert Bandura and Robert H. Walters, *Social Learning and Personality Development* (New York: Mcgraw Hill, 1962).

18. Wilbur Schramm and Donald F. Roberts, eds., "Children's Learning from the Media," in *The Process and Effects of Mass Communication*, rev. ed. (Urbana, IL: The University of Illinois Press, 1972), pp. 597–611.

19. *The Republic of Plato*, trans. Francis MacDonald Cornfield (New York: Oxford University Press, 1958), pp. 227–235. Plato's work was written in 387 B.C.

20. Hermann Ebbinghaus, *Memory: A Contribution to Experimental Psychology* (New York: Columbia University Press, 1913), trans. C. E. Bussinius. First published in 1885.

21. Margaret H. DeFleur, "Developing an Integrated Theory of Recall of News Stories," a paper presented at the annual meeting of the Association for Education in Journalism and Mass Communication, Baltimore, August 1998.

22. See, for example, Melvin L. DeFleur, Lucinda Davenport, Mary Cronin, and Margaret DeFleur, "Audience Recall of News Stories Presented by Newspaper, Computer, Television and Radio," *Journalism Quarterly*, 4, Winter, 1992, pp. 1010–1022.

23. W. R. Neuman, "Patterns of Recall Among Television News Viewers," *Public Opinion Quarterly*, Vol. 40, 1976, pp. 115–123.

24. E. Katz, H. Adoni, and P. Parness, "Remembering the News: What the Picture Adds to Recall," *Journalism Quarterly*. Vol. 54, 1987, pp. 231–239.

25. F. C. Bartlett, *Remembering* (Cambridge: Cambridge University Press, 1932).

26. B. Hoijer, "Television-Evoked Thoughts and Their Relation to Comprehension," *Communication Research*, Vol. 18, 1989, pp. 179–203.

27. R. J. Harris, *A Cognitive Psychology of Mass Communication*, 2nd ed. (Hillsdale, NJ: Lawrence Erlbaum Associates, 1994), pp. 25–26.

28. C. F. Cofer, ed., *The Structure of Human Memory* (San Francisco: W. H. Freeman and Company, 1976), pp. 105–106.

29. Marvin Spiegelman, Carl Terwilliger, and Franklin Fearing, "The Content of Comic Strips: The Study of a Mass Medium of Communication," *The Journal of Social Psychology*, 35, 1952, pp. 37–57.

CHAPTER 6

The Concept of Mass Society as a Contribution of Sociology to Media Studies

It was a remarkable new technology. It began in the laboratories of a university known for its technological developments. Then a young innovator developed it into a more efficient form that could be used to solve practical problems. Rather quickly, better and better versions were developed. Soon it was efficient and practical for wide applications. Few could imagine in its earliest days that it would be adopted worldwide and would change the economies and ways of doing business in all modern societies. All that was needed was to determine how best to use it. When that became clear, innovative entrepreneurs applied it to a host of practical problems, and fortunes were made.

What are we referring to here? The airplane? Computers? Atomic energy? Satellites? The Internet? None of those. It was the *steam engine*! (Its origins and applications to printing were discussed in Chapter 1.) Although its principles had been understood for many years, an essential technological component (condenser to cool the used steam, making it suitable for industrial applications) was developed and patented by James Watt in 1769. By the late 1700s, it was beginning to be used in Great Britain to pump out mines and run machinery in factories. Early in the 1800s, it was already driving the wheels of industry in many places—replacing animals, water wheels, and windmills as energy sources—and providing the first steps in the development of what would become *a totally new kind of society*.

Early in the 1800s, the new discipline of sociology had been founded by such luminaries as Auguste Comte (in France) and Herbert Spencer (in England). Others, such as Ferdinand Toennies (in Germany) and Emile Durkheim (in France), began their analyses of the great transformation in society that was occurring as the *Industrial Revolution*—initially based on steam power—began to take place.

What they saw was a decline of the *traditional society* in which people were linked by strong interpersonal bonds and open channels of communication, based on family ties, long-term friendships, and loyalties to local leaders. In its place, they saw the rise of the *urban-industrial society* in which unlike people were coming together to work in the new factories. It was a new society that became characterized by anonymity, a loss of strong informal rules for behavior, increasing social pathologies, lonely existence in a sea of people, and greatly reduced channels of interpersonal communication. In short, it was what came to be called a *mass society.*

As noted in earlier chapters, this change in society had profound implications for the way in which communication takes place. Replacing many of the open channels of interpersonal communication of the traditional society were those of the new *mass media.* At first it was the daily newspaper in large cities, followed quickly by the popular magazine distributed nationwide. Then, with the new twentieth century, it was the movies, followed soon by radio and then by television. In the years ahead, our media may include at least some features of the Internet and its World Wide Web. One by one, these media found their place in the mass society. Earlier, if people wanted news, advice, or amusement, they turned to their families, friends, and neighbors. In the new urban-industrial society, they turned to the media of mass communication.

Sociology has contributed significantly to our understanding of the mass society, an essential concept for understanding the processes and effects of mass communication. Indeed, even the term "mass," in the special sense that media scholars continue to use it, had its origins in the field. Moreover, many of the earliest research studies and attempts at theory building concerning the influences of mass communications were conducted by sociologists. Indeed, shortly before and after the second World War, the study of mass communication and its influences was one of the central research topics of sociology's most prominent scholars and researchers. That is not the case today, but sociology provided a number of truly basic concepts and theories that remain critical to the study of the processes and effects of mass communication.

Our previous chapter discussed the contribution of psychology to mass communication theory. It is easy to confuse the two fields. How are sociology and psychology different? One answer is that, although sociology and psychology share the use of the scientific method, and they sometimes study similar issues, their most basic concepts are quite distinct. As was indicated in Chapter 5, psychologists in one way or another focus on the *individual.* Their classic concerns have been the way in which the human mind works—trying to sort out relationships between *stimuli* and *responses* at the individual level. They do this in complex ways by investigating biological and cognitive factors that influence how people learn and show patterns of selective attention, perception, and memory—and how these and other factors influence their personal behavior.

Sociology is much less concerned with individual S–R regularities, or in ways in which biological factors or cognitive processes influence individual behavior. The central concept of sociology is *social organization*, which is a consequence of *interaction*—that is, activities that take place *between* people. By investigating the consequences of people relating to one another in patterned ways, sociologists study the nature of *human groups.* This is done by focusing not on the specific individual human beings who make up groups but on the regularities (and irregularities) of their patterns of interpersonal behavior that can be observed as their members interact.

Human groups range from tiny two-person pairs, such as dating couples or pals, whose members relate to each other informally, to very large groups with complex and formal patterns of organization. The latter would include such groups as a university, a corporation, an army, or a government bureaucracy. The largest group of all would be an entire society. By studying groups of many sizes and kinds, sociologists identify the basic features of all patterns of social organization.

The concept of social organization is not difficult to understand. One feature is a group's *norms* (shared rules for behavior that are supposed to be followed by all members). A second is a group's interrelated structure of *roles* (specialized parts played by members in distinct positions within the group). A third feature is a group's system of *ranks* (its levels or "strata," based on rewards, power, or status). The fourth feature is how members of a group enforce their pattern of organization through different techniques of *social control* (by applying various forms of rewards and punishments).

All groups have norms, roles, ranks, and controls. Those with effective patterns of social organization are characterized by *stability.* Those whose patterns are unstable or disorganized are often characterized by *deviant behavior,* with many unwanted consequences. These ideas are important, not only to the sociological study of groups, but also in trying to unravel the influences of mass communications—which often depict people deviating from accepted features of social organization in entertainment and other content.

Essentially, then, sociology, like psychology, emerged from philosophy during the 1800s. Philosophers had for centuries been interested in the nature of societies and their rules for behavior. For more than two thousand years, they sought answers to the question "what is a 'just' society?" That is, how can a society be designed and implemented so that everyone is treated fairly? Obviously, that question remains central even today—not only for sociologists but for everyone. Sociologists today focus much attention on this issue in studies of minorities, the poor, or others who do not enjoy the same benefits of society as the dominant majority.

Many answers as to the nature of a just society have been advanced during both ancient times and in more recent years. We noted earlier that Plato set forth his answer in his *Republic*. He described the way in which a city-state should be organized so that its citizens would receive fair treatment. This included ensuring that women and men were equal. He prescribed the way in which children should be educated (shielding them from harmful ideas in poetry and stories). He discussed the education of teachers and many other features of a just society. Above all, he explained the reasons why top leadership positions should be invested in philosopher-kings.[1]

Aristotle also produced important analyses of society. In his *Politics*, he discussed such issues as the nature and origin of the state, how it should be led, rights pertaining to property, democracy vs. oligarchy, constitutional government, and many other issues.[2] His works on political matters became central to the study of philosophy for centuries.

The nature of the "best" society, and who should be in charge, represents the most central part of the ancient concern with *doing* (human conduct) that, as we noted, preoccupied philosophers since the beginning. Many dozens of philosophers, from Greek and Roman times to the present century, produced treatises, analyses, and prescriptions about the ways in which societies should be organized to reach important goals. The number of thinkers who attempted to analyze this issue and offer their views is truly remarkable. Even a partial list of prominent figures includes such names as Polybius (204–122 B.C.), Cicero (106–43 B.C.), Augustine (354–430 A.D.), Aquinas (1226–1274), Machiavelli (1469–1527), Hobbes (1558–1679), Locke (1632–1704), and Rousseau (1712–1778).

In Chapter 4 we noted that, by the end of the 1700s, a new form of societal organization (democracy) began replacing older forms (monarchy). It had been advocated by philosophers for centuries. During the 1800s, other alternatives to existing orders were proposed. Among those with such plans was Karl Marx, whose prescriptions for the just society turned out to have a truly significant influence on the world. One of the appeals of Marxian proposals for reorganizing society (through revolution) was its promise that many of the injustices of the ages—poverty, inequality, and oppression—would be swept away as the new social order came into being. His ideas did not catch on immediately, but by the twentieth century they had become a commanding reality for many millions of people. Still other versions of what society should be like came into being—under the direction of such figures as Adolf Hitler, Benito Mussolini, Joseph Stalin, Fidel Castro, Saddam Hussein, Slobodan Milosevic, and many less well-known counterparts. The nature and organization of society, then, has been a matter of profound concern for human beings since philosophy began.

A useful perspective on the contributions of sociology to the study of mass communication can be attained by contrasting the characteristics of *traditional* society—which existed before industrialization and mass media came along, with those of *urban-industrial* society, which developed during the nineteenth and twentieth centuries. It was out of this transition from *Gemeinschaft* to *Gesellschaft* (German terms for "traditional" vs. "urban-industrial" societies) that a need for the field of sociology became apparent. The new field developed as a means of assessing and understanding the implications of the emerging social order for human beings. The key ideas from classic sociology for the study of mass communication, then, are related to the master concept of *industrialization*. These include role specialization, social stratification, migration, urbanization, and social diversity.

Briefly, "industrialization" refers to the change from a society in which the population is overwhelmingly engaged in agriculture to one in which manufacturing (and later the provision of services) predominates. As factories developed, and as a host of supporting industries and services grew with them, the division of labor became increasingly elaborate. That is, there was an increase in *role specialization*. That, in turn, led to a great increase in *social stratification*—that is, an increasingly complex "layering" of society with people in many different socio-economic classes characterized by differences in income, power, status, authority, and lifestyles.

In addition, as a result of the increasing availability of jobs and opportunities in the emerging industrial society, people *migrated*, especially from farms and villages to the city, throughout the nineteenth century. Because jobs were available in factories and related service industries, people also migrated from one country to another as well as from farms to towns and cities, and from one region of a country to another. That process continues even today. With many kinds of different people brought together, the society came to be characterized by *great social diversity*. That is, unlike people had been brought together—people with different languages, customs, religions, and political beliefs. They developed greatly different needs, tastes, interests, and outlooks based on such factors as age, income, gender, race, ethnicity, and cultural background. All of these factors have produced *audiences of great diversity* for mass communication today.

THE TRADITIONAL SOCIETY: THE GEMEINSCHAFT

To appreciate how different contemporary societies are from those that characterized human life before industrialization, it is useful to compare the two. Long before contemporary mass media were even dreamed of, human beings lived in what are usually called *traditional societies*. A term developed for this type of traditional society was *Gemeinschaft*. It was first used in the late 1880s by the German sociologist Ferdinand Toennies. As a young man he saw what was happening in his home province of Schleswig-Holstein in Germany. It had in the past been an agricultural area of small villages, much like it had been since the Middle Ages. As industrialization increased, however, great changes were taking place. It was becoming what he came to call a *Gesellschaft*.

Life is clearly different in the traditional *Gemeinschaft* society compared with what it is in the industrialized *Gesellschaft* world. Communities in traditional societies are small, and few strangers are present. Often, the inhabitants never travel any great distance from where they were born. They have little or no contact with ways of life different from their own. Traditional societies are usually characterized by a single lifestyle—one that all the inhabitants understand very well. There is no clash of cultures. Only one prevails. All members understand fully the customs, beliefs, and other shared aspects of living that are followed by all.

Shared Informal Rules for Behavior

Because the culture is so clear and binding in the traditional society, significant conflicts are uncommon. People are taught from birth the rules for behavior and for relating in acceptable ways to others in the tribe or village. It is rare for a person to violate the norms—the accepted ways of behaving—and risk the wrath of other members of the community. Communication takes place by word of mouth as people pass on gossip, tidings, advice, decisions of leaders, and even entertainment in the form of folk tales and stories.

The norms in traditional society consist of many *folkways*—well-accepted rules that govern the manner in which people relate to each other in everyday routines. Folkways are simply convenient guidelines and mutually understood expectations that people use in day-to-day matters, such as when greeting each other, serving meals, dressing, buying, selling, trading, and even speaking. In contrast, *mores* in such a society are rules that govern more critical aspects of life—where deep-seated values are at stake. Mores such as "though shalt not steal," "thou shalt not covet thy neighbor's wife," and so on express powerful injunctions that existed in traditional societies, even long before the time of Christ. Even today, such mores, even if unwritten, provide highly effective guidelines preventing deviant behavior. If they are violated, social rejection or severe punishments are sure to follow.

Obviously, contemporary societies also have folkways and mores, but they often become ineffective as guidelines for conduct. In traditional societies, few dare to go against the rules for "proper" behavior. The social expectations of the folkways and mores, and the harsh punishments that were meted out for serious violations, were sufficient for controlling conduct. There was little need for elaborate written codes of formal laws, a system of courts, police, fines, and jails. However, in more complex societies, even in early ones, such as in Rome, the development of legal codes was needed—and for much the same reasons as in more modern societies.

A Restricted Division of Labor

The concept of a *division of labor* was developed more than two centuries ago by Adam Smith, the intellectual founder of modern capitalism.[3] He used the phrase to refer to the different types of jobs people perform in the work force. Later, the idea was adopted by sociologists to refer to almost any kind of distinct social roles and their interrelationships that people play in any kind of human group, whether work-related or not. The division of labor (in the sense of work) in the traditional society was very restricted. While there were specialists, such as people who make tools, wagon wheels, or people who provide religious leadership, there was no great diversity of occupations or of economic levels. Most people were farmers or in some cases fishermen. Today, in truly primitive societies, the division of labor is even more restricted. Men are hunters and the women gatherers, with each gender having clear-cut responsibilities.

In traditional societies, then, there are no stockbrokers, government bureaucrats, used car salesmen, TV repair persons, news anchors, brain surgeons, school principals, or others in highly specialized occupations. The important point is that in a society with a restricted division of labor people are *similar to each other* in the sense that common concerns and problems are widely shared. An important point is that this makes it easy for them to understand their neighbors and to communicate with them effectively.

Also in traditional societies, the bonds between people are close. Because most do rather similar work, raising crops, fishing, etc., they share a common set of beliefs, skills, interests, and values. Among families who have lived together for many generations, their members know each other well, and they have strong ties to each other. Some of those bonds are created by intermarriage. Others are based on traditional loyalties to a leader. Still others may be inter-family friendships that were originally established by earlier generations but are still regarded as binding. These social ties make interpersonal communication especially open and effective.

A Social Order Based on Trust

As a result of the above conditions, among the members of a traditional society there exists a higher level of *personal trust* than what we have in contemporary urban life. To understand better the kinds of bonds and the level of trust between people in a traditional society, consider the case of a family of farmers in such a society that needs a new wagon. All they have to do is to promise the wagon-maker that they will pay for it when their crop comes in and after they sell it. The parties shake hands on the deal, and the wagon-maker begins its construction. The wagon is delivered, and later, when the new owners sell their crop, they pay fully and without question. In a traditional society, it would be unthinkable to dishonor one's word or a promise made by one's family.

Such trust prevails in all promises and agreements. If a horse is sold, the buyer has confidence that the animal has not been stolen and that its state of health is just what the seller claims. If a marriage is arranged and approved by the families, it is assumed that all concerned have been honest and that neither party will back out. While there can be the occasional rogue in a traditional society, such trust and honor in relationships are the rule.

In the more modern society, such verbal promises and agreements do not work very well. A new and more complex system for ensuring compliance had to be developed. Emile Durkheim referred to it as *restitutive law*, based on *formal contracts*. If agreements are abrogated, the state steps in—providing courts for lawsuits, in which restitution can be gained for the injured parties. If one sets out to buy a truck, for example, there are binding contracts to be signed and credit arrangements to be made. If the terms are violated, serious legal issues arise.

A Limited Need for Media

In traditional societies there is no need for mass media. Contact with the outside world is unimportant, and all the news, entertainment, and instruction that is required is passed around among the inhabitants by word of mouth. There is no need for a constantly changing popular culture, such as a flow of new kinds of music, information about celebrity personalities, the latest dance steps, or innovative fashions in clothing. For recreation, people play traditional games that they invent themselves. They sing traditional songs, eat traditional foods, and dress in ways that have been followed for many generations without annual changes in fashion.

Are there still communities of this kind? Indeed there are. People in remote parts of the world still live in traditional ways. But, with the increasing spread of the media to even very isolated areas, such ways of life are rapidly disappearing. When a television set comes to an inaccessible agricultural village in China or to a hut in the center of the Amazon rain forest, the people who live there see a world that they never dreamed existed. At that point, change begins. The remarkable artifacts and very different ways of life that they see on their screens among people in more developed societies often seem very attractive to those who have lived in simpler ways. Indeed, such a flow of information, bringing new ideas, innovative products, and nontraditional values can alter a traditional culture in a short time. One of the great questions of our time is whether this is good or bad. That issue will be addressed later (in Chapter 22, "Cultural Imperialism Theory"). Ultimately, it depends on one's point of view and personal feelings about preserving existing cultures, but it is happening at an increasing pace, and the media play a central role.

INDUSTRIALIZATION AND THE EMERGENCE OF SOCIOLOGY

As the 1800s began, it was clear to a number of scholars in France, Germany, and England that fundamental changes were taking place, brought about by the spread of new factories. New towns were being developed at sites where resources for the factories were available—water-wheel power at first, then coal for steam, and access to transportation routes by water and rail. Existing cities were also changing with the new economic order. As people came from villages, farms, or from other countries to find work in these businesses and industries, it seemed clear that the older traditional society was being replaced by some kind of new social order. It was very important, the early sociologists felt, that this new type of society be studied systematically and, if possible, be shaped and guided by better understandings that could benefit people.

A Science of Society

Specifically, during the early 1800s, the question arose as to whether it would be possible to develop a *science of society*—that is, a systematic study of the emerging social order based on some version of the methods of observation and explanation that were being so successfully used in other fields. If that could be done, some thought, such a science would be more effective in answering questions about how a "just" society should be organized, reformed if needed, and led. Using the scientific method in such a way seemed attractive, at least compared with continuing to rely on the traditional methods of personal insights and formal logic that had long characterized philosophy. When first proposed, however, the idea seemed doomed to failure. Critics asked how scientific methods could be used to study something as complex as human social conduct? Most people in the established sciences dismissed the idea as unworkable and perhaps even silly.

The origins of sociology as a named field, separate from philosophy and attempting to develop as a science of society, is usually traced to the writings of Auguste Comte. Many consider him the father of the field. His work *The Positive Philosophy*, published in parts between 1830 and 1842, discussed ways in which problems in a society could be analyzed by studying social phenomena *scientifically* in order to come up with solutions.[4] His term "positive philosophy" meant a search for "knowing" based on the observational features and logical procedures of science.

Comte also discussed the structure of modern society, during the time when the Industrial Revolution was getting well under way. He was especially impressed with the part played by *specialization*—what Adam Smith had called the division of labor. He did not see it as a problem. On the contrary, it was this, he felt, that held society together and enabled it to function as a whole—much in the way that the separate organs of a human body work together to enable a person to function effectively. Although his writing can be difficult to decipher, he put it this way:

> Can we conceive of [a more remarkable situation than] the regular and constant convergence of an innumerable multitude of human beings, each possessing a distinct, and, in a certain degree, independent existence, and yet incessantly disposed, amid all their discordance of talent and character to concur in many ways in the same general development, without concert, and even consciousness on the part of most of them, who believe that they are merely following their personal impulses?[5]

Essentially, then, as Compte saw it, *role specialization* was the "social glue" that made the society work. In a stable society, each person played a specialized part that provided some service or consequence to others, and that role activity helped to stabilize the whole.

But what would happen if there was *too much* specialization? As Comte saw it, if people became *too diverse* in what they do and how they relate to each other, there could be real danger that society would become *disorganized*. Such a condition would cause the society to lose that interdependency of roles that bound it together in the manner in which the organs in a human body contribute to its stability. Thus, he maintained, if a society became *overspecialized*, people would act in ways that would drive people apart. As he put it:

> [I have indicated... the mischievous consequences of overspecialization]. In decomposing we always disperse; and the distribution of human labours must occasion certain individual divergencies, both intellectual and moral, which require permanent discipline to keep them within bounds.[6]

As it turned out, this idea—that increasing diversity among members of a society would have negative consequences—was one of the most important ideas that came out of early sociology. Eventually, it was one of the central ideas that gave rise to the concept of a *mass society*—one composed of unlike people with limited meaningful social relationships with each other, barriers to effective interpersonal communication, and with limited concern for those around them.

As the nineteenth century progressed, more and more changes were taking place. The Industrial Revolution was very clearly transforming human relationships in major ways—especially in England, France, and Germany, where there were large cities and factory towns. These changes continued to capture the imagination of sociologists who came after Comte. In England, for example, in 1876, Herbert Spencer wrote extensively about the expanding division of labor. He emphasized the mutual dependency that was developing between people performing different roles:

> [Society] undergoes continuous growth. As it grows, its parts become unlike; it exhibits increase of structure. The unlike parts simultaneously conduct activities of unlike kinds. These activities are not simply different, but their differences are so related as to make one another possible. The reciprocal aid thus given causes mutual dependence of the parts. And the mutually-dependent parts, living by and for one another, form an aggregate on the same principle as an individual organism.

Spencer believed passionately that it would be wrong both ethically and economically to *interfere* in the natural progress of society. Therefore, he recommended, in the strongest possible terms, a policy of *laissez faire* (no interference) in virtually any form of social life—especially by government. By not interfering in any way, he felt (anticipating Darwin) that the *fittest would survive* in every kind of activity. This would provide effective leaders and, in the long term, be the best way to improve society. Thus, he was little concerned that overspecialization would pose problems—and, if it did, he would have been against doing anything about it.

From Gemeinschaft to Gesellschaft: Contrasting Social Orders

As discussed earlier, the German sociologist Ferdinand Toennies also saw that great changes were taking place as the modern urban-industrial society was emerging. He was not so much interested in the technologies of the factories and industries that had been developed as he was in what industrialization was doing to people. He analyzed relationships between those living in both the older social order and the new one that was developing as industrialization proceeded. He saw that the old traditional social order that had prevailed in village life had been based on strong emotionally based ties between people. They related to each other in family networks, they had traditional loyalties to one another that had been established through generations of friendships, and their fealty to their local aristocracy had been continued over long periods. As was noted earlier in this chapter, he called this type of social bonding, and the social order that it produced, a *Gemeinschaft*—which translates loosely into "a common unity based on reciprocal binding sentiments... which keeps human beings together."[7]

In contrast, Toennies also saw a new kind of social order arising from the urban-industrial society that was developing. In modern German, the term *Gesellschaft* (actually) means "business company." As in business, the basis of this new order was the formal and legally binding *contract* that defined relationships between people. In the earlier social order, a transaction such as a sale of a crop or animal, or the terms of employment, was negotiated informally between the parties and then sealed with a handshake. A person's word was sufficient, and people lived up to the agreements that they had made without question. If they did not, they would be disgraced in their community. In the new social order, that element of trust and dependability was vanishing. To make sure that an agreement was honored, it was necessary for the parties to sign a *contract* that had the formal enforcement powers of the state behind it. That is precisely what people do in such societies when they buy a car on payments, obtain a mortgage, or even accept employment.

The significance of these ideas of major social change was that the informal *web of trust* was disappearing in human relationships as the urban-industrial society continued to develop. People were increasingly *anonymous*—that is, "isolated" from each other in terms of social ties that were close, meaningful, and emotionally significant. Thus, as Toennies saw it, the individual in modern society was not only more and more obligated by the formal obligations of the contract but also slowly was losing those "reciprocal binding sentiments" that characterized the foundation of the earlier social order.

Anonymity and Anomie

In France, near the end of the century (1893) Emile Durkheim added important elements to this emerging view of the urban-industrial society. In his work *The Division of Labor in Society*, he pulled together many of the ideas of earlier sociologists, such as Comte, Spencer, and Toennies, into an explanation of how the conditions of the new urban-industrial order were changing both society and the individual. Like Comte, he understood that the division of labor, with reciprocal role relationships, held society together. It was the source, he said, of *social solidarity*. Even though the people in such a society did not know each other, or even if they did not even like each other, their individual contributions through their specialized activities stabilized the society.

On the downside, Durkheim maintained, was the fact that in a highly specialized social order, people did not share the same beliefs and commitments. The farmer had little in common with the operator of a machine in a factory. That person, in turn, was very unlike a nurse in a hospital, who was still different from a carpenter. It would be difficult for such unlike people to develop meaningful social bonds. Indeed, they would have so little in common that it might even be difficult for them to engage in an extended conversation. In other words, great *specialization* led to increased *anonymity,* a condition of psychological isolation for individuals in society.

Psychological isolation brought about by great social heterogeneity would lead, Durkheim felt, to a condition of *anomie.* This, he explained, is a condition of society in which its norms are no longer effective. They are neither shared nor seen as important, because people do not care about others around them who are seen as unlike themselves. The term translates awkwardly into "a condition of normlessness." As this becomes a characteristic of a social order, more and more people engage in *deviant behavior*—activities not effectively inhibited by the existing norms. In that case, the older social controls, such as the critical opinions of others, become ineffective. Formal controls have to take over—more laws, police, courts, fines, and jails—to maintain order. Thus, he saw the need for systems of *restitutive* law.

Generally, then, but the end of the 1800s, sociologists had put together a compelling picture of the emerging urban-industrial society. It was a society in which factory work was rapidly replacing agricultural pursuits. It was one in which diverse people had flocked to new industrial cities to work on assembly lines, or to perform tasks alongside of others who were not like them and about whom they cared little. It was a society in which older ties based on family, long-established friendships, and traditional loyalties did not bind people together. Social bonds of that type had been replaced by the contract. In such a situation, people were increasingly isolated socially, anonymous to each other, and relatively unchecked by traditional and shared social norms. These were all ideas that would provide the intellectual foundation for the concept of a "mass" society.

THE CONTEMPORARY URBAN-INDUSTRIAL SOCIETY: THE GESELLSCHAFT

Are these ideas from classic sociological theory valid today? Many would say yes—at least in part. It is very clear that life in the urban-industrial society today is very different than it has been at any other period of history. Above all, contemporary populations are characterized by great *diversity* and consequently a certain loss of *trust*.

Diversity and a Loss of Trust

In modern society there are few counterparts of the family in the traditional society who seals the deal for the wagon with a handshake. As suggested, if you need to buy its contemporary counterpart (say a pickup truck), you visit an auto dealership or a used car lot. If you proposed to the people who work there that they allow you to drive away with a vehicle on the basis of a handshake and a verbal promise to pay in the future, they would think that you were some kind of nut. After selecting the truck you intend to purchase, there would be discussions of your credit rating and your down payment and ability to pay monthly. Documents to be signed would outline the problems that you would face if you failed to meet the schedule of payments. Thus, instead of a handshake, a formal and legally binding *contract* would spell out in detail the rights, duties, and obligations of both seller and buyer.

This movement from verbally binding promises and handshakes to legally binding formal contracts that define relationships between people has turned out to be one of the major characteristics of the contemporary urban-industrial society. Contracts are not backed up solely by conceptions of personal honor and beliefs about trustworthiness. As we explained, they are regulated and enforced by the state through a body of what Durkheim termed *restitutive laws*. But even greater changes in norms were needed. Thus, as the industrial order developed, increasingly complex formal systems of *laws* became common, replacing reliance on folkways and mores.

Formal Systems of Control

As has been discussed, under the Gesellschaft conditions of the mass society, the means of controlling behavior are very different than they are in a more traditional setting. Because people do not share a single common and unifying culture, there is no one set of shared folkways and mores that serves as an effective guide to conduct. Different categories of people with different goals compete with each other for advantage. Familiar examples are management vs. labor, black vs. white, farmers vs. city dwellers, and the well-to-do vs. the poor. When one group gains, the other often loses. Competition between categories can easily lead to conflict. Too often, conflict leads to aggression. Aggression can be dangerous. In fact, competition, conflict, and aggression are common in urban-industrial societies. In such a society, there must be a much greater reliance on police, criminal laws, courts, fines, and prisons to keep order.

The Decline of Interpersonal Communication

In summary, then, people in contemporary urban-industrial societies frequently feel that others around them are different from themselves, often unpredictable, and potentially dangerous. For that reason, casual social contacts are limited, and many people prefer to remain anonymous. When people are wary of each other, they are much less likely to communicate readily. Children are warned not to talk to strangers. Adults tend to avoid any kind of revealing self-disclosure to other adults whom they do not know. Even eye contact with people on the street is discouraged. People from very different backgrounds feel that they have little or nothing in common—which indeed may be true. Few people feel completely comfortable in engaging in casual conversation with strangers on elevators, in stores, on the subway, or in other public places—assuming that it may lead to negative outcomes.

An important consequence of the development of this type of social order is that, when trusted interpersonal channels of communication become less available, other channels are needed to replace them. People still need a great deal of practical information, advice, entertainment, and news. If trusted interpersonal advisors are not available, if recreation cannot be found among family and close friends, and if the person-to-person networks for news and gossip are closed, then other means of getting such information must be used. In modern societies, these were conditions that made the print, broadcast, and other media so readily acceptable and useful. They became *substitutes* for the interpersonal channels that served people effectively in the traditional society. This feature of the mass society will be discussed in Chapter 15 (which presents the Media

Information Utility Theory). This theory explains the circumstances that lead people to be much more dependent on the mass media as sources for practical information that they need, rather than on family members, friends, and others, such as is the case in the traditional society.

THE THEORETICAL CONCEPT OF THE "MASS"

Many of the features of modern urban-industrial societies were incorporated by sociologists into a theoretical concept that they termed the "mass." It was developed to describe the basic or essential nature of urban-industrial social order. The term also became standard for referring to our contemporary media. It played a key role in the development of the first theory of the process and effects of mass communication. That theory, presented in Chapter 9, came in recent years to be called the Magic Bullet Theory. Now discredited and abandoned, nevertheless, it is of historical importance, not only because it was the first but also because it incorporated the conception of the mass as a major description of the urban-industrial society.

Mass communication expanded greatly as the 1900s began and also with the new media of the twenty-first century. It is important, therefore, to look systematically at the classic sociological conception of the "mass," especially as it was applied in developing some of the first theories of "mass" communication.

Psychological Isolation in the "Mass"

The most widely quoted definition of the "mass" is that developed by sociologist Herbert Blumer in 1946. In this instance, he was not considering the concept in connection with mass communication but in terms of how earlier sociologists had portrayed the way in which modern society was developing as a result of the great social changes that had taken place during the Industrial Revolution. The mixing of people and cultures that resulted from migrations, urbanization, and the changing social stratification, he stressed, were resulting in the isolated nature of individuals in the populations of modern societies. That is, the mass:

> has no social organization, no body of custom and tradition, no set of established rules and rituals, no organized group of sentiments, no structure of status roles, and no established leadership. It merely consists of an aggregation of isolated individuals who are separate, detached, anonymous.[8]

THE "MASS" AND THE MEDIA

In 1953, Eliot Friedson discussed the relationship between this sociological conception of the mass and the audiences of mass communication. Perhaps the closest fit between the terms "audience" and "mass," he maintained, can be seen in the case of going to the movies. This relationship, Friedson points out, was analyzed in an article by Herbert Blumer in 1936. Friedson summarized the idea in the following terms:

> In attending to movies, members of the audience are anonymous, heterogeneous, unorganized and spatially separated, and the content of the movies is concerned with something that lies outside the local lives of the spectators.[9]

Linking the idea of the mass to the concept of "audience," then, reinforced the idea of "mass communication." Thus, the concept of "mass" has survived in modern times. And, more important, it brought with it a conception of audiences that persists in the thinking of at least some segments of the public. As later chapters will show, communication scholars no longer think of audiences in this way (as a "mass"). Nevertheless, the term has persisted in the social sciences. By 1959, sociologists were still defining the mass and mass society in the following terms:

> Modern society is made up of masses in the sense that 'there has emerged a vast mass of segregated, isolated individuals, interdependent in all sorts of specialized ways yet lacking in any central unifying value or purpose.' The weakening of traditional bonds, the growth of rationality, and the division of labor, have created societies made up of individuals who are only loosely bound together. In this sense, the word "mass" suggests something closer to an aggregate than to a tightly knit social group.[10]

Other scholars, especially Europeans, have offered somewhat different interpretations in more recent years. Their key idea has been that the *large numbers* that make up the mass makes communication between them difficult. While this is consistent with the concept of anonymity and isolation, it seems, for some writers, to produce a dangerous or menacing situation:

> [Large numbers turn] industrious people into a dangerous, rioting, frame-breaking mob. The normal channels of communication being disrupted, that mob appeared to steady and wealthy citizens like Frankenstein's monster. One of the very few voices that denounced that image was Lord Byron in his first parliamentary speech at the House of Lords on the twelfth of April, 1812. 'You call these men a mob,' he told his peers, and yet they are the workers who produce your wealth, the servants who ensure your comfort, the soldiers who fight for your freedom. The concept of the mass thus stems from the inability to recognize a workable communication organization in a very large group.[11]

In summary, then, in the classic concept of the mass, each person in society is said to be a sort of isolated unit in a state of psychological anonymity with respect to others. This means that they are in a very *impersonal* environment. Under these conditions, they are presumed to be virtually free from informal binding social obligations, and from the kinds of controls people exercise over each other when the opinions of others count heavily. This, or course, makes networks of interpersonal communication difficult to maintain, and it reduces the degree to which people control each other on the basis of opinions, norms, and shared standards of behavior.

EARLY INTERPRETATIONS OF THE EFFECTS OF "MASS" NEWSPAPERS

The earliest assessments by sociologists of the influences of mass communication were that *they were powerful indeed*. For example, by the late 1800s, when the daily (so-called "mass") newspaper had come into wide use, scholars of the time were convinced that this new form of human communication had truly *great power*. The noted French jurist and sociologist Gabriel Tarde was convinced that they had a profound influence, even on peoples' conversations. In 1898, he wrote that:

> We shall never know and can never imagine to what degree newspapers have transformed, both enriched and leveled, *unified in space* and *diversified in time* the conversations of individuals. Even those who do not read newspapers but who, talking to those who do, are forced to follow the groove of their borrowed thoughts.[12]

Tarde believed that, in some ways, the newspaper was a *threat* to society. In his role as a judge and criminologist, he saw the medium as a destructive element leading youth astray. He observed that students were reading crime stories in the newspapers of his time and that this was having a corrupting effect on them. It would be far better, he believed, if they would spend their time in libraries that would provide healthier mental nourishment.

> But it is the trashy and malicious press, scandal-mongering, riddled with court cases, that awaits the student when he leaves school. The little newspaper, supplementing the little drink, alcoholizes his heart.[13]

Other social scientists of the period saw things differently and were convinced that there were equally powerful, but more favorable, effects of the new type of newspaper. For example, early in the 1900s, Charles Horton Cooley, a distinguished sociologist, used two concepts to describe their influences—*enlargement* and *animation*. The idea of enlargement, as Cooley explained it, referred to an expansion and improvement of the human mind. Newspapers, he wrote, have brought about a major changes in human nature. As he put it:

> They make it possible for society to be organized more and more on the higher faculties of man, on intelligence and sympathy, rather than on authority, caste and routine. They mean freedom, outlook, indefinite possibility.[14]

The reason for this change, Cooley noted, was that in earlier times communication took place mainly by word of mouth or, at best, via slow and limited postal facilities. Most people had little knowledge of events and affairs that were taking place at any significant distance beyond the immediate area or region in which their home, farm, or village was located. Thus, at the time, there was no counterpart of what we now think of as "news." With the arrival of the common newspaper, kept up to date by the telegraph and other means, people's understanding of events farther away expanded greatly. Cooley interpreted this as a truly profound effect. He wrote:

> People are far more aware today to what is going on in China, if that happens to interest them, than they were then to events a hundred miles away.[15]

Thus, he saw the new medium as having powerful, but on the whole very positive, consequences. The papers that regularly brought news of the outside world, he believed, resulted in both an enlargement and quickening of the human mind.

Within a short time, however, new ways of generating valid and reliable knowledge about human behavior would be developed by social scientists. These new strategies would permit both psychologists and sociologists to investigate the influences of mass communications through empirical research. It began in the 1920s, when methods and procedures for conducting quantitative research were adapted from their earlier use in the agricultural and biological sciences. This brought a transformation in the way knowledge was being developed about individual conduct and social life. In particular, statistics and survey methods based on representative sampling provided the strategies for the study of many kinds of human activities. Among them were influences of mass communication. As this trend continued, empirical and quantitative research on the effects of mass communications—based on the adapted rules of science, incorporated into the study of human conduct and social life—began to reveal more valid conclusions about the process and effects of mass communication. The broad interpretations of the effects of the media provided by such observers as Tarde and Cooley were no longer as relevant.

During much of the 1900s, it was sociologists—and to some degree social psychologists—who took the lead in studying the mass media. Survey and experimental methodology had been refined to a point where such social scientists could test hypotheses about the influence of specific kinds of content on specific kinds of audiences. By mid-century, however, scholars interested in the systematic study of the mass media began to establish the field of media studies as a separate discipline. As the number of universities offering formal degree programs focusing specifically on media studies increased, research on the process and effects of mass communication in many ways shifted from the social sciences to the new *discipline* of mass communication. In any case, the field of sociology left a legacy of research findings and theory that are now an important part of the foundation on which mass communication research and theory building developed and now rests. One of the most important of these contributions was the theory of mass society—from which, as noted, the term "mass" media is derived.

THE THEORY OF MASS SOCIETY

The concept of the mass and its interpretations of the nature of urban-industrial social order, especially as it differed from the earlier traditional society, can be brought together into a formal theory. This theory represents a summary and consolidation of the conclusions of a number of sociologists of the nineteenth and twentieth centuries who observed those changes in their lifetimes. While it may or may not accurately describe all urban industrial societies today, it provides a valuable and interesting perspective on the social conditions within which contemporary mass media exist.

The Theory of Mass Society: A Formal Summary

1. *Social diversity* in society increases as a result of the mixing of unlike populations through migrations, the growing complexity of the division of labor, and the development of distinctive socioeconomic levels of reward, power, consumption, and lifestyles.
2. Increased diversity *erodes consensus* concerning a central set of traditional cultural norms and values, reducing their effectiveness in maintaining conformity through informal social controls and resulting in an increase in the incidence of deviant behavior.

3. As informal controls become less effective, the use of formal controls replaces them, in the form of contracts, litigation, laws, police, and prisons—and, as a result, relationships within the society become more *impersonal.*

4. Competition between diverse people leads to an *increase in conflicts* between unlike segments of the population, who pursue mutually unattainable goals and who are unable to resolve their differences through informal communication, negotiation, and accommodation.

5. As conflict increases, open and easy communication between people as a basis for maintaining consensus and social cohesion in society becomes *increasingly difficult*, leading to distrust, prejudice, alienation, social rejection, and personal isolation.

6. **Therefore,** a "mass" society develops, composed of *socially isolated individuals*, with fewer and fewer meaningful interpersonal bonds that can serve as the basis of open and informal channels of communication.

The Mass Society as an Abstract Model

It requires no stretch of the imagination to see that there has never really been a true and total *mass* society, and in this book there is no assumption that it exists today. It is true, however, that modern *Gesellschaft* societies are very different from the older *Gemeinschaft*-type, pre-industrial ones and that they do indeed have at least some of the features of the mass. Obviously, in the modern city, people are not entirely anonymous or without ties to others. Modern sociologists are fully aware of this, and their research tracks the ties and interpersonal influences that do exist between people. Today's citizens in urban-industrial societies get to know at least some of their neighbors. They establish relationships with at least some people at work, at school, in churches, and elsewhere. Members of their families may live in the same city and visit often. People join numerous voluntary organizations, clubs, and associations. Therefore, an entire population of totally anonymous people, with no social obligations to others, would be difficult, or more likely impossible, to find.

In spite of its sometimes unrealistic assumptions, however, the theory of mass society has value. It was developed in its time as an *exaggeration*—as a kind of *abstract intellectual model* that could be used for comparing traditional and modern societies. Sociologists sometimes refer to such models as "ideal types." This does not mean "ideal" in the sense of desirable. Instead, it refers to a deliberately formulated conceptual pattern that can aid in understanding what is taking place in a real-world situation.

Constructing abstract "models" is common in science. Examples are the computer models of hurricanes or tornados that are used by meteorologists. These models do not reflect all of the characteristics of a real hurricane or tornado. They are abstractions that emphasize, or even exaggerate, the critical aspects of such storms. Nevertheless, they can help in trying to predict how real ones will behave. Similar models are generated by oceanographers when they study the flow of huge ocean currents, by physicists who develop models of atomic structures, and so on. For sociologists of the late nineteenth and early twentieth centuries, studying the changes brought by the Industrial Revolution, the concept of the mass society was an abstraction (a model) that could be used to help interpret many of the important trends and conditions that were making the new and emerging urban-industrial societies different from more traditional communities.

Mass Society and Audience Diversity

If it can be assumed that large cities in the United States today do indeed have at least some of the characteristics that are set forth in theories of the mass, it is little wonder that citizens believe themselves to be among diverse people and in anonymous, impersonal social relationships. Today's urban populations are very heterogeneous, with many social classes, lifestyles, ethnic and racial categories, religious beliefs, political affiliations, values, tastes, interests, and other factors. Sociologists study these differences among social categories and individuals constantly to develop understandings of how they influence the human condition in society today.

It would be difficult for individuals to get all information that they need in a diverse society solely through interpersonal communication, such as from neighbors. If they have moved to the city from a small town, as many have, it is immediately clear to them that life is very different in the urban setting than in the more traditional communities in which they grew up. While no city in the United States today has all of the *Gesellschaft* characteristics included in the theoretical concept of the mass society, that abstract model does help to explain why it is that people in urban-industrial societies often turn to mass media to obtain information or gratification that they need, rather than more to neighbors or even friends and family.

Generally, then, in the development of theories of mass communication, many of the basic concepts developed and studied intensively by sociologists are essential. The great diversity of modern audiences is quite clearly a result of all of the factors noted above. Those differences have indeed resulted from the remarkable changes that took place in the transition from traditional to urban-industrial society—from Gemeinschaft to Gesellschaft.

Notes and References

1. Plato, *The Republic*, trans. by Francis M. Cornford (New York: Oxford University Press, 1945). Plato wrote the original work toward the end of the fifth century and possibly the early part of the fourth century before the birth of Christ. Exact dates unknown.
2. Aristotle, *Politics*, trans. by Benjamin Jowett (New York: Oxford University Press). The original was produced during the fourth century before the birth of Christ. Exact dates unknown.
3. Adam Smith, *An Inquiry into the Nature and Causes of the Wealth of Nations* (Chicago: University of Chicago Press, 1976), pp. 7–25. First published in London, 1776.
4. Auguste Comte, *The Positive Philosophy*, trans. by Harriet Martineau (London: George Bell and Sons, 1915). First published in France between 1830 and 1842.
5. *Ibid.* p. 292.
6. *Ibid.* p. 293.
7. Ferdinand Toennies, *Gemeinschaft und Gesellschaft*, trans. and ed. by Charles Loomis (East Lansing: Michigan State University Press, 1957), p. 47. First published in German in 1887.
8. Herbert Blumer, "Collective Behavior," in A. M. Lee, *New Outline of the Principles of Sociology* (New York: Barnes and Noble, Inc., 1946), p. 186.
9. Eliot Friedson, "Communication Research and the Concept of the Mass," *American Sociological Review*, 18, 1953, pp. 313–317. See also Herbert Blumer, "The Moulding of Mass Behavior Through the Motion Picture," *Publications of the American Sociological Society*, Vol. XXIX, 1936, pp. 115–127.
10. Leonard Broom and Philip Selznick, *Sociology*, 2nd ed. (Evanston, IL: Row Peterson, 1959), p. 38. The quote within this passage is from Kimball Young, *Sociology* (New York: American Book, 1949), p. 24.
11. Robert Escarpit, "The Concept of 'Mass,'" *Journal of Communication*, 27, 1977, p. 45.
12. From Terry N. Clark, ed., *Gabriel Tarde: On Communication and Social Influence: Selected Papers* (Chicago: University of Chicago Press, 1969), p. 304.
13. Clark *Ibid.* p. 265.
14. Charles Horton Cooley, *Social Organization: A Study of the Larger Mind* (New York: Schocken Books, 1962), p. 81. First published by Charles Scribner in 1909.
15. Cooley, *Ibid.* p. 82.

CHAPTER 7

James Bryce's 19th Century Theory of Public Opinion and the Press

James Bryce was a British political philosopher who traveled extensively throughout the United States during the 1880s. The purpose of his travels was to study and write about the American democracy—which was at the time still a rather new and unique form of government. It had withstood a civil war, and it seemed to be doing well. Moreover, it was different from other democracies that had developed elsewhere. In a multivolume work, Bryce set forth a theory of the *formation, nature, and power of public opinion* in that democracy. His theory emphasized a central role for newspapers (which were the only news media of the period). Today, as new communications technologies have been added to the role that newspapers played in Bryce's time, they have greatly increased the degree to which politicians and voters can contact each other.[1] It can be argued that this has resulted in an increase in the power of public opinion and consequently of the press (news industry generally).

In this chapter, Bryce's theory, which he described in lengthy prose and examples, has been formalized into twelve related propositions. From them, a "therefore" theorem can be logically derived—a prediction indicating that (if the propositions of the theory can be regarded as correct) significant implications follow for public opinion in a society in the contemporary age—where multiple channels of mass communication are now in place.

While theories of public opinion have always been relevant to the field of mass communication, for reasons that are not clear, James Bryce has remained a relatively obscure figure among media scholars. To correct that shortcoming, his theories of the relationship between media and public opinion, which are now seen as seminal, are included in the present text.

As noted, Bryce developed his theory more than a century ago, when only the traditional newspaper provided news reports to the public on a daily basis. However, the concepts and conclusions that he set forth continue to have merit for understanding the relationship between public opinion and the (greatly expanded) "press" in contemporary times. In specific terms, the first goal of this chapter is to set forth, in summary form, a formalized version of Bryce's theory of public opinion. Its second goal is to explain how his descriptions of the formation and functions of public opinion provide insights into many features of our contemporary political processes and the ways in which these are linked to modern versions of the news media.

Grounds will be presented for concluding that Bryce's theory concerning the nature and functions of public opinion in the American democracy is now of *greater importance* than it may have been during his time. This may be the case because the many new media play an expanded role in linking the public with policy makers. As will be explained, Bryce described how the newspaper played a central part in both the formation and expression of public opinion. In addition, in the 1880s, there were few (or no) means available to measure or otherwise assess the nature of any public's opinions on any issue with any accuracy. Bryce recognized, however, that the power of public opinion in shaping the structure and functioning of the American government was of great importance.

The renewed relevance of Bryce's theory has come about because of two factors: The first is the great expansion of channels of mass communication delivering news (e.g., radio, TV, the Internet) that now exist but did not exist in his time. These provide a sharply increased level of *surveillance of political leaders* on the part of the public. In addition, today's constituents can easily *make their personal views known* to their leaders via modern interpersonal communication media (e.g., fax, telephone, polls, email, and express mail). These can provide politicians with a more thorough understanding of the nature of public opinion on any issue in terms of how voters perceive their positions and actions. In many ways, then, the great increase in communication channels has expanded the meaning of the ancient tradition of *vox populi*—providing a much closer link between constituents and those engaged in political decision making.

An equally important factor that increases the importance of Bryce's theory today is our contemporary means of *assessing* public opinion. Polls, focus groups, and other assessments taken by various research groups and agencies now reflect with reasonable accuracy the feelings of various publics on almost a daily basis. The results of such assessments are often transmitted back to the public by news media within hours of their completion. Moreover, an army of media pundits in talk shows, news programs, and editorial columns now discuss and dissect the merits of, as well as public reactions to, proposals and policy decisions of political leaders. Many of the faces and voices of these sages are as familiar to Americans as those of the people next door. In the present chapter, then, Bryce's nineteenth-century theory of public opinion and the press will be set forth, and its relevance in today's media-saturated democracy will be discussed.

When the general nature of Bryce's original theory has been made clear, the next section of the chapter will provide a brief sketch of James Bryce the man. Following that will be a summary of the goals and methods he used in, what we would call today, his large-scale (qualitative) research project on the nature of the American democracy. The next section will explain his conclusions about the unique nature of the political process in the United States. Then, a section will set forth in formal terms (as a set of related propositions) his theory of the formation, functions, and power of public opinion within that political process. Finally, as suggested above, some of the reasons why Bryce's theory may be *more important* today than it was at the time he developed it will be discussed by explaining how new media appear to have increased its significance.

BACKGROUND

James Bryce was born in Belfast, Ireland, in 1838, into a family of very modest circumstances. He was the first of the five children of James and Margaret Bryce. A short time after James was born, the family moved to Scotland where his father—a teacher of mathematics and geology—took a modest post at Glasgow High School. James, who attended that school, was a bright child and soon earned prizes in Latin and Greek studies. His family recognized his potential, and at the age of 15 they sent him back to Ireland, where for a year he attended the Belfast Academy. At 16 he returned to Scotland and entered Glasgow University. He was a brilliant student, and he impressed his mentors with his easy command of Latin, Greek, mathematics, logic, and rhetoric. Three years later, James tried for a scholarship at Oxford, which was a great challenge for a youth with his background. However, he performed very well on the highly competitive entrance examinations, and as a result he was instantly admitted to Trinity College at Oxford. The only difficulty he faced was that he refused to conform to religious requirements that were in force at the time. Nevertheless, he was admitted.

While at Oxford he easily won a number of important prizes and competitions. Bryce was, in short, an outstanding and brilliant young scholar who became deeply interested in the analysis of political issues and systems. Before leaving Oxford, he wrote a work titled *The Holy Roman Empire*.[2] His work was published in 1864. It was a sweeping study of change in societal institutions during the period of the universal Christian monarchy in Europe. The book won him widespread recognition and acclaim as a scholar, as well as important prizes.

To earn a living after leaving Oxford, Bryce became a barrister. He lived in London during the time of the American Civil War. His legal work brought him into contact with a number of highly placed and influential men. These individuals helped him to develop political aspirations. As a consequence, he accepted several appointments as a member of important government commissions whose task were to investigate different problems and conditions in British society. By 1870, he was in his early thirties and was well established and highly respected as an intellectual. He had prospered financially as well as intellectually from his legal work, and he became a lecturer in law both at Oxford and in London.

In mid-life he continued to develop as a distinguished scholar. Over the years, his works became both widely known and highly regarded by political scientists of the period. Because of his reputation as a political philosopher, he was honored with a peerage and became Lord Bryce, Viscount of Dechmont.

Later in his life (in 1907), Bryce became the British ambassador to the United States. It was a most appropriate appointment because his in-depth study of life in the United States had provided him with a deep understanding of the American people, their culture, political systems, and even their shortcomings and problems. He was greatly admired in this country, and he served in his diplomatic post with distinction. He died in 1922, just after the end of World War I, at the age of eighty-four.

BRYCE'S IN-DEPTH QUALITATIVE STUDY OF THE UNITED STATES

Bryce made a decision early in 1870 to visit the United States. As a result, he spent much of that year in this country. As a student of politics, the young American democracy held a considerable fascination for him. Consequently, he decided to travel widely throughout the country to learn first hand about its people, politics, and culture. Today we might call such an enterprise a large-scale and systematic qualitative research project.

Bryce made three trips to the United States in just over a ten-year period, beginning in the early 1880s. During each of his trips, he traveled for months, from one end of the United States to the other. He went east to west, north to south, and throughout the heartland of the country. People liked him very much, and he accepted numerous invitations to stay in their homes. He met with educators, business people, politicians, and many other categories of influential citizens. He constantly interviewed people that he met on trains and encountered in hotels, barber shops, restaurants, and in hundreds of other sites. With his open and likable personal manner, he easily established rapport with ordinary working people. The same was true of those in positions of power and affluence. Throughout his travels, he made extensive notes about the ideas, beliefs, attitudes, and values of the Americans he met. It seems likely that Bryce's study of the United States was one of the most thorough of any large-scale qualitative analysis of a society that has ever been undertaken.

The American Commonwealth

Bryce published his three-volume *The American Commonwealth* in 1888.[3] It soon became a work of particular importance to students of American politics and government. It was a detailed analysis of the general culture, the politics, and other social features of the United States, as these existed in the late nineteenth century. This important work has often been favorably compared with the earlier work by Alexis de Tocqueville (1805–1849). His *Democracy in America*, published a half century earlier, covered many of the same topics.[4]

If Bruce's book on the United States were to be published today, it would be recognized as a very lengthy and well-organized qualitative research report. The first volume provided a detailed description of the American Constitution. It explained the formal structure of the federal government of the U.S. and how the system was designed to function. The volume also made comparisons with European systems. The second volume was devoted to state and local government. It discussed both their positive features as well as their shortcomings. In his analysis, Bryce included a focus on political parties and so-called "machines." He described in detail the inevitable corruption that was part of American politics at the time.

Most important for the present chapter is the third volume. Here he presented his analysis of the nature and role of public opinion in the American politics. He set forth both his theory of the formation of public opinion as well as his conclusions about the powerful influences that it had on American politicians. In this third volume, he described how public opinion was assessed by politicians and others at the time. Again, this was prior to the development of polling techniques.

The Role of Public Opinion in Government

To understand Bryce's contribution to understanding the nature, functions, and development of public opinion, one must begin with his conception of its significance in the affairs of government. That perspective can be gained from his explanation of the role of public opinion in the three different types of democratic systems.

Bryce maintained that public opinion has been the *principle and ultimate power in all forms of governments at all times*. Even those that were entirely despotic, he maintained, were ultimately tolerated by their citizens. That toleration, he said, was a very basic form of public opinion. Even in great empires of the past that had been ruled by ruthless tyrants, who were backed by powerful military forces, he pointed out, leaders remained in power only through the indirect consent of those governed. After all, he noted, such military forces were small compared with the total number of citizens of such nations. A determined multitude could have displaced them if they were determined to do so. That seldom happened, he suggested. The reason was that people in such societies believed strongly in *authority*. Their desire for a stable and established order was a more powerful force than their desire for change. Even under conditions that were the very opposite of democracy, he believed, public opinion is the most important factor in supporting the political system.[5]

In democratic systems, Bryce explained, public opinion plays a more central role. He maintained that essentially there are only three forms of government that incorporate principles of democracy in one way or another. Each is based directly on public opinion.

The earliest were *primary assemblies*. Essentially, these were tribal systems in which the entire people participated in governance. They "met, debated current questions, decided them by votes, and chose those who were to carry out its will."[6] The source of political power in this type of government is simply the will of those who are present and who vote. Public opinion in this system shapes political decision making in a very direct way and at a very basic level. Few such societies remained, even in Bryce's time. One form that is still in existence at the local level in the twenty-first century is the traditional town meeting system that is still common in New England. It closely resembles the primary assembly form.

The second type of government incorporating democratic principles consists of a body of persons who have been elected and sent to office to "represent" responsibly the interests of those who place them in those positions. This is the basic idea of a *chamber of deputies*, often referred to as a parliament. In such a system, public opinion is most visible during elections. Representatives are chosen on the basis of their proclaimed stands on major issues. After they are in office, public opinion is still important, but it tends to remain in the background. Those who have been elected are expected to resolve conflicts by debating wisely and by making decisions that meet the needs of the majority—while protecting the rights of minorities. Those representatives are expected to choose people objectively for executive positions to carry out the functions of government in the best interests of the country and generally provide for what they believe to be the wishes of the majority. Public opinion is obviously the foundation of this system of government. However, the majority of citizens do not have to insert themselves into the process on a frequent basis. "They give these representatives a tolerably free hand," Bryce wrote, "leaving them in power for a considerable space of time to act unchecked, except in so far as custom, or possibly some fundamental law, limits their discretion."[7] A good example of this form of democratic government is the English parliamentary system. Elections are not called on a regular schedule but only when there are considerable shifts in public opinion or when crises occur that require them to vote in new representatives.

According to Bryce, there is still a third system that represents a compromise between these two—one of *popular sovereignty*—in which public opinion is far more apparent and it plays a more direct role in political decision making. In this system, the government is organized so as to apply the principle of primary assemblies to a large country. In this case, a legislature is elected but only for a short term. Moreover, checks and balances limit the power of the several branches of government to prevent any one from being in a position to control any of the others. Representatives who are elected can be voted out of office at the end of their term—keeping them insecure in their positions of power. Obviously, this is the way in which the federal and state governments in the United States are organized. Each of the main branches of government—the legislature, the executive, and the judiciary—have to share power in such a way that none can control the others. Moreover, those who serve can be removed by means of the ballot at the end of their short terms.

THE ROLE OF PUBLIC OPINION IN THE AMERICAN DEMOCRACY

In the government by popular sovereignty that prevails in the United States, Bryce maintained, the balance of power between the executive, legislative, and judiciary branches weakens all three. As he put it:

> The Senate, for instance, may refuse the measures which the House thinks necessary.... The President may propose a treaty to the Senate and the Senate may reject it.[8]

This passage was written well over a century ago, but it has a remarkably modern ring. When the effectiveness of government is limited by the structural balances designed in this system, Americans speak of *gridlock*. Today, this could easily be a description of the workings of the executive branch versus the Congress at a time when there are heated debates over crime, health care, foreign wars, Supreme Court appointments, welfare, Social Security, immigration, and intervention in the affairs of other nations.

Bryce also outlined the role of the federal judiciary in this system. He explained that it is the courts that must deal with questions of the Constitution. Nevertheless, he pointed out, its judges lack power in any real sense to influence most of the decisions of government. The reason is that they make their decisions within a framework of *litigation*. As a consequence, they play no part in the initial formation of policy. They can only reshape interpretations of laws that are already in place:

> ... in many cases, the intervention of the courts, which can act only in a suit between parties compels the courts to decide, because each of the conflicting parties is within its legal right.[9]

Most Americans are reasonably well aware of these features of the formal structure of their government. Many learn about how the system works in high school civics classes. What they may *not* have learned, however, is that the structure allows public opinion to exert unusual power in the American system of popular sovereignty. At the time, this was a major contribution by Bryce. He was able to explain why the formal structure of the system—with only limited authority held by any of the three branches—leaves a *vacuum of power*. In effect, he noted, that vacuum is filled by public opinion. As he put it in dramatic terms:

> Towering over Presidents and State governors, over Congress and State legislatures, over conventions and the vast machinery of party, public opinion stands out in the United States as the great source of power, the master of servants who tremble before it.[10]

Politicians elected to public office in the United States, he wrote, are particularly at the mercy of changes and shifts in public opinion. This is because Americans hold their elections on a regularly scheduled basis and far more frequently than is the case in other forms of democracy. To stay in office in such a system, an elected official must constantly be aware of the feelings, beliefs, and convictions of voters concerning the constant flow of topics and issues that come up. If that official is out of step in such a system, Bryce believed, he or she would run a serious risk of being voted out of office.

DETERMINING PUBLIC OPINION IN THE LATE 1800s

One of the features of the American political system in the late 1800s was that public opinion was very difficult to assess. Polling methodology did not exist. It would not be available until the 1920s.[11] In some dramatic situations, the nature of popular opinion was abundantly clear—as when riots broke out or when lengthy petitions were sent to members of Congress. At other times it could be assessed when angry mobs took to the streets, when public figures were hanged in effigy, or when torchlight parades provided clear statements as to the nature of how the public felt about an issue. While Bryce understood that only too well, short of such dramatic situations, it was not possible to gauge public opinion with any degree of accuracy. He had no confidence in any such attempt.

> How is the will of the majority to be ascertained except by counting votes? How, without the greatest inconvenience, can votes be frequently taken on all the chief questions that arise? No country has yet surmounted these inconveniences. [The] machinery for weighing and measuring the popular will from week to week or month to month has not yet been and is not likely to be invented.[12]

Even getting accurate reports back to voters on the actions of legislators was difficult because the means were limited. For most citizens the newspaper was the only source available to find out about the decisions and activities of their representatives in Washington. Sometimes those papers chose to publish such reports; sometimes they did not. Essentially, then, compared to today, limitations on information technology inhibited active citizen expression of views to legislators, and it also limited feedback from those in office to their constituents.

Because of these communications limitations, the activities of a person elected to Congress or the state legislature were much less visible—under less public scrutiny—than they are today. Without polls, understanding the dimensions of opinion on any important issue was difficult. The politician had to use the few indicators that existed at the time. To assess how the public viewed an issue, they had to rely on various leaders of associations, such as Chambers of Commerce, farmer's groups, unions, and the like. Often, such individuals wrote letters to their political representatives or presented their ideas in speeches. These became accepted as keys to the feelings of the rank and file. Journalists not only reported on the views of such spokesmen (women were seldom involved; they could not vote at the time, in any case, and had little voice), but they also added their own interpretations. Thus, what was reported in the newspapers was accepted as a guide to how the majority or a significant segment of the public felt about an issue.

Bryce did not believe that these sources were the only reliable indicators of prevailing public opinion. However, he did recognize them as important factors in shaping its nature. He recognized a "bandwagon effect". Perhaps shaping the ideas of later theorists, he saw that public opinion is influenced by those who are most outspoken. Those who make their views forcefully known provide an early form of the basic propositions of the contemporary Spiral of Silence Theory (see Chapter 24).[13]

> Opinion makes opinion. Men follow in the path which they see others treading: they hasten to adopt the view that seems likely to prevail. Hence every weighty voice, be it that of a speaker . . . or a newspaper, is at once the disclosure of an existing force and a further force influencing others.[14]

Thus, an individual's opinion is shaped and influenced as a consequence of interactions with others. Again, possibly influencing later theorists, he recognized that some individuals serve in the role of what later came to be called "opinion leaders." (See Chapter 13, "The Two-Step Flow of Communication Theory.") These are influential people who appear knowledgeable about an issue. Some speak for associations and make public presentations to groups. Others write in newspapers about (and interpret) the sentiments of the electorate.

Bryce was convinced that public opinion starts with *individuals*. He analyzed at some length how a particular person begins to adopt a specific viewpoint and how that individual's initial position on an issue is modified and reshaped into versions that eventually become widely shared. This individual opinion formation and modification, he thought, was the real *starting point* for the development of more widely shared public opinion. That is, he moved from the *individual* to the *collective* level, explaining that public opinion begins as a view that is similar among many individuals to become patterned into a shared or collectively held view. At that point it becomes a powerful social force shaping the political system. He developed a detailed explanation of this process of public opinion formation at both the individual and collective levels. It is that process that is in many ways the most important of his overall theory of its nature and functions.

BRYCE'S STAGES IN THE FORMATION OF PUBLIC OPINION

What is actually meant by "public opinion"? Moreover, how does it exercise its power? These were questions directly faced by Bryce. To answer them, he developed an elegant, if lengthy, explanation of the process by which public opinion is formed and an explanation of its ability to shape the political process. These explanations can be summarized briefly in order to provide a foundation for developing Lord Bryce's theory in a more concise form as a set of basic formal propositions.[15]

As was the style of scholars in the nineteenth century, Bryce set forth his theory of the formation and functions of public opinion in a lengthy descriptive and multi-chapter essay, abundantly illustrated with examples and commentaries that were relevant to his time. By summarizing his ideas and dropping passages that have little current relevance, Bryce's descriptions of the nature of public opinion, and how it controls government, can be summarized into four basic stages of the process.

Stage One

The first stage in public opinion formation, said Bryce, involves several basic steps, and it begins at the individual level:

> The simplest form in which public opinion presents itself is when a sentiment spontaneously rises in the mind and flows from the lips of the average man upon his seeing and hearing something done or said.[16]

In other words, individual opinion begins with perception of a topic, situation, or event that can potentially—in time—become a focus for the formation of public opinion. Such a topic can range from a policy adopted by government to an action on the part of a candidate for office. When the person perceives that, it can lead to an emotional reaction prompting the individual to discuss that interpretation with others. In other words, the process of formation of public opinion starts within an interactive and interpersonal context.

However, said Bryce, that is only the beginning of the process, and it involves more than merely a personal reaction followed by discussion of the topic with others. He recognized the part played by the mass media (newspapers in his time). It is usually the media that bring the initial information about the topic to the attention of the individual.

> A business man reads in his newspaper at breakfast the events of the preceding day. He reads [about a tariff policy or an election in New York]. These statements arouse in his mind sentiments of approval or disapproval, which may be strong or weak according to his predilection [regarding tariffs or the candidate]. They arouse also an expectation of certain consequences likely to follow.[17]

In other words, the topic or issue around which the individual begins to form an opinion is first encountered in the media. That happens before the person can discuss the topic with others. He also recognized that individual personality differences (what he called "predilections") play a significant part in shaping the person's initial interpretations as well as his reactions of approval or disapproval. Even in its initial stage, then, public opinion has an *affective*—that is, an "approve" or "disapprove"—dimension.

The individual's initial reaction of sentiments and expectations, Bryce believed, were not based on conscious reasoning. They were more basic reactions, that is, impressions formed on the spur of the moment. These, however, provide the basis for the next step. Once again, he explained, the individual turns to the media to seek clarification. Much depends on what is found there. The reader's initial impressions and feelings are either strengthened or are not confirmed by what he reads. Indeed, they may even be contradicted. The major point, however, is that the media play a central role:

> He turns to the leading article in the newspaper, and his sentiments and expectations are confirmed or weakened according as he finds that they are or are not shared by the newspaper writer.[18]

As the process continues, both discussions with others and what is encountered in the media about the topic continue to play a part in the complex process of the formation and crystallization of opinion:

> He goes down to the office in the train, talks there to two or three acquaintances, and perceives that they do or do not agree with his own still faint impressions. In his counting-house he finds his partner and a bundle of other newspapers which he glances at; their words further affect him, and thus by the end of the day his mind is beginning to settle down into a definite view.[19]

Basically, then, in this first stage, a media report on the topic provides the individual with an initial affective reaction—which is shaped by personality factors. Then, as a result of discussions with others, and also encountering interpretations provided by the media, the individual has begun to formulate a definite view regarding the topic.

Stage Two

The second major stage in public opinion formation takes place within a more collective framework. This, explained Bryce, takes public opinion formation beyond an individual reaction and makes it a shared or *collective* phenomenon. He states that a parallel process has been taking place in the minds of other individuals. This has not escaped the notice of journalists, and it becomes the focus of newspaper reports. In fact, journalists begin to influence each other.

> The evening paper has collected the opinion of the morning papers, and it is rather more positive in its forecast of results. Next morning the leading party journals have articles still more definite and positive in approval or condemnation and in prediction of consequences to follow; and the opinion of ordinary minds, which in most such minds has been hitherto fluid and undetermined, has begun to crystallize into a solid mass.[20]

Today, we would call this the influence of media pundits, who help to clarify the dimensions of public opinion. They influence not only the public but also each other. Bryce felt that this was a legitimate role for the journalist and the newspapers.

Stage Three

Bryce's third stage describes how, through a process of debate and controversy, public opinion becomes more clearly *divided* into those who are *for* and those who are *against* an issue. As controversy begins, those who favor a policy or a particular candidate debate it with others who do not. Through this process of conflict, the positions on either side are clarified.

> The effect of controversy is to drive the partisans on either side from some of their arguments, which are shown to be weak; to confirm them in others, which they think strong; and to make them take up a definite position on one side.[21]

As a result of this type of exchange—through both interpersonal interaction and arguments presented in the media—public opinion concerning the topic or candidate has become more clearly structured into those who "favor" and those "oppose." Those on each side now know their positions, and they understand the arguments that support them. Today, of course, this is precisely the kind of public opinion structure that is measured by pollsters. Their reports indicate the proportion of those contacted who either "approve" or "disapprove" of a policy, politician, candidate, or topic.

Stage Four

In a political system based on popular sovereignty, it is in the final and fourth stage of the process that public opinion exercises its ultimate power. Voters, said Bryce, come to the ballot box, not only with their individual predispositions (that have initially played a part in shaping their opinion), but also with the influences from other sources that have been brought to bear on them. These can be acquaintances, the media, or their political party. If Bryce were to reformulate his theory today, he might add the influence of what sociologists call *reference groups*—such as trade unions (not many existed in his time), peers, family, and neighbors.

Bryce believed that it was the *vote*—the major political factor—that was shaped by public opinion. It was those votes, after all, that most influenced the entire political process. Casting one's vote for or against a candidate or proposition reduced complex issues to a simple act:

> Bringing men up to the polls is like passing a steam roller over stones newly laid on a road; the angularities are pressed down and an even uniformity is given which did not exist before. When a man has voted he is committed; he has therefore an interest in backing the view which he has sought to prevail. Moreover, opinion, which may have been manifold till the polling, is thereafter two-fold only. There is a view which has triumphed and a view that has been vanquished.[22]

In summary, then, Bryce's explanation of the formation and functioning of public opinion begins with an initial surge of sentiment in the individual and unfolds through a complex set of exchanges between the person, other individuals, various groups, and the media. Finally, it results in a vote.

BRYCE'S THEORY IN MODERN TERMS

Bryce did not believe that the individual's personal judgment and reasoning played much of a part in the formation of public opinion—and consequently in shaping person's vote. He was convinced that the greater influence on the process came from outside sources. This interpretation is not consistent with the basic political theory used by the framers of the Constitution. As they saw it, in the system of popular sovereignty that they designed, individual voters examined the candidates and issues both thoroughly and objectively. They then reached their voting decisions by the personal exercise of reason and made their choices on the basis of enlightened self-interest—but in such a way that the common good was served. Bryce did not believe that this theory played any significant part in the realities of politics in the United States:

> There are persons who talk, though very few who act, as if they believed this theory, which can be compared to the theory of some ultra-Protestants that every good Christian has or ought to have, by the strength of his own reason, worked out for himself from the Bible a system of theology.[23]

The factors that shaped individual opinion, and in turn public opinion, which ultimately determined the outcome of the vote, said Bryce, had little to do with rational examination of issues or candidates. What actually shaped private as well as public opinion were personality factors ("individual predispositions"); conversations that the individual had with others, such as family, friends, and acquaintances; the views of groups with which the voter was affiliated, especially his or her political party; and, of course, the reinforcing interpretations presented by newspapers. It was precisely these factors that came under investigation by social scientists half a century later, using the methods of science to permit the quantitative study of such shapers of individual voting behavior. A prominent example is the classic study of the 1940 presidential election, *The People's Choice*, which probed the influences of family, friends, and acquaintances, plus party and media.[24] (See Chapter 13.)

Since that classic study, the factors that determine an individual's vote have been systematically investigated by political scientists who have produced a huge body of research on the election process. As a consequence, each of the influences discussed by Bryce have become standard factors in explaining how a person's vote is shaped.[25] Contrary to the ideas of those who shaped the Constitution, in none of these studies was there evidence that during the months prior to an election voters engaged in the rational personal process outlined in democratic theory. The overall conclusion that emerged from this large body of studies was that initial decisions for whom to vote tend to be made on the basis of individual (personality) predispositions and as a result of communicative exchanges with family, friends, and acquaintances. In addition, the evidence seems clear that political propaganda presented by the media sways few votes from one side to another. What it does provide is a *reinforcing* function.[26] In general, then, the factors and variables identified by Bryce in the late 1800s were precisely those that were later uncovered and confirmed by a large body of meticulously conducted empirical research that has accumulated over a number of decades.[27]

BRYCE'S THEORY OF PUBLIC OPINION: A FORMAL SUMMARY

As noted, Bryce set forth his theory in the expository style commonly used in the late nineteenth century. It was one of lengthy descriptions, using numerous illustrations and many quotations and anecdotes. These were intended to help the reader of the time understand what was being laid out as well as to confirm the validity of the generalizations being expressed. The social sciences were barely in their formative stage. They were not yet based on empirical studies and, indeed, were not yet even universally called "sciences." In Bryce's time, therefore, no scholar set forth theories in terms of sets of concise formal propositions. This form came from the model of the physical sciences. It was philosophers of science who eventually persuaded social scientists to use this kind of formal theory expression.

At present, however, it is appropriate to try to set forth theories in the form of succinct propositions that are linked together in a coherent system.[28] The great advantage of doing so is that the basics of what is being explained are clear. Moreover, logical inconsistencies can be revealed, and the use of deductive logic can (hopefully) predict testable research hypotheses.[29] By recasting Bryce's theory of public opinion in this form, it can be expressed as a rather complex set of formal propositions.

Stage One: The Formation of Initial Individual Positions

1. Individuals attending to the media encounter a *report* on a topic of potential political significance (issue, event, policy, situation, or candidate), and each person forms an initial and personal interpretation.
2. These initial interpretations are *affective reactions* of approval or disapproval with variations in intensity that are products of each individual's initial predispositions.
3. The individual checks his or her initial interpretation against *those of others* in conversations and through exposure to additional media reports and interpretations.

Stage Two: Early Crystallization of Shared Opinions

4. By the processes indicated in stage one, *many individuals* have formed and have begun to stabilize their initial positions toward the opinion topic.
5. At this point, the way various kinds of people feel about the topic becomes an object of intense *speculative analysis* and reports by publicists, journalists, and media commentators.
6. Subsequent media reports on these views help people who attend to them identify positions of approval or disapproval that are *shared* by various segments of the public.

Stage Three: Controversy and Final Structuring of Opinions

7. Public debate, reported by the media, begins as positions are advocated and their bases are explained by various *spokespersons* for different sides and interests.
8. Controversies follow and are reported in the media as the differences between the positions of those who take *opposite sides* are identified. This serves a reinforcing function for those who have taken a position.
9. As these controversies continue, the points of difference and the arguments for and against are *sharpened* by spokespersons for each position, leading to a clear structuring of the views and beliefs of those who are on opposite sides.

Stage Four: Public Opinion Shapes the Political System

10. Various *reference groups* play a part in shaping not only personal and shared opinion positions regarding the topic but also the positions of political candidates who favor or disfavor possible policies toward that topic.

11. As the debates mature, these differences in positions toward the topic become the *central issues* in campaigns for election in which candidates must make known via speeches and the media their proposals and intentions regarding the topic.

12. In the end, the political system is shaped at the *ballot box* when candidates sympathetic to the largest number of citizens who hold a clearly structured opinion prevail over their opponents.

This is obviously a complex theory, but it provides a clear description and explanation of a lengthy process. The central explanation that emerges from these propositions is that public opinion is first influenced at an individual level by personality factors and then by party affiliations, plus discussions with family, friends, and acquaintances. It is then reinforced by media interpretations. A major point is that public opinion is the *ultimate power* in a system of popular sovereignty such as exists in the United States. Bryce concluded that, because candidates come up for election, the political process is shaped at the ballot box—concluding a long and complicated process of awareness, discussion, debate, controversy, and final opinion-structuring.

BRYCE'S THEORY TODAY

As has been explained, Bryce emphasized the ballot box as the central point of the power of public opinion.[30] He did so because in his time communication between voters and those in office was both painfully slow and severely limited. Few channels existed whereby the electorate could make their views on a topic known directly to an officeholder, most of whom were located far away in the nation's capital or the state assembly. In much the same way, few trustworthy systems existed for legislators wanting to assess public opinion on any issue. There were, as noted, no polls as we know them today. However, local political bosses at the ward level did make efforts to understand the feelings of their party members. They even used voter's subscriptions to newspapers that expressed different views as a means of revealing at least *some* of their inclinations. These limitations on the flow of information each way were the reason that Bryce saw the ballot box as the major means by which the power of public opinion was expressed.

A logical inference that can modernize Bryce's theory can be drawn from the propositions stated above. Basically, it is in the form of a *theorem* (that is, a conclusion that can be reached by logical inference from stated premises). Its major premise is Proposition 12. That proposition sets forth the predictive statement in the formal version of Bryce's theory. That same proposition is a logical conclusion drawn from the previous eleven statements. If Proposition 12 is correct, it describes both the political situation of Bryce's time as well as our own. From that premise, the following theorem can be derived:

> If the volume and rate of transmission of messages between voters and an incumbent **increases dramatically**—far beyond that which existed in the pre-polling days of Lord Bryce—it will greatly increase the power of public opinion over that official.

In other words, if the two parties can communicate more effectively (than in Bryce's time) then public opinion becomes a more powerful force shaping the political system. This would be the case because of the following two conditions: (1) Faster and more detailed communication *to voters about the politician* would provide those voters with much greater knowledge of his or her characteristics, positions, and activities. If they like the person and approve of what he or she is doing, then the politician remains in office. If not, he or she is voted out. (2) An enhanced flow of information *from voters back to the politician* will reveal to that official much more reliable and comprehensive information about the electorate's views and wishes than was possible in Bryce's time. That knowledge can shape the politician's behavior so as to conform more closely to voters' wishes. If these conditions prevail, the power of public opinion over an elected official *increases dramatically* over what it was earlier.

Precisely those two conditions have come about. Modern media obviously can keep voters informed on a daily basis about the behavior of those whom they have elected. Moreover, the number of channels have increased greatly that can provide information about constituents to the office holder. Polling is now timely, sophisticated, informative, and accurate. Every candidate running for office employs independent pollsters to provide them with information about their constituents. Focus groups add depth to refine the information gained from polls.

Today, television, radio, and the Internet provide extensive campaign news coverage in addition to the print media. Political reporting and campaign advertising have greatly expanded. Consequently, voters now receive far more information about candidates far more quickly than in earlier times. In our contemporary media-saturated society, therefore, the powerful force of public opinion that Bryce described so clearly has been greatly enhanced, and it can descend on the politician not just at election time but virtually every hour of every day.

> As a result, modern politicians have become slaves to public opinion, and what voters profess to want—the unpopular vote [by a politician], made out of conscience—has become an immensely difficult act. All this is only slightly less true of the executive branch, a body so intimate with its electorate that the voters know their President's preference in undergarments, and their President—according to a newly leaked memo by his pollster—knows not just the issues, but the precise phrases that most excite the voters.[31]

Generally, then, adding the theorem that takes into account the increased flow of information provided by new media, and recognizing the influence that it has on politicians, makes Bryce's theory remarkably modern.

The addition of the theorem of enhanced communication does not represent a major change from the original theory. Although it was formulated in the 1880s, a major feature of Bryce's theory is its *emphasis on the role of mass communication.* It was, as he explained, the newspaper that initially brought the opinion topic to the attention of the public. It was to the newspaper that they turned to reinforce their interpretations of their initial positions. Media pundits (print journalists in Bryce's time) analyzed and reported to their readers the nature of opinion emerging among various segments of the public. It was the newspapers, then, that clarified the positions of various groups, reported on debates, and made the positions of candidates known. In other words, even though there was only one medium playing a major part, Bryce's theory was in many ways a *media-dependent* explanation of the formation and functioning of public opinion.

The new media of modern times, as well as advanced polling technologies, then, have brought significant changes in the flow of information between politician and constituent. In addition, the mass communication system today includes professional communicators and interpreters who were not part of the process in Bryce's time. When any new political issue arises, a horde of print and broadcast reporters, public relations consultants, pundits, publicists, spin doctors, special correspondents, speech writers, lobbyists, and others jump into action, busily concocting messages for public consumption. The voter can turn to this rich variety of would-be opinion shapers to assess his or her initial interpretations against the views of others. Thus, in contrast to the simple system of Bryce's time, this army of professional communicators produces a broad range of attempts to influence the "hearts and minds" of the electorate—hoping that this will shape their views and actions. Thus, the functioning politician is no longer a remote figure in Washington, D.C., or in the state assembly. He or she is a familiar face and voice appearing with great frequency in the media coming into the home. That familiar figure's views and actions can be studied not only in the daily newspaper but also with a flick of the TV remote control, a finger on the keyboard, or by turning on the car radio during the daily commute.

In other words, the political process is no longer a genteel debate of issues brought to public attention after the fact by newspapers. It is no longer conducted behind closed doors or in the relative obscurity of legislative chambers in a far-off capital. Today, the intensity of the movement of information between the relevant parties has increased enormously:

> Modern Washington is wired for quadrophonic sound and wide-screen video, lashed by fax, computer, 800 number, overnight poll, FedEx, grassroots mail, air shuttle and CNN to every citizen in every village on the continent and in Hawaii too. Its every twitch is blared to the world, thanks to C-Span, open meetings laws, financial disclosure reports and campaign spending rules, and its every misstep is logged into a database for the use of some future office-seeker.[32]

The overall conclusion, therefore, is that Bryce's theory is even *more* relevant today than during the time he developed it. A virtual army of communicators now creates a vast flow of information between constituents and politicians using contemporary technologies. The addition of the theorem concerning such communication makes Bryce's theory remarkably contemporary. If public opinion was, as he put it in the 1880s, "the great source of power, the master of servants who tremble before it" today it, has become by a staggering force created by the new media of communication that goes both ways. That force can sweep away the most entrenched politician who may seem invulnerable. Moreover, few who are in office can ignore the readily obtainable views of their constituents. Thus, by adding the theorem concerning the greatly expanded ease of communication that the information revolution has provided, Lord Bryce's media-based theory about the great power of public opinion in our system of popular sovereignty is brought back to center stage.

Notes and References

1. This chapter is based in part on Margaret H. DeFleur, "James Bryce's 19th Century Theory of Public Opinion in the Contemporary Age of New Communications Technologies," *Mass Communication and Society*, Vol. I, No. 1, October 1998.

2. James Bryce, *The Holy Roman Empire* (Oxford: Oxford University Press, 1864).

3. James Bryce, *The American Commonwealth* (London: Macmillan and Co., 1888).

4. See J. P. Mayer and Max Lerner, eds., Alexis de Tocqueville, *Democracy in America* (New York: Harper and Row, Publishers, 1966). The original work was first published in France in 1835 as *La Democratie en Amerique*. It was revised thirteen times by its author.

5. See Chapter LXXVII, "Government by Public Opinion," pp. 14–23.

6. Bryce, *Ibid.* p. 25.

7. *Ibid.* p. 25.

8. *Ibid.* p. 29.

9. *Ibid.* p. 28.

10. *Ibid.* Vol. III, p. 25.

11. Susan Herbst, "On the Disappearance of Groups: 19th and Early 20th Century Conceptions of Public Opinion," in Theodore L. Glaser and Charles T. Salmon, eds., *Public Opinion and the Communication of Consent* (New York: The Guilford Press, 1995), p. 92–93.

12. *op. cit.*, p. 20.

13. See Elisabeth Noelle-Neumann, *The Spiral of Silence* (Chicago: University of Chicago Press, 1984).

14. *Ibid.* Vol. III, p. 35.

15. It must be made entirely clear that Lord Bryce never set forth his analyses in such simple terms. Indeed, some may regard it as an injustice to his treatise to attempt to reduce it to propositional form in spite of the benefits of clarity and convenience that result. In any case, if the theory as summarized in this manner contains misinterpretations, they are entirely the responsibility of the author of this paper.

16. *Ibid.* Vol. III, p. 3.

17. *Ibid.* Vol. III, p. 4.

18. *Ibid.* Vol. III, p. 4.

19. *Ibid.* Vol. III, p. 4.

20. *Ibid.* Vol. III, p. 5.

21. *Ibid.* Vol. III, p. 5.

22. *Ibid.* Vol. III, p. 5–6.

23. *Ibid.* Vol. III, p. 7.

24. Paul F. Lazarsfeld, Bernard Berelson, and Helen Gaudet, *The People's Choice: How the Voter Makes Up His Mind in a Presidential Election* (New York: Columbia University Press, 1948).

25. During the late 1950s and the 1960s, a number of significant works on the determinents of individual voting were published by Angus Campbell and a number of his associates at the Survey Research Center at the University of Michigan. See Angus Campbell, et al., *The Voter Decides* (New York: Harper and Row, 1954); Angus Campbell, et al., *The American Voter* (New York: Wiley, 1960); and Angus Campbell, et al., *Elections and the Political Order* (New York: Wiley, 1966).

26. D. R. Kinder and D. O. Sears, "Public Opinion and Political Action," in G. Lindzey and E. Aronson, eds., *The Handbook of Social Psychology*, 3rd ed., Vol. 2, (New York: Random House, 1985), pp. 659–741.

27. For an excellent and up-to-date summary and synthesis of the relationship between public opinion and voting behavior, see Stuart Oskamp, *Attitudes and Opinions*, 2nd ed. (Englewood Cliffs, NJ: Prentice Hall, 1991), esp. Chapters 12 and 13, pp. 292–342.

28. The most influential work in the philosophy of science influencing the development of social science theory along these lines is Richard R. Braithwaite, *Scientific Explanation* (Cambridge: Cambridge University Press, 1953); see also the following two works: Ernst Nagel, *The Structure of Science* (New York: Harcourt, 1961) and Abraham Kaplan, *The Conduct of Inquiry: Methodology for Behavioral Science* (San Francisco: Chandler Publishing Company, 1964).

29. For an exposition of the nature and advantages of theories formulated as sets of systematic and linked axiomatic propositions, see George Caspar Homans, "Contemporary Theory in Sociology," in Robert E. L. Faris, *Handbook of Modern Sociology* (Chicago: Rand McNally and Company, 1964), pp. 951–977.

30. Contemporary political scientists and journalism scholars are debating the relationship between modern public opinion polls and democratic theory. See, for example, Katherine A. Bradshaw, "The Misunderstood Public Opinion of James Bryce," *Journalism History*, 28, 1, Spring 2002, pp. 16–25.

31. Michael Wines, "Who? Us? Washington Really Is in Touch. We're the Problem," *The New York Times*, The Week in Review, October 16, 1994, p. 1.

32. Michael Wines, *op. cit.*, p. 1.

CHAPTER 8

Walter Lippmann's 1920s Theory of Unintentional News Distortion: Implications for the Nature of Public Opinion and Public Policy

Walter Lippmann was an influential early twentieth-century scholar, journalist, and political philosopher who wrote prolifically about the relationship among newspapers, public opinion, and the democratic process. Born in 1889, his best-known work, *Public Opinion*, was published in 1922. He continued as an active intellectual until his death in 1974. In contrast to many classical writers of earlier years who undertook similar goals, Lippmann used a clear, concise, and very readable writing style. However, his basic ideas are scattered through a huge body of books, articles, and other writings that he produced over more than a half century. This makes it difficult to bring them together into a simple summary. Nevertheless, because his explanations of the relationship among public opinion, the press, and public policy in a democratic system remain so central to understanding those issues today, it is important to try to identify his central set of propositions and set them forth in formal terms as the basic assumptions of his theory. That is specifically the goal of the present chapter.

Essentially, Lippmann's theory, reconstructed in that manner, explains how the press *distorts reality* in news reports read by the public. That distortion is *unintentional* on the part of journalists, who strive for accuracy and who sincerely want their reports to represent "the truth." But, as Lippmann points out, because of the ways in which the press operates, "news is not truth." A consequence of this non-deliberate distortion is that the news audience's conceptions and the resulting public opinion, formed on the basis of information provided by the press, *can be seriously flawed*. In particular, public opinion—formed on the basis of such information—can, in turn, have powerful influences on the conduct of government. Thus, the flow of information he describes cannot produce public policy founded on an accurate factual information base.

Recasting his explanations into a formal summary may go beyond what Lippmann would have accepted. Hopefully, however, it will show how his ideas—formulated early in the 1900s—still have validity and relevance as we move on into a new century. The purpose of this chapter, then, is to try and pull together, in brief form, the essential propositions that Lippman advanced to explain why and how newspapers (or other news media today), which routinely strive for accuracy in what they report to the public, can seldom achieve that goal.

As suggested above, bringing Lippmann's propositions together into a single systematic theory may commit a transgression that he would have found disturbing. He embedded his explanations and theses in a long list of books, essays, editorials, news reports, opinion columns, and other writings prepared over his entire lifetime. Moreover, he illustrated his ideas abundantly with references to persons, policies, events, and situations that were easily recognized by the news-following public at the time (but which have been all but forgotten by later generations). Sifting out a set of formal propositions from this multitude of sources and accounts, therefore, strips them of the rich context within which Lippmann discussed his ideas. The justification for doing so is that it will make his ideas more accessible. While this may pose the risk of distorting what he "really meant," nevertheless, his explanations of how the press creates flawed "pictures in our heads of the world outside" remains as a truly important contribution. His theory is critical to understanding the complex relationship among (1) the mass-communicated news industry, providing ways in which citizens gain (flawed) information about what is taking place in their society; (2) how that process can influence the opinions they develop from the news they receive; and (3) how that unrealistic public opinion can have implications for, and be an influence on, the political process of decision-making in contemporary American society.

BACKGROUND

Walter Lippmann's name is well known by scholars in the field of mass communication. Few contemporary writers, however, would include him in a list of major theorists who have tried to explain an important aspect of the process and effects of mass communication. Most are aware that in the early 1920s he wrote an important book titled *Public Opinion*. Many can recall the catchy expression "the world outside and the pictures in our heads" from that book. (Actually, it is the title of the first chapter.) It is an easy-to-remember phrase that describes his view of the functions of the press in society in creating our personal understandings—that is, *social constructions of reality*—about what is happening around us. Beyond that, however, most students of mass communication would be unable to set forth a systematic account of the propositions and basic premises that make up his complete explanation of why the news we receive is inevitably distorted. Even fewer are aware of the great volume of his other publications.

Beyond his expression about pictures in our heads was his contention that *we cannot assume* that "news and truth are two words for the same thing."[1] Indeed, he makes it quite clear that news and truth are *not* he same—and *cannot be*, given the way news is gathered, processed, and disseminated by the press. This important idea was addressed throughout his writings. If examined as a whole, they reveal an underlying theory of how and why the news gets unintentionally distorted—in spite of efforts on the part of conscientious journalists to be both objective and accurate. As has been noted, Lippmann never developed his theory systematically—that is, as a set of related formal propositions—because during his lifetime, mass communication theories in that form were never a part of his craft. He was a superb and almost unbelievably prolific journalist who wrote for an intelligent public. However, for students and scholars today, his ideas are in danger of being sidelined to obscurity, not because they are difficult to read, but because his most critical insights can be difficult to tease out of his voluminous writings.

If Lippman had a single passion, it was that *a democracy sorely needs accurate news*. He pointed out in many places throughout his lifetime that a democracy cannot survive if its news media provide false accounts—either by deliberate and calculated misrepresentation or unwittingly because of the limitations and realities of the news process. Few would deny that point of view today in an era when the news is dominated by *spinmeisters*.[2] By the turn of the new millennium, that is, as the 2000s started, the public was growing very tired of scandal-driven feeding frenzies on the part of the press, with the pronouncements of professional image polishers, with legalistic hair-splitting, and with deliberately misleading press conferences.[3] Frantic battles for the allegiance of the public were in progress between mud-slinging political parties, the executive and legislative branches, and partisans on all sides. Shaping public opinion was seen as the key to victory by everyone involved.[4] The control of information—correct, biased, or just plain false—was seen as critical in shaping that opinion. News accuracy and the credibility of the press were casualties in the process, and the validity of what was presented by the spokespersons of all concerned was in serious doubt. Today, therefore, Walter Lippmann's pleas for accuracy in news, set forth just after World War I and repeatedly until the time of his death, are perhaps even more important than they were in his time.

Walter Lippmann: The Man

Walter Lippmann was born of middle-class parents in New York City on September 23, 1889. After an uneventful childhood and adolescence, Lippmann entered Harvard University in 1905. He graduated with his bachelor's degree in 1909. He briefly continued in school—doing graduate work in philosophy. He studied for a year with George Santayana and was influenced by William James—two of the most distinguished philosophers of the early twentieth century.

Lippmann wrote prolifically for nearly sixty years and became one of the most respected political analysts and commentators of the early and mid-1900s. He received many recognitions and honors, including two Pulitzer Prizes. He served on the Board of Overseers of Harvard University. He was a member of Phi Beta Kappa as well as the American Academy of Arts and Letters.[5]

As a scholar and writer, Walter Lippmann is difficult to classify for several reasons. Clearly he was a journalist, and for most of his life he earned his living as an editor and columnist. However, as a result of his extensive analyses of American politics, he was, and remains, highly regarded by many as a political scientist. Others see him as a philosopher with a special interest in the political issues of his time. However, while political events were his main intellectual focus, he held no public office, and he was not a spokesperson for any political party. As a combination journalist and political philosopher, he remained in the "private station" to offer opinions, moral judgments, commentary, and interpretations of American society for more than half a century. Perhaps the best characterization of Walter Lippmann should not be based on how he made his living but on what he wrote. From that point of view, he was an astute and honored scholar of American political life and, for present purposes, a theorist of the role of the press within that context.

Lippmann's Early Career

In 1913, when he was just twenty-four years old, he helped to found, and became assistant editor of, *The New Republic*—which came out with its first issue in November 1914. The new magazine became an important voice for liberal views and interpretations of the society of the time. Lippmann served in the military as a captain in the intelligence branch during America's participation in World War I. This gave him an advantageous position for commentary on the events of the period.[6] The early decades of the twentieth century were ones of great social change in the United States. Industrialization, urbanization, and immigration were replacing earlier, more tranquil ways of life.[7] The turmoil created by World War I was one of the most cataclysmic in Western society. It was followed by the rapid changes in lifestyles of the 1920s and in the 1930s, especially during the economic catastrophe of the Great Depression. As politicians sought to cope with these events, *The New Republic* provided Lippmann with a respected medium within which to state his views. He quickly became a very influential voice in American politics.

> Born in the Victorian tranquilities of 1889, he was stirred by the ferment of the Progressive era and became a socialist before he left Harvard in 1910. His socialism soon evaporated in any dogmatic form; but it left behind a residue in the shape of a belief in the necessity for rational planning and purpose to master the incipient chaos of modern society. He was one of the first Americans to read Freud, and this doubtless contributed to his sense that he was living in an age of transvaluation of values.[8]

Lippmann, through his writings while at the magazine and in direct discussions, made an impression on President Woodrow Wilson, who is said to have drawn on his ideas when he conceptualized his post–World War I settlement plan (Fourteen Points) and the League of Nations. In fact, Lippmann served briefly (in 1917) as an assistant to Newton D. Baker, who was secretary of war during the conflict. In 1919, President Wilson included Lippmann in his team that conducted negotiations for the Treaty of Versailles.[9]

A Focus on the Importance of the Accuracy of News

Walter Lippmann began to write books almost as soon as the ink was dry on his Harvard diploma. The year before the Great War was to begin in Europe, he had already published *A Preface to Politics* (1913). Following that, he managed almost a book a year for a decade, in addition to his voluminous newspaper and magazine pieces. In 1920, his *Liberty and the News* was published. Two of its chapters had already appeared in *The Atlantic Monthly*. It was a small but thoughtful work that assessed the American press and called attention to the need for accurate news, better training of journalists, and improved accuracy in reporting on government. He also addressed the difficulties of reporting on complicated questions to a public intolerant of complex writing and the need for newspapers to remain financially viable. Above all, it was an appeal for *objective journalism*. Lippmann forcefully advocated, in a plea to maintain the viability of democracy, that journalists should not take sides or slant their accounts but should strive for *accurate, balanced, and factual reporting*. In this early work, he was very critical of his colleagues in journalism, to say the least, and he lashed out at those who failed to report the news accurately:

> Just as the most poisonous form of disorder is the mob incited from high places, the most immoral act the immorality of a government, so the most destructive form of untruth is sophistry and propaganda by those whose profession it is to report the news. The news columns are common carriers. When those who control them arrogate to themselves the right to determine by their own consciences what shall be reported and for what purpose, democracy is unworkable.[10]

Two additional themes of contemporary interest stand out in Lippmann's early writings. One is his cry for better training for journalists. The other is bringing colleges and universities more effectively into the monitoring of the actions of government. In 1920, journalism had a very limited presence on college and university campuses. A few scattered programs had been started, but formal study to become a journalist was an idea whose time had yet to come. Lippmann made a plea for systematic training of those who gathered and processed the news:

> In a few generations it will seem ludicrous that a people professing government by the will of the people should have made no serious effort to guarantee the news without which a governing opinion cannot exist. . . . [It is also inconceivable] that they provided no genuine training for the men upon whose sagacity they were dependent . . .[11]

Lippmann also hoped that a way would be provided for more effective monitoring of the records of government. He would have been delighted at the development of what has today become *computer-assisted investigative reporting*, in which the actual records of various federal and state agencies—kept in electronic form—are available to specially trained journalists and scholars who can obtain them through "Freedom of Information" legislation at both federal and state levels.[12] He applauded early attempts to conduct statistical analysis of government activities, but he had no way of knowing that computers were coming or that journalists would be able to use them in their watchdog function to analyze the performance of politicians and public agencies. Nevertheless, he foresaw the value of such activities:

> Records and analysis require an experimental formulation of standards by which the work of government can be tested . . . Some have already been worked out experimentally, others still need to be discovered; all need to be refined and brought into perspective by the wisdom of experience. Carried out competently, the public would gradually learn to substitute objective criteria for gossip and intuitions.[13]

Later Career

Between 1929 and 1931, Lippmann served as editor of the New York *World*. All during the 1920s he wrote editorials for the paper. He often commented in those pieces on the relationship among the news, the distortions that were all but inevitable due to the nature of the news industry, and the influence that such misrepresentations could have on public opinion—and ultimately on public policy. In 1931, however, he began serving as a columnist for *The New York Herald Tribune.* The column was syndicated and appeared in more than 250 American newspapers and those in twenty-five countries.

In all, Lippmann authored the eleven books listed below between 1913 and 1955.[14] The best known, as was noted earlier, was his work entitled *Public Opinion,* published in 1922. It is still regarded as a classic. At the time, each of his books was widely read, and together they offer remarkable insights into the American political process:

> *A Preface to Politics* (New York and London: Mitchell Kennerly, 1913)
> *Drift and Mastery* (New York: Henry Holt, 1914)
> *Stakes of Diplomacy* (New York: Henry Holt, 1915)
> *Liberty and the News* (New York: The Macmillan Company, 1920)
> *Public Opinion* (New York: The Macmillan Company, 1922)
> *The Phantom Public* (New York: Harcourt, Brace and Company, 1925)
> *A Preface to Morals* (New York: The Macmillan Company, 1929)
> *The Method of Freedom* (New York: The Macmillan Company, 1934)
> *The New Imperative* (New York: The Macmillan Company, 1935)
> *The Good Society* (Boston: Little, Brown and Company, 1937)
> *Essays in Public Philosophy* (Boston: Little, Brown and Company, 1955)

As his fame grew, Lippmann traveled to many parts of the world. He won Pulitzer Prizes in both 1958 and in 1962. During his time on the magazine, and later while serving as an editor and columnist, he wrote literally hundreds of pieces that brought him additional recognition. As Rossiter and Lair note:

> His four thousand columns add up to perhaps four million words; his ten books of political philosophy, dozen books of comment on men and events, scores of contributions to *The New Republic,* two thousand or more editorials in *The World,* and nearly three hundred articles in nearly fifty magazines add up to more words than that. This vast output of a half-century is a monument to his creative genius.

In Lippmann's first book, *A Preface to Politics* (1913), he embraced at least some of the ideas of socialism. In books that came a short time later, *Drift and Mastery* (1914) and *The Good Society* (1937), he abandoned his socialist leanings and became anti-Marxist. He did, however, remain committed to an international role for the United States and strongly attacked isolationist sentiments.

In his own interpretation of his activities, Lippman concluded that he had led two lives. One was the more abstract life of a philosopher that permitted him to assess within his moral standards the unfolding events of his time. The other was the more practical life of a journalist that permitted him to apply those standards to the realities of daily political decisions and consequences. Walter Lippmann died on December 14, 1974, at the age of 85.

The majority of his writings addressed events and issues of his time as these unfolded in daily occurrences. Most of the names of persons, and the specific issues that concerned him, were important to the public and the government at the time he wrote about them. However, in retrospect, they seem obscure because one reads them decades after they occurred, and few remember the details of the events or the persons involved. Nevertheless, interspersed within this avalanche of words are passages that remain significant today. It is these insights—set forth in timeless conclusions and principles about the nature of journalism and of the press—that provide the foundation of what is, in this work, being called Lippmann's *theory of unintentional news distortion.*

THE ESSENTIAL PROPOSITIONS OF LIPPMANN'S THEORY

By reviewing the body of Lippmann's writings, a number of basic assumptions can be identified that led him to the conclusion that there would inevitably be a limited correspondence between the views of issues and events obtained by the public by reading newspapers and the realities on which those stories were based. He saw this outcome as a natural consequence of the way that journalists gathered their stories, made decisions about how to process them, and about which stories should be placed where in the newspaper that finally reached the public. That process begins with assumptions about how the press monitors the environment.

The Surveillance Function

The press, Lippmann noted, constantly observes the events of the physical and social environment in order to select, from those, stories that may be worthy of reporting to the public. There are not enough reporters in the world, he explained, to witness everything that takes place—even if they all worked twenty-four hours a day. Nevertheless, little of importance escapes the notice of the press. This is because they use systematic procedures: " . . . the range of subjects these comparatively few men manage to cover would be a miracle indeed if it were not a standardized routine."[15] What journalists do is not unlike the strategy of hunters after big game, who monitor water holes and other places where their quarry is likely to be found. Thus, journalists routinely develop *observation posts,* he explained, at points in the environment where newsworthy stories are likely to be encountered:

> Newspapers do not try to keep an eye on all mankind. They have watchers stationed at certain places, like Police Headquarters, the Coroner's Office, the County Clerk's Office, City Hall, the White House, the Senate, the House of Representatives, and so forth. They watch [or employ others to watch] 'a comparatively small' number of places where it is made known when the life of anyone . . . departs from ordinary paths, or when events worthy of telling about occur.[16]

Today, we would refer to this activity as a *surveillance function,* in which journalists from the various media of contemporary times constantly monitor local, regional, national, and international events. Surveillance, in other words, is organized around a great variety of "beats" to obtain information about anything about which a potential news report can be prepared. Stated more formally as the first proposition in a summary of Lippmann's theory of the distortion of the news, this activity can be characterized as the following assumption:

1. The press systematically *monitors* events, people, and situations occurring in the physical and social environment to identify potential news stories (the "surveillance function").

The Oversupply of Available News

One of the problems facing every newspaper, Lippmann explained, is that there is too much potential news every day about which to inform the public. Inevitably, those who prepare the content for the daily paper must *choose* among many topics that could be reported. This problem is, in part, one of complexity of the sources. For example, reporting on government in a complete and detailed sense is impossible. Reporters can try, Lippmann said:

> But the news from which he must pick and choose has long since become too complicated even for the most highly trained reporter. The work of the government is really a small part of the day's news, yet even the wealthiest and most resourceful newspapers fail in their efforts to report 'Washington.' The highlights and sensational incidents are noted, but no one can keep himself informed about his Congressman or about the individual departments by reading the daily press. This in no way reflects on the newspapers. It results from the intricacy and unwieldiness of the subject matter.[17]

The solution to this problem that is practiced by the press is based on *selectivity.* Different editors, developing the daily agenda for different papers, will use different criteria to select what they will print. Some stories are chosen for inclusion in the newspaper because they will *interest their particular kinds of readers.* Some journalists will select serious stories and provide their readers with what they need to know in order to act as responsible citizens. Others, with a different type of reader, will select those stories that are exciting or titillating:

> There are no objective standards here. There are conventions. Take two newspapers published in the same city on the same morning. The headline of the one reads, 'Britain pledges aid to Berlin against French aggression; France openly backs Poles.' The headline of the second is 'Mrs. Stillman's Other Love.' Which you prefer is a

matter of taste but not entirely a matter of the editor's taste. It is a matter of his judgment as to what will absorb the half hour's attention that a certain set of readers will give to his newspaper.[18]

Thus, the process of distorted reporting of reality is based in part on *selectivity*. In early versions of what we now call both Gatekeeping and Agenda-Setting theories (see Chapters 11 and 12), Lippmann noted that "Every newspaper when it reaches the reader is the result of a whole series of selections as to what items shall be printed, in what position they shall be printed, how much space each shall occupy, what emphasis each shall have."[19]

Therefore, the editor's judgments of what will serve the needs of his or her readers can be stated as the second assumption in a summary of Lippmann's theory:

2. To prepare the news that it will report, the press *selects*, from the abundance of possible stories, an agenda consisting of those stories that the news personnel believe will be of importance, or of interest, to the populations of readers that they serve.

Limitations on Resources

There is an additional set of factors that play a deciding part in shaping the news over which the editor will have limited or no control. The paper has to come out *on time* and *within its budget*. Otherwise, it would go out of business. Thus, there are always limitations, not only on time but also on manpower, that any editor can allocate to a particular report. If a story is truly significant, the editor may send reporters to investigate. However, as Lippmann pointed out:

Necessarily he cannot do that often. For those investigations cost time, money, special talent and lots of space. To make a plausible report that conditions are bad, you need a good many columns of print . . . News which requires so much trouble [to obtain] is beyond the resources of the daily press.[20]

Time and fiscal limitations, then, result in a lack of correspondence between the actual events that have taken place in reality and the reports that are gathered and processed in the newsroom. This is not a deliberate distortion but one that is an unavoidable consequence of the system that operates in a profit-oriented capitalistic economy.

Another outcome closely related to the fiscal and time limitations facing the press is distortions that are a consequence of dependence on what were called "press agents" and "publicity men" in Lippmann's time ("public relations practitioners" today). He noted that in New York City the newspapers had determined that just before World War I there were about twelve hundred who were regularly employed and regularly accredited.[21] These publicity men were serving the interests of an enormous variety of organized groups and personalities. He pointed out that, in any situation that arises, the facts are not simple, and there can be a great deal of ambiguity. This means that press agents make their choices of what information to pass on to the press.

The publicity man does that. And in doing it, he certainly saves the reporter much trouble, by presenting him a clear picture of a situation out of which he might otherwise make neither head nor tail. But it follows that the picture which the publicity man makes for the reporter is the one which he wishes the public to see. He is censor and propagandist, responsible only to his employers, and to the whole truth responsible only as it accords with the employer's conception of his own interests.[22]

Thus, much of what appears in the daily newspapers about the activities of organizations or celebrities has its origin in their public relations efforts. This is inevitable. Gathering and processing the news is under both time and fiscal constraints, leaving reporters *dependent* on news conferences, press releases, and handouts. Because of this symbiotic relationship, public relations practitioners are able to control the part of the "pseudo-environment" pertaining to their employer that will be presented to the public by the press.

The third proposition in a summary version of Lippmann's theory of the unintentional distortion of the news, then, is essentially a statement of these limitations and their consequences. Simply put, this assumption states that:

3. Many factors beyond the control of those in charge (time, money, technology, or opportunity) *limit the ability* of the press to investigate, describe, and transmit full details of all events and situations that come to their attention.

The Moral Obligation to Be Accurate

In spite of these difficulties, Lippmann maintained, reporters and editors for the most part try their best not to present reports that are biased, subjective, or false. This is a critical matter because it is only by knowing the truth that human beings can make rational choices with respect to issues of government. Journalists basically practice this moral obligation, knowing that if they deliberately provide false information, it attacks the very foundations of democracy:

> The theory of our Constitution, says Mr. Justice Holmes, is that truth is the only ground upon which men's wishes safely can be carried out. Insofar as those who purvey the news make of their own beliefs a higher law than the truth, they are attacking the foundations of our constitutional system. There can be no higher law in journalism [than to tell the truth].[23]

However, because of the limitations and constraints noted in proposition three, journalists must select their agenda on the basis of what they regard as important and what they believe their readers will attend to and understand. Thus, that agenda will necessarily be limited. The newspaper is not always able to report stories in full, to investigate them in detail, or even to check completely on their accuracy. Thus, a fourth assumption indicates the dilemma in which the press sometimes finds itself. It can be summarized in the following proposition:

4. Because of these factors (in assumption 3), news reports are often characterized by *selectivity, omissions,* and *distortions* in spite of efforts by many journalists to be objective, fair, and factual.

The fourth proposition was well illustrated by a set of events that took place in Cincinnati, Ohio, in March 2001. Timothy Thomas, a young black man, was shot by a white officer while fleeing. When news of the incident was presented on television and in the local newspaper (*Cincinnati Enquirer*) the African-American community in the city was indignant. It appeared to many African Americans to be a totally unjustified shooting and a clear indication that the police were "out of control" when it came to abusing blacks. In fact, outrage grew to a point where one night mobs of black youths stormed through the streets of the city, breaking windows, looting, and shooting at the police and white residents. Bricks smashed the windshields of cars with white drivers. One white woman was dragged from her car and beaten before she was rescued by people near the event. More than one hundred homes and businesses were set on fire. In short, it was a chaotic riot by enraged participants.

Journalists from national media prepared reports of the event for newspapers and network television, but their accounts were often very different from what had taken place in the streets (the world outside). For example, the *New York Times* version indicated that "groups of young black men had alarmed whites."[24] Presumably that was true. Most citizens would have been "alarmed" by what had actually taken place—to say the least. The *Los Angeles Times* was supportive of the rioters with its comment that the riots provided an "undeniable sense of relief" for the city by bringing its racial problems into focus.[25]

Many of the national news media, talk shows, and commentators providing accounts of the events for readers, viewers, and listeners across the nation portrayed the Cincinnati Police Department as a sort of "gun-happy killing machine" that had accumulated a dreadful record of unjustified shootings of young black men.

Later, a careful review of the facts showed a different picture. Data assembled by the *Enquirer*, the local paper that did take the time to investigate the situation with care, showed that 78% of those whom the police had shot at were black. However, exactly 78% of those who had been arrested in recent years for violent crime were black. Moreover, black officers made up 25% of the force, and 25%

of the shootings over the period were by black cops. Finally, the city's rate of police shootings was actually lower than that of a number of cities of comparable size in the region.[26]

In other words, the national news media badly distorted what had happened in Cincinnati. There was no attempt on the part of many who portrayed the city and its police force in very negative terms to check on the facts. They simply did what any busy journalist has to do when faced with deadlines and limited access to factual information. They quickly reviewed other published news reports—which happened to be badly distorted—and incorporated those versions into their own accounts. In addition, in some cases, the values and biases of those preparing those accounts influenced what they selected and reported.

The "Pseudo-Environment" as Consequence

The above four assumptions, if true, provide the basis for deriving a fifth statement. Lippmann made this consequence clear in the title to his first chapter in *Public Opinion*—"The World Outside and the Pictures in Our Heads." He discussed in detail and profusely illustrated how news stories that appeared in the press at the time often provided people with very misleading interpretations of what had taken place in their world. When that happens, the behavioral choices that they make are based on false or at least misleading assumptions:

5. When audiences construct their own meanings from the daily agenda of news reports, the "pictures in their heads" constitute a pseudo-environment in that they often have *limited correspondence* with the facts that occurred in reality ("the world outside"), leading people to believe and behave in ways unrelated to the original events or situations.

That certainly had been the case in Cincinnati, both for the African Americans who reacted aggressively to the initial news reports and for others around the country who condemned the Cincinnati police force on the basis of what they read, viewed, or heard on national news media.

It was this realization that news reports can create false interpretations—*a pseudo- environment*—that so deeply disturbed Lippmann. He understood completely that our system of democracy rests ultimately on public opinion. That lesson had been made elegantly clear several decades earlier by Lord James Bryce (see Chapter 7). In the late 1880s, in his classic work *The American Commonwealth*, he described public opinion as the most formidable of all political powers: "Towering over Presidents and State governors, and the vast machinery of party, public opinion stands out in the United States as the great source of power, the master of servants who tremble before it."[27] Moreover, like Bryce, Lippmann realized fully that the press was the central player in the process by which public opinion was formed, changed, and exercised. Both scholars agreed that those processes took place because of what people encountered in news reports. Because of the distortions in those reports, distortions that appeared to Lippmann to be unavoidable, he was deeply concerned that the press as he knew it was not serving his country well. In a passage that is remarkably current, he concluded that:

> The press, in other words, has come to be regarded as an organ of direct democracy, charged on a much wider scale, and from day to day, with the function often attributed to the initiative, referendum, and recall. The Court of Public Opinion, open day and night, is to lay down the law for everything all time. And when you consider the nature of news, it is not even thinkable.[28]

The bottom line is that, when officials who develop public policy, make political decisions, or promulgate laws make use of public opinion as a guide to achieving their objectives, they can be using a flawed foundation for their actions. As a consequence, that which they formulate may also be flawed. That conclusion can be summed up in a sixth "therefore" proposition:

6. **Therefore**, those flawed beliefs provide the basis for the formation of public opinion concerning the events and situations reported by the press—and that, in turn, guides the formation of *potentially flawed public policies* concerning those events and situations.

The foregoing six propositions can be brought together into a formal statement of Lippmann's theory. Taken as a whole, they provide a description and explanation of the ways in which the "pseudo-environment" of flawed beliefs is created by the public as the "pictures in their heads of the world outside," as that public attends to the reports of the press. The theory also notes the consequences for public policy that can result.

LIPPMANN'S THEORY: A FORMAL SUMMARY

Strictly speaking, Lippmann's news distortion theory pertains to the newspapers of his time—although in retrospect it is also applicable to all of the news media that came later. As put together in this chapter, the theory was developed directly from his work, most of which was written in the early part of the twentieth century. Radio was in its infancy, television was still an undeveloped concept in the minds of a few engineers, and the Internet was not even a dream of writers of science fiction. In broader perspective, however, it can be seen as his version of a much older and more general theory, drawn from Plato's Allegory of the Cave, which explains the role of all of the mass media in presenting "social constructions of reality" to the public—that is, *meanings people construct for the world in which they live and which they use as guides to action.* In that sense, Lippmann's theory is as modern as today's network newscast, radio bulletin, or online news summary—all of which distort reality in much the same ways and for much the same reasons as the newspapers of Lippmann's time. His writing also outlined what we now refer to as the "gatekeeping" process of the press as well as the "agenda-setting" function. These would be rediscovered and given their current names in later years.

At present, with a vast expansion in the media of communication, with the venerable newspaper still playing an important role, with news magazines providing weekly summaries, with network news reports several times a day, with twenty-four-hour reports available on CNN, with CSPAN, cable, satellite, and the Internet constantly available, the factors that led to distortion in Lippmann's time *are still there*! They continue to shape the news, public opinion, and ultimately political action. In any case, the five propositions suggested above can be brought together into the following formal statements:

Lippmann's Theory of Unintentional News Distortion

1. The press systematically *monitors* events, people, and situations occurring in the physical and social environment to identify potential news stories (the "surveillance function").
2. To prepare the news that it will report, the press *selects*, from the abundance of possible stories that come to its attention, an agenda consisting of those that the news personnel believe will be of importance or of interest to the populations of readers that they serve (now called "gatekeeping").
3. Many factors beyond the control of those in charge (time, money, technology, or opportunity) *limit the ability* of the press to investigate, describe, and transmit full details of all events and situations that come to their attention.
4. Because of these factors (in proposition 3), news reports are often characterized by *selectivity, omissions,* and *distortions* in spite of efforts by many journalists to be objective, complete, fair, and factual.
5. When audiences construct their own meanings from the daily agenda of news reports, the "pictures in their heads" constitute a *pseudo-environment* in that they often have limited correspondence with the facts that occurred in "the world outside," leading people to believe in ways unrelated to the original events or situations (now seen as a result of "framing").
6. **Therefore**, those flawed beliefs provide the basis for the formation of public opinion concerning the events and situations reported by the press—and that, in turn, guides the formation of potentially flawed public policies concerning those events and situations.

AN EMPIRICAL TEST OF THE THEORY

In August of 1920, Lippmann decided to put his conclusions to the test by conducting what we would classify today as an empirical study. His purpose was to demonstrate how inaccurate the news could be. Along with co-author Charles Merz, he conducted a complex research project and published its results in a forty-page article in *The New Republic.* The goal of the study was to compare actual events of the Russian Revolution with contemporary accounts of those same events that had appeared in the *New York Times.* By 1920, two years after the Armistice of World War I and the end of the major phases of the Bolshevik takeover of Russia, Lippmann and his co-investigator were able to obtain factual accounts of what had actually happened during that period. They examined each set of facts carefully from the historical record and discussed each in some detail in the article. In summary, what was analyzed can be seen in the following brief quotation:

> The reliability of the news is tested in this study by a few definite and decisive happenings about which there is no dispute. Thus there is no dispute that the offensive of the Russian army under Kerensky in July 1917 was a disastrous failure; no dispute that the provisional government was overthrown by the Soviet power in November 1917; no dispute that the Soviets made a separate peace with Germany at Brest-Litovsk in March 1918; no dispute that the campaigns of Kolchak, Deniken, and Yudenich were a failure; no dispute that the Soviet Government was still in existence in March 1920. Against such salient facts the daily reports about Russia are measured.[29]

Using a procedure that we would classify today as a content analysis, Lippmann checked the daily reports offered by the *Times,* detail by detail, as these events unfolded, against the actual factual record. He found glaring inconsistencies, errors, and distortions. In other words, the readers of the *Times* had been *badly misled.* The newspaper had created a flawed intellectual pseudo-environment that provided its readers with a view of the events that did not provide them with valid foundations of facts with which to make personal decisions at the time about the Russian situation.

Lippmann did not, however, castigate the *Times.* He regarded it as one of the world's best newspapers. Indeed, he selected it for his analysis for that very reason. He wanted to show how the process of producing the news, even by a respected newspaper, inevitably led to flawed social constructions of reality—*inaccurate pictures in our heads.* In explaining how this could happen, he noted that the newspaper was totally dependent on its sources, and it was those sources who were submitting information that was incorrect. He did, however, upbraid journalists for being so easily misled:

> From the point of view of professional journalism the reporting of the Russian Revolution is nothing short of a disaster. On the essential questions the net effect was almost always misleading, and misleading news is worse than none at all. Yet, on the face of the evidence there is no reason to charge a conspiracy by Americans. They can fairly be charged with boundless credulity, and an untiring readiness to be gulled, and on many occasions with a downright lack of common sense.[30]

Today, there is little interest in those details of the Russian Revolution, and Lippmann's 1920 study of its events of 1917 and how they were reported has faded into obscurity. However, at the time he saw fully how poorly Americans understood that upheaval and how their opinions about it did not correspond to reality. The important point, then, is that the study confirmed his view that informed public opinion cannot exist without access to accurate news and that the press does not create pictures in our heads that correspond point by point to realities in the world outside.

> It is admitted that a sound public opinion cannot exist without access to the news. There is today a widespread and growing doubt that there exists such an access to news about contentious affairs. This doubt ranges from accusations of unconscious bias to downright charges of corruption, from the belief that the news is colored to the belief that the news is poisoned.[31]

This recognition that, even in the most conscientious of newspapers, reports to the public often do not portray events as they actually take place was to provide the central thesis in what the present authors have termed Lippmann's *theory of unintentional distortion of the news.*

The danger, Lippmann pointed out, in failing to recognize that "news is not truth" is that people make decisions about their actions *not on the basis of what actually exists* but on the basis of *what they think exists.* This principle, that if a person believes something to be true, he or she will act as though it were true, is as old as philosophy itself. Lippmann placed it into the context of the politics of his time:

> In all these instances [of people acting on the basis of false beliefs], we must note one common factor. It is the insertion between man and his environment of a pseudo-environment. To that pseudo-environment his behavior is a response. But

because it *is* behavior, the consequences, if they are acts, operate not in the pseudo-environment where the behavior is stimulated, but in the real environment where action eventuates.[32]

DISCUSSION

This chapter summarizes into a brief set of six formal propositions the major ideas that Walter Lippmann developed over six decades. Such a drastic summarization obviously cannot do justice to the richness of his original writings, or the full value of his insights into the ways in which the press, of both his time and the present, serves as the window on the world for the citizens of our society. His theory is remarkably modern. Our contemporary news media are still bound by the limitations that he listed, and, as a consequence, the "pictures in our heads of the world outside" that our press continue to help us develop *are still flawed.* Thus, Lippmann's declaration that "news is not truth" remains as a valid principle.

Perhaps the major factor that makes this present summary acceptable is that it would require a painstaking review of thousands of pages of his original writings to sort out the basic propositions on one's own. However, another justification for such a summary is that it is important not to lose sight of the founders of the field of mass communication theory. In many respects, then, Lippmann was an intellectual giant on the shoulders of whom many contemporary theorists stand. Stephen Lacy pointed out that the time has come to develop more formal theories in this field.[33] One way of doing this is to adopt the strategy of the present author—to revisit the ideas advanced by distinguished scholars of the past and attempt to transform their writings into such a format. Although Lippmann is seldom mentioned in mass communication texts as a major theorist, or he is given only a few lines in contemporary works on such theories at best, it turns out that he was indeed a major contributor.

There seems little doubt that Lippmann's theory has what research methodologists call *face validity.* It just "seems right," and its essential correctness seems intuitively obvious. Moreover, his own remarkable research (for its time) on the relationship between the events of the Russian Revolution and reports in the *New York Times* showed that it was supported by carefully conducted observations. The facts and the news reports made during the period when those events were taking place had little in common. The news, in other words, was seriously distorted.

While he never developed his theory in the way it is presented in this chapter—and he probably never thought of it in quite those terms—it does have the features that research specialists list as important. It is a set of interrelated propositions that provide an explanation of why news reports are often less than complete and accurate. When taken together, the set of assumptions set forth above lead to a logical prediction that can be checked against empirical research results. Thus, even if Lippmann did not put his theory together in the way it has been presented above, his insights deserve to be recognized for the contribution that they continue to make to our contemporary understanding of the functioning of the press, its role in the formation of public opinion, how policy making can be influenced by those opinions, and the pitfalls that can take place in the process.

Notes and References

1. Walter Lippmann, *Public Opinion* (Harcourt, Brace and Company, 1922), p. 358.
2. Howard Kurz, *Spin Cycle: Inside the Clinton Propaganda Machine* (New York: Free Press, 1998). See also Bob Clark, "Inside Washington: Journalist Examines Spin Doctors Cleaning Up Clinton," *The Boston Herald*, March 22, 1998, p. 61; and Jonathan Broder, "Monica Talks at Last and Spinmeisters Tremble," *Newsday*, August 9, 1998, p. B04.
3. Anonymous, "Testing of a President," *The New York Times*, December 11, 1998, p. A32.
4. Ann Scales and Brian McGrory, "Public Opinion Seen as Key Player in Impeachment Drama," *The Boston Globe*, Friday, September 11, 1998, p. A1.
5. Clinton Rossiter and James Lare, *The Essential Lippmann: A Political Philosophy for Liberal Democracy* (New York: Random House, 1963), p. 553.
6. Gilbert A. Harrison, "Foreword," in Walter Lippmann, *Early Writings* (New York: Livewright, 1970), p. vii. (Gilbert Harrison was the editor-in-chief of *The New Republic*.)
7. Melvin L. DeFleur, William V. D'Antonio, and Lois B. DeFleur, "Urbanization and Industrialization," *Sociology: Human Society*, 4th ed. (New York: Random House, 1984), pp. 569–613.
8. Arthur Schlesinger, "Introduction," in *Early Writings, Op. Cit.*, p. ix.
9. Clinton Rossiter and James Lare, *The Essential Lippmann: A Political Philosophy for Liberal Democracy, Op. Cit.*, p. 553.
10. *Ibid.* pp. 4–5.

11. Walter Lippmann, *Liberty and the News* (New York: Harcourt Brace, 1920) pp. 14–15.
12. Margaret H. DeFleur, *Computer-Assisted Investigative Reporting: Development and Methodology* (Mahwah, NJ: Lawrence Erlbaum Associates, 1997).
13. *Ibid.* p. 92.
14. Clinton Rossiter and James Lare, *The Essential Lippmann: A Political Philosophy for Liberal Democracy, Op. Cit.*, p. v.
15. Walter Lippmann, *Public Opinion, Op. Cit.*, p. 338.
16. *Ibid.* p. 338.
17. Walter Lippmann, *Liberty and the News, Op. Cit.*, pp. 89–90.
18. Walter Lippmann, *Public Opinion, Op. Cit.*, p. 354.
19. *Ibid.* p. 354.
20. *Ibid.* p. 347.
21. *Ibid.* p. 344.
22. *Ibid.* p. 345.

23. Walter Lippmann, *Liberty and the News, Op. Cit.*, p. 12.
24. John Leo, "The Media Run Riot: Coverage of Cincinnati's Violence Misses the Mark," *U.S. News and World Report*, April 30, 2001, p. 17.
25. *Ibid.*
26. These data are summarized by John Leo, *Op. Cit.*
27. James Bryce, *The American Commonwealth* (London: The Macmillan Company, 1888–89), LXXVII, p. 29.
28. Walter Lippmann, *Public Opinion, Op. Cit.*, p. 363.
29. Walter Lippmann and Charles Merz, "A Test of the News," *The New Republic*, August 4, 1920, pp. 1–40.
30. *Ibid.* p. 3.
31. *Ibid.* p. 3.
32. *Ibid.* p. 15.
33. Stephen R. Lacy, "From the President," *AEJMC News*, 31, 6, September 1998, pp. 2 and 22.

The "Magic Bullet" Theory of Uniform Effects

It was widely held, as the twentieth century began, that the new mass media—radio and the movies—were going to destroy our moral standards by their depictions of unacceptable social behavior. By the 1920s, the new radio stations began transmitting popular music—*jazz*, which some claimed would stimulate strong sexual urges in young men. A woman attending a social event unchaperoned with such a man would clearly be vulnerable, especially if they traveled in his automobile. The motion pictures, especially during the 1920s, seemed especially menacing. They showed gangsters committing crimes, people in speakeasies consuming illegal liquor, and even couples in bedrooms where the women were shown in their undergarments. These depictions, some feared, would sweep away the sexual prohibitions and other standards of decency in society, leaving it in a state of moral ruin.

THE MAGIC BULLET THEORY AS POPULAR EXPLANATION

The theory of mass communication that much of the public entertained during those early times—and in many ways one that at least some people still use to interpret the influences of mass communication today—is simple. It goes like this: If a form of attractive but unacceptable behavior is depicted in a movie or a television program, it can be assumed that everyone who sees it will be stimulated to adopt—or at least accept—that form of behavior in his or her own personal conduct. In other words, the media are assumed to have *direct, powerful, immediate*, and virtually *universal* effects on their audiences. As a consequence, many citizens *fear* the media and long for someone to *control* them—by screening out content of which they do not approve. They are not sure who should do the screening, or exactly what should be allowed or forbidden, but they are convinced that the mass media are directly responsible for *controlling what people think* and in many ways *how they behave*.

This kind of thinking is a modern version of the very first theory of the effects of mass communication, which was developed by social scientists a century ago when the newspaper was in its golden age—long before other popular media came along. In the last part of the nineteenth century, and well into the twentieth, newspapers were thought to be very powerful and able to sway their audiences almost at will, bringing them to believe and behave in ways dictated by those who controlled their content. When the movies and radio first came along, such thinking continued to prevail for them as well. The remarkable propaganda successes of World War I seemed to prove that such thinking was correct. Support for the war effort, and hatred of the Axis powers, especially Germany, was successfully and deliberately fostered by the newspapers of the time.

In summary, this early theory assumed that a message delivered by the mass media will reach *every eye and ear*, that it will have *immediate and powerful effects*, shaping the thoughts and conduct of *all who receive it*. In a metaphorical sense, then, the media message is like a "bullet," penetrating the consciousness of everyone in the entire audience and shaping both belief and behavior. For that reason, the theory is called (in retrospect) the *magic bullet theory*. However, it was not called that at the time. Only in recent years have scholars assigned it that name. In addition, it was never set forth in concise terms as a set of related propositions, as it is at the end of this chapter.

When viewed in light of our current understanding of the process and effects of mass communication, the magic bullet theory can seem quaint and naive. We know now that the media can achieve effects—sometimes powerful ones. However, that does not occur often and then only with some people and under very specific kinds of conditions.[1] That was not understood in the late 1800s and early 1900s. Only after a significant accumulation of research on media effects over several decades, showing a more factual picture, were more realistic theories developed. We know now that mass communications certainly do not have the great power to influence all people uniformly that was thought to be the case as the nineteenth century closed and the twentieth began.

The present chapter looks closely at that now-abandoned theory. A legitimate question is *why do that*? Why should a now-defunct theory be included in this book? One answer is that, as mentioned, many members of the public continue to believe that the media routinely have such powerful and universal effects—even though they are wrong. A more important answer is that the magic bullet theory provided a *starting position for both research and the development of more adequate theories*. It stimulated scholars and researchers of earlier decades to study its predictions to see if they held true in the real world of media influences on populations (see Chapter 1). When they did not find such "magic" influences, researchers were forced to formulate different, more realistic explanations to replace it. Thus, by stimulating research, it provided an important "jumping off" point for developing more contemporary theories of mass communication.

Human Nature and the Social Order

There is another lesson to be learned from an examination of the magic bullet theory. It is that theories of mass communication do not exist in an intellectual vacuum. Any theory of the influences of the mass media must be consistent with accepted views of the *basic nature of human individuals* and the *fundamental features of the social order* in which the media operate. Thus, valid theories of mass communication must be based on valid underlying explanations of psychological and social reality. For example, several of the previous chapters have discussed what we know today about how people "socially construct" versions of reality, how they cognitively process information internally, and how they understand and are guided by the social order in which they live. Modern theories of the process and effects of mass communications must be consistent with that foundation.

As it turns out, the magic bullet theory *was consistent* with what scholars of that time believed about human nature and the social order. As will be seen, these interpretations are not the same today as they were a century ago, when the magic bullet theory prevailed. Moreover, they may change in the decades ahead. The second lesson, therefore, is that theories of mass communication are *embedded in more general theories of human nature and the social order*. That is very well illustrated by what social scientists believed about humankind a century ago.

A review of the underlying intellectual foundation on which the magic bullet theory rested illustrates extremely well the relationship between basic interpretations of the human condition and a theory of mass media. As will become clear, far from being a naive theory at the time, it was completely consistent with sophisticated explanations of human psychological functioning and the organization of society *that seemed fully valid* to scholars of the late nineteenth and early twentieth centuries. However, when those basic theories were replaced with more contemporary versions and became obsolete, the Magic Bullet Theory became obsolete along with them.

Basic Behavioral Paradigms

What were those general explanations that helped shape the magic bullet theory? There were a number that were current during the last decade of the nineteenth century and the early part of the twentieth. The ones to be examined are *paradigms* that seemed at the time to explain important aspects of human behavior and the nature of the urban-industrial society. A "paradigm" is a very broad and general theoretical formulation that provides an interpretation of a whole range of related events. An example of such a paradigm is Darwin's *theory of evolution*, with its explanations of the origin of species and the animal characteristics of human beings. That basic paradigm had a significant influence on the psychology of the time. In addition, a number of sociologists developed interpretations of the social order that came to be incorporated into the *mass society model*—a paradigm reviewed in Chapter 6. Also playing a part was the paradigm that provided the foundation for *psychoanalysis*, a general explanation that human behavior is motivated by *unconscious instincts* that motivate biologically based sexual drives. In the sections below, the intellectual foundations of the magic bullet theory of media effects are reviewed very briefly in order to indicate the sources of the theory's assumptions and to provide an example of how any such formulation is developed in ways that are consistent with more general explanations of human nature and the social order that are accepted at the time within the scientific and scholarly community.

NINETEENTH-CENTURY VIEWS OF HUMAN NATURE

The 1800s were a century of great change in the ways in which scientists and scholars viewed human beings. Up to the beginning of that century, few Christians challenged the explanation of the origins of humankind as set forth in the Book of Genesis. It was in itself *a paradigm*—an explanation of the origins and nature of humankind. For centuries it had been completely accepted that God had created men in His own image and then women from a rib of Adam. This meant that human beings were *very different* from other living creatures and *vastly superior*. After all, they were a special work of God. Unlike other living beings, they were endowed with an *immortal soul* that survived after death of the body. This made human beings capable of *salvation* to a very satisfying afterlife—if they had lived according to ways prescribed by scriptures (and a much worse fate if they had not). Few thought otherwise for many centuries.

A *second paradigm* that was brought forward from the 1600s was the conception of human beings as both *rational* and capable of exercising *free will*. Perhaps no philosopher had been more important in establishing the principle that human beings exercised reason in making their behavioral choices than Rene Descartes. Writing during the 1600s, he provided a foundation of systematic beliefs about the ability of human beings to exercise logic. He even used the human capacity to *think* as proof of his own existence.

> But what, then, am I? A thinking thing, it has been said. But what is a thinking thing? It is a thing that doubts, understands, [conceives], affirms, denies, wills, refuses, that imagines also and perceives.[2]

His famous dictum, *I think—therefore, I am*, is one of the best-known "sound bites" to emerge from the period. His reasoning was that, "If I doubt, I think; if I think, then I exist—*cogito ergo sum*."[3]

The conception of human beings as rational, logical, and capable of exercising enlightened free will did not challenge the basic Christian paradigm. Indeed, it complemented it by attributing to humankind noble qualities that no animal could possess. Moreover, it appeared to be very true in the 1700s, when great advances were made in science, philosophy, and the arts. The period came to be characterized as the Age of Reason. Human beings by this time, then, were seen as truly exceptional. Created by God to be like no other creature and endowed with a remarkable conscious mind that could reason systematically. This placed them in a category that no other living form could even approach.

But just after mid-nineteenth century, a very different paradigm explaining the origins and nature of humankind stunned the conservative Christian world. It was the *theory of evolution* offered by Charles Darwin. His interpretation stated that human beings came into existence not as a special project conducted by God but as a consequence of an enormously long process of *mindless biological adaptation*.

Then, late in the 1800s, a second contrary paradigm was advanced that openly contradicted the conception of humankind as rational and endowed with free will. It appeared to contradict the idea that human beings could make rational choices about their behavior. It stated that, in many cases, rationality and reasoning played only a minimal part in shaping conduct. Human beings were said to be driven by *unconscious drives and urges,* over which they had little control and of which they are essentially unaware. It was developed by several founders of the field of psycho-analysis during the late 1800s, and it was prominently publicized early in the 1900s by Sigmund Freud. It was to become enormously popular.

Human Beings Are Animals Driven by Instincts

Perhaps no set of ideas ever provided a greater challenge to established thinking about the origins and nature of human beings than the works of Charles Darwin. In his 1859 book, *On the Origin of Species by Means of Natural Selection*, he set forth a totally new paradigm. Human beings, he maintained, are complex animals that developed from simpler forms through a process of biological selectivity, adaptation, and evolution.[4] The work created an intellectual firestorm that continues burning even today.

As was noted earlier, for centuries the Christian churches had been teaching that God created the heavens and the earth and that He finally got around to creating human beings. He designed them to look like himself (at least the males), and he created woman a short time later so that the species could survive. That made human beings a truly special kind of creature and very different from all the others on earth. In particular, they were equipped with a *soul* that could exist after the body expired. That really set them apart from animals.

Upsetting this type of explanation, Darwin indicated that human beings developed from simpler forms, such as monkeys and apes—who had themselves developed from still simpler forms. This happened because over a very long period some creatures became more and more able to solve problems more effectively than the animals with whom they were competing. He described a process of "natural selection" in which those creatures least able to adapt did not survive. Only the best and brightest went on to perpetuate their species. This included human beings. This principle came to be called "the survival of the fittest," although that phrase did not originate with Darwin. Before Darwin published his famous treatise, Herbert Spencer, the British philosopher, theorized that a process of social evolution would produce the *best society* when those individuals most capable of success beat out the losers for positions of dominance and control.[5]

For present purposes, explaining the origins of the Magic Bullet Theory, the importance of Darwin's work lies in identifying the *animal nature of human beings* and their reliance on *inherited patterning of their behavior*. To account for the elaborate patterns of much of animal behavior—such as in defense, reproduction, and migration—the concept of *instinct* was developed. This idea was discussed in Chapter 6, but its importance in developing a theory of mass communications needs to be made clear. The instinct concept proved to be a very convenient one. An instinct was defined as an *inherited* mode of adaptation. For example, all salmon (not just some) swim hundreds of miles up rivers to spawn, returning to the very place where they were born. They are said to be guided by inherited guidance systems that are included in their genetic structure. The same is true of migratory birds and butterflies. Virtually all animals are thought to have instinctual patterns of behavior. Thus, these internal guidance systems are said to be *universal* in the species—a part of every similar animal's biological makeup. In other words, instincts are *inherited* and do not have to be learned, and they explain *complex* forms of behavior.

This idea caught on quickly and was used to explain human behavior as well. As the 1800s came to an end, the idea of human instincts came to be widely accepted. We were said to have instincts for mating, mothering, building shelter, engaging in wars, and for many other forms of complex activity. As was noted earlier, psychology texts at the beginning of the 1900s had long lists of human instincts that students in psychology courses of the time had to memorize and regurgitate on exams.

The idea of a biologically inherited force uniformly driving the behavior of all members of the species is still popular with the public. Many laypeople today speak of human instincts such as "mothering," in spite of the fact that it is scarcely universal. Some mothers abandon, beat, or even deliberately kill their babies. Another popular one is "survival." It would be hard to show that it was either inherited or universal. The fact that members of some military groups (kamikazes) and entire religious cults have deliberately committed suicide does not fit with the basic instinct concept. Moreover, there are also high suicide rates among teenagers, the elderly, and in certain other segments of the population. "Survival," therefore, is not some blind and uncontrollable force that we all inherit. Whether we survive or die at our own hands depends on a number of factors having nothing to do with our inherited genes.

While the public may continue to entertain the idea of instincts, among behavioral scientists a belief in such unwitting, biologically based motivations is no longer regarded as having any place in explaining human conduct. There do not seem to be any complex activities that are universal, inherited, and acquired without learning. In fact, by the end of the 1920s, academic psychologists had totally abandoned the concept of instinct to account for complex forms of human behavior (substituting learning in a cultural environment).[6] Only Freudian psychoanalysts have retained the idea in their paradigm, and perhaps it is because of this that the idea lingers on in popular thought as well.

For present purposes, the importance of the instinct concept was that it was incorporated into the Magic Bullet Theory. This happened for two reasons. One was that psychologists had conceptualized human behavior in S—R terms—that is, for a human act, a *response*, to take place, there had to be a *stimulus* that triggered it. When the S—R formula was expanded to S—O—R, this became the more complex idea that *response* (R) to the *stimulus* (S) was shaped by characteristics and conditions of the *organism* (O). Instinct provided a convenient characteristic of the organism that could shape the nature of the response. Thus, in terms of reactions to stimuli provided by the media, human beings were said to *react uniformly*. Thus, people were seen as animals with a set of uniform and inherited instincts over which they had little control. When they were exposed to stimuli provided by media content, presumably they responded automatically and unthinkingly. If that were really true, it would give enormous power to those who controlled the media!

Human Beings Are Driven by Unconscious Urges

As noted, another new paradigm emerged from the new field of psychology—more specifically, from psychoanalysis, as a mode of treatment for those suffering from mental problems. Perhaps no view of human nature (as essentially developed around instincts) was more influential as the nineteenth century closed and the twentieth began than the psychoanalytic theories of Sigmund Freud.[7]

In 1885, Freud—who was a physician—became deeply impressed by certain discoveries of Dr. Jean-Martin Charcot. Dr. Charcot had found that disorders such as paralysis (of an arm) could be caused *mentally*—as opposed to biologically—and they could sometimes be relieved by *hypnosis*. Freud tried out the idea and found that it did sometimes offer relief from pain. Even earlier, he discovered that people could be relieved of physical symptoms by a "talking cure" that discharged pent-up emotional blockage caused by events earlier in life that the person could not (or would not) recall. From a background of such observations that he encountered in his practice, Freud went on to develop a theory of *psychoanalysis*—a remarkable new paradigm that offered a nontraditional view of the human mind. Many of its concepts became household words in Western countries.

Freud described human psychological functioning as taking place at two levels—the *conscious* and the *unconscious*. The psyche (mind) was said to be organized around three major components—the *superego*, the *ego*, and the *id*. The superego is roughly equivalent to what we would call the "conscience" in everyday language. It is that part of the psyche in which are stored the learned moral norms that one ideally should follow in choosing actions. The ego, a second component of the psyche, is the conscious part of our mind that monitors, chooses, and directs our immediate behavior. The ego makes *choices* with reference to either the superego or a much more mysterious part of the psyche, the id. The id was defined as a reservoir of deep-seated instinctual needs that motivate us unconsciously. Freud felt that many people secretly want to engage in forms of behavior that are strongly disapproved of by society.

An important feature of the id is the biologically based *libido,* which refers to unconscious *sexual instincts* that we inherit at birth and cannot change. Such instincts, Freud emphasized, are often the motivations—unknown to us at the conscious level—that drive our behavioral choices. This is a complex picture, but the basic idea is that Freud and his followers described a radically new way of viewing human beings and their conduct. The main motivators are said to be a number of sexual and other inherited instincts that shape much of our behavior at an unconscious level.

Freud's version of psychoanalytic theory eventually became much more elaborate.[8] It was expanded into explanations not only of human nature but also of civilization as well. It is far too complex to be set forth in detail here. What is important for present purposes is that it helps in understanding at least one feature of what became the magic bullet theory. Freud and other psychoanalytical psychologists stressed the *unconscious* and *non-rational* aspects of the human mind as powerful influences on conduct. He also showed that human beings could be very *suggestible* at an unconscious level. Those truly were new ideas, and they became very well known by the public. The implication for developing a theory of mass communication is this: *If those who control the media can design messages that appeal to these unconscious motivations, suggestible people will act according to these needs and drives.* If that takes place, then the media can have truly great power over their audiences.

Thus, two of the intellectual foundations of the Magic Bullet Theory were the paradigms of Darwin and Freud. One paradigm stressed the animal nature of human beings and their dependence on biologically based instincts. The other used the concept of instincts and added unconscious urges and drives to engage in forbidden activities over which people lacked conscious and rational control. These paradigms were a part of the theoretical framework within which people began to interpret the power of the mass newspapers and later other media.

NINETEENTH-CENTURY VIEWS OF THE SOCIAL ORDER

Looking beyond paradigms that tried to explain individual behavior solely on the basis of internal motivations, sociologists of the time understood that human conduct was more than just a matter of inherited urges and drives. As was indicated in earlier chapters, a different paradigm developed from their studies was that human conduct was often shaped by *shared social expectations* (norms) that were understood within a group concerning the requirements for acceptable conduct. These were imposed on people by the groups and communities within which they had relationships with others. For example, at least some adult males may want to have sexual relationships with very young girls. However, the shared requirements for conduct imposed by society do not permit them free access to such youngsters—a fact of which they are undoubtedly aware and which laws make clear. They must rein in their urges and live by the moral and legal norms that society has imposed. In other words, this paradigm states that *behavioral control comes from without as well as within.*

Sociologists study the patterning and consistency of these socially imposed rules for behavior and the degree to which they are effective in limiting deviant conduct. In a stable and well-understood community or society, few people can ignore or violate those shared social rules. The norms and expectations for acceptable conduct are clear, deeply established, and universally enforced.

Sociologists understood very well that this had been precisely the situation in *traditional societies*—the small tightly knit *Gemeinschaft* communities that existed before the beginning of the Industrial Revolution (Chapter 6). As was explained, when the 1800s began, factory towns started to exist. Sociologists saw a new kind of social order arising in which the conditions of life were changing. The emerging *Gesellschaft* society was very unlike the traditional community. At first, some sociologists saw the new developments in positive terms. Their analyses were devoted to describing how the society was changing and how the new social order produced stability as a result of its increasing complexity. Initially, during the first half of the 1800s, the key idea that they developed was that society was a kind of increasingly complex "organism" whose parts functioned well together to keep it in equilibrium.

Society as Organism

Virtually all of the sociologists of the nineteenth century saw a close fit between what was happening in society as industrialization proceeded and the structural or design features of an *organism.* That did not mean that they believed that a human society was a plant or an animal. It meant that a human society had all of the characteristics of an organism and could indeed be described in those terms. That is, like any organism, a society is made up of *parts*, and those parts function together as a *system.* Moreover, the parts are mutually *dependent* on each other, and the whole is *more than the sum of its parts.* In addition, like other organisms, it undergoes a process of evolution. If it is true that those are the critical features, sociologists believed, then human society can indeed logically be regarded as a special kind of organism.

A key factor in any organism is its degree of *specialization.* We noted earlier that this was a major observation of those who developed the concept of the mass society. People were engaging in more and more specialized activities in the workplace. Auguste Comte, a French philosopher and sociologist, saw great *harmony* and *stability* in the specialization that was increasing in society.[9] Essentially, Comte saw how all the different occupational and other roles performed by people in a society fit together into an overall system, making it possible for the society to function smoothly as a whole, even though the people performing the actions do not plan this deliberately.

This idea, of many people performing specialized tasks that fit together into a smoothly functioning organic whole, had great intellectual appeal to a number of nineteenth-century scholars. For example, the British social philosopher Herbert Spencer, a second major founder of sociology, saw an important principle in this increasing elaboration of specialization that made it possible for society to function as a special kind of organism.[10]

Sources of Social Pathology

The significance of the organism concept as applied to society as a whole was that it provided a possible basis for diagnosing *social ills,* following the example of biology as a foundation for medicine. It appeared that sociology, providing an understanding of the ways in which the (societal) organism functioned normally and smoothly, offered a possible route for understanding how *social pathologies* might develop. This was in many ways a continuation of the ancient search for the "just" society that had started with philosophers. With new understandings of social organization as the basis for social solidarity and an efficient social order, it would be possible to identify those social conditions which had failed, causing *disorder* and thereby becoming the source of social ills. In other words, problems like alcoholism, crime, divorce, child abuse, and even poverty, all of which had previously been considered as failures of individual human beings, might now be seen as failings of the social order.

It was for this reason that conditions such as overspecialization, the loss of respect for traditional folkways and mores, and the increasing need for effective formal systems of social control were so closely studied by the early sociologists. The influence of the mass media came to be a part of this search. It was entirely possible, such scholars thought, that *the mass media had become a source of social pathology.*

The Era of Crowds

To sum up, the picture of society that was being put together by social scientists near the end of the nineteenth century can be described in the following terms: As industrialization continued, unlike people migrated to cities and their populations grew. The division of labor expanded hugely, creating great diversity in lifestyles. As a result, urban people became increasingly *unlike each other.* This led to *anomie,* a condition in which the social norms were increasingly unclear. Because of these trends, certain social pathologies were developing. The inhabitants of modern societies were becoming increasingly anonymous, socially isolated, and unresponsive to the opinions of others about their behavior. If these trends were indeed correctly assessed, the social organization of the emerging society was more like that of a *crowd* than a community.

The idea of a society as a kind of "lonely crowd" began to gain wide acceptance among social scientists. For example, in 1895, the French sociologist Gustave Le Bon described the emerging organization of society as an *era of crowds.* He was concerned because he had come to believe that people who have few or no social ties to each other—the inhabitants of the mass society—had gained the power to make collective decisions, guided only by their *unconscious desires.* In such a situation, public opinion is not based on rationality, even as it becomes a much more powerful force than it ever had been earlier.

To try to understand the political implications of the emerging society, Le Bon developed an elaborate analysis of the nature of crowds. By "crowd" he did not mean what we would think of today when we use that term to refer to a bunch of people gathered in a casual way—such as collected at a street corner to watch a parade. He was concerned with the deteriorating links between people incorporated in the mass society, especially when individual behavior is motivated primarily *by the unconscious.* For example, like the psychoanalysts, he discussed the place of instincts as well as the unconscious in the behavior of the inhabitants of modern society:

> Crowds, doubtless, are always unconscious, but this very unconsciousness is perhaps one of the secrets of their success. In the natural world beings exclusively governed by instincts accomplish acts whose marvelous complexity astounds us. Reason is an attribute of humanity of too recent date and still too imperfect to reveal to us the laws of the unconscious, and still more to take its place. The part played by the unconscious in our acts is immense, and that played by reason very small.[11]

This view of the modern citizen's decisions as driven by his or her unconscious, with little contribution from reason, rationality, or social relationships, seemed to Le Bon to have very disturbing implications. A major political change had occurred in Western societies with the decline of monarchy. As a result of the American and French revolutions, great political power had been placed in the hands of ordinary citizens. A century earlier, political decisions were made by powerful rulers. The opinions of the masses counted for very little. Now the fate of governments and their leaders depended on decisions of thousands of individual voters making their choices on the basis of unconscious forces. As Le Bon put it, "The divine right of the masses is about to replace the divine right of kings . . . The destinies of nations are elaborated at present in the heart of the masses and no longer in the councils of princes."[12]

Obviously, Le Bon's analysis of crowds and their significance for the political process had incorporated the new perspectives on human nature that were being developed, based both on Darwin's theories of evolution and those of the psychoanalytic school of psychology. An additional key idea that Le Bon stressed, and worried about, was that the psychological isolation of the individual in a crowd results in *a great increase in suggestibility.* According to prevailing interpretations, if traditional norms and individual reason do not guide behavior, this leaves only the unconscious. If this is the case, and if reason does not filter incoming ideas, then *suggestions coming from an outside source* can sway and motivate the person to act, often in ways that would not be the case if the person were completely isolated from such suggestions. Le Bon saw this as a particularly dangerous state, and it has significant implications for understanding the *fear of the mass media* that came to be generated during the period. It seemed clear that a potent message in a newspaper article would be quite capable of suggesting a course of action to a suggestible individual that would be irresistible.

THE MEDIA AS SOURCES OF PERSONAL AND SOCIAL PROBLEMS

What do all of these various paradigms about the psychological nature of the individual and changes in the social organization of society mean for understanding the Magic Bullet Theory of the effects of the mass media of the time? The answer is that they came to be seen as increasingly important in understanding how media content could lead people into forms of conduct that were *personally and socially destructive.* The role of the new mass newspapers in promoting personal deviance and social ills was the subject of much concern to thoughtful people of the period, and they began to voice their concerns. In particular, it began to seem clear that newspapers, because of their constant reporting on crimes, suicides, scandals, sexual misconduct, and other forms of destructive behavior, were serving as models for youth to emulate.

The Evils of the Mass Press

As the popular newspapers developed in the urban-industrial society, their news stories often reported crimes, arrests, and trials. The growing number of stories about stabbings, beatings, rape, murder, and other gross misconduct that came to peoples' attention through the newspapers seemed to suggest that such behavior was on the increase—enhancing peoples' feelings of possible danger from others. As such views became more common, sociologists became more concerned about the influences of newspapers.

To illustrate how the popular newspapers of the late 1800s came to be blamed for societal ills, the writings of the French sociologist Gabriel Tarde offer a clear example. He was a distinguished jurist whose opinions were widely respected. Tarde was convinced that more traditional institutions in society—the church and the family—were losing control over young people.

He charged that newspapers, due to their content, had become a source for promoting serious personal and social problems among suggestible juveniles. These problems included suicide among minors, increasing use of alcohol, and, in general, a rising rate of juvenile delinquency and crime.

Tarde conducted careful studies of the crime reports from a number of European countries, where he found a similar picture. There was, he said, "a growing perversity of youth" that he openly blamed on the newspapers. As background causes, he cited a number of social trends and changes. Specifically mentioned were "an increase in general irreligion . . . an exodus from rural areas to the cities . . . and above all, the contagious scourge of alcoholism."[13]

But it was the newspapers Tarde identified as the more immediate cause of youthful problems. He pointed out that children were not turning to libraries, to respectable meetings where learning could take place, or to artistic societies to improve their minds. Instead, sadly, they were using alcohol and reading newspapers.

> . . . it is the trashy and malicious press, scandal-mongering, riddled with court cases, that awaits the student when he leaves school. The little newspaper, supplementing the little drink, alcoholizes his heart. . . . No less frightening . . . is pornography and slander, which have become the twin breasts nourishing the newspaper. The *Chrionique judiciare* [the court reports from which newspapers got their information] alone has caused more crimes through the 'contagion of murder' and of theft, which it instigates, than the schools could ever prevent. For not a murder is committed but the press becomes aroused . . .[14]

The opinions of Gabriel Tarde were highly respected. He was a distinguished judge and the author of authoritative works on a number of sociological topics. His analysis of the role of the newspaper in promoting juvenile crime and other problems influenced many other European intellectuals who were saying much the same thing: Mass newspapers filled their daily editions with stories of crime and depravity. That these stories were a major factor in the deterioration of moral standards was widely accepted. This theme brought together the concerns of scholars who had been describing the problems generated by the new views of human nature and the negative features of the great social changes brought about by industrialization. By the end of the century, then, newspapers came to be seen by thoughtful members of the public as causes of many of the ills in society. The magic bullet theory seemed right on target and a very sound explanation of how the mass communications were *harming the human condition*.

New Media in a New Century

In the early years of the twentieth century, totally new media would be developed to provide entertainment, news, and other information to mass audiences. Their content would in many respects follow the same patterns as that which had enabled newspapers to develop and prosper. The emphasis would be on entertainment and popular culture. The now venerable newspaper would go through a period of "yellow journalism" (at least in major cities) in which entertaining the public was seen as far more important than careful and truthful coverage of the events of the day. The movies, which were in their infancy as the century began, quickly became the favorite weekly entertainment of millions. Radio became a household medium during the 1920s. Our more modern media are logical extensions of these beginnings.

While this was happening, the Magic Bullet Theory did not disappear. It came under attack by academic researchers who began to question its assumptions in the 1930s and especially when their findings showed that its predictions made no sense. However, the public *continued to believe that powerful and dangerous mass media were having negative effects on society*. For example, the movies in the 1920s began depicting young people engaging in activities that shocked the older generation brought up believing in the Victorian code of morality. Young women in short dresses, with "bobbed" hair and wearing makeup like common harlots, were shown smoking and drinking. The radio was saturating the airwaves with a dangerous form of popular music called "jazz." It was clear that society was close to collapse. As one newspaper report put it in 1922:

JAZZ RUINING GIRLS, DECLARES REFORMER

[Chicago, January 21]—Moral disaster is coming to hundreds of American girls through the pathological, nerve irritating, sex-exciting music of jazz orchestras, according to the Illinois Vigilance Association.

In Chicago alone the association's representatives have traced the fall of 1,000 girls in the last two years to jazz music.

Girls in small towns as well as the big cities, in poor homes and rich homes, are victims of the weird, insidious, neurotic music that accompanies modern dancing.

The degrading music is common not only to disorderly places, but often to high school affairs, to expensive hotels and so-called society circles, declares Rev. Richard Yarrow, superintendent of the Vigilance Association.

The report says that the vigilance society has no desire to abolish dancing, but seeks to awaken the public conscience to the present danger and future consequences of jazz music.[15]

What, then, does one do when popular music pouring from one's radio speaker is having such destructive effects? What steps can one take when shameless behavior is openly depicted on the movie screens? For many the answer has been to pressure the industries involved to "clean up their acts." That sometimes works, as it did for the movie industry during the 1930s. Failing that, an appeal can be made to politicians to intervene with censorship. That is not likely to happen in any real sense, due to a troublesome First Amendment to the U.S. Constitution.

Such problems continue to disturb many people even today. The Magic Bullet Theory seems to them to say about all that needs to be understood about the effects of the mass media. Today's version may be much modified from the one prevailing at the beginning of the twentieth century, but essentially it is alive and well in the minds of a multitude of ordinary people who serve as the media's critics.

THE MAGIC BULLET THEORY: A FORMAL SUMMARY

Listed below are the principle assumptions and predictions that express the ideas of the magic bullet theory as it was developed late in the nineteenth century. Keep in mind that it was *never put together* in this way at the time. This particular version was developed for the present text after an extensive review of both technical and popular writings about the real and suspected influences of the mass media during the last decades of the 1800s and early 1900s. As a theory it has *long since been abandoned* by scholars and researchers. No counterpart of its predictions could be found in reality, and it has been replaced by more realistic interpretations. Nevertheless, as it existed at the time, it could have been stated in the following propositions:

1. People in "mass" society lead *socially isolated lives* with very limited social controls exerted over each other because they are from diverse origins and do not share a unifying set of norms, values, and beliefs.
2. Like all animals, human beings are endowed at birth with a *uniform set of instincts* that guide their ways of responding to the world around them.
3. Because people's actions are not influenced by social ties and are guided by uniform internal instincts, individuals attend to events (such as media messages) *in similar ways*.
4. People's inherited human nature and their isolated social condition leads them to *receive and interpret* media messages in a uniform way.
5. **Therefore**, media messages are like symbolic "bullets," striking every eye and ear, and resulting in effects on thought and behavior that are *direct, immediate, uniform*, and, therefore, *powerful*.

Even though it has been abandoned by media researchers and theorists, the Magic Bullet Theory has historical importance. It was with this kind of explanation that systematic interpretations about the effects of mass communication began, based on what seemed to be valid biological, psychological, and social science at the time. But equally important, it remains, in modified form, the standard way of thinking about mass communication for many citizens. For parents worried about the influence of television on their children, the Magic Bullet Theory does not seem that far off the mark. Even among some people in media professions—like advertising, public relations, or even journalism—there can be found the naive assumption that if it appears in the media, then large numbers of people will have seen or heard it and that they will be influenced by its message. For many media critics, it provides a foundation for their charges. Fortunately, as many of the chapters that follow will show, explanations of the process and effects of mass communication are far more complicated than those that the Magic Bullet Theory provides.

Notes and References

1. Melvin L. DeFleur and Margaret H. DeFleur, "Using the News Media to Commit Crimes Against Humanity; A Case Study of Powerful Effects," (unpublished paper).

2. Rene Descartes, "Meditation II: Of the Nature of the Human Mind; and That It Is More Easily Known Than the Body," Part IV of the *Discourse on Method,* first published in 1637. See Rene Descartes and Cartesianism, "The World, Rules, and Discourse on Method," *Britannica Online.*

3. Errol E. Harris, *Fundamentals of Philosophy* (New York: Holt, Rinehart and Winston, 1969), p. 151.

4. Charles Darwin, *On the Origin of Species by Means of Natural Selection* (New York: D. Appleton, 1873). First published in England in 1859, this sixth edition contained additions and corrections.

5. Herbert Spencer, *Social Statics* (New York: Appleton-Century-Crofts, 1850). The original edition was published in England in 1850. See also Herbert Spencer, *First Principles* (New York: Appleton-Century-Crofts, 1892), first published in 1862, and Herbert Spencer, *The Principles of Sociology* (New York: Appleton-Century-Crofts, 1910). First published in 1876–1896).

6. Robert E. L. Faris, "The Instinct Theory in Human Behavior," in Chapter 2 of his *Social Psychology* (New York: The Ronald Press Company, 1952), pp. 13–27.

7. A. A. Brill, ed. and trans., *The Basic Writings of Sigmund Freud* (New York: Modern Library, 1938).

8. Ruth L. Munroe, *Schools of Psychoanalytic Thought* (New York: The Dryden Press, 1955).

9. Auguste Comte, *The Positive Philosophy,* trans. by Harriet Martineau (London: George Bell and Sons, 1915), Vol. 2, p. 289. First published in France between 1830 and 1842.

10. Herbert Spencer, *The Principles of Sociology* (New York: D. Appleton, 1898), p. 452. First published in England in 1876.

11. Gustave Le Bon, *The Crowd; A Study of the Popular Mind* (New York: The Viking Press, 1960), p. 7. First published in France in 1895.

12. *Ibid.* p. 16.

13. Gabriel Tarde, "Criminal Youth," Reprinted in Terry N. Clark, ed., *Gabriel Tarde: On Communication and Social Influence* (Chicago: University of Chicago Press, 1969), p. 261. First published in *Revue pedagigique,* February 1897.

14. *Ibid.* p. 266.

15. Quoted from Melvin L. DeFleur and Everette E. Dennis, *Understanding Mass Communication,* 4th ed. (Boston: Houghton Mifflin Company, 1991), p. 456.

CHAPTER 10

A Selective and Limited Influences Theory

While media such as newspapers, magazines, movies, and home radio were in wide use in the U.S. by the mid-1920s, systematic research on the process and effects of mass communication within a science perspective did not begin until the late 1920s and early 1930s. One of the reasons was that, before that time, media scholars had little in the way of scientific research tools to use in addressing the issue of media influences. That is not to say that earlier scholars were uninterested in newspapers or other media that played a part in shaping political or social behavior. During the last decades of the 1800s, or early 1900s, as the present text has explained, intellectuals like James Bryce, Walter Lippmann, Charles Horton Cooley, and Gustave Le Bon began to write thoughtful essays discussing the role of newspapers in political and social life. Some claimed that the newspapers of their time had great power. Others concluded that they did not.

Walter Lippmann's 1919 investigation of newspaper stories about the Russian Revolution appears to be the first empirical study of a mass medium. It was a primitive content analysis with a very narrow focus—but at the time he had little else in the way of methodology with which to conduct his study. The epistemology of statistics, based on probability, was being developed in the agricultural sciences and other fields, but before the 1920s it had not been brought into the social sciences. Sophisticated research methods for the study of behavior—experimental designs, sample-based surveys, systematic content analyses of media messages, and longitudinal observational studies—also came along but a bit later. Even by the end of World War II, the question of how much influence media had on whom was still very much a subject of debate.

By the early 1940s, research findings had begun to accumulate, but in some cases they yielded contradictory conclusions. As sociologist Joseph Klapper put it:

> The figure of the pen as mightier than the sword has been modernized by social observers who have claimed that the mass media are more powerful than the atom bomb. Other social observers have scoffed. As the more fearful have pointed to the impressive successes of various propaganda campaigns, the more phlegmatic have pointed to the impressive failures of other campaigns. Neither group has [been able] to find evidence to support its position.[1]

But between the late 1920s and the mid-1940s, the debate over media power began to take a new turn. Media scholars made fewer claims based on speculation, logic, anecdotes, and opinion. Increasingly, they reached their conclusions on the basis of *evidence uncovered by empirical research.* It was a slow and uncertain process at first. The early projects undertaken were uncoordinated with each other, focused on unrelated goals and sometimes based on methods and techniques that were unsophisticated. Nevertheless, as research evidence began to accumulate, it became increasingly clear that the *powerful influences (Magic Bullet) theory was simply inadequate* to describe and explain the effects of mass communications on audiences.

As the present chapter will explain, both the advancement of basic knowledge about the human condition provided by the social sciences and research findings from early media studies seriously challenged the Magic Bullet explanation. The conclusion that the mass media reached every eye and ear uniformly, bringing about immediate and universal effects, was simply *wrong.* A very different explanation was needed to replace it.

An important set of developments, making it possible to conduct systematic research on the processes and effects of mass communication, was that new and basic insights concerning human nature had been discovered and verified by research in both psychology and sociology. Psychologists had abandoned their explanations of human conduct based on inherited instincts—which essentially assumed that all human beings were more or less alike in the genetic factors that motivated and shaped their behavior. As was discussed earlier, that type of explanation was founded on the evolutionary theories of Charles Darwin, who had made a strong case that human beings were simply very complex animals that shared many biological and behavioral characteristics with other creatures arrayed along the phylogenetic continuum. Replacing such explanations were new theories of learning, motivation, perception, attitude, and other behavioral predispositions that explained how each human being is a *unique personality,* different from others, and his or her attributes are developed through socialization in a complex social and cultural environment.

Sociologists, on the other hand, were learning of the importance of various kinds of social groupings and *differences among different categories of people* who made up a population. In understanding social behavior, therefore, much depended on the location of the individual within the social structure. For example, where the person was in the ranking system of society helped shape his or her ideas on conduct. Each socioeconomic class was characterized by distinct lifestyles. Being raised as an upper-class person produced a different human being than being raised poor at the bottom of the social structure. The same was true of being a member in various kinds of groups—either as a child or as an adult. Those in the military, for example, developed a different outlook on life and different patterns of behavior than, say, those in a prison or in a fundamentalist religious community. It became increasingly clear that *unique subcultures,* existing in a variety of such social categories and groups, were truly significant sources for learning how one should think, believe, and behave.

As new behavioral paradigms were being developed in these basic social sciences, and as research methods used in each—experiments, surveys, attitude measurement, longitudinal studies, etc.—became more and more sophisticated, media researchers were able to use these conceptual and methodological tools to press forward the scientific study of the process and effects of mass communication.

A brief review of what was taking place within both psychology and sociology, as the context within which media studies emerged, can be helpful in understanding the directions taken by early mass communication research. Those developments, in turn, provided keys for understanding how theories changed in the study of media influences.

PSYCHOLOGY DISCOVERS THE IMPORTANCE OF INDIVIDUAL DIFFERENCES

During the first half of the twentieth century, psychologists made great strides in discovering how individual differences in personal cognitive organization had a profound influence on human behavior. Early in the century, the theories of Sigmund Freud and other psychoanalysis provided perspectives that seemed to explain many seemingly inexplicable features of human conduct. Repressed memories of early childhood experiences, sexual fantasies, emotional attachments to parents of the opposite sex, and even the nature of dreams were said to shape the choices people made in their lives. Not all psychologists subscribed to Freud's theories, but they clearly represented a new direction away from the explanations of the past. A major feature of the new psychology was an emphasis on *differences* that prevailed between individuals within a given population.

The Basis of Individual Uniqueness

Even in the late 1800s, as the new field of psychology was developing, it became clear that patterns of *attention* differed greatly among human beings. As discussed in Chapter 5, in classic experiments, Wilhelm Wundt and a host of later investigators demonstrated that differences in attention patterns could influence response patterns. Using a variety of so-called "brass instruments," Wundt was able to demonstrate that variations in levels and patterns of attention influenced the way and speed with which experimental subjects responded to stimuli in laboratory settings. Clearly, attention was not a factor uniformly distributed among human beings.

Early in the 1900s, the development of ways to measure *intelligence* was another accomplishment. The measurement of "intelligence quotients" (IQs) using various kinds of tests was routinely accomplished even by the time of World War I. It was clear that IQ was a truly important psychological characteristic that was far from uniform from one individual to the next. Those who scored high in such assessments made different behavioral choices than those who scored lower. All racial and ethnic populations appeared to have the same general or average level of intelligence—and each had a statistically normal distribution, with half of the population at various points below and above the median. However, individuals within these distributions varied greatly. One research project from Army studies produced findings that were startling at the time of the discovery. It was found that African Americans, who had been raised and had gone to school in the North, scored significantly higher on IQ tests than whites who had similar years of schooling in the South. It was obvious that the social environment, and not inherited characteristics, had produced different outcomes. Findings such as these challenged prevailing assumptions about the natural or inborn abilities of the races.

The basis of *perception* came under psychological investigation with special scrutiny during the 1920s. The Gestalt psychologists were able to show how human beings attended to stimuli, processed them psychologically, and interpreted their meanings in characteristic ways. While they sought general patterns and principles, it was clear that there was great *variation* among individual persons in how this psychological task was achieved. That is, people attributed meanings to both simple and complex stimuli in a variety of ways.

The measurement of differences in individual predispositions was another area in which great advances were made. Central to this was the study of *attitudes*. Attitudes were said to be important influences on action. A negative attitude or a positive one was thought to forecast how a particular individual would relate to the object of the attitude. L. L. Thurstone, Rensis Likert, and many other psychologists developed systematic ways to provide quantitative assessments of people in terms of such predispositions to accept or reject, to like or dislike, various features of their physical, social, and cultural environment.

The study of *learning* and *forgetting* also revealed truly significant individual differences within human populations. While *on average* people in every population seemed to be as able to learn at the same rate and level, there was great variation and diversity from one individual to another. Some individuals acquired new forms of behavior or stable habits quickly and easily, while others were much slower to learn. Beginning early in the twentieth century, the study of learning became one of the central focuses of psychology. Differences in intelligence remain a central issue for study even today.

Psychological Factors in Audience Behavior

One of the first things that became apparent, as social scientists turned research attention to the mass media, was that patterns of attention, perception, learning, and retention *varied greatly among audiences.* It was clear, almost from the beginnings of systematic mass communication research, that some people read, understood, and were influenced by newspapers, magazines, or books in distinct and different ways. When movies became a reality, the same pattern was evident. People attended to and interpreted films in different ways. The same generalizations came to be applied to radio, to television, and today, of course, to the use of the Internet.

"Individual differences" in psychological background and personal cognitive organization, then, are at the heart of ways in which people attend to and interpret mass communications. These differences are directly linked to personal interests, habits, preferences, and tastes that are products of prior learning experiences. Thus, as is the case with fingerprints and DNA, no two people are psychologically identical. Each person represents a distinct profile of likes and dislikes, needs, motivations, acceptances and avoidances, prejudices and loyalties, and so on. Thus, when people process any kind of information, including mass media content, *individual differences in psychological organization and functioning will be determining factors in how the individual responds to that information.* That generalization has become a central feature of assumptions that are now made about the process and effects of mass communication.

SOCIOLOGY DISCOVERS THE IMPORTANCE OF SOCIAL FACTORS

As the sociologists of the nineteenth century saw industrialization and urbanization in the Western world changing the social order from traditional to mass societies (*Gemeinschaft* to *Gesellschaft*), they assumed that individuals were increasingly being cut off from traditional social ties. They were becoming what David Reisman would characterize, decades later, as a "lonely crowd."[2] That is, people were assumed to be leading lives of personal isolation, anonymity, and anomie—even though (as Durkheim had maintained) they were held together in their society by their interlocking role activities and dependencies. We noted in Chapter 6 the theoretical model of the "mass society" that emerged from this type of analysis.

From Social Uniformity to Social Diversity

In more modern times sociologists changed that model. As they began uncovering the factual nature of modern societies, they had to abandon the concept of the mass society. Beginning in the 1920s, a different view of modern society began to replace it. However, it remained clear that the urban-industrial social order was one of *great diversity*. At first, that diversity was interpreted as the foundation of the "lonely crowd" idea. Large numbers of immigrants had poured into the United States, making its residents culturally dissimilar to each other. Diverse people relocated from farms and villages to cities. Moreover, the Industrial Revolution had greatly expanded the division of labor. Their differing roles in the occupational labor force, their income, level of educational attainment, and their occupational prestige, it was assumed, effectively identified where people fit into very different socio-economic strata (class levels), which further isolated people from each other.

Generally, then, modern societies were characterized by a large number of *distinctive social categories*. That is, people could be classified in a variety of ways, based on religion, ethnicity, occupational position, educational attainment, racial identity, nationality of origin, political affiliation, economic worth, and so on. These social and cultural characteristics, it was believed, were what made individuals *very different from each other*, bringing each person to respond to various features of his or her environment in totally individualistic ways—including the mass media.

The Discovery of Subcultures

What had not been apparent to the sociologists who had studied and analyzed these new social categories of people was the fact that *within each* of the major groupings their similarities brought them together. Thus, poor Italians of Catholic faith and immigrant background, who lived in a particular neighborhood and worked at modest jobs, *all had similar lifestyles.* They all faced similar problems, which they tended to deal with in similar ways. This often led them to behave in parallel and predictable ways. In the same manner, white upper-middle-class people who had moved to affluent suburbs at the edge of the city were also drawn together, facing the same problems, having similar interests, and *developing similar lifestyles.* Members of such categories, then, developed somewhat uniform patterns of thinking and action as they collectively coped with their environment. These patterns came to be called *subcultures.*

Generally, then, it soon became clear that much of the behavior of a given individual was linked to *social category membership.* Members of such categories tended to share a set of distinctive norms, rather uniform beliefs and mutually expected patterns of action. Sociologists began to study and describe those lifestyles as they observed such categories as blue-collar assembly line workers, street corner youths in the central city, prison inmates, families living in middle-class suburbs, teenagers in high school, young black males in blighted neighborhoods, upper-middle-class professionals, and so on. The unique ways of life and belief structures of these local subcultures explained a great deal about why one person would study hard, postpone gratification, and struggle to succeed, while another would gain status and prestige by carrying out deviant behavior or engage in criminal activities.

Social category membership in many cases, then, corresponded to a subculture in which an individual participated, shaping many of the person's preferences and choices. The implications were that *patterns of interpersonal ties and social relationships that people have with each other, plus their location within a complex set of social categories, are critical factors in explaining their behavior in a variety of settings.* This complex principle helped explain the individual differences psychologists were finding in patterns of cognitive processing, perception, learning, predispositions, and all the rest. As social scientists and other researchers turned their attention to the mass media, it also became an important principle that would play a key part in developing theories concerning the process and effects of mass communication.

With the individual differences and social categories paradigms in place, thinking about mass communication took a new turn. The earliest investigators were social scientists who saw that the media being developed could bring critical influences on populations. They designed research and developed theories that they hoped would lead to better understandings of the influences and functions of the media in modern society. It was not an easy task. A huge accumulation of research evidence would be required before the influences of mass communication would be adequately understood. Moreover, these efforts did not begin in a vacuum. The print media had long been in existence, and many intellectuals had speculated about their influences on individuals and society. Thus, there was already in place a body of opinions and speculative conclusions about the power of the media to influence the thoughts and actions of individuals who attended to their content. As it turned out, much of that body of ideas would prove to be largely incorrect, and much of it would have to be swept aside before research would provide more valid answers.

WORLD WAR I PROPAGANDA AS AN INFLUENCE ON MEDIA THEORY

In retrospect, the Magic Bullet Theory now seems counterintuitive and even naive. How was it, then, that those who tried to understand the influences of the mass media of the time were so seriously misled? Why did they assume that newspapers, and even the brand new motion pictures of the period, had such power to influence people in similar ways? One reason, as has been discussed earlier, was the explanations of the human condition and the mainsprings of human conduct that prevailed during the late 1800s. Such factors as instincts and assumptions about the isolation of the individual in the new industrial society predicted a uniformity of action among human beings.

However, another major source of beliefs about the power of mass communication to shape and control the beliefs and behavior of individuals was the experience provided by the use of the media for propaganda purposes in World War I. In fact, there are grounds for concluding that the beginning of theory development concerning the influences of mass communication began as a result of the efforts of propagandists during that time. It does seem clear that those efforts played a part in alerting social scientists to the potential power of mass communications to influence entire populations.

World War I was a global conflict in which entire nations—not just soldiers on the battlefield—took part. It was a war in which factory and farm production, as well as morale and political support among people at home, were as important as victories in the trenches. That is, the military might of both the Axis and the Allied powers depended not only on the willingness of families to sacrifice their young men but also on the motivation of civilian workers and farmers who were producing the necessities of war. It was quickly realized, on both sides of the conflict, that if those civilian contributors could be discouraged, it could hamper their commitment and their productivity. By the same token, if they could be strongly motivated, remain deeply patriotic, and work even harder with increased dedication to the cause, that enthusiasm could provide a significant advantage that might well influence the ultimate outcome.

The Need for Propaganda

As the Great War started, it was quickly realized that the answer to getting populations to make significant sacrifices and dedicate themselves vigorously to war effort was to *disseminate effective motivational messages.* This required the controlled use of every available medium to transmit messages continuously to large audiences. Such messages had to be designed to show the vicious and brutal nature of the enemy and the pure and noble characteristics of one's own side. Between 1914 and 1918, professional communicators on both sides went to work to accomplish this goal with a vengeance:

> Carefully designed propaganda messages engulfed the nation in news stories, pictures, films, phonograph records, speeches, books, sermons, posters, wireless signals, rumors, billboard advertisements and handbills. Top-level policy makers decided that the stakes were so high and the ends so important that they justified almost any means. Citizens had to hate the enemy, love their country and maximize their commitment to the war effort. They could not be depended upon to do this on their own. The mass media of communication available at the time became the principal tools for persuading them.[3]

It was a time of public innocence regarding the nature of propaganda. Even the word was virtually unknown by most people. As a consequence, these efforts did not come under public suspicion, and they were enormously successful as *media-generated constructions of reality.*

Later, after the war, the role of the propagandists was strongly criticized. Much of what they had claimed was patently false. Neither the Axis nor the Allied leaders or soldiers were the brutal monsters portrayed in the propaganda, but entire populations on both sides had learned from these messages that the enemy was truly evil and that all righteous people had valid reasons to hate them. They also learned that their own cause was just, that God was on their side, and that the great sacrifices they were making were required in order to save humanity.

Propaganda's Remarkable Success

In short, *propaganda worked—and to a remarkable degree.* As it turned out, the Allied Powers, and especially the British, were particularly effective in the use of propaganda, but the Germans had their own experts who were also successful. The persuasive messages transmitted by both sides reached their intended audiences directly and easily because virtually everyone was, understandably, vitally interested in the progress and outcome of the war. Moreover, on both sides, the simple and repetitive messages of the propagandists were not resisted and were widely understood in precisely the ways intended by their designers.

Because these mass-communicated efforts were so successful, a belief was generated following the war that the *mass media could readily control the beliefs and behavior of the multitude.* The propaganda messages did indeed seem like "magic bullets" that reached every eye and ear to produce relatively uniform results immediately in all who received them. These were, of course, the basic propositions of the Magic Bullet Theory, which was discussed in Chapter 9. It was presented there as a set of formal and interrelated propositions. While, as was made clear, the theory was never put together in that systematic way at that time, the basic ideas of that theory were well understood as World War I came to a close. The great lesson offered by the overwhelming success achieved by propaganda during the war was that *the media had great power to influence the beliefs and behavior of virtually everyone in their audiences.* Thus, the underlying ideas of the Magic Bullet Theory appeared to be valid.

EARLY MOVIE RESEARCH SEEMED TO SUPPORT THE MAGIC BULLET THEORY

Another source of support for the belief that the media have great power came from a large-scale research project conducted by social scientists a few years after the war. The project has come to be called the Payne Fund Studies. It was a series of investigations of the effects of the movies on children.[4] A case can be made that it was with this investigation that the field of mass communication research in an empirical sense most effectively got its start. As noted, its focus was on the movies. Radio was just becoming a home medium, and it did not seem all that powerful.

However, by the 1920s, the film industry had been thriving in the United States for more than a decade. Indeed, the movies had become the recreation of choice for citizens of virtually every category, and the average family attended more than once a week. Kids could get into a Saturday afternoon matinee for only a dime. Among those going to the movies on a weekly basis were approximately 17 million children under the age of fourteen.

Why the Movies Seemed Powerful

The content of the movies of the late 1920s, and the influences they were suspected of having on children, began to disturb many thoughtful people—parents, teachers, educators, and religious leaders. The reason was that films were routinely presenting depictions of crimes being committed, of people drinking alcohol (during a time of prohibition), of men and women together in bedrooms, and of gangsters who had fast cars and even faster girlfriends. Indeed, by the late 1920s, some films were even showing females in their undergarments—at a time when the majority of the population had barely emerged from the Victorian era of conservative dress and morality.

Many critics deplored this type of movie content and concluded that the youth of the nation were at risk—that they were being influenced to adopt lower moral standards and to emulate the unacceptable behavior shown in the films. However, adding to the concerns of the public, as W. W. Charters—a distinguished media scholar of the time—noted, the influence of the movies was *poorly understood*:

> Motion pictures are not understood by the present generation of adults. They are new; they make an enormous appeal to children; and they present ideas and situations which parents may not like. Consequently, when parents think of the welfare of their children who are exposed to these compelling situations, they wonder about the effects of the pictures upon the ideals and behavior of the children. . . . In short, just what effect do motion pictures have upon children of different ages?[5]

It was becoming increasingly clear that answers were needed. Motion picture producers were coming under pressure to "clean up" their portrayals, and they were increasingly anxious about possible intervention and control by government. It is important to note that the content of films was *not protected by the First Amendment* at the time (that would not become the case until the 1950s). This meant that politicians could step in and literally shut down the industry if the public demanded it.

As was explained earlier, another factor in this set of developments was the increasing sophistication of the social sciences. New tools for research had been developed in the form of attitude scales, experimental designs, survey techniques, and inferential statistics. It was now possible to conduct research making use of quantitative measurements, scientific samples, well-crafted experiments, and probability theory for decision making. Armed with new concepts, new understandings of the individual and social nature of human beings, plus an increasingly sophisticated methodology, a number of social scientists were eager to study the influences of the movies using these tools. However, there were no government agencies providing grants for behavioral research, and a major barrier was where to find the funding to support such efforts.

Large-Scale Research Begins

In 1928, these elements came together to launch the first truly large-scale study of the influences of a medium of mass communication. William H. Short—executive director of the Motion Picture Research Council—proposed to a group of social scientists and educators that they conduct a series of scientific studies aimed at uncovering the *influence of movies on children*. He had obtained a commitment from a private philanthropic foundation—the Payne Fund—to cover the rather considerable expenses. As a result, a number of prominent scholars in psychology, sociology, and education agreed to design and conduct specific types of studies.

The efforts of these researchers continued over three years. The scope of the project was impressive. Thirteen specific studies were undertaken between 1929 and 1932. Their findings were published in ten volumes in the early 1930s. Under investigation were issues such as the following: (1) the content and themes of 1,500 films, (2) the frequency of attendance by different age categories of children (average was once a week), (3) the retention of factual information from films, (4) the influence of films on childrens' attitudes toward selected racial and ethnic categories and toward selected social issues, (5) the capacity of films to arouse childrens' emotions, (6) how seeing certain types of films interrupted childrens' sleep, (7) the influence of films on standards of morality, (8) the relationship between exposure to films and specific forms of conduct—including delinquency and crime.

Each of the studies involved hundreds of subjects, or even thousands in some cases, and the findings seemed clear. The overall conclusion was that the movies were having *strong influences on children*. There is no need to set forth in full detail the conclusions of this massive project. A summary of the results can be found in W. W. Charters' overview volume.[6] What is significant about all of this research is that what these early media investigators concluded seemed to reinforce the basic ideas of the Magic Bullet Theory—*the movies had powerful influences on children*. Understandably, the public became alarmed, and the entire effort played a part during the 1930s in the imposition by the movie industry itself of a rigid "code" governing what content could be shown in films.

Controversial Results

Following their publication, however, two things happened regarding the Payne Fund studies. One was that the research methods used in the film studies received harsh criticism from some academic research specialists. Some of the projects were, in fact, not up to the methodological standards that had recently come to be expected in the social sciences. However, the public was not in a position to understand such criticisms and did not take them seriously. They dismissed the methodological debates as unimportant. They saw them as arguments about fine points of navigation that were taking place while the ship was sinking. It seemed clear to most citizens that the movies were offering objectionable content and that all children who attended were at risk.

A second challenge to the conclusions from the Payne Fund studies came from additional research that began to accumulate in the years that followed. Increasingly, their conclusions, which many saw as paralleling the assumptions of the Magic Bullet Theory, came under increased scrutiny. Eventually, however, that theory was abandoned. But the demise of the Magic Bullet explanation did not take place quickly or as a result of one or two dramatic research efforts. What happened was that as systematic research on mass communication slowly began to accumulate, beginning in the late 1930s, the idea that all members of an audience reacted similarly and immediately to a mass-communicated message was increasingly seen to have significant flaws. Eventually, the Magic Bullet Theory had to be replaced with one that was more consistent with the facts.

The new theory, which eventually came to be called the *Selective and Limited Influences Theory*, was also never set forth at the time as a set of interrelated formal propositions. Nevertheless, it became increasingly understood by those who were conducting media research that the audiences, toward whom a particular radio broadcast, newspaper story, film, or other form of mass communications were directed, *attended selectively* and that the influences of particular forms of content on their ideas and behavior were *clearly limited*.

THE MAGIC BULLET THEORY IS DISCREDITED

Four studies can be mentioned that were conducted during the late 1930s and early 1940s that offered challenges to the earlier Magic Bullet Theory and ultimately caused it to be discredited. One was a study of a dramatic radio play depicting an invasion of Earth by Martians—to which many people responded in an extreme way. Another was an investigation of a series of radio programs intended to raise tolerance of a number of ethnic groups within the American population. A third sought to understand why people selected particular stories to read from their daily newspaper and ignored others. Still a fourth was conducted by the U.S. Army in the early years of World War II, in an attempt to influence newly drafted soldiers' commitments to the war effort and their attitudes toward the enemy.

The Invasion from Mars: Individual Differences and Selective Audience Responses

In October 1938, the United States was invaded by dreadful creatures from Mars, who wreaked havoc in the New Jersey area where they initially landed and began a deadly poison gas assault as they moved toward New York City. At least that was what some six million Americans heard on the night of October 30, as they listened to a radio play presented in a "you are there" news style. It was a dramatic adaptation of the H. G. Wells 1896 novel *War of the Worlds*, which had described similar events. It was a clever and creative radio play designed for Halloween entertainment and presented by the CBS Mercury Theater On The Air—a popular weekly broadcast.

The play, like the novel on which it was based, was a masterpiece. Authentic-sounding actors played parts as astronomers, high-level political authorities, journalists, military leaders, and victims of the Martians. In the short time of an hour's broadcast, the invaders were fought fiercely, but for Earthlings it was a losing cause. Even bombing the invaders from the air did no good. The Martians prevailed, and Earth was clearly doomed. At the end of the program listeners heard only a lone radio voice, plaintively asking, "Isn't anyone on the air? Isn't there anyone there?"

As an immediate result of the broadcast, at least a million terrified people reacted in panic. Telephone switchboards all over the country were swamped. However, many listeners did not check with local authorities by phone—or anyone else—to see if the broadcast was genuine. In fact, most who panicked did not even switch their dials to other radio stations to see if things there were normal. Among those who were frightened by the broadcast, some blindly threw grandma, the kids, and a few groceries into the car and headed for the hills to get away from the Martians. Others simply hid in their basement, cried, or gave up, praying for their survival. In the days that followed, the radio network came under intense criticism for what had taken place.

Seeing an opportunity to study panic behavior on a large scale, Professor Hadley Cantril, a social psychologist at Princeton University, quickly organized a research project to try to determine why some members of the audience were so strongly influenced by the broadcast while others were not.[7] This researcher and his associates were social psychologists, and they were not routinely or specifically interested in the influences of mass communication. Their focus was on the panic behavior that followed the broadcast and not on the media content that triggered it. They sought to understand (1) the extent of the panic; (2) why this particular broadcast frightened a large number of people, while other fantastic plays on radio did not; and (3) what personal characteristics of (individual differences among) audience members caused the Mars broadcast to frighten some listeners but not others.

It was the last question, regarding the *selective influence* on some members of the audience who attended to the play, but not on others who also heard the broadcast, that actually addressed an important issue in mass communication. That is, out of some 16 million who attended to the program, only 1 million had panicked. That pattern of selective influence did not fit the predictions of the Magic Bullet Theory. If that theory was correct, then *all* who heard the broadcast should have responded in a uniform way. Cantril and his associates did not put their project together as a search for evidence on the validity of any theory of mass communication. As noted, their interest was in what cognitive factors motivated some people to panic in response to the radio play. Yet by re-examining what they found, it is clear that their results offered a direct and serious challenge the Magic Bullet Theory.

The researchers conducted in-depth personal interviews with a total of 135 carefully selected individuals, beginning shortly after the broadcast. Of those interviewed, 107 were selected because the broadcast had actually frightened them. The remaining 28, who had not been frightened, served as a comparison or "control group" so that their differences could be identified. While this study was limited in scope, and the persons interviewed cannot be regarded as a representative sample of the population as a whole, the results offer significant evidence regarding the limitations of the Magic Bullet Theory.

Essentially, the researchers found that there were important individual differences between those who checked to see and then decided that the broadcast was a clever play, and those who thought that it was a genuine news broadcast. One important difference was the listener's *religiosity*—that is, strength of religious beliefs. Those with strong beliefs were much more likely to think that the invasion was real—an act of God—and a clear sign that "the end was near." Assessments were made of listeners' personality characteristics that seemed to distinguish those who were frightened from those who were not. For example, those who were susceptible to panic were more likely to be characterized by emotional insecurity, various phobias (irrational fears), limited self-confidence, and a belief that their lives were controlled by mysterious powers. Thus, *individual differences* in personality traits, that is, in psychological makeup, was identified as an important factor in shaping how people attended to and responded to this particular radio program.

Overall, the researchers concluded that the most important personal factor was *critical ability*—the kind of "common sense" one needs to check out an unfamiliar situation. That factor appeared to be the most important variable that separated those who panicked from those who did not. Additionally, the *social context of listening* was also related to whether a person would panic. If a person tuned in at the request of frightened friends, it was more likely that he or she would believe the event was real. Other social relationships also separated the susceptible from those who sorted out the situation correctly. A listener who heard the broadcast together with other members of the family or friends, who were skeptical and who checked with someone by phone or who switched to other stations, were not strongly influenced.

Seen from the perspective of mass communication theory, then, these findings were clearly *inconsistent* with a magic bullet interpretation, in which all who attend to a mass communication are immediately and equally influenced. Instead, Cantril's results revealed very *selective* patterns of attention, interpretation, and influence. Some people attended without checking to see if it was real, but others did not. Some thought the Martians had landed, but others did not. Some went into panic, but others did not. Each of these modes of response was related to various personal and social characteristics of the listener. In other words, the entire body of research findings suggested a more selective and limited audience response to the broadcast, rather than a uniform and universally powerful one.

It must be kept in mind, however, that one research project is not enough, either to support or depose a deeply established theory. Cantril's study seemed to offer a significantly new way of looking at the process of mass communication and its effects, but it would take more than a single study to reformulate the thinking of social scientists, media scholars, and members of the public who still had the lessons of World War I propaganda before them. However, as additional studies accumulated, it became increasingly clear that a new theoretical perspective was needed to understand the influence of the media.

Social Categories That Shape Selective Media Attention

By the 1930s, radio was a widely used mass medium. At the end of that decade, a radio receiver could be found in virtually every home and in almost all recently manufactured cars. Moreover, stations all over the country were linked into several networks.

In 1940, Paul F. Lazarsfeld, a pioneer in media research, used radio to achieve a pro-social goal. He studied responses to a series of programs designed to increase the acceptance of, and tolerance toward, several ethnic groups (e.g., Italians, Poles, and so on) in the United States. A number of programs were broadcast, each focusing on a different nation of origin:

> The purpose was to teach tolerance of other nationalities. The indications were, however, that the audience for each program consisted mainly of the nationality group that was currently being praised. There was little chance for the program to teach tolerance because the self-selection of each audience produced a body of listeners who heard only about the contributions of a country which each already approved.[8]

Observations such as this openly challenged the idea that audience response was immediate, direct, uniform, and powerful. Evidence was making it increasingly clear that people attended to the media in very selective ways. That is, personal traits and characteristics played a part, and the social categories into which people could be grouped were also a factor. As research continued to accumulate, and as the social sciences increasingly unraveled the ways in which personal traits and social category memberships influenced virtually all forms of behavior, the foundation was in place for a new theoretical perspective emphasizing the selective nature of attention to media content and its limited influence on members of the audience.

Factors in Attention to News Stories

Another study that contributed to that foundation was research by Bernard Berelson—a well-known social scientist. Again, just before America's entry into World War II in 1941, he studied how people paid attention and were influenced by information encountered in the media. More specifically, he studied the role of *print*, as well as other media, in informing people about important public issues of the day—and thereby playing a part in shaping public opinion. He studied "two representative groups living in a small Midwest county notable for its conformity in opinion to the country as a whole. Both groups were selected as typical of their country in most respects."[9]

Personal interviews revealed what led people to attend to coverage of specific topics and events around which public opinion was formed. Prominent among them were two factors. One, of course, was the nature of the topic itself. Some were simply more prominent or important to virtually everyone than others (e.g., in the 1940 presidential election, assessing the contribution of Franklin Roosevelt's New Deal to ending the Great Depression was an important topic). In other words, some topics reported in the press attracted a great deal of attention because of their significance at the time.

The second factor influencing selective attention was what Berelson called the *personal predispositions* of members of the audience. That is, each individual has social characteristics that predispose the person to be interested in certain kinds of topics and less interested in others. As Berelson explained:

> By this we mean the whole complex of social characteristics—income, occupation, age and sex, religion, group memberships, and so forth—which inclines people confronted with public issues to respond in certain ways and not in others. . . . Predispositions tend to increase the recognition of [arguments the person favors] and decrease the recognition of unfavorable arguments.[10]

Essentially, Berelson was referring to predispositions based on membership in various kinds of *social categories* into which people could be classified—whether by ethnic identity, as reported by Lazarsfeld, or with respect to the lengthy list of memberships and classifications provided by Berelson. It was becoming clearer that such social identities play a central role in shaping patterns of attention to the mass media.

Army Film Studies: Different Effects on Different People from the Same Content

On December 7, 1941, airplanes from Japanese carriers suddenly and unexpectedly attacked American naval vessels and other military targets in Pearl Harbor, near Honolulu. They reduced a number of battleships and other vessels of the U.S. Pacific Fleet to ruins and devastated various bases and installations, with a significant loss of life. The next day, President Roosevelt called a special session of Congress, declaring that December 7, 1941, was "a date that will live in infamy." He announced that a state of war existed with Japan and the other Axis countries that were its allies.

It was a trying time for the United States, which was poorly prepared to enter a full-scale war of worldwide proportions. There was an instant need to rebuild the Navy, greatly accelerate war production, and, above all, add millions of young men (and some women) to the armed services. It was a time of great patriotism. Early on, thousands and thousands of young people dropped what they were doing and volunteered for one of the military services. For those men who did not volunteer, the draft brought them into the armed forces. Few resisted; virtually everyone shared a conviction that the country now had a highly significant moral mission to fight back and defeat despicable enemies. The problem was how to gear up to do so as quickly as possible.

To turn citizens into soldiers in the least possible time, the U.S. Army set up recruit training camps in all parts of the country. Some 15 million young men and several thousands of young women went into the military service. In recruit training they were taught about military matters, such as close-order drill, the use of weapons, proper wearing of uniforms, whom to salute, and all the rest. Then they were sorted into various special assignments that the Army needed. Some became cooks, clerks, or copilots; others became signal specialists, combat medics, or truck drivers, and so on. Others were assigned to fighter or bomber groups, artillery or tank units that would confront the enemy. Large numbers went to infantry units that would directly engage the enemy on the battlefield.

It was with the latter categories that the Army was especially concerned. Those who would see combat faced the most critical and dangerous tasks. Their motivation and commitment to the war was absolutely vital. Immediately it became apparent to Army officials that many of the people entering the service actually had very little knowledge about what had led up to the war or why the U.S. had become involved. Most had heard of Pearl Harbor, of course, but beyond that they had little knowledge of Japan, its industrial capacity, its recent history of war in China, or its objectives in attacking the American bases at Pearl Harbor. Similarly, many understood that Germany had been at war with England since 1939 and had overrun Europe, but they knew little about the Nazis, the *Wehrmacht* and its *Blitzkreig* tactics, the *Luftwaffe* and the Battle of Britain, and so on. It was necessary, the high command of the Army believed, that they be taught the basics of these recent events and issues so that they would understand *why they had to fight*. Only by teaching these new soldiers what their enemies were like, and the evil nature of what they had done, could they expect to increase the recruits' dedication and raise their morale to press on with a long and difficult war.

To accomplish these multiple objectives—teach a body of facts about the enemy, establish a belief in the right of the American cause, and generally increase motivation to pursue the war, the Army had a series of motion pictures produced. The series was called *Why We Fight*. Each film showed some aspect of the war, presenting much factual material, and each included persuasive content intended to accomplish the Army's objectives. Aside from their general use as part of military training, several of the films were systematically shown to a group of recruits in experimental settings to evaluate whether the motion pictures achieved the objectives—to see what influences they had on these recruits.

One of the most interesting features of these film studies is that there was no problem of selective attention and exposure. The recruits were simply marched to the building where the films were shown. They then viewed them under the watchful eyes of tough sergeants. No one went to sleep, read a magazine, munched on popcorn, or whispered to his buddies. Afterward, under the same close supervision, the recruits filled out questionnaires assessing the influence of the films. The result was a very "clean" experimental situation. The recruits all attended to the stimulus in a uniform manner (not unlike the audience behavior that had been assumed by the Magic Bullet theory). Afterward, assessments were made to see if the films had a direct and immediate influence on their audience. That is, the beliefs and feelings of the recruits were measured by the tests of factual material and by the various opinion and attitude scales used in the experiment.

The results were clear—but in many ways they were disappointing. The soldiers did *learn a lot of factual information* from the films. In the movies they saw the military might that the Germans had developed and what the Japanese had done at Pearl Harbor. Thus, most understood better the nature of the enemy that they faced. However, the films had little influence on the general opinions about allied nations and virtually no influence at all on the motivations of the men to serve as soldiers during a long war to come. Thus, in many ways the films *failed* in their most basic mission, to raise the morale and the commitment of the recruits.

What the researchers did uncover, of more lasting significance, was the *variability* of the influences among the recruits who saw the films. One factor producing that variability that stood out was *intellectual ability*. The soldiers had been assessed on this variable by the Army with standard IQ-type tests. Not surprisingly, those who earned the highest scores (indicating greater intellectual ability) learned more factual information than those who had performed lower on the test. Similarly, *educational attainment* separated those who had greater opinion shifts from those who did not. The better educated showed larger shifts in opinions about both the enemy and the allies than those with lower levels of schooling (perhaps because they understood the content of the films better). Overall, the effects of the films can be summarized in the following terms:

> Increased educational attainment led to increased levels of initial knowledge. However, it also led to learning more factual material from the film. On opinion change, the more complex the issue and facts concerning it, the more likely that opinion change would be primarily among the more educated men. Those of lower levels tended to change their opinions on issues of lesser complexity, less well supported by the facts, and on issues that more educated men found difficult to accept.[11]

The Army film studies showed clearly that the effects of mass-communicated content were both *selective* and *limited*. Because the soldiers were required to go to the films, and they had to attend closely once they were in the theater, selective attention was ruled out as an influence on the variability among the effects of what they viewed. The results showed that individual variations in personal traits and characteristics (individual differences) among the members in the audience played a key role in the influences achieved by a mass-communicated message.

Overall, from the research of the late 1930s and early 1940s, the idea of selective and limited attention on the part of the public came to be seen as an important factor limiting the power of the media to influence people equally. In addition, research showed clearly that both personal and social characteristics brought about selective and limited influences even when variations in attention were not a factor. As a result, a new theory had to be developed to replace the magic bullet theory, which simply had to be abandoned totally by this time (although it remains in the minds of many members of the public as they discuss the influences of the media even today). It was replaced by what can be called the Selective and Limited Influences Theory—a formulation that emerged from the early research cited in this chapter, plus other studies that also made a contribution.[12]

THE SELECTIVE AND LIMITED INFLUENCES THEORY: A FORMAL SUMMARY

As the 1940s moved on and additional research accumulated, it became clear to research scholars studying the media that *different kinds of people selected different kinds of content from the media and interpreted that content in different ways.* The body of research had been conducted within the framework of science, and making use of the conceptual paradigms and methodological tools of the social sciences, that led to this understanding. As a result, this principle was increasingly understood within the research community, if not among the general public. That is not to say that the media have no influences on people. As theories to be presented in later chapters will show, they very definitely do but not in the way that was assumed at an earlier time.

As has been explained, at the time when the theory's central ideas became clear, it was never formulated systematically as a as a set of formal and interrelated assumptions from which logical prediction could be drawn. In retrospect, however, the propositions of the theory can be summarized in the following terms:

1. People in contemporary society are characterized by great psychological diversity, due to learned *individual differences* in their psychological makeup.
2. People are also members of a variety of *social categories*, based on such factors as income level, religion, age, gender, and many more. Such categories are characterized by *subcultures* of shared beliefs, attitudes, and values.
3. People in contemporary society are not isolated but are bound together in webs of *social relationships* based on family, neighborhood ties, and work relationships.
4. People's individual differences, social category subcultures, and patterns of social relationships lead them to be interested in, attend to, and interpret the content of mass communication in *very selective ways.*
5. **Therefore**, because attention to media messages is highly selective and interpretation of content varies greatly from person to person, any specific mass-communicated message will have only *limited effects on an audience as a whole.*

As research continued into later decades, there was no return to the outmoded conception of the past—the idea that people reacted to powerful media immediately and uniformly. The variables and factors in paradigms that had been developed in the basic social sciences to explain human conduct at the individual and collective levels continue to provide conceptual frameworks guiding further investigation of the influences of mass communication.

Even today, although the Theory of Selective and Limited Influences does not address many aspects of the mass communication process, it *remains unquestionably valid.* In addition, it does hold true—even though it may not fit the beliefs of contemporary families who remain concerned about the influence of television on their children. Many in the public "just know" that tragic shootings in schools are a direct result of depictions of violence seen in the movies, on TV, in video games, or via the Internet. However, beginning in the late 1930s, the scholarly and research communities, armed with effective methodologies, moved beyond opinion, speculation, and *a priori* conclusions that were not based on empirical evidence. Thus, beginning about the time of World War II, an accumulation of research findings has provided the foundation for reassessing the power and influences of mass communications.

THE ACCUMULATION PROCESS: THE "ADDING UP" OF LIMITED INFLUENCES

The fact that a specific episode of mass communication content seldom has an immediate and powerful effect on an audience—and that those influences can be selective and limited—does not mean that significant influences never occur from what people encounter in the media. On some occasions, and under certain conditions, messages presented by the media can have powerful influences on people. This may seem like a contradiction. That is, the selected and limited influences theory predicts that few people will be significantly changed in terms of their beliefs, attitudes, or behavior as a result of receiving *a particular message* from the media. However, what can be called Accumulation Theory indicates the opposite—that under certain circumstances, mass communications can change people's ideas and actions in major ways. In other words, both of these theories can be correct *depending on certain features, conditions, and circumstances that are present.*

The following example can illustrate the point: What would be the likelihood today that the United States would undertake to invade a small and impoverished country about the size of Louisiana, located on the east coast of Africa? This country has never been a threat to the United States or even to its neighbors. It had no effective military force, no oil, no missiles, no weapons of mass destruction, and not much of anything else of value. Given those features, it does not seem too likely that people would see such an invasion as justified. However, in 1993, then President George Bush (Sr.) sent a powerful military force to *Somalia* to subdue those who were in positions of power. The majority of people in the United States applauded, as did much of the rest of the world.

An important question is this: How could that come about? What could possibly lead most Americans to see such a military invasion as a justified act? Looked at from a mass communication perspective, it seems likely that public approval was in many ways a result of what the media had been presenting concerning Somalia. It was a time when conditions in that poor country were in turmoil. A number of "warlords" were fighting each other, disrupting the stable life of the country. Their conflicts prevented people from raising their crops, and as a result many in Somalia were starving. The warlords blocked efforts by international humanitarian organizations to deliver food and relieve their plight.

The population's misery caught the attention of news media. As a result, night after night, Americans saw on their television screens, as well as in other media, pictures of pathetic, hungry people in Somalia. They saw little children who looked like walking skeletons, with the bloated bellies of the starving. They saw adults with stick-like limbs who had nothing to eat but leaves. It was truly painful to watch, and it caused a surge of compassion among Americans and among people in other nations as well. When the United States invaded in order to alleviate the misery, people all over the world applauded.

Looking at this situation from a mass communication standpoint, what was presented to American audiences were *repeated portrayals of suffering people that were consistent, persistent*, and *corroborative.* That is, the situation presented by the media was uniformly portrayed in the same basic way by all of the media over a lengthy period. Moreover, it was universally deplored. No one used the media to proclaim that these pathetic people deserved their plight or that it would be wrong to try to help them. The condemnation of the warlords was uniform. No one took their side to defend or justify their actions.

Under those three conditions, then, there was an accumulation over time of beliefs and attitudes that the United States should "do something" to relieve the situation. That did not happen as a result of a single message but as an *accumulation of minimal influences* that eventually "added up" to widespread approval for the military action.

On a less dramatic note, there are many such themes, topics, or issues that have been treated in a similar way by the media, with an accumulation of minimal influences that have led to change. For example, public service announcements have for many years advised people to wear seatbelts when in their automobiles. That theme has also been emphasized in local news reports that describe serious auto accidents. Often, the fact that the occupants of damaged vehicles were not wearing seatbelts is mentioned in the story—along with the fact that they were either killed or seriously injured. As a result, there are now few people in the population who are not aware of this advice, and the use of such belts has increased greatly over a half century.

Another long-term influence has been on the dangers of starting forest fires. A cartoon-like character (Smokey the Bear) has been seen by Americans in various media for many decades. Smokey's message is known by almost everyone (*"Only YOU can prevent forest fires!"*). In fact, that message is so well established as part of the American culture that many citizens were deeply disturbed when the Forest Service planned to start back fires deliberately in an effort to contain some blazes that had gotten out of control.

Another important example is smoking. Only a few decades ago, few paid much attention to the hazards of smoking. Then, the Surgeon General cited research showing its harmful effects. This idea became a frequent topic in media presentations. As that went on over a long period of time in a consistent, persistent, and corroborative way, the rates of smoking gradually fell in the U.S. Today, people understand the risks, and laws are now in place that have altered where smokers can pursue their habit. Another example of an effect "adding up" is the use of the media to persuade people to exercise. Much the same is taking place today as the nation has recognized that it has a problem with obesity.

THE ACCUMULATION OF MINIMAL EFFECTS THEORY: A FORMAL SUMMARY

Generally, then, the media can indeed have what amount to powerful effects—but almost never as a result of a single message. Instead, such influences more often occur over a long period of time. If that takes place, the content they present must be *consistent, persistent,* and *corroborative.* This feature of media influences can be expressed in propositions as follows:

1. The mass media begin to focus their attention on and transmit messages about a *specific topic* (some problem, situation, or issue).
2. Over an extended period, they continue to do so in a relatively *consistent* and *persistent* way, and their presentations *corroborate* each other.
3. Individual members of the public increasingly become aware of these messages, and on a person-by-person basis, a *growing comprehension* develops of the interpretations of the topic being presented by the media.
4. Increasing comprehension among the audience of the messages supplied by the media begins to *form or modify* the meanings, beliefs, and attitudes that serve as guides to individual behavior regarding the topic.
5. **Therefore**, as individual-by-individual changes in beliefs and attitudes *accumulate*, new shared norms emerge, resulting in widespread changes in audience behavior toward the topic.

Generally, then, a strong case can be made that mass communications do not have the immediate, uniform, and powerful effects that media scholars once thought they did. As knowledge accumulated in the social sciences, the influences of the media, and how they come about, slowly became increasingly clear. Individual differences and the influences of social and cultural conditions brought people to attend to mass communications selectively. It became clear that their influences of any particular message they received was seldom more than minimal. At the same time, however, if the media presented a particular topic or situation persistently, consistently, and in a corroborative way, there could be an accumulation of those minimal effects that could bring significant changes in people's beliefs, attitudes, and behavior.

Notes and References

1. Joseph T. Klapper, *The Effects of Mass Communication* (Glencoe, Il: The Free Press of Glencoe, 1960), p. 12.
2. David Riesman, *The Lonely Crowd* (New Haven: Yale University Press, 1969).
3. Melvin L. DeFleur, *Theories of Mass Communication*, 3rd ed. (New York: David McKay Company, 1966), p. 113.
4. W. W. Charters, *Motion Pictures and Youth: A Summary* (New York: Macmillan, 1933).
5. *Ibid.* p. v.
6. W. W. Charters, *op. cit.*
7. Hadley Cantril, *The Invasion from Mars: A Study in the Psychology of Panic* (Princeton, NJ: Princeton University Press, 1940).
8. Paul F. Lazarsfeld, "Effects of Radio on Public Opinion," in Douglas Waples, ed., *Print, Radio and Film in a Democracy* (Chicago: University of Chicago Press, 1942), p. 69.
9. Bernard Berelson, "Effects of Print Upon Public Opinion," in Douglas Waples, *ibid.* p. 43.
10. *Ibid.* p. 49.
11. Shearon A. Lowery and Melvin L. DeFleur, "Experiments with Film: Persuading the American Soldier in World War II," *Milestones in Mass Communication Research*, 3rd. ed. (White Plains, NY: Longman, 1995), p. 156.
12. For an extended discussion of this type of theory, see Melvin L. DeFleur and Sandra Ball-Rokeach, "Theories of Selective Influence," in *Theories of Mass Communication*, 5th ed. (White Plains, NY: Longman, 1989), pp. 168–201.

Gatekeeping Theory

The world is a big place, and there is a lot going on. Every day thousands, even hundreds of thousands, of events take place in local, regional, national, and international areas that are potential candidates for news stories. Originally, providing news about these events was a problem only for the daily newspaper—there were no other media providing such reports for citizens. Later, during the twentieth century, when the broadcast media, and then to some extent the Internet, began to be used to deliver news to the public, the plethora of potential stories also became a problem for them. Today, the flow of news continues, and decisions have to be made by those who manage the media about *what to select and present to the public.*

The problem inherent in this situation is that any given medium—whether it is the daily paper, a radio or television station, or an Internet news service—can present only a *limited number* of stories in the space or time that it has available.[1] Thus, any of these news channels can provide only a very selective picture of what is going on.[2] How, then, do those who produce a newspaper, or the content of one of the other media, *decide* on the stories that they will select to be presented to the public? More specifically: (1) What is the process used by news media for *observing the many potential stories* from which their daily offerings can be selected? (2) What are the *criteria used to screen potential stories* from those available to decide which ones to offer or reject? And, finally, (3) what are the *consequences of using those criteria* for the audience? It is with these questions that Gatekeeping Theory is concerned.

The concept of "gatekeeping" is by no means confined to the practice of gathering and disseminating a selection of news stories via a mass medium. The process of examining a pool of many items, applying a set of criteria, and then selecting from that pool a final smaller number for some treatment is found in a number of fields. Examples are applications to colleges and universities, where some individuals are selected and allowed in—if they meet certain criteria. Another is emergency rooms in hospitals, where the injured or ill are examined and decisions are made regarding whether to send them to surgery, a critical care unit, or to some other treatment. Still another is in the process by which articles submitted by authors are reviewed for publication in scientific journals. Those that meet the criteria used by the editor are published; others are rejected. The list could go on and on. Wherever there is a large number of candidates from which a few must be selected, some form of gatekeeping is essential.

Gatekeeping has a special significance for journalists as well as for their audiences. Obviously, the process of examining a huge number of potential stories, discarding many, while selecting a limited number to present as "the news of the day"—and placing these particular ones before the public—is an enormously important process for those who receive the content.[3] Many years ago, even before radio became a news medium, the humorist Will Rogers put the problem in an everyday perspective: he claimed that "All that I know is what I read in the papers." In more sophisticated terms, he meant that his "social constructions of reality" concerning the world of daily events were based almost exclusively on what was selected and presented to him by the newspapers of his time. They were his "window on the world," through which he had a view of what was going on—but one that was shaped and restricted by the selections of stories that newspaper editors of that period chose to present.

Today, even though we now have available other news media, we are still in many ways at the mercy of those who pick the stories that they decide to present so that we can be informed. In much the same terms that Will Rogers used, we could now say that "All that I know is what I read in the papers, hear on radio, view on TV, or see on the Internet." Thus, our window on the world has expanded, to be sure, but the media still define and restrict what we can learn. That is, they still provide us with the information (accurate or flawed) that we use for our daily "social constructions of reality."

As we explained in Chapter 3, the basic principle—that we engage in a communication process to develop our constructions of reality—was realized as far back as the time of the ancient philosophers, who concluded that "knowing" (the world around us) is dependent upon communicating with other people and not on sensory impressions alone. In 1920 the same issue was linked to mass communication in colorful terms by Walter Lippmann, when he noted that the proper function of the press was to provide "pictures in our heads of the world outside" (see Chapter 8). Gatekeeping, as the present chapter will explain, is a critical part of that process.

BASIC NEWS FUNCTIONS OF THE PRESS

The idea that newspapers (and now other media) have a responsibility to keep an eye on what is going and report it accurately to the public goes back to the era of the Colonial Press. Early in the 1700s, that responsibility was taken seriously by Peter Zenger, a printer and editor of the *New York Weekly*. In 1734 he was arrested and imprisoned on a charge of *seditious libel* (printing false statements intended to overthrow the government). He had openly criticized William Cosby, the Crown-appointed governor of New York for some of the government's official policies. In fact, what he had printed was *true*! Because of that, when he went to trial, a jury of his peers found him *not guilty*—much to the annoyance of Governor Cosby. The press, that jury decided, has a responsibility *to present the truth* and should therefore be *free* to monitor the activities of government and report them accurately to the people.

Zenger was by no means the first to argue for freedom of speech and the press. John Milton made a forceful argument for such freedoms as far back as 1644 in his response to criticism for printing an essay in support of liberal divorce laws. His prose is archaic, but the point he makes is the same:

> And though the winds of doctrine were let loose to play upon the earth, so Truth be
> in the field, we do injuriously by licensing and prohibiting to misdoubt her strength.
> Let her and falsehood grapple; whoever knew Truth put to the worse, in a free and
> open encounter?[4]

Actually, Milton's plea to the Crown was largely ignored at the time. However, less than a century later, the Zenger trial became an important event that helped establish the concept of the "freedom of the press" in the new nation that came into existence. The idea that the press should be free to exercise *surveillance* over government and that it had a responsibility in its reports to alert the public of potential or real wrongdoing came to be called the "watchdog" function of the press.[5] As time went on, that idea came to be extended to the view that the press has a responsibility to monitor virtually the *entire social environment* in which it operates and to report to the public items of importance and interest that came to their attention.

In more modern terms, the watchdog obligations of the press to the public that it serves had been broadened to include additional communication activities, which have come to be called the three functions of the press. In 1948, political scientist Harold D. Lasswell identified these as (1) *surveillance* of the environment, (2) *correlation* of the parts of the society in responding to the environment, and (3) *transmission* of the social heritage from one generation to the next.[6] When they exercise these three functions adequately, they perform well in alerting the public to the important events and situations that are taking place.

The Surveillance Function

The surveillance function means that the press has a corps of reporters and other professional observers that constantly monitor what is going on in the world. In the United States, special attention is paid to various "beats," such as Wall Street, the Pentagon, and the Congress. At a local level, it would be such beats as City Hall, police headquarters, area businesses and industries, sports teams, entertainment producers, and so on—which the news media have learned are frequent generators of important, or at least interesting, stories. This provides a truly important service as well as many benefits to the society. As sociologist Charles Wright puts it:

> One positive consequence of such surveillance is that it provides warnings about imminent threats and dangers in the world—about, say, impending danger from a hurricane or from a military attack. Forewarned, the population can mobilize and avert destruction. Furthermore, insofar as the information is available to the mass of the population (rather than to a select few), warnings through mass communication may have the additional function of supporting feelings of egalitarianism within the society—everyone has an equal chance to escape from danger. A second positive consequence is that a flow of data about the environment is instrumental to the everyday institutional needs of the society, for example, stock market activities, navigation and air traffic.[7]

Obviously, there are other consequences of the surveillance function to individuals and to society as well. The media, through news reports, can bestow or take away *personal prestige*; they can *disrupt social stability* by disseminating information that disturbs people (e.g., urban riots); and, finally, they can *mislead the public* when the news is controlled by individuals who shape it for their own purposes (e.g., unscrupulous individuals, public relations *spinmeisters*, and so on).

Correlation of Events in the News

The additional functions described by Lasswell are also important as obligations to the public. For example, the function of "correlation" is required to help people understand the *relationship between events*. For example, if there is a significant rise in the price of gasoline or heating oil, the public needs to understand *why*. It is not enough just to release news stories that document the sharp increase in costs per gallon. The press has an obligation to report on related events and issues that help place the situation in perspective. Thus, the public needs to know if a hurricane has disrupted supply, if the oil industry is "price gouging," if OPEC has reduced the international flow of crude oil, if there has been a breakdown in or sabotage of the pipelines that deliver petroleum to various areas of the country, if truck drivers who deliver gasoline or heating oil have called a strike, if the federal government is trying to solve the problem, and so on. Only by correlating these various aspects of the situation can the public understand more fully what is happening and reach conclusions as to what, if anything, they can do about it.

Transmitting the Social Heritage

News is, after all, *history in the making*. Today's news stories become a chronicle of the events that have taken place—a record of those issues, occurrences, and events that contribute to the development of the society and its culture. There is a critical requirement that those records be both accurate and inclusive. Future generations will turn to those accounts to gain a perspective on what took place earlier in their society. Reading contemporary accounts in the press of the Civil War battle of Gettysburg, or seeing newsreel footage of the assault on Iwo Jima, for example, enriches our understanding of what actually took place. Such reports can expand and flesh out the explanations that appear in history books. The same is true of other kinds of significant events. Reading newspaper reports about the sinking of the *Titanic*, for example, can make the loss of 1,500 people seem more personal and real—at least compared with drier historical accounts. Indeed, historians often consult the press reports of the time when they try to analyze and understand a particular event from the past.

As these three functions indicate, there is a heavy responsibility on those who review the flow of potential news stories into their newsroom to include the most significant among them in their paper, broadcast, or Internet release. This is part of the "fourth estate" obligation of the press—to serve as watchdogs of the public interest and to keep the public informed accurately about important things that are taking place. In the process of selection of the daily news, then, which stories will help the public in recognizing real or potential dangers? Which stories will help people relate various aspects of a situation so as to understand the whole more completely? And, finally, which will provide a thorough and accurate account of the important events of the day so that future generations can understand them? These are the questions that must be faced daily by those who screen and select what will be reported in the daily newspaper, news broadcast, or Internet release. Some do it well; others do it poorly.

The activity of editors in the newsroom, reviewing the stories that become available and selecting those as the content of their daily offerings, came to be called "gatekeeping" as a result of a classic research article by David Manning White, former dean of the College of Communication at Boston University. His article was published in *Journalism Quarterly* in 1950.[8] The article explained that one of the main sources for those who make these selections are the accounts arriving at the newsroom via the so-called "wire" services (telegraph). Many came in every day, and a special "wire service editor" had the task of selecting those that were to be included in the daily newspaper. In other words, those that were selected for the list of daily offerings to the public were allowed through that particular "gate." For those that went into the wastebasket, the gate remained closed. Gatekeeping also applies to other sources of candidate news stories from which editors must select. Those who generate potential news stories may be reporters, syndicates, press public relations persons, freelance writers, and so on. In each case, a decision must be made as to whether the story will get through the gate. Gatekeeping, then, is a general and complex process that depends on using many different types of criteria to sort and select stories from many sources.

THE ORIGINS OF THE CONCEPT OF GATEKEEPING

Where did the metaphor of a "gate" and "gatekeeping" come from to describe the selection and screening process that takes place every day in the newsroom, or its equivalent in other media? The term originated from a practical study conducted during World War II by social psychologist Kurt Lewin. He was not interested in mass communication or the selection of news. He had been asked by the National Research Council to develop an understanding of the process by which typical American families *selected the foods that they prepared and consumed at home.*

It was an important issue at the time. During the war, a number of foods were in short supply because they were needed to feed the armed forces of more than 15 million military personnel—a matter of very high priority. Examples of foods that were in short supply were the traditional cuts of meat that were normally purchased for home use—steaks, roasts, pork chops, etc. The government wanted to get the public to reduce their use of these meats and shift to others that remained in good supply (e.g., liver, heart, kidney, and other "organ meats"). These were not in high demand and were generally considered by the public as less desirable, even though they were adequately and equally nutritious. How, then, could ordinary families be persuaded to select and prepare these "organ meats," especially when it meant a significant change in methods of preparation and food consumption?

The first step was to understand the process by which typical families selected the foods that they prepared and brought to their tables. It was Lewin's study of this process that led him to develop the concept of a "gate" and of a "gatekeeper."[9] Briefly, he conducted a number of experiments and other studies on typical families to learn how they selected foods from home gardens (popular during wartime) or from those that they purchased. He developed a thorough understanding of the channels by which foods from these two sources reached the family table and how decisions were made to select some and reject others. He found that several criteria—price, availability, perceived desirability—played key roles. By applying these criteria, decisions were made by homemakers as to which foods were selected to finally appear on the family table. As he put it:

> This example [of using criteria] indicates that a certain area within a channel might function as a 'gate': The constellation of the forces before and after the gate region are decisively different in such a way that the passing or not passing of a unit through the whole channel depends to a high degree on what happens in the gate region. This

> holds not only for food channels but also for the [word-of-mouth] traveling of
> a news item through certain channels in a group, for movements of goods, and the
> social locomotion of individuals in many organizations.[10]

Lewin saw that there were many kinds of "gates" and that *specific criteria* were used to determine which items were let through and which were kept out. It was a simple idea and consistent with common sense, but the concept provided a clear way to refer to criteria to screen candidate items of almost any kind so that they could be further processed.

Lewin went on to focus on the *persons* who applied the criteria and made the decisions about opening the gate—or keeping it closed. In his food studies he found that these were (not surprisingly) mainly housewives but that the criteria they used varied from one cultural group to another. The major point of this part of his conclusions is that the characteristics and mode of action of this person needed to be understood:

> In case a channel has a gate, the dominant question regarding the movement of
> materials or persons through the channel is: who is the gatekeeper and what is his
> psychology?[11]

It was this question, in particular, that led journalism scholar David Manning White to look at the American *newsroom* and try to understand the gatekeeping process in the selection of the daily stories to be disseminated to the public. Conducting his investigation in 1949—a time when newspapers were still the dominant medium from which the public obtained its information about current happenings—he realized that the first task in studying this process was to determine just who served in the capacity of a gatekeeper.

He saw immediately that this was not a simple issue. There were, in fact, a number of gates. He gave the example of press coverage of a Senate hearing on a proposed bill for federal aid to education—an obviously important public issue.

> At the hearing there will be reporters from the various press associations, Washington
> correspondents of large newspapers which maintain staffs in the capital, as well as
> reporters for local newspapers. All of these form the first 'gate' in the process of com-
> munication. They have to make the initial judgment as to whether a story is 'impor-
> tant' or not.[12]

White went on to note that this was only the first step. Additional gatekeepers played a part in shaping the story and deciding what to emphasize or ignore or, indeed, whether to run the story at all.

To gain a more complete perspective on the role and functions of a gatekeeper, White selected a particular editor in a newspaper who actually performed gatekeeping duties. He then made a thorough analysis of what stories that individual allowed through the gate, which ones he tossed into the wastebasket, and, even more important, *why* he let some through but not others.

> Our 'gate keeper' is a man in his middle 40s, who after approximately 25 years of
> experience as a journalist (both as a reporter and a copy-editor) is now the wire
> editor of a morning newspaper of approximately 30,000 circulation in a highly in-
> dustrialized mid-west city of 100,000. It is his job to select from the avalanche of
> wire copy daily provided by the Associated Press, United Press and International
> News Service what 30,000 families will read on the front page of their morning
> newspapers. He also copy-edits and writes headlines for those stories.[13]

The editor, "Mr. Gates," as White called him, cooperated fully and not only saved all his rejects but also explained (in writing) why each was denied access into the pages of the paper.

By analyzing the reasons "Mr. Gates" used to reject a story, White was able to gain a perspective on the *criteria* that were being used in the screening process. One thing was clear: for the most part, these were (as White put it) "highly subjective value judgments." For example, Mr. Gates did not like sensationalist stories and would not select them. He tossed aside those that he felt were "pure propaganda." He also rejected those that he judged to be "poorly written," "dragged-out," "vague," "full of too many figures and statistics," "repetitious" (of earlier stories), "not in good taste," or simply "not interesting." In his final selections, space was a very important criterion. Newspapers have a "news hole," which consists of between 20% and 25% of their total space that they can actually devote to news. The rest is advertisements, comics, and other non-news content.

Obviously, a study of one gatekeeper at work selecting stories for only one week in 1949 cannot provide a full understanding of how the process works or what criteria are used to select and present today's news. Nevertheless, White's initial study of the process opened the research door for a number of other investigations of how news stories are screened, judged, selected, modified, and presented to the public by all of the media that are used to disseminate reports of current events.

OPENING THE GATE: CRITERIA FOR SELECTING THE NEWS

What features of a news story do editors, news directors, and others who control the flow of stories look for as criteria for opening or closing the gate? Basically, they are after stories that will *interest* as well as *inform* the public. But they are also concerned about the financial welfare of the medium that they manage. In making their selections, they use what has come to be called the "news perspective."

The News Perspective

The news perspective is a subculture of criteria and beliefs, loosely shared by journalists, that they use for selecting the daily flow of stories that will achieve the goals, not only of the public, but also of those who operate media. As David Altheid explains, it is a "complex of economic, organizational, and personal factors that determine the biases and the slants built into news reporting."[14] In each newspaper, or other medium, the criteria for selecting stories reflect the concerns and practices not only of *reporters*, who initially select and draft accounts, or the needs of the *public* for accurate and complete knowledge about events, but also those of *management* who are responsible for the financial "bottom line" of the medium. Above all, they are conscious of what they believe their audience will want, because they realize that they have to remain in business. The news perspective, then, provides a general framework for making decisions about the merits of a particular story regarding these several considerations. Thus, whether that story will get through the gate in today's news market depends not only on what it will contribute to the public but also on what it will contribute to the medium.

As a result of this perspective, there is a remarkable uniformity in the news topics that are covered by the daily press in the United States. There are only minor variations from one newspaper to another in the specific stories that will be found on the front page, in the business section, the sports page, and so on. The same is true of television news—either at the national level when networks are compared or at the local level when the stations in a particular city are contrasted. If one network news report opens with a story about the latest political scandal in Washington, the same story is likely to lead in the others. At the local level, if a gruesome murder or major fire is the lead story, the same events are likely to be covered in much the same way by the rival stations. A similar situation exists in news delivered over the Internet.

Clearly, the need to generate revenue from advertisers plays a prominent role in the way a paper or broadcast is organized. To survive financially and to make a profit, considerable space and time have to be devoted to these commercial messages. Moreover, a considerable amount of entertainment content is needed to attract and retain subscribers or loyal viewers. Thus, even in their selections of basic news stories, the entertainment factor remains prominent. This has been the case since the modern mass newspaper was started by Benjamin Day in the 1830s. His focus on crime—and even fictitious events that he invented, rather than just hard news, political reports, and economic information—was his the strategy for attracting the largest possible number of readers who would see the advertisements. Near the end of the 1800s, William Randolph Hearst provided a refinement of that strategy with his focus on "yellow journalism." These news formats effectively captured, entertained, and held the attention of the audience.

By the beginning of the 1900s, the "news perspective" meant—simply put—selecting news stories not only for their historic, economic, or political importance but also as a means of pleasing newspaper subscribers and readers. As editor Will Irwin put it in 1911:

> We will give the public what it wants, without bothering to elevate the commonwealth. If we find that people prefer murders, then murders they shall have.[15]

Just before World War II, newspaper scholar H. H. Hughes reviewed the development of the news perspective as it had been used since Benjamin Day started his paper, and up to his time. He summarized the relationship among advertisers, newspapers, and their audiences in succinct terms—noting that papers often had to exaggerate their numbers to survive:

> What the advertiser bought was circulation, and his money paid the costs of publishing the paper. Sales of the newspaper to readers barely paid for the ink and newsprint paper. But to make advertising space worth paying for, there must be wide circulation. The circulation liar was an inevitable phenomenon in a period when, to survive, it was necessary to boast. Circulation was achieved through the news columns.[16]

In many ways, our current media follow in the footsteps of the newspaper pioneers. Today, to accomplish much the same goal with respect to the television, radio, or Internet audience, the concept of "infotainment" plays a large part in the selection and treatment of news reports. Those stories that pass through the gate are likely to have some feature or slant that will provide entertainment as well as information, so that the audience will enjoy reading or hearing about it. By the 1980s, television became the main source for news for the American public, and it followed the same formula.[17]

As the various factors to be considered in selecting news stories converged, a general similarity emerged in what the media presented to the public. That is, newspapers became quite similar in their array of stories from one city to the next. Radio news emulated what was reported in print. Television stations adopted policies that made their news programs virtually identical to their competitors.

Taken together, this overall similarity was a consequence of the *news perspective* that had developed and become a binding tradition over nearly two centuries of American journalism. Every day, those who gathered, processed, and presented the news hoped for a lead story that would result in a contemporary version of what William Randolph Hearst said that he wanted his readers to remark when they opened their morning newspaper and saw the first headline. He told his editors that the ideal story would cause the reader to say "Gee Whiz!" (Today it would be "Wow!" or perhaps "Awesome!")

Even though the language might be different now, the principle remains. Those who manage the medium want riveted attention and an expression of great interest. An ideal story today might concern a prominent and respected figure who has engaged in shocking behavior that titillates or outrages the audience, or that triggers other strong reactions among them. Thus, in recent years, disclosures about O. J. Simpson, about Bill Clinton and Monica Lewinski, or about Michael Jackson took precedence as criteria for being passed through the gate over a report about even the most significant accomplishments of science (e.g., mapping the surface of Mars and deciphering the human genome). This practice continues to annoy critics of the news industry, but their complaints fall on deaf ears for the most part.

What is going on here? Why are these news media following such similar patterns? There are a number of answers. First, as was already noted, *financial survival is at stake.* The news industry is increasingly competitive, and the advertising revenue pie can only be sliced into a finite number of pieces. While the number of local newspapers that are published has declined steadily over many decades, the number of alternative sources offering news to the public (and for advertisers to use) has expanded greatly. Radio came on line as a news source during the 1920s, along with weekly news magazines. These reduced dependence on the daily paper for both audience and advertisers. Then television news made truly significant inroads. Today the number of websites on the Internet that offer news summaries, or even extended analyses, is legion. Almost all of these sources are dependent in major or minor ways on advertising revenue. Thus, the stories that are carried on these many channels must have content that can attract and hold the attention of those who turn to them to find out what is happening.

Given the financial competition and the resulting news perspective, a major question is this: What kind of content will attract and hold the attention of the largest number of people in a potential audience? That is, what specific aspects or features of a story will make it *newsworthy*—so that it will be read, heard, or viewed by the largest possible number of people? The answer is that a story must have as many as possible of a list of features that journalists refer to as *news values.* These are aspects of stories that over many decades have proven to have the best chance of attracting the attention and holding the interest of audiences.

News Values as Gatekeeping Criteria

As the news perspective developed over many years, journalists determined what features of a story will usually make it a worthy selection to get through the gate and to what degree. That is, depending on content, stories can vary in their level of newsworthiness. This means, simply put, they can differ in their potential interest level for the intended audience. This is judged by the gatekeeper who makes the decision whether to let them through the gate or not. The greater the number of these features, the more likely it is to be passed through to find a place on the pages of the paper, an allocation of time in the broadcast, or a spot on the website.

The criteria for making judgments about newsworthiness are traditionally called "news values." These have become a central part of the subculture of many working journalists, and they can readily recognize them at all stages of story preparation, processing, and dissemination. Generally, reporters try to include them in their reports. Editors, news directors, and webmasters scan candidate stories flowing into the medium to determine if enough of these values are included. Not every journalist uses these criteria, but many do. Summarized briefly, the news values listed below illustrate the concept.

IMPACT.   This refers to the number of people whose lives or circumstances will be influenced by the events of the story. For example, if a train is derailed and one person was killed, the story may have some newsworthiness. However, if the same train is derailed and 100 people were killed, the newsworthiness of the story is greatly enhanced. Or, if a storm strikes and the electricity goes out in one neighborhood, that is not particularly newsworthy. However, if a major power grid shuts down and an entire region and thousands of people are without electricity, that is truly newsworthy.

PROXIMITY.   A story about an event occurring locally is generally more newsworthy than one that is about a similar event that happened far away. For example, the train wreck that killed 100 people would be enormously newsworthy if it occurred in the immediate area. It would rivet the attention of nearly everyone. A similar wreck that took place a thousand miles away would still be newsworthy but not to the same degree. If it took place in a country on the other side of the globe, it would be still less newsworthy, and many in the audience might not be all that interested.

TIMELINESS.   Journalists have learned that it is important to get news reports to the public while they are "fresh." Stale news can be a problem. One reason is that it might cause the audience to turn to another source that is able to get the information to them more promptly. A long-term tradition in journalism is that the source that can "scoop" the competition has the best chance of attracting the largest audience. This has resulted in efforts to cover "breaking news"—that is, rapid reports about events that are just now taking place. These are thought to have a special appeal to the audience, making them especially "newsworthy."

PROMINENCE.   Stories about individuals who are very familiar to the public—politicians, sports figures, entertainers, etc.—have much higher news value than those who are obscure. Thus, the affair between President Clinton and Monica Lewinski created a journalistic counterpart of a shark feeding frenzy when the story first broke. It was incredibly newsworthy. In a similar way, the murder-related activities of O. J. Simpson, the Kennedy airplane crash, Michael Jackson's interest in young boys, the Mike Tyson rape charge, and the death of Princess Diana provided fodder for the grist mill of the news media for long periods. A story of identical events that took place among people whose names were not recognized by the public would have made the back pages.

CONFLICT.   Struggles of one side against the other command attention. Thus, if a major airport plans expansion, and those who live or work nearby believe that it will create unwanted conditions, a conflict will be generated that can generate news stories for a long period of time. The conflict perspective provides interesting stories when clashes are reported between environmentalists and developers, unions and management, racial groups, citizens of a neighborhood and the police, food producers using gene modification or cloning and organic enthusiasts, and so on. A new story about a bitter divorce between two prominent entertainment celebrities is a gatekeeper's dream.

CURRENCY.   Stories reporting on issues that are in the spotlight of public concern are of higher news value than those dealing with issues that people care little about. Thus, if Congress passes new legislation that helps seniors pay for prescription drugs, news reports are likely to be widely read—not only be seniors but also by their children. Or, if stories suggest that the price of gasoline and heating oil are once again going to rise significantly, the attention of the audience will be assured. A story reporting on a change in regulations for the way in which government monitors wool exports, however, will probably have only limited news value.

THE BIZARRE.   Stories about bizzare topics have high news value. A sure winner was a human interest TV story that reported on a lady's dog that can ride a tricycle. Reports of UFOs, Bigfoot, and unexplained events in the Bermuda Triangle have long provided interest. Alternatively, reports of an image of the Virgin Mary that was seen on the window of a bank at a certain time of day also had considerable news value. Perhaps even more interesting was a story from a small New Mexico community, where a woman who was frying a tortilla to make her husband a burrito was astonished to see a clear image of Jesus on the reverse side when she flipped it over. The story captured extensive press attention. The tortilla was placed in a glass case on a velvet pad. Because the event was widely reported in the area, thousands passed through the couple's home just to see it. Some claimed that it had healing power.

GATEKEEPING THEORY: A FORMAL SUMMARY

In summary, news gatherers of many kinds constantly feed into editorial offices, newsrooms, or website managers a huge number of stories about what is happening out there in the community, region, society, and world. There is so much going on, however, that far more stories are generated than can be included in any medium's daily news presentation. Therefore, some system for *screening* and *selecting* must be in place to sort out what will be reported to the public and what will be ignored. At the same time, to remain competitive and profitable—which is defined largely by audience size—stories must be selected that are of interest as well as importance to those who read, listen, view, or surf the medium. That process of screening and selecting through the uses of complex criteria has come to be known as *gatekeeping.*

As explained, the term "gatekeeping" was first used in this way (to label screening, decision making, and selecting) as a result of a study conducted by psychologist Kurt Lewin for the government during World War II. The federal government sponsored research designed to determine how homemakers could be persuaded to buy, prepare, and serve to their families cuts of meat that were not needed to feed the armed forces. He studied how decisions were made about what to purchase, prepare, and serve. He used the analogy of a *gate*—letting certain products through to the family table and keeping others out. Lewin reasoned that knowing whom the gatekeepers were and the criteria they used in making their selections would provide essential information for designing persuasive campaigns directed toward those gatekeepers to increase the selection and consumption of less popular foods during the war. As this research came to be widely read, the term "gatekeeping" came to be applied to a variety of decision-making functions, including the flow of news.

Thus, only four years after World War II ended, David Manning White realized that the editor in charge of the wire service—who selected many of the stories that would appear in the daily newspaper—was acting as a "gatekeeper." He decided to make a study of an editor actually exercising the gatekeeping role ("Mr. Gates"), focusing on how such decisions were made. In an article that he published in 1950, he spelled out what he discovered. Since that time, gatekeeping has come to be seen as an important part of the "news perspective"—the entire set of considerations and selection criteria that are part of the process by which news is collected, judged, processed, and disseminated on a daily basis. The basic propositions of Gatekeeping Theory, which explains that process, can be summarized in the following terms:

1. In exercising its "surveillance" function, every news medium, whether newspaper, radio, television, or, in some cases, the Internet, has a *very large number* of news stories brought to its attention daily by reporters, wire services, and a variety of other sources.
2. Due to a number of practical considerations, only a *limited amount of time or space* (the "news hole") is available in any medium for its daily presentations of the news to its audience. The remaining space must be devoted to advertising and other content.

3. Within any news organization, there exists a *news perspective,* a subculture that includes a complex set of criteria for judging a particular news story—criteria based on economic needs of the medium, organizational policy, definitions of newsworthiness, conceptions of the nature of the relevant audience, and beliefs about fourth estate obligations of journalists.

4. This news perspective and its complex criteria are used by editors, news directors, and other personnel who *select a limited number* of news stories for presentation to the public and encode them in ways such that the requirements of the medium and the tastes of the audience are met.

5. **Therefore,** personnel in the news organization become *gatekeepers,* letting some stories pass through the system but keeping others out, thus limiting, controlling, and shaping the public's knowledge of the totality of actual events occurring in reality.

Today, Gatekeeping Theory remains a valid explanation of one of the major aspects of the process and effects of mass communication. It will remain important as long as the American news media operate in their present form—with a commitment to advertisers to maintain as many in their audiences as possible. That commitment is to their owners and shareholders to make a profit and to their audiences to make their content as interesting as possible, while also offering coverage of those events that are judged to be important.

There are two major consequences that flow from the reliance of the media on the news perspective and the gatekeeping process. A negative view is that the use of news values—similar patterns of news selection from one paper to another, from one television report to another, and so on—tends to *trivialize* the news. The emphasis is often on content that *entertains,* rather than informs. This bothers many critics of the news industry, who charge that making use of the scarce pages or time in the "news hole" for *infotainment* can deprive the public of information that may be of great benefit to them. An illustration would be where a story high in the news values described above displaces an account of new medical findings that could help those who suffer from a particular, but perhaps relatively rare, disease. Although they may be small in number, those afflicted might benefit greatly by knowing that a new medical procedure had been developed to alleviate their condition. If it were a choice between using scarce space for that story and one about a sex scandal concerning a prominent person that would titillate and amuse almost all of their readers, it is likely that there would be no contest at all. The story high in news values, such critics charge, would easily win out.

A more favorable view of the contemporary press is that, because the advertising industry makes such heavy use of (and essentially pays for) the media, Americans are served by an enormously complex news industry. As a result, the public gets relatively free an abundance of channels that provide rich accounts of what is going on in the world. They can choose to read, listen to, view, or surf a broad selection of media that report on those events in ways with which they feel comfortable. To be sure, the accounts that are presented have been screened and selected on the basis of criteria that not all would agree are ideal. But, nevertheless, most major stories of importance do find their way into the press in one medium or another. Moreover, the overwhelming majority of journalists retain a strong sense of "fourth estate" responsibilities to the public. They try to provide information on political, social, economic, and other issues related to the well-being of society. In fact, most do their best—within the constraints of the news perspective outlined above—to provide the public each day with reasonably clear "pictures in their heads of the world outside."

Notes and References

1. F. Beard and R. L. Olsen, "Webmasters as Mass Media Gatekeepers," *Internet Research: Electronic Networking Applications and Policy,* 9, 3, 1999, pp. 200–211.

2. T. Barton Carter, "Electronic Gatekeepers: Locking Out the Marketplace of Ideas," *Communications Law and Policy,* 3, 3, 1998, pp. 389–408.

3. Gatekeeping takes place in virtually all media in the world. It is by no means confined to the United States. See M. S. Roberts and P. Bantimaroudis, "Gatekeepers in International News: The Greek Media," *Harvard International Journal of Press/Politics,* 2, 2, 1997, p. 62–76; L. P. Husselbee and G. H. Stempel, III, "Contrast in U.S. Media Coverage of Two Major Canadian Elections," *Journalism and Mass Communication Quarterly,* 74, 3, 1997, pp. 591–601; H. D. Wu, "Investigating Determinants of International News Flow: A Meta-Analysis," *Gazette,* 60, 6, 1998, pp. 493–512.

4. John Milton, *Areopagitica* (Oxford: Oxford University Press, 1940). First published in 1644 in England, this is a reprint edited by Sir Richard C. Jebb.

5. See Chapter 2, "The Development of Free Press Theory," in: Timothy W. Gleason, *The Watchdog Concept* (Ames, Iowa: Iowa State University Press, 1990), pp. 15–38.

6. Harold D. Lasswell, "The Structure and Function of Communication in Society," in: *The Communication of Ideas*, ed. Lymon Bryson (New York: Harper & Brothers, 1948).

7. Charles W. Wright, *Mass Communication: A Sociological Perspective,* 2nd ed. (New York: Random House, 1975), p. 11.

8. David Manning White, "The 'Gate Keeper': A Case Study in the Selection of News," *Journalism Quarterly*, 27, 1950, pp. 383–390.

9. Kurt Lewin, "Forces Behind Food Habits and Methods of Change," *Bulletin of the National Research Council*, CVIII, 1943, pp. 35–65.

10. Kurt Lewin, "Group Decision and Social Change," in Eleanor H. Maccoby, Theodore M. Newcomb and Eugene L. Hartley, *Readings in Social Psychology*, 3rd ed. (New York: Holt, Rinehart and Winston, 1958), pp. 197–211.

11. *Ibid.* p. 198.

12. David Manning White, *Op. Cit.,* p. 383.

13. David Manning White, *Ibid.* p. 384.

14. David L. Altheide, *Creating Reality: How TV News Distorts Events,* (Beverly Hills: Sage Publications, 1976), p. 1.

15. Will Irwin, "The American Newspaper," *Colliers Weekly*, 46, January 21, p. 18.

16. H. H. Hughes, *News and the Human Interest Story* (Chicago: University of Chicago Press, 1940), p. 16.

17. John P. Robinson and Mark R. Levy, *The Main Source: Learning from Television News* (Beverly Hills: Sage Publications, 1986).

CHAPTER 12

Agenda-Setting Theory

As was explained in the previous chapter on Gatekeeping Theory, the news media must select on a daily basis a limited number of the stories that flow into them from many sources. But once the reports to be presented to the public have been winnowed out, selected, and suitably prepared, editors, news directors, and web masters are then faced with the task of arranging them into a final format that they deem suitable to present to their audiences. Obviously, some stories are *more important or more newsworthy* than others.

In the case of newspapers, the really important ones belong on the front page—or even, as editors say, "above the fold," accompanied by a large-font headline. Similarly, in news broadcasts, some stories are identified as "our lead story tonight" and are the first to be reported—often with more time devoted to them than others that will come later in the program. The same principle prevails in the case of online news. Some are given more space or a more prominent position in the website than others.

There are, of course, other news accounts that clearly do not belong on the front page or in the earliest stage of the broadcast. Still, they may be seen as relatively important. If that is the judgment of editors or news directors, they wind up a bit farther back in the presentation—perhaps on page two—or second in the broadcast. In other words, stories judged to be of somewhat lesser importance or interest are positioned less prominently. Those with very limited importance or newsworthiness occupy the back pages, or the last part of the broadcast.

Many stories must be diverted to specialized sections of the paper or broadcast—such as "business," "sports," or "real estate." Even in those sections, however, some stories are more important than others, and a hierarchy must be decided upon. Which ones should come first? Which should follow in second place, and which can be placed closer to the end of the section or broadcast? These are important issues in producing the daily report.

Gatekeeping, then, is not enough. A second important task for those who gather, process, and disseminate the daily news is to make decisions about the *prominence of the position* of each story—to decide where it belongs within the format of the daily presentation. Thus, those who design each news broadcast, newspaper, or online site must decide on the organization of their daily *agenda*.

The term "agenda" in common usage refers to the list of topics that are to be discussed in a meeting. It can also refer to the issues that some group feels are important. In the case of the news media, both of those meanings are part of the agenda-setting process. That is, agenda setting by those who manage news presentations includes both deciding on which stories to let through the gate and in what order to present them in the medium. A theory regarding decisions as to where the story should be located in the news report—giving it greater or lesser prominence—is called the Agenda-Setting Theory.

The process of selecting media content and then designing an agenda format for its presentation to audiences has been studied within somewhat distinct issues, or frameworks. One framework—the original and most studied—is the relationship among (1) the organization (agenda) of the overall news report, (2) audience beliefs about the relative importance of the issues encountered in those reports, and (3) how those audience beliefs about relative importance influence the political process (the so-called *policy agenda*). That is, the agenda set by the news media is said to be a major influence on the beliefs of the audience about the hierarchy of importance of the issues and topics reported by the press. In turn, those issues that come to be regarded as important by the public become the agenda of concerns of policy makers. These may be government officials (e.g., political candidates, elected legislators, and judges) or others who have a voice in influencing policy directions (e.g., clergy, spokespersons for social movements, and educators). Thus, the agenda-setting process within this framework is a significant part of the *political process*.

In a broader sense, however, there is a second framework. That is, the media also set other agendas. In particular, through their entertainment function, and by providing what can be called "collateral instruction" (unintended lessons), they select and emphasize certain *behavioral themes*—that is, depictions of human actions that express or emphasize particular norms, values, and beliefs (see Chapter 24). Such themes can become an influence on the social constructions of reality developed from media entertainment content on the part of their audiences. An example would be this: If the actors that appear in soap operas, motion pictures, or other dramatic content are frequently shown consuming alcohol, this behavior might come to be seen as a correct and normative form of behavior on the part of the attending public. In a similar way, themes of resorting to violence, such as the use of guns to settle disputes, the frequent use of vulgar language, or engaging in sex without commitment, all illustrate themes that can be a part of the agenda in a movie or television drama, whereby they can provide collateral instruction.

If such presentations are very frequent on the entertainment media agenda, they can come to be seen as representing *norms of conduct* that are acceptable and approved by people in general. A closely related idea was developed as the Cultural Norms Theory (of media influences) by DeFleur in 1970.[1] If this is the case, the media have played a part in setting the public's *agenda of beliefs* (their social constructions of reality) about the normative appropriateness of such behavior. This consequence has long been feared by critics of the media and in many ways by members of the public who deplore depictions of violence, the use of guns, out-of-marriage sex, smoking, dirty language, the consumption of alcohol, and so forth on the part of the entertainment media.

In the presentation of entertainment formats, the counterpart of setting the political policy agenda (that is, a part of the news theory) is the *development of a social movement* that has the goal of changing public beliefs and behavior. A social movement is an organized effort on the part of people to alter some condition of social life. Mothers Against Drunk Driving (MADD) provides an obvious example. Legislators sometimes heed public demand for prohibitions regarding such matters as smoking, violence, guns, and the rest, but it is difficult for them to enact laws that limit either news or entertainment media content. In fact, such attempts often die when the judiciary proclaims that they transgress the First Amendment provision for freedom of speech. Thus, in a parallel sense, Agenda-Setting Theory applied to the entertainment media may help understand how the public can come to believe that certain kinds of media content can bring about an increase in unpopular conduct. That, in turn, can shape the agenda of groups who seek change through the development of social movements.

Thus, Agenda-Setting Theory (plus the older Cultural Norms Theory) helps to understand three important aspects of mass communication and their functions in society. It helps in understanding the complex relationship among *news media treatment of issues, public beliefs about those issues,* and the *policy concerns* of leaders regarding those same issues. A recent example has been the flow of news reports covering the acceptability of same-sex marriage in some states. Those reports helped shape public opinion about such unions and political actions that led to movements for a constitutional ban. In addition, it can help clarify the relationship between forms of behavioral norms depicted in media entertainment content, audience acceptance of those norms, and the goals of social movements among other citizens that seek to accept or condemn such behavior.

THE ORIGINS OF AGENDA-SETTING THEORY

The phrase "agenda-setting function of the mass media" is usually attributed to communications scholars Maxwell McCombs and Donald Shaw. This was the title of a research article that they published in 1972. Their seminal study offered empirical evidence on the relationship between the *prominence* (positioning in time or space) of stories reported by news media (newspapers, news magazines, and network television) and the attribution of *importance* of those issues by their audiences. Essentially, they found that stories that were emphasized by the press by being placed in prominent positions in their formats were regarded as *more important* by audiences than those that were given positions of lesser prominence. In the immediate years following the publication of the McCombs-Shaw article, this relationship between media emphasis and audience beliefs was referred to as the *agenda-setting hypothesis*. In later years, as research supporting the general idea accumulated, it was more commonly called the Agenda-Setting Theory of the Press.

This set of assumptions—that the media set the public's beliefs about the relative importance of issues reported in the news—aroused considerable research interest. A large number of investigators undertook studies of the ways in which the press emphasized certain kinds of issues. These concerned such matters as abortion, police brutality, civil rights, social security, and a host of others. Of special interest was not only how these issues were interpreted by the public but also how the resulting public opinions had an influence on policy makers. The result was a body of research findings that constitute the evidence related to the Agenda-Setting Theory. Today, that theory has been widely studied, and it is important and valid among those generated by media scholars and researchers.

Forerunners of the Concept

However, like many significant ideas, the Agenda-Setting Theory of the press did not arrive on the intellectual scene full-blown with the publication of a single article in 1972. A long list of earlier contributors laid the intellectual foundation. For example, the idea that the views of the public play a significant role in shaping the policies of government has been understood for centuries. In ancient times, Plato discussed the issue his *Republic*. Others who analyzed the nature and influences of public opinion over the centuries include such luminaries as Machiavelli (1513), Hobbes (1651), Rousseau (1762), de Tocqueville (1885–1840), Bryce (1888), and Lippmann (1920), to mention only a few.

We noted earlier the view of Bryce concerning the link between reports in the press, opinions formed by newspaper readers, and the influences of their opinions on government policy makers. In Chapter 7 we noted that he described it in dramatic terms in his classic *The American Commonwealth*:

> Towering over Presidents and State Governors, over Congress and State Legislators, over conventions and the vast machinery of party, public opinion stands out in the United States as the great source of power, the master of servants who tremble before it.[2]

We also noted that Bryce laid out in great detail the ways in which individual newspaper readers formed their opinions on issues of the day (no other news media were available). He explained that the "leading article" (on the newspaper's agenda) was a potent factor in the formation of the individual's interpretation of what important things were taking place that day. Thus, the individual's opinion was formed in an interplay among the reader's own predispositions and beliefs, the opinions of others with whom he discussed the issue, and the manner in which the topic was reported in the press. As others reached similar views, Bryce explained, public opinion as a collective process was developed.[3]

Early in the twentieth century, as was explained in Chapter 8, the relationships among the press, its readers, their opinions, and public policy were discussed at considerable length by Walter Lippmann.[4] In particular, it is clear that he understood both the gatekeeping and the agenda-setting processes (although he did not name them). In a clear statement of both processes, he noted:

> Every newspaper when it reaches the reader is the result of a whole series of selections as to what items shall be printed, in what position they shall be printed, how much space each shall occupy, what emphasis each shall have.[5]

The Chapel Hill Study

More recently, as we have noted, the term *agenda-setting* and the basic ideas of what is now termed Agenda-Setting Theory were discussed in a small-scale investigation of voters in Chapel Hill, North Carolina. The authors, media researchers Maxwell E. McCombs and Donald L. Shaw, focused on political news. The occasion was the presidential election of 1968 (Richard Nixon vs. Hubert Humphry). The goal of the study was to find out how voters in such a community made decisions during the campaign as to which of the issues that received extended news coverage were of various degrees of importance in their minds. News reports of political issues in the media received locally were identified, with specific attention to their positioning in the news reports. A survey of voters in Chapel Hill was conducted to determine which of the issues that were covered by news media the subjects thought to be important. The idea was to gather empirical evidence to see if the *prominence* assigned to a news story (in terms of its location in the medium) was related to the degree of *importance* of that issue in the minds of voters.

As it turned out, there was a high correspondence between the amount and kind of attention to a political issue by the news media and voters' judgments about its level of importance. Those issues that received the *most prominent positions* in the press were seen as *most important* by the voters. The conclusion was that the press had a strong influence on the issues that people would attend to most and discuss among themselves. In other words, the *agenda of the press became the agenda of attention and discussion* among those who followed the news about the campaign.

It is important to note that McCombs and Shaw did not claim that, in its role as the public's agenda-setter, the press shapes the thinking of the public—that is, they did not maintain that the press has a strong influence on the kinds of beliefs and opinions that readers and listeners form on the basis of what is presented. Their conclusions were more modest—and in line with those of Bernard C. Cohen, who in 1963 concluded that the press "may not be successful much of the time in telling people *what* to think, but it is stunningly successful in telling its readers what to think *about*."[6] McCombs and Shaw were convinced, however, that the emphasis placed on issues in news reports—through prominent or less prominent positioning—did bring the public to "think about" such issues in different ways, depending on where in the report the press presented them. They quoted sociologists Kurt and Gladys Lang, who in 1966 had written:

> The mass media force attention to certain issues. They build up public images of political figures. They are constantly presenting objects suggesting what individuals in the mass should think about, know about and have feelings about.[7]

By the mid-1990s, more than one hundred research studies reporting empirical evidence had been published on the agenda-setting process as it influenced public interpretations of issues presented in the press. Included among those publications were a number that focused on how the resulting public opinion influenced the public policy agenda—that is, how political leaders *reacted* to what the public was concerned about. This topic came to be an important and closely related mass media research question.

Sociologists James W. Dearing and Everett M. Rogers have summarized much of the research related to both of these two traditions.[8] They note that influences on the public policy agenda have been a topic of central concern by political scientists. Less well studied, they note, has been the issue of how agenda-setting decisions are made by those who manage the media. By 1996, they could identify only twenty studies that focused specifically on the criteria used to decide whether a particular story is awarded greater or lesser prominence in a news report. They state that:

> A variety of factors, including personality characteristics (of the decision makers), news values, organizational norms and politics, and external sources affect the decision (as to what makes news).[9]

In addition, they note that, in many cases, a story is given prominence because of the source from which it was obtained (e.g., the White House, a respected scientific journal, the *New York Times*, or a well-conducted public opinion poll).

In any case, from classic writings, from a body of more recent research findings, and from the scholarly contributions of a number of social scientists and communication specialists, a clear set of generalizations has emerged. Essentially they are these: The press provides, on a daily basis—as a result of the gatekeeping process—a list of news reports for the public to read, hear, view, or contact online. Some of those stories are judged, by those who make the relevant decisions, to be especially important or in some other way especially "newsworthy." Those stories are placed in the most *prominent positions* in the newspaper, magazine, broadcast, or website. That much seems abundantly clear—although the exact basis by which those decisions about prominence in the news format are made remains less than clear.

What happens next also seems reasonably clear. Agenda-Setting Theory assumes that, due to the different levels of prominence afforded the issues reported in the press, the public receiving these messages will form it's own hierarchy of beliefs about their relative importance. Moreover, there will be a correspondence between the level of importance assigned to an issue in a story reported in the news media and the level of importance of that issue as interpreted by the public. More simply put: It is assumed that those issues that are reported in a prominent manner in the medium will be considered important by the audience. Those that are less emphasized in the format (farther back in the paper, broadcast, etc.) will be seen as less important.

There is considerable support for this conclusion in many empirical studies that have been carried out. That was certainly the case in the study by McCombs and Shaw. The voters they studied had a similar ranking of importance as did the media for the issues that were reported.[10] Many others have reached similar conclusions. An example is a study of the influence of crime reports in the press on the public's fear of crime in three major cities in the United States. Margaret T. Gordon and Linda Heath studied the prominence given to crime stories in the major newspapers in Chicago, Philadelphia, and Los Angeles. Their measure of prominence was the percent of the "news hole" occupied by crime stories in these papers. (The "news hole" is that portion of the paper devoted to actual news—as opposed to advertising, entertainment features, etc.) Generally speaking, they found that the greater the prominence given to such stories, the greater the fear of crime on the part of readers.[11]

Finally, the third issue is the ways in which the opinions of the public, presumably formed on the basis of the relative prominence of issues and topics in the news reports, have consequences for *policy makers*. This remains somewhat less clear. However, it has been accepted—literally for centuries, as we have noted—that public opinion is the foundation of decisions in government. That seems especially true in democracies, where policy makers are elected and serve at the pleasure of the public, because (obviously) they can be voted out of office if the policies that they produce are unpopular. Some scholars maintain that public opinion is the chief and ultimate power in all governments at all times. For example, in Chapter 7 we noted that James Bryce concluded that even governments that appeared to be entirely despotic were ultimately *tolerated* by their citizens. This, he maintained, was a very basic form of public opinion. Even great empires ruled by tyrants backed by strong military forces, he pointed out, remained in power only with the indirect consent of the governed. Military forces were usually very small compared with the total populations of such nations, and a determined multitude could have displaced them.[12]

Generally, then, from a background of philosophical and scholarly writings, both ancient and modern, and from research that has accumulated over many years, the basic topics that are addressed by Agenda-Setting Theory can be summarized in the following terms:

Those in charge of designing the format for the day's newspaper, news broadcast, or news website use *a variety of criteria* to decide how much space or time will be devoted to each story. In doing so, they decide where each report will be placed in the format—as the lead story, on the back pages, or somewhere in between. The result of exercising these criteria by news personnel is a ranking of *prominence* of the stories included in the day's report. That level of prominence for each story indicates the degree of emphasis that the designers of the news report have awarded to each specific issue or topic. Members of the public, who read, listen to, or view these reports, from that organization of topics, form their own conceptions of the relative importance of each of the stories disseminated. Thus, each member of the news audience (unwittingly) develops a *ranking* in his or her own mind of the importance of the issues and topics covered in the stories contained in the daily media reports.

Taken together, these conceptions of relative importance constitute an important feature of public opinion regarding each of the topics that have appeared in the press. That collective opinion may be highly structured around a particular consistent view or hopelessly divided among many conflicting versions. Public opinion that is consistently structured around a particular view becomes an important (indeed powerful) influence on those in charge of the policy agenda. A failure to take public opinion into account in the formation and administration of public policy can mean that those currently in office may find themselves replaced by others after the next election.

But what does research reveal about these basic features of the agenda-setting process? That is, what has been discovered about the *criteria* used for setting the agenda on the part of news personnel? Is there convincing evidence that the relative prominence given to issues in news reports does indeed bring about a ranking of importance on the part of the public? And, finally, does a well-structured and concerned public opinion actually have a strong influence on the policy agenda? Answers to these questions are important in assessing the value and importance of the Agenda-Setting Theory.

FACTORS USED IN SETTING THE NEWS MEDIA AGENDA

There is an old saying in the legal profession: When asked "what is the law?" the answer is often "whatever judges say it is." A somewhat similar principle prevails within journalism. One might ask, "what is news?" Obviously, the answer is "whatever editors [and their counterparts in other media] decide it is." While there may be wisdom in such a definition, an important question remains unanswered. That is, how do they decide? What considerations, criteria, requirements, or other factors are weighed in the minds of those who select the news stories of the day and place them in different positions of prominence in the various media?

There is no simple answer to that question—no straightforward "check-list" of criteria that are uniformly applied by all news format designers in the various versions of "the press." There is, of course, the underlying requirement that whatever is covered and disseminated needs to attract the attention and interest of the *largest possible numbers of readers, listeners, viewers, or surfers.* In other words, there is a fundamental requirement—underlying all other considerations—to keep the profits coming in. But given that requirement, there is flexibility in how it can be achieved. After all, the news agenda of the *New York Times* is not identical with that of the *National Enquirer,* but each manages to stay in business.

Traditional News Values

The features that make a story "newsworthy" in general—at least in the minds of journalists—were discussed in some detail in Chapter 11 (on Gatekeeping Theory). These same values serve as criteria not only for letting a particular story through the "gate" but also for deciding *where it should be placed* in the format of the news report. They are by no means the single or most important set of criteria, and they may not be unifrmly applied, but they do play a part in the considerations of editors and others who make decisions about the "newsworthiness" of a particular story and the prominence it should receive.

Summarizing briefly, in Chapter 11, it was explained that these news values include the following features of a story: *impact,* referring to the number of people whose lives or circumstances will be influenced by the events reported; *proximity,* the fact that a story about an event occurring locally is generally more newsworthy than one that is about a similar event that happened far away; *timeliness,* meaning that it is important to get news to the public while it is "fresh"; *prominence,* which in this context means that stories about individuals who are very familiar to the public have much higher news value than those who are obscure; *conflict,* indicating that there is public interest in struggles of one side against the other; *currency* implies that issues that are in the spotlight of public concern are of higher news value than those dealing with one-time issues that will soon fade away; and, finally, *the bizarre* can be counted on to be a sure winner.

Other Considerations

Decisions about where to place a story in the daily news presentation are not made solely on news values. They are made on the basis of many complex and pragmatic considerations. Many of these were developed over long periods of time, yielding strategies and practices for presenting the news to the public in such a way that the medium (1) survives economically and (2) serves many of the needs of the public. These criteria and considerations for setting the news agenda are partly derived, then, from strategies and practices that have developed over two centuries in the print media and many decades in broadcast news. Listed below are some of particular significance.

AUDIENCE COMPOSITION. No medium speaks to all citizens. The composition of the population in the area served by a medium can influence the agenda developed by a news medium. Audiences are studied closely to determine what will work best with whom. Conscious decisions are made, in part, then, on the basis of beliefs about what major segments of a particular medium's audience will find interesting, important, amusing, insulting, titillating, and so on. That principle is as old as the decision of Benjamin Day to feature crime news prominently in his *New York Sun* in the 1830s.

Capturing audience attention, then, with anything that might be seen as "sensational" remains an important criterion. That may not appeal to more serious citizens, but there are large numbers of others. For that reason, a sensational story regarding unusual sex practices in an otherwise quiet New England community can easily earn a prominent place in a newspaper or in a television newscast. For example, in the summer of 2000, police in a small Massachusetts town raided a building in which about two dozen people in different rooms were engaging in sado-masochistic sexual practices. One woman was arrested for spanking another woman with a wooden spatula. Others were also taken in for questioning and/or arrest. In all cases, these were consensual acts, but the paraphernalia (whips, chains, spiked gloves, and so on) discovered by the police were described at great length in local news media. Participants' photos were printed. An enormous controversy erupted as to whether the police acted properly in their intervention. Prosecution was discussed as it could be related to an archaic feature of Massachusetts law concerning "Crimes against Chastity, Morality, Decency and Good Order."[13] News audiences loved it.

Religion and race can also be criteria for story placement in some cases. To illustrate, a newspaper in a heavily Catholic community is not likely to emphasize favorable news stories about groups that seek to legitimize abortion. A television station that serves a population with a preponderance of African Americans is not likely to make its lead story one that features the remarks of a spokesperson for a group advocating the elimination of affirmative action. John Pollock and his colleagues assessed the coverage of sensitive issues in cities with varying population characteristics and found that *the nature of the audience* was a significant influence on what the media chose to present.[14]

DISPLACEMENT OF "OLD" BY FRESH ISSUES. Another traditional consideration—which also finds expression in the news values used in the gatekeeping process—is *timeliness*. There is a constant flow of new issues that must be covered by the news media. Because this is the case, old issues must be crowded out. For example, in the summer of 2000 (and again in 2005 and 2007), gasoline prices soared in the United States. Intense public interest in that issue made it necessary to assign fresh stories to the front page or the lead position in the broadcast. That made it necessary to reduce attention to other issues, such as severe droughts in the Midwest and forest fires in the West, which had been seen as very important a few weeks earlier. Another example that was of great interest to those living in the Northeast was the 2002 Senate race that was developing between former First Lady Hillary Clinton and Rudolph Giuliani, the mayor of New York City (who later dropped out to be replaced by Congressman Rick Lazio). Interest in the race virtually died as news coverage of the gasoline crisis occupied prominent positions. Accounts of the race were moved to the back pages or their counterparts in the broadcast news media.

JOURNALISTS' COMMITMENT TO THE PUBLIC'S NEED TO KNOW. In all fairness to journalists, they also make decisions on the basis of what they feel the public *should* know—even if the issue is neither exciting nor inherently interesting. In their capacities as watchdogs of the public interest, they feel it is important to give prominence to stories that expose such issues as corruption in high places, mismanagement by public officials, or misbehavior by persons charged with the public trust. For that reason, a story about clergy charged with sexual abuse will find a prominent place. The same will be true of a teacher who has abused or had sexual relations with a student; a lawyer, banker, or CEO who embezzled money; tainted food products imported from China; or a policeman who accepted payoffs. Each is likely to earn a prominent place on the agenda.

DISPLACEMENT BY "KILLER ISSUES."   Stories about events that simply drive other important reports off the media agenda—or move them to positions of lesser prominence—have been called "killer issues."[15] Examples from recent years would be the impeachment troubles of President Clinton, caused by his relationship with Monica Lewinski; the O. J. Simpson trial for the murder of his wife; John F. Kennedy, Jr.'s plane crash, which killed three people; Martha Stewart's trial and jail sentence; Michael Jackson's trial for sexual misconduct with young boys; and political controversies about the role of Americans in Iraq. If one attended to television news, or to the print media, during the times when these issues were prominent, one might have concluded that there was simply little else going on in the world.

BELIEFS ABOUT AUDIENCE BOREDOM AND APATHY.   Still another traditional criterion is derived from the conviction on the part of journalists that the public is simply not much interested in a particular issue. For example, voter apathy and fatigue can be a factor in political reporting that results in a particular story being assigned to a non-prominent position. As political contests drag on, the latest claims, pronouncements, or charges by a candidate can come to be regarded as repetitious and boring. Moreover, issues sometimes become "stale," even though they may, in the long run, be important. Thus, debates over campaign financing, what to do about Social Security, or immigration policy can elicit yawns if they have appeared over and over in the news.

STANDARD NEWS PRESENTATION PATTERNS.   In terms of their overall format, both newspapers and broadcast news have over many decades worked out standard patterns into which they insert whatever stories make up their offerings for the day. For example, local television news is offered to the public in standard ways around the country. The "news team" is made up of a more or less attractive anchor woman, a mature and wise-looking man who serves as a co-anchor, plus a male sports commentator and a weather person. In presenting the news, they engage in "happy chatter" with each other. Their clothing, hairstyles, and so forth have been carefully selected with the advice of a consultant. The desks and background against which they are shown have been carefully designed to look impressive. Major local stories are often introduced by one of the anchors, who then switches to a "standup" (a reporter in the field with a microphone) who describes what is going on—while images of the (fire, wreck, crime, trial) are shown to the audience. For other local items, the anchor introduces the story to the reporter in the field, who than turns to a "package" (an individual or individuals interviewed at the scene). This may be a police officer, a fire chief, a neighbor who saw it happen, or a relative of the victim. The broadcast ends with a lightweight, sometimes amusing, "human interest" piece of soft news. Advertisements are slipped into the format on a more or less regular schedule. In addition, at various points during the broadcast, brief messages claim that this particular news channel is the very best in the area. Whatever actual news items have gotten through the gate that day are presented in this overall traditional agenda.

FOLLOWING THE LEADER.   Certain prestigious newspapers and broadcast news organizations have clear advantages that place them at the top of their profession. For example, the *New York Times* is located in the city that is the center of the commercial, financial, and entertainment power structure of the nation. Nothing can take place on Wall Street, in the nation's major banking systems, or in the offices where decisions are made about the production of movies, television programs, magazines, books, and major online offerings without the news reaching the *New York Times*. The city is also the center for many of the nation's largest advertising and public relations firms—which produce a constant flow of releases and promotions that wind up in the pages of the *Times*. In the nation's capital, the *Washington Post* is at the center of the federal government—the White House, the Congress, the Pentagon, the State Department, and the various agencies that are most involved in national affairs. Again, similarly, in the world of broadcast news, New York City is the location of the major television networks, which compete vigorously to deliver the first accounts of breaking stories. Each of these media is served by a large and complex network of reporters and other sources in the field.

Because of these advantages, it is not possible for a newspaper or television station located in, say, Tupelo, Mississippi; in Walla Walla, Washington; or in Camden, Maine; to be the first to present a major news story of national significance. The news media serving those communities have no options but to monitor—and place conspicuously on their daily agenda—what comes out of New York and Washington. It is for that reason that local newspapers and television stations play "follow the leader" in developing their agendas.

THE PUBLIC'S AGENDA OF BELIEFS ABOUT ISSUE IMPORTANCE

Receiving the daily agenda of the press are its readers, listeners, viewers, and online news enthusiasts. There seems little doubt that there is often a correspondence between the issues that media present in prominent positions and the level of importance that the public assigns to those issues. Numerous research studies have confirmed this conclusion.[16] But beyond that simple correlation lies the question of what else the public believes, understands, or feels about those issues—that is, in addition to the idea that some seem more important than others. Specifically, how do the members of these audiences put together what Walter Lippmann called "pictures in their heads of the world outside"? That is, given the daily tidal wave of information that flows over the nation from its complex news sources, what *social constructions of reality* are achieved by those who attend to the news and then form various kinds of qualitative opinions about the issues presented? Do all members of the public react in a uniform way? Or are there distinctions and variations in the responses, assessments, and conclusions of different segments of the public?

The Attention Requirement

Obviously, patterns of attention are the first consideration. As previous chapters have made clear, different kinds of people differ in the amount of time and energy they devote to following the news. At one end of the spectrum are "news junkies," such as senior citizens who read their newspaper in the morning from one end to the other. They are likely to subscribe to a weekly newsmagazine. They view both the local television and network news reports after supper and may even catch the latest TV report before retiring. On the other end of the continuum are young people who have little interest in what is going on outside their own sphere of friends and activities. They do not read newspapers or weekly newsmagazines, and they are unlikely to follow local or national television news. Some might catch a few headlines when surfing the Internet, but they are unlikely to seek details.

Somewhere in between these extremes are the other news consumers. Among all categories of race, religion, and ethnicity, it is the middle class—who are more educated, more affluent, and more involved in politics—who will attend to at least some of the news, especially that which is of personal interest to them. They are likely to own more than one television set, subscribe to a cable or satellite service, receive a weekly newsmagazine, receive a daily newspaper, and be connected to the Internet. However, their busy schedules—pursuing businesses and professions, raising children, and managing complex households—do not leave as much time for attending to news as is the case with seniors. But they do attend.

At the lower end of the socioeconomic structure are those with limited education and less income. They are less likely to subscribe to a newspaper or a weekly newsmagazine. They may view news programs on their television set, but they do so less often and to a much lesser degree than do the seniors or even the middle class. A much smaller proportion of them own a computer—and an even smaller segment is online. This does not mean that they are not interested in what is going on. It does mean that they get much of their information and understanding of events that interest them through interpersonal sources—from those among them who do attend to the media and transmit information about what is happening by word of mouth, thereby serving as "opinion leaders." (See Chapter 13 on the Two-Step Flow of Communication.)

Interest as a Prerequisite

For all of these groups and categories, a key element shaping patterns of attention is *interest*. If a particular news story, whatever its position in the media's agenda, does not present an issue or topic that interests a member of the audience, it is likely to receive little attention and will thereby have little influence on the thinking of the individual. Those that do speak directly to the interests of a person are far more likely to be examined in detail and to play some part in shaping what the individual thinks—or at least what he or she *thinks about*. This pattern of selective and limited influences was discussed at length in Chapter 10 (the Selective and Limited Influences Theory).

But how are the interests of a person shaped? Social scientists have researched and analyzed this issue for a very long time. Briefly stated, a person's interests are a product of demographic factors, location in the social structure, level of education, participation in particular subcultures, and unique patterns of past experience. To illustrate, a retired senior Hispanic male with a college education and a comfortable income—who participated in the business subculture for many years and who served in combat in the armed forces—will immediately be interested in news reports that relate to his particular background. In contrast, a single mother in her thirties—who may be a member of the same minority but who is employed in a routine job and struggling on a limited income to raise her child—will not be interested in the same stories as her senior male counterpart. They may view the same television agenda of the daily news, but what they take away in their thoughts and evaluations is very likely to be quite a different personal agenda based on what they attend to.

Shaping What People Think, or Merely What They Think About?

While the relationship between interest and attention has been well established, a very important question remains much less clear. That is, does the news agenda simply provide people with a list of more or less prominent issues *to think about*? Or does that agenda of differential emphasis *actively influence* their beliefs, attitudes—and possibly their behavior? An oft-quoted answer to that question is that from the 1963 statement of Bernard C. Cohen (cited earlier). He maintained that the press "may not be successful much of the time in telling people what to think, but it is stunningly successful in telling its readers what to think *about*."[17]

While that idea has been widely discussed and accepted, is it really correct? Or are there grounds for concluding that—at least with some issues, some of the time, and with some people—it does not work that way? To illustrate that question, an example of particular issue of prominence on the news agenda can be reviewed. In 1997, a well-known case of "police brutality" came to national attention when a black man named Rodney King was beaten by white officers in the Los Angeles Police Department. A videotape of the incident (filmed by an amateur who happened to be nearby) was shown over and over on national television. The incident was unusually high on the news media agenda over a long period of time. That tape could be seen both immediately following the incident as well as for months afterward, both during and after the trial of the officers. Indeed, it was still being seen three years later, in the summer of 2000, when the issue of police brutality was on the news agenda once again. The consequence of having this issue placed prominently on the media agenda was that it created a wide division in public opinion. Many citizens supported the police; many others denounced them. What was missing in this outcome was evidence that the audience was merely led to "think about" the actions of the victim and the police. On the contrary, the opinions that were formed were deeply held and sharply divided.

In fact, several subsequent incidents of "police brutality" caught on tape further reinforced the depth of those two views. In the summer of 2007, several policemen were photographed kicking and beating a man who had shot an officer. That film was also very prominently placed on the media agenda. Again, public reaction was mixed. Few simply sat back and said, "Gee, that is an important issue. I will think about that." What happened was that strong opinions were influenced. Many citizens concluded that the police should not be chastised for what they did—given the very bad behavior of the perpetrator. Others became deeply concerned and more entrenched in their belief that the police in many cities are "out of control."

Even before the Rodney King incident made the top of the media agenda, the issue of police brutality was studied by a team of journalism scholars at Northwestern University. A sample of 428 subjects, randomly selected by random-digit dialing, was polled regarding various social issues—including police brutality. Those who had been exposed to a local television investigative series regarding police brutality changed their opinions about the issue after seeing the Rodney King news presentation. The results were statistically significant, indicating that they did not just *think about* the issue but formed very definite opinions.

Given such examples, what is the best conclusion that can be reached as to whether or not an item placed prominently on the media agenda will significantly influence the beliefs, attitudes, or behavior of those who attend to it? Perhaps the best inference is this: An influence on the entire news audience is *highly unlikely*. One simply cannot assume a Magic Bullet Theory (Chapter 9) explanation of uniform effects. It is far more likely that influences will be *selective and limited* (Chapter 10). By the same token, however, there is no reason to conclude that items given prominence on the media agenda will uniformly have *no influence* in changing what people think about an issue. That conclusion is simply a reverse form of the magic bullet idea—a Blank Bullet Theory. Thus, the best assumption seems to be that *on some issues, some people, some of the time, will sometimes form opinions or change some of their ideas* when the media present those issues in prominent ways on their agenda. Thus, the nature of the "pictures in their heads of the world outside" that members of the news audience will develop will depend on their particular patterns of interest and attention—which are determined in complex ways.

THE PUBLIC'S ISSUE AGENDA AND THE POLICY AGENDA

An important question is this: If a particular issue, presented prominently by the press, does capture the attention of a large segment of the news audience, and if the members of the public come to hold strong and reasonably similar opinions about it, how does that situation capture the attention and shape the actions of those responsible for public policy? This is the issue of the relationship between the *public's agenda* (presumably influenced by the press) and the *policy agenda* (presumably influenced by public opinion).

The fact that politicians are sensitive to public opinion can be assumed. What cannot be assumed is that public opinion toward an issue has been solely shaped by the press. That idea is based on a *simple linear model* of the relationship among the news media's agenda defined in terms of prominence, a corresponding public's agenda of the importance of issues, and the agenda for action that is developed by those in charge of shaping or administering public policy. Such a linear view would look something like this:

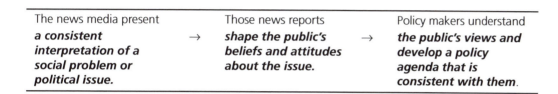

The news media present **a consistent interpretation of a social problem or political issue.**	→	Those news reports **shape the public's beliefs and attitudes about the issue.**	→	Policy makers understand **the public's views and develop a policy agenda that is consistent with them**.

The problem with such a linear model is that it is much too simple—indeed, so simple as to be completely *unrealistic*. The factors that bring large numbers of people to hold a particular view—a consistent public opinion—toward a problem or issue are many and complex. News stories about that topic prominently reported in the press will be only one factor that helps people shape their beliefs about it. People's ideas about any situation that disturbs them are almost always derived from many sources. Just as humanists and others declared that "Man does not live on bread alone," those who study the agenda-setting function of the press should note that "Man does not think on the basis of news alone." (Politically incorrect language to be sure, but the expression gets the point across.) People's evaluations and beliefs about a public issue or problem are shaped by what they learned as children, ideas encountered in the entertainment media, interpretations posed by religious leaders, views expressed by their neighbors, opinions obtained from work associates, attitudes prevailing in their family, and so on. Attending to news stories in the press, then, may be an important factor, but it is one that is mediated by a host of other sources of information and influence.

The Emergence of a Significant Problem of Public Concern

The first thing that must happen if an issue is to become one of public concern—to get on the policy agenda—is that citizens must become *aware* that a problem exists. That is, some condition must come to be present in the society that begins to disturb a significant number of people (e.g., high cost of health care, abortion rights, same-sex marriage). It is in creating awareness of such conditions that the press has a clear role—but one that it shares with others. In discussing the development stage of *social problems,* DeFleur describes the awareness process in the following terms:

> Once causal factors begin to produce a situation with the potential to disturb large numbers of people, journalists, political leaders, moral spokespersons, leaders of powerful interest groups, educators and other concerned citizens are likely to publicize it. It is thus likely to come into public awareness.[18]

Many social problems have troubled Americans for a long time (alcoholism, drug addiction, poverty, environmental damage, health and smoking, and so on). At an earlier time, these underwent an awareness process. In more recent years, people have become increasingly aware of still others (hate crimes, excessively expensive prescription drugs, obesity, sexual misuse of immigrant women, stalking children via the Internet, and so forth).

It is clear that news reports are a principal channel by which awareness of such issues is created among the public. Spokespersons for various policy groups provide press releases, interviews, research reports, and other messages that receive more or less prominent positions in the news, depending on who originates the message. If the president is the spokesperson, the prominence of the message is assured. Similarly, the surgeon general, governors, and other officials who are regarded as highly credible are provided a conspicuous forum by the press. In this way, in many situations, *it is the agenda of the policy makers that establishes the agenda of the news media*—and not the other way around.

A Circular System of Mutual Influence

At the same time, little would happen if the public simply ignored what was being disseminated by the news media about an issue. What this means is that there is a second necessary condition in the development of a social problem that will eventually have an influence on the policy agenda. That second condition is that *the public must disapprove.* There must be a significant consensus that "this is wrong and something needs to be done." If public opinion is hopelessly divided, unclear, or not yet formed, it is highly unlikely that the views of citizens will have any significant influence on the policy agenda. Similarly, a condition, issue, or problem about which public feelings are unclear is one that will be of lesser interest to the press. Stories reporting on issues about which the public is simply not aroused may take place—but the accounts are likely to be found on the back pages or near the end of the broadcast. There is a kind of systematic relationship, then, among the press, the public, and policy makers that shapes the level of prominence given a news story, its definition by the public, and the likelihood that it will be the subject of policy concern.

To illustrate the point, today there is debate about the wisdom of allowing states to impose their sales taxes on items that are purchased via the Internet. It is an issue that has sometimes been prominent in the news—but not frequently. Some spokespersons claim that the lack of such taxes poses an unfair advantage for local merchants who sell the same products. State government officials often decry the loss of sales tax revenue in their budgets and the reduction in funding programs that results. Others, however, maintain that encouraging e-commerce will bring more benefits than losses—creating an increasing number of jobs and an improving economy—like a rising tide that "will lift all boats." The public, looking on—reading and viewing news reports on the issue—remains in a state of indecision and confusion. Some disapprove; others approve; still others yawn. Until the majority of citizens disapprove of the current situation and want such sales taxes, it is highly unlikely that public opinion on the issue will have any influence on the policy agenda. That will not happen in the case of any issue or problem until the public demands that the issue be addressed. DeFleur puts it this way:

> The turning point is reached when enough people express a degree of moral outrage and say, figuratively, 'Enough is enough; we want something done about this.' At this point they are willing to provide the resources; programs for change are designed and set into place; organized, collective attacks on the problem begin.[19]

Precisely this sequence took place in a number of major problems that were discussed prominently in the press over the last several decades. The environmental movement created awareness of pollution through the press. That aroused the public to demand that "enough is enough." New laws and regulations of many kinds against emissions and other pollutants were the result. These were actively reported by the press. The damages on health created by smoking is another conspicuous issue. The outrage of the public has been reflected in terms of banning certain advertisements, restricting smoking in many public places, and government-led lawsuits against the tobacco industry. Portrayal of violence in television has long been one that aroused the public. The V-chip and rating systems were the policy outcome. Currently, the problems of widespread obesity as well as illegal immigration are frequently on the news agenda. Whether this will influence the policy agenda remains to be seen.

Thus, the relationship among the prominence of issues in the news, the agenda of importance assigned to those issues by the public, and the hierarchy that they achieve on the policy agenda is not a simple linear one. Each of these agendas is influenced by the other in complex and circular ways. Sometimes one of the three takes the lead; at other times, that same one simply follows. Overall, they constitute *a system of mutual influence* that comes to address, discuss, define, assess, and provide action regarding a constant flow of social problems and issues.

THE AGENDA-SETTING THEORY OF THE PRESS: A FORMAL SUMMARY

The above discussion addresses a number of considerations that were never a part of the original formulation of the theory explaining the agenda-setting function of the press. As that was laid out in the original article by McCombs and Shaw, it focused on the ways in which different levels of prominence given to issues in print and broadcast news reports would result in a parallel hierarchy of beliefs about importance on the part of those who attended to the stories. Moreover, it is that original "hypothesis" that has been extensively researched over the years—resulting in considerable consensus that the outcome predicted can usually be found in empirical studies. Much additional research is needed to assess the implications of this emerging theory, especially with respect to ways in which the resulting public's agenda of importance has an influence on the policy agenda. Is the linear model (set forth above) a correct description of the direction of that influence? Or is a systematic relationship between the three agendas more realistic? That question remains to be resolved. In any case, the original theory of agenda setting—relating the issue of prominence in reports by the press and rankings of importance by the public that attends to them—can be stated in the following propositions:

1. The press (news media, in general) *selects* a number of issues, topics, and events from its continuous surveillance of the of the environment to process and report daily as "the news."
2. Because of limited space and time, and because of journalists' convictions as to what is "newsworthy," many issues and topics are *ignored* and do not become part of the news.
3. The press gives each of the news stories selected greater or lesser *prominence* in its reports by assigning it a particular position, or giving it more or less space or time, in its print or broadcast news presentations.
4. The selection of stories presented, with their different levels of prominence, space, and time, forms the *news agenda* of the press.
5. **Therefore**, when the public attends to these news reports, they will perceive the order of prominence assigned by the press in its agenda of stories and will use it to decide on a parallel *personal ranking of importance* of the issues and topics that make up the news.

Notes and References

1. Melvin L. DeFleur, *Theories of Mass Communication*, 2nd ed. (New York: David McKay Company, 1970), pp. 129–139.
2. James Bryce, "Government by Public Opinion," *The American Commonwealth* (London: Macmillan, 1888–1889), pp. 14–23.
3. See Margaret H. DeFleur, "James Bryce's 19th Century Theory of Public Opinion in the Contemporary Age of New Communications Technologies," *Mass Communication and Society*, Vol. 1, No. 1, October 1998.
4. Walter Lippmann, *Public Opinion* (New York: Harcourt, Brace and Company, 1922).
5. Walter Lippmann, *Liberty and the News* (New York: Harcourt Brace, 1920), p. 354.
6. Bernard C. Cohen, *The Press and Foreign Policy* (Princeton: Princeton University Press, 1963), p. 120.
7. Kurt Lang and Gladys Engel Lang, "The Mass Media and Voting," in Bernard Berelson and Morris Janowitz, eds., *Reader in Public Opinion and Communication,* 2nd ed. (New York: Free Press, 1966), p. 466.
8. James W. Dearing and Everett M. Rogers, *Agenda-Setting* (Thousand Oaks, CA: Sage Publications, 1996).
9. *Ibid.* p. 17.
10. Maxwell McCombs and Donald Shaw, "The Agenda-Setting Function of the Mass Media, *Public Opinion Quarterly,* 36: 176–187.
11. Margaret T. Gordon and Linda Heath, "The News Business, Crime and Fear," in Dan A. Lewis, ed., *Reactions to Crime* (Beverly Hills: Sage Publications, 1981), pp. 227–251.
12. James Bryce, *Op. Cit.,* Ch. LXXVII, pp. 14–23.
13. Cindy Rodriguez, "1976 Case Seen as a Key to [name of community omitted] Sex Party Charges," *The Boston Globe*, July 17, 2000, p. B1.
14. John C. Pollock, James L. Robinson, Jr. and Mary C. Murray, "Media Agendas and Human Rights: The Supreme Court Decision on Abortion," *Journalism Quarterly*, 55, 3, Autumn, 1978, pp. 544–548, 561.
15. See Hans B. Brosius and Hans M. Keppler, "Issue Competition in the Agenda-Setting Process of German Television," *International Journal of Public Opinion Research*, 7, 3, 1995, pp. 211–231.
16. The research literature supporting this conclusion has been summarized by James W. Dearing and Everett M. Rogers, *Op. Cit.,* pp. 49–53.
17. Bernard C. Cohen, *Op. Cit.*
18. Melvin L. DeFleur, *Social Problems in American Society* (New York: Harper and Row Publishers, 1983), p. 6.
19. *Ibid.* p. 8.

The Two-Step Flow of Communication Theory

The phrase "news diffusion" refers essentially to the process of spreading by word of mouth fresh and timely information about recent news events or situations through a number of individuals. In that sense, its social and psychological dynamics may be little different from those involved in the spread of rumors and gossip. Such interpersonal transmissions have probably been a feature of social life for some 45,000 years—since human beings first learned to speak and use oral language. Certainly we know that complex tidings and items of news were passed on through oral transmission long before writing became available to provide the foundation for the first primitive "news media." Before that, hundreds of generations of our ancestors engaged in oral transmission of rumor and gossip. They also developed techniques to enhance the capacity of human memory for transmitting complex messages about important events in that manner. For example, epic poems, such as the *Iliad* and *Beowolf* provided structured accounts of battles and adventures for audiences that heard them from individuals who had committed thousands of their lines to memory.

In earlier chapters, we noted that, in pre-literate, pre-media, and pre-industrial societies, social ties between individual members and between families in clans, tribes, and villages were deeply established. It was these links that constituted the channels through which the flow of information took place by interpersonal transmission. Local news, gossip, and rumors moved through those "grapevines," much as they do today in modern organizations or neighborhoods where people know each other. News from afar was another matter. Without news media as we know them, information from "outside" was brought to the attention of local people by *visitors* of one sort or another—travelers, troubadours, itinerant peddlers, and others who were in contact with the world beyond the immediate area. When they arrived at a local site, such individuals passed on what they knew in what amounted to *centers for oral distribution of the news*—local marketplaces, coffee houses, inns, taverns, fairs, and other locations where people came together.

Today, the spread of news by oral channels remains a very real part of our lives. Just as the American colonists learned that "the British are coming" through an interpersonal process initiated by Paul Revere, their contemporary counterparts learned in a similar manner that "President Kennedy has been shot in Dallas," "the space shuttle disintegrated," "terrorists have hit the World Trade Center and the Pentagon," "we have bombed Baghdad," and so on. Dramatic tidings, then, still spread quickly by word of mouth.

An important difference today, compared with the pre-media era, is that the process of oral transmission of the news is almost always a *secondary flow of information* that takes place after the basic information has been presented via television, radio, newspapers, or, in some cases, the Internet. The process, in other words, is a *two-stage* one—with the initial release of the news story in mass media followed by a word-of-mouth diffusion spreading a basic summary to those who have not yet learned about it. The discovery that interpersonal communication—spreading of information by word of mouth—continues to play an important part in the overall mass communication process came as a surprise to the team of researchers just before World War II. They were studying the part played by mass media in a U.S. presidential election. It was a time when social scientists had become convinced that the members of modern, urban-industrial (Gemeinschaft) societies were characterized by *anonymity* and *limited direct personal communication* between each other that did not provide for much interpersonal flow of news. People in such societies were thought at the time to be like impersonal atoms, separated from each other without meaningful close ties to their fellow citizens. As noted earlier, these were said to be the characteristics of the "mass society"—that is, populations living in the urban conditions that had emerged with the Industrial Revolution. It was that mass society model that provided the underlying conceptual view of human societal relationships on which the Magic Bullet Theory came to be based (Chapter 9). Thus, at the time, the mass communication process was thought to be *direct, powerful, and immediate, with messages striking every eye and ear in a similar way and having virtually universal effects on their audiences.*

As has been explained in previous chapters, that type of thinking underwent a drastic change over the years because the Magic Bullet Theory was not supported by evidence from research. One of the most important of those studies was one that uncovered a clear link between mass communication and interpersonal communication. It was that research project in which the two-stage movement of information—the interpersonal flow of messages—from a limited number of those attending closely to the media to others in the society became clearly apparent. That research provided the basis for the theory of the Two-Step Flow of Communication—the topic of the present chapter. The research was conducted shortly before the bombing of Pearl Harbor by the Japanese brought the U.S. into World War II.

THE PEOPLE'S CHOICE PROJECT: THE SEMINAL STUDY

In 1940, a large-scale study of how voters make up their mind in a presidential election was conducted in Erie County, Ohio. The contest pitted incumbent Franklin D. Roosevelt, the Democrat's candidate, against Wendell Willkie, the Republican's nominee. A major focus of the research was on the part played by the mass media in presenting information about the candidates and the issues. At the time, print (specifically newspapers and magazines) played a prominent part in election campaigning, along with radio—a newer but well-established medium. (Obviously, television and the Internet were not yet realities.)

An important question under study was the relative contribution to the voters' decisions made by the political campaign messages that those media transmitted. Also studied were a number of additional variables that could potentially shape a voter's decision—the person's religion, socioeconomic status, urban vs. rural residence, type of employment, and several other factors. A detailed report on their project was published as a book (*The People's Choice*) in 1944 by sociologists Paul Lazarsfeld, Bernard Berelson, and Hazel Gaudet.[1] Second and third editions, with citations of subsequent studies and additional interpretations, were published in 1948 and 1968, respectively. These reports described in detail the objectives, research methods, findings, and their implications for understanding how voters made their decisions during a presidential election campaign. The researchers stated the goals of their project in the following terms:

> We are interested here in all those conditions which determine the political behavior of people. Briefly, our problem is this: to discover how and why people decided to vote as they did.[2]

As will be explained, two quite different sets of findings were revealed by the research project. One was how the media of that time had (or did not have) an influence on the vote decisions of various categories of people. That was the major thrust of the project. The findings related to this objective revealed a great deal about that issue. Indeed, in spite of the great changes in the American society and its media since that time, in many respects those findings *still provide valid guides* to understanding the influences on voters of the mass-communicated political messages provided by the two major political parties during presidential election campaigns.

A second set of findings came as somewhat of a surprise to the researchers. It was the *serendipitous* (unexpected) discovery that one of the main sources of information people received about the campaign and the candidates was neither the print media nor radio but *other people.* Many of those who were interviewed in the samples indicted that their vote decision was influenced significantly by what they heard in conversations with friends, relatives, fellow workers, and others—people who had paid closer attention than they had to what the media were providing.

There was, in other words, a *two-stage flow* of political information taking place that had not been anticipated by the researchers. More specifically, some individuals in Erie County (the site of the study) attended much more closely to the political messages that the opposing parties transmitted via the media than did the majority. Those better-informed individuals then transmitted the content and their interpretations of those messages by word of mouth to others, who had not encountered them via the media. This form of interpersonal communication was found to have played an important part in shaping the vote decisions of many of those who were interviewed. That combination of mass communication and interpersonal transmission was labeled the *two-step flow of communication* by the research team. It provides the foundation for the theory discussed in this chapter.

Background: The Presidential Election of 1940

In 1940, the United States was still trying to get beyond the devastating Great Depression that had characterized American life during the 1930s. The incumbent president was Franklin Delano Roosevelt, who had been first elected in 1932. He was a very popular figure and had been re-elected for a second term in 1936. Shortly after assuming office, he began trying to cope with the near-collapse of the economy that came after the 1929 dramatic decline of the Stock Market. For example, in 1932, unemployment in the U.S. reached record highs, with 15 million Americans out of work (in a much smaller population than now).

The Depression brought difficult times to rich and poor alike. The rich lost a great deal, but many families had nothing to eat, and their children had no shoes. Hundreds of thousands of people wandered around looking for any kind of work. Unlike today, there were no federal welfare programs to assist them. Workers in every category suffered. Farmers could not sell their crops and had to allow them to rot in their fields—while people were going hungry in the cities. Factories closed and laid off their workers because people had no money to buy their products. People lost their homes and farms because they could not pay their mortgages when they no longer had their incomes. It was by far the worst financial crisis in the history of the United States. Even today, with the country in a difficult financial situation, it is difficult to imagine the stresses of those earlier times, but they left an indelible mark on an entire generation. The children of the Great Depression not only had to cope with those difficult economic conditions, but just as they came of age they had to confront World War II.

During his first and second terms during the 1930s, Franklin Roosevelt initiated a great many changes in the American political system in order to get the country back to a sound financial condition. In 1932, shortly after taking office, he headed off a crisis in banking. Local banks had run out of money and feared that large numbers of depositors would suddenly demand cash. That would cause the banks to collapse. To avoid that calamity, Roosevelt declared a national "bank holiday" of several days, which allowed the institutions to replenish their supplies by borrowing from the Federal Reserve. During subsequent years, he brought into existence what was termed a "New Deal" for the American people. It was a complex political program, with a number of new federal projects and agencies.

President Roosevelt was able to get the Congress to pass and endorse such radically new ideas as Social Security (enabling people to save modestly and receive income during their retirement years) and the Works Progress Administration (the WPA), which put many to work on government-sponsored programs. Other programs helped farmers. Many public works projects, such as new dams, court buildings, and post offices, were funded by the federal government to provide employment. Thus, it was during the Roosevelt administration that a number of contemporary federal welfare programs and other government interventions came into existence to provide help for those in desperate circumstances. To pay for all this he "primed the pump" by having the federal government borrow large sums to finance many types of efforts designed to restore prosperity. Those who benefitted loved all of it—and especially their president. Conservatives of all kinds deplored it and despised Roosevelt as fiscally irresponsible.

One of the major problems with these changes was that they really did not work all that well. They had only a short-term and limited influence at the time in terms of solving the problems that the Depression had brought. Indeed, in spite of the reforms of the New Deal, by 1940 the nation was sliding back into high rates of unemployment and other financial difficulties. Moreover, Roosevelt was running for an unprecedented *third term*. No American president had ever done that, and there was some question as to whether the Constitution permitted it. All of this gave the Republicans hope that, with just the right candidate, they could retake the White House.

Bypassing several well-experienced politicians, who could have been effective candidates, the Republicans nominated Wendell Willkie. He was what politicians call a "dark horse"—a political unknown but one with impressive personal credentials. Willkie was raised in humble circumstances, on an Indiana farm—as opposed to Roosevelt's patrician background in elegant and wealthy surroundings. From that humble beginning, Willkie had worked hard to become an outstanding success in the business world—which was greatly admired by Republicans. At the time of his nomination, he was the head of a huge public utilities company. There was no doubt that he was an impressive candidate—a man of great personal charm and high intelligence, as well as a proven and capable business administrator. He was an excellent speaker and a political moderate. Republicans believed that voters would find him engaging and (hopefully) an attractive alternative to Roosevelt.

It didn't work! Roosevelt won his third term in a landslide. It was a remarkable victory indeed—and for the Republicans, it was a total disaster. In the Electoral College, where presidential elections are actually decided (as opposed to the popular vote), Roosevelt won a remarkable 449 votes, as opposed to only 82 obtained by Willkie. However, Roosevelt was gracious. He liked Willkie and asked him to serve his administration in important roles and missions, which he did. Roosevelt even discussed a possible joint ticket with Willkie if he decided to run for a fourth term in 1944. However, Franklin Roosevelt died during his third term.

Erie County, Ohio: The Site of the Study

One of the major problems for the researchers was selecting a site to conduct their election study. They wanted one small enough to allow a sample of people to be interviewed every month, that is, several times as the election campaign unfolded. That ruled out a strategy based on a national sample. In the end, after considering many such sites, they chose Erie County, Ohio. It is an area that had some 43,000 people (at the time). It is located on Lake Erie, about midway between Toledo and Cleveland.

Erie County had a number of features that the researchers felt were important. Sandusky is the principal city, with a population (in 1940) of 25,000. Three newspapers were published in the city. In addition, many residents subscribed to the *Cleveland Plain Dealer*. (Newspapers at the time were a main source for news.) It was also something of an industrial center—which meant factory workers would be in their sample. In addition, it was an active agricultural area, with a significant number of farm families. There were no radio stations in the county, but people received broadcasts from nearby Cleveland and Toledo. In addition, there was one additional feature of Erie County that truly intrigued the researchers. In every presidential election during the 1900s, voting patterns in Erie County had mirrored closely those of the nation as a whole.[3]

THE UNIQUE DESIGN OF THE STUDY

As it turned out, their study of how people make up their minds for whom to vote was one of the most detailed and sophisticated survey research efforts ever completed on that topic. It remains, even today, a model of social science research conducted with meticulous care. One of the reasons why it stands out is that the investigators developed a unique research design—one that permitted repeated interviewing of a sample of six hundred carefully selected respondents but which also allowed for assessments of any possible influences that those repeated interviews might have had on their vote decisions.

The Problem Posed by Repeated Interviews

That potential influence (of repeated interviews) worried the researchers. It was regarded as a major consideration that could contaminate the results. Many people, it was feared, would become much more interested in, and sensitive to, the unfolding election campaigns of the candidates if an interviewer came to their home several times (once a month). The interviewers intended to question them on those occasions about for whom they intended to vote, what political media messages they had attended to, and from what source had they received them. The researchers were concerned that repeated interviews could increase their attention to the campaigns and candidates and thereby skew subsequent research results. A way to assess any influences caused by such repeated interviews had to be devised. To overcome the problem, the researchers developed and used what has come to be called a *panel design*.

The Panel Design

As noted, their innovative research design called for repeated interviews with six hundred residents of Erie County, Ohio. This "main panel" (actually a carefully selected stratified sample) was interviewed *once every month*—a total of seven times—beginning in May of 1940 and continuing until just before the election in November. To assess the effects of these repeated contacts, the researchers interviewed four additional "control panels"—that is, four *different sets of six hundred* carefully and similarly selected subjects who had not been interviewed previously. Interviews with a different one of these control panels were conducted in May, July, August, and October. As noted, this was done to determine if the repeated interviewing of the "main panel" was influencing its members in making up their minds for whom to vote. In each of these occasions, the findings from the main panel were compared carefully with those from one of the control panels (whose members had not been previously interviewed) to see if there were major differences.

As it turned out, there actually were no statistically significant differences. The repeated interviews of those in the main panel yielded data that were *essentially the same* as those in each one of the four control panels on each occasion that such a comparison was made. Thus, the use of this clever design allowed the researchers to study the main panel repeatedly over time without biasing their results. This was a considerable advantage over the usual survey procedure, in which subjects are interviewed only once at a particular point in time.

THE RESULTS

As noted, there were several different types of results found by the investigators. One set was consistent with the goals that were originally being pursued by the project. That is, they indicated how the media had influenced the vote intentions of various categories of people in several different ways. Generally speaking, those who were higher in the social class system (socioeconomic status, or SES) of the county were more likely to vote for Wendell Willkie, the Republican candidate, than for the Democrat, Franklin Roosevelt. It came as no surprise that SES was one of the factors that served as a "predisposition" shaping vote intentions. Another finding that was fully anticipated was that those who identified themselves as members of the "laboring class" were less likely to vote Republican.

In addition to social-class identifications, both religion and age were predisposing factors. Simply put, Catholics were inclined to vote for Roosevelt, while Protestants were more likely to favor Willkie. In addition, older citizens favored the Republican candidate, while those who were younger were more likely to vote for the Democrat. Again, these results provided few surprises.

The Effects of the Media Campaigns

Among the major effects of the media-presented campaign messages on voters who were making up their minds was a process that took place in *stages* or *steps* as the campaign continued. That process reveals the influence of the media-transmitted political messages—campaign propaganda, if you will—about the candidates, their records, their proposals, and their characteristics. These include newspaper stories, magazine articles, and radio-presented speeches.

In many ways, there is reason to believe that things today still work in the ways that were found. Specifically, the researchers assessed three types of general influences of the media campaigns that played a greater or lesser part in helping to shape the voters' final decisions. They termed these *activation, reinforcement*, and *conversion*.

ACTIVATION.   This was a complex multi-stage process that explained how political campaign propaganda presented by the media influenced voter intentions. In summary:

1. Media-presented propaganda initially *arouses interest* in the election and the candidates. That is, as mediated messages explaining the candidate got people's attention, that began to increase their interest.
2. Increasing people's interest levels *increased their exposure* to further media information about the candidates. Thus, there was a kind of circular effect—attention raised interest, which, in turn, raised exposure, which then raised interest even further.
3. As attention and interest increased, voters *became more selective* regarding what they attended to. Essentially, they began to select political messages consistent with their predispositions.
4. Finally, votes *crystalized*. At some point, people made up their minds for whom they would vote, and there were only a few who changed those decisions later.

REINFORCEMENT.   A very important issue for political parties in elections is this: if a person has already made a decision to vote for a particular candidate, it is essential to *reinforce* that decision and keep the person from straying to the other side. Indeed, fully half of the voters in Erie County had done that. They had already decided that they would vote for the candidate of their party, whomever he was, even before his nomination in the convention. Election propaganda, then, was designed to prevent such people from switching sides. This a less dramatic outcome of a media political campaign, but it is one that must be achieved if a candidate expects to win.

CONVERSION.   It is the hope of every candidate that his or her campaign propaganda and messages will convert voters from their previous intentions to vote for their opponent and sway them to their own position. Indeed, many people see election propaganda as designed to do precisely that. The only problem with that idea is that it really does not work. Very few indeed switch sides because of campaign messages they encounter in the media. That was clearly the case in Erie County. There were only about eight percent of all voters who made such a change over the time in which the repeated interviews were conducted Moreover, these were people who were less sure of their earlier intention.

Radio as a New Medium

Another issue of importance at the time was the relative role of radio versus newspapers (which were in their "golden years" in terms of newspaper subscriptions per household). As it turned out, radio had only recently become an important medium in election campaigning. While newspaper accounts conveyed little about the personalities of the candidates, hearing them speak on the radio provided another dimension. In this case, both candidates were effective orators, but people had come to know Roosevelt's soothing voice very well. He had made very effective use of the radio during his two terms in office, and he had a comfortable and friendly speaking style.

THE DISCOVERY OF THE TWO-STEP FLOW OF COMMUNICATION

As noted, the six hundred voters in the main panel (sample) were contacted month after month. They were compared on four occasions with one of the similar (control) samples who were interviewed in the same way. As has been explained, the idea was to determine if the repeated interviewing of the main panel had changed or influenced them is some way. This panel design served the project well. It was found that, in each such comparison, the main panel and the comparative or control sample did not differ in any statistically significant way.

But as the interviewing of the samples continued, the researchers kept encountering something that they had never anticipated. When the interviewers asked how the subjects had learned something about one of the candidates, the researchers fully anticipated that they would identify *one of the media as sources of their information*—perhaps a newspaper story about the candidate, a magazine article, or a speech heard on the radio. But in a great many cases, subjects kept mentioning another source of information from which they had obtained both information and interpretation. That source was not the media. *It was other people.*

As it turned out, the people in Erie County talked to each other a lot about the candidates and their campaigns. Conversations took place among friends, neighbors, families, fellow workers, and even among strangers in barber shops, beauty parlors, and markets. Those conversations provided a great deal of the information and interpretations that were important to the voters as they made up their minds. The bottom line is that, just as the researchers were well into their series of interviews, they had to reshape their thinking and strategy to take into account this unanticipated source of information.

What they found was that there were certain individuals—at all social levels in the county—who paid a great deal more attention to the media (and the campaign) than most of the others. Those well-informed people carefully read the newspaper stories and the magazine articles. They listened to the speeches of the candidates on the radio. It was these people who passed on to others—to those who paid less attention to the campaign messages—the information they had received. They also passed on their *opinions and interpretations*. It was for that reason that the researchers dubbed them "opinion leaders." These opinion leaders played a key role for the less well informed by providing information and interpretations about the candidates and the election in general. That flow of information and influence—from those in greater contact with the media campaigns who passed on information and interpretations to the less well informed—was labeled the *two-step flow of communication*. In that sense, the movement of campaign content from the media to the audience—in the case of election campaigns—takes place in two stages: (1) Opinion leaders attend closely and become well informed. (2) Then, by word of mouth, they inform and influence others who have not encountered the media messages of the candidates as directly.

While this two-stage phenomenon became apparent during the study of the 1940 presidential campaign, it is now understood that it is a more general situation that extends beyond presidential or other elections. That is, subsequent research has shown that such better-informed individuals who attend closely to the media often appear to act in this manner, not only in the case of election messages, but also in terms of other forms of content—such as news events, marketing, or even entertainment. Thus, those who transmit information obtained from the media and pass it on to others with their interpretations play a unique role in shaping the influences of mass communications for the larger audience.

THE NATURE AND ROLE OF OPINION LEADERS

Who are these people, and what factors are at work to bring them to serve as opinion leaders? What the Erie County researchers concluded was that opinion leaders are present in *every level of society*. At first, they wondered if people with higher status in the community were the ones who passed on information and influence to those who were lower in the class system.

Opinion Leaders Exist at All Levels

As it turned out, that was not the case. The investigators found that opinion leaders exist at all SES levels—among humble workers, the middle class, and those in upper levels as well. Thus, a factory worker was more likely to receive information that would influence his or her vote decision from another factory worker, rather than from some middle-class person at a higher socioeconomic level. Opinion leaders could be family members, friends, neighbors, or fellow workers who passed on their information and influences to others. Thus, there was no evidence that those higher in income, education, or other forms of social status were exerting their personal influence downward.

Another issue is the sheer volume of personal contacts. The researchers reported that, on any given day, ten percent more of their respondents had participated in discussions about the election than had heard a speech or had read something in a newspaper about the candidates or their issues.[4] In other words, interpersonal communication was a more widely used channel for the delivery of political information than were any of the media.

Mistrust of Media Campaign Propaganda

Opinion leaders also have another advantage over media persuaders. If they encounter resistance, they can quickly reshape their messages in a flexible way to overcome that resistance. That is not the case with media-presented persuasive communications:

> Neither radio nor the printed page can do anything of the kind. They must aim their propaganda shots at the whole target instead of just at the center, which represents just any particular individual. In propaganda, as much as in other things, one man's meat is another man's poison. This may lead to boomerang effects, when arguments aimed at 'average' audiences with 'average' reactions fail with Mr. X.[5]

Thus, one of the factors that made personal influence so effective in terms of shaping vote intentions was that people tend to trust people they know. They do not have such a high level of trust in the media-delivered promises and claims of politicians. If your neighbor tells you something about what he or she heard from the media about a political candidate and then expresses his or her opinion about the topic, it is not likely that you will attribute improper motives to what is being said. The same is true of friends, fellow workers, and so on. They are not immediately perceived as propagandists trying to influence your vote. The messages one encounters in the media or transmitted by politicians, however, face that barrier. Therefore, personal influence has a *credibility* advantage over media influence.

Overall, then, among the important findings of the Erie County study was that there was an interpersonal flow of information by word of mouth between individuals who attended closely to the media and then on to others who paid less attention. This two-step flow was important in that it appeared to have a significant influence on the voting decisions of many of those interviewed in the study. Simply put, personal influence was found to be more effective than media influence.

In summary, the Erie County study provided a turning point in developing explanations of the influence of mass communications on media audiences. Its results showed that the flow of information from media to audience does not take place as was described in the Magic Bullet Theory. Thinking about the ways in which information moves from the media to its audiences had to be revised. As Elihu Katz, who became a distinguished media scholar, put it in 1956, in an article based on his doctoral dissertation:

> Analysis of the process of decision-making during the course of an election campaign led the authors of the *People's Choice* to suggest that the flow of mass communication may be less direct than was commonly supposed. It may be, they proposed, that influences stemming from the mass media first reach 'opinion leaders' who, in turn, pass on what they read and hear to those of their everyday associates for who they are influential. This hypothesis was called 'the two-step flow of communications.'[6]

ADDITIONAL STUDIES

Insofar as the two-step flow process was not in the initial plan of study in the Erie County research and was an almost accidental discovery made during the conduct of the project, it was not as thoroughly investigated as other aspects of the investigation. However, following the publication of *The People's Choice*, a number of other studies of personal influence were undertaken. These were also conducted under the auspices of the Bureau of Applied Social Research at Columbia University. These studies did not focus on elections but on the process of personal influence in other kinds of situations and activities.

One investigation, completed in 1940, shortly after completion of the Erie County project, was sociologist Robert Merton's *Rovere Study.* It was a follow-up to the Erie County research intended to yield additional information about opinion leadership. It was conducted in a small town in New Jersey (named "Rovere" in the research report).[7] In that project, a sample of eighty-six residents were first asked to identify the names of people to whom they turned for information and advice on a variety of topics. Those source persons who were mentioned frequently by the initial sample were then located and interviewed. Although it was a small project, it revealed that opinion leadership was by no means confined to the election process. Opinion leadership and personal influence took place in many other ways.

A second investigation, called the *Decatur Study*, took place in 1945–46. It involved a somewhat different strategy. In a "snowball" approach, those identified as both receivers and providers of opinion leadership were interviewed. That is, people who claimed to have been receivers were interviewed, but those who claimed to have influenced others were contacted as well. The findings revealed clearly that such interpersonal contacts were an important influence in areas of decision making that were by no means confined to election campaigns. Opinion leaders influenced the decisions of others in *marketing* (what products and brands to buy), in selecting *entertainment* (which movies to see), and in *public affairs* (what were the important issues).

In addition, the investigators tried to extend the flow of information and influence *beyond the dyadic contact between opinion leader and receiver*—that is, to a longer chain of interpersonal exchanges. An important discovery using this approach was that those initially identified as opinion leaders were themselves often the receivers of influence from still others. What this revealed is that there were more stages involved in the flow of information and influence than just two steps. The two-step flow of information was now seen to be a *multi-step flow along a chain of interpersonal contacts.*

In still a third study, the focus was on interpersonal influences on decision making by *physicians* who chose to adopt new drugs to prescribe for their patients. This was a difficult project. There are not that many physicians to be interviewed in any one community. For that reason, the study was conducted in four Midwestern cities. Each physician was asked to identify three colleagues with whom he or she interacted socially on a frequent basis, talked with, and looked to for advice about their medical cases. When the subject indicated that he or she had been influenced by another physician to adopt a new drug, an audit was made in local pharmacies in the city to verify that the doctor had indeed started using a new medication. A great many other issues were involved in the drug study, but it was clear that there were opinion leaders among the physicians who had a significant influence on the medical adoption decisions of others.

These three studies confirmed the validity of looking at personal influence as an important factor in people's decisions, whether in marketing, entertainment, public affairs, or medical decisions. It was clear that it was a complex process, often involving word-of-mouth chains of multiple givers and receivers of personal influence. As the concepts of opinion leadership and the two-step flow of communication became more widely known, a large number of studies was undertaken by a variety of investigators to try and understand the processes better. These concepts were among the most widely studied by communication scholars during the 1950s.[8] Quite obviously, these findings were one reason why the Magic Bullet Theory had to be abandoned.

THE TWO-STEP FLOW OF COMMUNICATION THEORY: A FORMAL SUMMARY

Based on the findings of the *Peoples' Choice* research conducted in Erie County, plus the additional findings of major studies that followed up, the theory of the Two-Step Flow of Communication can be summarized in the following terms:

1. The mass media present a constant flow of information about a great variety of topics of interest and importance to people in contemporary society, but most people attend only *selectively.*
2. Some people at all levels of society *attend more fully* to the media than others and become more knowledgeable than their families, friends, or neighbors in certain areas of media content.
3. Among those who attend more fully are people who become identified by others as *opinion leaders*—persons like themselves but who are especially knowledgeable and trustworthy as sources of information and interpretation about certain topics of media content.
4. Such opinion leaders often *pass on* information they obtain from the media about specialized topics to others who have turned to them for information and interpretations about those topics.
5. **Therefore,** mass communications often move in *two stages*—from the media to opinion leaders who attend directly to media presentations about selected topics, and then by word of mouth on to other people whom they influence by their information and interpretations.

THE PROBLEM OF DISTORTION IN INTERPERSONAL COMMUNICATION

A question closely related to the idea that information flows from the media by word of mouth through interpersonal chains of tellers and retellers is this: *what happens to the accuracy of the content as this takes place?* The literature on the two-step flow of communication does not address this issue. Mainly, it has focused on the characteristics of opinion leaders and in what areas they exert personal influence. There is, however, another body of research that should be considered in trying to understand the *accuracy* of messages that are transmitted in this way. That is, if a potential opinion leader attends to a mass-communicated message and then transmits its content by word of mouth to a receiver, is that message likely to get distorted and lose accuracy in some pattern?

The basic concept within which a two-step (or multi-step) flow of information from media to mass needs to be considered is the general process of *interpersonal message diffusion.* In other words, an important focus on the process is not only what kinds of people do what to exert influence on whom but also what levels of *distortion and inaccuracy* can be expected in the content of the messages so exchanged. That process has been widely studied but not in the context of mass communication. As DeFleur put it in 1962:

> Recently, mass communication researchers within sociology have paid increasing attention to the social dynamics of the spread of information, influence and innovation through social systems. They have located and studied the characteristics of and relationships between opinion leaders, followers, influentials and other key individuals in the two-step flow of information, in the transmission of influence and in the adoption of new products or ideas. Lesser attention has been given to discovering what happens to communication content itself, in terms of distortion, change and misinterpretation that may occur when mass media messages are socially diffused through interpersonal networks of opinion leaders and followers.[9]

Over the next four decades, a number of studies of such oral diffusion of the news were published. By the mid-1980s, DeFleur was able to locate twenty-eight studies that had dealt with the topic in terms of empirical research. However, the pace of such research had markedly slowed and had almost halted by the beginning of the 1990s.[10] It is difficult to account for that change, due to the importance of news in the American society. With new media constantly entering the mix—first radio, then television, and more recently the Internet—the flow of information from those media to news audiences merits full attention.

An important model of what may happen to a news story as it flows from person to person in a word-of-mouth chain can be found in the study of *rumor.* The social dynamics of the spread of a rumor are very similar to those that are involved when a news story is transmitted through interpersonal chains. The classic analysis of patterns of change in the message content of a rumor is that of psychologists Gordon Allport and Leo Postman, who studied the process during the time of World War II—when it was an issue related to national security. In their research on actual rumors and those that were spread in laboratory-type experiments, they found three major kinds of changes (distortions) in the content of the message. Taken together, they called these an *embedding process.* They termed the three kinds of distortions *leveling, sharpening,* and *assimilation.* Briefly stated, these can be described in the following way:

1. *Leveling* is defined as follows: "As a rumor travels it tends to grow shorter, more concise, more easily grasped and told. In successive versions, fewer words are used and fewer details are mentioned."[11]
2. *Sharpening* refers to the reciprocal process. That is, certain central details remain in the story, becoming the dominant theme. The process has been defined as follows: "the selective perception, retention and reporting of a limited number of details from a larger context."[12]
3. *Assimilation* refers to the way in which items in the rumor are sharpened, leveled, or otherwise altered in accordance with interests, attitudes, cultural themes, stereotypes, etc. (among those involved in the telling and retelling). Thus, assimilation is what most people would think of as distortion—that is, substantial changes in actual content that take place as the story becomes embedded in the mind-sets of those involved.

One study that linked the issue of accuracy and distortion to the interpersonal flow of news by word of mouth was conducted by DeFleur and Cronin in 1991.[13] The three concepts were used in a comparative experimental study of the accuracy of recall of a news story of just over three hundred words. One version was presented to subjects in a televised account. The other was read by the subjects in a newspaper story format. In each condition, the story was then passed on through seven separate chains of word-of-mouth tellers and retellers. The results showed that subjects remembered the details of the newspaper version better than that presented by television. However, *a clear pattern of leveling* was noted in both cases.

Sharpening was also evident as many details were dropped. Nevertheless, as the story moved along this interpersonal route, it retained a coherent and more or less logical organization of the central ideas. It did not become a distorted jumble of random ideas or even one influenced by the personal characteristics of those in the word-of-mouth chains, as might be suggested by the study of rumor. Obviously a great deal of additional research is needed on this topic of interpersonal news distortion, as it may vary by the type of initial medium, the nature of the story, and the characteristics of those who do the word-of-mouth transmission. In any case, a body of research findings on the interpersonal transmission and patterns of distortion that can occur in the multistage flow of information needs to be integrated into the two-step theory.

Notes and References

1. Paul F. Lazarsfeld, Bernard Berelson, and Hazel Gaudet, *The People's Choice: How the Voter Makes Up His Mind in a Presidential Election* 3rd ed. (New York: Columbia University Press, 1948).

2. *Ibid.* p. 1.

3. In a personal discussion, Paul Lazarsfeld maintained some years later that this was not a major reason why Erie County was chosen. It was certainly a plus, he felt, but it was the remaining characteristics of the county that made it a good choice.

4. Paul F. Lazarsfeld, Bernard Berelson, and Hazel Gaudet, *The People's Choice: How the Voter Makes Up His Mind in a Presidential Election*, 3rd ed. (New York: Columbia University Press, 1968), p. 150.

5. *Ibid.* p. 154.

6. From Elihu Katz, "The Two-Step Flow of Communication," *The Public Opinion Quarterly*, Spring, 1957. Note: This article is an abridged version of a chapter in the author's "Interpersonal Relations and Mass Communication: Studies in the Flow of Influence" (unpublished PhD dissertation, Columbia University, 1956).

7. Robert K. Merton, "Patterns of Influence: A Study of Interpersonal Influence in a Local Community," in Paul F. Lazarsfeld and Frank N. Stanton, *Communications Research, 1948–49* (New York: Harper and Brothers, 1949) pp. 180–219.

8. For a list of such research reports completed by the late 1950s, see Elihu Katz, *Op. Cit.,* p. 348.

9. Melvin L. DeFleur, "Where Have All the Milestones Gone? The Decline of Significant Research On the Processes and Effects of Mass Communication" *Mass Communication and Society* Vol. 1, No. 1/2, Winter/Spring, 1998, pp. 85–98. Prepared at request of editor.

10. Melvin L. DeFleur, "The Growth and Decline of Research on the Diffusion of the News," *Communication Research*, Vol. 14, No. 1, February 1987, pp. 109–130.

11. Gordon W. Allport and Leo Postman, *The Psychology of Rumor* (New York: Henry Holt and Company, 1947), p. 75.

12. *Ibid.* p. 86.

13. Melvin L. DeFleur and Mary Cronin, "Completeness and Accuracy of Recall in the Diffusion of the News From a Newspaper vs. a Television Source," *Sociological Inquiry*, 61, 2, 1991.

Uses for Gratifications Theory

As previous chapters have explained, beginning just before World War II, two general principles emerged from early research on mass communication. The first was that audiences were *selective* because of a diversity of interests and tastes based on their social and cultural identities, and because of that diversity *not all members attended equally.* That idea was embodied in the Selective and Limited Influences Theory (developed retrospectively in formal terms in Chapter 10). That theory had made clear that the audience was *not passive,* with all members uniformly attending to whatever content the media happened to present. The assumption of a passive audience had been central to the defunct Magic Bullet Theory, which had been shown to be inconsistent with the facts. The second general principle was based on the realization that members of media audiences *actively select that content to which they want to be exposed.* For that reason, it became essential to understand *why* people sought out particular types of news stories, magazine articles, books, radio programs, and films to which they wished to attend, while ignoring other available content.

A major study of radio audiences provided a first step in providing answers to this second question. The answer that came was that individuals in the audience sought content that would provide them with various kinds of personal fulfillment, enjoyment, or satisfaction of various kinds of *needs.* Thus, audiences were selective not just because some people had different tastes and interests than others but because individuals were actively seeking content to which they wanted to be exposed in order to obtain different types of *gratifications for their personal needs.*

THE DISCOVERY OF THE ACTIVE AUDIENCE

The growing conviction that individuals actively seek out media content that provides them with personal satisfactions of various needs eventually led to a new explanation—which in the present text will be called the *Uses for Gratifications Theory.* As noted, it was the second general perspective that directly challenged the assumptions and predictions of the Magic Bullet Theory. Originally, the name attached to this second perspective phrased the label as "uses" *and* "gratifications." In the present text, that has been deemed much too broad, given the origins of the theory. Therefore, in an effort at refinement of the theory, the focus in the version presented below is on "gratifications" that are provided by attending to media presentations.

Such gratifications are said to be related to various *needs* and other motivations that bring people to seek amusement, enjoyment, diversion, etc. In that sense, the "uses" concept (a much broader idea) can best be viewed within a more pragmatic perspective. That perspective is presumably related to obtaining *practical information* from media content—such as where to get a job, rent a dwelling, buy a car, get bargains on food, or prepare for the weather. That type of "use" has in this text been treated separately in the Media Information Utility Theory (see Chapter 15).

The slow development of alternatives challenging the Magic Bullet assumptions should not be surprising. In the 1930s, the rapid growth of the mass media was still a relatively new phenomenon in Western civilization. At the beginning of the century, during the early years of the 1900s, when most adult citizens of the 1930s were children, there were no movies, and there was no radio to listen to (and obviously none of our more contemporary media). Then, suddenly, just after World War I, people began going to the movies regularly, and a decade later, during the 1920s, radio had become an almost universal household medium.

By the 1930s, the United States was about to become what we now call a "media society," in which mass communications began to play a central role in both the economy and in people's everyday lives. Indeed, that transition had clearly begun. The print media had long been widely established. During that decade, there were more than 2,500 daily newspapers published in the United States. Dozens of slick general-circulation magazines reached millions of subscribers on a regular basis. However, it was during the 1930s that the movies became immensely popular with people of all ages. More than twice as many films were produced and shown to large and enthusiastic audiences in pay-at-the-box-office theaters than is the case today. During that same decade, hundreds of radio stations went on the air around the country and were linked in nationwide networks. Millions listened avidly to the entertainment that they provided on a daily basis.

It has been noted that, before World War II (which began for the U.S. in 1941), relatively little empirical research had been conducted to learn about the effects of mass communications on media audiences. As was explained in the previous chapter, there had been a few noteworthy efforts, such as the famous Payne Fund Studies of the influences of movies on children[1]. There had also been a widely read study of how several million Americans panicked when they head a radio program called *War of the Worlds* on October 30, 1938.[2] By this time, however, radio was coming under increasing scrutiny. Many were wondering what its influences were on its audiences. It was from research on radio's audiences that the basic ideas for the Uses for Gratification Theory would be developed.

The Office of Radio Research and the Soap Opera Studies

Specifically, it was from the findings of several large-scale research projects designed to study the influences of *radio daytime serials*—the soap operas—that the gratifications theory would come. These radio programs got their colorful name because they were used as advertising vehicles by manufacturers of common household products, such as laundry soap. Even before World War II, these serial dramas could be heard daily in all parts of the country, thriving on national network radio. By 1942, there were *more than twenty* of these daytime programs on the air. The radio versions were basically the same in their format as those that can still be found on daytime television. They were plays in which the characters depicted had romantic relationships but also suffered numerous stressful situations with which they tried to cope.

By the early 1940s, the soap operas drew huge national audiences, mainly of housewives who listened faithfully every day. At that time women were more available to listen because a much smaller proportion of adult females were employed full time outside the home than is the case now. (About twenty-five percent of women over fifteen years of age had full-time jobs in 1940, compared with more than sixty-five percent today.) The daily soap operas offered the housewives of the time a very satisfying diversion—stories that they could listen to as they went about their domestic chores. As a consequence, nearly half of the adult women in the United States listened regularly to one or more of these stories every day!

The sheer size of these audiences astonished pioneer communication researchers. Nothing like them had ever been encountered before. The audience for a single episode of a soap opera on a single day sometimes exceeded the number of people who had ever seen a live performance of a Shakespeare play since they were first produced in the Globe Theater in the early 1600s. The communication researchers studying the radio serials felt that they must surely be having significant influences on the millions of women who listened to them.

To study this remarkable new media content, as well as others, a special institute was established in 1937 at Columbia University with funds granted by the Rockefeller Foundation. The new Office of Radio Research, as it was called, was founded and directed by sociologist Paul Lazarsfeld. Its mandate was to study the influence of radio on people's lives. The studies that would be undertaken by Lazarsfeld and his colleagues would focus on a variety of such influences. These would include not only what programs people listened to on their radios, such as soap operas, but also on the role of the medium in the society at large. For example, as discussed in Chapter 13, studies were conducted to assess radio's role in election campaigns, in which the use of the medium was becoming increasingly important.

By the early 1940s, the Office of Radio research had undertaken four separate studies of the daytime serials. These investigations were designed to compare women who listened regularly to soap operas, to other women with similar characteristics *but who did not listen*. The purpose was to see if regular listening to the soap operas made any difference in the women's lives. These were truly large-scale studies. One was a nationwide investigation that consisted of interviews with 4,991 farm women. A second consisted of a cross section of 5,325 rural and urban women in the state of Iowa. A third studied a randomly selected panel of 1,500 women who were interviewed in Erie County, Ohio. Finally, the fourth was an investigation that had been undertaken by the radio network CBS. Its results were made available to the Office of Radio research.[3] It was based on interviews with hundreds of women in three American cities (Syracuse, New York; Memphis, Tennessee; and Minneapolis, Minnesota). Even today, these investigations would be considered massive. Samples of 5,000 give very precise results, to say the least. Modern sampling theory has shown that accurate results can be obtained in nationwide surveys with as few as 1,500 respondents, if they are properly selected.

One of the problems Lazarsfeld and his colleagues faced at the time was that many scholars in more traditional academic disciplines looked down upon the whole idea of studying soap operas. It just wasn't done. Scholarly research was supposed to focus on serious issues and topics. Scholars who studied culture were expected to study *elite forms*—classical music, ballet, the theater, opera, or modern dance. Conducting research on why people listened to soap operas, or attended to any other form of *popular culture*, seemed intellectually thin and even trivial to many academics at the time.

Lazarsfeld and his colleagues felt differently. The researchers realized that a new kind of society was developing—what we now call the "media society"—in which mass communications transmitting popular culture to huge audiences were becoming a central feature of social life. It was important, they decided, to investigate radio thoroughly—the newest of the mass media—to see what influences it was having. They wanted to learn *why* the members of those audiences picked certain kinds of programs and what kinds of *satisfactions* they derived from the experience of listening. They also wanted to find out if that experience *influenced their behavior* in any way.

Characteristics of Soap Opera Listeners

In 1942, the basic findings from the four studies noted above were brought together in a summary report by psychologist Herta Herzog, one of Lazarsfeld's associates.[4] From that report, one thing was very clear. Judging from the samples studied, the soap operas on radio *did indeed have truly massive audiences*. Some forty-eight percent of the nation's housewives listened to one or more episodes every single day. An additional five percent listened some of the time. The remaining forty-seven percent did not listen. This made possible direct comparisons between women who were regular listeners and similar women who were non-listeners. These comparisons were expected to show a number of differences between the two categories.

It is important to note that the intellectual framework for the comparisons of listeners and non-listeners in this pioneering study was drawn from psychology. Not surprisingly, then, the research focused on *personality factors* for the most part—including individual differences in interests, levels of self-assurance, anxieties, need satisfaction, and so forth.

This early focus on psychological factors was to have a strong influence on the nature of the emerging theory.

ENTHUSIASM AND ACTIVE SELECTION.   One fact that struck the researchers immediately was the enthusiasm of the soap opera audience for specific radio stories. They found that the women whom they interviewed were *not passive listeners.* That is, they did not just listen to any program that happened to be broadcast at a particular time. Each had favorite stories that they specifically sought out and eagerly attended to for enjoyment. This led the researchers to the conclusion that the audience was *deliberately selective* in picking content that interested them. The concept of a passive audience simply had to be abandoned. Indeed, for some women, listening daily to their favorite serial was a central part of their lives.

Herzog illustrated how important such a radio play could be to a dedicated listener with an account of a young woman named Toni Jo Henry. This young woman had been convicted of murder and was on death row awaiting her execution. For Toni Jo, listening to the daily episode of her favorite daytime serial on the radio in her cell was the only joy she had in her dismal circumstances. To her dismay, however, she learned that her favorite soap opera was to be discontinued during the summer (a common programming practice at the time) and would not start again until September. But, also to her dismay, that would be *after her execution!* The producers of the play were informed of her distress, and they had a summary prepared of the episodes that would be broadcast during the entire next season. It was sent to Toni Jo. Whether this helped her to meet her Maker in a happier frame of mind is not known.

PERSONALITY CHARACTERISTICS.   Because they approached their studies as psychologists, the researchers (logically enough) tried to determine if soap opera listeners had a particular profile of individual personality characteristics. This was a difficult task because the survey interviews were rather brief and they focused on a number of other issues. Furthermore, procedures for assessing personality factors during brief interviews were not well developed at the time (or even today). For example, to assess "self-assurance," interviewers made subjective judgments about each respondent on the basis of what they observed while talking with her during the interview. (This would not be an acceptable procedure for such assessment today.) Not surprisingly, from these observations only minor differences were reported. The non-listeners were said to be somewhat more self-assured than the listeners. All subjects were asked how much they "worried." The listeners reported that they worried somewhat more than did the non-listeners. Overall, however, not much was revealed by these comparisons, and the personality characteristics of the two categories seemed rather similar.

INCOME AND EDUCATION.   Regular listening to the daytime serials was clearly related to the educational attainment of the women studied, as well as to their family income level. Among those at every income level (low, medium, and high), education was an important factor. Those with only a grade school education listened most and college-educated women the least. Those who had graduated from high school were in the middle. This link between income and education was found in both rural women in Iowa and in the nationwide survey. The most avid listeners, then, were the least educated women with the lowest incomes.

INTEREST IN PUBLIC AFFAIRS.   It must be kept in mind that, before television arrived, radio was a major source of news for most people. Evening news programs of thirty minutes were common—much as is the case of television today. Knowledge about elections, foreign affairs, and other public issues was presented regularly by network news organizations. An important question, therefore, was whether serial listeners, who attended to radio daily, would be better informed about public affairs than non-listeners. An alternative hypothesis would be that attending to the soap operas would draw attention away from news and public affairs programming. The data from the three studies that probed this issue supported that serial listeners had less interest in the news than non–serial listeners, although the differences were not great.

Overall, then, the researchers found some individual differences between those who listened regularly, or at least somewhat regularly, to the daytime serials and those who did not. Listeners tended to have more worries but less self-assurance. Listeners were lower in income, educational attainment, and interest in public affairs than were non-listeners. Yet the differences were rather minor, and it was not possible to attribute any truly powerful effects on their audiences related to attending to the daytime radio serials.

Major Conclusions: Seeking Gratifications by Listening

Central to the questions probed in the studies of the audience for the soap operas was what *satisfactions* the women obtained from listening. This turned out to be an important issue. Herzog used the psychological term "gratifications" in discussing this factor. She tried to determine if listening to the stories provided some sort of *fulfillment of basic needs.* For example, one of her hypotheses was derived from the idea that human beings have a basic need to associate with others—that is, to have meaningful social relationships. The question she studied was whether listening to the daytime serials served as a kind of *substitute* for being with other people, fulfilling that need while leading to less actual participation in groups.

To answer this question she compared listeners and non-listeners in terms of whether they attended church (a social activity) regularly. She also asked the two groups about participating in other kinds of social gatherings. She found that listeners and non-listeners did not differ significantly on this factor of social participation. Whatever gratifications the listeners were getting out of the radio plays, then, they were not a substitute for the satisfactions of actual social participation.

EMOTIONAL RELEASE.   What Herzog found regarding this psychological factor was somewhat unexpected. She found clear evidence that the listeners were using the experience to *obtain emotional release* by attending to the soap operas. That is, it was rewarding to listen to the troubles of other people portrayed in the plays. It made the listeners *feel better* by sympathizing with the actors who faced difficulties. Thus, when a character in one of the plays was ill, the listener felt a great deal of concern. When a baby was expected, the listener was excited by the prospect. When the listener vicariously enjoyed a portrayed incident, or cried over the problems confronting a favorite character, it released her own internal emotions and in many cases compensated for bleakness or troubles that might be present in their own lives.

WISHFUL THINKING.   Listening to the daily episodes provided more than emotional release for their audiences. Another form of gratification was *wishful thinking.* Listeners got vicarious satisfaction when their favorite character had experiences that they themselves had no opportunity to enjoy. A matronly housewife struggling with a weight problem, misbehaving kids, and a dull husband enjoyed imagining herself as an attractive, young, single woman having a romantic love affair with a handsome young man—like one of the characters in her favorite serial. While listening to an episode, she could pretend that it was her, with a svelte figure, dressed in expensive clothing and going to an elegant party in glamorous surroundings. By wishful thinking she could drive a fancy car, eat in an expensive restaurant, or even fly to an exotic destination with her lover in one of the new passenger airplanes.

GETTING ADVICE.   Still a third kind of reward listeners obtained from the stories was understanding how they could handle problems in their own lives by hearing how the characters in the plays dealt with theirs. Typical of what listeners gained was how to deal with a straying husband or how to relate to a sickly parent. After hearing how a favorite character handled such a problem in one of the serials, the listener would often adopt the same strategy. Getting along with a domineering mother-in-law or dealing with difficult children were other areas for which the plots and actors were regarded as providing advice.

Sometimes the advice obtained did not seem to the researchers to be particularly realistic. For example, one woman explained that she was happy that she had learned from her favorite daytime serial what do if she should unexpectedly come into a great wealth. The likelihood of this happening to the poorly educated, low-income, Iowa farm woman was remote, but nevertheless she felt good that she now knew what to do if it should happen.

Perhaps the most important conclusion yielded by the soap opera studies was that audiences for the daytime serials were very clearly *active.* The women who were studied had deliberately sought out *exactly the stories that they wanted to follow.* They tuned in faithfully every day to be sure that they kept up with the plots and followed the events portrayed by their favorite characters. This was very different from the idea of a passive audience accepting and responding to whatever the media happened to present.

In retrospect, the most important conclusion reached by the researchers was that the experience of listening to the plays provided their audiences with very *clear psychological gratifications.* The psychologists concluded that listening was "need-fulfilling." The women obtained emotional satisfactions by suffering vicariously through the problems depicted in the dramas and by sympathizing with the experiences portrayed by the actors. They lived richer lives in their own imaginations by pretending that they were living out many of the activities that they heard described in the episodes. Terms such as "escape," "diversion," and "fantasy" speak to the same idea and they came to be used in later discussions of gratifications obtained from the media.

As noted earlier, comparisons between women who listened avidly to the soap operas and those that paid little attention did not reveal much. Listeners were lower in educational attainment and in income, but they were not much different from other women in their level of social isolation or their interest in public affairs.

THE USES AND GRATIFICATIONS "PERSPECTIVE"

It was the findings from the daytime serial studies that led researchers to adopt what initially came to be called a *uses and gratifications perspective* in their studies of the relationship between mass communication content and those who attended to it. The term "perspective" was useful because a formal theory had not yet been proposed. Indeed, progress was slow in refining the ideas uncovered in the original research. A few studies were conducted during the last half of the 1940s on such issues as the satisfactions that children obtained from reading comics and the gratifications provided by the daily newspaper.[5] These added little that was new, but they were important because they expanded the gratifications perspective beyond radio and soap operas to include satisfactions obtained from other media. Thus, the "perspective" came to be seen as very general and not confined to a single medium or a specific kind of content. This was an important step in the development of the theory that eventually emerged.

What Children Obtain from Television

During the early 1950s only a few investigations were conducted within this new perspective. However, the pace picked up toward the end of the decade—particularly during the time that the American public was more fully adopting television. With the beginning of the 1960s, large-scale research began to be undertaken on the ways in which children (in particular) were using television and how it was having an influence on their lives. In 1961, Wilbur Schramm, a noted media researcher, along with his associates, published a book summarizing the results of eleven large-scale studies on children and TV.[6] Their results provided strong evidence that this particular audience was active, rather than passive, in terms of their uses of the new medium. Their theoretical perspective was clearly focused on uses as well as gratifications. Their work seemed to make it clear that television was not a "cause" that produced "effects" on passive viewers, as had been a major assumption of the Magic Bullet Theory. In trying to understand the relationship between children and television, Schramm and his associates maintained that the term "effects" was misleading:

> . . . it suggests that television does something to children. The connotation is that television is the actor; the children are acted upon. Children are thus made to seem relatively inert; television relatively active. Children are sitting victims; television bites them.[7]

Basically, they maintained, the older assumption of a passive audience was just wrong. Children selected and watched television programming in order to satisfy three needs. These needs were not arcane functions of the unconscious or some other obscure psychological motivation. They were simple requirements found in ordinary daily life. They were needs for *entertainment*, for *information*, and for *social utility.*

ENTERTAINMENT.   All human beings enjoy entertainment. Like adults, children enjoy seeing the adventures of exciting and attractive people on television. Schramm and his associates did recognize that being entertained was in a sense a passive experience, but selecting from the programs offered to obtain the experience was clearly goal-oriented and active. Once the content was selected, children "used" television to relieve boredom and escape from real-life problems. It was in that sense that the term "uses" was included in the original title of the perspective. On closer look, however, the more focused term "seeking gratification" implies much the same thing.

INFORMATION.   The researchers concluded that children clearly learned from television. This potentially could be deliberate, but it was more likely to be *incidental.* (This major concept was discussed in some detail in Chapter 5 (see also Chapter 24). That is, lessons were learned unwittingly while being entertained. For example, girls often viewed the hairstyles and the clothing of the women they saw on television, thereby learning unwittingly what was fashionable. Children also learned many other kinds of lessons that were not planned by either the media producers or the viewers. For example, both boys and girls gained an understanding from TV that it was appropriate to tip a waitress or a cab driver, even though they had never personally done so. By watching sports, boys learned how to swing a bat, throw a football, or to play the role of pitcher in a baseball game, even if they had never participated in such sports.

SOCIAL UTILITY.   Watching television with friends had other benefits. It was convenient and inexpensive. In particular, it furnished an opportunity for boys and girls to sit closely together. At school, or among peers, discussing television programs provided a universe of discourse—something to talk about among friends and to show that one was "with it."

Overall, the findings and discussions provided by this widely read research report seemed to confirm the validity of the emerging perspective. It did not result in a clear-cut statement of a theory as a set of propositions expressing assumptions and predictions, but it very clearly helped to focus attention away from the older assumptions of the Magic Bullet Theory.

A "RESEARCH TRADITION" DEVELOPS

By the early 1970s, quite a large number of studies had been conducted within the perspective. Indeed, many dozens had been reported, and they addressed a great variety of needs and satisfactions obtained from many kinds of media content. A strong emphasis continued on how children and others were influenced by television. By this time, a number of versions of the perspective had been proposed by various scholars and researchers.[8] While it was not yet formulated as a systematic set of statements that unambiguously specified its assumptions and predictions, research was accumulating that would aid in its clarification. As a result, with more and more studies offering additional evidence, a new descriptive phrase came into use. What had been a "perspective" came to be called the *"uses and gratifications research tradition."*[9]

Enough studies of the gratifications derived from exposure to media content had been published by the mid-1970s, in both the U.S. and in other countries, to merit a book devoted solely to the developing perspective. Two distinguished researchers, Jay Blumler and Elihu Katz edited a volume titled *The Uses of Mass Communication: Current Perspectives on Gratifications Research.*[10] The book brought together fifteen essays and research reports prepared by twenty-three social scientists and other scholars who were working within the emerging tradition. It cited more than 120 research reports based on the uses and gratifications approach. Within this volume, Katz, Blumler, and Gurevitch set forth in an essay what they termed a uses and gratifications "model," noting that no formal theory in the sense of systematic propositions stating assumptions and predictions had yet been developed:

> The common tendency to attach the label 'uses and gratifications approach' to work in this field appears to virtually disclaim any theoretical pretensions. . . . Nevertheless, this effort does rest on a body of assumptions, explicit or implicit, that have some degree of internal coherence . . .[11]

The authors went on to draw together from several sources a set of five assumptions that they felt provided guidelines for conducting uses and gratifications research. In much simplified form, these were as follows: (1) The audience is active. (2) The audience member links his or her need gratifications to [media content]. (3) The media compete with other sources of need satisfaction. (4) People are aware of their needs and can indicate them to media researchers.

(5) Judgments about the value of what people attend to [such as popular culture] should not be a part of research on uses and gratifications.[12]

These assumptions do not, and were not intended to, provide a formal theory. As Katz and his associates put it, they were intended to "explain something of the way in which individuals use communications, among other resources in their environment, to satisfy their needs and achieve their goals." Thus, while they did not set forth the theory in a refined form, they did provide a broad set of ideas that helped focus the emerging perspective.

DEVELOPING A FORMAL THEORY

In 1985, a second edited volume devoted solely to scholarly discussions and research reports on the types of uses and gratifications obtained from media content was published by Karl Rosengren and his associates. Titled *Media Gratifications Research: Current Perspectives*, it brought together the work of more than twenty authors who interpreted additional research on what was now being labeled a *theory* (as opposed to a "perspective," "approach," or "tradition").[13] The book cited more than four hundred articles, books, and other source materials relevant to uses and gratifications. A majority of these had been published after the earlier work by Blumler and Katz.

Identifying Basic Assumptions

Recognizing that there was a great lack of consensus as to the exact nature of the developing theory, the authors justified this vagueness as a natural outcome of the ways in which knowledge is developed in the social sciences (which includes the study of mass communication when the scientific method is used). It is a plodding process, they note, that does not develop logically in a simple linear manner:

> While enjoying popularity, media gratifications research has developed much like anything else in social science—slowly, and tending to plod along a relatively uncharted course. One of its redeeming features no doubt has been its longevity, much of which might be attributable to the flexibility of the approach and the reluctance of its practitioners to be fenced in, either through premature modeling or through external criticism.[14]

To assist in clarifying the nature of the emerging theory, Palmgreen, Wenner, and Rosengren reviewed the now huge research literature that had accumulated and sorted out what they considered the most important assumptions that characterized the investigations of how people were achieving gratifications by selecting and attending to media content. They stated them as eight propositions:

> (1) the audience is active, thus (2) much media use can be conceived as goal directed, and (3) competing with other sources of need satisfaction, so that when (4) substantial audience initiative links needs to media choice, (5) media consumption can fulfill a wide range of gratifications, although (6) media content alone cannot be used to predict patterns of gratifications accurately because (7) media characteristics structure the degree to which needs may be gratified at different times, and, further, because (8) gratifications obtained can have their origins in media content, exposure in and of itself, and/or the social situation in which exposure takes place.[15]

Obviously, this is a rather complex statement, and at first glance it can be difficult to understand. However, by looking closely it can be seen that the central ideas set forth are (1) *an active audience* that is (2) *goal directed*—that is, its members seek, select, and attend to media content that (3) provides some sort of *satisfaction for needs* or that provides some other type of *gratification*.

What Content, Needs, and Gratifications, and for Whom?

It was soon realized that the emerging theory left many questions unanswered. For example, if exposure to mass communication content is assumed to provide need gratification, answers are required as to "what content," "what needs," "what gratifications," and "for whom." Does each category in the audience—teenagers, elderly men, middle-aged women, the rich, the poorly educated, and so on—have the same or a different list of needs? That is, does "one size fit all"? Obviously, there can be no simple answer to that question, and much research remained to be done. There are also many kinds of media content—including instructional materials, news of public affairs, popular culture for light entertainment, and serious elite art, to mention only a few.

As answers were sought to this question, the developing theory began to get increasingly complicated. Seeking direction, media researchers turned to basic social science to gain insight into the relationship among the basic concepts of *needs, motivation, and conduct.*

The study of needs and their relationship to human motivation had been pursued by generations of psychologists, ranging from turn-of-the-century psychoanalysts through the more modem behaviorists, social psychologists, and humanists. Individual human beings were said by the spokespersons of these different branches of the field to have a list of various kinds of needs that had to be satisfied in order to lead a normal life. The lists varied from one branch of psychology to another.

A major influence on thinking about human needs was the seminal work by psychologist Abraham Maslow.[16] During the 1950s, just as the theory of uses and gratifications was starting to be developed, he described a "hierarchy of needs" said to characterize all human beings. At the lowest level, he maintained, are the basic needs for food and water. Others are more complex, such as the need for "security." Higher in the scale are socially acquired needs for "belongingness and love" and the need for "self-esteem." At the highest level is the need for "self-actualization."

Maslow's theories of universal needs emphasized their role in motivating human behavior. This touched off a great interest in associating various kinds of human conduct—including attending to mass communications—with underlying needs for different types of experiences that provided fulfillment and gratification. Communication scholars began to use these ideas to try to understand why people were active in preferring, selecting, and attending to specific kinds of mass communication content. Researchers studied many kinds of people in the hope that they could identify just the right list of both basic and acquired needs that led people actively to select and attend to media content in order to gain satisfactions. Some were named by the investigators. Others were needs that people themselves identified in non-technical terms when asked by the researchers. The needs that were identified in these ways were described in such terms as "fantasy," "diversion," "excitement," "relaxation," "surveillance," "consistency," "tension-reduction," "ego-defense," and dozens more.

A major problem was that each investigator came up with a different list, and no agreement was achieved on which ones were truly central, important, or realistic. In the end, the search for needs that were being gratified and that were common to all audiences was not successful. This did little to clarify the emerging uses and gratifications theory. On one hand, it did seem clear that people were selecting and using media content to obtain some sort of satisfactions, but it was difficult to pin down exactly what needs were being gratified in the process.

Alternatives to Need Gratification

All theories must be considered against alternative explanations for the same facts for which the theory tries to account. Psychologist William McGuire provided an interesting alternative answer as to why people attend in such large numbers to the content of the media. He paraphrased Henry David Thoreau, who noted that "the mass of men lead lives of quiet desperation."[17] McGuire suggested that most people in modem societies lead *dull and boring lives.* They may turn to the trivialities of media content, not to fulfill deep-seated needs, but as an alternative to their otherwise dreary circumstances.

> Perhaps the satisfactions that mass communication can offer to the person, pitiful though they may be, are better than the alternatives offered in the real life of quiet desperation that which many members of the public endure. The large proportion of their time that people choose to devote to media consumption is evidence that however illusory the gratification offered, it may be exceed . . . the satisfactions available in their actual world.[18]

Thus, an alternative to complex assumptions about deep-seated needs that explain massive media attention is the simpler explanation that people select the trivial experiences that attending to mass communications offer *because they provide a painless way to pass the time that is better than the boring alternatives that they have available.* There is no satisfactory way of telling whether this alternative is correct. Research has yet to answer this question. However, it does fit with the time-honored *principle of parsimony*, which has long been favored by scientists. That principle states that if two explanations for a particular phenomenon are available, it is the wisest to choose the simplest. By this standard, McGuire's explanation of selecting media content in order to experience something more interesting than boring alternatives makes a great deal of sense.

Another alternative to explaining media attention by referring to need gratifications is that obtaining such satisfactions constitute only one of the many "uses" of media content. In fact, it is important to note that the uses and gratifications theory is in many ways only marginally concerned with "uses." The focus is clearly concentrated on the *gratifications—that is, fulfillment or satisfaction of needs*—presumed to be obtained from exposure to content. In many ways, the approach could have more appropriately been labeled "uses *for* gratifications" rather than "uses *and* gratifications." Indeed, it is for this specific reason that the theory has the "uses for gratification" label in this book.

To explain more fully, there is another form of "uses" of media content that does not fit well into the gratifications tradition. For example, many people "use" factual information that they obtain from the media for solving problems associated with routine matters in daily living. For this behavior, explanations based on need gratification seem clearly inappropriate. More specifically, media content provides people with useful information that can be efficient and helpful in dealing with a host of commonplace problems and difficulties. For example, looking in the newspaper to determine what time the movie will start hardly seems to provide for deepseated need fulfillment. The same can be said about consulting the weather channel on TV to see if it will snow and make stressful the morning commute. Listening to music on an FM station while driving to work seems better explained by avoiding boredom than seeking deep-seated need satisfaction. Thus, all selections of media content cannot be explained with a complex theory of need gratification.

There are other forms of information that are media supplied that seem unrelated to psychological gratification. At an earlier time, before mass media, people got certain kinds of advice through interpersonal channels. In traditional societies, for example, daughters would turn to their mothers for advice on clothing, manners, personal hygiene, child rearing, and household chores. Young men would get information and advice from their fathers, uncles, or other male elders on how to deal with problems that they encountered regarding appropriate manly behavior, how to use existing technology, how to relate to members of the opposite sex, and generally what they should do in a variety of circumstances.

These customary sources from which people obtained such advice and information underwent change as urban-industrial societies developed. Today, few can still turn—or even want to turn—to those interpersonal sources for such information and advice. Instead, they find answers in the media. For example, women's magazines are filled with details about how to develop a better wardrobe, a slimmer body, or desirable relationships with males. Television ads show how to have more attractive hair or what household products to buy. Men's magazines and other media also provide practical information. Various ones explain how to catch more fish, how to have better success in developing larger muscles, or how to put together homemade furniture using basement workshops.

Even the common ads in the daily newspaper are sources of practical information on such matters as where the best buys can be obtained on mattresses, where to buy a suitable used car, or even how to contact others for a date. Turning to the media for such useful information does not require explanations based on complex need satisfactions.

Thus, a distinction must be made between using the media to obtain complex, need-based gratifications—or even to relieve boredom—and "using" the media to obtain practical information on how to deal with common problems of daily living. This difference has led in recent years to two separate theories. One is the Uses for Gratifications Theory, under discussion. The other is a (new) much simpler formulation, called Media Information Utility Theory. Discussed in Chapter 15, the latter focuses on ways people in contemporary societies have become dependent on media for information that helps in dealing with routine issues and common practical problems that are encountered in everyday life.

As noted earlier, the most important new idea in the Uses for Gratifications Theory was that people in audiences were *active* in exposure to the media. It was clear that audiences were goal oriented, exercising a great deal of personal choice in picking what media content to which they wanted to attend. Less clear was the answer to *why* they chose particular types of media content. Because of the psychological focus of the early investigations, answers were sought within a structure of individual personality characteristics of members of the audience. This led to a focus on human needs. This seemed logical because such needs are often thought to serve as *motivators*, explaining why people engage in many kinds of behavior—including attending to mass communications. Thus, individual needs and their satisfaction or gratification moved to center stage in the development of the emerging theory. Today, the basic ideas of the Uses for Gratifications Theory can expressed in a list of assumptions that, if regarded as true, lead to a logical prediction. Stated as a set of interrelated formal propositions, the theory can be summarized as follows.

THE USES FOR GRATIFICATIONS THEORY: A FORMAL SUMMARY

1. Audience members *do not wait passively* to attend to whatever forms of content and programming that the media happen to transmit.
2. Consumers of mass communications have *a structure of motivating needs* that they seek to gratify through various kinds of experiences.
3. Those needs have been shaped by the individual's *inherited nature,* as well as by his or her personal *learning experiences,* within a web of social relationships and social category memberships.
4. Their structure of needs leads audience members *actively to seek specific forms of media content* that can provide diversion, entertainment, respite, or other kinds of need satisfactions.
5. **Therefore**, members of the audience actively select, and then attend to, specific forms of media content *that provide gratifications that fulfill their needs.*

Today it is recognized that explanations in terms of needs and their gratifications focuses mainly on the individual person. It attempts to explain complex behavior almost solely on the basis of motivations, needs, and gratifications that take place within the psychological functioning of the individual. Such a perspective is not complex enough to aid in understanding many forms of behavior. It ignores the influence of *social organization* (norms, roles, ranks, and controls) that can have profound influences on individual behavior. The same is true of *culture* (shared beliefs and behavioral requirements) and social *relationships* (interpersonal influences).

All of these can be important factors in determining to what media content people will attend. For example, individuals may seek exposure to specific forms of media content because what they do at work requires it. People in one society, with a traditional culture, may decline to attend to media content from another culture that is in conflict with their beliefs. A devoted wife may elect to sit through a broadcast of a football game on TV solely on the basis that it pleases her husband if she shares the experience. The program itself may provide her with very little in the way of need gratification. Indeed, she may regard it as totally incomprehensible and boring. Similarly, a thoughtful husband may tolerate attending a sappy romance movie because he knows that his wife enjoys it. Thus, while some media selections may indeed be made on the basis of need gratification, other kinds of exposures are based on personal, social, cultural, and emotional considerations that guide people in what they choose to consume from the media.

Many criticisms, evaluations, and reviews of the Uses for Gratifications Perspective (and tradition) have been published over the years. Recently, for example, Ruggiero assessed its current state as we began the decades of the twenty-first century.[19] He summarized the main issues addressed in 196 scholarly publications that had appeared over more than half a century. He concluded that it remains a conceptualization that will continue to provide explanations for media-related behavior and directions for research in the future. In particular, he maintains that it will be important in understanding use of the Internet as it continues to take its place among the American media mix—just as it was for newspapers, magazines, radio, movies, and television. At the same time, he recognized that the concepts used in the formulation, as it has been portrayed in the past, have often been vague and methodologically naive.

The bottom line is that the Uses for Gratifications Theory is still under study and revision. Researchers continue to try to understand the needs that people have and how various forms of media content provide for their gratification. It is a difficult task and one not likely to be fully resolved in the near future. In the end, it may not matter. There probably will never be a single list of needs—trivial or profound—that every human being seeks to gratify with media content.

Locating an inventory of universal needs that are always satisfied by a list of corresponding universal gratifications will probably turn out to be as difficult as finding the proverbial Holy Grail. Yet, for all of its limitations, the Uses for Gratifications Theory does help in understanding the selections that people actively make from the media—particularly if other factors are taken into account. Overall, and at least in part, the theory has moved forward our understanding of why people turn to mass communication in such large numbers.

Notes and References

1. The Payne Fund Studies consisted of thirteen specific studies of the influence of the movies on children, which were completed during the late 1920s and early 1930s. See W. W. Charters, *Motion Pictures and Youth: A Summary* (New York: Macmillan, 1933). More recently, these studies have been summarized in Shearon A. Lowery and Melvin L. DeFleur, *Milestones in Mass Communication Research: Media Effects,* 3rd ed. (White Plains, NY: Longman, 1995) pp. 21–43.

2. See Halley Central, *The Invasion from Mars: A Study in the Psychology of Panic* (Princeton, NJ: Princeton University Press, 1940). See also Lowery and DeFleur, *op. cit.,* pp. 45–67.

3. This was a nationwide study of listeners of twenty different daytime serials that were being broadcast on CBS and NBC at the time (1940). The listening behavior of these women were followed for several weeks in order to understand their levels of satisfaction and preferences. No specific information is available on the nature of the sample, other than the fact that it was large. See Paul F. Lazarsfeld and Frank N. Stanton, *Radio Research, 1942–43* (New York: Duel, Sloan and Pierce, 1944), pp. 3–33.

4. Herta Herzog, "What Do We Really Know About Daytime Serial Listeners?" in Paul Lazarsfeld and Frank Stanton, *Op. Cit.,* pp. 3–33.

5. K. M. Wolfe and M. Fisk, "Why Children Read Comics," in P. F. Lazarsfeld and F. N. Stanton, eds., *Communications Research, 1948–49* (New York: Harper, 1949). See also B. Berelson, "What 'Missing the Newspaper' Means," in P. F. Lazarsfeld and F. N. Stanton, *Op. Cit.*

6. Wilbur Schramm, Jack Lyle, and Edwin Parker, *Television in the Lives of Our Children* (Palo Alto, CA: Stanford University Press, 1961).

7. *Ibid.* p. 1.

8. Jack M. McLeod and Lee Becker, "Testing the Validity of Gratification Measures Through Political Effects Analysis," in J. G. Blumler and E. Katz, eds., *The Uses of Mass Communications: Current Perspectives on Gratification Research* (Beverly Hills, CA: Sage, 1974).

9. E. Katz, J. G. Blumler, and M. Gurevitch, "Utilization of Mass Communication by the Individual," in J. G. Blumler and E. Katz, eds., *The Uses of Mass Communication: Current Perspectives on Gratifications Research* (Beverly Hills, CA: Sage, 1974).

10. J. G. Blumler and E. Katz, *op. cit.*

11. E. Katz, J. G. Blumler, and M. Gurevitch, "Utilization of Mass Communication by the Individual," in J. G. Blumler and E. Katz, *Op. Cit.,* p. 21.

12. *Ibid.* pp. 21–22.

13. K. E. Rosengren, L. A. Wenner, and P. Palmgren, *Media Gratifications Research: Current Perspectives* (Beverly Hills, CA: Sage Publications, 1984)

14. *Ibid.*

15. *Ibid.* p. 12.

16. A. H. Maslow, *Motivation and Personality* (New York: Harper, 1954).

17. H. D. Thoreau, *Walden: or Life in the Woods* (New York: Vintage Books, 1991), p. 9. First published in 1854.

18. William J. McGuire, "Psychological Motives and Communication Gratifications," in Rosengren, Wenner, and Palmgren, *Op. Cit.,* p. 169.

19. Thomas E. Ruggiero, "Uses and Gratifications Theory in the 21st Century," *Mass Communication & Society,* 3, 1, Winter 2000, pp. 3–37.

CHAPTER 15

Media Information Utility Theory[1]

P eople in contemporary urban-industrial societies, such as ours, make heavy use of the content of our mass media for a great variety of purposes. These range from seeking utilitarian information needed for routine decisions about practical problems to obtaining psychological gratification for complex and deep-seated needs. The information they use for these purposes includes checking the newspaper to learn when the movie starts at the local theater or even enjoying vicarious sexual experiences by viewing hard-core pornographic material on pay-per-view channels on cable television. It was the realization that people pick and choose, depending on their personal and social characteristics, that led to the formulation of the Selective and Limited Influences Theory (Chapter 10).

As has been discussed in earlier chapters, as research on this issue accumulated, "magic bullet" conceptualizations were discredited. In their place came the conclusion that audiences are *highly selective* in the ways in which they read newspapers, magazines, and books; pick movies; watch television; rent DVDs to see films on their television sets; or listen to the radio. For that reason, any single media message may influence the specific individuals who attend to it, but it can have little influence on the audience as a whole—most of whom do not attend to it. That conclusion is as valid today as it was many decades ago.

THE UNDERLYING PROBLEM: EXPLAINING SELECTIVITY MOTIVATION

Once it is realized that people are highly selective in what they choose from the media, it becomes important to try to explain *why*. That is, when people pick certain kinds of content and ignore others, *what is it that motivates their selectivity*? A major attempt to provide an answer to this question of motivation was the Uses for Gratifications Theory, set forth in the previous chapter. Emerging in the late 1940s from a substantial body of psychological concepts and research, this theory maintained that a significant factor leading to attention to mass communication content is the person's motivation *to fulfill deep-seated needs* through gratifications that can be obtained from specific forms of media content.

Viewed in this way, the Uses for Gratification Theory provides an important extension to the earlier Selective and Limited Influences Theory. The basic explanation was that people have different "needs" as a product of their personal experiences, their genetic inheritance, or their socialization within a particular culture. Therefore, the theory explains, they select different content to achieve gratification for those needs.

This turned out to be a very popular explanation that stimulated an enormous volume of research over more than a half century. That research focuses on different categories of human needs and how they motivate people to select different types of media content that will provide satisfactions and gratifications for those needs. This seems, at first glance, to be a very simple and intuitively obvious formulation. That is, needs provide motivation; selective exposure to media content provides gratification for those needs.

While the Uses for Gratifications Theory did provide a popular answer to the question of why people are so selective regarding media exposure, there are a number of unanswered questions about issues that are fundamental to this formulation. For one thing, it *assumes the existence of a similar structure of deep-seated needs within each person*. It then assumes that these needs are the prime motivational factors leading to media exposure. That structure of similar needs has been much discussed and debated. However, the exact number and nature of those fundamental human needs that are presumed to motivate selection and consumption of media content have never been agreed upon by behavioral scientists. It seems unlikely that they will reach consensus about that issue in the near future. Moreover, exactly how distinct *forms* of media content provide *specific patterns of gratification* for particular *kinds of needs* remains to be discovered. In short, the Uses for Gratifications Theory, focusing on one specific motivational concept, depends on variables that are difficult to define and (more important) to observe in an empirical manner.

In a very real sense, then, and in spite of its popularity, the Uses for Gratifications explanation is still under development regarding its basic underlying concepts. One of its major problems is the underlying logic that is used in directly linking needs to behavior. This problem is not restricted to this particular theory but is common to many kinds of psychological theories that purport to explain human motivation. This problem can be appreciated by examining certain *alternative motivational concepts* that could be used instead of "deep-seated needs."

THE LOGIC OF NEEDS-GRATIFICATION EXPLANATIONS

A close look at the underlying logic of the needs-gratification formulation indicates that it may be equally valid to attribute media content selection to certain other, rather different, motivational concepts. That is, attributing a form of behavior to an assumed underlying motivation can take many forms. As will be indicated, using the concept of "needs" is only one possibility among the alternatives available.

The logic used to explain a form of conduct by attributing it to any particular motivational mainspring, such as needs, goes something like this: (1) A distinctive *pattern of behavior* can be observed repeatedly among a population. (2) An *explanation* is required. A simple way of accounting for this regularity is to say that, (3) among the observed population, the activity being observed is motivated by an *invisible psychological factor* that drives the person on to engage in that pattern of behavior and that (4) engaging in that behavior *serves some purpose*, such as fulfillment, satisfaction, or (in the case of needs) gratification for the actor. In the case of "needs" as an "invisible psychological factor," the logic is straightforward:

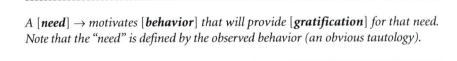

A [**need**] → motivates [**behavior**] that will provide [**gratification**] for that need.
Note that the "need" is defined by the observed behavior (an obvious tautology).

The problem with this logic is that there are too many unknowns. While the behavior (selecting specific media content) may be empirically observable, other features of the process are not. These include the human needs themselves (inferred from the behavior), presumably serving as a motivational engine—but hidden within the human psyche. Similarly, the process of gratification that is said to satisfy those needs can only be "inferred." As yet unknown is *how a specific form of media content provides precisely the (inferred) gratification that will satisfy a particular (inferred) need*.

Moreover, there is no consensus among psychologists as to the nature or origins of human needs. It is clear that the human body requires food, water, and at least some shelter from harsh elements (obvious "needs"). But beyond that, speculation and inference has gone in many directions. Freud, Maslow, and others have developed lists of needs—ranging from "libidinal drives" to "self-actualization."[2] But the logic on which they are based is precisely that indicated in the above diagram—a kind of "black box" interpretation that begins with observing behavior and then inferring (unobservable) motivational and gratification processes that are said to provide mainsprings of action. In short, in spite of extensive writings on the subject, there has never been consensus on the exact *nature* of needs, their *origins* (inherited vs. learned), and how a specific experience provides *gratification* for an assumed need. All that exists is a long list of conflicting and unrelated speculations and inferences.

ALTERNATIVE BLACK BOXES

Essentially, then, "needs" serve as a kind of "black box" that appears to produce an effect—but no one has been able to take the lid off that box to see its internal workings. A metaphorical parallel would be the primitive tribesman who discovers a pocket watch in the jungle. After much manipulation and observation, he is able to wind the watch and detect that the hands go around in sympathetic movement with the sun. That behavior is clearly observable. However, he has no idea what is inside the watch to produce that effect. He has no way to remove that back of the watch to observe what is inside. Nevertheless, an explanation is required. In the end, he explains it as either "magic" or there is a god within the watch who runs things—accounts consistent with his culture.

The same logic that is used in needs-explanations could be used to explain virtually anything. For example, Joe Suburban can be observed with great regularity mowing his lawn every Saturday. To explain this behavior, one need only postulate a "lawn-mowing need" that is gratified by pushing the machine back and forth. That particular black box is no different in its logical form than the one in the above diagram that is used to explain media selectivity based on needs gratification.

There are a number of alternative black boxes that could possibly serve as well in the above diagram to explain media content selection. These too have been used as explanations for various kinds of complex behavior by psychologists at one time or another. Two examples are *instinct* and *addiction*. Although these concepts may seem totally inappropriate for explaining behavior related to mass communication, at least one (addiction) has been so used. However, the logic on which both instinct and addiction are based is really little different from that used in need-gratification approaches.

We have already explained that, early in the 1900s, instinct provided a popular explanation of how human behavior is motivated. The concept was abandoned by the late 1920s. However, interestingly enough, it may now be making a comeback as a result of new interpretations of human genetics as a motivator of behavior. The second concept, "addiction," quite obviously is usually thought of in connection with drugs, alcohol, and tobacco. However, it is now being used by some writers to explain certain forms of media content selection. A brief look at both of these alternatives can help to understand the logical problem associated with theory construction using any such "black box" explanation.

Instincts

The term "instinct" is a concept rooted firmly in Darwinian thought. It has long been clear that certain forms of animal behavior (migrations, sexual attraction, nest building, etc.) can often be explained in this manner. At one time, psychologists sought "laws of behavior" that were universal along the phylogenetic continuum—a search for patterns of action that are common among all (or at least many) species, including *homo sapiens*. These seemed to offer opportunities for explanations in terns of instincts. Some still pursue this idea in their search for patterns of "language" communication among certain animals that parallel those found among human beings. Nevertheless, putting instinct into the black box to explain media content selection may seem truly far-fetched, because even in social psychology it is now considered totally obsolete. However, as will be discussed, it is currently undergoing an interesting revival in a very different discipline.

For decades, during the early twentieth century, the concept of instinct was invoked as an explanation to account for numerous forms of complex human activity. At the time, it had one distinct advantage as a black box. It was said to be based firmly in (highly respected) biology—as a *genetically inherited pattern* of behavioral predispositions. The idea was something like this: If a consistent pattern of human behavior was observed, it could be explained as the consequence of an underlying *inherited, unlearned,* and *universal* (among the species) motivational force—an inherited mainspring that guides complex patterns of action. It supposedly worked in ways similar to those found among animals that clearly do have such instincts. Early in the 1900s, such human behaviors as "motherhood," "home-building," "acquisitiveness" (accounting for saving money), and "pugnaciousness" (as a cause of war) were easily explained by attributing them to this motivational mainspring. Psychology texts of the time contained long lists of human instincts, said to motivate many kinds of complex behavior. These had to be memorized by psychology students preparing for exams.[3]

Eventually, the existence of a highly focused instinct came to be assumed for almost any form of patterned human activity—even actions and behavior that were unusual and very specific. For example, in its final phases of popularity, an instinct was said to exist to explain the observable human behavior pattern of putting little baby birds back in their nests when they had fallen out. This was an observable practice, so an explanation was required. A contemporary example might be that Joe Suburban has an "instinct" that drives his lawn-mowing behavior. However, partly because of such unlikely attributions, and mainly because no truly universal patterns of complex behavior could be identified, the utility of the concept began to come into question.

By the 1920s, instinct came to be critically re-examined by psychologists. It had become clear that there were no universal, unlearned, and inherited forms of complex behavior to be found among all human populations.[4] Such behavior as "survival" and "motherhood" were certainly not universal (some people committed suicide, and some mothers killed their infants). The only universals to be found were very simple reflexes, like eye blinks, knee jerks, and the like. Moreover, as the study of learning progressed, it came to be accepted that human conduct was far more likely to be a product of habits acquired by *learning,* and that these varied with socialization within a particular culture. As result, the Darwin-inspired concept of instinct was completely abandoned by psychologists as an explanation for complex human conduct (except for followers of Freud) by the late 1920s.

However, as youngsters might say today, *It's baaaaack!* Like the mythical phoenix, the instinct concept now appears to be rising from the ashes of its earlier dismissal by psychologists. In recent years, developments in molecular biology have revived interest in the idea. Following the discovery in the 1950s of the double-helix structure of DNA by James Watson and Francis Crick, increasingly detailed understandings are being uncovered concerning the nature of the chromosomes and genes that provide uniqueness among human beings and other living things.

More recently, extensive efforts have made it possible to map the molecular and even atomic structure of genes—the human genome. One assumption, of at least some of the biologists who spearhead this type of research, is that deep within the atomic (DNA) structure of the molecules that make up human genes, investigations will reveal *patterns that explain the nature of human instincts.* In short, they want to take the lid off the black box and look inside, find instincts, and see how they work.

> Having created a new science, they were racing on. They thought of the problem of instinct as an extension of the problem of inheritance. An instinct, like a gene, is a kind of memory, a gift of time. The gift confers enormous advantages on all those that possess it. We are born knowing a thousand things we could not reinvent in a lifetime if we started from scratch.[5]

At present, such research focuses on humble species, such as *drosophila,* the fruit fly, but the vision for the future is that even something as seemingly intractable to science as "free will" will eventually yield to research by molecular biologists as they try to "break apart each act of instinctive behavior into a series of steps they called 'atoms of behavior.'"[6] Whether or not such a search for an atomic explanation of instinctual behavior—presumably including attention to specific forms of media content—will ever succeed is anyone's guess.

The major point being made here is that, using the same logic as that of needs-gratification explanations, there are a number of black-box theories that can be invoked to account for the actions of human beings. The problem is that, at present, each suffers exactly the same limitations of the needs-gratifications approach to explain media behavior. What goes on in the black box *cannot be observed.* The uncomfortable conclusion is that one person's hypothesized black-box explanation is as good as another's, as to why people select and attend to specific forms of media content.

Curiously, the concept of instinct was never abandoned by journalists as well as much of the public. When asked why people engage in some specific pattern of behavior, a common answer is that, "*It is just human nature.*" If one looks at that explanation closely, however, it is a statement that human beings inherit a genetic makeup that motivates them to perform [whatever activities are under discussion]. Additionally, that explanation presumably applies to *all* human beings—regardless of age, gender, race, and so forth. That is about as good a definition of instinct as one could formulate. Thus, even though the concept was abandoned long ago by behavioral scientists as an explanation for patterned human conduct, it continues to be used in news reports, as well as in discussions among the general public.

Addictions

An even older black box that is used today to label the motivational forces behind certain kinds of repeated exposure to media content is "addiction." This term is increasingly being found today in news stories and even among some psychologists who try to explain *behavior related to the Internet.* Some use it to explain why some people extensively use video games. In another example, the term is currently being used in the press to label the motivation of individuals who obtain gratification from sexual content (for which the popular term is *cybersex*). It refers to getting sexual thrills by selecting and viewing pornographic content on one's computer screen via the Internet. Claims are made that this constitutes a "dangerous new addiction" affecting people from many walks of life. For example, a recent newspaper report posed the issue in these terms:

> The Internet is revolutionizing sexuality, said Al Cooper, clinical director of a sexuality clinic in San Jose, Calif. He told psychologists [at a professional conference] that cybersex is changing the definition of sexual compulsion [read 'addiction'] 'like crack cocaine changed the field of substance abuse.'[7]

Psychologists at the 2000 conference were told that the anonymity provided by the Internet, plus the great variety of fetish and fantasy content that can be found on erotic websites, create a "compulsive need" for cybersex. Moreover, this, they maintained, can damage marriages and relationships. Kimberly Young, a clinical psychologist reporting at the conference, is quoted as saying: "The pain that this can tear through a relationship is deep, and it is profound. And relapse is just a click away."[8] These "experts" (who do not represent the mainstream of psychology) recommended that those afflicted with a "cybersex addiction" (their term) should receive therapy. Young offers such "treatment" for a fee via the Internet through her (private) Center for Online Addiction.[9]

In invoking the concept of addiction to explain such forms of behavior, the logic is the same as with need and instinct. That is, a complex pattern of behavior is observed, and a ready (black box) explanation is provided by attributing it to an "addiction." However, in the case of this particular black box, the use of this concept to explain why people repeatedly select cybersex *seems particularly inappropriate.* The specific reasons for this judgment are explained in the section on the "medical model," which follows. The same could be said of explaining Joe Suburban's repeated behavior with the lawn mower as an "addiction." The basis of this judgment that such attributions are inappropriate is that the criteria for identifying an actual addiction do not fit even remotely well with the behavior that its users are trying to explain.

What, precisely, is an "addiction"? For one thing, attributing a form of behavior to an addiction defines the person involved as in the iron grip of a force that is *beyond his or her self-control.* This is very convenient for the individual involved. Conceptualizing motivation to select sexual (or other) media content in this way *relieves the actor of responsibility* for his or her behavioral choices because he or she is presumably totally unable to quit. Those advocating "therapy" for cybersex "addicts" suggest that all those afflicted have to do is "delete their Internet bookmarks to the erotic sites." The same applies to anyone who uses the Internet to excess. As noted, there are those who will offer "therapy" (for a price).

This "I am not responsible" interpretation of excessive Internet use has led one lawyer to plan a defense of his client in a criminal case around "Internet intoxication" (i.e., "addiction"). The lawyer's client, an eighteen-year-old from Cape Coral, Florida, wrote threats while in a chat room to a sixteen-year-old student from Columbine High School in Littleton, Colorado (where, in 1999, twelve students and a teacher were shot and killed in a highly publicized massacre). The attorney, Ellis Rubin, maintained that his client was "so addicted to the Internet that he lived in a 'virtual world' and should not be held accountable for the threat."[10] Lawyers critical of this strategy maintain that it appears to be the "Twinkie defense" of the cyberspace age (a strategy so named after a San Francisco lawyer who tried to defend his client on a murder charge by claiming that he had eaten so much junk food, like Twinkie cupcakes, that he should not be held responsible for his crime).

There is no doubt that excessive preoccupation with the Internet can cause problems. There are many individuals who spend so much time online that other aspects of their lives and their relationships with family and friends suffer. Such individuals do seem obsessive or driven in some manner. For example, a man writing to the *Straits Times* (of Singapore) reported the following:

> We were happily married for 20 years before she got on the Internet. She has had at least one cyber-lover that she says she fell in love with. She will have nothing to do with me any more. If I ask her a question about anything she snaps at me, as if I am wasting her time with stupid questions. I cannot talk to her any more, touch her, or have any oher contact with her. When I am home, she is always on the Internet chatting. . . . I don't know what to do but pray to God that she soon comes to her senses and realizes that she has a family that loves her more than her cyber-friends ever will.[11]

While the behavior described does seem obsessive, one must ask in such cases if there is a simpler explanation. That is, with respect to this, or similar cases, is the Internet behavior a *cause* or a *consequence*? That is, did the relationship between husband and wife deteriorate for other reasons—sending the wife to seek solice by getting online? In other words, what appears to be an "open and shut" case for Internet addiction may very well be a result of other *prior* factors—that is, pressures and problems in these two persons' lives. Again, the principle of parsimony should be observed—the simplest explanation is usually the best.

The idea that individuals are not responsible for their Internet usage because of an "addiction" has been challenged by other critics. For example, Jonathan Sidener, writing for the *Arizona Republic,* takes objection to the use of this term by newspapers—not only in this country but in others as well. He notes that there are very real addictions to substances that do create serious withdrawal symptoms. Excessive use of the Internet does not do this:

The Medical Model

The quotation above indicates that an important misuse of the term "addiction" to describe excessive use of the Internet or of video games is that such an application does not fit into a *medical model*—that is, a *biologically, based illness perspective.* When such a model is used, it makes the actor a *victim* who needs *therapy*—not criticism. In addition, as noted earlier, defining the cause of the behavior within such a model shifts the responsibility for escaping from the controlling "addiction" to some sort of *therapist* whose job it is to "cure" the person who has fallen prey to the dreadful condition.

Thus, the traditional meaning of an "addiction" is clearly based on a "medical" model, and it has merit for classifying certain specific forms of behavior. That model has long and correctly been used to explain the plight of people who engage in the excessive use of alcohol, narcotics, and (possibly) tobacco to a point where they truly lose control. To account for such behavior, the medical model was developed many years ago, and various kinds of therapists and treatments have been devised to get the victim out of the clutches of such addictions.

The opposite of this idea is the claim—supported by some—that there is no such thing as a true "involuntary addiction." This point of view is advanced by those who point out that people who drink excessively, use illegal drugs, or smoke too much voluntarily made the initial free choices that led them into their current pattern of behavior. Furthermore, such critics maintain, they continue to make such choices voluntarily, and they can exercise the same freedom of choice at any time to stop. That issue directly confronts those who describe viewing pornography as an addiction. Is such media content selection voluntary or involuntary? This "free-will" (and non-medical) model may be more appropriate to describe the excessive use of the Internet.

There are other clear reasons why explaining repeated viewing of pornography on the Internet (or attending to any other form of media content) in terms of an involuntary addiction is inappropriate and a serious misuse of the concept. A closer look at the origins of the addiction concept, and the way it is used to account for substance abuse, reveals that the term does have a clear meaning in the fields in which it originally developed—meanings that *disqualify it* as an explanation of Internet behavior.

An addiction, then, is by no means a mysterious black box. The technical meaning of addiction is that it is a strong urge that people feel *after their bodies have become accustomed to—and are physically dependent upon*—the presence of certain chemical substances. Thus, addictions are firmly rooted in biological processes. The substances involved that produce these organic changes can be alcohol, opiates, or other narcotics—or perhaps nicotine. Because of these changes in bodily functioning, an addicted person experiences great physical discomfort and pain when denied such substances. This distress is often referred to as *withdrawal symptoms.* They are very real and very distressing. The person having such experiences is strongly motivated to obtain the substance that will restore bodily homeostasis and bring relief.

The study of true addictions within a medical model has a long history. During the Civil War, for example, shortly after the invention of the hypodermic syringe in 1856, wounded soldiers were often given (newly discovered) morphine—a derivative of opium—to relieve the pain they suffered during and following amputations and other surgery. While pain was temporarily relieved, there were unsuspected side effects of these substances on their bodies. Many became physiologically dependent on the continued (and slowly increasing) use of the drug. The term that was used at the time to describe their condition was the "army disease." Today, it would be immediately classified as "drug addiction." Other citizens who had surgery or suffered from other painful conditions were similarly treated with narcotics. They also became dependent. By the early decades of the twentieth century, it was estimated that there were at least 250,000 such "medical addicts" who had by this means become dependent on opiate derivatives.[12]

Another important feature of a true addiction interpreted within a medical model is *psychological dependence.* This is not the same idea as appears to be involved in so-called "Internet addiction." In that case, the person achieves some sort of psychological satisfaction or gratification from engaging in the activity. In a true addiction, however, the situation is different. Psychological dependence is a condition that results when the addicted individual realizes exactly what substance will reduce his or her withdrawal symptoms. It requires an understanding that the distress (biologically based withdrawal symptoms), experienced when the drug wears off, can be replaced by feelings of well-being, or even euphoria, by further intake of that particular substance. This is not the same idea as believing that some *activity* (such as using the Internet) will reduce anxiety and discomfort. In the case of a true addiction, it is intake of the chemical substance that reduces withdrawal distress by modifying the biological conditions that gave rise to the problem.

That is not to say that people who habitually use the Internet do not gain enjoyment, satisfaction, or gratification from that activity. Undoubtedly they do so. However, the same could be said of fly-fishing, playing tennis, or bowling. Those activities also provide enjoyment, satisfaction, or gratification—but even among those who pursue them avidly, they are seldom confused with an "addiction."

Adding to the criteria for classifying a condition as a true addiction is a third feature that makes up a part of the medical syndrome. Addicts often develop a *tolerance* for the substance—and ever-increasing doses are needed, not necessarily to achieve a state of euphoria, but just to feel "normal." That is:

> Addicts experience both tolerance and dependence. According to the World Health Organization, *addiction* involves (1) an overpowering desire or compulsion to continue taking the drug, (2) a tendency to increase the dose, (3) a psychological and general physical dependence on the drug, and (4) detrimental effects on the individual and the society.[13]

The medical model for interpreting patterns of behavior has a long history. This important concept developed from Western society's experience with what came to be called "mental illness." Before the 1800s, there was no such "illness." People who were mentally deranged were simply referred to as "mad." The development of a medical model to explain behavior that society could not accept as "sane," and to make it appropriate to intervene with "treatment," took centuries.

Briefly, the idea was eventually developed as a means of understanding and dealing with the "mad." By the time widespread leprosy finally disappeared (by about 1500), and was no longer a basis for societal rejection, "madness" became the new category to take its place. At first, those so labeled were ignored, but eventually they came to be shunned, feared, and treated brutally. The "crazies" were simply put into prisons along with criminals and paupers or, in some cases, were transported through the canals and ports of Europe on vessels ("Ships of Fools") where for a fee they were exhibited for the amusement of the public. During the 1700s, "madhouses" were developed where those who were afflicted could be segregated to protect society. However, earlier interpretations of the causes of their plight still prevailed, and they were flogged, burned, starved, tortured, and worked to exhaustion to try to "drive out" the influence of demons, bad blood, Satan, or witches that had caused their problems. Later, after the medical model replaced such interpretations, "asylums" and special "hospitals for the insane" were developed where the afflicted could be both isolated from society and cared for in somewhat more humanitarian ways.

In summary, a close look at the traditional meaning of "addiction" as it came to be interpreted within a medical model shows that it is a very different idea than that currently being applied by some clinical psychologists and a large number of journalists to virtually any form of behavior that seems compulsive. This is unfortunate, because it is not a good black box to use to explain excessive use of the Internet, and it can be confusing to those who seek to understand true addictions to substances within a medical perspective.

SELECTIVITY BASED ON INFORMATION UTILITY

Aside from alternative black boxes and problems related to observing and defining needs, the Uses for Gratifications Theory clearly has other limitations. For one thing, it does not provide explanations of why people select many categories of media content that are simply and very obviously *unrelated to deep-seated needs*. Originally, that idea—that people turn to media for many other purposes—seems to have been recognized when the term "uses" (of media content) was included in the theory's traditional title. However, as the existing body of research and writing over the last half century indicates, virtually no attention has ever been given to practical "uses" that are unrelated to need fulfillment.

Because people pick and choose many kinds of media content that have little to do with complex needs, *a different type of theory* is required to account for more routine selectivity. One rather obvious explanation of such behavior is simply to assume that people use the media as a convenient source from which *to obtain information they can utilize to achieve practical goals or solutions to routine problems that characterize everyday life*. That is, they turn to the media for information that can be "helpful" but which cannot as easily be obtained from other sources. For example, people in modern society consult advertisements in the newspapers to find out where they can purchase a used car at the best price. They could drive around visiting various used car lots to compare prices but at considerable inconvenience. As another example, they may turn to broadcast weather reports to decide whether or not to water their lawn. Other media provide a quick and easy way to locate a suitable apartment to rent, to check the latest baseball scores, to scan opportunities for employment, or to find someone to wallpaper their bathroom. It would be quite a stretch to assume a complex need, instinct, or addiction for, say, used car purchases, weather information, or bathroom wallpapering.

Thus, the media provide the citizens of modern societies with a wealth of simple and practical information that is easy to find and useful in a variety of daily circumstances where decisions must be made to achieve simple goals. Advertisements are obviously one such source. "How to" TV shows are another. Magazine articles are still another. For example, even the most casual examination of many specialized magazines reveals that many are a kind of "instruction manual" providing practical lessons on various goals, hobbies, and interests. They instruct readers on how to take better photographs, plant tomatoes, select a suitable laptop computer, find an enjoyable vacation destination, raise better houseplants, or cook tastier meals. Men's magazines teach how to catch larger fish, make furniture in a basement workshop, tune up a car, and interpret the latest sports results.

Perhaps a case could be made that seeking out such information is motivated by complex needs, or other black boxes, and that obtaining it provides deep-seated psychological gratifications. However, an important dictum in science is the "principle of parsimony." As noted, what that principle teaches is that, when two or more explanations of a particular event or outcome are available, it is wisest to choose the simplest one. Thus, a theory attributing much selection of media content to practical and routine utilitarian purposes would appear to be a simpler explanation than available "black box" alternatives.

CHANGING SOURCES FOR UTILITARIAN INFORMATION

People have always required information to achieve simple and practical goals. However, the sources from which they obtain it have undergone change in modern times. The shift from a *Gemeinschaft* to a *Gesellschaft* social order was explained earlier (Chapter 6). As a consequence of that change, the *channels* through which people obtain useful information are very different today from what they once were.

In an earlier time, basic problem-solving information was obtained more or less directly from *other people* with whom a person had significant social ties. For example, if a young woman wanted to know the proper and best way to deal with a monthly bodily function or a problem like excess weight, she would be likely to turn to her mother or perhaps another trusted female relative. If a young man wanted to understand how to catch a particular kind of fish or how to repair a broken chair, he would ask his father, an uncle, or even a knowledgeable neighbor who had such expertise. Today, however, it is less likely that the needed answers will be available through such channels. The traditional ties between people that existed in village life, or among members of multigenerational rural families are simply less likely to be there. It is more likely that answers to a great many practical problems would be obtained from the mass media in one form or another.

Mass Media in Mass Society

In other words, a major reason for turning to media sources for utilitarian information is that we live in a society in which networks of interpersonal ties are less deeply established as they were in pre-industrial societies. As was explained in Chapter 6, in modern life people of many unlike backgrounds live in physical proximity to each other, but with extensive differences based on ethnicity, race, education, income, religion, and other characteristics. Such social and cultural differences pose barriers to interpersonal communication. This tends to inhibit the free flow of information between people, and it leads them to turn to other sources to get the information that they can use.

That is not to say that in contemporary "mass" societies we do not retain family ties and networks of friendships. Obviously, they are not completely absent. However, they are not as extensive and open as was the case in the older traditional societies, where people lived together in small communities generation after generation without mass media. Today, our relatives and friends are more likely to live in other parts of the city or even in other parts of the country. As a consequence, in large part, it is the mass media today that provide information that we use as a basis for making many kinds of decisions and for solving many kinds of practical problems in our daily existence.

Obviously, practical problems confront each of us every day, and we consult available sources for answers. To understand more fully how routine information is obtained and used by individuals, a simple and down-to-earth explanation is needed of where that person goes for such information and why. The simplest possible explanation is that individuals seek enormous amounts of information from media on a daily basis. Garden enthusiasts read horticulture magazines. Advice to the lovelorn is readily available from the newspaper. Radio talk shows supply opinions and assessments of public personalities and issues. Television teaches everything from how to install kitchen cabinets to what to buy mom for Mother's Day or ways in which to prepare a soufflé. The Internet is increasingly a source from which "how to do it" lessons can be obtained on a vast array of problems. Even lessons on how to make bombs can be found there. There is virtually no difficulty confronting people in modern life for which advice, answers, and lessons cannot be found in one of the media.

An Empirical Example: Companionship in the Classifieds

A concrete illustration of the functioning of the mass media in supplying useful information that can be used as a basis for decision making can be seen in a research project conducted by Merskin and Huberlie.[14] The study investigated advertising for potential romantic partners in daily newspapers.

Locating a potential mate for a young person of marriageable age was a well-established procedure in many traditional societies that existed before industrialization. For centuries there was considerable variation in the ways that traditional people formed community-sanctioned unions. Indeed, in many parts of the world, where traditional societies still prevail, some of those practices continue to be followed. In certain islands of the South Pacific, for example, the couple simply selected each other and then cohabited for an extended period before marriage to determine if they were compatible.[15] If everything went well, they were formally married. If not, new partners were sought until a suitable union was established. The community regarded this as a sensible and proper way to proceed. That can be contrasted with the practice in certain traditional Muslim societies that did not provide the participants with much choice. As a result of arrangements made between families, they were betrothed as infants and were formally married when they became of suitable age. In some cases, the couple had not seen or spoken with their bride or groom prior to the ceremony.[16] Perhaps even less romantic was the practice of the Yanomama Indians of the Amazon region in South America. They simply secured their wives by forcefully taking them from other tribes.

Today, in our present urban-industrial society, meeting other people in whom one might be potentially interested is one of the truly practical problems of daily life. How does one routinely go about identifying, meeting, and getting to know a suitable person to date, with whom to form a bond of companionship, possibly to live with or actually marry? The practices of traditional societies are scarcely the answer. In the absence of adequate information channels through interpersonal sources, the mass media have for some begun to supply utilitarian information. The Internet now provides ways to get acquainted and see if the participants are good prospects. Before the existence of the Internet, and even now, "personal" ads in newspapers and magazines supply information that can be useful in solving this problem. Thus, this form of media content has become increasingly routine and socially acceptable in recent years. Earlier, it was regarded as controversial, available only in offbeat publications that were not deemed suitable for family consumption. For example, publishing this kind of information was regarded as taboo among almost all newspaper editors and managers—even during the 1980s.

According to the findings of Merskin and Huberlie, a few newspapers began experimenting with personal ads in the late 1980s. However, adoption of this form of content accelerated after about 1990. By the early 1990s, the majority of American newspapers were including personal advertisements. Of the sixty-seven newspapers that were studied (a random sample of the 268 dailies in the U.S.), "...nearly four out of five (82.1%) were carrying personal advertisements. An additional seven, or 10.4% of the dailies, said they had plans to carry the personals within the next few months."[17] Furthermore, the decision to accept and offer to readers this form of media content by newspapers followed a classic "adoption curve" (see Chapter 18).

The provision of this type of information about potential intimate human relationships by daily newspapers is a clear illustration of the change that took place in modern societies from interpersonal sources of information to media channels. Earlier, such information would have been provided by parents, other relatives, close friends, acquaintances, neighbors, or perhaps the clergy. As the media took over this information function, however, interested parties need not do much more than consult their morning newspaper while eating breakfast or go online. Shopping for a companion, or even a potential mate, is not much more difficult than reading the ads to find out efficiently and easily where tomatoes are on sale or where one might rent a furnished apartment.

MEDIA INFORMATION UTILITY THEORY: A FORMAL SUMMARY

This explanation of the relationship between certain kinds of content of the mass media, the changing nature of society, and this type of selectivity exercised by audiences can be called Media Information Utility Theory. As can be seen, it is an attempt to explain the heavy use that contemporary audiences make of *practical* information—information not related to deep-seated needs—that they seek out from various media sources, attend to, and make use of for a variety of utilitarian purposes in urban-industrial societies.

This theory is intended to correct the confusing "uses" term currently found in the original name of the Uses and Gratifications Theory. Since that theory is almost exclusively concerned with a search for deep-seated needs that are gratified by selective exposure to media content and does not seem to address utilitarian uses, its name was changed in the present book to Uses *for*

Gratification Theory. This gives that theory a more defined focus—one that is consistent with a very large research literature on needs-gratification that has accumulated.

To provide for the host of selections of media content made by audiences that have little to do with deep-seated psychological needs and their gratification, the present theory was based in part on the Media System Dependency Theory (discussed by DeFleur and Dennis—see endnote 1) but modified and renamed the Media Information Utility Theory.[18] In this new form it attempts to explain the selection of, and attention to, many kinds of content routinely supplied by mass media—practical information that serves as a basis for dealing with problems people often encounter in daily life. In this sphere of human behavior, deep-seated needs gratification does not seem to be a readily applicable concept. The major propositions of the revised theory, therefore, can be summed up in the following terms:[19]

1. People in all societies make use of information acquired from others in order to make numerous decisions about numerous practical aspects of daily life.

2. In traditional societies, in which people are closely linked to word-of-mouth networks of extended families, deeply established friendships, and other long-term ties, they obtain utilitarian information mainly through interpersonal channels.

3. In urban-industrial societies, populations are greatly differentiated by race, ethnicity, occupational specialization, complex socio-economic classes, and other forms of social and cultural diversity.

4. Because of their far greater social differentiation, people in urban-industrial societies have fewer trusted word-of-mouth channels based on deeply established social ties through which they can obtain utilitarian information.

5. **Therefore**, people in urban-industrial societies turn to newspapers and other forms of mass communications for information for making many kinds of routine decisions, and the mass media provide them with a flow of utilitarian instructions, advice, and even role models through news, advertising, and entertainment content.

Notes and References

1. An earlier version of this theory, titled Media Information Dependency Theory, can be found in Melvin L. DeFleur and Everette E. Dennis, *Understanding Mass Communication*, 5th ed. (Boston: Houghton Mifflin, 1991), p. 3. For the purposes of this book, that theory title has been changed, along with a clear focus on utilitarian goals in selecting media content. The purpose is to make it distinct from the Uses for Gratification Theory, which almost exclusively focuses on deep-seated psychological needs to explain motivation for media content selection by audiences.

2. See, for example, Abraham H. Maslow, *Motivation and Personality* (New York: Harper and Row, 1970) and Sigmund Freud, *The Basic Writings of Sigmund Freud*, A. H. Brill translation (New York: Modern Library, 1900–1914 and 1938).

3. William McDougal, *An Introduction to Social Psychology* (Boston: J. W. Luce, 1908).

4. L. L. Bernard, *Introduction to Social Psychology* (New York: Holt, 1926).

5. Jonathan Weiner, *Time, Love and Memory: A Great Biologist and His Quest for the Origins of Behavior* (New York: Random House, 1999), p. 66.

6. *Ibid.* p. 84.

7. Erin McClam, "Online Sex Addiction on Rise, Specialists Say," Associated Press article in *The Boston Globe*, May 6, 2000, p. A12.

8. *Ibid.* p. A12.

9. (anonymous) "Hooked on your PC? Get Help Online for Internet Addiction," *Montreal Gazette*, June 4, 2000, p. W9.

10. (Fron Reuters), "Net Addiction to Be Issue in Columbine Case," *The San Diego Union Tribune*, January 16, 2000, p. A29.

11. (anonymous) From *The Straits Times* (Singapore), October 8, 1999, p. 11.

12. Charles E. Terry and Mildred Pellens, *The Opium Problem* (New York: Bureau of Social Hygiene, Inc., 1928), p. 41.

13. Nathan B. Eddy, Henry Halbach, Harris Isbell, and Maurice Severs, "Drug Dependence: Its Significance and Characteristics," *Bulletin of the World Health Organization*, 32, 1965, p. 722.

14. Debra L. Merskin and Mara Huberlie, "Companionship in the Classifieds: The Adoption of Personal Advertisements by Daily Newspapers," *Journalism and Mass Communication Quarterly*, 73, 1, Spring 1996, pp. 219–229.

15. John F. Peters, "Yanomama Mate Selection and Marriage," *Journal of Comparative Family Studies*, 18, Spring 1987, pp. 79–98.

16. Unni Wikan, *Behind the Veil in Arabia* (Chicago: The University of Chicago Press, 1982).

17. Merskin and Huberlie, *op. cit., p. 224.*

18. See Melvin L. DeFleur and Sandra Ball-Rokeach, *Theories of Mass Communication*, 5th ed. (White Plains, NY: Longman, 1989), pp. 297–326.

19. A related version of this theory and its implications appeared in Melvin L. DeFleur and Sandra Ball Rokeach, *Theories of Mass Communication*, 4th ed. (New York: Longman, 1984), pp. 240–250.

CHAPTER **16**

Modeling Theory

Modeling theory is an explanation that focuses on a *particular category* of effects of mass communication. As this chapter will indicate, this type of influence has long interested psychologists who study the effects of the media. Today it is regarded as a special case of *social learning theory*—a more general formulation that seeks to explain how people acquire new forms of behavior by observing other people performing them—either by observing them in real life or by attending to depictions embedded in the content of mass communications.[1] Sociologists have also studied ways in which people's behavior is shaped by what they observe in media depictions (see Chapter 17 on Social Expectations Theory). Sociologists, however, focus their attention on how people learn to act in groups and what kinds of behaviors are expected of members in different positions or roles within a group.

The two social sciences, sociology and psychology, are based on quite different paradigms—broad conceptualizations that guide strategies of investigation in their attempts to explain human conduct. We noted earlier that sociology focuses on relationships *between people* and the ways in which groups organize rules and expectations for their members' activities. Several types of social expectations become the focus in the field's search for clues as to how individuals shape their behavior. The other—psychology—looks *within the person*, focusing largely on products of learning, or sometimes genetics, to understand human actions. In review, then, psychologists develop theories that explain human behavior as shaped by what people have "in their heads." Their concepts include such factors as needs, attitudes, beliefs, gratifications, opinions, values, learned habits, and emotions.

The psychological paradigm provides the basis for what has come to be known as Modeling Theory. While the idea that people often imitate what they see others doing is an old one, as media research advanced, the term came to be applied to situations in which mass-communicated depictions, and especially visual representations, such as can be seen in movies and in television programs, show people performing a great variety of actions. Often these are "emulated," "imitated," or "adopted" by individual members of the audiences. These can be ways of relating to members of the opposite sex, modes of speaking, wearing various items of clothing, using distinctive hairstyles, or almost any other form of personal behavior.

The basic idea is that, when a member of the audience sees such an activity displayed, under a certain set of conditions, he or she may acquire, adopt, or emulate the depicted behavior. In this sense, the display in the media serves as a "model" for the member of the audience, and that person may "model" (that is, adopt) what he or she has seen. Thus, the term "model" is used in much the same way as in the fashion industry, where human models display various kinds of garments before audiences so as to encourage their adoption—that is, purchase and use. In media studies, Modeling Theory pertains to human behavior that is on display, rather than an item of clothing, and it is not a display deliberately designed to influence anyone.

The idea that audiences imitate what they see in media entertainment was an important finding in the early (1930s) Payne Fund Studies of the movies, discussed in previous chapters. Considerable attention was given to this type of influence on conduct from seeing the early films. At the time, Herbert Blumer asked more than a thousand youths to prepare written personal histories of their own experiences with movies and especially how the experience of seeing them had modified their behavior.[2] These subjects were college, junior college, and high school students, plus some office and factory workers. Each prepared a "motion picture autobiography," indicating what films they had seen and what they may have adopted from them in the way of new patterns of behavior.

These were carefully analyzed. Some of the main influences on females among these young people was the imitation of patterns for dress and beautification. Another, adopted by both males and females, was mannerisms—ways of walking, talking, gesturing, speaking, and so forth. Especially important, according to Blumer, were techniques of "love-making," which at the time (late 1920s and early 1930s) essentially meant flirting, kissing, and other forms of inter-gender conduct that did not include intimate sexual relationships.

There is no suggestion that those who design the media content that provides the modeled behavior deliberately set out to influence their audiences in a particular way, and there is no implication that the adopting person decides to imitate the model with planned and conscious intention. The display of modeled actions and their adoption can be a very subtle and unwitting process for both parties.

The broader explanation—the cognitive paradigm from which modeling theory in more modern terms was derived—is only one of many that have been developed to address the learning process. It is important in explaining the ways in which both animals and human beings acquire—that is, take up or adopt—new patterns of behavior. Understanding that process is of obvious importance to a large number of professional groups—teachers, parents, and many others.

The scientific study of learning began well over a century ago with the rote learning and memory experiments of Hermann Ebbinghaus.[3] Important pioneers in the field were Edward Thorndike, who focused on learning among animals, B. F. Skinner, Edward Tolman, Edwin Guthrie, and Clark Hull, each of whom developed somewhat different types of learning theories.[4] Today the study of learning, and ways to explain how it takes place, remains as perhaps the most central focus of psychology.

SOCIAL LEARNING THEORY

It is not often that a new theoretical perspective emerges that is purported to be a general explanation of why individuals adopt a broad range of new forms of human behavior. However, that precisely was the case when psychologist Albert Bandura developed the *social learning theory* during the 1960s. Bandura began to see a need for a different kind of explanation of how and why individuals acquire, adopt, and use (learn) certain patterns of overt behavior. Most of the learning theories from the past had emphasized a kind of mechanistic process with *direct and conscious experience* as the central factor in the acquisition of new forms of behavior.

That is, according to those earlier theories, the "organism" (person or animal) performs a new activity—possibly just by chance—and that performance brings some sort of "reward." That reward could be anything from relief from pain or hunger, or a more positive experience that brought some satisfying or pleasant condition. The theories maintained that, if performing an overt action in a particular situation consistently brought about some type of reward, then the probability that the activity would be repeated by the organism in similar circumstances is said to be *increased*—"reinforcing" the bond. If the organism then uses that action routinely in the same behavioral circumstances to gain the same type of satisfaction, a *habit* is said to have been established. That is, there is an increased probability that the action will be repeated. In this way, the reward that is usually a consequence of the action is said to provide *reinforcement of the habit*. These, then, were the central propositions and basic concepts of several learning theories over many decades.

A feature of the then-existing psychological explanations of behavior that troubled Bandura was the use of acquired *motivational forces* (within the person's psyche) to explain why a person undertook to engage in particular activities seeking rewards. As explained in the previous chapter, these motivations were said to be various learned *needs, drives,* or *impulses* that, in some cases, were presumed to operate below the level of consciousness. The problem, said Bandura, is that such explanations are *tautological* (logically circular). The same observations are used to identify the inner motivational impulse or other psychological determinate driving the action that is used to explain its consequences.

To refer to our earlier example (See Chapter 15), if we see Joe Suburban frequently mowing his lawn, we can explain that set of actions by postulating a "need or "drive" to engage in the activity. Then, when asked to explain how that motivational concept can be defined, the answer is that we can observe Joe engaging in the action, and that pattern of behavior defines the concept. Thus, both the conduct and its cause come to be defined tautologically by the same observable phenomena (mowing).

Or, in another example, if we observe a person who regularly behaves in hostile ways toward members of a particular minority, we can derive from those observations the conclusion that he or she has *learned and harbors a negative attitude* toward that category of persons (presumably a motivational factor). At the same time, if we have to explain to a friend why that person behaves in that hostile manner, we may state that it is because of his or her negative attitude. Thus, we have once again gone around in a tautological circle—using the same behavior to account for the acquisition of a motivational condition that we use to explain how it causes overt behavior. In questioning such explanations, Bandura put it in this way:

> The inner determinants often were inferred from the behavior that they supposedly caused, resulting in description in the guise of explanation. A hostile impulse, for example, was derived from a person's irascible behavior, which was then attributed to the action of an underlying hostile impulse.[5]

Bandura believed that a less tautological and mechanistic approach to learning was necessary and that the learned acquisition of inner motivational determinants was not an adequate way to explain the acquisition of patterns of conduct. His alternative answer was that learning takes place as a result of *observing patterns of behavior acted out by other people seen in a positive way—and understanding the consequences they have for those observed.*

Social Learning Theory, then, is an important key to understanding how people acquire new ways to respond to their environment. This type of learning takes place when an individual observes some kind of action performed by someone else and comes to understand that the behavior either benefits or punishes that observed person. If the observer regards the actor in a positive way, then he or she may acquire that behavior pattern if it appears to have positive consequences for him or her. Or the person avoids it in the future if those consequences are seen as negative. These features of the process may take place at a less than conscious level.

Observers can view other individuals acting out patterns of action in many contexts. They can do so as children on the playground, viewing what their peers act out. They can observe what siblings or parents do—and with what consequences. Or they can see actions and their consequences portrayed in media content. After making such observations, they can choose to adopt—that is, *imitate*—the activities that they see as bringing rewards, or they can elect to avoid those behaviors if they understand that they have negative consequences.

SOCIAL LEARNING FROM MEDIA DEPICTIONS AND REAL-LIFE SITUATIONS

While Blumer probed much the same issue in the Payne Fund Studies, the media had greatly expanded by Bandura's time. Moreover, a theory was needed that included both learning from media and acquiring behavior patterns just by seeing other people actually perform them. That is, he concluded that we learn many of our patterned actions by observing them directly in the overt behavior of others, as well as by seeing behavior portrayed in media. Particularly important as a source, then, are *visual media*—such as television or the movies, where depictions of people in action seem more realistic. Print media are less of a source. One can read descriptions of actions in a book or magazine, of course, or listen to someone describe or explain them in verbal terms on the radio, but these are not as rich in detail.

Specifically, then, *modeling* takes place when an actor carries out some activity that can be seen by that actor as an observer—either in real life or in a media portrayal. The obvious case is where a TV viewer or movie patron sees the action on a screen—as was the case in Blumer's time. The observer can not only see what is taking place but also assess the favorable or unfavorable consequences for the person performing the behavior in the depiction.

Modeling, in terms of learning behavior from media depictions, and in the sense discussed by Bandura, can be illustrated as it took place within a situation that was reported to the authors of this text *by a next-door neighbor.* The following is a description of what happened: The neighbor [whom we will call Mrs. Smith] was a middle-aged housewife who was also a conservative Christian. While she was not an outspoken critic of the use of alcohol, she had never tried any such beverages and knew little about them. Then, shortly after she and her husband had moved into the neighborhood, a small group of women who lived nearby called on her to get acquainted. She thought that was very nice and neighborly. She served tea and enjoyed meeting the women. Before leaving her home, the new friends invited Mrs. Smith to accompany them the next day on a shopping expedition at a nearby mall. She was happy to accept.

On the afternoon of the event, Mrs. Smith and the others went to the mall and rummaged through a number of stores, looking at various items and even buying a few things. Everyone seemed to be having a good time. Then, as the afternoon wore on, the leader of the group suggested that it was getting late. She also suggested that before they all went home they should make their usual stop at a nice cocktail lounge in the mall and have some refreshments. The other women were enthusiastic. Mrs. Smith was willing but a bit apprehensive. She knew little about such establishments and less about cocktails. She was not really sure what she should do there.

As it turned out, it was really not all that challenging. They all sat down in a booth. A nice young woman came to take their orders—just like in a restaurant. Each of the women ordered a different kind of cocktail. One ordered a Manhattan, another a martini, and still a third a tequila sunrise. Then, it was Mrs. Smith's turn. At first, she was at a loss. She did not want to reveal her ignorance of such worldly matters to the other women. But, having no real knowledge of any of those drinks—and reluctant to order an unsophisticated iced tea or a Coke—she felt very uneasy.

Then, suddenly, she remembered what she had seen on her favorite soap opera a few days earlier. Mrs. Smith recalled the female star of the show was an attractive young woman—a person whom Mrs. Smith thought it would be nice to be like. She remembered that the soap opera star and her boyfriend went to an establishment rather like the one she was in now to discuss their strained relationship. (The boyfriend wanted to dump her.) When the attendant in the TV soap opera came to their table, the young woman who starred in the play had said that she would have a "Brandy Alexander." Mrs. Smith remembered the name of the drink quite vividly because her brother's name was Alexander. With confidence, then, she simply said "I'll have a Brandy Alexander." As it turned out, it was a mild and pleasant-tasting concoction—a mixture of cream and brandy. She liked it. Later, each time the group went on another shopping expedition—and stopped to have a drink—Mrs. Smith had no problem. She just ordered a Brandy Alexander.

This simple encounter provides a clear example of Modeling Theory in action. As can be seen in the example, the modeling process proceeds in stages. Some form of behavior is acted out by a person—in this case, a drink order was depicted in a soap opera. Another person who faces, or will face, some sort of problem observes this activity conducted (that is, modeled) by an individual with whom he or she can "identify" (see as someone to be like). Then, because the depicted action appears to provide a solution to the observer's problem, he or she *emulates* (that is, imitates) the model. If trying the modeled behavior indeed does provide a solution to the problem, that is, a *reinforcing reward*, the imitated action will probably be repeated later in similar situations. That is, the action is likely to become a habit—a lasting part of the behavioral repertoire of the observer.

Obviously, modeling and emulation can take place in many contexts, from imitating an action seen in a real-life encounter to doing so for an action seen in a media portrayal, such as the soap opera scene just described. Modeling Theory, then, as used to explain media influences, focuses on the adoption of some pattern of behavior as a consequence of encountering it portrayed (modeled) in a media presentation.

Modeling Theory became one of the most popular focuses of research on media influences not long after the use of television became widely adopted in the United States. One reason why the theory came under special study was that it offered a possible explanation of how children learn to engage in aggressive acts by watching violence portrayed on television. That topic became a national concern during the 1960s and 1970s.

THE TROUBLESOME ISSUE OF TELEVISED VIOLENCE

Two major social changes, and one particularly significant set of events, took place in the United States during the 1960s that are relevant to the development of Modeling Theory. One was the introduction of television as a mass medium and its rapid adoption by the majority of American families. The resulting pattern of adoption over time formed a typical s-shaped curve (as will be described in Chapter 18, on the Diffusion of Innovation Theory). That is, a trickle of television broadcasts to homes to be received by innovators (who had purchased TV sets early on) began in a few cities in the last years of the 1940s, shortly after the end of World War II. However, great numbers of additional adoptions took place during the 1950s, as many stations came on the air. By the late 1960s the majority of all American homes had a TV set.

Two other changes also took place in the United States during that same period. One was an upsurge in rates of *crime and delinquency.* These rates rose sharply, especially among the young, creating a great deal of concern among the public. In addition, in several cities, instances of *civil disorder*—explosive urban violence—occurred. In a number of major cities in the United States, angry mobs engaged in destructive riots. Cars and buildings were burned. People were dragged from their cars and beaten, and widespread looting took place. Scenes of this violence could be viewed on television news broadcasts almost every night. The entire nation was deeply disturbed by the rise in crime and delinquency and greatly alarmed by the urban upheavals.

As these changes in TV acquisition and urban upheavals took place at the same time, many people began to believe that there was a causal link between them. That is, at least some made the inference that the violent behavior portrayed in television entertainment programming—increasingly available in homes—was in some way a *cause* of the increasing rates of crime and delinquency (*post hoc, ergo propter hoc*). The point is well illustrated by a letter that one citizen sent to the *New York Times* on December 12, 1963:

> The shooting of President Kennedy was the normal method of dealing with an opponent as taught by countless television programs. This tragedy is one of the results of the corruption of peoples' minds and hearts by the violence of commercial television. It must not continue.[6]

In addition, many came to believe that televised violence was somehow related to, or even responsible for, the civil disorders and violence in the streets. Generally, then, Americans became deeply suspicious of the new medium that had spread among them rapidly to bring moving pictures right into one's home. It came to be seen as a mixed blessing—perhaps creating more harm than good. No one really knew whether TV was causing increasing crime and delinquency or the occurrence of street violence in America by showing aggressive behavior in its programming. But many suspected that it was. That issue became a special focus of Modeling Theory.

The Rapid Adoption of Television

As noted, television was a new medium in American homes following World War II. Its technology had been fully developed (for black-and-white broadcasts) by that time, and manufacturers began to market receivers for home use (with small screens by today's standards). At first, broadcasts were available only in a limited number of cities, but by 1950, about eighteen percent of American households had a television set. Then, the situation changed rapidly. Transmitters began broadcasting TV programming in virtually all cities in the country, and everyone wanted a set. The rate of adoption suddenly soared. By 1960, television receivers were in well over eighty percent of households in the U.S. Then, the diffusion curve (see Chapter 18) began to level off, as set ownership was approaching saturation. By 1970, well over ninety-five percent of households had acquired a receiver. Today, virtual total saturation has been achieved. There are very few homes that do not have one or more TV sets.[7]

As the use of television spread, a great deal of violent programming could be found on the medium (which is still the case today). Moreover, children were spending more and more time viewing television. On average, in a typical home, the set was on for about seven hours a day. Many children were spending more time in front of their sets than they were in school class-rooms. As was the case many years earlier, when the movies were new, parents, teachers, and other citizens were troubled by what the youthful audience was seeing on their screens. A great deal of criticism emerged, arguing that what was being depicted was causing harm. Few thought that it was wholesome. Children, it was said, were seeing entirely too much violence. Fears were expressed that such programming unintentionally provided *collateral instruction* and that audi-ences received *incidental lessons* (see Chapters 5 and 23), from which children unwittingly learned how to engage in aggressive acts. Many made the inference that the violent content that could be seen in television broadcasts was a direct, or at least an indirect, *cause* of aggressive behavior among children. (Reasoning the other way—that aggression among children had caused the rise in television use and depicted violence—was an obvious non sequitur.)

Thus, by 1960, television had emerged as the most popular (but suspect) medium used by Americans. Children whose early years were being spent before the TV screen were being referred to as the "television generation." Many people were deeply concerned how that experience was in-fluencing them. By that time, movies were not seen as so much of a problem, even though many depicted similar violent behavior. Indeed, attendance at motion pictures began to fall as families stayed home to view programs on TV. For example, in 1946, just before the widespread adoption of home TV began, movie attendance had reached an all-time high, with 2.37 tickets sold every week at the box office (on average) for every household in the U.S. Going to the movies had long been very popular. By 1960, however, that figure had dropped precipitously to a mere 0.53 tickets per household per week. The movie industry was facing a crisis and was no longer widely be-lieved to be a major source for acquiring aggressive forms of behavior.

Increasing Rates of Crime and Delinquency

Between 1948 (during the time that television was being introduced to Americans) and 1957 (when it had been widely adopted), the nation experienced a forty percent rise in juvenile crime and delinquency. Then, as the medium was adopted even more widely and reached virtual satu-ration in American homes during the next decade, those rates showed even larger increases. Those increases were greatest among the young—the "television generation." To illustrate, data on crime and delinquency in the United States is regularly gathered by the FBI from the police in local communities. These are published in annually as the *Uniform Crime Reports*.[8]

According to the FBI's data, the number of juvenile arrests involving serious offenses rose almost eighty percent between 1960 and 1968. However, the number of juveniles actually in the population showed only a minor increase. These youths were, of course, the "television genera-tion," who were spending more time before their TV screens than they were in classrooms. Many of the offenses that were included in these statistics involved violent and dangerous behavior, such as aggravated assaults, or carrying or possessing weapons. For example, the number of youngsters under twenty-one who were arrested for robbery (considered a violent crime), rose fifty-six percent during the eight-year period—as attending to television became increasingly popular among the youthful audience. For those under eighteen, the corresponding figure was 33.3 percent. Even younger children (under fifteen) were performing such violent activities. Their percentage increase was 11.9 percent.

These trends were truly alarming. People all over the country began to turn to the federal government to ask if it could "do something." The public was clearly linking the violent content of television programs to these changes in the rates of crime and delinquency. In the Congress, their concerns were registering. For example, Senator Thomas Dodd, of Connecticut, put it this way:

> Glued to the television set from the time they can walk, our children are getting intensive training in all phases of crime from the ever-increasing array of Westerns and crime-detective programs available to them. The past decade has seen TV come of age. However, the same decade has witnessed the violence content in programs skyrocket and delinquency in real life grow almost two hundred percent.[9]

At the same time, a number of social scientists who were interested in the effects of mass media began to conduct research to see if they could document the link between TV violence and the rise in aggressive behavior among the nation's youth. Meanwhile, however, a third factor caught the attention of those who had begun to attribute a causal role to television.

Civil Disorders: The Rise in Urban Violence

While those media and crime trends were occurring, another set of events was taking place that deeply disturbed Americans. As was noted earlier, for a variety of reasons, a number of destructive riots had broken out in poor areas in American cities. As social scientists were able to determine later, much of what happened actually had nothing to do with the mass media. In large part, the events resulted from the resentments that existed among African Americans concerning their treatment in American society. At the time of the riots, the civil rights movement—and the federal legislation that the movement eventually brought about concerning job discrimination, voting, housing, education, and other issues—had not yet altered the conditions of life among much of the black minority in the United States.

For generations, African Americans had experienced a world of disadvantage, discrimination, and blocked opportunity because of their race. They had been assigned the lowest level in the social structure. They were labeled with insulting terms. They had been allocated only the most menial and poorly paid occupational roles. Many had fled from the South, where their conditions and opportunities at the time were the least desirable. Seeking better opportunities for themselves and their families, they had moved to cities in the North and West, hoping that life there would be better. While a few prospered in the urban centers where they relocated, *the majority did not*. Large ghetto-like areas developed in cities like Chicago; Detroit; Washington, D.C.; and Los Angeles. These areas were populated by frustrated people for whom living conditions and opportunities, for the most part, remained dismal.

It was within one such setting that an instance of dramatic violence began and captured the attention of the entire American population. Its events were displayed nightly to the nation in televised news broadcasts. The place was Watts, a district in Los Angeles. It was here that one of the worst urban riots in the history of the U.S. took place.[10] Watts was a community into which many poor Americans had moved. Most were African Americans who had migrated to the area seeking a better life. Others were recent arrivals into the United States. What they found was little better than what they had left behind. Young men in Watts were bitter and without work. Resentment and frustration were at high levels. As is the case in areas of poverty everywhere, crime and delinquency rates were high. The Los Angeles police force (which was almost completely white at the time) enforced the rules in Watts with relentless vigor—creating further resentments.

On August 11, 1965, into that setting two young black men drove their car through a thirty-five-mile-an-hour zone doing fifty miles an hour. They had been drinking. A white highway patrol office on his motorcycle then chased them with siren screaming and red light blazing. He was finally able to pull the vehicle over. The car and the motorcycle both stopped at a crowded street corner, and a large number of curious (mainly black) onlookers almost immediately surrounded the event. The officer was polite but firm. He made the two young men try to walk a straight line—which they clearly were not able to do. At this point, the crowd saw it as funny and were laughing and joking.

Then, suddenly, the mother of one of the young men arrived. It was actually her car. The officer politely released it to her. But then she began shouting at her son, strongly denouncing his misbehavior. The son responded by screaming obscenities at the officer (and another who had by then arrived in a car) claiming that it was all their fault. The officers tried to subdue the distraught young man and place him under arrest. He resisted vigorously. At one point one of the officers got out his club and struck the offender in his attempt to control him.

At that point, the scene began to change dramatically. While the officers were trying to subdue and handcuff the man, the people in the crowd started to turn hostile. The officers became apprehensive. One went to his car and produced a shotgun. That really made things worse. The situation was deteriorating rapidly. However, just at that time, additional officers arrived in another car to take charge of the offender. In trying to get him into their car, they appeared to treat him somewhat roughly. They pushed him into the backseat with their legs and knees because he was resisting so strongly. The crowd thought that the officers had kicked him, and that made many mad. The crowd then became vindictive.

Suddenly, a few rocks were thrown at the police. The officers then began to arrest some of the offenders. That brought even more hostility from what was now a much larger crowd that had assembled. At this point, the situation broke down completely. Shouts were heard to "Kill the bastards," and "Smash those white sons of bitches." Suddenly, a torrent of bricks, bottles, and stones were thrown at the police. They beat a hasty retreat to their cars as missiles rained on their vehicles, smashing windows.

After this happened, many in the crowd simply went home. However, many hotheads did not. A number of young males set out on a fury of destruction. Cars were set on fire. Store windows were smashed, and what was inside was quickly looted. These activities spread rapidly. Buildings were torched. A favorite target at first was liquor stores. Later, looting became more general. TV sets, furniture, kitchen appliances, and clothing were carried away. Women raided supermarkets, wheeling home carts laden with foodstuffs. That night, many additional buildings and automobiles were set on fire. When the firemen arrived to extinguish the blazes, snipers shot at them. The same thing happened to many of the police officers who were brought in to try to restore order. Innocent white people driving through the area, who had no idea about what had been happening, were dragged from their cars and beaten.

With some delay, the National Guard was called out to subdue the violence. It took six days, and at one point it required 13,500 troops. It was the worst case of civil disorder in the history of the United States. Before order was restored, thirty-four people had lost their lives and several thousand had been injured. Six hundred buildings had been set on fire, causing more than $40 million in damage. Watts looked like a bombed-out city from World War II.

This remarkable set of events was covered in great detail by television reporters. Millions of people all over the country saw "with their own eyes" what was taking place in Watts as they viewed their home receivers. The nation was in a state of shock. How could this happen? What had caused it? How could so many people be stirred to commit so much violence? Then, to make matters worse, during the same period, a number of other instances of copy-cat urban riots took place in Detroit, Chicago, and Washington, D.C. Clearly, there was some causal agent that was directly or indirectly playing a part in creating the problem. One very obvious and very visible candidate was *televised violence.*

THE SURGEON GENERAL'S REPORT

With the new medium under deep suspicion as an agent promoting violence and with the dreadful evidence of the urban riots, Americans appealed to their political leaders to "do something." Politicians managing the policy agenda and anxious about votes often rise to such occasions, seeking to address the concerns of citizens. Indeed there was such a person in the U.S. Congress who stepped forward to "do something." Senator John O. Pastore, of Rhode Island, was chairman of the Communication Subcommittee (of the Senate Committee on Commerce). In 1969, he took steps to establish a panel of distinguished behavioral researchers to advise Dr. William Stewart, the surgeon general (who was given the task of developing an extensive program of research, to be funded and coordinated by the National Institute of Mental Health, or NIMH).

The research was to develop evidence from new scientific studies to be conducted concerning the issue of television violence and its influences on children. The panel came to be called the *Scientific Advisory Committee on Television and Social Behavior.* Under the direction of psychologist Dr. Eli Rubenstein, it consisted of a number of distinguished academic researchers. Its task was to assemble evidence from the research projects to be conducted, plus other evidence from studies that had already published, of the influences of television on children, and to prepare a detailed report to the surgeon general on its conclusions. Senator Pastore persuaded his colleagues to appropriate a million dollars to support this extensive research effort. The basic task of the participating social scientists was this:

> To produce and evaluate a sufficient amount of hard data to answer definitely the question posed by the senator, *whether there is a causal connection between televised crime and violence and anti-social behavior by individuals, especially children.*[11] (Italics added)

By the early 1970s, all projects funded by NIMH had been completed, and the overall findings were brought together into a federal report that popularly came to be called the *Surgeon General's Report.* (Actually, it was a report prepared by the Advisory Committee *to* the surgeon general.) Then, when the report had been completed, Senator Pastore's Subcommittee on

Communications held public hearings concerning the results—giving everyone who might want to offer views or comments on the findings an opportunity to be heard. In the hearings, held in March of 1972, more than forty witnesses reported. They were from either the behavioral science community or from the media industries. They reported either on what their research had revealed or on their objections to the implications of the findings.

The research projects conducted included surveys of various kinds, laboratory-type experiments, and clinical studies. After spending three years (and a million dollars), reactions to the findings presented to the surgeon general were mixed. Essentially, what was finally concluded could be summed up as follows: *Some programming, some of the time, viewed by some youngsters can have some influences.*

This somewhat inconclusive result did not please everyone by any means. The problem was that the results did not reveal an overwhelming, clear, and straightforward causal relationship between televised violence and aggressive behavior among the nation's children. What was found was exactly what the summary statement described. Additional publications on the topic were prepared by the National Institute of Mental Health. One (*Television and Social Behavior*, Washington, D.C.) presented little that was different from Senator Pastore's project. In the end, the conclusions reached in these efforts by the federal government to provide an answer to the senator's charge (to get hard data on the link between TV violence and aggressive behavior), offended critics of television but delighted many who represented the industry.

RESEARCH FINDINGS CONCERNING TELEVISION AND VIOLENCE

In terms of how all of this national concern relates to modeling theory, an example of a research project conducted at the time can clarify the logical predictions that were made by the new theory that explained social learning influences of the media. As public concerns about rising rates and incidents of violence in the U.S. increased, a number of social psychologists and other scholars began to turn their attention to the issue. Those who did so began to explore the hypothesis that there might be a relationship between *seeing violence portrayed* in media content and *engaging in violent behavior* as a result. That hypothesis was obviously consistent with Modeling Theory, and it became the theoretical foundation for a number of later studies. Among them was what has come to be called the "Bobo doll study." (Actually, there was more than one, but the example described below illustrates the strategy and findings.)

The Bobo Doll Study: An Illustration

One of the most intriguing early studies of the relationship between modeled violence and aggressive behavior was conducted by Albert Bandura, Dorthea Ross, and Sheila A. Ross. It was published in 1961—several years before the Pastore–surgeon general projects.[12] It has become a classic and was one that caught the interest of social scientists interested in the TV violence debates. It was one of a continuing series of somewhat similar studies conducted by Bandura and his associates that assessed the influence on children's behavior of observing an aggressive model. Many people found the results of the Bobo doll experiments disturbing, and they showed the need for further research on the topic. The findings did little to calm fears about unwholesome effects on children of violence portrayed in both movies and on television.

At the time, research on the violence issue had barely begun. Bandura reported that a number of incidents of (what psychologists refer to as) "anecdotal" evidence suggested that the depiction of aggression by a model could shape the behavior of a person who observed it under certain conditions. For example, Bandura noted the following as an example:

> A recent incident (*San Francisco Chronicle*, 1961) in which a boy was seriously knifed during a re-enactment of a switchblade knife fight the boys had seen the previous evening on a televised rerun of the James Dean Movie, *Rebel Without a Cause,* is a dramatic illustration of the possible imitative influence of film stimulation.[13]

In a research report published in the same year (1961), Bandura and his colleagues, Dorthea and Sheila Ross, tested the hypothesis that *exposure to aggressive models will increase the probability of aggression on the part of those who are exposed.* To test this hypothesis, they chose a relatively complex experimental strategy—focusing on the potential link between modeled violence and aggressive behavior.

Note that this hypothesis contains several important (independent) conditions, concepts, and variables. These include *models behaving aggressively* (engaging in violent behavior) and *subjects observing those actions*, with the consequence (dependent variable) that those subjects viewing the models would show an observable *increase in their aggressive behavior*. These, of course, are the classic factors in Modeling Theory. To determine if Modeling Theory was supported, the experimenters had to design an experimental format—a controlled situation—that would include all of those variables and conditions. Then (as a dependent variable) the experimenters needed to assess the degree to which the subjects who had observed the models behaving aggressively had actually become more aggressive in their behavior.

The experimenters chose as their subjects forty-eight boys and forty-eight girls, who were enrolled in a nursery school. These were very young children, ranging in age from thirty-seven to sixty-nine months, with a mean age of fifty-two months (basically, three to six years old). Two adults, a male and a female, served as models. One supervising female experimenter actually conducted the experiment.

They divided the children into eight groups of six subjects each—with each experiencing somewhat different conditions. Some were "experimental" groups, who would experience conditions within which they observed modeled behavior. Among those, some did see a model behaving very aggressively. Another set of subjects saw a model that did not exhibit aggressive behavior. There was also a "control" group that received a neutral experience. These different experimental situations and controls made it possible to compare the conduct of those children who saw or did not see a model exhibit violent behavior.

One at a time, the subjects were placed in a room that contained a number of toys, including a mallet. The room also contained a so-called Bobo doll—an inflatable and rather crude representation of a human being—which was about four feet tall. Those in the experimental group *witnessed a human model behaving violently*. They saw him strike the Bobo doll with the mallet, punch it, kick it, and sit on it. The model in that condition also made aggressive verbal comments about the doll (e.g., "Hit him down," "Kick him," "Sock him in the nose," and so on).

After this exposure, the experimenter took each subject to another room where there were also a similar variety of toys for him or her to play with—including another mallet and a Bobo doll but no human model. The behavior of the subject toward these objects was observed for twenty minutes, and each was scored for aggression. The results of the experiment were rather straightforward. As Bandura and his colleagues reported:

> Subjects in the aggression condition reproduced a great deal of physical and verbal aggressive behavior resembling that of the models, and their mean scores [on this dependent variable] differed markedly from those subjects in the non-aggressive and control groups who exhibited virtually no imitative aggression.[14]

Needless to say, these rather clear results seemed to confirm the basic ideas of Modeling Theory. Violent behavior acted out by a model was imitated by those young subjects who saw that performance.

Limitations of the Experimental Approach

Later, Bandura and his colleagues conducted a number of additional experiments on the issue of models and violence. In some, the subjects did not see a live model but instead saw violent acts portrayed on a film. Even in these conditions, imitation took place. The bottom line is that there seemed to be clear evidence from this type of experiment that when children see violent behavior—as in a movie or on TV—*they often imitate it in their own conduct*.

Not all social scientists accepted Bandura's findings as solid evidence that television was the cause of rises in the nation's rates of violent behavior. They were reluctant to generalize from the artificialities of experimental settings to what takes place in "real life" outside the small group's laboratory. This is a continuing problem in experimental psychology. An experiment under artificial and controlled conditions, some say, is little more than a kind of *metaphor* that describes what people do with all of the controls in place, but in the greater complexities of real-life situations, people might behavior quite differently.

MODELING THEORY: A FORMAL SUMMARY

Nevertheless, from Bandura's Social Learning Theory, the violence experiments, and many other studies, a theory explaining modeling behavior can be induced. Its major propositions, as it pertains to the influences of mass communication content, can be expressed in the following propositions:

1. An individual encounters a form of action portrayed by a person (model) in a media presentation.
2. The individual *identifies with the model*; that is, the viewer believes that he or she is like (or wants to be like) the model.
3. The individual *remembers and reproduces* (imitates) the actions of the model in some later situation to handle a personal situation.
4. Performing the reproduced activity *results in some reward* (positive reinforcement) for the individual.
5. **Therefore**, positive reinforcement increases the probability that the person will *use the reproduced activity* again as a means of responding to a similar situation.

Obviously, as illustrated earlier in this chapter, modeling behavior is by no means limited to violence and aggression. It is reasonably clear that human beings do imitate many forms of human activity that they see exhibited by other people—whether on movie or TV screens or in real-life circumstances. In any case, Modeling Theory provides a clear example of basing an explanation of certain influences of mass communications of the psychological paradigm. Modeling Theory is now recognized as a well-tested and valuable contribution to the study of the process and effects of mass communications.

Notes and References

1. Albert Bandura, *Social Learning Theory* (Englewood Cliffs, NJ: Prentice-Hall, Inc., 1977).
2. Herbert Blumer, Chapter 3, "Imitation by Adolescents," in *Movies and Conduct* (New York: The Macmillan Company, 1933), pp. 30–58. This is one of the major reports from the Payne Fund Studies.
3. Hermann Ebbinghaus, *Memory*, trans. H. A. Ruger and C. E. Bussenius (New York: Teacher's College, 1913), first published in German in 1885.
4. The learning research and theories of these pioneers is summarized in: Ernest R. Hilgard, *Theories of Learning* (New York: Appleton-Century-Crofts, Inc., 1948).
5. Albert Bandura, *Social Learning Theory* (Englewood Cliffs, NJ: Prentice-Hall, Inc., 1977), p. 2.
6. Cited by Otto N. Larsen, ed., *Violence and the Mass Media* (New York: Harper and Row, 1968), p. 8.
7. For several decades, from 1950 to 2000, television usage continued to expand, but at an ever slower rate. As cable, satellite broadcasting, videotapes, and DVD were added, Americans spent more and more time in front of their sets. Today, the TV set is on somewhat over seven hours on a typical day. Many children spend more time watching television than they spend in school classrooms. For the pattern of TV adoption, see Margaret H. DeFleur, et. al., Chapter 14, "Understanding Mass Communication Media," in *Fundamentals of Human Communication,* 3rd ed. (New York: McGraw-Hill, 2004), p. 388.
8. See *Uniform Crime Reports* (Washington, D.C.: The Federal Bureau of Investigation, 1968), p. 117.
9. Quoted in Eve Merriam, "We're Teaching Our Children That Violence Is Fun," *The Ladies Home Journal*, October 1964, p. 44.
10. For a detailed description and explanation of what took place in Watts in August of 1965, see Melvin L. DeFleur, William V. D'Antonio, and Lois B. DeFleur, *Sociology: Man in Society* (Glenview, IL: Scott Foresman and Company, 1971), pp. 363–373.
11. See *Hearings Before the Subcommittee on Communications on the Surgeon General's Report by the Scientific Advisory Committee on Television and Social Behavior* (Washington, D.C.: U.S. Government Printing Office, 1972), p. 168.
12. Albert Bandura, Dorthea Ross, and Sheila A. Ross, "Imitation of Film Mediated Aggressive Models," *Journal of Abnormal and Social Psychology*, 66, 1966, pp. 3–11.
13. *Ibid.* p. 3.
14. Albert Bandura, Dorthea Ross, and Sheila A. Ross, "Transmission of Aggression Through Imitation of Aggressive Models," *Journal of Abnormal and Social Psychology*, 63, 3, 1961, pp. 575–582.

Social Expectations Theory

W e noted in Chapter 10 (Selective and Limited Influences Theory) that extensive research on the influences of mass communication content on behavior—conducted within the quantitative rules of the social sciences—began nearly a century ago with the Payne Fund studies. As was explained, these consisted of a series of large-scale investigations of the influence of motion pictures on youthful audiences.[1] The purpose of these projects was to try to determine if the movies—a relatively new medium of entertainment at the time—were having harmful influences on the nation's children.

Parents were concerned that their youngsters, who were going to the moves in large numbers, were learning (and possibly adopting) unacceptable forms of behavior shown in the films. They were alarmed that this new type of entertainment was showing such content as gangsters and their lifestyles, people committing violent crimes, patrons drinking (illegal) alcohol in speakeasies, and even women in their undergarments (even though those items of clothing covered the woman fully from the top of the bosom down to the upper hips). These were not seen as wholesome themes for youthful entertainment by the critics of the movies.

Kids of the era, of course, loved the movies. Some 90 million tickets to motion picture theaters were sold weekly during the last years of the 1920s—with almost half of them purchased by youths under fifteen. Going to the movies on Saturday afternoon had quickly become an established tradition among children (with parents gladly paying the dime that it cost for admission, just to get the kids out of the house for a while). However, no one really knew what the behavioral consequences were for the youngsters who saw the films.

The Payne Fund research focused on two forms of influence. The main one was on *cognitive effects*—that is, altering children's attitudes and beliefs. The other was on *codes for behavior*—by showing in movie plots and actions rules for conduct that the youngsters might be tempted to adopt. In contemporary research, those two distinct focuses on the effects of attending to mass communication content are still pursued in studies of media influences on their audiences. For example, in the same tradition, media researchers continue to search for cognitive influences of media-portrayed violence as a potential causal factor promoting aggressive behavior among youths. However, other scholars study the norms and codes of human groups—to see if those who observe depictions of them in the groups that are portrayed tend to adopt them as their own forms of conduct. The search for cognitive effects and the adoption of specific forms of behavior are pursued by those who use a *psychological* perspective. Those who try to understand the influences of group norms, role definitions, and other features of social organization do so within a *sociological* perspective.

ALTERNATIVE PARADIGMS FOR EXPLAINING BEHAVIOR

As the social sciences developed over the last century, psychology and sociology became the two disciplines that led the way in conducting research on the influences of mass communications. As was explained in Chapter 9 (on the Magic Bullet Theory), each of these fields of study emphasizes a quite different paradigm that guides its strategies of investigation. The one (psychology) looks *within* the person to understand human actions. The other (sociology) studies relationships *between* people to find clues as to how individuals choose ways to shape their behavior.

Conduct as "Inner-Directed": Psychological Explanations

In review, psychology is a discipline that seeks explanations for human behavior based on what people have "in their heads"—needs, attitudes, beliefs, gratifications, opinions, values, learned habits, emotions, and other internal psychological concepts. In other words, those developing the field seek understandings of conduct in terms of such *cognitive and emotional factors.* Much debated in earlier years was the source of such factors. At the beginning of the twentieth century, psychologists theorized that behavior was a product of "instincts." As was explained in earlier chapters, these were said to be *inborn* tendencies to behave in particular ways—tendencies that were inherited as part of one's genetic endowment. At the time, all human beings were thought to have a similar set of such instincts that guided their behavior. By the late 1920s, however, that concept came to be challenged. It was difficult to explain why some people killed themselves if they had a universal *instinct for survival*, or why some women had abortions or did away with their babies if they all had a uniform *instinct for motherhood.*

By the end of the 1930s, as was explained in earlier chapters, the concept of instinct had been largely abandoned in favor of accounting for "in-the-head" factors as products of various types of *learning*. Even today, however, the instinct concept remains as part of the conceptualization of some branches of psychology, such as Freudian psychoanalytic theory. Moreover, there continues a search for biological explanations on the part of some psychologists. They continue to maintain that at least some forms of behavior are determined at birth by genetic factors that shape what goes on inside people's heads. Most others, however, continue to seek answers to such questions by assuming that they are brought about by the learning process within a socio-cultural environment. All of these searches for the bases of internal cognitive and emotional explanations of human conduct have, of course, considerable merit, and psychologists continue that quest in contemporary times.

Conduct as Socially Controlled: The Influence of Groups and Cultures

Again, sociologists seek answers to how behavior is shaped in a different way. They do not look exclusively to internal psychological variables to explain human conduct. They certainly accept the ideas that many forms of behavior are a result of learning. But they make extensive use of a different paradigm that focuses on what happens *between* people. That is, they seek to discover *socio-cultural factors* that shape the behavior of members of groups. Essentially, these are behavior patterns that groups establish and practice routinely, indicating what forms of conduct are *expected* and *approved of* on the part of their members.

In other words, this paradigm assumes that "social expectations" of acceptable behavior are collectively held by members of groups. These expectations define which forms of individual and social interaction between members are approved, accepted, tolerated, disallowed, rewarded, or punished—that is, generally permitted under a variety of circumstances. For that reason, the central (or umbrella) concept of sociology is *social organization*. This term refers to *stable and predictable patterns of conduct* that are understood, shared, and expected of group members. Its opposite is *deviant behavior*—which is unexpected and unacceptable forms of action disapproved and rejected by members on the ground that they lead to group instability and disorganization.

Social organization, then, is a very general concept that refers to the "institutionalized" (that is, deeply established) rules of conduct that those who participate in a group are expected to follow if they intend to remain members. Deviant behavior refers to conduct and activities that are regarded as failing to follow those social expectations and are, consequently, unacceptable to—and usually punished by—the members.

For the most part, the Payne Fund studies and the great majority of research on the effects of mass communication that has accumulated over the subsequent decades have been based on the psychological paradigm. The Payne Fund series did incorporate some features of the sociological paradigm, as will be noted, but it was not central to the studies. The psychological paradigm continues to dominate even today. Thus, "attitude change" is still under study as an assumed dominant key to changes in conduct. Tendencies leading to personal violence learned from the media have been extensively investigated. As noted in Chapter 14, the psychological need-gratifications obtained from exposure to media content have also been topics of extensive research.

What has been learned using the psychological paradigm is impressive. Literally thousands of studies (including those of the Payne Fund series) have reached conclusions suggesting that the media do have at least some influences on cognitive and emotional factors that can play a part in shaping a person's behavior. Less fully investigated, however, are the social expectations factors that are depicted in the media and their influences on the behavior of their audiences.

The present chapter will present an explanation of behavior influenced by mass communications based on the sociological paradigm—*a theory of social expectations*—explaining that the mass media portray rules for, and definitions of, behavior that specify what patterns of conduct members of groups and people generally are expected to perform in a great variety of social circumstances. It is important to note that this is a theory that has only recently been formulated.[2] As such, it has yet to be assessed by a body of research evidence. Nevertheless, the theory does offer insights into many kinds of influences of mass communications.

THE SOCIO-CULTURAL PARADIGM

The most inclusive concept of the socio-cultural paradigm is the *human group*. As was explained in Chapter 6 (on the contribution of sociology) it is with that concept, in one way or another, that the field of sociology is concerned. It is a broad concept that includes both very small as well as very large numbers of people repeatedly acting together in patterns (e.g., a dating couple vs. an entire society). The foundation assumption concerning human groups is that people form and interact within all of them, regardless of size or complexity, *in order to accomplish some goal that they could not achieve when acting alone.* For example, they marry to have companionship, establish a home, have a socially approved sexual relationship, and in many cases to conceive children and jointly raise them. Those activities cannot be accomplished by persons acting alone. Or a number of people may form a large corporation to produce a product or service that allows them to achieve a financial goal. Obviously, a single person, acting alone, would find that impossible.

The Human Group as the Basic Concept

When groups are formed and people become members, interacting together to achieve their shared goals, that situation has profound influences on their conduct toward each other. It also influences in many ways how they respond to others outside the group. Because of the importance of this very basic concept, a summary of the ideas included in the socio-cultural paradigm must begin with a clear explanation of the fundamental nature of any human group.

First, a distinction needs to be made between the term "group," as used in sociological theory and research, and a related term, "social category." Strictly speaking, a human group is at least two or more people who relate to each other in some consistent way *over time within some pattern of social organization.* That is, they work out some set of stable and mutual understandings about how members are expected to behave as they interact with each other in pursuit of their shared goals. That is a very different idea than the way in which the term "group" is often used in common language. One often hears the term used to refer to people who share some common attribute— but who may not even know each other. An example would be "that group that makes more than $100,000 per year" or "the group that has less than a high school education." Another common usage is "minority group," used to describe persons with a common ethnic or racial heritage.

Technically, sociologists would refer to those persons (who may have little else in common) as "social categories." That is, people who have particular levels of income, those who did not graduate from high school, or those whose ancestors came to the United States from some particular part of the world can be "classified" into distinct categories insofar as they share those specific attributes. Virtually any attribute can serve as a basis for classification as a social category—left-handed banjo players, card sharps, alcoholics, vegetarians, college presidents, artists, and so on.

There are a host of different types of human groups—ranging from very small ones consisting of two close friends whose goal is to enjoy each other's company regularly to the U.S. Army, with hundreds of thousands of members and a relatively straightforward set of military goals. Some groups are "informal" (as in the case of "buddies"). Others are very "formal," in that their rules are set forth in written codes (as in the case of the Army). But both informal and formal groups, whether simple or complex, large or small, have *sets of rules* that are understood by their members. Sociologists refer to that pattern of expectations—those rules for conduct—as the groups' pattern of *social organization*.

"Social organization," then, is an umbrella term that is applied to a number of different types of behavior mutually expected of each other by group members. These are the stable patterns of conduct that group members develop and follow, so that their joint activities enable them to achieve their shared goals. As a way of indicating that these expected patterns have over time become accepted by the members of the group, sociologists often use the term "institutionalized." This indicates that each part of the pattern has become a *fully established* rule for conduct within the group and that is has the support of its members.

In the sections that follow, four such institutionalized forms of behavior that make up a group's overall pattern of social organization are briefly described and illustrated. These are its *norms, its roles, its ranks,* and *its controls.*[3] As will also be explained, mass communication content now serves as a major source from which children, and also adults, can learn and understand each of these features in many kinds of group patterns of social organization. They can learn what these are from media depictions—even if they have never in their lives actually participated in that particular type of group. It is specifically with that influence of media content that the Social Expectations Theory is concerned.

Norms as Guides to Conduct for Group Members

As noted, it is clear that, when people form and act within groups to pursue goals that they are not able to achieve alone, they work out and agree upon a set of *general rules* that all members will be expected to follow. Some of these rules govern such mundane matters as where they meet, how often, and at what times. Others may deal with more significant matters. There may be many such rules. How do they dress? How do they address each other: informally, with greetings like "Hey, man, whazzup?" (or the female counterpart), or do they use more formal modes, such as "Good morning, sir (or ma'am)?" Obviously, such general rules differ greatly from one type of group to another.

General norms provide *predictability* for people. They know what to do in a great variety of occasions; therefore, they also know what to expect from others. That is a very important idea. For example, when your telephone rings, if you are an American, you would normally pick up the receiver and say "hello." However, if you were in one of several Latin American countries, you would say "habla" or "digame" (that is, "speak"). In none of those places would you hum a tune, provide a biblical citation, or recite a small poem. Another common situation is when people are waiting for a bus or are in line at the supermarket waiting to be checked out. The rule is that you wait your turn. If another individual comes along and just pushes the front person away and "cuts in," it would arouse hostility because it is a gross violation of the general "wait your turn" norm. (It would be deviant behavior.) It would not matter if the person who "cuts in" was young or old, male or female, rich or poor, etc. All members of the American society are expected to observe that norm, and it provides a clear guideline as to how others expect you to behave when waiting in line to be served.

A great variety of general norms, then, are part of the ways in which people who belong to groups pattern their activities. Such norms exist in groups large and small, as well as in those that are formal (like the Army, with the rules clearly specified and often written down) or informal, where rules are just "understood." In either case, norms are a major component in the social organization of the human group.

Roles as Expectations of People Playing Particular Parts

While general norms apply to all members, another very different set of social expectations guides the behavior of *individual* members as they perform specialized tasks within a group. The term "role" is used to identify the activities of a person who is expected to behave in some unique but predictable way. Presumably, the term was derived from the theater, where a "role" is a specialized part in a play. In a similar manner, people play specialized "parts" in all groups. Consider, for example, a baseball team. Each member is expected to perform in a distinct manner. One will be a pitcher, another a catcher. Still others are first, second, or third basemen (or women), and so on. The point is that the person in each of the team's positions (roles) performs different actions, but *all are coordinated into an overall system.* Moreover, each member conducts his or her special activities in order for the group to achieve its major goal—in this case, to win the game.

The structure of roles within a group provides for great predictability. If each member understands well his or her role expectations and the role conduct of all of the other members as they play their specialized parts, the activities of the group can proceed smoothly. In the case of the baseball team, for example, once the pitcher throws the ball toward the batter, each of the other members of the team (actually both teams) knows well what all others on the field will do under a variety of circumstances. Each, then, has a kind of "map" is his or her head as to the likely activities of each player in each role in the entire system. It would be a total disaster if a member decided to play the role in some unexpected manner. For example, in the baseball team, if the pitcher did not throw the ball to the batter but tried to bean his teammate on first base, the goal wouldn't be achieved. Or if an outfielder just stood and looked at a ball that had been hit to his or her area of responsibility and just left it lay on the ground while smoking a cigarette, the game could be lost. Failing to perform the specialized duties of the role, in other words, would be a gross violation of the social expectations of the members (again, deviant behavior).

These ideas are not restricted to baseball teams. The same can be said about any other kind of group. Every family, group of friends, school, factory, crew on a Navy ship, or even a community or society has specialized roles. When played properly, according to the shared expectations of the members, the system "works," and (if there are no other problems) the group can achieve its goals. Roles, then, are an important component of the overall pattern of social organization of the group.

Ranks: Distinctions Among Members in Power, Prestige, and Rewards

Some of the roles that exist within a group are defined by members as more important than others. Consequently, groups usually reward those who play them well to a greater extent than is the case with roles that are of lesser importance. In the baseball team example, the pitcher plays the role that in many ways decides whether the team wins or loses. If the pitcher can strike out all of the members of the opposing team, it is likely that his or her team will be victorious. The others contribute in various ways, of course, but the pitcher has the greatest responsibility. As a consequence, pitchers often receive the most respect, and in many cases the highest salaries, on a professional team.

That principle—that there are differences in the kinds and levels of rewards provided for different roles in a group, according to their importance as seen by the members—provides a key to another important component of social organization. To illustrate, the officer in charge of the regiment has a greater responsibility for the outcome of the battle than do the privates who make up the rank and file. By performing the more critical duties associated with planning and leading the entire regiment, the military provides that person with a more prestigious title (such as colonel as opposed to, say, corporal). Playing that role also brings more pay, greater respect, and more privileges (such as a personal car and driver and better living accommodations) than are provided to other members of the group.

In this way, those who play different parts or who have some other attribute are "ranked" into various levels. While the idea of "rank" is well understood in military groups, this component of social organization exists in all human groups. In the traditional family, for example, the father traditionally had the position with the greater power and rewards, followed by the mother and then the children. Even among children, in historic times, first-born males were ranked above those who came later, and girls did not have the same rank as boys. In today's families, things are often different. The father and mother may share the same levels of prestige, power, respect, and other rewards, but children still occupy a lower level. Thus, there is still a ranking feature in the system.

If the group is large and if there are a number of members who have essentially the same rank—as in the military example with a number of officers, sergeants, corporals, and privates—the group is said to have a pattern of *social stratification*. That means "layers," such as might be found in a wedding cake or in a geological formation in which different layers of rock or soil have been deposited over the years. The term "social class" is often used to describe the "layers" of social stratification among ranks that exist in a community or society. Some people in the group have "more" of something that its members see as important than do others. It may be income, prestige, respect, power, material possessions, family background, a form of employment, educational attainment, or some other factor. Such criteria of rank are often some combination of social and economic factors (e.g., education, occupation, and income). For this reason, social scientists use the term Socio-Economic Status (SES) to label the person's or family's position in the community's or society's ranking system.

In any case, ranking criteria are used to define *levels* of social class in towns, cities, or countries. Those in the "upper class" have more—of whatever criteria are important to the group—than those in the "lower class." Others are seen as belonging to levels in between (as in upper-middle class, lower-middle class, and so on). An important point is that these well-understood SES levels provide guidelines to behavior. Those who are in the upper class often receive more deferential treatment than those who are identified at lower levels. This idea can be personally verified by going into a business (such as an expensive automobile agency, fancy furniture store, or an elegant restaurant) on two occasions. In one, to see what happens, dress in a very formal or even elegant manner. In the other, wear very casual, wrinkled, or even soiled or damaged clothing. The different ways in which you will be treated will be obvious.

In every human group, therefore, ranging from the largest and most complex to the smallest and most informal, some members have *more* of something that their members value. This *ranking* feature in the social organization patterns of group life is also a component that provides predictability, and therefore stability, in the ways in which members relate to each other.

Controls: Enforcing the Expectations of Social Organization

A final component of social organization is *controls*. What this refers to is the ways and techniques used by groups to ensure that their members adhere to the expected patterns of social organization that have been established to provide for predictability. This stabilizes the group and limits troublesome deviant behavior. Some social controls are *positive* in nature. These are used when members are rewarded in some way for following the rules in some highly approved manner. Others can be *negative*. These controls are applied when members "deviate" from the accepted social expectations and cause problems for the group. Positive rewards can range from words of encouragement and expressions of gratitude to certificates, plaques, and diplomas. In the workplace, they can include raises in pay, promotions, a more prestigious title, a reserved parking place, or a corner office. Even in the most informal group of peers, members receive signals of approval, words of praise, slaps on the back, thanks, or other positive sanctions when their actions have pleased other members.

There are a host of negative actions that make up the controls available to various kinds of groups. Negative sanctions for deviant behavior range from frowns and words of disapproval to truly drastic measures, such as the death penalty, used when violations of the rules have been truly severe. In a work environment, sanctions can range from getting unpleasant work assignments and being passed over for raises or promotions to being fired.

Social controls are a necessary part of group life. Departures from the institutionalized ways that are used by the group to provide for stability and predictability—that is, deviant behavior—is a source of conflict, strain, and significant barriers to the attainment of group goals. It is for that reason that people are rewarded or punished for their positive or their negative performance of the norms and roles of their group, or for their recognition of appropriate conduct implied by its system of ranks.

Clearly, then, the term "social organization" refers to an extraordinarily complex set of concepts and ideas. Each of the components—norms, roles, ranks, and controls—includes a great variety of behaviors and actions that groups use to try and ensure that their members follow the behavior patterns that have been institutionalized. The nature of these components, the ways people organize their group life, vary greatly in different types of groups. Nevertheless, each is characterized by a pattern of social organization that is understood by its members. If that were not the case, social behavior would simply be random and chaotic.

LEARNING EXPECTED PATTERNS: THE PROCESS OF SOCIALIZATION

How do members of groups come to learn and understand the pattern of social organization that prevails in their groups? Because such patterns are complex, acquiring a full understanding of the expectations prevailing in the various groups that characterize one's life is also complex. Sociologists refer to the process as "socialization."

Essentially, socialization is based on *learning*, but there is much more to it than that. Learning is only one part of the process. There also must be other people in the situation where that learning takes place. It is from those people that the person undergoing socialization can acquire and understand the accepted patterns of behavior. Those others *display* (*model*) *or explain* the behavior required, and they often provide rewards (social controls) when the individual newly acquires approved ways of behaving. They may also provide punishments if the learner does things wrong. Generally, then, socialization takes place when a person becomes a new member of a group and gradually understands, accepts, and behaves according to its accepted and shared patterns of social organization.

Every child born into a society must learn its ways. Indeed, it is a lifelong process. At first, the child has to acquire behavior patterns appropriate to his or age. These all change later as the person becomes a teenager, then a young adult, a middle-aged person, and on into old age. Other group members expect different behavior from individuals in each of these life stages.

Every person who enters a new group must undergo a period of socialization to function adequately as a member. For children, the process begins in the first years, when they learn that mother and father, or perhaps siblings, are different beings from whom different things can be expected. Gradually, they acquire the norms of their family. They begin to babble and then speak as they learn the rules of language. As they mature, they gradually understand more and more about what is proper or improper conduct. Things become more complex when the person must deal with groups outside the home—playmates, neighbors, and then school, and so on, into the richness and complexities of community and national life. In each group encountered, if they are to participate as members, they must internalize and follow its pattern of social organization.

In some groups, introduction to its requirements is systematic, deliberate, and demanding. The U.S. Marines, for example, socialize new members in "boot camp." Here, during a period of rigorous training, the recruit learns how to dress, speak, sleep, wear one's hair, and generally behave as required by the Corps. In addition, the new member learns the roles, the ranking system, and the social controls. He or she also learns to manage firearms and other tools of combat, plus a great many other features of this formal group. This socialization experience transforms the person from a civilian to a new identity as a Marine. Other groups may be less demanding, but they too often have formal training to prepare new members to function as full-fledged participants. Most socialization, for most people, however, is rather haphazard and random. For example, no one plans systematic exposure to the community as a whole as a human group. Indeed, most socialization takes place in an almost accidental manner as the person encounters various features of community life.

There are many sources from which individuals gain understanding of the social organization of groups—whether the individual is actually a member or not. Clearly, in some cases, other people systematically teach the person about the norms, roles, ranks, and controls by which a particular group conducts its affair. In other cases, the person has chance-like learning encounters from which understandings can be obtained. An important point, then, is that people often learn—or assume that they have learned—the patterns of social organization that exist in groups—even those of which they are not members.

LEARNING BEHAVIORAL RULES FROM MEDIA DEPICTIONS

Before mass media were available, and before formal schooling, socialization was a process by which older members of a clan, tribe, village, or other entity taught their ways of life to the young. Indeed, the new members of society had to acquire the rules for behavior that constituted not only the group's pattern of social organization but also the entire culture's—its shared beliefs, history, language, religion, technologies, and all other aspects of the way of life of the group. Later, much of this was handled by formal schooling. Even so, the influence of the family, friends, and neighbors continued to play a part.

Depictions of Codes for Behavior in Entertainment Content

When mass media came to societies, they were added to the sources from which young people could learn about groups. This was especially true with the visual media. Even the early movies—such as those studied in the Payne Fund research—had become sources from which children learned the social expectations that prevailed in many kinds of groups that were portrayed in the entertainment content. The films of the 1920s, for example, showed children the features of life in many kinds of groups.

Two examples of children learning general norms from seeing them depicted in films of the 1920s can illustrate the point. In one of the Payne Fund studies, the boys who were studied were asked what they had learned by seeing the films. One subject replied that he now knew that the man was supposed to light the cigarette of the woman—although he had not yet taken up smoking. Another had learned that, when he would become able to drive a car, he was supposed to open the passenger door for a woman entering the vehicle—and after arriving at their destination, he was supposed to go around and open the door for her. While these general norms have not prevailed into modern times—where some women are sometimes offended by such male behavior—they were clear guides to proper male conduct during the 1920s.[4]

There is little doubt that children today continue to see various forms of social actions portrayed in the entertainment content of the mass media—illustrating the norms that are followed. Even in television programming designed for a very young audience, the ways in which the children are portrayed provide lessons as to how kids relate to, speak to, obey, or ignore their parents. These portrayals provide youngsters with guides to conduct by illustrating clear depictions of family norms.

At a more general level, youngsters know what the norms require in great variety of groups of which they have never been—or probably never will be—members. For example, any boy knows that, if he were a private in the Army, he would be expected to salute when walking along and coming upon a commissioned officer. Most can also provide the correct answer when asked that, after making an arrest of a suspect, the police officer is supposed to say, "You have a right to remain silent . . . " (and supply the remainder of the Miranda phrases).

These are "collateral instruction" provided unintentionally by the media (see Chapter 23), and they are unwittingly learned as "incidental lessons" by their audiences, as discussed in Chapter 5 (Cognitive Processing: The Contribution of Psychology to Mass Communications Theory). Thus, while the child does not deliberately seek out instruction in television programs, movies, or other media content in order to learn the norms of groups, the lessons are there as an unintended part of the content produced, and they are learned in an unwitting way by their audiences.

In the same manner, media entertainment depicting people in a variety of social situations, acting out parts in groups, provides incidental lessons in the nature of *roles*—the specialized activities that people perform in groups as part of their pattern of social organization. An interesting example of such learning was noted in a research project that studied what children had learned about the nature of the labor force. The investigators asked children to explain the duties of a number of common roles in the labor force. Some were frequently portrayed on television (e.g., police officer, lawyer, doctor). Others were seldom seen on TV (e.g., electrical engineer, government clerk, accountant). Still others were commonly visible in the community (e.g., supermarket clerk, teacher, mail carrier). The question was, did television portrayals provide children with clear conceptions of roles that were not visible to them in their normal contacts in the community?

One finding from that study illustrates the point that TV provided very clear definitions of certain roles that were *not* seen in the community by the children. For example, the project was conducted among children who lived in a small community in southern Indiana. It was certain that there was no family in that community that *employed a butler*. However, most of the children interviewed could provide reasonably detailed explanations of the duties of a butler. They had acquired this knowledge from seeing depictions of the role in the movies and on TV. Similarly, many of the children were able to describe the expected behaviors of the participants in a criminal trial. They knew what to expect of a judge, the prosecutor, the defendant's attorney, and the jurors—even though none of the children interviewed had ever sat in a courtroom to observe such a trial.[5]

Much the same can be said about the depictions of both social ranking and the controls that groups use to maintain stability in the social expectations that make up their pattern of social organization. In media entertainment, portrayals and depictions make it clear who has more prestige, respect, power, income, and material possessions. Those high in the class structure are seen living in more luxurious dwellings, often with servants, driving expensive automobiles, dining in elegant restaurants, and so forth. Those at the lower end of the class structure fare much more poorly—with fewer material possessions and so on. These provide inescapable lessons as to who "counts," who is shown deference and respect, and other features of social ranking.

Abundant collateral instruction provided by media entertainment also makes it clear that those who misbehave are usually punished for their misdeeds. The sanctions portrayed range from raised eyebrows and frowns to the death penalty. These applications of social controls are entirely visible to children who go to movies, watch television, and attend to other media for entertainment. Again, they acquire understandings (correctly or sometimes incorrectly) concerning the social control consequences of deviant behavior.

Learning the Rules Through Incidental Lessons

In general, then, in their depictions and portrayals, the mass media provide a great deal of collateral instruction about the patterns of social expectations that make up the components of social organization in a variety of groups. By attending to media entertainment, a youngster can learn in an unwitting (incidental) manner how to behave when dining at an elegant restaurant, when serving in the military, when participating in a criminal trial, when acting as a member in a juvenile gang, or when serving as the secretary of the CEO of a major business—even though he or she has never participated in any of these things.

It is important to stress that this source of socialization is not a set of deliberate instructions planned and conducted by those who produce media entertainment. Those who produce such products have one major goal in mind—to make a profit. That is an approved and respected goal in the American society, with its political and economic system organized on the basis of capitalism. Moreover, as has been made clear, children do not go to the media in a deliberate manner to select content that will provide them with systematic instructions as to how various groups pattern their expectations. Chapter 10 (A Selective and Limited Influences Theory) has explained that audiences—including children—pick out what they want to read, view, or hear for other reasons. Chapter 14 (on the Uses for Gratifications Theory) has indicated that audiences often look for content that they will find enjoyable, rather than instructional. Again, Chapter 5 (on the The Contributions of Psychology) has noted that many of the lessons people learn from media content are "unwitting"—that is, not recognized or understood by those who receive them. Chapter 23 (on the Collateral Media Instruction Theory) will discuss how the producers of media content provide unintended lessons about people and many other topics. All of these processes and consequences underlie the acquisition of knowledge by media audiences about the patterns of socialization often prevail in many kinds of groups.

SOCIAL EXPECTATIONS THEORY: A FORMAL SUMMARY

These explanations and examples can be brought together in a theory that describes and explains the influences of media entertainment content as a major source for socialization—for learning about the ways in which members are expected to behave as members of groups. That theory includes the following propositions:

1. Various kinds of content provided by the media often portray *social activities and rules for behavior* in specific types of groups.
2. These portrayals are *representations of reality* that reflect, accurately or inaccurately, the nature of many kinds of groups in American society.
3. Individuals who are exposed to these representations receive *unintended collateral instruction* as to the nature of the norms, roles, social ranking, and social controls that prevail in many kinds of common groups.
4. The experience of exposure to media portrayals of a particular kind of group results in the *incidental learning* of the behavior patterns that are expected by others when acting as a member of such a group.
5. **Therefore**, these learned expectations concerning appropriate behavior for self and others serve as *guides to action* when individuals actually encounter, become members of, or try to understand such groups in real life.

Social Expectations Theory, then, is based on the socio-cultural paradigm that sociologists use to explain human conduct. In this perspective, behavior is interpreted as shaped by the anticipations of others in a group concerning the pattern of social organization that will be followed. That pattern identifies expected norms, roles, ranks, and controls governing the behavior of group members as they seek to achieve their shared goals. Social Expectations Theory, as set forth above, identifies the significant part played by mass communications in the socialization process in societies where media-provided entertainment content is widely attended to by young people. From media sources, they acquire conceptions of the social organization patterns of many kinds of groups. Even though they may never become members of those portrayed, they gain an in-depth understanding of how actual members are expected to behave under a variety of circumstances.

Notes and References

1. For a summary of the nature of these studies and what their findings seemed to indicate at the time, see Shearon A. Lowery and Melvin L. DeFleur, Chapter 2, "The Payne Fund Studies: The Effects of Movies on Children," in *Milestones in Mass Communication Research: Media Effects*, 3rd ed. (White Plains, NY: Longman, 1995), pp. 21–43.

2. A summary of the theory can be found in the following: Melvin L. DeFleur and Everette E. Dennis, *Understanding Mass Communication*, 6th ed. (Boston: Houghton Mifflin Company, 1998), pp. 472–475.

3. For a detailed explanation of the umbrella concept of social organization, see Melvin L. DeFleur, William D'Antonio, and L. B. DeFleur, *Sociology: Human Society* (Glenview, IL: Scott, Foresman and Co., 1971).

4. For a summary of the findings of one of the Payne Fund series that investigated the influence of films on social attitudes toward various racial and ethnic categories, as well as on behavioral norms, see Frank K. Shuttleworth and Mark A. May, *The Social Attitudes and Conduct of Movie Fans* (New York: The Macmillan Company, 1933).

5. Melvin L. DeFleur and Lois B. DeFleur, "The Relative Contribution of Television as a Learning Source for Children's Occupational Knowledge," *American Sociological Review*, 32, 5, October 1967, pp. 777–789.

CHAPTER 18

Media-Influenced Diffusion of Innovation Theory

The adoption by a group or population of an "innovation"—that is, something "new"—is a matter of concern to a number of academic disciplines and professional fields. For example, a variety of scholars study the process of *cultural diffusion*—that is, the spread from one society to another—of material artifacts, as well as various forms of belief, values, codes of conduct, and behavior. In traditional (mainly agricultural) societies, changes in people's way of life are slow. They seldom travel more than a few miles from their farms or villages, and contacts with "outsiders" are not common. Also, in such societies, there are far fewer "new" things being invented and few or no media to call them to attention. Thus, diffusion of innovation is less apparent. In the contemporary world of industrialized societies, however, worldwide travel is common, and there is a fast pace of inventions. Also, with "globalization" of mass communications, along with manufacturing and marketing, contemporary cultures change rapidly as people incorporate a constant flow of innovations into their lifestyles.

Social scientists are especially interested in innovations. Sociologists are concerned with the process by which *social change*—modification of codes of conduct, language, shared beliefs, and other social expectations, takes place within a particular group or society. Such changes occur when its members acquire new ways of behaving, believing, or of using some new form of technology that was not part of their earlier shared activities. Societal organization and class structures undergo change as people become acquainted with and acquire new ideas as to how such social arrangements should be maintained and viewed.

Cultural anthropologists recognize the importance of the diffusion of innovation. When the people of a society take up and incorporate into their way of life some new idea, belief, word, tool, or other solution to a problem—whether initially developed with their group or adopted from another society—their culture undergoes change. Many such innovations are acquired from "outside" as people contact others and they come to make up a part of the total of artifacts, technology, and practices that exist for a people.

Commercial and industrial organizations also have a keen interest in the diffusion of innovation. Those who manufacture goods for the marketplace or offer services to the public need to understand the ways in which consumers decide to make use of new solutions to their problems or new products that they might use. It is here that the media play a significant part in these activities, bringing to the attention of their audiences a constant flow of information about things and services that have become available. In each of these situations, people often make media-influenced decisions to adopt and use something that they have not used before.

Generally, then, for media scholars interested in understanding the process and effects of mass communication, the diffusion of innovation is of interest for three reasons:

(1) The use of *new media technologies* takes place through the adoption of innovation. For example, subscriptions to the (then new) daily mass newspaper increased in the American society over a number of decades from the 1830s to the 1920s, as its use spread to larger and larger numbers of families. (Subscriptions per household declined after that as the new broadcast media were adopted.) The same pattern of increasing use was true of the other mass media. Typical patterns of adoption characterized the spread over time of movies as entertainment, the acquisition of home radio sets, television, cable TV, and the Internet, as well as cellular phones and other more recent communication technologies.

(2) In addition, by making the availability of many kinds of innovations known to audiences through ads and other messages, the media play a significant role in *promoting* the adoption of new ideas, forms of behavior, and material goods. In other words, those who produce and advertise such goods and services depend on mass media messages to inform potential users of the nature and availability of their products and activities, and persuade them to purchase them.

(3) In a more subtle way, through unintended "collateral instruction" provided by the media—and resulting in "incidental learning" on the part of people in various parts of the globe who attend to media for entertainment—members of audiences often *unwittingly adopt* artifacts, ideas, beliefs, and forms of behavior that are depicted in the content. This can be disturbing to conservative people in those societies who do not approve of the changes such adoptions bring and who often see that process as "cultural imperialism" (see Chapter 22). That is, they interpret such media influences as a deliberate imposition of ideas and behavior patterns by the societies that produce the content—a practice that they believe is intended to dominate, exploit, change, or otherwise control their audiences. In other words, the ways in which innovations are adopted is of interest and of significant importance to a number of practitioners, researchers, and scholars insofar as it is a basic process leading to both social and cultural change, and an activity essential to the functioning of a market economy.

BASIC DEFINITIONS

The present chapter will focus on three issues: (1) the ways in which innovations of various kinds come to the attention of members of a group or society, (2) the pattern formed when a particular innovation is adopted by different categories of people, and (3) the role played by mass communication in the process. One problem in such an analysis of the processes of diffusion of innovation is *terminology*. When the study of innovations is addressed by distinct categories of social scientists, and by commercial practitioners as well as by media scholars, they do not always use a common vocabulary. In discussing the diffusion of innovation and the part played by media, therefore, it is important to provide clear definitions of exactly what is being considered. This requires careful definition of a number of concepts. That will be the first task. For the present chapter, then, the meanings of the concepts and terms needed for developing a theory explaining the diffusion of innovation within the mass communication context must be made clear.

Innovation

The most basic concept is "innovation." In their classic work, *Communication of Innovations: A Cross-Cultural Approach*, media scholars Everett Rogers and Floyd Shoemaker have provided a clear definition:

An *innovation* is an idea, practice or object perceived as new by an individual. It matters little, so far as human behavior is concerned, whether or not an idea is 'objectively' new as measured by the lapse of time since its first use or discovery. It is the perceived or objective newness of the idea for the individual that determines his reaction to it. If the idea seems new to the individual, it is an innovation.[1]

Given that definition, even such common objects as a form of popular music, a clothing style, the use of lipstick, an automatic rifle, a different code for sexual behavior, a set of religious beliefs, or even a slang term can seem to be an innovation to a person who has not encountered it before.

The Personal Adoption Process

A second concept and issue to define is the *personal adoption process*—that is, acceptance and use of some innovation by an individual. What is it that takes place at the individual psychological level when a person encounters and perceives something that, to him or her, seems "new?" The individual may seek further knowledge about the item, decide whether it has application in his or her situation, and, if so, then adopt and use it. Is the process of personal adoption *automatic* and *immediate* once the person becomes aware of the innovation? Does he or she readily accept it as part of his or her behavioral repertoire or set of useful artifacts? Or is the process of personal acquisition more complex? One of the purposes of the present chapter is to address those questions.

Within-Group Diffusion

A third concept to be defined is *diffusion* (of an innovation). What this term refers to is the pattern by which something new is taken up by members of a group or society. In many cases, at the group or societal level, an innovation will be taken up by at least some—or perhaps all—of its members. That is, its acquisition and use "spreads" as increasing numbers of people within the group adopt the innovation. However, an important question is whether all members who actually acquire and use a particular innovation do so at the same time. Or is a *characteristic pattern formed over time* as more and more of the members gradually (or swiftly) take up the new item? Thus, the term "diffusion" refers to the way in which more and more members take up the new item over some time span.

In addressing this issue, this chapter will focus on "within-group" diffusion. That is, within a given group, category of persons, or even a society as a whole, what *quantitative pattern* is formed over time as increasing numbers of members decide to adopt the innovation? Does a small number adopt it initially, and then more and more members take it up over an extended period? Moreover, do *all* members—that is, 100 percent—eventually adopt the innovation or only some lesser proportion? That pattern can be expressed graphically in the form of a curve. As will be explained, research has disclosed that a "typical" pattern, or quantitative *adoption curve*, is often found. That curve shows what proportion of members have acquired the innovation during any point or period along a time axis.

Between-Groups Diffusion

Note that "within-group" diffusion of innovation is distinct from that which takes place "between groups"—although the two are often related. For example, interest in a new form of dancing or listening to an innovative style of popular music (as was the case with ragtime, jazz, or rock) may initially spread through the population within which it was first developed ("in-group diffusion"). Often, however, people in other societies become acquainted with the innovation. If they begin to show a similar interest, and some members start to use the new form, it may then spread widely among members of that second society—that is, "between-groups" diffusion (sometimes called "intercultural diffusion"). As was noted, that process—of an innovation spreading from one society to another—has long interested cultural anthropologists, who try to determine the origins of a particular belief, artifact, practice, or technology that is present within a culture that they are studying.

An interesting example of intercultural diffusion is the case of Eskimos in remote and frigid northern regions who were using tobacco long before they were first visited by Europeans.

Those explorers who made those early contacts were astonished to find Eskimos smoking tobacco in ice- and snow-bound parts of the world, in which it was totally impossible to grow the plant. Initially, they thought that tobacco had spread from its origins in Central America up through the North American continent to the far northern regions. Eventually, however, it was discovered that was not the case. Because of high mountains, huge distances, difficult travel, and lack of contact between tribes, tobacco did not move northward in that manner.

The answer to the puzzle was finally figured out. Tobacco had become an item of trade and consequent inter-group diffusion between tribes and societies in far northern regions. Actually, this had taken place over several centuries—but not by contact with other indigenous people of North America. First, it had spread from Central America, where growing tobacco originated, up into North America, where Native Americans could grow and use it. Then, after European explorers arrived (essentially in the 1500s) and discovered the plant, tobacco crossed the Atlantic to England, where it was widely adopted. From there it spread rather quickly to other countries on the European continent. Not long after that, it diffused eastward into Asia, where it came to be routinely grown and used. In time, traders crossed the short strait between Siberia and Alaska and brought tobacco leaves to trade for furs with the indigenous people. The Eskimos liked it and rather rapidly adopted its use. Thus, tobacco had made that remarkable global "diffusion" journey clear around the world long before explorers actually encountered Alaska's native people.

Such society-to-society diffusion is an important process for two reasons. One reason is that it can greatly enrich the receiving cultures. Obvious examples can be seen when Americans sit down to eat pancakes, pizza, or pasta—or indeed many dozens of other foods that originated in Europe, Asia, or elsewhere. Americans also use dishes (pottery is an ancient invention), wear clothing made of cloth (weaving was invented by prehistoric people), and read books and newspapers (the technology of printing was first developed in Germany by Johannes Gutenberg in the 1500s). The list of cultural items developed elsewhere to be adopted and to become "American" could go on and on. If intercultural diffusion had not taken place, no one outside Scotland would have steam power, no one outside the United States would have airplanes, and no one outside France would be aware that tiny germs cause illness. In other words, the culture of people who live in most developed societies today include literally thousands and thousands of words, objects, behavioral codes, beliefs, and other features that originated elsewhere. This provides a great advantage. Because of this spread of innovations from one society to another, none is totally dependent on its own members to invent and develop the host of ideas and things that so enrich their cultures today. As anthropologist Ralph Linton noted:

> If every human group had been left to climb upward by its own unaided efforts, progress would have been so slow that it is doubtful whether any society by now could have advanced beyond the level of the Old Stone Age.[2]

The same is true of scientific fields and academic disciplines. For example, the relatively new field of mass communication makes use of statistical procedures, forms of theory development, research strategies, and measuring scales that were initially developed in other disciplines (e.g., statistical tests of significance, content analysis, attitude scales, and sampling procedures). Generally, then, the process of inter-group diffusion can greatly enrich the culture of the host group that adopts innovations from outside sources.

However, while inter-group diffusion often has obvious and enormous benefits, there is sometimes a darker side. It can be the basis of hostilities and resentments that can lead to truly serious consequences. For example, if some number of traditional and conservative people in the receiving society are disturbed by the consequences of the spread of a particular innovation—say, among its youth who encounter it in mass communications—they may bitterly resent its consequences and take steps to retaliate. They can interpret such diffusions as a deliberate and sneaky effort on the part of the originating society to create harm to, or even dominate, the adopting host. Precisely that was the case when conservative people in India found that their youths had adopted the Western practice of exchanging *Valentine cards*. They saw the practice as an unacceptable form of sexual expression among young people who were not married. They denounced the practice and blamed Western societies for the intrusion. Many such items that are common in Western societies are currently seen as unacceptable by conservative elders when youths encounter the liberal practices, values, and behavior codes common in the U.S. and Europe by seeing them depicted in imported popular culture and media entertainment.

BACKGROUND: INFLUENCES OF THE INDUSTRIAL REVOLUTION

Prior to the Industrial Revolution, societies and their cultures changed very slowly.[3] There were, of course, a few inventions. There were also items of culture acquired from other societies. Some, like gunpowder, were widely adopted. For the most part, however, it took decades for an invention or a new culture trait to move from one society to another. Then, as it did become available to the host society, it often took many decades, or even centuries, to come into wide use among its people. Thus, traditional and pre-industrial societies changed slowly indeed. Their ways of life and their social institutions remained relatively stable for very long periods of time.

For one thing, the rate of innovation within such a society was low. That is, few things were invented in nonindustrial societies. In addition, in societies without mass media, communication took place mainly by word of mouth. There were a few cities, of course, but most people lived in small villages and worked on farms. Only a very few traveled many miles from where they were born. Literacy was very low, and only a small number had contact with written materials. Even after the press became available and was widely adopted, literacy remained limited. Only the urbane and affluent elite could afford to buy the few books that were available. The same was true of the early newspapers and the few primitive magazines that existed. Obviously, these conditions did not lead to rapid and widespread diffusion of new things or ideas.

Beginning near the end of the eighteenth century, the Industrial Revolution started to change all of that. In both Europe and the United States, that revolution accelerated during the nineteenth and twentieth centuries. As this took place, the rate of invention increased sharply. Consequently, diffusion of innovations also increased greatly as new things became available. One reason was that the ability of people to read became commonplace. The increased use of mass communications brought new things to people's attention. For example, by the time of the Civil War, the proportion of the population that could read was increasing rapidly. One of the reasons was that during the nineteenth century, more young people went to school as more and more states adopted free (tax-supported) and compulsory primary school education.

With literacy increasing, a rising tide of mass communications soon followed. By 1834, the penny press, published daily, became the first mass medium capable of serving truly large numbers of ordinary citizens. The daily newspaper was soon supplemented by nationally circulated magazines. These were especially popular during the last half of the 1800s. It was also a time when instantaneous communication was beginning. The telegraph became a reality in the 1840s, just before the Civil War. The telephone soon followed (in the 1870s). Early in the 1900s, radio broadcasting and film were added. As these new media came into wide use, what had been a limited flow of information through the society by word of mouth became a flood via various media. The result was that news concerning the characteristics of a host of new products, perspectives, and ideas was made available easily and quickly to a huge population of potential adopters.

All during this period, significant social and cultural changes took place not only in the use of new technologies but also in basic lifestyles. Fundamentally altered were ways in which goods were produced, distributed, and consumed. A great advertising industry developed to sell the goods and services of the Industrial Revolution. Cheap amusements based on popular culture became an urgent necessity as armies of industrial workers were crowded into urban centers and had at least some income and leisure time. The demand for entertainment and news fired the growth of wide-reaching media empires. Print, film, and broadcasting in all their various forms expanded to meet those needs.

In these ways, the Industrial Revolution not only brought mass media and popular culture, it also altered the very organization of society. The factory system and related economic growth greatly expanded the social class structure. Differentiated social levels of income, status, and power were created by people's positions in complex commercial enterprises, industrial production systems, and governmental bureaucracies. Populations were mixed through migrations as people sought economic opportunity. They moved between countries, from farms to cities, and from one region of the country to another. The result was many kinds of unlike people living together in urban environments. This diversity reduced the free flow of information through informal channels based on friendship, traditional community ties, and kinship. The old order of the traditional society was disappearing. People were less guided by tradition, less tied to their neighbors, and less bound to their extended families. More specifically, people became increasingly *dependent on mass media* as a means by which they could become aware of new products, ideas, and other innovations.

A Vast Increase in Innovations

Beginning in the 1800s, the number of inventions being produced in industrializing societies greatly increased. All during the twentieth century, the number of innovations available rose sharply. That was especially true in societies like the United States. A tidal wave of new ideas, procedures, machines, and a host of other items of culture were constantly being invented. In all the developed countries, many were borrowed from other societies. This greatly increased flow of innovations and swiftly altered almost every aspect of life.

The Search for Explanations

An important question concerning these changes was *why* one new thing, practice, or idea would be widely adopted, while another would be all but ignored. For example, some forms of popular culture, like ragtime music and jazz, became instant successes and were immediately adopted by large numbers in the U.S. population as well as by people in other societies. Others, like Esperanto—a universal language proposed to unite all people on earth—were ignored by all but a few enthusiasts. That question—of why some spread and others did not—was seen as critical to understanding the dynamics of social and cultural change. A number of scholars at the time attempted to provide explanations. For example, as Gabriel Tarde, the French sociologist, posed the issue in 1890:

> Our problem is to learn why, given one hundred different innovations conceived of at the same time—innovations in the forms of words, in mythological ideas, in industrial processes, etc.—ten will spread abroad, while ninety will be forgotten.[4]

Tarde believed that the answer was in what he termed the "universal laws of imitation." He explained these "laws" by relating the characteristics of "things" to human "desires" through a process of "suggestion." He tried, in other words, to identify the human *decision-making process* that led people to adopt a specific innovation when it came to their attention. Unfortunately, while Tarde posed the issue in a unique way, his "laws of imitation" did not survive the test of time. They were based on psychological concepts that soon were regarded as outmoded. Moreover, he failed to recognize the connection between the adoption of innovation and the creation of public awareness of the item through the use of mass communications.

THE DIFFUSION OF HYBRID SEED CORN: THE SEMINAL STUDY

The basic theory of diffusion of innovation that is now relevant to the field of mass communication initially came from an unlikely source. Two rural sociologists, studying the diffusion of a new farm practice, developed the basic model. Early in the 1900s, rural sociology had been established as a practical academic field in the U.S. within (mainly) state-supported educational institutions. Their mission was to assist rural populations in improving their lifestyles and productivity. In particular, as so-called *land-grant institutions* developed their goals during the 1900s, they took on missions to conduct research on technologies and practices that could improve American agriculture. In addition, they employed "extension agents," who were specialists in various fields related to agriculture. These agents served as field advisers mainly to farmers to help them solve specific problems related to crops, animals, or related farming matters.

Many of these schools later became comprehensive academic institutions that closely resembled their more traditional counterparts. Early in the twentieth century, however, most of the land-grant institutions were called "colleges," with the term "state" added (as in Ohio State College). The remainder of the earlier titles "of Agriculture" or "of Agriculture and the Mechanical Arts" were dropped. Still later, during the decades following World War II, many of those titles were changed even further, and most of the land-grant institutions became complex "universities" (as in Louisiana State University). As these changes took place, the institutions organized their various academic departments internally into traditional "colleges" and "schools," such as a college of arts and sciences, or of education, a school of mass communication, or a college of agriculture (in which departments and other groups continued the basic agricultural mission). By the 1930s, most of these changes and consolidations had already been accomplished.

After World War II came to a close, an additional set of background conditions became important. American agricultural technology began to move forward rapidly. For example, new pesticides had been developed, and innovations came rapidly in the use of antibiotics to control animal diseases. Farm machines were greatly improved. New chemicals came into use to control weeds, and hormone supplements were developed to add to feeds so as to increase animal growth. As a result of these remarkable innovations, American farmers began to increase their productivity per acre and per worker at an unprecedented rate. Indeed, the production of food and other agricultural products became so efficient that great surpluses began to develop, and eventually government programs had to be devised that paid farmers *not to grow crops*. New federal programs severely limited the amount of acreage that they could place in production and still receive price supports.

One of the main factors in these developments that became evident was that farmers did not all instantly adopt the innovative marvels that resulted from the research. For example, even though a new way of plowing, a new kind of weed spray, or a new type of animal feed could be shown to improve productivity, farmers sometimes ignored, or at least resisted, adopting these new technologies. However, if a few farmers took up such improvements, and they obviously worked well, eventually many others would follow. Nevertheless, a situation that was troubling to the faculty in the state research institutions was that diffusion of useful technology was seldom universal. In particular, this frustrated the agricultural scientists who conducted research that could greatly improve farm technology and practices. Resisting their contributions, they felt, was not rational, and reasons why that resistance took place sorely needed study.

This problem of resistance vs. adoption of innovation, which had so interested Gabriel Tarde and other early students of social change, was to become an important area of study among rural sociologists. Several early investigations of the effectiveness of a communication medium—specifically, agricultural bulletins issued by the Federal Extension Service—in promoting new farm technologies were undertaken by rural sociologists. Though most of the resulting research reports were known only within limited circles, they suggested the importance of this line of inquiry. These relatively obscure studies indicated that the process by which farmers adopted new agricultural technology *included communication in one way or another.*

It was from this matrix of events that rural sociologists realized that the human problem of the diffusion of innovations was an important area of research that fit well with the goals and objectives of the schools of agriculture. As this line of inquiry progressed, it gained approval and support from academic administrators. In spite of earlier suspicion, and even negative assessments of their discipline, rural sociologists began to find ready acceptance for their research. One of the studies that was undertaken as a result of this acceptance took place at Iowa State University—one of the major land-grant institutions. It looked at *human factors* in the adoption of an important agricultural innovation.

One study in particular, completed by a professor of rural sociology and his graduate student, is now recognized as providing the foundation for what has become the Theory of the Diffusion of Innovation. This study, of farmers adopting an agricultural innovation, seemed, at first, quite unlikely to have any significance for the new field of mass communication studies. Nevertheless, it has become a classic among seminal research projects in the field.

The Innovation

One of the most important events in the improvement of agricultural technology during the years preceding World War II was the development of *hybrid seed corn*. The term "hybrid" refers to the offspring of any genetically mixed parentage. With respect to plants, it means crossing varieties of specific plants, like corn, with others kinds of corn that have an unlike genetic constitution. This is done by controlling *pollination*. (This is not the same as the more modern practice of gene modification.) If the parent plants are appropriately selected and cross-pollination is successful, the hybrids that are produced sometimes have a vigor and resistance to such factors as drought and disease that may not be found in the contributing strains. Just such qualities were present in the hybrid seed corn that was developed in the late 1920s at Iowa State University and at other land-grant institutions. Once perfected, the innovation was then produced and sold to farmers by commercial seed companies during the Depression years of the 1930s.

While such hybrid seeds undoubtedly have many advantages, there is one negative feature that must be considered. Hybrid seeds saved from a crop *will not reproduce exactly the same plants the next year*. Thus, farmers who had for generations reserved seed from their current crop, so as to plant another identical type of corn next year, could not do that with the hybrid varieties. They had to purchase new seeds each year for every planting. That, of course, represented a considerable expense—especially during the 1930s, which had been so economically difficult for farmers. Offsetting this economic disadvantage, however, was the fact that the use of hybrid seeds led to much larger crops of better overall quality—and with somewhat less risk to the perils of drought. Still, there was this trade-off, and it came to be an important factor as individual farmers considered adoption of the new seeds. Nevertheless, the benefits seemed so clear for the nation's food supply that during the 1930s the U.S. Department of Agriculture (through extension services, experiment stations, and other groups within the land-grant institutions) increasingly advocated the use of hybrid seed by Midwestern corn farmers.

By virtually any measure, hybrid seed corn was a great success as an agricultural technology. As a result of this new product, it has been estimated that between 1933 and 1939 acreage in hybrid corn increased from 40,000 to 24 million acres (about one-fourth of the nation's corn acreage).[5] As Ryan and Gross reported in 1948:

> The introduction of hybrid seed corn has been the most striking technical advance in Midwestern agriculture during the past decade. Although a few experimenters had been acquainted with this new and sturdier seed for many years, only since 1937 has it become a nationally important production factor.[6]

In spite of the fact that the use of this agricultural innovation had spread rapidly among corn growers in many parts of the country, relatively little was known about the *process of diffusion* on an individual-by-individual basis. By 1939, for example, seventy-five percent of the farmers in Iowa were planting hybrid seeds. Yet no studies had been made as to *why* such farmers had altered their traditional practice of saving seeds from year to year. What information did they receive, through what channels, and how did this influence their decision making?

The seminal study of the diffusion of innovation, which is now regarded as a classic, was conducted by Bryce Ryan and Neal C. Gross. Published in 1943, the study was designed by Ryan, who had been on the faculty of the Iowa State University in the department of rural sociology since 1938. His special area of interest was in processes of social change. He recognized that there were nonrational aspects of economic decision making that probably played a part in the diffusion of innovation. Neal Gross became Ryan's graduate assistant in 1941. It was he who gathered the empirical data by conducting interviews with farmers. He used the data in his master's thesis.

Purpose of the Study

As has been suggested, the principal focus of the study was to try and uncover the process by which an individual farmer decided to adopt and use the new corn seed.[7] That goal was stated by Ryan and Gross in the following terms:

> Analysis of this diffusion has a special significance in that it represents a farm trait which can almost unqualifiedly be termed a 'good (economic) farm practice.' The study of its spread may offer some factual knowledge of conditions attendant to the eminently successful diffusion of a rational technique.[8]

More specifically, a number of important issues were explored. For example, did the general condition of the economy play a part in the decisions of farmers to adopt and use this new type of seed? In particular, were farmers inhibited by the cost of the seed? On the other hand, were the decisions of some motivated by the prospect of larger profits? In addition, how did these farmers find out about this innovation? What were the channels of communication by which they *first learned* abut hybrid seed corn? What part was played by radio, printed media, personal contacts with salesmen, advice received from neighbors or friends, or communications from some other source? In addition, how important was each of those communication channels in the final decision by an individual farmer to adopt? Another issue was how long it took between awareness and action. That is, once the individual became aware of the new seed, did he start planting it right away, or did it take some time? If so, how much time lapsed before adoption? Finally, what was the *time pattern* by which the innovation spread widely among corn farmers? Did the curve of diffusion follow an "*s*-shaped" cumulative normal or give (such as was the case with the growth of a fruit fly population in a laboratory setting, as well as other phenomena studied in various fields), or what?[9]

Research Method and Strategy

To provide answers to these questions, Ryan designed a research project based on personal interviews with farmers who were raising corn. He selected two small communities, each about forty to fifty miles from Ames—the site of Iowa State University. Of the 259 farmers finally included in the study, each lived near either Jefferson or Grand Junction—which are quite typical of small Iowa "Corn Belt" towns. Each farmer studied (all were males) had more than twenty acres in production and was included in the sample only if he had been planting corn before hybrid seed became available. Thus, each respondent in the sample had been able to adopt the new seed as an innovation.

As noted, Neal Gross personally interviewed each of these respondents. Those interviewed were asked when they had begun their first use of hybrid seed corn (if they indeed were using it). In addition, they were asked to identify their earliest source of information about the new kind of seed and when that information came to their attention. The respondents were also asked to evaluate the importance of these sources. That is, how important were they in leading them to take up the practice?

FINDINGS AND IMPLICATIONS

What the researchers discovered was that deciding to adopt was not a quick decision. Among most, it took place on a gradual basis. Almost none of the farmers had suddenly changed his entire acreage from the older freely pollinated seed to the new hybrid. The majority had experimented—trying it out in a small area before making the change. An important background factor here may have been the general economic conditions of the nation. As noted earlier, during the 1930s the county was in the Great Depression. These were very bad times for farmers. Many had suffered financially during the early 1930s (before Federal farm support programs were enacted). While people in cities went hungry, many farmers could not sell their crops. With no one to buy them, they simply had to let them rot in the fields. During the mid-1930s, the Roosevelt administration developed federal programs to support agriculture, and conditions for farmers got better. Even so, paying a considerable amount of money for a new type of seed—even with the prospect of a more bountiful harvest—still seemed to many to be a gamble. Midwestern farmers were notoriously conservative, and given the economic difficulties of the time, it is not surprising that many held back on wholesale and immediate adoption.

Communication Channels for First Learning

By what means did these farmers first learn about the innovation? A number of different communication channels were involved. Some were word of mouth; others were via various media. Almost half of the respondents indicated that they first heard about the innovation from salesmen who worked for the seed companies. A lesser number, only 14.6 percent, named neighbors as their initial source. Another small number were informed by relatives. Among those who learned from media, some 10 percent first learned of the seed's existence from advertisements on the radio. In addition, 10.7 percent learned from farm journals. A small number learned from the university's extension service. Thus, both interpersonal and mediated communication played a part.

In terms of influencing the farmer's decision, not all of these sources were equally important. For example, *the most influential source* was neighbors. While they were not named with great frequency as the origins of their earliest information, their assessments and judgments were *trusted*. (See discussion of "opinion leaders" in Chapter 13, "The Two-Step Flow of Communication Theory.") In contrast, while seed company salesmen were mentioned as the most frequent source of initial information, they were not seen as equally trustworthy sources influencing the decision to adopt.

Time Between Learning and Adoption

The time period between first learning and making the decision to adopt turned out to be a lengthy one. For many farmers, several years passed between when they first heard of hybrid seed corn and when they actually began to plant it. In fact, the modal time period between learning and planting was between five and six years. What this implied was that many farmers knew a great deal about hybrid seed corn before they actually started using it.

Another complex relationship existed between time of first learning and the degree to which various interpersonal and media sources actually served as channels of information that were influential in the adoption decision. For example, seed company salesmen were the most active sources of information for the farmers who adopted in the early period—when they first learned of the existence of the new seed (from 1928 to 1935). Moreover, salesmen were also influential among the earliest adopters. These were farmers who acquired the innovation between the first of those years during which most adoptions were actually made (1935 to 1940). However, the influence of salesmen declined sharply later. For those who adopted late (after about 1936), salesmen played little part in their decision.

In terms of interpersonal channels, neighbors were important in two ways. In many cases, they were the ones who brought the seed to the attention of adopters, especially during the early 1930s. In addition, neighbors became increasingly influential during those years when the hybrid seed was actually being adopted. In particular, they were far more influential than salesmen during the last half of the 1930s. Generally, then, mass media—such as farm journals and radio ads—were not as important in promoting the adoption of this innovation as were interpersonal contacts. However, in the earlier period, before 1935, both played some part in bringing the innovation to the attention of the respondents.

The results made one thing clear. The processes of *interpersonal communication*, identified by Ryan and Gross as having been highly influential in bringing about the acquisition of this agricultural technology, did not fit earlier assumptions of scholars about how such diffusion took place. Some had suggested that it was a result of *random activity*. That is, the actors involved in the diffusion of an innovation—such as salesmen, county extension agents, relatives, mass communicators, or others in this case—were thought to encounter each other in some form of chance-like pattern, and the result was the adoption of the item. Clearly, that idea did not make sense in the case of the hybrid seed corn. What the researchers found was a web of relatively orderly interpersonal and media contacts. Within those established patterns of social interaction, neighbors and salesmen, as well as attention to mass communications, played the central roles in providing initial information about the innovation and defining it as an important one for those who would eventually adopt it.

It was that finding that made the Ryan and Gross study important. They had established that the diffusion of innovation appears to depend on some combination of well-established interpersonal ties plus habitual exposure to mass communications. It is for that reason that their study is now regarded as a milestone in the study of the diffusion of innovation. It became a classic and seminal study not because it revealed how a particular kind of corn seed came to be used by farmers in Iowa but in part because it focused on the *process by which diffusion of innovation takes place* to become a basis for social change. This idea challenged the explanations offered by earlier scholars, such as Gabriel Tarde, who had tried to identify that process in the 1890s. As was noted, his theory of the "laws of imitation" did not survive, due to the undeveloped state of sociology and psychology in his time. By the 1940s, however, the social sciences—utilizing the strategies and procedures common to other sciences—were able to identify the process of diffusion of innovation on an individual-by-individual basis. This enabled those sciences to incorporate research, such as that of Ryan and Gross, into the general body of concepts important to the study of social change.

For the contemporary field of mass communication, the hybrid seed study provided a foundation and conceptual framework for understanding the process of diffusion more generally. It identified a link between *awareness* of something new—often provided by information transmitted by mass media—and the *action* of adoption. Adoption can take many forms. It might mean purchases of an advertised product, modification of beliefs, or opinions advocated by an information campaign. It can mean changes of attitudes sought by persistent public relations efforts or other modifications of behavior that result from incidental lessons learned in attention to mass-communicated messages.

Since the time of the hybrid seed study, a very large literature concerning the diffusion of innovation has accumulated. As additional studies were undertaken, the boundaries between studies of the acquisition of new technology and the study of influences of mass communication began to merge. Indeed, by the early 1960s, there was keen interest in research by media scholars on the spread of innovations. For example, in 1962, in his definitive work on the process and effects of the diffusion of innovations, Everett Rogers reviewed 506 studies of diffusion.[10] The innovations under study by that time were diverse indeed—they included medical practices, agricultural technology, educational changes, birth control methods, consumer products, manufacturing techniques, and a variety of other inventions and changes.

Stages in the Diffusion Process

As the focus of scholarship shifted from pattern to process, increasing research attention was focused on the *stages* involved when individuals made decisions to adopt and use something new. As a result many of the concepts involved were clarified. For example, as was indicated earlier, Rogers defined an innovation in a very simple way as "an idea, practice or object that is perceived as new by an individual or other unit of adoption."[11] This definition has a number of advantages. Perhaps most important, it makes what the individual *perceives* the key to what constitutes an innovation. In other words, it matters little whether or not the item is "new" in some real sense. A person will regard it as an innovation if it *appears* to him or her as something he or she did not know about earlier. Moreover, Roger's definition is consistent with a variety of different types of studies of the diffusion process. Some are concerned with individual persons (such as farmers). Others focus on different kinds of adopters (such as nations, cities, organizations, and other kinds of groups).

Rogers was able to clarify the contribution of Ryan and Gross by identifying five major stages in the diffusion process. These stages were the *awareness, interest, evaluation, trial*, and, finally, *adoption*. In the first, the (potential) adopter learns of the existence of the innovation. In this stage, either the mass media or interpersonal contacts transmit the information about its existence to the attention of the potential user. This stage in the process was well identified by Ryan and Gross.

Rogers also addressed a question that remained controversial at the time—whether awareness of an innovation is created on a random basis or in some other way. This explanation was not supported by the findings from the Ryan and Gross study. For example, paying attention to media, or even interpersonal messages, about hybrid seed corn would have had little interest for the average city dweller. Such a person might have encountered the information by chance, but close attention would have been unlikely. In contrast, that information was important to a corn farmer in Iowa. Therefore, Rogers reasoned that awareness appears to be related to some kind of *significant interest* or *need*—one that might be satisfied by adopting the new product or technology.[12]

Specifically, then, if the individual becomes aware of the innovation, his or her *interest* may be aroused. If that is not the case, adoption does not occur, and the process ends with this second stage. However, if the person's interest has been aroused, mass communication channels as well as interpersonal contacts may play a major role. Interest can bring the individual to search actively and purposively for more information about the item. As Rogers noted, the selective use of media and other information sources guide behavior at this point.[13]

Then, once the individual understands the nature of the innovation, the third stage becomes important. At this point, the potential adopter has to *evaluate* whether it will actually meet the interest or need that he or she thought was important in the previous stage. Rogers refers to this as a sort of "mental" trial stage. Here the person decides whether the problem-solving advantages of adopting the innovation truly outweigh its disadvantages (costs, risks, effort, etc.).[14]

It is in the fourth, or "trial," stage that the innovation is often first used. In many cases, this is done on a small scale. Planting a trial plot was clearly the case among the Iowa farmers. They often planted a few of their acres in the new corn in order to compare the results with the full crop that they had been raising. But in many situations, for many innovations, parallel small-scale trials may not be possible. In these situations, the new item may be used temporarily before a final decision is made. An example is the common practice of taking a "test drive" in a new car before a final purchase decision is made. If such a small-scale or temporary use is not possible, many potential adopters will not pass through this trial stage.

The final stage is *actual adoption*. Here, the person has made his or her decision, and the innovation is acquired. When this takes place, the innovation is used on a more-or-less permanent basis as part of the individual's behavioral routines. At this point, the person becomes a part of the population who has adopted, and he or she is added to the diffusion curve.

Types of Adopters and the S-Shaped Curve

An additional issue addressed by the Ryan and Gross study was to identify differences among *types of people* who adopted the innovation at various time intervals along the accumulating *s*-curve. They identified what they called "innovators," who were the earliest adopters—in that they were the very first to try out the new seed. They also identified what they termed "early adopters." These consisted of a slightly larger number who began using the hybrid seed after seeing it demonstrated by the innovators. The next category was the "majority." These were the farmers who adopted the innovation in large numbers between 1940 and 1941. Finally, they defined "later acceptors" as those who did not take up the innovation until most of their neighbors were already using it. Thus, the study not only shifted attention from *pattern* to *process* as a major emphasis, but also the hybrid seed corn study identified *types of adopters* as a focus of concern.

As research accumulated on diffusion in later years, such differences between categories of adopters came to be intensively studied.[15] Rogers integrated the pattern, the process, and the types of people into a synthesis of adopter categories on the basis of a personality trait he termed "innovativeness." His classifications included "innovators" (the initial 2.5 percent who were first to adopt in the s-shaped curve), "early adopters" (the next 13.5 percent), "early majority adopters" (34 percent), "late majority adopters" (another 34 percent), and finally "laggards" (some 16 percent who were the last to adopt).[16] Each of these figures is a percent of the normal curve—which plotted in an accumulated manner forms an "*s*" shape. In addition, Rogers defined "diffusion" in a clear way that identified the major related concepts. As he put it, "Diffusion is a special type of communication. Diffusion is the process by which innovations spread to the members of a social system."[17]

As the hybrid seed corn study and a number of earlier studies have shown, diffusion takes place over time. As explained, innovations typically form an s-shaped curve as they are adopted within a population. For example, Figure 1 shows the pattern by which many innovations were adopted over time by the American population.

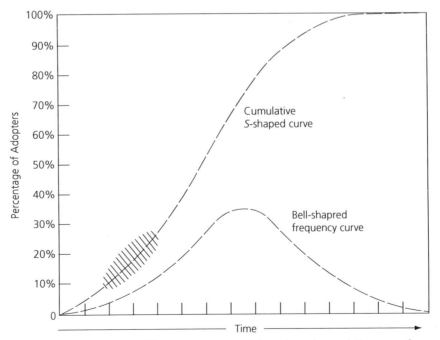

FIGURE 1   The bell-shaped frequency curve and the *s*-shaped cumulative curve for an adopter distribution.   *Source:* Everett M. Rogers. *The Diffusion of Innovations,* 4th Ed. (New York Free Press, 1983). P. 243.

The diffusion curve is one that accumulates slowly at first, as innovators start the process, then rises much more rapidly when early adopters and then the majority take up the item. Then it tapers off as late adopters are added. In its final stage, it flattens out due to non-adopters. Thus, that curve or distribution reveals the percentages of the relevant population of potential adopting units that have taken up the item at various points in time. As noted, these may be individuals or some other types of units—such as school systems, military forces, cities, or even national governments. However, as research began to accumulate, it became clear that different kinds of innovations diffused at different rates.

Eventually, as research accumulated, what was found was a *family* of different-appearing curves. For example, some innovations can sweep through a population of adopters very swiftly. This was the case with home television receivers between 1950 and 1960. Even under those conditions, they form an *s*-shaped curve, such as that identified by Rogers. Other types of innovations may take many decades to become widely adopted. That was clearly the case with daily newspapers as they were increasingly used between about 1840 and 1910. Even so, their diffusion pattern formed a more extended, but typical, *s*-shaped curve. Thus, the pattern of diffusion (whether swift or slow) will depend on the particular trait and the different characteristics of the types of people who become aware of its existence and potential value for their purposes.

CONCLUSIONS

As explained, it is widely recognized that the Ryan and Gross study was the classic and seminal study of the pattern and process of the diffusion of innovation. This is the case because it focused attention on the four major factors that are influences on the diffusion of an innovation. These are (1) a *specific innovation*; (2) processes of *interpersonal and mass communication* that create awareness of the item; (3) a specific kind of *group, population, or social system*; and (4) different *categories of individuals* who made decisions at various stages as the item diffuses through the relevant population. Furthermore, the study served as a beginning point that shifted scholarly interest from an almost exclusive concern with the *pattern* formed by diffusion through a population over time to the human personal *behavior* involved in the action of adoption.

For the field of mass communication, the hybrid seed corn study called attention to the relative role of media versus interpersonal channels in communicating awareness of the innovation. At the time, this was not a major objective of the Ryan and Gross study. They were interested in diffusion as a sociological phenomenon. For that reason, their research did *not* show that mass communications played a particularly important part in either informing the relevant population about the innovation or persuading them to adopt it. However, today, with the media greatly expanded, and for many kinds of innovations, that would not be the case. The media are now *far more significant* as sources of information to the populations that they serve.

One of the reasons is that, at the time of the study, mass communications played a relatively minor part in the lives of corn farmers in Iowa. The setting was a rural environment, which more closely resembled a traditional society where word-of-mouth communication channels were more important than newspapers and radio. In addition, a new kind of seed corn was not the kind of innovative product that would normally be advertised via the common mass media that were operative at the time. Thus, among the Iowa corn farmers, interpersonal channels—that is, salesmen and neighbors—were far more important channels of communication in bringing the innovation to the attention of potential adopters.

Other studies of the period supported what Ryan and Gross had found regarding interpersonal channels. The role of interpersonal communications was independently found by Lazarsfeld and his associates in the discovery of the two-step flow process (Chapter 13). As was discussed, this was found in the very different Erie County, Ohio, setting of the *People's Choice*. The same conclusions about the importance of interpersonal channels were reached by Katz and Lazarsfeld, Merton, and others, later in their pioneering research on *personal influence* in still other settings (also discussed in Chapter 13).

In more urban settings, then or now, in which one's neighbors may be total strangers, it would be unrealistic to expect to receive a great deal of information about some innovation by word-of-mouth communication. In such settings, family and friends may play a part, but neighbors are not as likely to be as important. Even people who live in the same building may have few contacts with each other, and such encounters tend to be far less frequent than between neighbors living on nearby farms. Indeed, there may be no contact with neighbors at all in the city environment. Also, salesmen pushing products do not have the same access to potential adopters in urban environments as they do with rural populations.

Generally, then, for city residents, the mass media serve as far more significant *sources of first learning* about new ideas, products, or services. They hear of a new cell phone, soft drink, or laxative from ads on television or the Internet. They encounter information about a new cholesterol medication or innovation in computer software from magazines devoted to their interests; they encounter new hairstyles or slang expressions in movies. Even those innovations related to their occupations or business will probably come to their attention when they read a newsletter or specialty magazine, rather than interpersonally from neighbors, family, or friends. Thus, in the urban environment, the ratio between interpersonal and mass media channels that bring information about innovations is likely to be drastically reversed from that encountered among rural residents.

MEDIA-INFLUENCED DIFFUSION OF INNOVATION THEORY: A FORMAL SUMMARY

From the above considerations and the extensive body of findings that have produced explanations of the conditions and process of the diffusion of innovations, the basic propositions of the theory can be set forth in the following terms:

1. The diffusion process begins with an *awareness stage* in which those who will ultimately adopt an innovation learn of its existence (often from the mass media) but lack detailed information about it.
2. Awareness is followed by an *interest stage*, during which those who contemplate adoption will devote increasing attention to the innovation and seek additional information about it. The media are often providers of some of this information.
3. In an *assessment stage*, such individuals use the information obtained to evaluate the applicability of the innovation to their present and future situations.
4. In a *trial stage*, a few of these individuals acquire and apply the innovation on a small scale to determine its utility for their purposes.
5. **Therefore**, in the final *diffusion stage*, a number of innovators actually acquire and use the innovation on a full scale. After that, increasing numbers adopt it, and the accumulation of users follows a characteristic "*s*-shaped curve" that starts upward slowly, then rises quickly, and finally levels off.

In a very real sense, then, it was the Ryan and Gross study of hybrid seed corn that provided the foundation for the development of this theory, as well as the flood of research that followed. The resulting accumulation of research greatly expanded our understanding of the process of the diffusion of innovations of all kinds—regardless of whether those who were potential adopters of the new item first learned about it from neighbors or other interpersonal channels, or from the mass media. The important contribution made by the Ryan and Gross study was that (1) there are *stages* in the diffusion process, that (2) *different categories of adopters* are involved in these stages, that (3) there a number of *channels* by which the adopters receive different influences, and that (4) the *s-shaped pattern* typically described the pattern of diffusion over time. These contributions are as valid today as they were in Iowa in the 1940s. They help in understanding how new traits spread through a relevant population of adopting units.

To illustrate the influence of this study, Rogers estimated by 1993 that more than 5,000 studies of the diffusion process and their patterns over time had been published.[18] Research on the patterns and process of diffusion of innovations have been pursued in such diverse fields as national development, public health, geography, marketing, the diffusion of media technologies, changes in manufacturing processes, educational innovations, new government policies, and dozens of others.[19]

Notes and References

1. Everett M. Rogers and F. Floyd Shoemaker, *Communication of Innovations: A Cross-Cultural Approach,* 2nd ed. (New York: The Free Press), p. 19.

2. Ralph Linton, *The Study of Man* (New York: Appleton-Century-Crofts, 1936), p. 324. (Quoted by Rogers and Shoemaker, *ibid.* p. 1.)

3. The following sections of this reading incorporate a number of ideas from Shearon A. Lowery and Melvin L. DeFleur, Chapter 6, "The Iowa Study of Hybrid Seed Corn," in *Milestones in Mass Communication Research* (White Plains, NY: Longman, 1995), pp. 115–133.

4. Gabriel Tarde, *The Laws of Imitation,* trans. by Elsie C. Parsons (New York: Henry Holt, 1903), p. 140; first published in Paris in 1890.

5. From a personal conversation with Bryce Ryan.

6. Bryce Ryan and Neal Gross, "The Diffusion of Hybrid Seed Corn in Two Iowa Communities," *Rural Sociology,* 8, 1, March, 1943, p. 7.

7. Insights into the ways in which this study was generated were provided to one of the authors in personal conversations with Professor Ryan.

8. Bryce Ryan and Neal Gross, *Op. Cit.*, p. 16.

9. Explanations and insights into how these issues played a part in planning the study were provided to one of the authors in personal conversations with Professor Ryan.

10. Everett M. Rogers, *Diffusion of Innovations*, 3rd ed. (New York: Free Press, 1963), p. 5.

11. Everett M. Rogers *Ibid.* p. 89

12. Everett M. Rogers *Ibid.* p. 103

13. Everett M. Rogers *Ibid.* p. 177

14. *Ibid.* p. 85.

15. See, for example, "Adopter Categories as Ideal Types," in *Ibid.* pp. 247–270.

16. Everett M. Rogers, *Op. Cit.*, p. 247.

17. Everett M. Rogers and F. Floyd Shoemaker, *Op. Cit.,* p. 9.

18. *Ibid.* pp. 38–86.

19. *Ibid.* pp. 38–86.

CHAPTER 19

A Theory of Audience and Media Dependency on Popular Culture

As the mass media developed in the United States, they came to rely heavily on popular entertainment content. This dependency was first established by the mass newspapers as they began their development in the 1830s. Unlike their colonial predecessors, their emphasis was less on serious news and more on reports on crime, scandals, human interest, and other kinds of entertaining stories that would capture and hold the attention of their readers.

Those early entrepreneurs understood clearly the importance of *numbers.* The characteristics of those who made up those numbers were largely irrelevant. It did not matter whether they were educated or poorly schooled; male or female; politically active or not; or if they were of a particular religion, political persuasion, occupation, or age. What did matter was that they could *purchase the common products* that were advertised in the newspaper.

The bottom line was that *large numbers of subscribers and readers* brought in *large revenues*—not so much from subscriptions or street sales but from *advertisers*, who wanted their messages seen by the largest possible numbers of potential consumers. To maximize those numbers, the content of the newspapers had to emphasize what the public liked to read about. This formula (*popular content attracts the attention of the largest audience, which brings in the money*) became the fundamental operating principle of each of the remaining media that developed in the United States early in the nineteenth century. Today it applies equally well, not only to print media, but also to radio, television, the movies, and in limited ways to the Internet. It will continue to apply as our media develop further in the future. If even newer media become a reality in the years ahead, they will still be governed by that basic principle. As they say, "There ain't no free lunch." That is, someone has to pay the costs. There are really no alternatives to that principle in a political democracy in which *capitalism*, with privately owned media, is the economic institution. Few want the government to operate the media and control their content.

Given that situation, and looking at our current media, few would disagree that their content—from what appears in the venerable daily newspaper to the latest offerings on the other mass media—is mainly a mixture that includes or even emphasizes various kinds of popular entertainment. People seldom turn to television, newspapers, magazines, radio, the movies—or indeed any of the major media—seeking sophisticated wisdom, intellectual enlightenment, or moral guidance. Serious information, and even some content of artistic sophistication, can be found in a few media sources, such as specialized magazines and journals, for the limited number who diligently seek it. However, the vast majority in the audience have little interest in acquiring complex knowledge from the media or in using mass media to raise their moral standards or to enrich their aesthetic experiences. Most people attend to mass communications for recreation, relaxation, diversion, or, arguably, needs gratification—and, in many cases, utilitarian purposes.

The term usually applied by scholars to the overwhelming majority of the entertainment content presented by the mass media is "popular culture." Included in that broad concept are various forms of music, talk shows on radio, romance and mystery novels, soap operas, motion pictures, spectator sports, much of what appears in many magazines, paperback novels, and that part of the content of broadcast and print news that is aimed at amusing the audience. The list could go on and on. Even a casual check on any of the mass media at any hour of any day would show that what is being presented to audiences is of limited artistic, intellectual, moral, or educational merit. It is aimed mainly at providing interesting *diversion* that poses few cerebral challenges to those who are attending. That statement is not intended as a criticism of the media but as a factual description of how they manage to stay in business and make profits. Collectively referred to as "popular" or sometimes *mass* culture, this type of content remains the overwhelming mainstay of modern media systems in the United States and in similar capitalistic democracies.

THE MANY MEANINGS OF "CULTURE"

It may be confusing to use the term "culture" to characterize the kind of content that is so overwhelmingly encountered via the mass media. The reason is that the term actually has many distinct meanings that have little to do with mass communication. Therefore, it may be helpful to review very briefly how the term "culture" is used with alternative specific meanings. This will help make clear exactly what is being discussed in a Theory of Media Dependency on Popular Culture.

Culture as a Design for Living

The term "culture" as applied to the collective human condition was first used in 1871 by Edward B. Tylor—an early anthropologist. The term appeared in the title of a two-volume work on what were then called "primitive" people.[1] The original meaning of the term, as described by Tylor, continues to characterize the ways in which anthropologists and other social scientists use it even today. That is, among such scholars, the concept of "culture" is defined as the *social heritage of a society*—its total "design" for conducting a collective life. Culture is not the same idea as "society." That term refers to *a large number of living people* who lead a common life—interacting in various ways according to a pattern of social organization and usually in a defined spatial area. Essentially, culture refers to what those people *believe, do, use,* or *produce*. In this sense, the culture of a society can be regarded as all of the things and ideas that its population makes use of. That includes all of its shared beliefs and rules; all of its symbolic usages, such as language and numerical systems; its values; its amusements; and its entire array of material objects and tools.

Culture, in this sense, represents *solutions*. Each generation passes on its "design for living" to the next. Its social heritage is made up of a body of techniques and technologies for handling problems of living. For example, our generation does not have to invent a language so that we can communicate. We need not invent ways to control fire or use the wheel. Those solutions were developed many thousands of years ago.[2] As time went on, clever people either invented or borrowed from others (who had invented them) ways to grow and harvest food, and use metals, pottery, and cloth. As more centuries passed, gunpowder came into common use, an understanding of both the human and the heavenly bodies was developed, steam was harnessed, and factories were built. In time, science flowered to offer still more solutions. Eventually, swift communication media, medical treatments, automobiles, airplanes, and computers were perfected. The mass media that we enjoy today were a part of this ever-increasing and ongoing *accumulation* of Western culture.

Clearly, the term "culture," used in this way, is enormously broad and inclusive. It encompasses everything that has ever been invented, borrowed, and then adopted to become a common part of what people use to deal with the problems that they face. It includes all the intellectual knowledge we store in libraries, the content of what we teach in schools, and the total of all technologies, techniques, and tools that have ever been produced and are present in one form or another in our society.

As is obvious, the term "culture" as used in this way in social science is so broad that it almost boggles the mind. For that reason, social scientists use another, somewhat more restrictive, concept. The term *subculture* focuses more narrowly on the way of life (social heritage) of some particular category of people in a complex society. These may be a social class; a regional population; a religious, racial, or ethnic category; or those in a particular occupation. For example, in the United States, there has developed what many social scientists refer to as "middle-class culture." It includes all of the physical things (houses, lawns, cars, clothing styles, foods), along with shared values, patterns of recreation, beliefs, and practices that make up our middle-class (typically suburban) way of life.

To illustrate, it includes a shared belief that it is important to *postpone gratification* in the interests of long-term reward. It is this shared belief that motivates middle-class people to make short-run sacrifices so that longer term goals can be achieved. Those whose way of life corresponds to this subculture usually continue into college and even into graduate programs, rather than terminating their education before or right after high school. They aim at higher levels of employment and larger incomes than lower levels of education would provide. They save for their eventual retirement or for their children's forthcoming college expenses. In contrast, those lower in the SES system have lifestyles that tend toward more immediate gratification. They are more likely to get a job right out of high school so that they can buy a car, a stereo, or a TV, and they enjoy other immediate rewards. In other words, they tend to spend their income as soon as they receive it, for more *immediate gratification*, rather than invest or save to accomplish long-term goals.

Other categories in modern societies follow distinctive lifestyles (subcultures) with their own sets of beliefs and practices. These include various occupational categories (physicians, lawyers, truck drivers, construction workers, artists, and so on). Also included are various kinds of ethnic and minority categories. Thus, the shared beliefs of African Americans are not identical to those of Native Americans. Each of the major regions (e.g., New England, the Deep South) also tends to have somewhat distinct subcultures.

As can be seen, the use of the term "culture" with the associated meanings just described, has little to do with the content of the mass media. As any social scientists would agree, the mass media and their content make up only one feature of the general American culture. They would also agree that those who can be identified as members of various subcultures may have different tastes for and patterns of usage of distinct types of media content. However, as will be made clear, the idea of "popular" or "mass" culture is quite different.

High Culture

Another use of the term "culture" focuses on artistic products, participation in and tastes of more "refined" activities among those who consider themselves apart from and somewhat superior to ordinary members of mass society. In popular terms, we sometimes refer to people who are "cultured." They are so identified because of their knowledge about and enjoyment of works of art, music, dance, literature that have been produced by highly skilled and talented artists, musicians, writers, and so on. Many of those works were produced by honored individuals—mainly Europeans—who died long ago. Those who produced "great literary works" generally lived during the eighteenth and nineteenth centuries—but seldom later than the early part of the twentieth century. "Classical" music is mainly a product of a few dozen composers of the last two centuries. The recognized "master painters" are mostly confined to men who worked in Italy, France, and in a few cases other countries during the same period. Few Americans are recognized as among this elite. Almost no one from Africa, Asia, or South America (or women) is included. A "cultured" individual would be expected to be familiar with, enjoy, and have high regard for the works produced by this somewhat limited number of persons.

Not only has there for many centuries been an admiration for what can be termed "high" or "elite" culture, but also there has been a conviction that what holds interest for common persons may be debasing, or even destructive—in particular for young and tender minds. This has often produced a clash between those who value high culture and those who prefer simpler forms. In ancient Greece, for example, the elite of the society were fond of plays, music, and poetry. They wanted their children to be exposed to artistic products of aesthetic and moral value that would have a positive influence on shaping their character. They were troubled by the possibility that their children would be exposed to more common stories and tales that would pose a threat to their minds. As was noted in an earlier chapter, in Plato's famous work *The Republic*, where he outlined the nature of the ideal city-state, Plato set forth his prescriptions for educating the young. As he put it:

> Then shall we simply allow our children to listen to any stories that anyone happens to make up, and so receive in their minds ideas often the very opposite of those we think they ought to have when they grow up?
>
> 'No, certainly not.' [replies Glaucon, who is being addressed].
>
> In seems, then, our first business will be to supervise the making of fables and legends, rejecting all which are unsatisfactory; and we shall induce nurses and mothers to tell their children only those which we have approved. . . . Most of the stories now in use must be discarded.[3]

If these ideas have a strangely modern ring, it is because the content of elite culture has always been regarded as beneficial and uplifting, while simpler forms of cultural content that children may encounter have often been both feared and rejected by those who are concerned about their influences on children. Today, much of what can be encountered in the mass media—portrayals of violence, mindless drama formulas, depictions of sexual excess, and vulgar language—cause the same reactions among those committed to high culture that their counterparts experienced in Plato's time.

Folk Culture

Still another use of the term "culture" is its application to the creative products of *traditional* people. Members of tribal or agricultural societies—as they existed (and in some cases still exist), independent of the processes of industrialization—produce many kinds of music, songs, poems, stories, dances, rugs, pottery, masks, and many other kinds of decorated objects. These are termed "folk" culture. Their styles and forms are often unique to a particular village or language community. The members of such groups use these products in activities that are a normal part of their everyday lives.

People in traditional societies all over the world have produced folk culture, and for many enthusiasts today it is regarded as a valuable art form. Examples would be the pottery traditionally made and used daily by particular tribes of Native Americans in the Rio Grande valley before contact with Europeans. Ancient pieces discovered in burial sites are treasured and command very high prices. Today, this type of pottery is still produced, but it is no longer made to be used for its original purposes. It is produced as objects to sell to tourists.

Another example of folk culture would be the stories, songs, and dances of earlier Americans who lived in remote and isolated areas in the Ozark mountains, or in coastal areas of Louisiana. These have long commanded the interest of academic folklorists who have attempted to record and preserve their original forms. Today, the music produced by such people has been popularized to be sold on cassettes and DVDs as "bluegrass," "Zydeco," or "Cajun." When that type of transformation takes place, what was genuinely folk art becomes little more than one more category of commercialized goods for sale.

Obviously, folk culture is seldom a matter of concern to students of mass communication. Some aspect of folk culture may occasionally be a part of a media presentation, but it is not thought to be controversial, an object of criticism, or particularly dangerous. Like high culture, it is of limited interest to the majority of people who make up the audiences for the mass media.

Popular Culture

There are two terms that can be interchangeably used to label the cultural products that appeal to "the masses." One is simply "mass culture," and the other is "popular culture." As sociologist Herbert Gans explains:

> The term *mass culture* is a combination of two German ideas: *Masse and Kultur*. The mass is (or was) the non-aristocratic, uneducated portion of European society, especially the people who today might be described as lower-middle class, working-class

and poor. *Kultur* translates as *high culture*; it refers not only to the art, music, literature and other symbolic products that were (and are) preferred by the well-educated elite of European society but also to the styles of thought and the feelings of those who choose these products—those who are 'cultured.' Mass culture, on the other hand, refers to the symbolic products used by the 'uncultured' majority.[4]

Some who wish to be politically correct avoid the use of "mass" to refer to this type of culture. The reason is that it is not a flattering term. It suggests a kind of collection of mindless dolts who have little appreciation for the finer things of life—a sort of undifferentiated mob, who know nothing of sophisticated art, music, literature, or other features of high culture. For those who do not wish to be so pejorative, the term "popular culture," or even more recently "popular arts," has become a less offensive way to refer to that which is enjoyed by the less-educated and less "refined" part of society.

But of what does such popular culture consist? It is a term that goes beyond the content of the contemporary mass media, because (as the quotation from Plato suggests) there was popular culture before there were such media. An example is the *circus*, which goes back at least to Roman times. During the nineteenth century in America, there were all kinds of amusements that were forms of popular culture to entertain the majority of citizens. During the 1800s, for example, modern spectator sports were invented. Football, baseball, and even basketball games came to be a part of popular culture. Before broadcast media were available, fans went to stadiums and ball parks to see the spectator sports action—or, if unable to attend, they could read about them in the newspaper. Other forms of popular culture during the 1800s included minstrel shows, vaudeville, rodeos, dances, skating rinks, and amusement parks with Ferris wheels and roller-coaster rides.

Today, the mass media are the most significant delivery systems for bringing most forms of popular culture to the public. As explained earlier, in many ways, that delivery began with the early mass newspapers, such as Benjamin Day's *New York Sun*, which, beginning in 1834, sold for only a penny on the streets of New York City. It carried reports of crimes, scandals, human interest events, and even stories that were later found to be hoaxes. The main idea, however, was that what was in the newspaper should be interesting and fun to read about. It worked, and the *Sun*, and later its rivals, proved to be very popular. Newspapers have carried on that tradition from the period of "yellow journalism" right to the present when similar content can be found in tabloids sold at the check-out stand in the supermarket.

As newer mass media became available—movies, popular magazines, comic books, tabloids, radio, television, and more recently the Internet—these became the channels that delivered an ever-increasing flow of popular entertainment to the masses.[5] Today, many millions of citizens are amused, diverted, and entertained by such forms as popular films, radio music stations, talk shows, television sitcoms, staged wrestling, soap operas, and all of the rest that can be found in the American mass media.

Media content is not the only form of popular culture, but it is by far the most available. If a definition were necessary, it would refer to a great variety of products, activities, and entertainment designed to amuse or serve as a pastime for large numbers of people, without making significant intellectual demands on them.

In summary, then, the term "culture" has many meanings. In its broadest sense, it refers to *everything that the people of a society use in their "design for living" and pass on to the next generation as their "social heritage."* Within that broad usage, somewhat distinct designs and heritages can be identified in complex societies as the "subcultures" of specific categories of people who share similar ways of life. Still another term is "folk culture." This refers to the creative products of traditional people, which may include music, songs, poems, stories, dances, rugs, pottery, masks, and many other kinds of decorated objects. Their styles and forms are developed by members of specific villages, regions, or language communities. Popular culture generally refers to the content of the several mass media, which offer simple forms of entertainment to large numbers of people without making intellectual demands upon them.

THE AUDIENCE'S DEPENDENCY ON POPULAR CULTURE

The further back the history of humankind goes, the less need there was for popular culture. The earliest human beings may have invented simple ways to amuse themselves when they were not hunting or gathering—which were demanding ways to exist, to say the least—and little is known of any leisure-time aspects of their day-to-day life. By the time of the Middle Ages, common folk worked at farming or at domestic chores from daylight to dark. They had virtually no free time. They had to prepare and preserve food, make clothing, and conduct all the tasks and chores by hand that we do with machines in factories today. If free time was sometimes available, it was spent on religious observations. Even in Western societies, prior to the Industrial Revolution of the 1800s, men, women, and children were preoccupied with chores, duties, and work obligations that left them with little time for entertainment. There were few channels to bring them much in the way of popular culture.

The Industrial Revolution and New Life Schedules

The development of factories and other aspects of industrialization altered the rhythms of life for millions of people who participated in the process—but not at first. For centuries, the vast majority of people had lived on farms. In that setting, their lives were governed by the daily rhythms of agriculture. This meant attending to crops and animals from dawn to dusk and performing household and other chores in the evening hours. There was very little in the way of leisure time. Even children had their responsibilities, and when not in school, they performed assigned tasks that were needed by the family. As was the case with the adults, there was virtually no leisure time that they could devote to diversions of their choice.

The arrival of the *steam age* and *factories* soon changed all that. A factory runs on a time schedule. Before electricity was available, so that the plant could have a longer daytime shift, work started as soon as it was light enough to see. It did not end until it became too dark. Men, women, and their children toiled during all the daylight hours at machines and other tasks to manufacture whatever the factory produced. The average age at entering the labor force was about 13 years. There was no concept of retirement, so people kept working as long as they were physically able to do so. Many simply died at their work stations. This was the condition of humankind in the early years of the industrial age. There was little possibility, given such conditions, that mass media would develop to provide diversion for the working masses during their leisure time. Even if they did have leisure time, they had no discretionary income to pay for amusements.

The miserable condition of working families during the early Industrial Age deeply offended Karl Marx as he began his scholarly career in 1841.[6] He saw the new economy and power arrangements of the emerging industrial society as an extension of those that had prevailed through the ages—in all of which a few dominated the many. It was a dreadful situation. Workers were used up by owners and managers, with little thought to their exploitation to make profits. They had about the same value as the resources of a coal mine. Moreover, Marx made clear, the culture of the societies undergoing industrialization were essentially supportive of the early economic forms of capitalism. That is, the established systems of law, art, religion, education, and even science offered little resistance to the continued development of early capitalism based on factory production, with more and more workers entering the system. It is little wonder that by 1848 Marx and his colleague Frederick Engels proclaimed that there was no hope for achieving social justice through reforms. A *total revolution* was the only possible answer. Their advice was "Workers of the world, unite!" [to displace the owners and manager class by means of a revolution] and that "The proletarians [workers] have nothing to lose but their chains."[7]

While revolutions based on the political philosophies of Marx did take place in the twentieth century, they were of little consequence for the development of popular culture. It was the growth of the mass media that fostered that development. What happened was that the plight of the working classes began to change for the better, and it continued to improve over many decades. That improvement could not take place until the conditions that offended Marx were altered to allow people *more leisure time.* Slowly, however, new conditions for the industrial worker did come. Publics in Western societies no longer tolerated child labor. Trade unions discovered their power and began to shorten both the work week and the number of hours worked daily. Payment for workers also improved, providing at least some discretionary income that could be spent on amusement. Moreover, in the U.S., mandatory schooling for children (based on a plan devised by Horace Mann of Massachusetts in 1834) was gradually adopted state by state. The idea also spread to other countries.

The result of these changing conditions was an ever-expanding pool of potential readers of newspapers, books, and magazines. It was this foundation—along with increased hours of leisure—that permitted the masses to spend time reading and participating in other early forms of popular entertainment. It created, in short, a *market* among the working classes for the production of popular culture that could make a profit—an essential requirement within a capitalistic economic system.

As the 1800s moved on, scientific discoveries in electricity and chemistry laid the foundation for the emergence of additional media—the telegraph, the telephone, wireless telegraphy, and photography. These, in the 1900s, would enable scientists and engineers to develop home radio, the movies, television, and (more recently) the Internet. However, these new technologies would have been quite useless if people in the society had no time or money to attend to them. The essential factors, then, were *leisure and discretionary income*, which increased decade by decade in the Western world.

In summary, social, political, and economic changes altered the nature of human life in industrial societies for the vast majority. These changes brought a great increase in time available for entertainment, as well as required increases in discretionary purchasing power, needed to purchase that entertainment. In addition, advances in science and engineering made our current media possible. Finally, the huge profits that could be attained from advertisers by the production of various forms of media content to provide the masses with simple entertainment fueled the production of an ever-increasing flow of popular culture in media content.

Filling Leisure Time

Imagine, for a moment, what working- and middle-class families would do if they did not have movies to attend or to view on their home TV screen, or if they had no other television fare to watch, radio to listen to, paperback novels or other print materials to read, or the Internet to preoccupy their time. Most now work only eight hours a day, and for only five days of each week. After their evening meal, and making allowances for transportation, there are at least four hours in each work day to fill. Then there are the weekends, with at least ten hours per day that are not preoccupied with eating or other routine household matters. All of that adds up to some forty hours per week that are left over as *leisure time*—roughly the equivalent to full-time job. To be sure, some of that time can be spent in talking with grandma, correcting the kids, going to church, mowing the lawn, or chatting with neighbors. However, even with a generous allowance for such activities, there would still be about twenty hours left over—something like a half-time job.

The question is, what would people do with that leisure time if they did not have the media? Some might go to church, visit with family, or attend various kinds of live performances. The majority, however, would probably just sit at home, bored out of their minds. Even by the early part of the twentieth century, however, there were newspapers, magazines, and books to read; radio programs (with soap operas, ball games, comedy shows, and evening dramas) to listen to; and the local neighborhood movie (and later the drive-in) to attend. By the beginning of the twenty-first century, the range of media offering popular culture content had greatly expanded. The typical television cable system offers somewhere around one hundred channels or more, from which one can select anything from MTV to the latest sitcom. Movies can be rented from chain outlets to view—either on the TV set or on the home computer. Indeed, each of the media—print, broadcast, and online—has greatly expanded the choices available, ranging from hard-core pornography to the latest release from the Disney Company.

In short, life today in the American society, or in similar modern societies the world over, is one in which the media present a daily tidal wave—a virtual *tsunami*—of popular culture from which its citizens can choose. And choose they do. The average time during which the television set is on in American homes has expanded steadily from about four hours a day during the late 1950s, when the medium first entered the majority of homes, to the present, when the set remains on for an average of well over seven hours a day. Online usage has been soaring in the last several years, with ever-increasing proportions of the population owning a home computer linked to the Internet. To be sure, there have been various patterns of growth and decline within the media industries as one or another of the traditional forms prospers or declines. The overall pattern, however, is an ever-expanding availability of popular culture presented by the media as a whole. In parallel, there has been an ever-growing pattern of attendance to this kind of content on the part of the public as their leisure time and expendable income have increased.

MEDIA DEPENDENCY ON POPULAR CULTURE

While the public has become more and more preoccupied with popular culture as a means of filling leisure time, the media themselves are almost totally dependent on using their time, space, and technology to deliver unsophisticated content to the majority in the audience who will find it entertaining. To illustrate, imagine a situation in which you wake up one day to find that the American mass media have totally changed their programming and editorial strategies. Popular culture has been abandoned. Your morning newspaper no longer has reports of crimes, fires, auto accidents, the latest escapades of celebrities, or scandals involving public personalities. Gone too are human-interest accounts—such as one in which a single lady finds a snakeskin from a four-foot boa constrictor in her fifth-floor apartment.[8] Instead, the newspaper has provided verbatim reports of speeches made by several senators debating the latest budget proposal for funding the Commission on Agricultural Policies. The paper also includes a lengthy account of a performance of an obscure opera composed by Scott Joplin early in the 1900s, a discussion of the relative merits of three Impressionist painters from the 1890s, and a review of a recent performance of Don Quixote, a ballet based on the writings of Cervantes. There are no crossword puzzles, advice from Dear Abbey, comic strips, or stories about the latest baseball, basketball, or football games.

In frustration, you turn on your TV to try and find something that interests you. What you find is only a panel of talking-head historians reviewing the political issues that might have made a difference in the Eisenhower vs. Carter election, a lecture on the merits of industrial bonds vs. common stocks as long-term investment prospects, a sermon on moral problems related to failing marriages, and a discussion of how increasing your exercise can provide a healthier lifestyle. Radio is much the same. It carries no popular culture. You notice too that all the movies being shown are art films, foreign-language movies, or documentaries on serious topics. Turning to the Internet, all you can find is technical information for engineers, listings of the Wall Street stock exchange, and a few reports about changes in the curricula in a few major divinity schools.

How long would such media remain profitable? The obvious answer is somewhat less than a heartbeat. Advertisers who now provide huge sums to push their wares via the mass media would stop paying immediately for such boring content. Without those revenue streams, virtually no media would be left. Perhaps a few specialized newsletters—paid for by churches or particular political groups—would still be available. Their content would focus on their own organizations and events. Only a few subsidized broadcast programs that were not dependent on advertising earnings would survive. The movie industry would soon be flat broke. The Internet might survive on government funds—but in a form mainly devoted to exchanges between scientists—which is exactly what it was when it started. The point is that *big numbers count* in maintaining the media. If the numbers of subscribers, listeners, viewers, surfers, or payers at the box office decline sharply, profits quickly disappear. If that should happen, the media could not survive in their present form.

In short, mass media in the United States are in a state of almost *total dependency* on advertising to earn their way. To attract advertisers, they must attract audiences—the bigger, the better. They cannot attract audiences by delivering high culture. That kind of media content can be presented to a minority, but only if it can earn its way through appropriate advertising to such people. The overwhelming majority that make up audiences want to be entertained with unsophisticated content that makes few intellectual demands and provides diversion—in short, the kinds of popular culture that one finds any day, during any hour, on any medium in the United States.

CRITICS' VIEWS OF THE CONSEQUENCES OF KITSCH

There is a host of critics of popular culture, and they have a long list of complaints. They sometimes use a colorful German word to describe the characteristics of much popular culture. The term is *kitsch*, which refers to trashy, garish products that are in bad taste and have no redeeming artistic merits. Originally the word was a label for the kind of objects that one might find in a low-level carnival—a small stuffed animal won for tossing baseballs accurately, a pillow that has "Niagra Falls" on one side and "Mother" on the reverse. The term was adopted by media critics, however, to apply to such products as "whodunit" detective novels, sex magazines, the music of the latest pop star, soap operas, game shows, and comic strips. Perhaps the ultimate form of kitsch would be a painting of Elvis Presley—on black velvet.

It is not just that popular culture is in bad taste, according to its critics, or that it lacks the artistic merits of products classified as high culture. They also maintain that popular culture has a number of truly negative consequences that pose significant problems for the society. Some of these charges include the following: (1) Popular culture *mines* high culture for themes, which is destructive and debasing to elite art, music, literature, and drama. (2) It *diminishes the stature* of real-life heroes by creating media-made celebrities who make no true lasting contributions to human life. (3) It is mass-produced for profit, which needlessly *raises the costs* of consumer products to the public. And (4) it often provides models for *deviant behavior*, such as violence, crime, sexual excess, and vulgar language. Do these charges have merit? Perhaps; it all depends on one's values.

Mining, Debasing, and Detracting from High Culture

As noted, a frequent complaint about popular culture is that it detracts from the value of high culture. When an exciting movie or television action play is available—showing cars and buildings blowing up, sexy women and men scantily clad or fully naked grinding in bed, macho heroes gunning down the forces of evil, and so on—it may be difficult for many in the audience to see that the thoughts, plots, characters, and adventures of a more literary work have greater merit. Because of limited education, or disinterest in sophisticated material generally, the offerings of elite plays, novels, ballets, and so on often cannot command the attention of the majority of people. In fact, they may seem downright dull. The same is true of music. The pounding beat and screaming lyrics of the latest popular hit can seem far more exciting than a performance of an opera in Italian or of a symphonic work by one of the great masters. Popular culture, then, simply "crowds out" high culture.

Another way in which popular culture defeats high culture is through "mining." An example is a print ad that was used early in the 1990s by a particular brand of pasta sauce to promote its products. The ad consisted of two pictures, side by side, with a catchy description of the merits of the product below. In fact, there were two versions of the product, the "original" and the "chunky." In the two pictures, the "original" showed the Mona Lisa, much as Leonardo DaVinci had painted her, slender and with her enigmatic smile. However, she was holding a jar of the pasta sauce. The other was a different version of the Mona Lisa, holding a jar of the "chunky" sauce. However, the one holding the "chunky" product was a very fat depiction of the Mona Lisa—also with an enigmatic smile, to be sure—but with a double chin, fat arms, and a very bulbous bosom. Did it catch one's eye and make clear that there were two versions of the sauce? Indeed, it did. At the same time, critics would claim, it both *mined* and *debased* the original example of high art for what many would regard as a shallow commercial purpose. On the other hand, it did call attention to DaVinci's painting, which might cause some who were uninformed to ask about it and learn where it came from—possibly advancing the agenda of high culture. But that would not be likely.

Popular culture, then, focuses the public's attention on its products and presumably keeps interest in more sophisticated art forms low. In addition, it makes use of classic cultural products by transforming them into shallow versions. This happens in advertisements, as in the Mona Lisa example, but also in television drama, movies, music, and even comic strips where themes, plots, and melodies are "borrowed" from classical sources and disseminated to media audiences in various forms of popular culture.[9]

Diminishing the Stature of Real-Life Heroes

It is not difficult to demonstrate how popular culture focuses attention on and creates media-made celebrities. It is this consequence that brings some individuals to public attention—makes them renowned, even if their only contribution to humankind is only to be entertaining. They become "heroes" to the masses, largely because they are so defined by enormous media attention.

There are, of course, genuine heroes. Individuals who, through meritorious accomplishments or heroic acts, have made remarkably important contributions to human existence but who receive no recognition whatsoever from the overwhelming majority of the public. Consider, for example, Phylo T. Farnsworth. Do you recognize him? Are you familiar with what he did to benefit humankind? How about Francis H. C. Crick? What was his significant accomplishment? Or how about William Crawford Long? Does his contribution leap to mind? Perhaps the name

John Gorrie is more familiar. What did he offer to human existence that was important? In contrast, consider the following names: Marilyn Monroe, John Lennon, Elvis Presley, John Wayne, and Babe Ruth. Most Americans have at least some familiarity with these personalities and can explain who they are (or were) and why they are considered important.

Let us compare the accomplishments of the individuals in the two lists. First, those whose names are little known but whose accomplishments clearly place them in a special class:

Many people fail to recognize the name of Philo T. Farnsworth, even though he was the inventor of television as we know it. As a youth, he designed and patented the electronic circuits by which television systems transmit and display the pictures that people all over the world enjoy as they tune in to their favorite form of popular culture. Was this contribution worthwhile?

What about Francis H. C. Crick? His accomplishments may not have leaped to mind. He, along with James Watson and Maurice Wilkins, received the Nobel Prize for Physiology or Medicine in 1962 for the discovery of the molecular structure of DNA. This is the chemical structure of genes and chromosomes that control the inheritance and life functions of animals, including human beings. Because of their work, the human genome has now been mapped, providing keys to correcting and controlling many kinds of illnesses that afflict humankind. The contribution that this discovery will make to human existence is truly profound.

Does the name William Crawford Long ring an immediate bell? His contribution to human existence was the discovery of a way to perform surgery on the human body in such a way that the patient feels no pain. In 1842, in Jefferson, Georgia, he successfully cut out a large cancerous tumor from the neck of one of his patients after putting the person to sleep with *ether*. The patient recovered nicely. Dr. Long received very little recognition for his accomplishment until more recent times, but if you have to go to the hospital for surgery, try to remember that your owe Dr. Long a debt.

John Gorrie is similarly a person whose name or contribution is unlikely to be recognized. However, whenever you go to your refrigerator to get a cold one or to take out food that has been kept from spoiling because of the low temperature, or even to turn on your air conditioner, you might think of him. As early as 1842 he was able to design a device that cooled rooms in hospitals. By 1851 he had patented a machine, based on the principles we use today, for mechanical refrigeration. He made no profit from his invention and received scant recognition, even though his contribution to human life and comfort has been truly significant.

On the second list are a famous female movie star, who because of extraordinary media attention came to be thought of as a sex goddess of the movie screen. Marilyn Monroe rose to fame during the late 1940s and the 1950s. Her face was recognized all over the world. She died by her own hand in 1962.

John Lennon was a prominent member of the world-famous British rock band The Beatles. Although they were popular in great Britain, they took the world of popular music in the United States by storm starting in the early 1960s. They became television stars as well as recording artists. Their style prompted many imitators. The Beatles made an especially strong impression on the young, personifying an emerging counterculture of hedonism, uninhibited sex, and experimentation with drugs. By 1970, it was over, and the band broke up. In 1980, John Lennon was killed by a fan in New York.

Elvis Presley was, of course, an American invention. With a unique style and clothing, he was an immensely popular performer beginning in the mid-1950s. Dubbed the "King" (of rock and roll), he represented a cross between country music and the emerging rock style that even now continues in popular music. He had millions of enthusiastic fans who eagerly purchased the more than 100 popular hits in which he performed. Not only was his musical style widely imitated, but so was the way he wore his hair. Millions mourned his death in 1977.

John Wayne was a "macho" and enormously popular movie star whose performances on the screen, often in Western movies, provided popular entertainment for Americans for many decades. He became a kind of definition of what it meant to be "manly."

What about Babe Ruth? What were his contributions to humankind? Actually, he was an American baseball player who served on a team called the New York Yankees during the late 1920s and early 1930s. During that time, he performed well. He had the highest batting average during several seasons. He also accumulated a record number of home runs. Moreover, he set a record of "most runs batted in" (hitting the pitched ball in such a way that runners already on base could get "home"). These important accomplishments ensure that Americans will remember his name in the years to come.

Essentially, then, the media provide a "status conferral function."[10] The principle is this: *If a person is important, then surely he or she will receive a great deal of media attention.* That seems logical enough. But by the same token, *if a person receives a great deal of media attention, then he or she must surely be important.* Clearly that attention, so significant in the conferral of status, is through media-transmitted popular culture. In that sense, popular culture emphasizes celebrities but ignores, or even diminishes, the recognition of individuals who have truly contributed to human existence.

Needlessly Raising the Cost of Products

Those who create popular culture do not do so for the sake of art. They are motivated in a quite different way than those who produce high culture. That is not to say that high culture artists enjoy poverty—which many of them have experienced over the ages. Their motivation is not to seek riches but to gain recognition. They are driven to perform, paint, sculpt, write, choreograph, and otherwise create products that will survive critical examination by those who make up the sophisticated cultural elite.

The manufacture of popular culture, on the other hand, is done for money. Those who star in sports, the movies, music, television sitcoms, and all the rest are among some of the highest paid people in modern society. The amount of money paid to an outstanding sports figure, a movie star, or a popular writer of mystery novels, for example, can stagger the imagination—at least when compared to a concert pianist, a successful poet, or a recognized painter.

Actually, only a few popular culture performers make astronomical incomes. For most who work in the industry, money still provides their motivation through reasonably well-paid salaries. It is clear, however, that it is not artistic acclaim but salaries and bonuses that drive the producers of the media's daily diet of infotainment news, magazine fare, reality shows, game shows, films, pop and talk radio shows, and so on. But while their may lack international acclaim and their incomes may be modest, the amount of popular culture that they generate on a daily basis—grist for the mills of the media—simply boggles the mind.

Added together, the total amount of money paid to media stars and to the faceless drones who create the constant flow of popular culture is simply staggering in an overall sense. No estimates of that amount are available, but it is clearly in the billions each year. But who pays for all of that? The answer is obvious: anyone who buys an advertised product at the supermarket, at an automobile dealer, or at any other retail outlet, whether in a traditional store or via the Internet. A very considerable part of the cost of the product or service that is purchased can be traced back to the *advertising budgets* of both the manufacturer and the retailer.

Some critics see the production of mass culture within a Marxian perspective—as a means by which those in the business community can maintain political power and exploit the public. Dwight MacDonald, a well-known critic of popular culture, put it this way:

> Mass Culture is imposed from above. It is fabricated by technicians hired by businessmen; its audience are passive consumers, their participation limited to the choice between buying and not buying. The Lords of *Kitsch*, in short, exploit the cultural need of the masses in order to make a profit and/or to maintain their class rule.[11]

While such criticism are both interesting and challenging, such critics fail to make clear how the American economy could exist, at least in its present form, *without* popular culture and advertising. As was discussed in Chapter 18, information about products obtained through media advertising is an essential part of the process by which products are purchased by the consuming population. Aside from innovations, vigorous advertising stimulates sales for existing products, which in turn keeps a labor force employed to manufacture, distribute, and retail those products. Indeed, these are the very processes that have produced abundant economies in the Western world. In short, while some people deplore it, *popular culture linked to advertising is a necessary condition within a capitalistic economy.*

Finally, portraying the media audience as "passive," as in the above quotation, misses the point that was stressed in previous chapters—that the audience is clearly "active" and that its members engage in a great deal of selectivity (Chapter 10). Their selections may be little more than between one soap opera and another, or between staged wrestling and a game played by a commercialized sports team, but those who make them are scarcely passive, accepting any kind of content that is "imposed from above."

Providing Models for Deviant Behavior

In Chapter 3, an important contribution of philosophy was discussed in terms of the social construction of reality. That same idea appears in more recent times in the work of Walter Lippmann (Chapter 8), who identified the function of the press as one of "creating pictures in our heads of the word outside." It is also an underlying theme in other theories (e.g., Modeling Theory, Social Expectations Theory, and Cultivation Theory—Chapters 16, 17, and 24). The basic idea is that in its depictions of lifestyles and human behavior in popular culture, mass communication offers unintended (collateral) lessons on what kinds of actions people will tolerate, expect, or condone. Through incidental learning, critics maintain, those collateral lessons become guiding maps for conduct for individuals who are falsely led into committing acts that are, in fact, not tolerated.

In recent years, there have been widely publicized incidents of individuals using firearms to kill innocent people. These have occurred on college campuses, in post offices, in restaurants, in other kinds of business settings, in high schools, and even in grade schools. In an immediate jump to a conclusion, critics have maintained that these are instances of individuals imitating what they see on television (or alternatively in the movies, computer games, and so on), where such behavior is routinely depicted in popular culture. That conclusion is regularly followed by demands that television, the movies, etc., must be better controlled and that such portrayals must be barred.

While there has been an enormous amount of research in the social sciences, starting as far back as one may wish to look, there has yet to emerge a consensus that such depictions do indeed drive individuals to commit such acts. Some scholars have concluded that there is sufficient evidence to indicate that those who watch a lot of television are more prone to violence and aggression. Others deny that this is the case. Still others point out that some of the most violent young males—such as youthful gangs in central cities—actually view little television, because they spend their time on the streets with their companions.

At the same time, these influences of popular culture remain an open question. There is reason to believe that depictions of ordinary Americans in movies, TV dramas, and other forms of popular culture do provide collateral instruction for young audiences in many countries that have few local movie or TV production facilities. In those countries, youths greatly enjoy popular culture entertainment content produced in the U.S. Under those circumstances, with few other ways of learning about ordinary Americans, young people who attend to such entertainment form flawed and negative beliefs about what people who live in the United States are like. (This issue is addressed at length in Chapter 23.)

The bottom line here is less than clear, but the evidence seems to lead to a *tentative* conclusion. Popular culture depicting violence, drug use, and sexual activities probably has limited effects on young people raised in stable American homes where they receive clear moral guidance. It may have an influence on other kinds of individuals. Such media content may influence more marginal persons who have problems in adjusting to conforming lifestyles and are without adequate role models or behavioral controls. In contrast, in other countries, where American popular culture is the only source for learning about people who live in the U.S., it may have more pronounced influences on their beliefs (see Chapter 23).

Generally, then, some of the conclusions of the critics of *kitsch* may have validity. Others may not. In the intensely competitive effort to produce a constant flow of advertising and popular culture, the themes and content of high culture may inspire imitators among those who churn it out day after day. Whether this harms the nature and uses of high culture can long be debated.

In the case of heroes, however, it does seem clear that popular culture pays virtually no attention to those in science, engineering, medicine, or other intellectual fields who bring truly important advances to society—accomplishments that make people's lives richer, safer, healthier, and more comfortable. A list of hundreds of names of unknown people could be compiled who have done that, without the slightest recognition by the manufacturers of popular culture. Those elevated in status by media attention tend to be those who offer exciting forms of entertainment that have little to do with the more serious advancements of the human condition.

As to whether the preparation and use of popular culture to attract attention to advertisements has positive benefits or negative costs is also an open question. There seems little doubt that the costs of both advertisements and their presentation in media is very expensive. Those costs are obviously passed on to the consuming public, raising the price of virtually everything that is purchased and consumed. At the same time it would be difficult to imagine modern life without advertising. That has been tried in such places as the (now-defunct) Soviet Union and in contemporary societies like Cuba and North Korea, but the lifestyles of the people who live in such places has little appeal to the Western world. People would not know what was available or what ways one product has features that others lack. While many of the claims of advertisers may be spurious in some way, their messages clearly do *encourage consumption.* That, in turn, stimulates the economy in obvious ways. It may be better to have an economy based on popular culture and advertising than one that offers far fewer jobs and economic benefits. Much depends, in this debate, whether one can accept an advertising-driven consumer economy or one based on some other kinds of principles.

Finally, the jury is still out concerning the benefits or problems created by the mass media, with their frequent depiction of unacceptable behavior in popular culture. Does such entertainment contribute positively to society, or does it stimulate crime, delinquency, drug use, overheated sex, or other problems that the public finds unacceptable? There is little doubt that such content is abundantly present in the forms of entertainment widely attended to by the public. There is no clear consensus, however, whether it is a truly causal factor in stimulating deviant behavior.

POPULAR CULTURE THEORY: A FORMAL SUMMARY

The ideas presented in this chapter are complex and do not lend themselves easily to a simple summary statement. The factors involved range from the principles of capitalism through the nature of several forms of culture and include the increasing dependency of the population on simple forms of exciting entertainment. The consequences of this conjunction of factors are also complex. Nevertheless, and at the risk of oversimplification, the following set of assumptions and propositions appear to express in summary form much of what has been discussed:

1. Our privately owned media, functioning within a capitalistic economic system, are dedicated to *maximizing their profits* by presenting popular culture that will increase circulations, numbers of viewers, and other audience sizes.
2. This locks them into an economic dependency on attracting and holding *the attention of the largest number of people* who make up their potential media audience, regardless of their level of artistic tastes.
3. The members of the audience rely on the media to offer a broad range of entertainment content to fill an *ever-increasing amount of leisure time*, but it is content that makes limited intellectual demands on its consumers.
4. To maximize profits from advertising, subscriptions, movie admissions, or direct sales, the media manufacture and disseminate *an endless and complex flow of kitsch*—popular culture products with limited redeeming artistic value but which command wide attention among the audience.
5. **Therefore**, the economic forces and consumer taste systems driving the media result in a constant production and dissemination of *kitsch*. The consequences may or may not be exploiting and driving out high culture, elevating the status of media-created celebrities, diminishing or obscuring the recognition of real-life heroes, exploiting the public economically, and providing guidelines for those who choose to engage in deviant behavior.

Notes and References

1. Edward B. Tylor, *Primitive Culture* (London: John Murray, 1871).
2. Ralph Linton, *The Tree of Culture* (New York: Alfred A. Knopf, 1955), p. 8.
3. From *The Republic of Plato*, trans. by Frances M. Cornford (London: Oxford University Press, 1954), pp. 68–69.
4. Herbert J. Gans, *Popular Culture and High Culture* (New York: Basic Books, 1975), p. 10.
5. For a summary of mass culture content from 1941 to 1990, see James L. Baughmen, *The Republic of Mass Culture* (Baltimore: The Johns Hopkins University Press, 1992).
6. See *Karl Marx: Selected Writings in Sociology and Social Philosophy*, trans. by T. B. Bottomore (New York: McGraw-Hill Book Company, 1956).

7. Karl Marx and Frederick Engels, the *Communist Manifesto* (Chicago: Charles H. Kerr & Company, 1947), p. 60. First printed in England in the German language in 1848.

8. This did happen in New York City in mid-June of 2000.

9. An example from the comics is two cartoon strips that appeared in the *Boston Globe* on June 20, 2000. One quoted the philosopher Santayana (without naming him) and made a joke of the passage. The other displayed two cartoon versions of paintings by Picasso and made fun of them. Both represent blatant examples of "mining" high culture.

10. This reciprocal principle was first set forth by Paul Lazarsfeld and Robert Merton in their essay on "Mass Communication, Popular Taste and Organized Social Action," in *The Communication of Ideas* (New York: The Institute for Religious and Social Studies, 1948). A more available source is Wilbur Schramm, *Mass Communications* (Urbana, IL: University of Illinois Press, 1960), p. 498.

11. Dwight MacDonald, "A Theory of Mass Culture," in Bernard Rosenberg and David M. White, eds., *Mass Culture: The Popular Arts in America* (Glencoe, IL: The Free Press, 1957), p. 59.

CHAPTER 20

The Creeping Cycle of Desensitization Theory

This theory seeks to explain the following: Why, in the face of constant criticism, does the content of this country's mass media continue to evolve toward what appears to many to be *increasing triviality*, *decreasing levels of taste*, and *ever-lowering moral standards*? For more than a century and a half, this trend has been deplored by a long list of respected critics—by preachers from the pulpit, professors at the podium, and politicians on the political platform. It has also been castigated by a host of citizen's groups concerned about rising crime, looser sexual norms, more widespread use of dirty language, the erosion of family values, and the welfare of children. They have spoken out against what they see as a "vast wasteland" of kitsch—trivial newspaper stories, offensive popular music, mindless content of broadcasts, trite movie plots, the use of swear words, offensive advertising, and disgusting sites on the Internet. They are deeply saddened by the use of the technological marvels of modern communication for what they believe to be shallow, meaningless, and even harmful purposes. Yet, in spite of these protests—bitter at times—the print, film, recording, broadcast, and computer media, critics maintain, are slowly but constantly pushing on and on to lower cultural tastes, behavioral norms, and moral standards.

Why is this happening, critics ask, not only in the United States but in other countries as well? Are the mass media being controlled by amoral managers who are determined to lower the quality of life of their audiences? Is this a deliberate plot to alter and degrade the sensitivities of decent people—to get them routinely to accept mindless drama, to accept violence as an approved way of settling disagreements, and to have them regard sexual encounters out of wedlock as having little more meaning than having lunch together? Is this an attempt to bring people to use an expanded vocabulary of disgusting four-letter words to color their everyday speech?

At least some of the critics seem to accept the idea that those who make the decisions about media content are doing just that. They see them as *irresponsible* at best and decidedly *immoral* at worst—hiding behind First Amendment protections for the goal of profit. Each of the masters of the media, from those who decided on the content of the early mass newspapers to the contemporary decision makers who determine what will be presented in film and broadcast media worldwide, has been denounced by at least someone who wants a more responsible communications environment.

Or is there something else at work here? Are there impersonal factors and forces in the American society, and in others similarly organized, that have produced the present situation *without any deliberate intent* (on the part of those who control the media) to lower tastes and abandon moral standards? That, precisely, is the explanation that is offered in the present chapter by the Creeping Cycle of Desensitization Theory. That theory places the changes in intellectual level of media content, as well as the norms concerning triviality, violence, sex, and vulgar language, into a context of economic, political, and cultural factors. Functioning together, the theory explains, these factors have made it *inevitable* that, over the last 120 years or so, those who have controlled the media have had to make these changes in content in order to make profits and (essentially) to enable them to survive financially. If they failed to do so, they would have had to go into bankruptcy and would have had to close down their newspapers, movie studios, television networks, and websites.

To put it mildly, that would have distressed the American public who enjoy and use their media. Thus, the theory concludes, what has been taking place is not a result of evil individuals making irresponsible decisions, but it is a product of a social-political system within which contemporary media operate in a highly competitive capitalistic socio-political environment.

These conclusions are not new. The distribution in the American population of such factors as education, income, and discretionary purchasing power has long been understood. It has also been understood that it is these impersonal factors that produce what we see in a newspaper, a film, on television, and elsewhere in the media. Again, what drives media producers to offer their wares to the public in the way they do is *the profit line*. That has not changed over the years. For example, in 1966, DeFleur put it in these terms:

> The type of entertainment content that seems most capable of eliciting the attention of the largest number of audience members is the more dramatic, low-taste content. Films, television plays, newspaper accounts, or magazine stories that stress physical violence, brutality, sexual gratification, earthy humor, slapstick, or simple melodrama appeal most to those whose educational backgrounds are limited. Their prior socialization has not provided them with sensitive standards for appreciation of the elite arts or for judging the cultural, educational or moral merits of a given communication within complex frameworks. In the affluent American society, it is this type of audience member who is by far the most numerous. He has the purchasing power in sufficient abundance so that his confined influence on the market is overwhelming. He is in full possession of the media.[1] [There are politically incorrect references to gender in this passage by today's standards, but this was the norm at the time.]

Stated simply, then, what the Creeping Cycle of Desensitization Theory predicts is this: As long as the factors listed in the above quotation remain in the economic system of the U.S., and as long as there is no strong and effective control over content by government or some other agency or group, *the trend toward greater transgressions of conservative norms will continue in the mass media* as the years ahead unfold. Indeed, that change is likely to increase for the same reasons that it started in the first place.

Thus, if this theory is correct, in the future, our media will turn to increasingly trivial content, higher levels of violence, more explicit sex, more depictions of crime, and an escalation in the use of vulgar language. There is every reason to believe, furthermore, that the same thing will happen in societies that have similar political and economic systems. To understand the basis of that prediction, one needs to see what social and economic conditions in society provide the theory's basic assumptions. In the sections that follow, those conditions will be described within the context of each of the several mass media.

THE CYCLE BEGINS WITH THE DAILY NEWSPAPER

As has been explained in previous chapters, newspapers were a part of the American society a full century before independence was gained from Britain. However, they were neither available to, nor much read by, ordinary citizens. They were printed on presses not much different from that used by Gutenberg centuries earlier. They survived financially from the payment of subscriptions (not from limited advertising in the preindustrial economy of the time). Their content was of interest mainly to the well educated and financially affluent. They did play an important part in spreading information about the excesses of the British government prior to the revolution. Even more significantly, they played a key role in establishing freedom of speech and of the press in the United States. By the time that the U. S. Constitution was written, government interference with the content of the press (short of certain specified illegalities) was essentially set aside as an issue. However, after the nation was founded, newspapers changed very little for several decades. It was not until the 1830s that a remarkable set of events brought on the first years of the Age of Mass Communication.

Benjamin Day and the *New York Sun*

Reviewing from earlier chapters, it has been explained that during the 1830s, five factors came together in New York City that were to provide the beginnings of both the Age of Mass Communication and the foundation of what will be termed the "creeping cycle of desensitization." Those factors, in one form or another, have been a part of the context within which the American mass media have operated since that time.

Factor one was *a new source of power*—specifically, the steam engine—that could be used to drive many kinds of machines, vastly increasing the capacity of factories to produce products. An additional such application was to the Napier cylinder press, which in 1830 was refined by Robert Hoe. The steam-driven rotary press revolutionized printing, making it possible almost overnight to turn out a remarkable 8,000 copies of a newspaper sheet every hour. The old hand-operated press could print only a couple of hundred per day at best.[2] This new printing technology was a major factor permitting the Age of Mass Communication to begin.

Factor two came in the form of a *new type of newspaper*—one intended not for a small list of well-educated and affluent subscribers, as had been the case with American papers up to that time. The new newspaper was designed for a humbler audience—working people who had learned to read but for whom the daily paper was as much a form of entertainment as enlightenment. It was, of course, the *New York Sun*, founded in 1833 by Benjamin H. Day, a printer who saw that the new steam-driven press could produce an almost unlimited number of copies every day.

Factor three was *a new way of making a profit* on such a newspaper. Day decided to give his paper away virtually free! He charged only a penny for a copy—which almost anyone could afford, but which would hardly recover the cost of the ink. However, he realized that New York City was a center of retailing and services in the growing nation. The new factories in the Northeast were producing goods for consumers as never before. Day saw that stores and service suppliers needed more effective ways to *advertise*. While advertising had long played at least some part in the revenue stream of newspapers and early magazines, Day saw that if he could sell thousands of papers a day, he could greatly increase the exposure of the public to advertisements. That would enable him to charge much higher fees for space, supporting the paper financially and producing a high profit margin. Thus, by pricing his paper for only a penny, he did, in fact, greatly increase its circulation. That was very appealing to advertisers who wanted their messages to be seen by large numbers of people—and they were willing to pay for that outcome.

Factor four was *literacy*. More and more people were acquiring the ability to read—at least at a basic level. The United States, in the early decades of the nineteenth century, was scarcely a society of well-educated citizens. Yet the concept of free, tax-supported, and mandatory education—introduced by Horace Mann in Massachusetts—was swiftly spreading among the states. Children were gaining a foundation of reading, writing, and arithmetic that would enable them to participate more effectively in the democratic political process as well as in the emerging industrial order. Thus, while literacy rates were still relatively low in the 1830s and 1840s, they were increasing rapidly—especially in major urban centers like New York City. A large and literate audience, in other words, was developing for a new medium—a popular newspaper designed for everyday people. Thus, what came together in Benjamin Day's innovation was exactly that—a cheap newspaper, made possible by financing it through advertising, that could be rapidly produced to be read by a large number of people who could read its content and readily afford its low price.

Only one factor remained. The *content* of that new mass medium had to be consistent with the tastes and interests of these new kinds of readers so as to expand and retain the largest possible audience. As noted earlier, the limited circulation colonial newspapers devoted most of their space to "serious" information. They carried reports of debates in political circles, the opinions of learned citizens, essays on morals and manners, and accounts of commercial transactions that were mainly of interest to the business community.

Benjamin Day realized that this was not what the majority of people wanted. He believed that they would like content that was more *entertaining*. Therefore, he dropped the high literary standards of earlier papers and developed a witty style that made his stories fun to read. He emphasized the "human side" of the news. He hired George Wisner, the first professional newspaper "reporter," to attend the early morning sessions of the police court, where the troubles of pickpockets, pimps, and prostitutes picked up during the night were aired. Wisner wrote a lively "Police Office" column every day, with accounts that ordinary New Yorkers enjoyed reading.

One reason that readers responded so favorably was that there wasn't much else in the form of entertainment in the lives of simple people at the time. Day ran reports of scandals in high places, sensational events such as murders, human situations with pathos and humor, and even completely false accounts about exciting events that never actually happened. Such content was much more entertaining than dull reports of speeches in high places. As a result, by 1839, only six years after its founding, the daily circulation of the *New York Sun* had reached a remarkable 50,000. It was an astounding achievement and a true revolution in newspaper publishing. Day's success quickly spawned a number of imitators and rivals who competed for readers. The Age of Mass Communication had begun.

In summary, the combination put together by Benjamin Day included (1) a new *technology*, (2) a new approach to *making a profit*, (3) a new kind of popular *entertaining content* (4) available at *very low cost* (5) to a *very large audience* characterized by *limited tastes and interests*. Today, in the increasingly competitive world of mass communication, that combination is still one that can spell success or failure. If Day had decided, in the face of his critics, that he should change his objective from making a profit and use his newspaper to elevate the cultural tastes of his readers—by giving them more reports on the arts, providing detailed reports about the political events that were shaping the nation and information on the factors that were influencing the economy—it is likely that his paper would have foundered in a few months.

It is not difficult to show how exactly that fate lies in wait today for those who may wish to use a mass medium to try to elevate the tastes and understandings of its audience. For example, in the year 2000, news producers of a television station in Chicago decided that the time had come to present "responsible" news to their audience. To do just that, station WGBM offered a 10:00 p.m. local news show, hosted by Bill Curtis and Carol Marin (serious and experienced broadcast journalists). The idea was to focus in depth on "serious" events in the area. The show would not present the usual list of auto wrecks, burning buildings, police shootings, sexual transgressions, and sordid crimes. Instead, it would focus on such matters as price-fixing of milk, labor-management controversies, complexities facing local political leaders, and so on. The stories were longer and went in to greater depth than the usual offerings on the evening local news. As it got under way, the show was applauded, not only by civic leaders and serious segments of the public, but also by other journalists. However, almost immediately, its ratings were so low that advertisers lost interest. It did not "earn its keep," and the show lasted for only eight months.

From the time of Benjamin Day forward to the present, then, American mass media have operated in a very specific context *not of their own making*. They function in a highly competitive capitalistic economic system—one in which the approved goal of making a profit is a basic and compelling fact of life. To make that profit, it is essential that the content they supply be appreciated, enjoyed, and valued by those who attend to the medium, so that their numbers can be maximized. Thus, the economic and political context within which the mass media in the United States operate boils down to three major features of the society. These are (1) *economic capitalism*, (2) almost-complete *freedom from government restraint* regarding content, and (3) a public whose norms of taste and sophistication of interests are, for the most part, *low and limited.*

These three factors were at work when Benjamin Day founded the *New York Sun*, and they remain in place in today's mass media markets. As will become clear, it is these conditions that provide the central assumptions of the theory set forth in this chapter—the propositions that taken together lead to the logical prediction made by the Creeping Cycle of Desensitization Theory—a forecast that the content of mass communications in America will continue to show the trends that have characterized their past. In sections that follow, those trends will be illustrated in terms of newspapers, movies, the recording industry, comic books, television, and newer digital media.

Adoption of the New Type of Newspaper

All during the last half of the 1800s, the daily newspaper was steadily being adopted in cities across the country by a rapidly growing and increasingly literate American population. The new medium had no direct competitors as sources of up-to-date information about current events. The spread of telegraph wires throughout the nation after the 1840s brought stories to newspaper editors at unprecedented speed via the "lightning lines." Interesting events in the nation were unfolding—the Mexican, Civil, and Spanish American wars; the opening of the West; gold in California; numerous technological innovations; and great debates over Darwin's remarkable new explanations of the origins of human beings. It is little wonder that newspapers thrived.

In 1850, for example, two households in ten in the American society subscribed to a daily newspaper. By 1890, however, that figure had shot up to six in every ten households, *a three hundred percent increase.* By the end of the century, well over 2,500 dailies were being published in the United States. Indeed, as the 1900s began, newspaper subscriptions per household reached a peak. Many families subscribed to more than one daily paper. By 1910, the figure was 1.36 per household.[3] This meant one paper in the morning and another in the evening. It was, after all, the only source of news swiftly delivered that was available. As the 1800s ended, then, the newspaper was not much different than it is today:

> By the end of the century, the newspaper was a technologically sophisticated and complex mass medium. Their publishers had at their disposal a rapid telegraphic news-gathering system, cheap paper, linotype, color printing, cartoons, electric presses, and, above all, a corps of skillful journalists. The newspaper had settled into a more or less standard format, much like what we have today. Its features included not only domestic and foreign news but also a financial page, letters to the editor, sports news, society reports, 'women's pages,' classified sections, and advice to the lovelorn. Newspapers were complex, extremely competitive, and very popular. Furthermore they had no competition from other media.[4]

The Trend Continues: The Era of Yellow Journalism

Between 1880 and 1900, the number of newspapers (that is, titles) more than doubled in the United States. Virtually every city and town of any size had at least one daily, and almost every small community had a weekly. As a result of their remarkable success, papers became so profitable that they generated intense competition in most cities. The key to increasing profit levels during the period was precisely the same as it is today—get more people to attend to the medium so that the ads are seen by greater numbers.

Efforts to increase and to dominate circulation in urban markets intensified during the late 1880s and continued well into the new century. What touched off increasing competition was the fact that the curve of adoption of the newspaper use was reaching saturation (see Chapter 18). There simply were no significant numbers of households left that had not yet subscribed to a daily paper. This situation led to a struggle as to *which among the available newspapers* people would buy and read. Because of this battle for circulation—particularly in the great cities where the largest numbers of subscribers lived—the American newspaper came to be redefined. What happened was another change in the nature of the "news" that was placed before the public on a daily basis. The circumstances of this change illustrate perfectly the underlying economic, political, and cultural factors that produce the Creeping Cycle of Desensitization.

As the nineteenth century closed, then, the United States was in every respect a society founded on competitive capitalism and private ownership. Earning a profit was highly valued in this system—as it is today. Essentially this meant providing the public with a product that they wanted and for which they would willingly pay (a basic principle of capitalism explained by Adam Smith).

As we have noted often, the key to the changes in newspaper content was the money earned from advertisers—just as had been the case with Benjamin Day in the 1830s. Those earnings could be maximized only by increasing the number of subscribers to the paper. Thus, the larger the circulation, the more the potential for profit. However, increasing circulation meant offering subscribers less serious news and more of what they wanted to read about. This business formula was fully understood at the time. For example, in 1909, a piece in the *Atlantic Monthly* explained the relationship among circulation, advertising revenue, and newspaper content:

> A newspaper is a business enterprise. In view of the cost of the paper and the size of each issue, tending to grow larger, every copy is printed at a loss. A one-cent newspaper costs six mills for paper alone [6 tenths of one cent]. In other words, the newspaper cannot live without its advertisers . . . [thus] it must be remembered that the advertisers exert an enormous power. If a newspaper has such a circulation that complete publicity can be secured only by advertising in its columns, whatever its editorial policy may be, the question is solved.[5]

It was within that context that the concept of "yellow journalism" developed. It was, in many ways, an extension of the strategy used by Benjamin Day and his competitors in the earliest era of the penny papers, with their emphasis on crime, human interest, and humor. Leaders of this movement were Joseph Pulitzer and William Randolph Hearst. By 1890, for example, Pulitzer had succeeded in building the circulation of the Sunday edition of the *New York World* to more than 300,000, a truly remarkable number at the time.

> To accomplish this record, he combined good reporting with an emphasis on entertaining accounts of many kinds. His strategy placed an emphasis on disasters and melodramatics, sensational photographs, and comic strips—all to intensify reader interest. Pulitzer also crusaded against corrupt officials, for Civil service reform, and for populist causes, such as taxes on luxuries, large incomes, and inheritances. He pioneered the use of color printing of comics in newspapers, Which did much to spur the circulation of his Sunday editions.[6]

Pulitzer soon had a formidable competitor. William Randolph Hearst had taken over control of the San Francisco *Examiner* from his father in 1887. In only two years, he had successfully built up its circulation by publishing lurid sensationalism. Moving swiftly, in 1895 he purchased the *New York Morning Journal*. He was able to build it into unprecedented circulation by printing sensational stories on crime (the Lizzie Borden case provided copy for weeks). He then expanded rapidly, and by the turn of the century he had put together an astonishing empire of 150 newspapers in the United States. His strategy was very simple. His newspapers printed news that the public found fascinating. Their content focused on stunts, sensational accounts, bizarre events, sexual disclosures, and in many cases stories that really never happened at all!

There were various kinds of fake stories. Some had no foundation in fact whatsoever, and were total fabrications. Others were grossly exaggerated versions of some event that had taken place but were reworked to make them more sensational and startling. One reporter of the time noted that faking—that is, "publication of articles absolutely false"—was common:

> It will probably be a revelation, as disagreeable as startling, to these people to know that often there is not even a foundation of truth in the double-leaded articles with flaming headlines published in both the daily and Sunday papers.[7]

Essentially, then, Pulitzer, and in particular Hearst, redefined the American urban newspaper. The large metropolitan newspapers came to be preoccupied with content that pressed the cutting edge of quality to a new low. They provided less and less "serious news" as they focused on crime, sex, sob stories, exposes of sin, disclosures of corruption in high places, sports, dramatic photographs, misrepresentations of science, and fake stories—indeed, anything that would attract additional readers. There is little doubt that the innovations in style and content brought in by Hearst and his competitors in New York influenced American journalism—not only of that period but, in many ways, also the contemporary press.

Public Reactions to the Yellow Press

By the first decade of the 1900s, scores of critics were raising a howling chorus of protests about the content of the big city newspapers, and the trend to lower quality was temporarily halted. It was not only a reaction to yellow journalism as such but also to the negative influences on their readers that newspapers were assumed to have. Those who controlled and produced the major urban papers were vilified by many intellectuals because their influences on their readers were thought to be powerful. (See Chapter 9, on the Magic Bullet Theory.) There were four elements to this negative reaction. That is, it appeared to critics of the time that (1) major newspapers were filled with trivialities, rather than serious news; (2) the stories published emphasized such matters as brutal crimes, suicides, and sexual scandals; (3) outright distortions of truth were common in the press, providing readers with false versions of what was taking place in their society; and (4) such newspaper content created harmful influences on their audiences.

Even the more thoughtful of the publishers of the period were concerned about the harmful influences of newspaper content on their audiences. For example, in 1841, when the new type of cheap daily newspaper was still in its infancy, Horace Greeley maintained that the new type of newspapers were:

> . . . willing to fan into destroying flames the hellish passions that now slumber in the bosom of society. The guilt of murder may not stain their hands; but the fouler guilt of making murderers surely does.[8]

Indeed, there seemed little doubt that this new phenomenon in the world—the cheap and sensational daily newspaper—was at the bottom of many of the current ills of society. For example, by the late 1800s, the French jurist and social scientist Gabriel Tarde (whose works were widely read by social scientists in the United States) regarded the newspaper as a direct stimulus causing criminal behavior among youth. He believed that the influence of the sensational daily newspaper was every bit as damaging as that of the excessive use of alcohol. As was noted in an earlier chapter, writing in 1897, Tarde blamed the press for stimulating cowardice and weakness of character among the young offenders that came before the courts:

> But it is the trashy and malicious press, scandal-mongering, riddled with court cases, that awaits the student when he leaves school. The little newspaper, supplementing the little drink, alcoholizes his heart.[9]

In addition, the lords of the press were seen as deliberately lying to the public by distorting the news to make it more entertaining to read. For example, political scientist Graham Wallas, writing just prior to World War I, deplored the fact that ordinary citizens had their thoughts about their nation shaped by the unreliable popular press. Their understanding of what was taking place, he maintained, was seriously distorted:

> Much of it is due to conscious propaganda by the vested interests, for, though the average citizen may be aimless, careless and thoughtless, the controllers of newspapers, especially of the sinister American or British journals whose writers are apparently encouraged to 'color the news' as well as their comments on the news, in accordance with the will of a multi-millionaire proprietor, know pretty exactly what they are doing.[10]

Over nearly a century, then, the cycle unfolded. Newspapers became increasingly sensational, preoccupied with entertaining rather than enlightening the public. The cutting edge of content was pushed toward ever more reports of sex, crime, corruption, and fake events.

Eventually, however, people tired of sensational and misleading newspapers. A reaction set in, slowing the cycle. People wanted a more responsible press. Understanding that, and faced with growing opposition, journalists retreated into an "objective" style that supposedly separated opinion from fact and that gave space to both sides of controversial issues.

Contemporary News as "Infotainment"

Today, all of the media delivering news are locked in intense competition because of the explosive growth of the number of news communication channels available. Americans can learn what is going on from newspapers, news magazines, radio broadcast, cable and satellite television, the Internet, and even cell phones. With the news delivery pie cut into so many pieces, the competition to attract audience attention to advertising by reporting the news has become truly brutal. Seeking the largest possible audiences, journalists absolutely must produce stories that interest the public. The days of in-depth, extended but boring reporting of detailed facts about a significant news event may have almost come to an end. It is little wonder, then, that fewer sources remain for "serious news."

To be sure, journalists still present some serious information, but the majority of stories in a daily paper or broadcast absolutely must have entertainment value. Journalists need to attract and hold audience attention and create satisfaction with their product, even if what they report is not particularly important to the state of the society. If they do not, ratings and circulations go down—spelling economic doom for the medium. For this reason, the term "infotainment" came into use during the 1990s to describe the new style that journalists have had to adopt to keep their profit levels high enough to stay in business. Obviously, this is not really a completely new phenomenon. It was noted that the trend toward news as entertainment began with the penny press in New York City in the early 1830s. However, it remains a clearly present feature of the news today.

Stories about public figures involved in sexual misconduct provide great entertainment. A good illustration of news as infotainment is a series of six stories, starting on January 16, 2002, that appeared in a newspaper in Providence, Rhode Island. The stories concerned a police investigation that eventually resulted in the arrest of seven allegedly gay men on misdemeanor charges. The newspaper reported they had engaged in sexual activity at an adult video store in a nearby town. One of the stories, on page one, described the alleged behavior in detail and included photos of the men. Other stories gave their ages, home addresses, and occupations or employment status. One of the men, a public official, committed suicide a few days later. These news reports led to a significant controversy. A group of gay activists confronted the newspaper and made accusations that the reports were "salacious and unbalanced" and that the coverage of the events were driven by "homophobia."[11] When such controversies arise about whether or not the stories of this type should have been published, newspaper officials often maintain that "the public has a right to know" and that such a story clearly constitutes "news." There is no such "right to know" in the U.S. Constitution, but journalists maintain that it does exist.

An interesting activity is to keep track for, say, a week, while viewing national or local news on TV, to make note of the number of stories devoted to (1) crime in some way or (2) the reported activities of "celebrities" (popular media personalities, sports figures, etc.,) that in no way are truly important. The local newspaper offers a similar interesting possibility. Few indeed are stories that report events or situations that are really important to the public. The media might again point out that the public has a "right to know" which celebrity was arrested for drunken driving, who has strayed sexually, which among such people are getting a divorce, etc. One problem is, of course, that there are actually very few news events on any given day that really are important, and the TV report or the local paper has to fill its pages with something.

But what of the future? One prediction is that as communication technology continues to add channels from which the public can select—intensifying the competition even more—it may be increasingly difficult in the future to tell the difference between news and entertainment.

CONCERNS ABOUT INDECENT MOVIES

Movies arrived as the nineteenth century came to a close. Various inventors and scientists had been trying to solve the problem of making photographic images "move," or at least *seem* to move. Actually, the principles involved in perceiving motion from a series of rapidly presented stimuli had been understood for many decades. Psychologists studying the functioning of the human senses had long known that, when presented with a series of carefully crafted drawings or photos, in which each frame showed the subject in a coordinated but slightly advanced position, a person would see them "moving" smoothly. That experience was based on a phenomenon known as *visual lag*, or *visual persistence*. The physiological basis of this phenomenon is that the neural system of the eye (rods and cones) *retains* an image that had just been seen for a fraction of a second, even after the image itself has been withdrawn. If a new image is then quickly superimposed, the two merge together in the person's visual experience. Thus, when a series of such still figures or photographs—changing quickly in succession—is seen, it seems to the viewer that a single image is moving smoothly.

It became possible by the 1870s to take photographs of just such a rapidly changing series of events, like a horse running or a couple dancing. If the pictures were bound together in the form of a booklet, a person swiftly riffling through those photos sees the image in what appears to be full and smooth motion—just like a motion picture.[12] The work of a photographer of the period with the unusual name of Eadweard Muybridge is usually credited for making that discovery.[13] Such booklets with pictures or drawings later became fascinating toys for children.

But discovering a new visual principle is not the same as developing a new mass medium. It was entrepreneurs in several countries seeking ways to make a profit by applications of the principle that led the way to motion pictures as a form of popular entertainment. Inventors, including the famous Thomas Edison, whose lab developed a practical motion picture camera and projector, were motivated by profit. They wanted to make money by offering the public an entertainment experience for which they would be willing to pay. For that reason, when practical cameras, projectors, and flexible roll film finally became available early in the twentieth century, they were used to create motion pictures as entertainment products. Several ways of viewing were tried, but the theater model soon prevailed. By 1904, a few crude theaters were showing brief films. They were a novelty, and people were fascinated with them.

The industry matured quickly. By 1910, there were an estimated 10,000 motion picture theaters in various cities in the U. S. Typically, they charged a nickel for admission (hence the popular term "nickelodeon"). That same year, estimates indicate that some 26 million patrons attended—about one-fifth of the American population. It was a system as old as the circuses of Rome (pay at the box office to be admitted—then enjoy the spectacle).

The success and swift adoption by the public of this new form of amusement can only be characterized as remarkable. A new entertainment industry quickly came into existence to supply the films. Due to favorable weather for filming, production soon came to be located in Hollywood, which up to that point was a drab village just outside the fringes of Los Angeles. By the early 1920s, literally hundreds of movies were produced annually. Movie theaters became larger and in some cases ornately decorated. The earliest movies attracted mainly poor residents of inner cities. But by the1920s, with more elaborate theaters and feature films, they became the favorite popular entertainment of most of the American public. At this time, the movie industry sought ways to attract larger and larger audiences—to make even higher profits.

The creeping cycle of desensitization is well illustrated by what happened in the early development of the motion picture. As will be shown, in their search for profits just after World War I, studios began to produce content that attracted more and more movie fans but which conservative segments of the public found objectionable. Unprotected by the First Amendment (at the time), movies that crossed the conservative line came to be banned, and theaters were often closed by local police and other groups. To solve this problem, within a few years the studios "cleaned up" their own house with a restrictive "code" (the Hayes code for film production and distribution). However, when profits dropped sharply as television was adopted, the code was soon abandoned, and motion pictures once again began to incorporate content than many people found objectionable. Today movies are characterized by dirty words, violence, and sexual scenes that would have sent earlier generations into a frenzy.

As the movies advanced their production technology, techniques for production with special effects and better photography came swiftly. The "star" system was established, and movies soared in popularity. Their profits also soared. To give some idea of what the movies meant to the public, even before the 1920s, the salaries paid to popular performers provide a clue. For example, one of the earliest stars was a pretty young woman named Mary Pickford. Her first appearances in films were early in the century (1907). By the time the U.S. entered World War I (1917), she had become one of the best-known entertainment personalities in the nation and indeed in much of the world. The public loved her and lined up at the box office to see a movie with her in a starring role. Because of her value to filmmakers, Mary Pickford's pay rose in a startling pattern. Movie historian Douglas Gomery notes (see Table 1) that, over a ten-year period, her salary increased 1,500 percent.[14]

TABLE 1 Annual Salary Paid to Mary Pickford	
1907	$100 per week
1910	$175 per week
1914	$1,000 per week
1915	$2,000 per week
1916	$10,000 per week
1917	$15,000 per week

The popularity of the movies was by no means confined to the United States. Several countries in Europe had begun to produce films—until World War I intervened and they had to stop or reduce production. Quickly, American studios took over the world market. Later, the same economic and political conditions, plus the huge demand for the entertainment provided by the films, had essentially the same result in countries in which capitalism prevailed and government censorship was limited. The basic principle of film industries, except in dictatorships, was *give the people what they want.* However, movie content that was popular with the public was often considered by responsible authorities and conservative groups to be bringing about unwanted consequences, contributing to social problems. In Great Britain, for example, the National Council on Public Morals issued a report in 1917. It was the conclusion of the Council that motion pictures were (1) very popular, (2) were having profound influences on their audiences, and (3) had become a significant factor in creating negative effects—especially on youth:

[There may not yet be] sufficient realization of the strong and permanent grip which the picture palace has taken upon the people of this country. [The lure] of the pictures is universal. . . . moving pictures are having a profound influence on the mental and moral outlook of millions of our young people—an influence the more subtle in that it is so subconsciously exercised—and we leave our labours with the deep conviction that no social problem of the day demands more earnest attention.[15]

During the 1920s, then, the motion picture matured into a complex, wildly popular, and enormously profitable mass medium. It was a form of entertainment ideally suited for the urban-industrial society—enjoyable, cheap, easily available, and making few or no intellectual demands on its audience. To meet to the increasing demand, a number of studios in Hollywood were churning out hundreds of films every year, devoted to a dozen or more basic genres, ranging from interpretations of literary classics to Westerns and slapstick comics.

Given the fortunes to be made, it is little wonder that *intense competition* developed among the studios that were producing these films. Success in attracting the public was a certain route to almost incredible riches. To illustrate, in 1920, 1.6 movie admissions tickets were sold every week for each American household. This meant that almost 40 million people were attending on a weekly basis. However, a decade later, by 1930, the number of tickets sold had soared about 3 tickets for every households. The number of people paying at the box office weekly had increased to more than 90 million.[16] Everybody was going to the movies. For the studios it was as though the gates of heaven had opened and a waterfall of gold was pouring out. (By contrast, today less than 0.1 movie tickets are sold at box offices per week for every American household.)

In a span of a mere twenty years, then, the movies as popular culture assumed a truly significant place in the lives of Americans. The only alternative forms of immediately available cheap media entertainment were newspapers and magazines—which had limited appeal for many. There was also the wind-up Victrola and, in some homes, the piano. Home radio was just getting its start. Scheduled broadcasting began for the very first time in Pittsburgh in November of 1920. Even by 1930, the end of the decade since its inception, only about forty percent of households had a radio.[17] It would be decades before television would arrive.

Thus, the movies were a readily available, cheap, and easy solution for the family that wanted a night out together to enjoy an entertaining experience. It was fun for the kid who wanted to go with his or her pals to an event on Saturday afternoon. Admission was only a dime. It was an ideal solution for the teenager or young adult who needed an inexpensive but acceptable way to get together with a member of the opposite sex for a date. In fact, it was a very enjoyable experience for almost anyone, young or old, who wanted to escape from their humdrum life to live vicariously for an hour and a half in a world of fantasy. The movies seemed wonderful, appealing, glamorous, and enjoyable for virtually everyone.

The Movies of the 1920s Transgress Prevailing Moral Norms

As the decade moved on, some in the public began to take a new and more critical look at this wonderful new medium. Conservative elements in the society began to see movie content that concerned them deeply. For example, the films were depicting the life of gangsters—portraying them with easy but tainted money, fast cars, and even faster women. Many saw that these were portrayals of a glamorous image, not of disgusting evil-doers. Their fear was that such portrayals could cause youngsters to want to imitate such lifestyles. Even worse, the gangsters used guns to "bump off" their opponents—and even to do battle with law enforcement officials. These were not wholesome lessons in good citizenship, designed to instruct America's youth in modes of socially accepted conduct.

Local governments were the first to act. They were quite free to ban certain movies at the time. The First Amendment to the U.S. Constitution was finally ratified by 1791, but movies did not exist. It was not until 1915 that a court test came as to whether its provisions applied to the content of films. That year, the Supreme Court ruled that the cinema was a "business, pure and simple, originated and conducted for profit" (*Mutual Film Company v. Ohio*). Thus, *movies were not protected* by the First Amendment, and there was nothing that prevented local communities from banning a particular motion picture. If the good citizens of the local censorship committee felt it was not acceptable for their community, local police departments were called upon to prevent the showing of a particular film. Many did so with vigor, and across the country such actions became more and more common. This created great anxiety in the movie industry. A *reaction was setting in* to their new lower standards. It would not be until 1952 that the Supreme Court would reverse itself on this matter. The court ruled in the case of a movie with a religious theme—one that the state of New York had banned on the grounds that it was sacrilegious (*The Miracle*).[18]

As the 1920s moved on, demands to "clean up" the movies grew louder and louder. Always sensitive to the policy agenda of the public, and sources of votes, members of Congress spoke out, assuring the good citizens in their districts that their concerns were being heard—that "they felt their pain." Proposals were made to hold congressional hearings, focusing on the possible corrupting influences of the movies and ways in which the industry might be controlled. Angry editorials appeared in the local press. Preachers warned their flocks that sinful things were to be seen at the local picture palace. Academics entered the controversy. As has been explained in earlier chapters, between 1927 and 1929, a massive research project on the influences of motion pictures on youth was undertaken by a team of distinguished social scientists (the Payne Fund studies). Its findings seemed to confirm the worst fears of movie critics. The research showed that children were being influenced in a number of negative ways.[19] Parents reacted with deep concern.

The Motion Picture Producers Association's Code

Finally, those many voices were heard by the movie industry itself. The studios had gone too far in attempting to maximize their audiences. In developing a protective strategy, the producers got together, formed an "association" (the Motion Picture Producers Association of America, Inc.). They decided that they had better clean up their own house—before it was cleaned for them.

To do this, they adopted a strategy that has since become common—as noted, they devised a "code." It was a lengthy set of standards for production that their motion pictures would have to meet before they could be shown to the public. Since the producers owned not only the studios producing the films but also the system for their distribution and exhibition in local theaters, they were in complete control. Motion picture theaters in the United States could exhibit only the products sent to them by the controlling studios (a practice known as "vertical integration"). This was later declared by the courts to be monopolistic and illegal.

To devise the code, they hired Will Hayes, a former postmaster general. Under his direction, a complex set of written rules was formulated: *A Code to Govern the Making of Motion Pictures.* Each member of the association agreed to its standards.

To say that motion pictures produced under the new rules were "wholesome" is to put the situation mildly. In its statement of General Principles, the Code set forth the following:

1. No picture shall be produced that will lower the moral standards of those who see it. Hence, the sympathy of the audience will never be thrown to the side of crime, wrongdoing, evil or sin.
2. Correct standards of life, subject only to the requirements of drama and entertainment, shall be presented.
3. Law, natural or human, shall not be ridiculed, nor shall sympathy be created for its violation.[20]

Various sections of the Code included detailed provisions for depicting such subjects as law, sex, vulgarity, obscenity, profanity, costumes, dances, religion, locations, national feelings, titles, and special subjects. Each of these sections set forth strict rules for filming portrayals. A remarkable list of events, words, situations, actions, and interpretations were specifically forbidden from appearing on American screens. If movies were being produced and available for viewing when the Pilgrims stepped off the *Mayflower* in 1620, they would have immediately approved of the Code. It was truly puritanical.

Beginning in 1930, then, under the provisions of the Code, the motion pictures seen by American audiences were no longer a threat to anyone's morals, even by the strictest standards. This was the era of cute little Shirley Temple, singing "The Good Ship Lollipop." It was a time when audiences flocked to see Fred Astaire and Ginger Rogers dancing glamorously in a tuxedo and a long gown. People laughed at the antics of the Marx Brothers, Laurel and Hardy, and the Three Stooges. They marveled at *The Wizard of Oz* and at *Snow White and the Seven Dwarfs*. Many adventure stories or literary classics were brought to the screen. Nowhere in any commercial screen in America was there shown a nude breast, a person sipping booze, or a criminal who went unpunished. If there had been, the public would have been outraged. Indeed, when Clark Gable (in the role of Rhett Butler in *Gone with the Wind*) turned to Vivien Leigh (playing Scarlett O'Hara) and said "Frankly my dear, *I don't give a damn*," his use of this vulgar word created a chorus of criticism.

In spite of these strict rules, and contrary to the fears of some, the motion picture industry thrived during the time the Code was in force. In particular, as the country entered the years of the Great Depression, there was understandable concern about profits. But the hard times made no difference. Receipts at the box office did not diminish. In fact, they increased. Even in the 1940s, when the tragic events of World War II came, the sale of tickets to movies remained high. On average, over the two-decade period (1930s and 1940s), there were 2.5 such tickets purchased at the box office every week for every household in the United States. The film industry seemed impervious to economic problems. Americans just could not get enough of the movies. Hollywood became the glamour capital of the world, the studios were wallowing in profits, and movie stars were being paid astronomical salaries beyond the wildest imaginations of ordinary people. Everyone just continued to go to the movies.

Today, virtually all restrictions on the use of foul language and the depiction of graphic sexual scenes in films have disappeared. Contemporary movies regularly have characters using four-letter dirty words and expressions that were simply unthinkable in earlier times. Movies today regularly show naked couples writhing in bed while engaging in coitus. By the twenty-first century, the sight of naked female breasts in films had become commonplace. Even full frontal nudity is not uncommon, for both males and females. As the century has progressed, in some cases movie audiences can view naked female genitals as well as those of males.

While such increasingly graphic portrayals in earlier times were not to be found in movie theaters, the arrival of television began to change drastically what people could see in their homes as television was swiftly adopted by American families.

The Challenge of Television

Almost overnight, following World War II, the motion picture industry began to be in financial trouble. By 1950, television stations were going on the air in almost all major cities all over the country. Millions of people were buying the remarkable new boxes. They were the marvel of the age because they had screens that showed moving images right there in the home. They were expensive, to be sure, and the screens were small—hardly larger than the size of a man's wallet. The pictures were black and white and often less than clear. *But they moved!* The diffusion curve soared. Within a span of only ten years, ninety percent of American homes had a TV set. By then they offered larger and clearer pictures. Programming that had been on radio since its beginning quickly moved to television—soap operas, sports broadcasts, comedy shows, evening drama, and news. The same was true of advertisers. Suddenly radio was in deep financial trouble along with the movies. TV was where the action was for advertisers.

Families no longer had to drive to a theater and buy tickets to see pictures that moved. If they wanted cheap entertainment, all they had to do was turn on their TV sets at home. It was free. They could view popular comedians, cop dramas, soap operas, musical shows, sports events, amateur hours, children's shows, and many more. Everything came via over-the-air broadcasts at first. Then, community antennas and early cable systems quickly expanded the number of channels that people could receive. Screens became even larger, and color finally arrived. That really made a difference. Television was rapidly becoming the dominant medium of the nation.

Receipts at the motion picture box office plummeted. By 1960, the movies were in serious trouble. There were only about 0.75 tickets sold per week per American household—a drop of more than 300 percent compared with an all-time high of 3.0 in 1930. It was a disaster. Indeed, as the trend continued, sales at the box office continued to decline. By 1970, things were even worse. There were only about 0.3 tickets sold per week per household—another drastic drop. (There are even fewer today.)

Desperate to meet this competition, the movie industry turned first to *technology*. Screens got much wider, sound systems more elaborate, and color more natural. It made no difference. Ticket sales remained down. At one point, an old technology—stereopticon photography—was tried. It had been used in the late 1800s, when people looked through a special optical device to see still photos in three dimensions. Studios adapted the system to produce and exhibit movies that audiences, using odd red and blue glasses, could see in three dimensions. It made no difference and was soon abandoned. Studios seeking to regain profits turned more aggressively to foreign markets to help their profit line. That had some success, but it produced resentments in parts of the world where conservative standards for entertainment continued to prevail (see Chapter 22, on Cultural Imperialism).

As it became increasingly clear that much more drastic steps were needed to salvage the industry, filmmakers began to dump the earlier restrictive *Producer's Code*. It did not happen over night. The studios were not sure what the public would accept, but they began to experiment with increases in violence, explicit sex, and vulgar language. By this time, however, the movie audience was mainly younger people who were less bound by the more restrictive norms of the past. The older folks stayed home, watched TV, and fewer and fewer went to the movies.

As the years moved on, the motion picture producers pressed the cutting edge of normal transgression onward, hoping to lure people back to the theaters with higher and higher levels of things that many in their audiences wanted to see—more violence, more crime, more and more dirty words, and increasingly revealing sexual portrayals. There were protests. Religious leaders devised "advisory codes" for their parishioners to use to select the movies they would pay to see. The idea was that patrons could first check the film against its rating in the advisory code and then decide for themselves if they wanted to see it. The Catholic Legion of Decency offered a six-level code, ranging from *"morally un-objectionable for general patronage"* on down to *"condemned."* The movie industry, pressed by both Congress and various spokespersons for various segments of the public, agreed to label their films with their own advisory codes. These were subsequently modified from time to time. In an early version, films rated "X" (for a high level of objectionable sexual content) became increasingly popular among the young. Later, that code was dropped, and a new one—linked to age of the patron, rather than film content—was adopted. Films rated "G" were *"suitable for general audiences."* At the other end of the scale were those rated "NC-17," which meant that *"no one under 17 was to be admitted."* In 1990, this was changed back to "X."

In fact, the new codes made little difference. The association's code of 1930–50 had prevented movies with controversial themes and depictions from even being *produced*. The news ones were supposed to serve merely as *advice* to parents and others about content that they might find inappropriate. For the most part, people who went to the movies paid little attention—and for understandable reasons. Few patrons checked on the rating before selecting what they wanted to see. After paying at the box office and getting seated in the theater, an announcement on the screen might proclaim that the movie they were about to view was rated in a particular category. Few people at that point decided to get up and leave and demand their money back.

The movie makers simply had to try a more effective strategy to make profits. The result was that they turned to depictions and portrayals that had been strongly prohibited under the old *Code.* Increasingly, sexual love making was filmed in more detailed and realistic ways. Nude breasts became much more common. Levels of violence soared. The language spoken by the actors became increasingly dirty. By the end of the twentieth century, four-letter words were as common in the films as they were among the most foul-mouthed male youths hanging out on the street corner. Many older movie patrons were embarrassed by what they heard in the theater or on their TV screen as a movie was playing. The younger patrons either did not care or loved it.

Even today, as noted earlier, there are few lines in the sand that are not being crossed—indeed, not many are left. As noted, by the beginning of the new millennium, total frontal female nudity, with all intimate body parts visible, were being seen on American screens. The same was true of graphic lesbian scenes of nude love making (e.g., both appeared in the film *Eyes Wide Shut*). However, there was still a strong reluctance to show total male nudity with erect genitalia, to depict the full details of oral sex, or display serious love making by homosexual males. By 2002, however, other lines were crossed. The film *Goldmember* (rated PG-13) was, according to movie critic Richard Corliss, basically "toilet humor," including a scene where one actor urinates into the mouth of another. Also included to amuse the children, he notes, were gags about penis size, excrement, and farts. In his opinion, a number of such recent films (aimed at children) are "gross-outs." They:

> … The film Goldmember (rated PG-13) was, according to movie critic Richard Corliss, basically "toilet humor," including a scene where one actor urinates into the mouth of another. Also included to amuse the children, he notes, were gags about penis size, excrement, and farts. In his opinion, a number of such recent films (aimed at children) are "gross-outs." They are analogous to pranks played on a teacher by obnoxious children. Corliss identifies the unlucky victim of the pranks as America's children. They are victims, he surmises, in that their exposure to dirty jokes and naughtiness has lost the almost forbidden allure that it had when this sort of humor was shared secretly, whispered in private by older cohorts. It was part of a child's social development, a rite of passage. Today, these ribald scenes have become commonplace, available for children to view and share publicly in theaters and homes. Any sense of mystique or secrecy that may once have accompanied these jokes has been swept away. [21]

Today, with first-run movies shown not only in theaters but immediately becoming available in DVD form, the mechanics of viewing are changing. Many relatively recent movies can be seen on pay-per-view cable channels as well. Thus, the convergence of film and television, and even the computer screen, has become a reality, and the creeping cycle is by no means restricted to motion pictures. Will the cycle for movies continue? Given the trends of the past, the best guess is a definite "yes." With almost every depiction that offended audiences in earlier times now becoming common, there are few lines left to cross.

THE OUTRAGE OVER COMIC BOOKS

During the 1940s, a new medium came to alarm the American public. It was the *comic book*. Defining comics as "new" would not be entirely accurate. Cartoon-like drawings have been around in one form or another for a very long time. They existed in the form of wood-cut drawings even before the printing press came in the mid-1400s. Later versions were the crude political cartoons of early newspapers. However, the *comic strip*, as a special feature of the daily newspaper, came into its own in the last years of the nineteenth century. In 1894, a full page of strips, published in color, appeared in Joseph Pulitzer's *New York World*. In 1896, to meet the competition, William Randolph Hearst brought out an eight-page weekly supplement to *The Morning Journal*. The comics were in full color, with continuing characters, including the famous "Yellow Kid" (from which the term "yellow journalism" came). The comics were immensely popular, and they remain so today.

A new form of comics came, to the delight of children, beginning in the 1940s. The *comic book* was a crudely printed magazine-like publication containing little drawings in color, along with limited text that told simple stories (plus the inevitable ads). At first, their content seemed harmless enough. The earliest ones were simply reprints of comic strips that had already appeared in newspapers.

It was soon realized that there was some real money to be made in producing these booklets for kids. By the mid-1930s, a number were on the market. Many were about cute animal characters, some of which inspired Disney's animated cartoons. A different type soon came along, including

Detective Comics (1935) and *Action Comics* (1938)—in which *Superman* made his debut to punish the wicked and restore justice. Other superheroes with unusual capacities soon followed. By the beginnings of the 1940s, these publications had gained an immense following. For example, in 1943, comic books were selling 18 million copies per month, bringing in $72 million to their publishers in the United States—a third of all magazine sales for the entire nation.

As the 1950s began, comic books became even more popular. In addition, because kids swapped them among themselves, those millions of copies directly sold were reaching a huge secondary audience (two-step flow). Many children spent most of their waking hours reading comic books. As public awareness increased concerning their contents and possible negative influences on children, serious questions began to be raised. Social scientists undertook studies of their popularity and possible influences. Professional groups of physicians, psychiatrists, and psychologists placed the topic on their agenda. In a short time, the comic book became a topic of considerable public debate. Hearings were held by an increasing number of local political groups.

As a result, some of these publications increasingly came to be seen by many adults as *a dreadful menace* to the mental health and moral behavior of children. There seemed to be a clear intuitive basis for these concerns. There were some categories that caused little concern—the cute animal comics aimed at young children and those with love-romance themes that were popular among teenage girls. However, two other types truly alarmed parents and others. These were the *crime* comics and those portraying *horror* themes. These booklets were filled with vivid colored drawings and dialogue that appeared to many to have seriously crossed the line of acceptability as content for children and youths. Plato clearly would have banned them.

The crime comics vividly portrayed criminal acts, such as murder, robbery, kidnaping, torture, and beatings, along with blood and gore. Also, in many ways, they bordered on pornographic content. Women were often depicted in scanty and sexy undergarments, as having unusually large breasts that were scarcely concealed by what they were wearing. The boys called them "headlights." Other women were seen being tied up, struck in the face, threatened with ice picks about to be stabbed into their eyes, and in other less than wholesome situations. The horror comics were filled with ghoulish pictures and morbid content. They were also often dramatically pornographic.

As public outcry continued to rise concerning these kinds of comic books, the industry tried to calm fears with a "code." This familiar strategy did not cause the criticism to cease. No one took them seriously. The codes were changed often, had no true restraining value, and were often ignored, even by the publishers themselves. Many local groups, including some from various levels of law enforcement, made attempts to reduce the sale of these materials in their communities. That didn't work either. The industry had high-talent legal counsel that fought such efforts with vigor and success on First Amendment grounds.

In the end, however, the comic book industry met its nemesis. Dr. Frederic Wertham was senior psychiatrist for the Department of Hospitals in New York City. He served in that capacity for twenty years before undertaking a detailed, systematic, and thorough clinical study of the nature and influences of comic books on children. He was a distinguished expert in medico-legal cases who frequently testified before state and federal courts, including the U.S. Supreme Court. In his practice and professional capacities, he had been able to observe the problems, behavior, beliefs, and ideas of an enormous number of troubled children. In particular, he became interested in those who were avid comic book readers. He held in-depth interviews with hundreds. It would be hard to imagine a professional medical expert who had more impressive qualifications.

In 1952, his book *Seduction of the Innocent* was a powerful indictment of the industry that had flooded the country with crime and horror comics. He spelled out in detail what that industry was publishing, why that content was so fascinating and harmful to children, and the nature of the negative effects he believed that it was creating. The book was written in an engaging and easy-to-read style. He provided details of his testimony on comic books before a long list of government bodies and professional groups, explaining in dramatic terms the nature of his conclusions. For example, he described his testimony at a U.S. post office hearing (to determine if comic books should continue to be sent through the mail) in the following way:

> I had to give a psychiatric analysis of what constitutes obscenity. By way of comparison with nudity in art and photography, I introduced comic books which I called obscene. I pointed out that the picture of a nude girl *per se* may be the opposite of obscene, as compared to one of a girl in a brassiere and panties about to be tied up,

gagged, tortured, set on fire, sold as a slave, chained, whipped, choked, raped, thrown to wild animals or crocodiles, forced to her knees, strangled, torn apart, and so on.[22]

As more and more communities began to try to slow or stop sales of their product, the comic book industry fought back with every legal strategy their lawyers could devise. But it was a losing battle. Within a decade, the number of comic books being printed and sold was a fraction of what it had been. The generation that had consumed them with great glee matured and went on with their lives. The generation that followed became preoccupied with television—which was then the newest medium. Even so, Wertham's book undoubtedly played a major part in the demise of the comic book. His work was widely read, and it remains something of a classic even today. If television had not come along to replace comic books, however, the story might have unfolded in a different way. In this case, the cycle was not repeated. It was not because comic book publishers had a change of heart and made personal decisions to stop what they were doing, but because a challenger and other conditions not under their control (a new technology) changed the economic conditions that had previously supported their industry.

CONTROVERSIES OVER VIOLENCE ON TELEVISION

Televison arrived in American homes almost overnight. Broadcasting had begun in a limited way in a few cities by 1949. Between 1950 and 1960, as noted earlier, ninety percept of American householders acquired a set. Although the earliest ones were primitive by today's standards, over the next three decades the technology of television improved rapidly—cable, color, size of screens, satellite signal delivery, VCRs, DVDs, pay-per-view movies, links to the Internet, and all the rest. But it was not the technology that troubled Americans during television's years of swiftly increasing adoption. It was what children were seeing on their screens. Parents and others were startled by reports on what came to be called the "TV Generation"—children who were now growing up in front of the tube.

Some of the conclusions made public by government officials and academic researchers were particularly troubling. For example, Newton Minow, who served as chairman of the Federal Communications Commission during a part of that period, maintained that television was a "vast wasteland." He further stated that, by the time most children reached the first grade, they would have spent the equivalent of three school years viewing television, and by the time they were eighteen, they would have spent more time with TV than time spent in school.[23] Studies made by academics indicated that children's TV shows contained more violence than those aimed at adults. According to the American Psychological Association, the typical child of the time would see more than "8,000 murders on TV and 100,000 acts of violence during his or her lifetime."[24]

Another factor that was deeply disturbing to Americans during the late 1960s and the 1970s was the *alarming rise in the rate of violent crime*—as was noted earlier. For example, in 1968, the number of violent crimes reported to the FBI (by local authorities) for each 100,000 inhabitants was 298. (These included such transgressions as murder, rape, robbery, and aggravated assault, among others.) However, by 1979, that number had soared to 535—an unprecedented 79.5 percent increase.[25] Moreover, in 1979, more than half of the persons arrested were under twenty-five years of age. In other words, youths and juveniles were committing far more of the robberies, burglaries, and motor vehicle thefts than could possibly be accounted for by their numbers in the population. The public was very aware that these changes had followed a significant increase in televised and other media-portrayed violence.

How did ordinary citizens interpret this change? They understood it in terms of the logical fallacy *post hoc, ergo propter hoc.* That is, when one set of events closely follows a previous set, it can be concluded that the first must have caused the second. The public's reasoning was simple: During the 1960s, television offered ever-increasing amounts of violence and crime in its programming. The nation's youth spent more and more time viewing TV. Then there was a great increase in violence and crime on the streets. In addition, there were destructive riots in many urban centers and the tragic assassinations of President Kennedy in Dallas and his brother Robert in Los Angeles. To the public, it all seemed linked to the newest mass medium.

Criminologists, of course, understood the change in different terms. It was a time of great migrations of poor people from rural areas of the nation to urban centers. Beginning in the late 1950s, and continuing into the 1960s, the struggle for civil rights was bringing about frustration, urban unrest, and demands for change among minorities. Youngsters raised in the conditions of the urban ghetto—in poverty, with one-parent families, blighted neighborhoods, street gangs, and many other difficult conditions—had neither the same opportunities that others enjoyed nor the same constraints on them that had been in place at an earlier time in a rural environment. These were the conditions that led to urban violence and rising crime. Nevertheless, televised violence did seem to many citizens to be an important causal factor driving young people to commit transgressions, and a large body of research was undertaken to study this possibility. But social scientists were unable to agree that the linkage was shown convincingly.

The Presidential Commission on Violence

For the general public, however, the research controversies among social scientists were irrelevant—arguments about fine points of navigation while the ship was sinking. The alarms raised by television's many critics were a call to action. Politicians once again marshaled to the cause. In 1968, President Lyndon B. Johnson signed Executive Order 11412, creating a *National Commission on the Causes and Prevention of Violence*. The commission was composed of thirteen distinguished citizens, whose task it was to have experts assemble and interpret all available evidence as to what was bringing about the great increases in violence in America.

Part III of the commission's report focused on *Television Entertainment and Violence*. A large number of studies by social scientists, summarized in the report, seemed to reveal that there were short-term and long-term effects of excessive violence in the media among those who were exposed.[26] The general conclusions offered in the report were these:

1. The weight of social science stands in opposition to the conclusions that mass media portrayals of violence have no effect upon individuals, groups, and society.
2. To the extent that mass media portrayals of violence have effects upon individuals, groups, and society, it is a variety that most persons would deem costly and harmful to individuals and society.
3. The direction of effects of mass media portrayals of violence is to extend the behavioral and attitudinal boundaries of accepted violence beyond legal and social norms currently espoused by a majority of Americans.

Conclusion 3, above, suggests the basic idea of the Creeping Cycle of Desensitization Theory. That is, increasing violence in the media leads to greater acceptance of such content—that is, *desensitization*—on the part of Americans. Although the theory was never formulated in those terms at the time, the findings of the commission appear to be consistent with its explanation.

The media did not receive the commissions's report with meek acceptance. Indeed, the major TV networks and the National Association of Broadcasters answered public concern with three basic assertions.[27] Essentially, they claimed:

1. "... there is no conclusive evidence that violence on television causes viewers to behave violently." (That causal relationship has never been established beyond controversy, even today.)
2. "... the industry will sponsor the research to determine the relationship between violence and violent behavior." (They failed to do this in any serious way.)
3. "... the industry [promises] to reduce the amount of violence on television." (This did not happen. Indeed, there was evidence that levels of violence increased.)

Senator Pastore's Million-Dollar Project

A second major federal effort to probe the influence of TV on behavior was undertaken in 1969. It has since come to be called the "Surgeon General's Report." As was explained in Chapter 16 (on Modeling Theory), it was a report prepared and submitted *to the U.S. surgeon general*. The report summarized extensive hearings before the Subcommittee on Communication of the Committee on Commerce of the U.S. Senate. The project had been initiated by Senator John O. Pastore, of Rhode Island, for the purpose of sponsoring research and hearing witness testimony regarding the influence of television on social behavior. A number of the witnesses appearing before the subcommittee were from the networks or various media-related associations. However, the majority of the several dozens of witnesses who provided testimony were social scientists who had conducted research on the relationship between media violence and behavior. Many of these investigators had been funded to conduct their studies by the subcommittee itself (with an appropriation of one million dollars). In addition to the twenty-three projects funded by the controlling advisory committee, nearly 500 additional research studies on the issue were examined, summarized, and interpreted.

The bottom line was that much of the evidence suggested that viewing a great deal of violence on television may have predisposed some children under some conditions to engage in some kinds of violent acts. If that seems like a vague statement, it is. After all the hearings, testimony, research, and report writing, the issue remained mired in controversy.

The reports from both the Violence Commission and the Commerce Subcommittee did not provide answers that were completely clear. In the minds of many, political concerns clouded the conclusions. Industry spokespersons claimed that ultra liberal social scientists were trying to lynch the industry. Many researchers felt that the government was too protective of the media. Indeed, while Surgeon General Jesse Steinfeld concluded that there was evidence of a causal relationship, a headline in the *New York Times* on January 11, 1972, stated unequivocally that the report concluded "TV Violence Unharmful to Youth."[28]

CONTROVERSIAL CONTENT ON COMPUTERS

In more recent years, computers have offered many opportunities to present controversial material in digital form to audiences. One way is by providing online vicarious sexual experiences and pornography in a variety of forms. Another is providing opportunities, particularly to youngsters, to engage vicariously in violent behavior by playing video games. Both of these experiences are widely available, and both are widely condemned. Moreover, both appear to have been following the pattern of the Creeping Cycle of Desensitization.

Pornography and the Internet

Pornography is as old as human civilization. Sexual depictions appear in ancient Greek and Roman art, and erotic material has been presented in every age to those who want it via virtually every medium that was capable at the time of transmitting words, pictures, or sounds. Today, pornography is a multibillion-dollar entertainment industry. The Internet, our most contemporary medium, is now a major transmitter of erotic material. At first it was a highly restricted tool for scientists, supported by the federal government, so that researchers engaging in projects relevant to national defense concerns could exchange scientific data. By the 1990s, it had become a full-blown medium that ordinary people could use to receive almost any kind of information that one could imagine. The World Wide Web made available literally millions of sites, web pages, databases, and other content that could be captured with a few keystrokes on a keyboard to appear on the screen of a personal computer at home. Much of it was informational and utilitarian. However, as has been the case with other media, there was money to be made by presenting content that provided thrills and excitement with content that transgressed prevailing conservative norms. Prominent in this category was vicarious sex. Pornography transmitted over the Internet, including content portraying children engaging in sex or being used for sexual gratification by adults, quickly became a huge money-maker.

What is different about pornography on the Internet is that it comes directly into the home without the barriers and hurdles that have existed with other media. Earlier consumers of pornography had to buy their erotic materials at "adult bookstores," attend "blue movies" at stag parties, pay to get into porno theaters, or rent tapes from the "adult" section of the VCR rental store. It became a bit easier when pornographic movies became available on pay-per-view cable. In all these channels, however, fees of some sort are charged, and it is not easy for children to gain access to them.

Things changed as the 1990s began. The number of pornographic sites on the Internet soared. There was a lot of erotic material that was free. Individuals could post dirty pictures of themselves or others with few restrictions. Such content was easily available to anyone. Much of it could be viewed by any child who had the skills of getting online.

It was this ready availability of erotic content to children that became the center of a controversy. Parents, educators, and other concerned segments of society raised a howl of protest. They maintained that the nations's children were being harmed. Congress soon got into the act.

Politicians always want votes, and when they see an opportunity to act on behalf of disturbed citizens, they do not hesitate. In 1966, Congress passed the Communications Decency Act. Simply put, it made it a federal crime to place any so-called "adult" material online where children could gain access to it. Many conservatives in the society, deeply concerned over "family values" and the welfare and morals of children, applauded.

Almost immediately, the new law bumped into the First Amendment of the U.S. Constitution. Those who opposed the act felt that it had gone too far. These were not necessarily people who were advocating pornography. There were other kinds of problems with the new law. For example, it made it impossible to use such terms as "breast" in websites. Medical discussions of breast cancer would have been off limits. There were many other unintended problems along these lines. The act, in the minds of many, was framed in too broad a way to be allowed to prevail. Others believed that there should not be any limitation of the right to say or present any kind of content whatsoever in the media.

Almost immediately, therefore, the Communications Decency Act was challenged. In 1997, the case came before the U.S. Supreme Court. The result was that certain portions of the act were struck down. As far as conservatives were concerned, it was a tragic defeat. For example, a news report from Pascagoula, Mississippi, that appeared in the New Orleans *Times Picayune* in August of 1997 included the following observations:

> Our nation is moving away from God and suffering a moral decline like a ship that is lost at sea. Congress and the president have taken steps to correct this problem, but their efforts have been blocked by the Supreme Court . . . The court's decision is unfair and not in the best interests of our country. The entertainment industry is making millions of dollars appealing to the baser qualities of people, while juvenile crime, teen pregnancies, date-rape, and violence in our schools are becoming ever-increasing problems . . . Our country is at a great risk of losing forever the traditional family values on which our nation was founded. A constitutional amendment is needed to force the entertainment industry to clean up its act.[29]

Within a short time, the Congress acted again. The Child Online Protection Act was passed in 1998. It narrowed the restrictions of the earlier legislation to commercial websites and defined indecency in more specific terms. However, a federal appeals court stopped enforcement of this new law. Other laws were also passed, essentially limiting what libraries and schools could allow to appear on their computers. Currently, controversies and legal confrontations continue. The final outcome is difficult to forecast.

What is not difficult to show is the increasing use of the Internet for vicarious sexual experiences. As we noted earlier, experiencing sex in cyberspace has been called an "addiction" by some. In a conference of a group called the National Council on Sexual Addiction and Compulsivity (in the year 2000), using the Internet for vicarious sexual gratification was termed a "growing epidemic."

> Research shows that an estimated 15 percent of Internet users have visited online sex chat rooms—online person-to-person discussions—or pornographic sites. A study presented at the conference [of the National Council noted above] found that almost 9 percent of people who use the Internet for sex spend more than eleven hours a week surfing for erotic content. The numbers were nearly equal for men and women, countering the widely accepted view that an overwhelming majority of cybersex participants are men.[30]

It seems clear, therefore, that the Internet, like the print, broadcast, and film media before it, is showing the same pattern concerning what the public will accept, what conservatives want to prevent, what profit making demands, and what the Constitution protects. It is difficult to predict where this trend will eventually lead. Perhaps, as the cutting edge of technology continues to move forward, it may be possible, in the not too distant future, for those who enjoy vicarious erotic experiences transmitted online to view them in three-dimensional space. Possibly these experiences will include the sounds, smells, and other sensory experiences that are found in the actual performance of physical acts.

Video Games

Electronic games were first developed in the 1960s, long before the desktop computer appeared on the market. They were used mainly by engineers and computer experts for their own amusement. Typical at the time were electronic chess, blackjack, and backgammon (none had video). In the 1970s, more sophisticated versions were developed with video displays. At first, most were in arcades. But as technology advanced, especially during the 1980s, versions were marketed on the (then) new compact disks to be viewed on television screens and eventually on the monitors of desktop computers. It was these versions that were especially attractive to children. Today, in addition to the desktop computer, special devices for viewing the games are commonly used. Some are handheld; others are more complex (e.g., PlayStations). While these entertainment products are used by many adults, they are especially popular among preteen boys.

Many of the earlier games had themes of violence. This increasingly became the case as an expanding market for these products developed. During the 1990s, revenues from such games exceeded $10 billion annually. Today, with worldwide sales, it is far greater. Typically, the player can manipulate virtual characters and futuristic weapons to blast dragons, invaders from outer space, or just plain bad guys. The concerns of critics is that children using these entertainment devices—in which they play the part of a person who can kill off villains or anyone else—are providing *collateral instruction* on how to perform and make use of such acts of violence.

In Chapter 5 the nature of "collateral instruction" embedded in media content was explained (see also Chapter 23). As was explained, the concept of "incidental learning" from that teaching was introduced by Wilbur Schramm in 1961—long before video games arrived.[31] He was concerned with the lessons children unwittingly obtained from viewing violence on television. At the time, and indeed today, children view television programs or other media content solely for entertainment. They are not seeking "lessons"—they just want to have fun. Moreover, those who produce the content that the children see do not intend to "teach" their audiences. However, what that content often provides (incidentally) is instruction in the techniques and circumstances for performing violent acts. In this way, *social learning* takes place.

Social Learning Theory (as explained in Chapter 16, Modeling Theory) is a general psychological perspective that explains how people acquire many kinds of knowledge, habits, beliefs, and performance techniques by *imitation*. That is, they see such actions acted out by others and learn how to perform them. In the case of video games, they learn even more directly—by actually manipulating the virtual characters, weapons, and so on.[32] Social Learning Theory has been widely tested and well supported for decades. Thus, the concerns of the critics appear to have merit. There seems little doubt that contemporary video games in which the player performs violent acts does have the capacity to teach children some very nasty incidental lessons.

In spite of the possibility that children can learn antisocial attitudes and behavior from such entertainment products, those who produce and distribute them are not subject to any effective controls over what they make or sell. No one, other than parents, have any real way to slow down, stop, or otherwise interfere with what content children see when they use these products. The First Amendment poses a formidable obstacle for any who would try to suppress any form of public communication. Thus, this communication industry, like all others in the United States, operates within the capitalistic system, essentially protected from interference. Profits must be made, and this means getting ahead of the competition. The alternative is bankruptcy. The pressure is on, therefore, to get ahead of the competition by giving users more and more of what they will enjoy—and pay for.

Are such games becoming more violent, more realistic, with collateral teaching of lessons of greater concern? For the most part, the earlier video games presented unrealistic situations. The graphics portrayed such themes as invaders from outer space to be repelled by the player with futuristic weapons that do not actually exist. While they did depict opportunities for the player to engage in violence, they could easily be recognized as fantasy—lowering the possibility of providing unwanted incidental lessons.

But what about a much more realistic game? How about having the young player armed with a *baseball bat*, able to wander around an American city shown on the screen in remarkably realistic detail? How about presenting the player with opportunities to smash people over the head with the bat and suffer no consequences, or engage in other truly violent behavior? In October of 2001, RockStar Games released an entertainment product called Grand Theft Auto III, to be used with PlayStation 2. It was filled with such opportunities. Only two months later this video game had sold 635,000 copies. Made available for rent through Blockbuster, it almost immediately became its leading rental. It is not possible to pin down the number of people who have played this game since that time—but apparently it is a great many. A later version (Grand Theft Auto: Vice City) became the best-selling video game in the United States in 2002. A child playing this game can earn extra points for hiring a prostitute and more for having sex with her, then beating her to death and taking back the money paid to her for her services. While the video game industry provides a simple set of ratings (based on age), merchants seldom enforce them, many parents know nothing of them—or don't care. Thus, children as young as six can play the part of the actor in the game and engage is virtually any form of violence one can imagine.

Two questions can be asked about this type of entertainment product. First, does such a game cross an important line in media depictions of violence? Second, does it represent a clear example of the Creeping Cycle of Desensitization? There are no conclusive studies, with hard empirical evidence, to answer either of these questions. However, a closer look at the content of this video game—the experiences that it provides for its players—may suggest some tentative answers.

The game, Grand Theft Auto III, takes the player into a (virtual) American city in a remarkably realistic way. It has a "mature" rating (whatever that means), but, again, there is no way to enforce age restrictions on who can buy, rent, or play it. The graphics are superb. The player is depicted on screen in almost photo clarity as a young male with neatly trimmed brown hair, dressed casually in a leather jacket and olive-colored jeans. He holds a baseball bat. The player can have him walk around in the city and engage in a remarkable variety of violent and illegal activities. His virtual environment has very real-looking cars, rooms, buildings, plants, other people in conversations walking by him, and so on. The player, guiding his virtual surrogate, can commandeer a police car, be a bank robber, be a mob hit man, be a car highjacker, or be virtually any kind of ruthless thug—carrying out truly dreadful acts. One recent report by a person playing the game for the first time provides an example of the experiences it provides:

> The world you roam is stunningly realistic, shadowy and gritty. When you drive beneath a streetlight, a pool of light reflects on your car. When you pass people on the sidewalk, you hear snippets of their conversation: 'Damned foreigners.' 'Got any doughnuts?' If you jostle them, they glare at you. . . .
> I walk around the streets with my bat until I spot an old lady and decide to see what happens if I hit her. She falls down. A pool of blood forms around her. A police officer arrives. In a panic, I hit him repeatedly until he appears to be dead.[33]

Is this harmless fun? Or is there some serious collateral instruction here providing incidental lessons within the context of this entertainment? The people of Australia appear to believe that this is the case. The game has been banned there on the grounds of its graphic violence and the lessons it teaches. Thus far, no such action has been taken in the United States. Moreover, for reasons explained earlier, it is not at all clear that there are any legal grounds for doing so. However, one thing is clear. Many parents and other people are unlikely to accept this latest entertainment product from the video game industry as harmless fun. Indeed, in the minds of critics, it does appear to have crossed an important line in the depiction of violence. Whether the controversy will die down and similar games become the standard is anyone's guess. If the theory presented in this chapter has merit, however, that is likely to be the case.

ADVERTISEMENTS CROSS THE LINE

In 2003, in the never-ending quest for profits, the advertising world produced and aired TV and radio commercials that many people have found offensive. For example, the Miller Brewing Company, seeking to enhance its share of the beer market, began airing a commercial called "Catfight." Its content was sexy women, scantily clad, who were engaging in a kind of mud-wrestling match. Chris Reidy, a writer for the *Boston Globe* described the situation in these terms:

> Beer ads with sexual imagery are hardly new. But in their desperation to spur sales in a flat market, some beer companies striving to reach their core audience of young men—young men raised in a culture of reality television and R-rated movies—have pushed the boundaries of taste to get their message across.

> . . . In a spot titled 'Catfight,' two women turn Miller Light's old 'tastes great-less filling' argument into a brawl that ends in a mud-wrestling match. During the wrestling, much clothing is shed, and the cleavage of the combatants is exposed.[34]

The commercial was condemned by a number of (mainly older) people. Their argument was that children see this content when they watch television. Critics point out that such TV content offends parents who are trying to teach their children caution and responsibility.

Other beer companies have also used sex as a selling strategy. During the previous summer, another attempt to sell beer with sex appeared to many to have crossed the line, and it resulted in a considerable controversy. It was a radio station promotion for Samuel Adams beer. It was produced and aired for the Boston Beer Company. It appeared to involve two people having sex in New York City's St. Patrick Cathedral. The company later apologized and changed its ad strategies.

There is little doubt, then, that in the news, entertainment, and even advertising worlds, standards of what is acceptable and in good taste will continue to change. The norms of taste and morality are likely to continue to give way in situations of fierce economic competition. Protected by the First Amendment of the U.S. Constitution (originally designed to protect political speech), there is little to hold back the Creeping Cycle of Desensitization. As the young become increasingly willing to accept open sexual depictions, a greater emphasis on violence, increasing portrayals of crime, and more and more dirty language in their entertainment, news, and advertising content, the cycle will continue to evolve.

THE CREEPING CYCLE OF DESENSITIZATION THEORY: A FORMAL SUMMARY

The concepts, variables, conditions, generalizations, and changing standards that have been discussed in the sections above can be brought together into a theory that both describes and explains major trends in media content in the United States. The same pattern may also be found in certain other countries that have similar political and economic institutions. What has been set forth is a repetitive pattern bringing about changes in media content. Those changes began with media presentations that were consistent with conservative norms of society—at least for a time. They then progressively became more sensational. Sexual depictions became increasingly explicit. The level of violence in drama and other content increased. There was an increase in the use of four-letter words and other vulgar language. This was not a phenomenon restricted to a single medium but a pervasive pattern that can be observed more widely in almost all of the media—print, film, broadcast, and digital—that deliver news, entertainment, and advertising messages to the public.

Critics have often attributed these changes to greedy and ruthless people who operate, direct, and decide on what a particular medium will offer to the public. Conspiracies are seen. Charges are made that media moguls are attempting to get rich, even at the cost of public decency and morality. Some see it as a great betrayal—taking advantage of the First Amendment protections of free speech (originally intended to protect political dissent) for the crass purpose of enriching profits (at the expense of morality and good taste). Fears arise concerning the welfare of children. The media are identified as causal agents in the rise of crime, delinquency, looser moral standards, and other ills of society.

The present chapter presents one explanation of why the American media—and indeed those of some other countries that have similar economic and political systems—have seen a particular pattern over time in their media content. That explanation attempts to show that what happens to news and entertainment products in a society is in many ways shaped by the social, economic, and political conditions that create demand among certain audience categories for certain kinds of media content. The basic propositions of that theory can be expressed in the following terms:

1. The communication industries producing entertainment and other content, such as newspapers and magazines, radio, television, popular music, the Internet, and video games, do so within a system of economic capitalism, in which *making profits* is an essential and highly approved goal.

2. Making a profit on mass communication content follows the classical principles of competitive and *market-driven capitalism*—keeping costs down while offering a commodity, service or experience for which a maximum number of people will pay to use or enjoy.

3. The types of products that attract the *largest number of paying customers* are often those that emphasize socially controversial themes, such as sensationalism, sex, crime, violence, and vulgarity.

4. In the United States, due to the protections of the First Amendment to the Constitution, there are *few legal or political restraints* on what content such media products can contain and be presented to the public.

5. What is acceptable in the content of such mass communication content is largely left to *audience tastes and the cultural norms* that define what various categories of people will or will not tolerate.

6. The largest audience category providing the largest profits from most such products are *young people* who care less for the conservative tastes and restraining cultural norms than do older people (whose numbers are smaller) as they actively seek pleasure and excitement.

7. For that reason, producers of media content—seeking ever-larger profits in a highly competitive economic but protected environment—will constantly *increase depictions of sensational topics*, sex, crime, violence, and vulgarity until a sufficient number of the public, or various leaders, protest strongly.

8. **Therefore**, if the outcry threatens their industry, the producers will stop, or even temporarily reverse, their transgressions of norms. But in a creeping cycle of desensitization, the producers will move the *cutting edge of transgressions forward again* as soon as the public protest becomes muted.

Notes and References

1. Melvin L. DeFleur, *Theories of Mass Communication* (New York: David McKay Company, Inc., 1966) pp. 156–157.

2. For a detailed history of the printing press, see James Moran, *Printing Presses: History and Development from the Fifteenth Century to Modern Times* (Berkeley and Los Angeles: University of California Press, 1974).

3. These figures are from U.S. Bureau of the Census, *Historical Statistics of the United States* (Washington, D.C., 1960) Series 255.

4. Melvin L. DeFleur and Everette E. Dennis, *Understanding Mass Communication,* updated 6th ed. (Boston: Houghton Mifflin, 1996), pp. 86–87.

5. (anonymous) *Current Literature*, V. 46, 1909, p. 47.

6. *Ibid.* p. 88.

7. J. B. Montgomery McGovern, "An Important Phase of Gutter Journalism: Faking," *Arena*, V. 19, 1898, p. 240.

8. Horace Greeley, *The Tribune*, 1841.

9. Gabriel Tarde, *Selected Papers on Communication and Social Influence,* ed. by Terry N. Clark (Chicago: The University of Chicago Press, 1969), p. 265.

10. Cited by Harry Elmer Barnes in "Graham Wallas and the Sociopsychological Basis of Politics and Reconstruction," Chapter 36 of *An Introduction to the History of Sociology* (Chicago: The University of Chicago Press, 1948), p. 711.

11. See Chris Reidy, "Less Taste, More Willing," Boston Globe (Business Section) January 25, 2003, p. C1

12. For summaries of the events leading to the invention of the movies, see the following: Brian Coe, *The History of Movie Photography* (New York: Zoetrope, 1982); Raymond Fielding, *A Technological History of Motion Pictures and Television* (Berkeley: University of California Press, 1967).

13. See Kevin McDonald, *Eadweard Muybridge* (Boston: Little Brown, 1972). Also: Gordon Hendricks, *Eadweard Muybridge* (New York: Grossman, 1975).

14. Douglas Gomery, *Movie History: A Survey* (Belmont, CA: Wadsworth, 1991), p. 39.

15. *The Cinema: Its Present Position and Future Possibilities*, Report of the National Council of Public Morals, [of Great Britain] 1917. Quoted in Garth Jowett and James M. Linton, *Movies as Mass Communication* (Newbury Park, NJ: Sage Publications, 1980), pp. 67–68.

16. See U.S. Bureau of the Census, *Historical Statistics of the United States: Colonial Times to 1957* (Washington, DC: Government Printing Office, 1960).

17. See U.S. Bureau of the Census, *Historical Statistics of the United States: Colonial Times to 1970* (Washington, DC: Government Printing Office, 1989).

18. John L. Halting and Roy P. Peterson, *The Fourth Estate*, 2nd ed. (New York: Harper and Row, 1983), p. 9.

19. The Payne Fund studies were a massive research effort conducted between 1927 and 1929 to understand how the motion pictures were influencing children of the time. Large-scale projects investigated what ideas children were learning about society, their attitudes toward minorities, general conduct, influences on delinquency, emotions, manners, morals, patterns of sleep, and many more. Thirteen volumes were published. A summary of what was found overall can be found in: W. W. Charters, *Motion Pictures and Youth: A Summary* (New York: The Macmillan Company, 1933).

20. Motion Picture Association of America, Inc. *A Code to Govern the Making of Motion Pictures: The Reasons Supporting It and the Resolution for Uniform Interpretation*, 1930–1955, p. 3.

21. Richard Corliss, "This Essay Is Rated PG-13," *Time*, July 29, 2002, p. 70.

22. Frederic Wertham, M.D., *Seduction of the Innocent* (Mattituck, NY: Amereon House, 1953), pp. 297–298. This work was reprinted in 1973.

23. Newton Minow, *Abandoned in the Wasteland: Children, Television and the First Amendment* (New York: Hill and Wang, 1996).

24. Glen S. Sparks, *Media Effects Research* (Belmont, CA: Wadsworth, 2002), p. 74.

25. See: *Statistical Abstract of the United States, 1980* (Washington, DC: U.S. Bureau of the Census, 1981), Table 302.

26. Robert K. Baker and Sandra J. Ball, *Violence and the Media: A Staff Report to the National Commission on the Causes and Prevention of Violence* (Washington, DC: U.S. Government Printing Office, 1969), p. 375.

27. *Ibid.* pp. 7–8.

28. An excellent summary and assessment of the nature and findings of the Surgeon General's Report can be found in: Robert M. Liebert, Joyce N. Spratkin, and Emily S. Davidson, *The Early Window: Effects of Television on Children and Youth* (New York: Pergamon Press, Inc., 1982), pp. 67–135.

29. © 2014 NOLA Media Group, L.L.C. All rights reserved. Used with permission of the Times-Picayune and NOLA.com.

30. Erin McClam, Associated Press, "Online Sex Addiction On Rise, Specialists Say," *Boston Globe*, May 6, 2000, p. A12.

31. Wilbur Schramm, Jack Lyle, and Edwin Parker, *Television in the Lives of Our Children* (Stanford, CA: Stanford University Press, 1961), pp. 75–78.

32. Albert Bandura, *Social Learning Theory* (Englewood Cliffs, NJ: Prentice Hall, 1977).

33. Joanna Weiss, "Connecting with Your Inner Thug; Grand Theft Auto III Gives You an On-Screen Crime Spree—and Too Much Fun," *The Boston Globe*, January 13, 2002, pp. E1 and E5. (This reporter provides a website for viewing a gallery of ten screen shots from the game: www.boston.com/globe/ideas.)

34. Chris Reidy, "Less Taste, More Willing," *The Boston Globe*, January 25, 2003, p. C1.

CHAPTER 21

Critical Cultural Perspectives: Interpretations of Media Influences on Individuals and Society

C ultural criticism of the process, content, and influences of mass communications is not a theory in the same sense as those that have been set forth in most of the other chapters in this book. However, it is a *perspective* used by many scholars in the field. The reason that it is not a theory in the same sense as those in other chapters is that the assumptions on which such criticisms are based have not been derived from a body of factual evidence assembled through the use of the scientific method. Because of this, the conclusions that are reached by those using this type of critical analysis are not intended to serve as guides to further empirical research aimed at evaluating the theory. However, such perspectives do provide important ways of assessing the process and effects of mass communication.

The assumptions about the nature of human individuals and the social order on which the perspective is based, and which are made by those who engage in cultural criticism, are taken *a priori* as valid—that is, as "obviously true." In that sense, they are seen as needing no quantitative research findings to testify to their validity. Nevertheless, such assumptions can be identified. When this has been accomplished, the basic ideas of cultural criticism—as an approach to analyzing, understanding, and criticizing the process and effects of mass communication—can be brought together into a related set of formal propositions. Thus, the purpose of this chapter is to identify the assumptions of the cultural critics concerning mass communication, to set them forth systematically, and to identify their logical consequences—*as those consequences are seen by such critics.*

At the end of the chapter, therefore, these propositions will be stated in summary form in much the same manner in which the formal theories developed in earlier chapters have been set forth. Whether those scholars who have developed the body of comments, claims, arguments, and conclusions currently termed "cultural criticism" of the mass media will agree that this is an accurate summary may or may not be the case. Nevertheless, it is the purpose of the present chapter to try to set forth in reasonably simple and understandable terms what cultural criticism is all about when this activity is applied to the process, content, and influences of mass communications.

CULTURAL CRITICISM: THE GENERAL BACKGROUND

There are two important features in the background of the cultural criticism perspective that require explanation: First, it is *very general in what is examined*. Cultural critics address a very broad range of topics and issues, including mass communication. They are concerned with the nature of contemporary society and how its conditions and features produce influences that can be unfavorable for many kinds of people—particularly those who are in some way disadvantaged.[1] Second, as has been indicated above, it is *not based on a scientific epistemology*. That is, those who practice this form of commentary and analysis do not proceed from, or base their conclusions on, scientific evidence gathered by an empirical process. Given that, the purpose of this chapter is to attempt to explain the foundation of assumptions that are used by these scholars in their criticism of issues and topics broadly but with a particular focus on those that are related to the mass media.

Cultural Criticism as a General Intellectual Activity

But, more specifically, just what is cultural criticism? That is not a simple question that can be answered in a sentence or two with a straightforward definition. To explain cultural criticism, it is necessary to begin with a brief review of its complex intellectual heritage. That will help in understanding its procedures as well as its origins. Within that context, the next step will be to look more specifically at the ways in which those who practice cultural criticism have turned their attention to the mass media in contemporary society.

First, then, the present section will review briefly the *very broad and general idea of cultural criticism*. Following that, another section will discuss the *intellectual foundations* of that activity. Only after these broader strokes have been placed on the canvas will it be possible to discuss *cultural criticism of the mass media* and their influences on populations—as one of the many features of modern societies that are criticized by this body of scholars.

A PLETHORA OF PERSPECTIVES.   Today, engaging in cultural criticism is a popular activity practiced by a great many kinds of scholars who are located in a great many academic fields. For the most part, these are in the humanities or the social sciences, and many are associated with very liberal political perspectives and agendas. Many share a strong concern for the disadvantaged in society. Disadvantage may be defined in terms of ethnicity, poverty, race, gender, sexual preference, or political power, among other categories.

Another background feature that has led to a broad range of scholars becoming interested in cultural criticism is that *there is so much in life today that can be criticized*. The rewards of contemporary society—income, power, status, opportunity—however defined, are not equally distributed among citizens. It is the sincere hope of many cultural critics that such inequities can be identified and addressed. Thus, there are many intellectual perspectives and many criteria that can be used for finding fault with many aspects of contemporary culture and the social order.

One issue that has not been addressed in any detailed sense by contemporary cultural critics is *what should be done about* the conditions they see as unsatisfactory. In recent times, few have offered any new plan for society or for any major reorganization of the social order that would alleviate what they discuss as problems. That was certainly done by Karl Marx—perhaps the greatest cultural critic of all time—who, shortly after the mid-1800s, advocated that the industrial society of his time be swept aside by a revolution so that his vision of a classless society could replace it. Few cultural critics today have offered any alternatives to his sweeping vision.

Perhaps the most readable and easily understood explanation of this broad and general perspective is that of Arthur Asa Berger, who, in his insightful book *Cultural Criticism: A Primer of Key Concepts* (1995), described it this way:

> Cultural criticism is an activity, not a discipline per se. . . . That is, cultural critics apply the concepts and theories [of many fields] in varying combinations and permutations, to the elite arts, popular culture, everyday life and a host of others. Cultural criticism is, I suggest, a multidisciplinary, interdisciplinary, pandisciplinary, or metadisciplinary undertaking, and cultural critics come from, and use, the ideas of a variety of disciplines.[2]

Berger's explanation describes cultural criticism as an activity of breathtaking sweep and generality. The concerns of cultural critics with the media is only one small segment, so to speak, of that broad range. However, before focusing on the media more specifically, two other features of cultural criticism need to be discussed. Specifically, many of its scholars use a number of *labels and terms* that are by no means familiar to outsiders. In addition, their *writing style* can sometimes seem difficult to understand.

PROBLEMS POSED BY UNUSUAL LABELS AND TERMS. Because cultural criticism cuts across so many topics and disciplines, it has developed a number of distinctive ideas and concepts that have been given specialized names—unique labels for ideas apparently understood within a group of like-minded scholars but not necessarily familiar to people outside those circles. It is clear to anyone trying for the first time to read what some of the critics write that many of these unique and unusual terms are not well understood by those who are not a part of a particular subdiscipline. Indeed, many people who are not critical cultural theorists often complain that people engaged in this kind of analysis seem to use terms that are simply unintelligible to otherwise intellectually capable people seeking to understand what they are saying.

To illustrate the issue of unfamiliar labels, consider such words as *hermaneutics, deconstruction, postmodernism, phallocentric, defamiliarization, and dialogical.* Quite obviously, these are not common topics of discussion at the average breakfast table or even in serious conversations at lunch among the well educated. It is easy, therefore, to dismiss the conclusions advanced by various kinds of cultural critics as unintelligible—and therefore unimportant. That would be a mistake, because much of what the cultural critics say may be important. The bottom line here is that their conclusions can be complex and often difficult to interpret, but in many ways they may provide important insights into the nature of modern life.

A COMPLEX WRITING STYLE. There are many who are unsympathetic to cultural critics, not only on the grounds that they use obscure words, but also because their overall writing style can sometimes seem impenetrable. Among the unsympathetic, some claim that cultural critics write in this manner for the deceptive purpose of protecting weak ideas. The charge is that if someone from the outside attacks obscurely written conclusions, the cultural critic can always claim that the person simply "failed to understand" what the critic was saying. Thus, both obscure terms and an unfathomable writing style, say some, provide convenient camouflage for ideas that cannot stand the light of day on their own.

Whatever the final answer to this accusation, there are at least some grounds for concluding that writing by cultural critics can at times be very difficult to understand. To illustrate, we can look closely at the term "postmodernism." It is a common one used in the analysis of trends and conditions in society that can be criticized. In the writings of some cultural critics, however, it can illustrate the problems outsiders sometimes have in understanding their discourse.

At first glance, the term "postmodernism" would not seem all that difficult to interpret. It could be understood as an *intellectual perspective* needed to analyze and understand certain conditions in "postmodern" (or, as they are sometimes called, "postindustrial") societies. Those are societies that have undergone changes beyond those that developed in factory-based economies during the Industrial Revolution of the nineteenth and early twentieth centuries.

One problem here is that the term "modern" can be confusing. There was, after all, a clear transition in Western societies from the Middle Ages into a much more enlightened period before the Industrial Revolution. That is what some call the "modern" period, which followed the Renaissance. During those times, before the Industrial Revolution, great advances began to be made in science. Philosophy blossomed, and remarkable transitions from monarchies to democracies took place in several Western nations.

Later, however, many claim that the Industrial Revolution brought another kind of "modern" society. In Europe and other parts of the West, factory production slowly replaced agriculture as the principal form of work. People moved from farms to factory towns to sell their labor. Gradually, large cities developed with heterogeneous populations. Life became increasingly impersonal, bureaucratized, anomic, and anonymous. (This was the transition to "mass" society—from *Gemeinschaft* to *Gesellscahft*—that was discussed in Chapter 6.)

But in more recent times, a different social order and way of life has emerged. For example, in the United States and in Europe, we are no longer classic industrial societies—in which people with blue collars work in factories using steam-driven machines to produce "things." Today, many "things" are produced by automated and computerized production systems that require only a few technical operators. Such automated machines now produce goods at far higher rates of productivity than was ever the case during the earlier industrial era.

That transition in the industrial process brought great changes in what people do for a living. That is, in this "post" industrial era (of automated production), far more people are employed in "service" industries than in producing goods in factories. In such jobs, they provide *assistance* to people in a great variety of ways. The majority in the labor force work in jobs providing people with educational, tourist-oriented, health-related, financial, retail, recreational, and other kinds of services. Not that many people still work in factories for hourly wages using machines to produce goods. (Much of that is done overseas, where labor is cheap.) In this new kind of "service" work, many say, we have become an "information" society. The manipulation of numbers in data files and words in message content are far more common than working at machines in factory settings. It is for this reason that this new way of life is sometimes described as "postmodern" society.

But how do we get from that type of postmodern society to the term "postmodern*ism*"? What does the "ism" mean? The answer is that it is convenient for writers and analysts to invent a term to label a particular *intellectual approach*—a kind of mindset—toward a particular topic, or a *mode of analysis* emphasizing certain central values. This makes is easy for those who advocate the mindset to talk to each other or for people needing to discuss its overall ideas to refer to them in a collective sense. Obvious examples are "rac*ism*" (a mindset that persons of African American heritage are not equal to those of Caucasian descent) and "radical femin*ism*" (a belief that drastic changes are needed in society to promote the status, power, and rewards allocated to women). Thus, the suffix "ism" is a convenient way to construct such a term. Other obvious examples have long been used in political discourse. For example, the Communist organization of government and the ideological commitments upon which it rests represent an intellectual approach usually referred to as "Communism." People today can also discuss and write about "multiculturalism" and "globalism" as a complex of intellectual ideas.

In general, then, adding an "ism" to a broad set of related ideas creates a linguistic convenience—a label whose referent is a mindset incorporating complex beliefs, attitudes, and concepts concerning some condition or social arrangement. It is in this same way, then, that the study and criticism of the features and organization of postmodern society can conveniently be called "postmodernism." It is an intellectual orientation used by those who describe, and often criticize, the conditions prevailing in this type of postindustrial society.

But, returning to the issue of complex writing styles, how well do cultural critics explain to others these ideas about postmodernism and other terms that are important parts of their vocabulary? Some say *badly* and maintain that the critics explanations are dreadfully unclear. For example, one scholar in the cultural criticism tradition defined the meaning of "postmodernism" with this passage:

> It self-consciously splices genres, attitudes, styles. It relishes the blurring or juxtaposition of forms (fiction-nonfiction), stances (straight-ironic) moods (violent-comic) cultural levels (high-low). . . . It pulls the rug out from itself, displaying an acute self-consciousness about the work's constructed nature. It takes pleasure in the play of surfaces, and derides the search for depth as mere nostalgia.[3]

Will this passage be readily understood by the casual reader? That is not likely. For one thing, this description obviously suffers from the writing sin of *anthropomorphism* (attributing human qualities and activities, such as "relishing," being "self-conscious," and "taking pleasure," to an inanimate and abstract idea—postmodernism). Whatever postmodernism is, it does not have such human qualities and experiences. But aside from that, the definition does appear to illustrate the point that scholars in this tradition sometimes fail to make their ideas entirely clear. Perhaps there are meanings in the passage that outsiders just can't seem to grasp. Or, as some faultfinders suggest, such obscure language may be just a convenient cover for murky and weak ideas.

Whatever the answer to the above issue, criticism of various features of contemporary culture should not be rejected out of hand just because they are expressed awkwardly. It is beyond dispute that cultural criticism has produced a body of writings that has triggered lively debates, close inspection of contemporary culture identification of practices, and conditions that warrant thoughtful consideration—but not many proposals for useful reorganization of society to correct the problems.

An Ideological Epistemology

We noted earlier that the assumptions used and the conclusions reached by cultural critics are derived from *ideological* rather than empirical sources. What this implies is that, for those who practice cultural criticism, the premises from which they reason appear to them to be *truths that are self-evident*. More specifically, this means that the basic propositions accepted by the majority of cultural critics have not been induced from a body of research findings obtained from empirical observation and testing in the world of research.[4] Moreover, the conclusions that they reach—reasoning from those *a priori* premises—are also seen by such critics as *truths* that require no additional empirical verification. In this sense, the epistemology of cultural criticism is obviously quite different from that used in developing theories through a scientific strategy and then assessing their validity by using an empirical research methodology.

A PRIORI TRUTHS AS A BASIS FOR EXPLANATION. But is this a serious deficiency? Perhaps. Perhaps not. It can be noted that, in the search for valid knowledge over the centuries, this dependence on *a priori* truths, accepted as self-evident, has at times been a common epistemological strategy. For example, the devout Christian has never needed scientific research to support his or her commitment to the proposition that God created humankind in His own image—along with the heavens and earth and all the living creatures of the world. For Christians, that self-evident truth has been revealed in sacred documents and teachings. Such propositions require no scientific studies—only an act of faith—to validate them. It was this difference in epistemologies that led to the conflict between science and religion, such as those surrounding the works of Charles Darwin.

This does not imply that cultural criticism has a religious base. Quite the contrary: The cultural critic accepts a number of specific assumptions provided in the secular writings of charismatic intellectuals. These are taken as "givens" that need no empirical verification. As this chapter will explain in later sections, one very important source of such *a priori* assumptions is the writings of Karl Marx, along with a number of more recent interpreters and extenders of his analyses. The essential point here is that these propositions, for those who are cultural critics, need no empirical verification to be accepted as true.

THE *A PRIORI* ASSUMPTIONS OF SCIENCE. A second essential point that needs to be made here is that discussing this feature of the epistemology of cultural critics is not intended as a criticism. All who seek knowledge begin with *some set of* a priori *assumptions*. For example, those who demand a scientific epistemology as a basis for understanding the human condition *accept the proposition* that the most valid way of obtaining reliable knowledge is by gathering and analyzing empirical evidence concerning whatever is under study. Science begins with an accepted conviction *(an* a priori *truth)* that the world of phenomena is an *orderly* one. A second conviction is that the orderly arrangements among whatever is under investigation can be *identified and understood*. Still a third is a commitment to the proposition that *empirical observation* (via some form of sensory input) is the accepted way of assembling data.

Using those *(a priori)* postulates of science, however, is only one way of analyzing individual and social behavior. One can begin with alternatives and then reason to conclusions. Therefore, it is not the intention of this chapter to maintain that cultural criticism is less worthy than scientific investigation because it is based on different *a priori* assumptions or that ideological-based interpretations are without merit. Indeed, cultural criticism can provide provocative interpretations and challenging conclusions that can raise serious questions about the nature of social reality, including the process and effects of mass communications.

THE INTELLECTUAL ORIGINS OF CONTEMPORARY CULTURAL CRITICISM

The second general background consideration required to understand cultural criticism, and eventually how and why it concerns mass communication and the mass media, is to look closely at its *intellectual foundations or origins*. It is those origins that reveal the nature of the *a priori* truths that are accepted as premises from which conclusions can be reached by those practicing cultural criticism. Today, there is a very lengthy list of scholars, intellectuals, analysts, and writers who have contributed to the body of information developed within this perspective. It would be impossible in a brief chapter to do justice to this immense body of writings by attempting to summarize the works of all of them. Instead, the focus will be on the *early* origins of cultural criticism, its foundations—but ones that retain their significance today.

Karl Marx as Cultural Critic

It is not difficult to make the case that Karl Marx was one of the most notable cultural critics of all time—and perhaps the most influential of the last two centuries. Indeed, his ideas literally changed the world, and his influence is still with us. It is true, however, that in one sense his influence has declined. Today, Marxism (there is that "ism" again) is no longer a political philosophy that provides the central ideas for truly powerful systems of government.

Nevertheless, contemporary cultural criticism is in one way or another still based on the conclusions and interpretations of the problems of nineteenth-century industrial society that Marx set forth in his writings. Others have added to the body of "givens" initially established by Marx. Over the nearly century and a half since Marx first published his *Das Kapital* (1867), a host of additional intellectuals, interpreters, and writers have re-examined, reinterpreted, elaborated on, and extended his basic ideas. This extensive body of writings makes up today what constitutes the intellectual activity, basic assumptions, and evaluative pronouncements of cultural criticism.

Thus, current scholars who engage in such criticism have clearly gone beyond the foundation that Marx provided. Nevertheless, their intellectual perspective still reflects his central ideas. In spite of the additions to and extension of Marxism in various intellectual spheres, then, he remains the dominating figure providing the basic *a priori* assumptions shaping the thinking of the majority of cultural critics.[5] Berger maintains that this is particularly true of those in Europe.[6] They continue to criticize postmodern society, in the Marxian tradition, attacking many disquieting conditions in contemporary capitalistic societies.

Since the ideas of Karl Marx represent such a central point of departure that is easily recognized in the premises, logic, and conclusions of contemporary critical scholars, a very brief review of his ideas is important. Indeed, it would be difficult to understand even the most basic ideas of cultural criticism without a grasp of at least the fundamentals of the interpretations Marx developed concerning early Capitalism.

MARX AND THE NINETEENTH-CENTURY INDUSTRIAL ORDER. It is not difficult to see that, in many ways, Marx wrote in response to two major developments in Western society—the establishment of *factory production* and a commitment to *Capitalism*. Factory production was not new. Water and wind power had been used for some time, in a primitive way, to produce goods with machines. But factories were transformed and hugely expanded beginning in the early 1800s with the application of the steam engine to power their machines. Steam engines were also applied to rail and water modes of transportation—both of which facilitated the movement of raw materials to factories and finished goods to markets.

The other development that prompted Marx to criticize the emerging industrial society was Adam Smith's work *An Inquiry into the Nature and Causes of the Wealth of Nations.* In that classic work, first published in 1776, Smith systematically laid out the principles of Capitalism. Producing goods for markets was not a new idea, but Smith effectively laid out the rules of an impartial economic system based on the use of both labor and machines in the production and distribution of goods for the central purpose of maximizing profits.

As a consequence of these two developments, by the middle of the 1800s, great changes had taken place in England and in other Western countries undergoing the process of industrialization. What was taking place was the development of an entirely new kind of "modern" social order—what Ferdinand Toennies would come to call the *Gesellschaft* (Chapter 6). The urban-industrial society, based on factory production, was replacing the older, more traditional social order (the *Gemeinschaft*), which was based on subsistence agriculture, or on aristocratic land ownership. Marx saw that the changes taking place were creating dreadful conditions, particularly for those who were now selling their labor for wages in the factories. He spoke out vigorously to criticize those conditions and to offer an alternative vision for a more humane society.

INHUMANE CONDITIONS IN THE CAPITALIST SOCIETY.   What was it that Marx saw that led him to be so critical? The answer is the conditions imposed on those who worked in the new industries. The early period of Capitalism was, by today's standards, a truly dreadful one of inhumane conditions for factory workers and their families. By the mid-1800s, the new economic order was well developed. It was not a time characterized by great sympathies for the working class. Workers who had left the land to labor in the new factories were not seen by their employers as complete human beings. Those who owned and controlled the means of production saw them collectively as "assets," an *impersonal resource* to be used in their drive to make profits. "Labor," according to Adam Smith, was a feature of production that was to be "exploited" (that is, used efficiently) in the search for maximum profits. To achieve the highest profits per monetary unit invested, production costs had to be rigorously controlled. This meant that labor was to be "used" efficiently, in the same way a seam of coal or some other raw material was used efficiently as a part of the production process.

A central principle of the capitalistic system was that, above all, labor costs had to be kept *as low as possible* if profits were to be maximized in competitive markets. This meant that workers had to be paid enough so that they did not actually starve and could continue to work—but no more. In addition, their pay had to provide for bare subsistence for their children. Otherwise, there would be no continuing supply of workers. But to raise pay beyond that level for any kind of "humanitarian" consideration was regarded as economic folly—on the grounds that it would reduce profits.

It was not a matter of anyone deliberately trying to be cruel. Capitalism was an *abstract system* with its own unique set of rules. Those who followed those rules were successful; those who ignored them were not. The people who actually owned the new factories were often (absentee) "investors," who played no part in setting the rules. All they cared about was the greatest possible return on the money that they had placed at risk. They had no interest in the introduction of humanitarian concerns or altruistic values into the production process. Limiting labor costs was simply one of those strategies that was necessary so that the highest possible level of profits could be made on whatever was being produced and marketed.

MARX'S VISION OF A NEED FOR NEW TYPE OF SOCIETY.   Karl Marx began as a journalist but was expelled from both Germany and France because of his radical writings. His remaining life was spent in London. By the time Karl Marx sat down in the reading room of the British Museum to write his famous criticisms of Capitalism, the Industrial Revolution was very well developed with all of the conditions for workers described above. He saw firsthand how the workers in the mid-nineteenth century lived so miserably and how their labor contributed to the profits earned by those who owned or controlled the means of production. It was abundantly clear to him that the lives of working people were inhumane. Indeed, there is no doubt that they lived in dreadful conditions. They worked from sunup to sunset, six days a week. If the owners and operators of the factories could have figured out a way to introduce artificial lighting, they might have extended that working day.

To put it mildly, factory workers were poorly paid. Consequently, they were poorly fed, poorly clad, and poorly housed. If they became ill, that was just too bad. Workers who became ill lost their jobs. If that happened, they and their families were in dire straits, to say the least. There were no welfare systems or other provisions to provide for them—only a few religious charities. Without funds to pay for care and with the limited health knowledge of the time, they received little or no medical attention. Illness was common, and life expectancy was short. Even children had to work alongside their parents in the factories just to keep everyone in the family alive.

ADVOCATING A VIOLENT REVOLUTION.   Marx was appalled by these conditions. He tried in every way to speak out against them. It was in this sense that he became one of the most visible and successful cultural critics of all time. Like his more modern counterparts, he brought into his writings a number of terms that he felt were necessary to get his ideas across. In his *Communist Manifesto*, published with Frederick Engels in 1848, he brought new terms into the English language. He used the French term *bourgeosie* to refer to "the class of modern capitalists—owners of the means of social production and employers of wage-labor." Similarly, he used the label *proletariat* to refer to "the class of modern wage-laborers, who having no means of production of their own, are reduced to selling their labor-power in order to live."[7]

But Marx went beyond just criticizing and complaining. The *Communist Manifesto* was a *blueprint for a new society.* It was a "call to arms"—a declaration that there should be a restructuring of society through a violent revolution:

> [The Communists] openly declare that their ends can be attained only by the forcible overthrow of all existing social conditions. Let the ruling classes tremble at a Communist revolution. The proletariats have nothing to lose but their chains. They have a world to win. Workingmen of all countries, unite![8]

In this document, Marx openly advocated a *political revolution* that was, as he saw it, needed to develop his new vision of society. He set forth a detailed design for such a social order. It was to be based on the proposition that people would work and receive benefits "from each according to his abilities and to each according to his needs." Above all, it would be a society in which the owners of the means of production would be pushed aside—violently if need be. The factories and other means would be *collectively owned* by the workers, and all would contribute what they could, and all would share in what was produced.

The Worldwide Spread and Continuing Influence of Marxism

The ideas of Marx seemed very attractive to many of the poor of the world—not only in industrial societies where the labor of workers was "exploited" for profit, but also in agricultural societies where people had long been dominated and used by those who owned the land. His ideas also appealed to many intellectuals and leaders who thought it essential to make a revolution happen to correct the ills of the industrial society. Thus, by the twentieth century, the political and economic theories of Marx played a very prominent role in shaping the world's political events and governing systems. Certainly, in the late Soviet Union, founded on Vladimir Lenin's interpretations, Marx's theories were at center stage, especially during the Russian Revolution of 1918. The rise of the USSR, its part in World War II, and the Cold War that followed were profoundly influential events shaping much of what took place on the world stage during the last half of the 1900s. Similarly, Mao Zedong's interpretations of Marx determined the destiny of China following World War II. The political systems of many smaller and less powerful nations—Cuba, North Korea, and a number of less developed countries—were also shaped by similar political philosophies. Thus, the daily lives and destinies of literally billions of individual human beings were influenced and directed by Marxian interpretations, beliefs, and values. It is little wonder, then, that the concepts, conclusions, values, and beliefs of Marx continue to influence many cultural critics.

For the most part, those societies that were founded on the ideas of Marx have not worked out all that well. Their leaders often had to adopt harsh means to keep their populations in control. Their secret police, repressive measures, enforced conformity, and gulags (prisons) did not uniformly produce happy workers in social orders in which each contributed "according to his ability" and received "according to his needs."

What Marx did not take into account is that human beings are not all the same. Indeed, individually, they are greatly different. Some are motivated by altruism, to be sure. But others are driven by monetary greed. Some are willing to be submissive and work for the benefit of others, but some have a lust for power and seek ways to dominate other people. Some are ambitious, others lazy. Some adhere to the laws and norms; others engage in deviant behavior. And so it goes. If all human beings were alike and were willing to work in a cooperative manner to play a part in developing a fair and supportive society for everyone, the society envisioned by Marx might have worked. In many ways, it was a remarkable vision. Today, however, those Marxist societies that remain tend to be gross parodies of what he envisioned. Most are repressive regimes controlled by force by clever but ruthless individuals who use intimidation to retain their power.

In the early decades of the twentieth century, the ideas of Marx were extended, reinterpreted, and applied to social and political analyses by many scholars who were sympathetic to his basic ideas. Most prominent among these was a group of social analysts at the University of Frankfort, in Germany. An Institute for Social Research was founded at the university in 1923 by Max Horkheimer. It was a Marxist-oriented center (not devoted to empirical research). Horkheimer and others (T. W. Adorno, Erich Fromm, Herbert Marcuse) took up the task of interpreting, within a Marxian perspective, social relations characterizing contemporary capitalist society. It was in many ways this group that founded the contemporary intellectual perspective that came to be known as "critical theory." They focused on criticisms of large corporations, problems for individuals and society brought about by new technologies, and generally the continuing influence of industrialization on degrading the lives of human beings—especially those who are in some way disadvantaged.

THE CULTURAL SUPERSTRUCTURE OF CAPITALISM

Marx was convinced that the economy of a society—essentially its system of production—was its most central feature. It was more important than its political system, because an economy based on either agriculture or industrial production could exist in several kinds of governmental arrangements. It was on the foundation of the *economy*, he maintained, that the society organized its political system to support and complement the means of production. Thus, it was critical, he believed, that the economy be supported by the society's structure of laws and all its other institutionalized cultural activities, such as art, science, and education. Those features of a society's culture must generate and disseminate agreed-upon "truths," constantly supporting the economic means of production. He referred to this organization of norms, beliefs, and values as the *cultural "superstructure"* of a society.

The Need to Support the Status Quo

It was this conviction that led Marx to conclude that the messages and interpretations provided by virtually all features of the cultural superstructure of the capitalist societies were *deliberately designed and controlled* to be supportive of existing political arrangements by those who owned and controlled the means of production. In a stable society, its members must be reasonably accepting of its political arrangements, more or less content with their place in its ranking system, and remain willing to work. To achieve that, all of the teachings of all of its institutions must proclaim the society to be a *desirable* one. Indeed, they must define it not only as an acceptable society but as *the best one possible.* If some of the cultural institutions in a society—say, education and the church—were constantly to criticize and denounce the economic system, the society would not remain stable. People would become discontented and demand change.

The Mass Media as Cultural Superstructure

But how do the mass media fit into this complex picture of *a priori* assumptions, class struggles, revolutions, forms of government, and cultural superstructure? The answer, provided by cultural critics, is that the media play a central role in *fostering the approval and acceptance of people of the existing system of Capitalism.* Keeping people happy with their economic and political system is clearly an important goal for those who remain in control of that system. In contemporary terms, people in a society like that of the United States must believe (1) that their political system—democracy, as practiced in the U.S.—is the best of all possible arrangements and that it provides maximum benefits for its citizens. Similarly, (2) its economic system—Capitalism—must be seen by the rank-and-file as the only reasonable and correct economic order among the alternatives—providing opportunity and rewards for those who work and invest within it.

Among those institutions that generate messages and interpretations about the merits and advantages of contemporary American society, none plays a more prominent role than the mass media. They produce news, instructional information, and entertainment products in the form of popular culture—movies, music, television programming, and so on. In a society like the U.S., it is clear that the themes, plots, depictions, and portrayals that these media present are *supportive of*, and not in opposition to, the existing economic and political systems.

Marx had no idea that mass media, beyond the newspapers of his time, would develop to become an important part of the cultural superstructure of contemporary society. He had no way to anticipate that the content of the media—the news, information, and entertainment that they disseminate—would be an important factor in shaping people's interpretations of their lives. He could not foresee that their *social constructions of reality*—based on the media's depictions of the benefits and the shortcomings of their society's economic and political systems—would be shaped by collateral instruction embedded in the content of media. *But that is precisely the concern of many cultural critics today.* They see the content that the owners and controllers of the media generate as a crucial element shaping the cultural superstructure of society today. The result, they say, is that the lessons embedded in that content are *a means to control the masses.*

But what do the movies, television programs, and other media content provide in the way of collateral instruction providing incidental lessons about the nature of the American society? The fact is, claim the cultural critics, that the messages in the popular culture provided by the media subtly tell the public that: (1) They live in a great society—one that provides them with the freedom to speak out and with a part to play in the political process through their individual votes. (2) It is the best of all possible economic and political systems, with welfare support for those in trouble and with equal opportunities for those who want to try to get ahead and prosper through hard work and rational planning. And (3) it would be the worst kind of folly to replace the system with anything else.

But the facts, say the critics, are quite different. If you are a minority person, the doors of opportunity are not as open to you as they are to others. Your vote may amount to little or even be prevented in subtle ways. And, lacking access to media, your voice is unlikely to be heard at the seats of power. If you are a woman, the "glass ceiling" may block your access to upward mobility in the workplace, and decisions about your body and its reproductive system may be made by older white males. If your sexual preferences are not those of the majority, you may be stigmatized and disadvantaged by ways in which you are labeled and portrayed in the media. Thus, say cultural critics, life in the United States is very good indeed, as long as one is (1) male, (2) white, (3) affluent, (4) educated, and (5) successful. The media will demonstrate in their content that you represent the "ideal American." If you are something else, however, the media will portray you in much less positive terms.

Public Unawareness of the Role of the Media

Most Americans, say cultural critics, have no insights or awareness of the part played by the media as an important element in the cultural superstructure of their society. They have little understanding, say such critics, of how those media constantly disseminate and reinforce favorable and widely accepted ideas about the merits of the American capitalistic system and its military-industrial complex.

It is not that they cannot grasp the principle. For example, most Americans believe fully that people in the totalitarian countries are manipulated by their governments—that their beliefs, attitudes, and values are a product of what those governments have chosen to present to them in newspapers, magazines, films, radio, and television. However, they do not believe that this could happen in the enlightened countries of the West, where there is little or no direct government control over media content. For example, Berger notes that the Soviet Union exercised tight control over culture and the arts (including mass media) to convince citizens that their political and economic system was a very model of the best that could exist:

> The notion that culture and the arts are ideological tools of ruling elites who use them to brainwash the masses is very close to the Stalinist theory known as *zhdanovism*. This theory argued that works of art should be characterized by 'socialist realism'—heroic truck drivers giving apples to rosy-cheeked children, heroic coal miners with rippling muscles working 100 hours a week for the good of the people, and so on. The purpose of art, according to this theory, was to support the Soviet state directly, by showing how wonderful life would be when Communism had been fully realized.[9]

The Media as Eager Volunteers

In spite of the lack of concern or recognition on the part of most Americans, the critics conclude, much the same thing takes place in the United States. The media strongly support the government and the economy. It is true that, at all levels, government is constrained by the First Amendment to the U.S. Constitution and cannot directly censor the press or insist that the entertainment industry tailor its offerings to support the *status quo*. Nevertheless, the critics maintain, the press and entertainment industries *voluntarily* act in concert to promote and reinforce public beliefs that life in the United States is *special*—with freedom, fairness, open opportunities, and political equality for all. By any criteria, however, the critics point out, that is not the case.

But why, one may ask, would the media do this voluntarily? The answer, say the cultural critics, is that *it is in their best interests to do so.* Those who own and control the media have huge advantages for profit within the economic and political structure of the American society. They want to keep it that way. Millions can be made on a single movie. Profits from newspapers are greater than an investor can earn on almost any enterprise—other than the illegal drug trade, a chain of houses of prostitution, or selling swampland for home sites in Florida. Other media, while competitive, are similarly earners of significant profits. In recent decades, consolidation of ownership among major media companies has produced great economic empires that make the profits of the robber barons of the 1800s look like those of kids operating lemonade stands.

In short, as a part of the cultural superstructure of the United States, the American media voluntarily play a key role in *supporting the status quo of the political system and economy.* It is an effective way to protect their power and profits. To attack the existing arrangements of government or instill discontent with existing economic arrangements would be counterproductive. Such acts would reduce opportunities to make maximum profits for those who own and control the media. Thus, there is no need for government bureaus of censorship, regulating newspapers and dictating to movie studios, radio stations, or television stations who might not send out favorable views of American society. The media are quite eager, the cultural critics say, to do that on their own.

It is not an easy task to bring together the complex ideas that have been discussed in this chapter into a propositional list. Nevertheless, to try to provide an overview of this complex body of scholarship, it is important to make such an effort. As has been indicated, many of the ideas, analyses, commentaries, and criticisms of these scholars have been written in terms whose meanings may not be clear to everyone, and their writing style can often seem difficult to penetrate. Reducing their major assumptions and conclusions to a brief set of propositions, therefore, is a risky endeavor at best.

The focus here is not on cultural criticism broadly. That is far too large a body of writing to try to pull together. The assumptions set forth below are mainly relevant to criticism of the *mass media and their content.* In general, then, the major propositions and conclusions of cultural criticism, focusing on the mass media, their content, and their influences are these:

THE BASIC PROPOSITIONS OF CULTURAL CRITICISM OF THE MEDIA

1. Cultural criticism is a broad activity conducted by a variety of scholars who use many criteria to call attention to *numerous flaws* they believe exist in postmodern societies, including their systems of mass communication.

2. The assumptions about human nature and the social order that they use as premises for reasoning to the conclusions they reach are derived from *ideological sources*—that is, *a priori* conceptions of truth, as opposed to empirical observations made within the rules of science.

3. A major source of their *a priori* assumptions concerning the nature of postmodern societies, and the part played by their media, is based in large part on the nineteenth-century conclusions of *Karl Marx,* but in many cases these have been modified by his later interpreters.

4. An important assumption originally set forth by Marx is that the economy of a society is the foundation on which its other features rest and that a *cultural superstructure* (which includes its media) supports and reinforces beliefs by the masses in the necessity and superiority of that economy.

5. In postmodern societies, with postindustrial capitalist economies, the mass media play *a central part* in supplying audiences with a range of content intended to convince them of the positive features of established political and economic arrangements.

6. **Therefore,** those who control the media in postmodern societies *voluntarily shape mass communication content* (news, entertainment, and other information) so that it will protect their enterprises and power and maximize their profits, in the classical tradition of Capitalism.

Notes and References

1. For example, for a concern with changing patterns of hostility toward blacks in American society promoted by televised news reports, see Robert M. Entman, "Modern Racism and the Images of Blacks in Local Television News," *Critical Studies in Mass Communication,* 7, 4, December 1990, pp. 332–345.

2. Arthur Asa Berger, *Cultural Criticism: A Primer of Key Concepts* (Thousand Oaks, CA: Sage Publications, 1995), p. 2.

3. Todd Gitlin, "Postmodernism Defined, at Last!" *Utne Reader,* July/August, 1989, p. 56.

4. For an informative essay on some of the nonscientific methods of analysis used in cultural criticism, see Horace M. Newcomb, "On the Dialogic Aspects of Mass Communication," in Robert K. Avery and David Eason eds., *Critical Perspectives on Media and Society,* (New York: The Guilford Press, 1991), pp. 69–87.

5. Newcomb points out that "Among the most important and successful [critical] studies are those based in Marxist theory." *Ibid.* p. 70.

6. Arthur Asa Berger, *Op. Cit.,* p. 41.

7. Karl Marx and Frederick Engels, *The Communist Manifesto* (Chicago: Charles H. Kerr & Company, 1947), p. 12. First published in German in 1848 and in English in 1850.

8. *Ibid.* p. 60.

9. Arthur Asa Berger, *Op. Cit.,* p. 45.

CHAPTER **22**

Cultural Imperialism Theory

Entertainment products that are popular in the United States are distributed throughout the world. Even in tightly controlled countries, where religious and other strong leaders frown on such behavior, people regularly listen to American popular music, hear news from the United States, see American films, and view television programs produced in the U.S. A major reason is that such countries lack the facilities needed to produce media entertainment content (movies, TV programming, etc.). But the local countries clearly do have the technologies to *transmit* such media content to their populations—and those people want it. Therefore, those countries must *import* what their audiences consume—and most of it comes from the U.S.

The forms of entertainment that such people attend to often depict goods, conduct, ideas, and general ways of life that are very different from those that exist in the receiving countries. Some of those in charge of the media in those countries receive these popular culture and other media products warmly; others denounce them and see them as a form of "cultural pollution."

In the popular entertainment products that move from the United States to people in other societies, various versions and features of American life and culture are shown. Media depictions inevitably include American political concepts, male-female and parent-child relationships, household appliances, clothing, hairstyles, use of alcohol, fast foods, and even slang expressions. As these are encountered by audiences in other countries, they often offer alternatives to the traditional beliefs, practices, and goods of the receiving societies. For many in those societies, these may seem attractive. That is, these depictions can pose *models* for cultural changes that the receivers may wish to accept or acquire. In fact, as a huge body of research from a variety of fields has documented, many forms and features of American culture have become adopted in countries outside the U.S. The same can also be true of media content originating in other developed societies, such as in Western Europe. In the present chapter, however, the focus is on the United States and elements of its culture that may be seen as desirable by populations in other types of societies.

But what is this process by which people in one society adopt ideas, forms of behavior, and material items from another? What brings it about? As discussed in Chapter 18 (on the Adoption of Innovation Theory) there is little doubt that change occurs in all societies as people invent new cultural artifacts or practices, or acquire them from other societies. That has been true since prehistoric times. In recent years, however, the mass media appear to play a major part in the process by bringing new items and forms of culture to people's attention. That seems particularly true among the less developed societies ("developing" societies, in more politically correct terms). Their populations often adopt many items and practices that have not been a part of their traditional ways of life. Those changes may be trivial, such as influencing a person's musical preference, or they may be profound, as when a population sees media depictions and develops a desire to change its religion, political system, or even overall lifestyle.

In terms of this role of the mass media, there are two very different explanations that can account for the wide adoption of elements encountered in entertainment products that are produced in the United States and then distributed worldwide to audiences around the globe. One explanation is that this is simply a contemporary form of *cultural diffusion*. As was explained in Chapter 18, this process has long been studied by anthropologists. It focuses on the spread of cultural items from one society to another—a process that has been going on since the dawn of human existence (again, see Chapter 18). As noted earlier, here is how it works: People in one society come into contact with people from another. People in one society see some cultural artifact or practice in the other society that seems desirable. They then bring that item or practice into their own society, and a few begin using it. In time it is adopted widely by the majority of their people to become a part of their culture. In that way, cultural items "diffuse" from one society to another. Thus, the process of intergroup cultural diffusion is a relatively simple explanation of social and cultural change. People in one society have something attractive; people in another society want it, and they adopt it—and both have played a part.

A more complex alternative to the diffusion explanation of social and cultural change is *Cultural Imperialism Theory*. Here, people in one society are seen as more developed and advanced, and consequently more economically powerful, than those of certain others. The people in a powerful society, and especially its leaders, are said to have a desire to exercise *hegemony* over the less developed people—that is, to dominate them in various ways. Presumably, to do this, they deliberately set about to produce and export products—in particular, media entertainment products—that will be seen as desirable by those whom they want to influence. Because of the process of collateral instruction (Chapter 23), such exported products are capable of changing ideas, values, and lifestyles among those who receive them in ways wanted by those in the dominant society. The receiving society does not produce these products—or really need them—but in a sense, some say, they are "forced" on them by the producing society (read U.S.) through clever marketing or in other sneaky and subtle ways. Thus, the changes brought about enable the exporting powerful society to exercise *hegemony* over the less powerful receivers.

The basic postulates (*a priori* assumptions) of the cultural imperialism explanation of social and cultural change have been derived by scholars (who take this view as correct) from the political and economic theories of Karl Marx. As was explained in the previous chapter (Critical Cultural Theory), one of his most fundamental conclusions was that, in a capitalistic economic system, a limited number of powerful owners and managers of the means of production *exploit* (that is, make use of) workers as a means to maximize profits. Profits in such a system are the ultimate goal, and other features of the culture are shaped to assist in their achievement. Thus, Marx maintained, bodies of law, education, and even religion and art (a cultural superstructure) are developed in such ways that they serve the purposes of the powerful.[1] As was explained, these ideas have been applied to those who own and control the mass media and who produce and distribute their products for profit. Cultural imperialism theory, then, is a complex approach used by some scholars to explain the use of American films, TV programming, and other media content worldwide by the U.S. in order *to gain power and exercise hegemony over other people*.

In the sections that follow, two alternative ways to describe and explain the worldwide distribution and use of American entertainment products disseminated by mass media will be discussed. However, an important question must be addressed first. That is, has such a flow of cultural items actually taken place? Specifically, have movies, television programs, popular music recordings, and other entertainment products produced in the United States come to be commonly used and adopted by people in developing countries? This has been indicated in previous chapters, but if so, how is it that they have become available to so many people around the world? If this is indeed the case, a later question will be this: What has been the influence and effects of this flow?

AMERICAN POPULAR CULTURE BECOMES GLOBAL

As has been noted in earlier chapters, worldwide distribution of American popular entertainment products actually started long ago. Early in the 1900s, the dissemination of American popular music began throughout many parts of the globe. First it was ragtime, followed by jazz, then swing, rock, and so on. The same was true of early films. There were several factors that accounted for these early starts. For one thing, much of the technology that made contemporary mass communication possible was initially developed in the United States. That includes the phonograph, photography, consumer electricity, the practical motion picture camera and projector, flexible roll film, scheduled radio programming, televison, cable systems, satellite delivery, and even the telephone and many features of the Internet. Other technically advanced countries played a part, of course, but the most significant source of such innovations was the United States.

The Early Distribution of American Movies

Early in the 1900s, as has been discussed in chapter 20, a remarkable new medium, motion pictures, was rapidly becoming a source of popular entertainment in the United States. As the century began, Thomas Edison and his associates had developed a practical technology for producing and exhibiting pictures that seemed to move. Fledgling studios in Europe were also beginning to produce movies, but the new industry was especially successful in the U.S. By 1910, some 10,000 primitive theaters (nickelodeons) in American cities were bringing in $90 million a year in box office ticket sales. Going to the movies was cheap and great fun. An export market was quickly established to send them to other countries where people wanted to see them. This was highly successful because in most of those countries there were no production facilities whatsoever.

Then came World War I. It began in 1914, and it disrupted almost everything in Europe. Motion picture studios producing popular films were shut down as both the Central Powers and the opposing Allies concentrated on their war efforts. Their workers went to the armed forces and in many cases their materials and cameras were used in other ways. Less developed countries still had few or no movie industries. The U.S. did not enter the war until 1917, and its movie makers remained in full production. Indeed, Europe's preoccupation with the war left a *vacuum* in world distribution of films. That vacuum was quickly filled by American producers and distributors.

After the war was concluded, well-established systems for marketing American motion pictures worldwide remained in place and expanded steadily. By then, Hollywood studios had become the dominant producers of this form of entertainment product, and they also controlled global distribution. As the film industries recovered in other Western nations, their products were added, but American films had already established the business and financial systems that enabled them to continue to dominate foreign markets. In many ways that remains the situation even today. No wonder, then, that people in developing societies continue to see American films. When television was added, a parallel system of exporting TV content was developed. It served those countries that had broadcasting capacities but limited or no content production facilities. Once again, entertainment media content was imported mainly from the United States.

The Global Reach of American Popular Music

Another American entertainment product that quickly spread throughout the world—and continues to spread—is popular music. As noted, it began in the U.S. with ragtime. It was the first form of popular music (as opposed to folk, religious, classical, and traditional) to capture the attention of large numbers of Americans, both young and old. Ragtime had an exciting shady connotation because it had started in what were then delicately called "sporting houses." In the late 1800s, these houses of prostitution were common in ports up and down the Mississippi River. In such establishments, seamy pleasures were provided for men working on the docks and on boats—men who had money jingling in their pockets. There was a concentration of such houses in New Orleans, the great port city that transhipped the products of mid-America and the South to far-off places in the world.

To entertain the customers in the sporting houses, there was more than the purchased embraces of young ladies. Since, at the time, there were no record players or juke boxes, each house had a piano played who played catchy tunes for the customers, who drank whisky before and after receiving the other services. These piano players were mainly talented African Americans who made use of the rhythms and folk music of the poor black people among whom they had been raised. Using that musical background, they developed a new style. As its unique beat became standardized, the music came to be called "ragtime." By the beginning of the 1900s, it had swept the nation in the form of sheet music for the home piano (there were few record machines or other ways for families to hear it). Tunes such as Scott Joplin's *Maple Leaf Rag* led the way, and soon others were being pounded out on pianos in the homes of white middle-class Americans—who probably did not even suspect where the music had originated.[2]

Within a decade or so, people tired of ragtime. But shortly after World War I was over (in 1918) and the 1920s began, a new form of popular music once again swept northward from New Orleans. This time it was a group of young white musicians who originated it. They called it "Dixieland Jazz." By any standard, it was strange. It had a very fast beat, with each of the instruments seeming to go off on its own—but with a combined "syncopated" sound bringing it together in a way that was very catchy and exciting.[3] Jazz quickly spread from its origins in New Orleans to New York, where it was offered as an attraction in fancy night clubs. Within a decade, it had swept the nation, and in virtually every town and city young people danced to its fast beat. Older generations deplored it and proclaimed that it was morally insidious. Public leaders denounced it, calling it a growing menace to the purity of young women.

A major appeal of jazz, and the many forms of popular music that followed it, was that it was "modern." As such, it had an inherent appeal to youth. From their perspective, it represented a way to cast off the restraining rules of the older generation and escape into a new personal freedom. As "new things" arrived—cigarettes early on, lipstick, then prohibited substances, new words, blue jeans, bikinis and other clothing, bodily adornments, new dance steps, male-female freedoms, or even more democratic parent-child relationships (and so on almost endlessly)—the young were eager to adopt them. Among youth such items or practices are perceived as ways in which they can express their freedom and escape from the controlling bonds of tradition.

Thus, "new things" are an adventure—a means of going beyond what parents or controlling others try to impose. They allow an expression of individuality as well as independence. Each generation invents new terms for such things, such as "in," "hot," "neat," "hip," "with it," and "cool." These labels identify which things qualify one as *modern* and *emancipated* in this sense. Peers who lag behind in adopting the new things are defined as "weird," "nerds," geeks, "dweebs," or by other less-than-flattering labels and are excluded from in-groups that see themselves as superior.

The mass media play a key role in depicting and disseminating "new things" that have the quality of being "modern." That was true of Dixieland Jazz as the 1920s began. Young sophisticates in New York, Paris, and Rome enthusiastically danced to its beat. From there it disseminated outward until youth in towns and cities in far-off places were doing the same—much to the despair of their elders. The same was true of later versions of popular music—from swing, boogie-woogie, and the twist, to hip-hop and all the rest.

The media have delivered many other modern things—even lifestyles—through their enticing depictions. For example, a young woman from Taiwan explained to the authors that she regularly attended American-produced films when she was in high school in her country. Taiwan has no extensive or well-developed movie production system, and their cinemas regularly exhibit American films. She also regularly viewed television programming of the kind popular in the U.S. on her family's TV set. Shortly after her arrival in the United States, she reported the following as influences on her life brought about by seeing depictions of American family life in movies and television sitcoms.

> For me, who was leading a controlled and regulated life in high school, America represented absolute freedom. Freedom was applied to everything. It appeared that living in the U.S. fit the true definition of freedom itself, with no restrictions existing there. I guess the most enviable thing was the freedom of teenagers, like me. They seemed to do whatever they wanted, not caring about the rules or opinions of their parents or teachers. It was a breathtaking idea, to be free from the tight controls constantly imposed on me, in what I said, the way I said it, what I wore, where and when I went, with whom, and so on.[4]

It may be a search for individual independence and freedom, then, that serves as a major motivation for youth who adopt, or want to adopt, "modern" ways and things that they see depicted in American entertainment products.

The Role of Technology

Having the necessary technology to make use of a cultural innovation is a prerequisite. For example, as jazz spread around the world, advances in recording technology were an important factor. The swift diffusion of this form of popular music could not have taken place if recordings had not been marketed for the recently developed windup Victrola. With that technology in place, however, it caught the fancy of young people in many countries in Europe, Latin America, and even Asia.

To be seen as modern in the 1920s, one had to dance to jazz. Thus, within a decade, this form of American popular culture had diffused worldwide. Later, when home radio developed, it became still another medium by which popular music spread to be adopted by young people in many parts of the globe. Then, as even newer forms of popular music appeared, they also diffused to many other countries.

The worldwide dissemination of popular entertainment products produced in the United States continued with the arrival of television. The United States was a frontrunner in the development of this technology. Available in the 1940s, but held back by World War II, the adoption of home TV sets took place rapidly during the 1950s. By 1960, the vast majority of American households had a set. By 1980, only in the most remote places was there no TV (Fiji finally caught up in the early 1990s). Once sets were acquired, and as the technology of video recording of broadcasts matured, hundreds of situation comedies, game shows, cop-and-crook dramas, children's shows, soap operas, and other forms of television fare were stored on studio VTR tape. These were ready and waiting in the vaults of television producers in the U.S. until markets developed overseas. As noted above, these were added to the entertainment products fed into those foreign markets where they could easily be rebroadcast to audiences with receivers. This was especially convenient in less developed societies that wanted to offer television programming to their populations but lagged far behind in production facilities.

Other new technologies played a key role in the spread of American products. The arrival and wide adoption of the VCR for home use in the 1980s, and later DVDs and cable, enhanced ways in which such programming (as well as movies) could be viewed in peoples' homes. The distribution of programming by satellite transmission—foregoing the need for a wired infrastructure in less developed nations—added another dimension. People in remote areas can now receive an elaborate menu of news, movies, and television entertainment originating in the U.S. directly in their homes, just as easily as people anywhere else.

Multinational Corporations Produce and Market Entertainment Products

With the necessary technology in place by which people could use the various forms of mass-communicated popular entertainment, it was also necessary to make the products available to them—that is, to provide ways for them to purchase, rent, or otherwise view them in one form or another. In some countries, this is the role of government—in the sense that they own and control broadcast facilities and even motion picture theaters. In such settings, bureaucrats decide who sees or hears what. Some such countries produce their own films and television content, but most do not. A few have native popular music stars, but most do not. Where local facilities are lacking or limited, those who control media in tightly regulated countries are dependent on Western—and especially American—products. They have to have some sort of content to show on their TV systems and in their cinemas. Their people demand it. The best that they can do is to preview what is transmitted and censor those that they do not want their populations to see or hear. A few do that—most do not.

In other, less tightly controlled countries, private enterprise provides the services. But, whatever the political and economic basis of the infrastructure, it was the coming together of the technology—the production and the marketing of movies, TV programs, and recordings that completed the link between producers and consumers of American popular culture.

Today, radio and television programming (broadcast and cable), movies, popular music, along with newspapers, books, magazines, and even theme parks are produced and distributed globally by a small number of mass media conglomerates.

> Over the last decade, much of the world's media business has been swallowed up by seven giant global companies—AOL Time Warner, Disney, News Corporation, Viacom, Sony, Bertelsman and Vivendi. Four are American, one is Japanese and one is French.[5]

While not all of these multinationals are American-owned, virtually all produce their entertainment content in the United States. Hollywood is still the center of the movie industry, while New York is where most television entertainment programming is produced. Most of what these media portray depicts life in the United States.

In the countries receiving these exports, a number of critics of the ideas and depictions of alternative ways of life these conglomerates bring to their society attribute them to a *government-industry conspiracy* on the part of the United States. The fact is, however, that these are global private enterprises that are independent of links to any government. By no means are they dedicated to a mission of deliberately spreading American culture across the globe. Their goal is simple and straightforward. They want to *maximize their profits*—and the fact is that they are indeed enormously profitable. One reason is this: Once the costs of making a movie, a TV series, or any other form of media content has been recovered—say, in the U.S.—there are no further production costs and only minor costs involved in distributing it to eager customers and audiences around the world. The profits derived from such extended distribution go directly to the bottom line. If they can get five million people in the U.S. to see a movie, they make a profit and production costs are paid. Then, if they can get five hundred million people to see it in other countries, even if only a modest sum is made on a single person, their profits truly soar. Moreover, the distributers and exhibitors in those countries also make profits by airing or showing the content on their systems. Thus, everybody wins—except for the ultimate receiving audiences, who may be seriously misled by what they see, read, and hear.

There are several other media that also operate worldwide. With mergers and consolidations increasingly common, the situation changes quickly over time. Media scholar David Demers has identified what he calls the "global media dozen"—the twelve largest media corporations.[6] These organizations market their products in countries of all kinds, regardless of their internal political systems. According to Demers, these dozen corporations collectively sell an almost unimaginable $137.4 billion dollars worth of movies, recordings, TV programs, and other media content to billions of consumers and audiences every year.

Why have these organizations merged and consolidated to become so large? The answer to that question is not difficult. These are *private enterprise systems operating within the rules of capitalism and dedicated to making a profit.* They are neither owned nor controlled by government in any sense differently than is the case with any other privately held, profit-oriented businesses. The reasons for which countless mergers have produced these giants lies in the basic nature of capitalism. Once that economic system is in place, certain inevitable results follow. The fundamentals were set forth by Adam Smith in his classic work.[7] As he indicated, the most basic rule of capitalism, then or now, is to maximize profits. This means minimizing costs and producing as efficiently as possible. But an important factor that can limit profits is *competition.* Competition works for the consumer but against the producer. If competitors are making the same product, then prices must be lowered to maintain market share. That helps consumers. However, profits decrease as competition increases.

There are only a limited number of ways to avoid this dilemma. One is illegal cooperative arrangements to control prices—a dangerous way to go. However, by *merging* with the competition, larger amounts of raw materials can be bought from producers for less and administrative costs can be reduced. Greater efficiency is achieved with fewer labor and production costs. Thus, consolidation can correspondingly increase profits. The answer to why they have become so large, then, is that they achieve *economies of scale*—which is the same economic principle that brought supermarket chains, fast food franchises, and home repair giants to replace mom-and-pop grocery stories, family hamburger stands, and local hardware stores. Only if competition is eliminated altogether and a monopoly is achieved (where prices can be raised at will) does this harm the consumer.

It is because of these fundamentals of capitalism, then, that consolidation has taken place in media industries ever since chain ownership of newspapers began in the 1800s. All during the 1900s, publishers, broadcasters, and movie producers came together in increasingly large corporations and conglomerates. While critics worry about the consequences in terms of a few being able to control the thoughts of many, the process of consolidation is likely to continue.[8] If it does, it will eventually produce a smaller and smaller number of multinational corporations that dominate all forms of media content shown everywhere on the globe. That thought may be disquieting to many.

Obviously, the early role of the United States in the realm of producing and exporting mass-communicated popular entertainment products did not take place overnight. It was the result of a host of historical, political, cultural, and economic developments and events that came together. These included an early worldwide taste for popular music; developments in technology, such as the success of sound recordings for home use; the adoption of motion pictures and home radio; and finally the spread of television—with its insatiable need for a continuing flow of content that people find interesting and entertaining.

As these forms of entertainment became increasingly available, and as people around the world acquired the means of using them, it is scarcely surprising that companies, corporations, and other kinds of organizations were created to market such products to those willing to pay for them. It was these simple economic facts, more than any kind of "political conspiracy" among those seeking power, that brought into place the existing systems of production and distribution of American entertainment and other media products. Profits, then, are the economic engine that now brings mass communication content produced in the United States to people in Iran, Bangladesh, Nigeria, Bahrain, Fiji, and virtually everywhere else on the planet via the highly consolidated marketing systems that are now in place.

The question is, how can this worldwide flow of cultural items from media conglomerates in powerful countries to many less developed countries be interpreted? As mentioned earlier, one way is to view the process within the classic "it-takes-two-to-tango" framework of cultural diffusion—a process that has resulted in social and cultural changes through the intergroup adoption of innovations from other societies since prehistoric times. Another way to interpret it is more complex—to see it as a result of a deliberate "imperialistic" effort by one dominant country, namely the United States, to exercise *hegemony* over the less powerful. That interpretation requires a set of assumptions concerning "exploitation" that essentially are drawn from Marxian theory. In the sections that follow, both of these explanations will be set forth.

THE PROCESS OF CULTURAL DIFFUSION

It should not be surprising that items of culture that are invented and developed in a country that has a *high rate of innovation* will often spread to others that have very low rates. There are, in fact, great differences among countries in the degree to which they develop innovations. In that respect, the United States is very clearly the most innovative country in the world. To illustrate, the U.S. Patent Office currently issues more than 100,000 patents per year. Some go to citizens of other countries (who seek the significant protections of a U.S. patent). Others go to Americans who have developed something new. The dominant role of the United States as innovator can be seen in the fact that in any recent year about 60 percent of all patents granted have gone to individuals and corporations in the United States. All other countries in the world combined were awarded the remaining 40 percent. The only country that even comes close to the U.S. in this index of innovativeness is Japan, with about 20 percent of all such patents year after year.[9] What this implies is that there will be a flow of items from the U.S. to other countries that is far greater than the reverse, simply because more new items are available to be adopted by those receiving populations.

We noted earlier that a somewhat similar situation exists in the world of entertainment. For many decades, the U.S. has by far exceeded any other country in the production of motion pictures, television programming, popular music, and other items of popular culture. On those grounds alone, without any consideration of political issues such as hegemony, it is to be expected that people who want entertainment products and have difficulty in obtaining them from producers in their own countries (that have low rates of such innovation) will import many items of popular culture from the United States. The fact is that they do so in abundance.

An important question is this: How can movies, television programs, and other entertainment products produced in a Western country, such as the United States, spread so easily to, and be accepted in, so many types of countries in the world—countries that have very different traditions, languages, religions, and customary practices? The process by which items developed in one culture are imported and accepted by people who have a very different culture has long been one that has fascinated social scientists. The reason is that it provides an important key to understanding *social and cultural change*. This is because any culture is an accumulation of items that originally were invented internally, plus those that came in as innovations from outside and then were widely adopted by the people of the society to become a part of their way of life.

As cultural items come from outside, change takes place. It is very clear that such *intergroup diffusion* (movement from one society to another) of cultural artifacts and practices has been going on for many centuries before mass media could even be imagined. One of the great debates that developed within that branch of anthropology that studies cultures of prehistoric people concerns the presence of many identical items of culture among many different kinds of people. Early in the history of anthropology, there were two views: One was that each item was *independently invented* by the people who used it. The other view was that many of the artifacts in a particular ancient culture were obtained by *a process of intergroup diffusion*. That is, many items were invented by one people and were passed on to another as the two came into contact. That, specifically, is what cultural diffusion is all about.

Cultural Diffusion in Prehistoric Times

Specific examples of cultural diffusion in truly ancient times are provided by two artifacts that were found to have been possessed by certain prehistoric people. One is *sea shells*, and the other is *amber beads*. Painstaking studies of the living sites of an upper paleolithic people of the central Russian plains were completed by anthropologists over many years.[10] These ancient human beings were hunter-gatherers who lived between 20,000 and 26,000 years before the present. They hunted woolly mammoths, among other animals, on the great plains. They had both winter and summer camps and bases.[11]

These prehistoric people had a number of what anthropologists came to call "exotics," that is, items that were not at all common to their local region. Some, indeed, had to come from very long distances. An excellent example is *sea shells*.[12] Note that the central Russian plains are about as far as one can get from any ocean. Yet many sea shells were found among the living sites of these Stone Age people. There is no way in the world that this can be explained by the theory of independent invention. Such sea shells had to be obtained by a process of trade or some other form of contact with others who possessed them. People living near the sea could easily gather shells, then trade them for other items with nearby people. Those people, in turn, could trade them for items that they wanted from others still farther away. One alternative to the trade explanation might be by assuming that they were items of plunder as one people raided another. But trade is by far the most likely explanation, as there is little evidence of warlike conflict among the paleolithic people of the time. By means of contact and exchange, then, sea shells could travel over enormous distances. It would undoubtedly have been a very slow process, but it is a perfect illustration of the process of cultural diffusion.

Amber beads provide a second example from the same people. These ancient human beings had a number of decorative objects that they used as portable art and personal jewelry, which they made for themselves from locally available material (ivory, bone, etc.). However, they also had amber beads. The significance of amber beads is that there simply is no source of such exotic material anywhere near where they lived. They had to get either the finished beads or the unfinished amber from others—indeed, the only sources were nearly a thousand miles away. Thus, even from very ancient times, there are very clear examples of the movement of items of culture from one people to another that can only be explained by a kind of "it-takes-two-to-tango" theory. Certainly in earlier times, both parties played an essential part in the exchange.

The Diffusion of American Popular Culture Today

A major problem with existing cultural imperialism interpretations is that they view the process of cultural change from only one perspective—a one-sided or "push" interpretation that sees more developed societies "forcing" their products on the hapless populations of less-developed countries. It may certainly be true that those in well-developed countries who produce entertainment products, items of popular culture, consumer goods, or any other kind of material things to make a profit are anxious to penetrate foreign markets. The capitalistic system, stressing the virtue of profits, encourages that strongly. Furthermore, a government that assists in promoting global trade for profit is also devoted to the same goals. Those values are widespread in the industrialized countries. It would not be good government policy to prevent citizens from exporting what they produce (unless it is drugs or children). However, while such producers and their government may not be seen as some sort of evil conspiracy to dominate other people, the idea of a government making it easy for its nation's industries to export products in order to benefit the economy is hardly a radical or even conspiratorial idea.

On closer look, then, one of the major theoretical problems for those devoted to conspiracy theories derived from Marxian postulates is that they overlook the "pull" aspect of the diffusion process. That is, they see what happens within a traditional country that receives the exported products of a more developed one only as "cultural pollution." What is not included in such Marx-based theories is that the populations of the receiving countries—like the ancient hunter-gatherers who had shells and amber beads—may actively *want* and *seek* what the exporters have to offer. The fact is that they often find those products and the ways of life associated with them as attractive, fun, and fulfilling—and the older ways as less desirable. If such is the case, the adoption of innovations from outside the traditional country is as much spurred by eager inhabitants within the receiving society as it is by aggressive outsiders determined to force things on them to achieve cultural imperialism. As one media scholar has recently noted:

> . . . . the 'media imperialism' thesis—at least in those versions that assume the unmediated transmission of ideology from metropolitan centre to peripheral receiver— has come under increasing pressure in recent years, with mounting evidence of its theoretical and empirical inadequacies. One result of a growing skepticism has been the attempt to investigate the actual conditions of reception and consumption of cultural products in the context of popular cultures.[13]

Thus, a "push-pull" interpretation of cross-border transmissions of popular culture has come about through investigations of what happens on the receiving end. What this change in thinking amounts to is similar to what happened when the old Magic Bullet Theory (Chapter 9)— which is a "push" explanation—fell into disrepute in the United States. As a result of empirical investigations of the audience, it was replaced by the general Selected and Limited Influences Theory (Chapter 10)—a "takes-two-to-tango" theory. A similar explanation needs to be made with respect to the diffusion of American popular culture on a global basis. This is the case because it would be naive to assume that audiences in less developed nations are totally *passive*—that they are people incapable of exercising judgments, people without individual preferences and interests, simply absorbing whatever "magic bullets" come their way via mass media.

Magic bullet assumptions about those receiving audiences does them a serious injustice. It is *their* interests and preferences that determine what media content *they* will select and consume from what is available. The Selective and Limited Influences Theory is just as applicable to people in other parts of the globe as it is to individuals in Western societies like the United States. Indeed, it is insulting to those populations to assume that they are mindless dolts on whom ideas and values can be dumped by some sort of conspiracy of American profit-driven corporations supported by a power-hungry U.S. government. Moreover, when local authorities in the less-developed countries decry the diffusion of popular culture to their populations, with claims of deliberate "cultural pollution," "McDonaldization," and "Americanization," they do their own people a serious injustice. In what way is popular culture being "forced" on them? Those people at the receiving end are as essential a part of the process as those at the initiation end. *It does indeed take two to tango.* A "push" theory, based on Marxian and Magic Bullet assumptions, totally fails to take that into account.

An excellent example of this two-sided "push-pull" or "two-to-tango" theory can be seen in the case of Iran. It is a country that is especially (officially) hostile to the United States. It is not a society into which there can be an easy penetration of entertainment products produced in the U.S. or other features of American popular culture. Indeed, there exist solid walls of import regulations that prevent such intrusions. However, as will be explained, the population of Iran is not one made up of mindless robots into which ideas, values, and cultural products can be forced by conspiratorial outsiders. Iranians appear to know what items of popular culture and of other cultural items they want, and they take active steps to obtain them.

What are some of the characteristics of Iran that make it an appropriate example to illustrate the "push-pull" or "two-to-tango" explanation? In summary, the situation is this: Until the late 1970s, Iran was ruled by Mohammed Reza Shah Pahlavi. The Shah had set the country on a course of Westernization. This was resented by many conservative and deeply religious citizens who were strongly committed to the values of Islam. With their support, the Shah was deposed in 1979 in a revolution inspired by Ayatollah Khomeini, a charismatic religious leader with unrelenting hostility to all things Western—and particularly those originating in the United States. As a result of the revolution, the country became the Islamic Republic of Iran, and Shiite clerics took over all forms of political and economic power. Since that time, strong efforts have been made by the mullahs in charge to preserve Islam and the traditional Iranian culture.

To say the least, from the point of view of many Iranians, their efforts have not been an unqualified success. The religious leaders nationalized all industries, banks, and other economic interests. The result was that the economy foundered. Many Iranians now live in poverty. Health care and standards in areas outside major cities are now very low, illiteracy is high, and the country has an enormous foreign debt. Petroleum is its major export, but Iran must import much of its food, machinery, even gasoline, and other necessary goods.

An example of the two-factor basis of social change in this traditional society can be seen in the case of the automobile. Traditional or not, people in Iran need cars. Iranians, like the rest of us, require basic transportation beyond the traditional donkey, horse, and camel. So what is the situation of automobiles in Iran? Importing Western autos was not allowed by the ruling authorities, so to meet the needs of the people, a government-owned factory was developed to produce cars.

The automobiles produced are quite unlike those common in developed societies. The *Pakyan* is a small car based on a 35-year-old British design that was marginal to begin with. According to many in Iran, it has not improved with age. Indeed, it is the subject of many local jokes. For example, "Why does the *Pakyan* come with heated rear windows?" (Answer: to keep your hands warm while pushing it.) Or, "How do you get a *Pakyan* from zero to 60 miles per hour in only 15 seconds?" (Answer: push it off a cliff.)[14] Nevertheless, as noted, in Iran people need transportation, so it sells well.

Even so, cars do not fit in well with the traditional religious values of the mullahs and are accepted by them reluctantly. In particular, automobiles are seen by religious authorities as a menace to the virtue of young people. They are concerned that unmarried couples may drive around in them without proper chaperones. So, any car that appears to be used by youth for romantic activities is suspect, and the ever-vigilant "morals police" are always on the alert.

Compounding the Iranian situation on the "pull" side is age. An older generation can still be enthusiastic about their memories of the 1979 revolution, in which ties to the West—and especially the United States—were cheerfully severed and celebrated when the mullahs took over. However, large numbers of people in Iran have no such memories. Fifty percent are younger than 20, and they appear to lack the religious fervor needed to keep the revolutionary flame vigorously alive. Indeed, many of them look to the West for ideas, products, and entertainment experiences that they see as desirable. For that reason, the rate of adoption of American entertainment and other products is very high.[15] A former Iranian, who is now a professor in the U.S., returned to Iran for a visit during the mid-1990s. He noted the intrusion of Western (and especially American) culture:

> . . . it was quite fascinating for me to experience personally the prevalence of American symbols, media, and products practically everywhere. Even in remote villages, one could easily use the American dollar in lieu of the Iranian currency (Rial) to purchase products. Satellite receiving dishes were on the rooftops of millions of Iranian homes, where families could gather around their [TV sets] and view *Oprah, Donahue, America's Funniest Home Videos, Hard Copy,* and *Growing Pains.* . . . Pepsi Cola and Coca Cola were the most popular soft drinks; Winston and Marlborough [cigarettes] were displayed by peddlers at practically every street corner; movies such as *Dances with Wolves* and *Silence of the Lambs* were circulating on videocassettes; *Pinochio, Mickey Mouse,* and other Disney icons were visible in a variety of formats—from T-shirts, to books, to videos; American pop singers, such as Michael Jackson, Madonna and others (whom I had never heard of) were known to the youth . . .[16]

It is easy to see this situation from the two perspectives noted above: One is that of the conservative religious leaders in the country who deplore this invasion of Western culture and see it as threatening the very way of life and the spiritual values for which they led the revolution. From this perspective, the intrusion of American entertainment products and other features of popular culture is an unwanted and polluting invasion—one that seems designed by evil people in the U.S who have set out to destroy the very culture that they, the clerics, are determined to preserve.

From a different perspective—that of the fifty percent who are younger than twenty—the old ways are not as attractive as the American model. They want the goods, fun, and in some cases even the values that they see portrayed in the movies, in television programs, and in other forms of communication that they receive from outside their borders. They see no vast conspiracy on the part of a foreign government, media-managers, and producers of consumer goods who are determined to control their ideas, their markets, and (eventually) their political system. They just want to drink Coca Cola, wear funny T-shirts, enjoy movies, listen to popular music, and keep out of the hands of the morals police. In fact, if their country were to open up to the importation of automobiles produced in the industrialized societies, the factory that produces the venerable *Pakyan*, with its ancient technology, would go out of business virtually overnight.

Thus, the process that some see as "cultural pollution" is as much generated from *within* the borders of traditional societies, such as Iran, as it is by outside aggressive capitalists working vigorously to promote their products. What is irrelevant, then, is the premise of some "evil conspiracy"—a complex assumption that there exists a mix of a powerful government, working in concert with producers of popular culture and other products, whose goal is to undermine the authority of traditional leaders. Such an idea is simply not needed to explain what is taking place.

A simpler explanation, following the venerable *principle of parsimony*, can suffice. Thus, the old saying that "it takes two to tango" is probably an accurate, if metaphorical, underlying perspective on which a theory of cultural diffusion can rest. That "push-pull" perspective was true of the prehistoric hunter-gatherers of the central Russian plains who willingly acquired sea shells and amber beads from trading partners many thousands of years ago. There is no need to assume that some evil conspiracy was in place at that time, aimed at "cultural pollution" and "hegemony" by getting people to want sea shells and beads. Those ancient receivers found those items interesting and desirable—so they acquired them. The same process can explain what is taking place today in countries like Iran, where people like various items that they encounter from sources outside their country and deliberately and knowingly adopt them.

The Reverse Flow: Cultural Diffusion to the United States

Just as was the case with the ancient people who acquired seashells, there is a constant flow of cultural artifacts, ideas, practices, and other cultural items from the outside into the American culture. Indeed, even the most casual glance at the lifestyles of typical Americans reveals how their daily lives depend on inventions, innovations, and other forms of culture that originated elsewhere. Even the most common items of daily use have been imported at some point in time to become part of the culture: leather, metal, cloth, grains, the wheel, domesticated animals, law, printing, glass, pottery, rugs—the list is almost endless. All have become standard features of American culture. Every time an American eats a taco or a pizza, prepares a sausage for breakfast, or goes to a Japanese, Chinese, or French restaurant, he or she is making use of items that arrived through a process of cultural diffusion.

While these examples entered what is now the American culture at some time in the past, the process continues. For example, a number of young American women now paint various parts of their bodies with henna, a dark red vegetable dye. Some wear a jewel in their nose or have some other part of their anatomy pierced so as to wear a metal ring. These cultural artifacts came into the youth culture only recently. Those familiar with such practices believe that they began when an attractive young woman from India won the title of Miss Universe in the early 1990s. She used a nose jewel as a personal adornment, and much attention was given in the media to that fact at the time. Today, a limited number of movies from India shown in the U.S. are the source of many such items that are adopted by youth in an effort to be "distinctive" or perhaps "modern."

Every year, many cultural artifacts and practices from other countries are adopted by Americans. These include ever-changing women's fashions, children's toys (Pokemon), forms of amusement (karaoke), conceptions of harmonious home decorating (feng shui), furniture designs (chinoiserie), and a long list of others. It would be difficult to identify some conspiracy of government and industry in the countries of origin of these cultural artifacts and products— some coalition that is bent on dominating the people of the United States. The Cultural Diffusion Theory seems adequate to explain how the items made their transition. The complex assumptions of Cultural Imperialism Theory do not seem applicable.

Thus, a major problem with alternative explanations based on assumptions of imperialism is that they view the process of cultural change from only one perspective. They postulate a "push" interpretation that sees more developed societies "forcing" their products on the less developed. It may certainly be true that those who produce entertainment products, items of popular culture, consumer goods, or any other kind of material things to make a profit are anxious to penetrate foreign markets. The capitalistic system, stressing the virtue of profits, encourages that strongly. Furthermore, a government that is designed to promote trade for profit is also devoted to the same goals. It would not be good government policy to prevent citizens from exporting what they produce (again, unless it is drugs or children). However, to go beyond these facts and postulate that producers and their government have formed some sort of unsavory alliance to dominate other people requires very complex assertions that may not be necessary.

Generally speaking, then, Cultural Diffusion Theory can be expressed in the following set of formal propositions:

CULTURAL DIFFUSION THEORY: A FORMAL SUMMARY

1. The people of a particular society invent, develop, and adopt an artifact, a form of behavior, or a belief that for them solves some problem of living in a way better than what they had before.
2. These inventors come into contact and communication with people from a second society—one that lacks that particular item or artifact.
3. Those in the second society who do not have the item observe it and conclude that it could solve a problem for them, or otherwise serve them, in a way better than what they currently have.
4. This creates a desire, need, or determination to obtain the item in question on the part of people in the second society. They take measures to acquire it, and it becomes adopted by members of their population.
5. **Therefore,** in a process of cultural diffusion, the item in question moves from one society to another and, in many cases, through a number of similar transitions to additional societies, where in each case it becomes a part of the adopting society's culture.

Cultural Modification and Resistance to Change

When new items are adopted by a population from outside sources, they can quite obviously modify the host culture. It is this feature of social and cultural change that lies at the heart of accusations of "cultural pollution." Many conservative leaders in societies around the world become bitter about what they see as "Americanization" of their traditional way of life. In France, for example, the arrival of a chain of fast food restaurants specializing in hamburgers was seen as an assault on a culture in which food holds a special place. In French-speaking parts of Canada, even the incorporation of English language words, as in signs on businesses, was seen as threatening. In such countries, special "language police" and censorship policies have been developed to prevent such "pollution."

Many examples can be noted. In China, for example, Santa Claus and his reindeer have become popular in urban areas—much to the distress of some authorities. Most Chinese are not Christians, and Christmas does not have the significance it has elsewhere. Another example can be seen in India, where a problem appeared in New Delhi, on February 14, 2002:

> Gangs of Hindu nationalists accosted couples holding hands, burned Valentine's Day cards, and blocked access to gift shops and restaurants yesterday, trying to keep people from celebrating what they called an invasive Western tradition. As more than 40 police officers stood watching, the nationalists, wearing scarves and headbands in the sacred Hindu color of saffron, blocked tourists, and shoved anti-Valentine's Day handbills at them. Traditional Indian society does not approve of public displays of affection between the sexes, including hand-holding.[17]

There is little doubt that those in other countries who want to preserve their cultural traditions try their best to keep such intrusive practices out. Their fear is that such cultural modification weakens the established way of life, traditional beliefs, and possibly their own control over their populations. Their efforts to freeze their culture in place, however, are probably doomed to failure. Cultural diffusion has been a fact of human existence for a very long time.

In contrast with this "diffusion" explanation is an alternative—a theory of "hegemony"—which we have noted is essentially based on assumptions drawn from the writings of Karl Marx. An important difference between "diffusion" theory and the one based on Marxian postulates is that the latter also incorporates, in an analogous way, the original meaning of the concept of "imperialism." For this reason, that concept needs to be understood in detail because it is such a central part of the alternative theory. The section that follows discusses and explains the nature of the term's original and classic meaning.

THE TRADITIONAL MEANING OF "IMPERIALISM"

The term "imperialism," in its traditional sense, meant the establishment of some measure of political and economic dominance and control by a more powerful country over less powerful people, for purposes of exploitation. The word is derived from "empire" and the power and authority of an "emperor." In its original meaning, imperialism referred to hegemony (dominance) established by *military means,* as aggressive societies conquered other unwilling people in the process of building empires. For example, Rome established a huge empire by using its legions to conquer the less powerful areas in both Europe and Africa. The Romans then made use of them for its own purposes. In some cases, that meant enslaving their inhabitants or using them in other ways as workers. The dominated people also provided the Romans with valued materials and goods very cheaply.

Empire building in that sense began early and continued for many centuries in many parts of the world. Indeed, it continues even today. Spain undertook the process in the 1500s, dominating many indigenous people in the New World. In the 1600s and 1700s, the British and other European powers established worldwide empires of colonies as they pursued mainly economic goals. Such colonies were kept within these empires by military means. In the late 1700s, the British lost control of one set of their colonies that became the United States, even though they sought to stop that loss by using military power. In the 1840s, the United States took over by military means a number of land areas (that are now included in southwestern and western states) following a war with Mexico. Later, it gained other territories (e.g., the Philippines, Cuba, and Puerto Rico) as a result of a war with Spain. Thus, imperialism has long been a concept associated with domination by military force, conquest, and subjugation. In that sense, it has long had a very negative meaning.

Ample grounds for the term's negative meaning can be found in what took place in the twentieth century as empires were established by military might. The Japanese set out in the 1930s and 1940s to establish their "Greater East-Asia Co-Prosperity Sphere." That long name identified a number of subjugated nations in Pacific areas from which the Empire of Japan obtained raw materials and markets for Japanese goods. As did Rome, they also enslaved workers. Some went to their factories to play a part in the production of war materials. Others were enslaved as "comfort women" to provide sexual services to Japanese soldiers. The Germans, during the Nazi era under Hitler, also set out—often in very harsh ways—to establish an empire in Europe to serve what they referred to as the "master race." They enslaved workers to serve in their factories that produced war goods. And, as is well known, they executed millions of those whom they regarded as *untermensch*—people they defined as lesser forms of humanity, such as Jews, Gypsies, and others. The late Soviet Union also dominated by military means a number of countries in various parts of Europe and Asia in order to expand their sphere of political and economic control.

Overall, then, the term "imperialism" has had a very unsavory meaning for a long time, implying force, domination, and often brutal exploitation of victims of conquest by those who have the power to subjugate them. In more recent times, that original and very negative meaning for "imperialism" has found its way into discussions of mass communication. By using the term in an analogous way, a number of contemporary scholars have incorporated it into their interpretation of the flow of entertainment products from the United States (and in some cases other Western societies) to people in less developed parts of the world.

Other scholars feel that this analogous use of the term is inadvisable, even objectionable. That is, labeling the movement of cultural items from one society to another, using the harsh term "imperialism," brings a particular, and very biased, interpretation into the analysis of a process of social exchange. In the minds of some writers, it transforms the meaning of the term from a scientific concept into a politically radical slogan. As one distinguished scholar has put it:

> Like 'development,' 'imperialism' and 'colonialism' are charged terms with different meanings to different people. Perhaps the most stereotyped is imperialism. It is clearly

pejorative, full of political implications and ideological assumptions. So successful has the attack of the Left been on imperialism that admitting to being an imperialist falls in the same category as being a racist or fascist.[18]

Whether one wants to view the process by which one country accepts and makes use of another's media and entertainment products as "cultural diffusion" or as "cultural imperialism," then, depends upon one's political orientations. For those who see the cross-border spread of some item of culture as a process of cultural diffusion, the process is not interpreted as a deliberate means of achieving hegemony. For others, who begin with different underlying assumptions—based on the original meanings of imperialism, plus additional assumptions that are based on postulates drawn from Marx—it is a way in which a powerful society achieves dominance over a hapless population that is less developed.

Non-Military "Imperialisms"

For those who prefer the imperialism interpretation, there are a number of assumptions as to how hegemony is achieved. The use of the media is only one such way that has become possible in relatively recent times. Several other non-military means of achieving domination were used earlier. Conquest by armed force was only a first step. After that, the ideas of the conquered population had to be controlled so as to accept their situation. Those populations had to see their subjugation as an *advantageous situation*, in which the dominating power was providing benefits. For centuries there were two traditional ways in which such an outcome can be shaped by non-military means. One was through *education,* and the other was through *religious conversion.* Both were used effectively by colonial powers. In more recent times, *tourism* has been added to the list.

In more recent years, all of these strategies have come under criticism. Some critics see cultural imperialism as an outcome when educators establish formal systems of education in the dominated societies. Others point to religious groups who send their missionaries to less developed countries to get them to abandon their native beliefs and adopt those of Western powers—a process that has been in place since the voyage of Columbus. Still others note the influences of tourists on social and cultural change within societies where visitors flock.

EDUCATION.   In most modern societies, education is seen as an essential process that benefits both individuals and the society as a whole. For that reason, it is defined as "good." Indeed, when the colonial powers established formal schools for children, and even universities, in the territories that they controlled, responsible people almost everywhere applauded. What a beneficial thing to do—to enlighten youth in less fortunate nations. After all, in the industrial societies, formal schooling is the key that opens the door to advancement.

> Educators, school administrators, and teachers stress the enlightening function of the school; they claim that formal schooling is an important component of a life-time process of education; teaching youth not only an understanding of important phenomena but also the process of learning itself . . . [it is] a key to higher incomes and status, a step toward success in a competitive and success-oriented society . . . For those who are poor, this last function is held to be particularly crucial, for social mobility may mean the difference between lifelong poverty and access to the consumption society.[19]

To object to efforts to lift less fortunate people into a more abundant way of life by providing formal education would seem heartless. However, some scholars claim, formal schooling, designed and provided by controlling powers over those who are being controlled, is, in fact, a strategy by which hegemony can be maintained.:

> Our thesis is that educators, social scientists, and historians have misinterpreted the role of Western schooling in the Third World . . . We argue that far from acting as a liberator, Western formal education came to most countries as a part of imperialist domination. It was consistent with the goals of imperialism: the economic and political control of the people in one country by the dominant class in another. The imperial

powers attempted, through schooling, to train the colonized for roles that suited the colonizer.[20]

Education in dominated countries, then, provided for a class of colonials that were able to manage local governments (established and supervised by the stronger society). They could also serve as managers for local enterprises—mines, farms, and plantations—that were providing raw materials to be exported to the more developed society. Finally, in some societies, they could serve as minor officers in military colonial regiments that served the needs of the predominant society. Looked at from that perspective, formal schooling, designed by colonial masters for conquered societies, may not seem to merit the same level of applause that it appeared to deserve when viewed from other viewpoints. However, labeling those who have reached out to less developed societies in efforts to help educate their populations may not deserve the harsh meanings that are embedded in the term "imperialism."

RELIGION.   Whether Spain, Portugal, and other European powers deliberately used religion as a means to dominate conquered people to extend their hegemony remains a question. The Church at that time was very powerful. In many ways, that power superceded that of existing states, and it held sway over secular monarchs. A case can be made, therefore, that it was the religious leadership, especially Rome, that sought domination—and not the nations that used their military power to conquer others. In any case, religious missionaries were regularly sent to conquered people to convert them to religions that prevailed in Europe. Their native religions were all but wiped out as permanent institutions and churches were quickly established in the new lands.

In more modern times, religious groups from the United States have played a somewhat parallel role. In the Philippines, for example, the Spanish had established Roman Catholicism, beginning in the early 1500s. But following the Spanish-American War in the late 1800s, it was the Americans' turn. In 1898, the American Bible Society, along with a similar group from Britain, began actively reshaping the beliefs and orientations of the indigenous people. They saw their activities as a civilizing mission:

> The Americans set up YMCAs, gave courses and lectures, published magazines, and organized wholesome recreation like volleyball. Mission schools provided an industrial education, aiming to 'save souls' but also to promote social transformation and humanitarian reform. Missionaries [saw themselves] as 'advanced agents of civilisation' trying to end slavery, polygamy, and cannibalism, and cope with—what they saw as—the generally dirty, lazy and immoral Filipinos. Such was "the white man's burden".[21]

In many countries that became colonies, then, religious systems were established following military subjugation. This served to calm those who had been conquered and to bring them to believe that they should abandon their indigenous faiths and reorder their lives around the dictates of the new beliefs. It worked remarkably well, and in those countries that eventually threw off the political domination of European powers, the religious systems they established are still in place.

One may evaluate those efforts to convert native populations to Christianity as undesirable—as "imperialism" in its negative sense. Yet it is unlikely that the missionaries who went to serve in far-off places were agents of governments intent on domination. They undoubtedly thought of themselves as helping people who would benefit spiritually from their ministries.

TOURISM.   A century ago, travel to foreign lands and exotic places was only for the privileged few. But by the end of the twentieth century, millions from increasingly affluent middle classes were traveling swiftly from the more developed countries to those that offered interesting sights, such as native customs, uncrowded beaches, and possibly interesting ruins. Tourists take with them complete models of their way of life. They transport items of clothing (blue jeans, bikinis, and shorts), new slang, epithets, vulgar words, and demands for entertainment, services, foods, and beverages that are not a part of the traditional cultures in the countries that they invade.

> It is perfectly legitimate to compare tourists with barbarian tribes. Both involve mass migrations of peoples who collide with culture far removed from their own. There is, however, one major difference. The old Golden Horde (a Tartar Empire led by Genghis Khan's successors) was a nomadic, non-monetary people which threatened

the settled urban civilizations of Europe. Today, the pattern is reversed. Tourists come from the industrialized centres, but this time it is they who are fanning out through the world, swamping apparently less dynamic societies, including the few pre-industrial ones that still remain.[22]

There is little doubt that any country that receives thousand and thousands of tourists every year will find that those visiting bring with them items of culture that the people of the host country find attractive and which they will adopt. One may ask, however, if this is a deliberate strategy on the part of the countries from which those tourists come. Is it a means to develop a relationship of hegemony with those that they visit? It would be difficult to make that interpretation. These encounters may more closely resemble those by which seashells and amber beads found their way to the Russian plains in prehistoric times than they do a deliberate plan by industrial countries to control those that provide hospitality to tourists. This kind of transmission looks more like a "two-to-tango" situation, as opposed to a deliberate form of imperialism.

In any case, in these non-military ways, traditional cultures have been and continue to be modified or even replaced by those of Western nations. But whether one classifies that as analogous to the harshness of traditional imperialism or not, there is now an easier way to expose the people of less developed societies to the cultures of the Western world. Using the mass media represents an effective and efficient way to show people artifacts and practices that may seem desirable to them—features of the cultures of the more developed societies that they may wish to adopt.

Mass Communication as Imperialism

According to many scholars, an effective way to achieve hegemony is by distributing mass-communicated entertainment products to societies where gaining economic and political influence is an objective. That requires no military conquest, teachers, missionaries, or tourists. All that is needed is that the necessary technologies (TV sets, VCRs, DVDs, radios, cinemas, etc.) are in place in the receiving society. As noted earlier, many critics of the United States maintain that its government and a group of communication industries follow a deliberate policy of using the mass media to dominate people in less developed countries. They are said to do this by controlling the channels of communication that deliver news and entertainment, distributing their popular culture throughout the world. In particular, by exporting motion pictures, television programming, popular music, and other forms of entertainment products to less developed societies, a special kind of influence is achieved.

A complex set of events led to such interpretations of media imperialism. Those events can be seen in three areas of scholarly concern that have emerged over recent decades about the role of the media in international communication. One is a body of research and analysis from the 1950s and 1960s that led to the conclusion that mass media were a very important factor in *national development*.[23] The media were found to be useful agents in bringing new technologies and rapid social change in those societies that valued these goals—establishing, of course, markets for American technology and other products.

Another scholarly focus was on an often heated debate that started within UNESCO during the 1970s and continued through the 1990s, protesting the domination by Western organizations of the *flow of news* that emphasized events in the developed societies and ignored what was happening in much of the rest of the world.[24] Many third-world leaders see this as a form of domination and have long fought for significant changes.

A third, and possibly more significant, topic of scholarly debate and study that has contributed to imperialistic interpretations of the influence of mass communication is one that we have already discussed in some detail—the predominance in foreign markets and heavy use of American entertainment products, particularly *films, television programs*, and *popular music*.[25]

Using the mass media to engage in cultural imperialism is said to be especially insidious and effective. It is insidious in that what the media deliver is often eagerly welcomed by many in the receiving society. This push-pull situation is effective because such entertainment products portray attractive ways of life and material goods that can be attained only by adopting them from the advanced nations. This is said to motivate those in the less developed societies to reject their more traditional cultures and adopt the goods, norms, beliefs, and general ways of life of Western societies. In the minds of critics of the process, this is a very undesirable outcome.

Traditional cultures, such critics maintain, have served their people effectively for millennia. Replacing them with lifestyles modeled after those of the Western societies is both foolhardy and morally unjustified. For those who encourage the adoption of Western ways, the opposite is the case. Little harm is seen in providing products that people enjoy. Obviously, creating demand increases the markets for consumer goods produced in the more advanced societies. It also is said to weaken the authority of traditional leaders and governments in the receiving societies who cannot deliver these popular products. These consequences, say the producers and distributors of popular entertainment products, are not their problem.

CULTURAL IMPERIALISM THEORY: A FORMAL SUMMARY

Cultural imperialism theory, in the foregoing sense, can be summarized in a set of five somewhat complex propositions. It has not been formalized in this way by its many advocates, and it is unlikely that all those who espouse these views would agree to each of its basic assumptions as set forth below. Nevertheless, it does express many of the concerns of those who see a new world order—a new and bland "global village"—one that produces an "Americanized" or "McDonaldized" culture being formed on the basis of American entertainment products distributed globally via the mass media. In any case, the basics of Cultural Imperialism Theory, as generally understood, can be summarized in terms of the following five formal propositions:

1. The content of print and broadcast news, plus movies and television programming, produced by organizations in the United States and Europe is widely distributed *throughout the globe*, including non-Western and "developing" countries.
2. Citizens who live in such societies have only *limited choices* for media-provided information and entertainment outside those brought to them by Western global distribution systems. (Local systems lack resources.)
3. Those in less developed societies who receive the content produced and distributed by those global systems are exposed to what many in the audience perceive as *attractive alternatives* to their own material culture, values, and traditional ways of life.
4. Such audiences are *tempted to adopt, or do adopt*, the goods, services, values, and lifestyles that they see portrayed in the Western media, which creates both political unrest and markets for goods that can be exploited by Western powers.
5. **Therefore**, the developed societies deliberately *engage in cultural imperialism* by distributing media content that systematically undermines and replaces traditional beliefs, values, and lifestyles, leading people to prefer the political systems, material goods, and perspectives of Western populations.

In many respects, both Cultural Imperialism Theory, as formalized above, and the alternative Cultural Diffusion Theory are closely linked to the Adoption of Innovation Theory (discussed in Chapter 18). Both of the two alternatives address the process by which a new item of culture (such as something seen in a particular movie, TV show, or heard in a popular music composition) comes into a society from outside. Such products are *innovations* in every sense. Neither of the two alternative theories attempts to explain the details of the process and patterns by which such a new item is taken up within the society by some portion of the receiving population to be incorporated into their culture. That is precisely what the Adoption of Innovation Theory attempts to do. However, both the "imperialism" and the "diffusion" theories focus on the issue of how the item *initially comes to the attention* of the receiving society in the first place— that is, by forceful "imperialistic" activities or by a voluntary "diffusion" process.

Whether one accepts the explanation of the arrival of some new feature of culture offered by one or the other of these theories is a matter of one's personal values, preferences, and political commitments. The "imperialism" explanation requires complex assumptions drawn from both the writings of Karl Marx and from the Magic Bullet Theory. The "diffusion" account is more parsimonious in that its basic postulates are much simpler. But whatever account one accepts, there is no denying that such transfers of cultural items have important consequences. Because of such movements, traditional cultures undergo change when popular entertainment products bring depictions of new ideas, artifacts, values, and practices to the relevant receiving populations. Conservative leaders in such societies, dedicated to maintaining the "purity" of their indigenous ways of life, deplore such changes. It should not be surprising, therefore, that they denounce them and label them with pejorative terms, such as "pollution," "Americanization," "McDonaldization," and the like. Even the term "imperialism" is an example of such pejorative labeling. In any case, both theories attempt to address an important part of the contemporary process of social and cultural change. The issue of whether such media-based cultural change is good or bad can only be decided on the basis of personal values.

Notes and References

1. The writings of Karl Marx and his collaborator Frederich Engels are voluminous. Marx began developing his theories in his writings as a journalist in the early 1840s. He brought his major interpretations of history and his critical analysis of capitalism together in his famous work *Das Kapital*, which appeared in1867. He produced many other works before his death in 1883. See T. B. Bottomore, *Karl Marx: Selected Writings in Sociology and Social Philosophy* (New York: McGraw-Hill Book Company, 1956).

2. See Melvin L. DeFleur and Everette E. Dennis, "The Development of Popular Music and the Recording Industry," in: *Understanding Mass Communication*, updated 1996 edition (Boston: Houghton Mifflin Company, 1996). pp. 452–491.

3. *Ibid.* pp. 464–468.

4. From a class project paper prepared for the author by a female graduate student from Taiwan who had recently arrived in the U.S.

5. *The Economist*, Vol. 363, No. 8272, May 11–17, 2002, p. 16. See also: Vol. 363, No. 8274, May 25–31.

6. See David Demers, *Global Media: Menace or Messiah* (Spokane, WA: Marquette Books, 2009)

7. Adam Smith, *An Inquiry Into the Nature and Causes of the Wealth of Nations* (Buffalo, NY: Prometheus Books, 1991), first published in 1776.

8. For an insightful analysis of how these trends have been taking place in many regions of the world, see Alan B. Albarran and Sylvia M. Chan-Olmstead, *Global Media Economics: Commercialization, Concentration and Integration of World Media Markets* (Amer, Iowa: Iowa State University Press, 1998).

9. See "Number of U.S. Patents Granted, by Inventor Residence, Inventor Sector and Year of Grant, 1963-98," *Congressional Information Service*, 2002.

10. Timothy Champion, et. al., *Prehistoric Europe* (New York: Academic Press, 1984).

11. T. Douglas Price and James A. Brown, *Prehistoric Hunter-Gatherers: The Emergence of Cultural Complexity* (New York: Academic Press, 1985), see especially p. 184.

12. Olga Soffer, *The Upper Paleolithic of the Central Russian Plain* (New York: The Academic Press, 1985) for more detailed information concerning seashells and amber, see "Social Networks," 435–442.

13. J. Martin-Barbero, *Communication, Culture and Hegemony: From the Media to Mediation*, trans. by Elizabeth Fox and Robert A. White (Newbury Park: Sage, 1993), p. 10.

14. These examples are based on an excellent article on Iranian automobiles by Niel MacFarquhar. See *The New York Times International*, March 17, 2002, p. 12.

15. As an example, a well-known basic American text in the field of mass communication (Melvin L. DeFleur and Everette E. Dennis, *Understanding Mass Communication*, 7th ed., originally published by Houghton Mifflin Publishers of Boston) was recently translated into Persian, to be used in Iran for classes in media studies.

16. Yahya R. Kamalipour, *Images of the U.S. Around the World: A Multicultural Perspective* (Albany: State University of New York Press, 1999), pp. 24–25.

17. From the *Boston Globe* (via AP), February 15, 2002, p. A12.

18. Martin Carnoy, *Education as Cultural Imperialism* (New York: David McKay Company, 1974), p. 25.

19. Martin Carnoy, *Education as Cultural Imperialism* (New York: David McKay, 1974), pp. 1–2.

20. *Ibid.* p. 3.

21. Annabelle Sreberny-Mohammadi, "The Many Faces of Cultural Imperialism," in Peter Golding and Phil Harris, eds., *Beyond Cultural Imperialism: Globalization, Communication and the New International Order* (Thousand Oaks, CA: Sage Publications, 1997), p. 54.

22. L. Turner and J. Ash, *The Golden Hordes: International Tourism and the Pleasure Principle* (New York: St. Martin's Press, 1976), quoted in Sreberny-Mohammadi, *Op. Cit.*, p. 63.

23. See Wilbur Schramm, *Mass Media and National Development* (Stanford, CA: Stanford University Press, 1964).

24. Pradip N. Thomas, "An Inclusive NWICO* Cultural Resilience and Popular Resistance," in Peter Golding and Phil Harris, eds., *Op. Cit.*, pp. 163–174. *[New World Information and Communication Order].

25. Yahya R. Kamilpour, ed., *Images of the U.S. Around the World* (Albany: State University of New York Press, 1999).

CHAPTER 23

Collateral Media Instruction Theory

I n Chapter 2 (Introduction to the Origins, Nature, and Uses of Theories) the processes by which new theories are developed and tested were explained. As noted, there are two major sources from which specific mass communication theories have been put together in initial form. As was also explained in Chapter 2, most of the theories presented in the present text and that are now available to scholars trying to understand mass communication today have been derived from *empirical data* obtained from research projects that make use of scientific methods (see pp. 25–26). For those who use this approach, such theories offer both *descriptions* and *explanations* of the process, causes, and effects of mass communications. They also serve as *guides for further research.*

As was also explained, other theories have been derived from *a priori assumptions* that are a part of a particular ideology—assumptions that are simply accepted from the start as "true" (see pp. 26–28). Examples are Critical Cultural Theory (Chapter 21) and Cultural Imperialism Theory (Chapter 22). As was explained in Chapter 2 (see pp. 27–28), these theories are not based on empirical data. They have been developed from the writings of social critics, such as Karl Marx and others, to provide an intellectual foundation for assessing and criticizing the nature and consequences of mass communications in contemporary societies. As noted, while they are not founded on observed data, they can offer important insights into what their authors see as problems with, and objectionable features of, the nature, processes, and effects of mass communication in modern times.

The present chapter is an attempt to provide an example of a new theory that has been derived from empirical data. These data were obtained from a large-scale study of the influences of mass communications on youthful audiences in a number of countries. As will be explained in detail in later sections of the chapter, the study focused on the beliefs and attitudes concerning the ordinary people who live in the United States that were held by 1,313 teenage high school students in twelve countries in different parts of the globe. The purpose of that study was to describe and explain the *negative beliefs* about ordinary Americans that are held by the majority of these youths—who enjoy and are heavily exposed to American movies, TV programming, and news content. The high school subjects studied all have access to these products because they are exported to their countries and transmitted by their media to entertain and inform their local populations. This takes place because most of those countries have very limited (or even no) film or TV entertainment production facilities (or global news organizations) of their own. Thus, imported American mass communications are seen on local movie and television screens, to receive entertainment and news information.

As was explained in Chapter 2 (see p. 20), a theory derived from empirical observations consists of a set of *concepts* that are linked together in a number of *related propositions* that make up the way the theory is stated in formal terms. These concepts name and identify various kinds of factors, situations, or categories of events that have a part in the theory. More precise theories make use of quantitative concepts, that is, *measurements of variables* (such as beliefs and attitudes in the present case) or other measurable factors. When these concepts are linked into a set of interrelated formal propositions, the theory that results can offer both a concise tentative explanation as to how certain effects of the media come about as well as logically derived predictions as to what should be found if further research can be accomplished to see if the theory has validity.

In the remaining sections of this chapter, then, the background of the empirical study of the 1,313 teenagers, the methods used to obtain the data, and the concepts and the propositions that make up the formal theory are set forth. Essentially, the new theory is an attempt to explain why the majority of the young people studied, who are routinely exposed to U.S.-produced and exported media products, have such negative attitudes toward and flawed views of the ordinary people who live in the United States. That is, the theory looks at the unintended contribution that American-produced media content contributes to that outcome.

BACKGROUND

Learning is a process that takes place not only in families and classrooms but in a variety of other contexts as well. One of the most important among these is mass communication. Whenever people attend to a film, a TV program, or a news presentation, they unwittingly learn various things that they read, view, or hear about the topic. That is, as members of audiences, they normally go to the media for entertainment or information. However, once there, they unwittingly receive *unintended lessons embedded in the content* that is provided by the medium. For example, showing people smoking in movies was long considered by Hollywood producers of films as a way to portray the actors as sophisticated and glamourous. In fact, however, as we understand it now, such scenes also provided a subtle lesson for non-smoking young people. It showed them how they too could be regarded by their peers as more sophisticated and interesting. Consequently, many took up smoking. In a great variety of ways, then, many kinds of unintended lessons have long been included in what Hollywood, TV corporations, and the news media produce as content.

Clearly, those who produce such media products do not do so with the intention of systematically developing instructional content in order to educate their audiences. However, in fact, their reports, plots, depictions, and portrayals do include unintentional lessons for millions in the audiences who attend. An important point is that these U.S.-produced products are seen and enjoyed not only by Americans, young and old, but also by people in almost every country—even in remote regions of the world—where media content is available.

This widespread situation exists because such media content is produced and marketed worldwide by a number of multinational corporations as a means of gaining *profits*—which is a highly approved goal in a capitalistic society. As a consequence, learning about Americans and details about their lifestyles, as depicted in that entertainment and news content, takes place in all countries that offer U.S.-produced and locally imported media products to their populations. There is no U.S. control over such exports to make sure that what they depict does realistically and accurately portray the actual characteristics, values, and behavior of Americans. From what is offered, portrayed, or depicted in that media content, then, many millions of people can develop inaccurate and misleading understandings of the behavior, lifestyle, and values of ordinary Americans.

There is no doubt that U.S.-produced mass communications reach populations worldwide, whether those audiences live in sophisticated cities and towns in the U.S., in small villages in remote rural areas, or in the dismal slums of developing countries. Only in the most isolated regions of the world do contemporary people have no access to movies, TV programming, radio news broadcasts, and other media. That is the case because basic communication technologies, such as the cinema, telephone, phonograph, telegraph, newspaper, and radio were adopted long ago in virtually every country—with the possible exception of truly isolated regions in the Amazon basin, polar areas above the Arctic Circle, or in the deepest jungles of Africa. Thus, today, radio and television programming, motion pictures, and news information exported from the United States are all but universally available.

American media content, in the form of both news and entertainment, dominates in these transmissions. Again, media products produced in the United States are so widely seen, heard, and enjoyed because many less developed societies—indeed, the majority—have limited or no facilities of their own for the production of global news coverage, or visual entertainment, such as films and TV programs. However, local populations in those regions are as eager to receive news and to enjoy entertaining content as are the people in typical communities in the United States. As a result, local media systems worldwide pay well to import this content and provide it to their populations via their local transmitting media.

Obviously, few of these news and entertainment products are specially designed for local people in other countries. Indeed, most of what is developed, exported, and transmitted to audiences has been prepared initially by multinational corporations specifically for audiences in the U.S. However, as noted, easy profits can be earned by exporting these products widely to global markets. For example, once a product, such as a news story, movie, or TV broadcast, is produced for American media, the cost of exporting it to other countries is relatively little. The the production costs have already been recovered, and the profits obtained from such global dissemination can be great. Thus, various forms of media content depicting Americans are in high global demand, and they are easily available to and enjoyed by audiences in virtually every country.

In the case of motion pictures, for example, the exportation of silent, black-and-white movies produced in the U.S. began long ago—about the time of World War I. During that conflict, fledgling European media industries that had started to produce films were largely shut down or devoted to war efforts. Early on, then, Hollywood became the world center for the production of motion pictures as entertainment. As a result, the U.S. quickly dominated the world market for films. That remains the case today.

In the silent films, subtitles in local languages were easy to insert. Seeing people act out movie plots and dramas on a big screen was a completely new and truly exciting experience at the time. Nothing quite like them had ever been see before. Consequently, audiences worldwide enjoyed the exported films produced in the U.S. When sound, color, and local language dubbing or subtitles were added to the films, they were even more in demand. That domination continues today.

Similarly, TV broadcasting of news and other content became widely adopted in the U.S. during the 1950s, as the new medium was rapidly acquired by American families. As that took place, people in other countries also began to want and began to adopt the new magic box. Recorded broadcasts of American programs of all kinds were in great demand and were imported to provide information and entertainment for their local populations. As was the case with movies, if language was a problem, subtitles or even dubbing could be inserted. Again, such content was not often produced locally. Broadcasting stations had been quickly established, but again, few of those countries had established facilities for producing television entertainment or international news content. Consequently, the United States came to dominate the world market with its exported TV entertainment programming.

In many ways, the same can be said about news. Contemporary American television news organizations, such as CNN, ABC, and CBS, as well as press associations, operate worldwide. Their products are distributed to audiences in other countries, and they see much the same on their movie screens, television sets, and in their print media as what is seen by Americans in their home communities.

In the case of movie and TV entertainment, it is difficult for such youthful audiences to separate fantasy from reality. Teenage audiences worldwide see the behavior of Americans portrayed "with their own eyes," as they learn about them in news stories, view them on movie screens, and watch them in TV programming. They have no reason to believe that what they see is not a valid picture of the characteristics and behavior of the majority of ordinary people who live in the United States.

THE MAJOR CONCEPTS

The development of the theory to be presented below is based on three important concepts. One, collateral instruction, is new in this text. Another, incidental learning, was explained in Chapter 5 (see pp. 00–00). It is of less recent origin. It dates back to the early days of television. And a third, the social construction of reality, comes from ancient sources in the writings of Plato.

Collateral Instruction: Unintended Lessons Embedded in Media Content

The first of the three concepts that are central to the theory being explained, then, is the idea of collateral instruction. The term "collateral" has been borrowed from the military. In that setting, it is used to characterize accidental and unintended damage that occurs nearby when a military target is bombed from the air or is shelled by artillery. Often, in such occasions, "collateral dam-age" occurs to nearby people or to facilities in ways that are certainly not wanted or intended by those initiating the attack. This "collateral" concept has not been used before in developing mass communication theory. In the present text, then, "collateral instruction" refers to lessons presented to an audience in media content being produced—lessons providing instruction that is neither intended nor even understood by the producers of the content. That is, these lessons are not deliberately placed there by those who design, develop, and disseminate that content. Not only do they have no intention of producing instructional materials, but usually they also have no under-standing that they are actually doing so. Moreover, aside from news production, they have no concern whatsoever whether what they do produce is or is not factually correct. Their goal is solely to create media products that will attract and please their audiences (for the purposes of making a profit). However, these lessons are learned among youth and others in various parts of the world—audiences who enjoy American-produced media content. Thus, they unwittingly acquire beliefs about what ordinary American people are like from such collateral instruction as they view movies, TV dramas, and news stories depicting people who live in the U.S.

One example of such collateral instruction was mentioned briefly earlier—showing people smoking in movies to imply glamour and sophistication. A recent study of depictions of smoking in movies was conducted in Britain, and the research results were reported in *Lancet*—a major medical journal.[1] Exposure to smoking as depicted in movies was assessed among a total of 3,547 youths (ages ten–fourteen). These were youngsters who reported in a preliminary survey that they had never tried smoking. Then, the influence of exposure to films showing people smoking was as-sessed. A total of fifty recent movies was randomly selected, and the number of times actors were shown smoking in these films was carefully determined. Most of the original youths (seventy-three percent) were contacted a second time, thirteen to twenty-six months later. The research goals were to identify two things: One was to determine the number of the youths who had seen how many of these movies. The other, and a major goal, was to determine how many had since taken up smoking.

The results indicated that there was an unmistakable relationship between exposure to the movie-portrayed smoking and taking up the habit. The relationship was strongest for those youths whose parents did not smoke—indicating that the subjects were not influenced by their fathers or mothers. Those who produced the movies did not plan such collateral instruction, and the youngsters who took up smoking were not aware of the influence of the lessons they inciden-tally learned that were embedded in the films.

In recent times, the movie industry may finally be understanding that the collateral instruction that such content provides can have consequences. In 2007, changes in production policy, and even the rating system applied to movies for audiences, were under public discussion. The issue was whether to permit the showing of people lighting cigarettes and smoking in the films. As a strong antismoking movement has developed in the U.S., claims are now being made that this provided a negative influence on youths (read collateral instruction), and pressure has been placed on producers to eliminate such behavior from portrayals in films.

A second example of collateral instruction and incidental learning is provided by crime re-porting on local TV news in the U.S.—televised reports to audiences on what is happening in their community—viewed and enjoyed nightly by many millions of Americans. Typically, TV journalists report numerous local crimes, and often those who have been arrested are shown in handcuffs or in prison garb being led into the jail or courthouse. Also, "mug shots" of the perpetrators are routinely shown to the audience.

Unfortunately, as Robert Entman has noted, young black males are more often involved in such criminal behavior, for whatever reasons, than are their white counterparts. When these unflattering photos are shown to white audiences, Entman maintains, they can influence negatively the ways in which such viewers think about young black males:

> Mug shots make their subjects look guilty. Rarely flattering, the tell-tale gridlines behind the face or the combined portrayal in front and profile shots yield an impression of guilt based on hundreds of thousands of previous inter-textual memories of the image in news and fiction.[2]

Stated in terms of the theory being developed, then, these TV news presentations are providing collateral instruction that teaches their white audiences that young black males are truly dangerous people. Thus, as these unintended lessons are communicated, and as news audiences incidentally learn that such males pose a serious threat, the result may well be that existing racial stereotypes and prejudices shared among them can be reinforced. That can have significant consequences for race relations in the communities involved.

As previous chapters clearly indicate, the majority of mass communication research that has been published has been concerned with the effects of media content on people in the United States—and particularly on children. From the beginnings of research on the influences of mass media, a very large number of studies has been aimed at understanding whether their content in some ways promotes violence, immoral sexual behavior, or other negative effects, particularly among youths in the U.S. However, no media research in the past could be found that had focused on the concept of collateral instruction of people in other countries as it concerns the nature of ordinary Americans—lessons provided by media entertainment and news stories exported abroad.

Unwitting Incidental Learning by Members of the Audience

The process of incidental learning has already been introduced. It is a concept from the early days of television that was introduced by Wilbur Schramm and his colleagues. The term focuses not on the content of the media but on members of the audience. As described by Schramm, et. al., it refers to the process by which youths who attend to TV programs for entertainment (unwittingly) *learn* what a variety of situations and people are like as they view on their screens the plots, dramas, and characters that are presented.[3] In other words, on the audience side, flawed beliefs and images about the people and their behavior that are depicted in such media content are often unknowingly acquired by those who are exposed. As was explained above, in the 1950s, at a time when TV was a new medium, Wilbur Schramm and his colleagues coined the term to explain how those who attended to the new visual medium to be entertained could unknowingly ("incidentally") acquire distorted ideas and beliefs about the people and situations that were depicted. As they explained:

> Most of a child's learning from television, as we have said, is *incidental learning*. By this we mean learning that takes place when a viewer goes to television for entertainment and stores up certain items of information without seeking them. (italics added).[4]

Later, other scholars developed related ideas. For example, in Chapter 5, a theory of *social learning* was described (p. 75). It was developed by Alfred Bandura to explain how people learn from observing the behavior patterns of others.[5] Nevertheless, at the time, the concept of incidental learning as discussed above did move forward the level of understanding of the potential influences of TV. It provided an understanding as to how it could have a subtle influence on the beliefs and behavior of young people who viewed its content. Since 1961, however, when the concept was first advanced, only limited efforts have been made to use it in developing new theories that advance our understanding of the influence of television—or other visual entertainment media—on the ideas and behavior of youths.

The Social Construction of Reality

As was explained in Chapter 5, it was in the writings of Plato that the ways in which people develop conceptions of reality through processes of communication were described. His purpose, at the time, was to show that *sensory impressions* (as opposed to pure reason) were untrustworthy. In his allegory of the cave, he described a situation in which men viewing shadows on the walls of the cavern discussed the meanings of what they were seeing. A consequence of this communication was that the men came to believe that the shadows *were reality.* Plato held that these interpretations were so valid to the men that when one of their members (who had been taken outside the cave) was returned and then challenged those interpretations, they rejected his ideas as false—and they even might have killed him.

In more modern times, the ways in which popular newspapers can mislead readers was discussed by a number of early critics of the medium. Thus, the function of the news in distorting reality—the idea that media can thereby create false beliefs and images among their audiences—is by no means a new one. In 1922, for example, as noted in Chapter 4, in his classic book, *Public Opinion*, Walter Lippmann stated that the function of newspapers was to create for their readers "pictures in their heads of the world outside." Obviously, he was following the lead of Plato (but he did not indicate that). Lippmann noted that those media-provided understandings produced what he termed a "pseudo-reality" among newspaper readers. These were distorted interpretations of people and events reported in news stories—that is, flawed constructions of reality, obtained in a process of communication. These, he noted, often governed both the beliefs and actions of readers.[6]

The Importance of "Programmatic" Theory Development

Generally, then, from the large body of accumulated writings on mass communication, as well as from other more historical and classic sources, the set of concepts discussed above can be brought together in a new way to develop a theory about the nature and influences of media content on audiences. Obviously, it is important to develop new theories that can potentially advance our understanding of the processes and effects of mass communication. As this book indicates, many such theories are already available.

However, in a recent paper, DeFleur pointed out that one feature distinguishing mass communication research from other fields is that the development and testing of theory by media scholars is not "programmatic."[7] That is, unlike theory development in other fields—such as physics, biology, or chemistry—researchers conducting media studies seldom follow up on promising leads found by others in order to advance the frontiers of knowledge about the process and effects of mass communications. The present chapter represents an attempt to do that. That is, the chapter uses the concept of incidental learning, the ancient concept of the social construction of reality, and the newer idea of collateral instruction to develop a new theory that can help to account for misconceptions that are held in many countries around the world of the personal attributes and behavior of ordinary American people.

THE EMPIRICAL STUDY

As was noted, the present attempt to develop a new theory emerged from a large-scale empirical study by the author of this text and a co-author. The study concerned the beliefs and attitudes toward ordinary Americans held by teenagers in twelve countries.[8] This research addressed the issue of how global dissemination of media content as *popular entertainment products* can result in certain influences on young people of high school age in twelve countries located in three regions of the world. The purpose of presenting certain findings of that research in the present context is to provide an empirical basis for developing the new theory. It is clear that the audience for media entertainment worldwide consists mainly of the young. Older people who work and have many responsibilities spend less time with media and less attention to the latest movie, TV sitcom, etc. Figure 1, below, indicates that the young make up the vast majority of the populations of the less developed (nonindustrial) societies.

The objective, then, is to put together a formal theory that can explain why the teenage audiences of media content produced in and exported from the United States *consistently develop decidedly flawed and clearly negative beliefs* about ordinary Americans. Simply put, the findings indicate that the lives and activities of the Americans that they see depicted "with their own eyes" in U.S.-produced media content presents a very unrealistic picture.

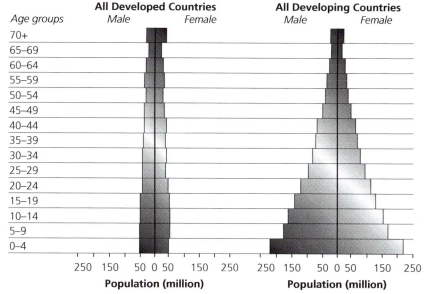

FIGURE 1 Population Pyramids   *Source*: "National Trends in Population, Resources, Environment and Development: Country Profiles." United Nations Department of Economic and Social Affairs: Population Division: Country Profiles, 2005.

While the empirical study from which the theory to be developed focuses mainly on entertainment and teenage audiences, its basic structure and its underlying assumptions may also be applicable to the process of production and distribution of other types of mass communication content. In particular, the theory may help in understanding the influences of *news about Americans* that is disseminated worldwide by major international news organizations. Those messages are more likely to be received and interpreted by adults rather than by the young, but at least some of the teenagers in those countries also attend. Thus, while the influences of news from the U.S. was not specifically under study in the research to be described, reports about people and events in the United States transmitted globally may also have unplanned and unanticipated negative effects on various kinds of audiences—including the young.

The basis for that implication comes from the ways in which the American journalists, and the news industries generally, select, process, and deliver their reports via international systems to foreign audiences. It is in many ways the same process that takes place in the production and dissemination of entertainment content. Obviously, news reports are not pure entertainment, but they too are selectively *designed, produced,* and *disseminated* globally for profit. Presumably, at least to their audiences, they represent what is "currently happening" among people who live in the United States. Those reports are then seen, read, or heard—and interpreted—by readers, listeners, and viewers in many other countries. In this way, they also provide collateral instruction. The point is that such information about Americans and their society *has consequences.* That is, what is reported internationally as "news" from the United States can often serve as unintended depictions of members of the general and ordinary American population in ways that do not represent their overall reality. Thus, while visual entertainment may play a central role, there is no doubt that certain kinds of news presented on TV, in print, or on radio can also play a part.

The reason for that conclusion lies in the way that a "newsworthy" story is defined. One feature of American journalism that frequently finds its way into such news reports is illustrated by the maxim that "*if it bleeds, it leads.*" Journalists, like other producers of media content, seek the largest possible audiences. They do so because profit lies in large numbers. The advertisers who support news media want their messages to be seen by as many potential customers as possible. To attract those maximum numbers, the content produced has to be exciting, attention-grabbing, and interesting to read, hear, or view. That is clearly the route to higher profits.

For those reasons, the daily flow of news stories presented to the world routinely emphasizes negative features of the lives and conduct of at least some people who live in the United States. Typically, those stories include spectacular murder cases and the court trials of the persons allegedly responsible. They routinely present dramatic reports about Americans who have behaved very badly as serial snipers. Another favorite gives extended news attention to shooters who kill young children in schools or innocent students in a university. Still others report on shootings in workplaces. (The collateral instruction: *Americans are violent.*)

Other news reports have featured American executives who have misused their positions to enrich themselves illegally. Another focus has been on politicians who have engaged in unacceptable practices while in office—accepting bribes or gifts from corporations and individuals in exchange for promoting their interests. (The collateral instruction: *Americans are criminals.*)

There have also been disclosures that a number of Americans, including clergy, have sexually abused many children. In addition, stories have been distributed about an immensely popular entertainer who was charged with sexual indecencies concerning children. (The collateral instruction: *Americans lack family values.*) Widespread news coverage has also reported that women teachers have engaged in sexual activities with young boys. (The collateral instruction: *American women are sexually immoral.*)

Noting that they repeatedly focus on such unusual events and situations does not imply that the news media should be controlled in some authoritarian way by the State or someone else to prevent the dissemination of negative news stories. If all that was reported were dull accounts and uninteresting information, the news industry would soon be out of business. Profits are essential in a capitalistic economy. Controlling the news media to reduce reports of negative actions by citizens or by government is the path of nondemocratic societies. This has recently happened in Russia, where the government has ruled that news stories about events in Russia that are broadcast over the state-controlled radio system must consist of fifty percent "good news" about the country.[9]

However, it is not difficult to demonstrate that such a constant flow of negative news reports of events, situations, and actions contributes to the interpretations on the part of audiences in other countries of the nature of ordinary Americans and their society. The empirical study of teenagers in twelve societies (to be discussed below) indicates that clearly. The data reveal that a constant flow of negative news content about people and events in the United States appears to present an unfavorable image of Americans—a flawed social construction of reality.

It does not take the proverbial "rocket scientist" to predict that such a constant flow of unfavorable images and depictions can serve as a major source for incidental learning—particularly for those who have *no alternative direct and objective sources of information* about the ordinary people who live in the United States. When that is the case, seriously incorrect and unfavorable beliefs and negative attitudes toward ordinary Americans are likely to result. This can be especially true when those who receive such media reports personally have (1) never met an American, (2) have never visited the United States, and (3) have few or no other reliable sources to learn what people who live in the U.S. are really like. It is precisely these three conditions that describe the majority of people who make up audiences for media content exported from the United States.

Essentially, then, it is not only the propaganda machines of hostile nations that regularly denounce American foreign policy, or criticize U.S. military activities to their populations, that are shaping the beliefs of youths in other countries about what ordinary and everyday Americans are like. Obviously, those foreign propaganda sources play an important part in shaping attitudes toward "official" America. However, a testable theory is that it is our own entertainment and news media industries that regularly provide people in other countries the clearest definitions of what you, your family, your friends, and the people in your neighborhood *are truly like as human beings.*

Perhaps a useful way to introduce the proposed theory that attempts to explain how the content of mass communication produced in the United States has negative consequences is to refer to a comic strip character that was once very popular in the U.S. The character was "Pogo," a small animal cartoon creature of less than realistic features. A phrase that Pogo used in commentaries on American life was that *"We have met the enemy, and they is us!"* To explain, while news may play a part as suggested, the media content that unintentionally produces the most negative views of the people who live in the United States is *entertainment* products, such as U.S.-produced TV programming and movies that are exported to be enjoyed by populations around the globe.

The bottom line, then, from the evidence to be presented is this: It appears that our entertainment products (and also news content) are unintentionally serving us as *media of collateral instruction* in many countries where they generate negative beliefs and flawed images (social constructions of reality) concerning ordinary people who live in the United States.

The Research Setting

Specifically, the empirical example used in developing the collateral instruction theory consists of research findings reported in the present authors' previously mentioned book, titled *Learning to Hate Americans*. In summary, these researchers conducted a study of *beliefs and attitudes toward ordinary Americans* that were held by 1,313 teenage high school students in twelve countries. These societies are located in three different regions of the world (Western, Muslim, and Asian). The study revealed that virtually all of those youths have ready access to and enjoy greatly the kinds of popular TV programming and movies that depict people who live in the United States. What they experience as audiences, as they attend to these entertaining products, is little different from what teenagers attend to in typical American communities. The findings from the study indicate ways in which that mass American media entertainment content has influenced the beliefs and attitudes of most of the youths in those dozen countries concerning the characteristics, conduct, and lifestyles of Americans. It is in this sense that "we have met the enemy, and they is us!"

As has been suggested, a major result of attending to these depictions of Americans is that these young people have formed *unrealistic beliefs* about the nature and lifestyles of typical people who live in the United States. Based on those flawed beliefs, their attitudes toward such Americans, for the most part, are *decidedly negative*. The authors conclude that, unfortunately, it is likely that those beliefs and attitudes provide an important foundation element in generating a "culture of hate" toward Americans among the current teenage generation (soon to be adults) who live in a number of those countries. In their research report, DeFleur and DeFleur suggest that such a *culture of hate* may in some situations be providing an important contributing condition for those who organize and conduct destructive activities against the U.S. and its people.

Stated simply, then, what this research project provides is a specific instance in which media industries have produced *popular culture*—that is, entertainment products—mainly in the form of movies and television content depicting Americans, that are distributed to many other countries. These countries make use of them to provide entertainment for their populations, mainly because they have few or no comparable production facilities or industries of their own. In particular, in virtually all regions of the world, then, those American-produced products are the principal media entertainment enthusiastically enjoyed by the youths studied.

The main objective for selecting this particular set of data is not to try to focus attention on the specifics of the results—the fact that teenagers in twelve countries have formed flawed beliefs about, and negative attitudes toward, ordinary Americans. The purpose here is to portray in general and theoretical terms the *stages in the process* by which that particular effect has come about. The theory being developed, then, attempts to describe and explain each of the following major steps in which mass media content is:

1. *selected, designed, and produced* in specific ways needed to make a profit,
2. then *disseminated* to countries around the world to enhance those profits,
3. where it is then *received enthusiastically by youthful audiences,*
4. who *attend to it* in a specific way for specific reasons,
5. which bring about a set of *unwitting but observable "collateral" effects* on teenage audience members,
6. which can have unanticipated long-range *consequences* for the U.S.

As has been suggested, once that multistage process is set forth within the context of a specific empirical example, the resulting theory may (or may not) be applicable to explain how other forms of content (specifically news), delivered to other kinds of audiences (older audiences), can bring about similar kinds of consequences. That, of course, will depend on further research by communication scholars—research specifically designed to assess this proposed theory against other bodies of empirical observations. In this way, theories derived from empirical data provide important guides to further investigation.

In the sections that follow, therefore, the first task is to provide a summary of the research project on the 1,313 teenagers that will be used to illustrate what they believe about people who live in the United States. That summary will indicate specifically (1) what *objectives* were sought by the study, (2) how the *data* were gathered, and (3) what *conclusions* were reached from the data analyses. Once those issues have been made clear, each of the steps or phases of the mass communication process by which these particular consequences resulted among this audience can be set forth as a set of *interrelated formal propositions*. As noted, each of those stages in that overall process has been already addressed in considerable detail by one or more of the theories discussed in previous chapters. The goal in this chapter, then, is to develop a new explanation of *specific* influences on audiences in the countries where the data were gathered and to provide a potential explanation of how features of mass communications played a part in bringing about the results.

The Basic Questions

The basic research questions initially addressed in the teenage project were these:

> First: *How do youths now in high schools in twelve countries in various parts of the world view ordinary Americans?*

That is, what do they believe about, and what are their attitudes toward, everyday people who live in the United States?

> And second: *How were these views influenced by exposure to mass communication content?*

The term "ordinary Americans" is used to refer to everyday people—persons and families who live in typical communities and neighborhoods in the United States. Note that assessing attitudes toward such persons is *a very different issue* than the ones typically addressed by the numerous polls and other observations that are frequently conducted in different countries. For the most part, those efforts have studied attitudes toward such issues as American foreign policy, the actions of the U.S. military (e.g., recently in Afghanistan and Iraq), the decisions of political leaders that have implications for people in other countries (e.g., global warming and illegal immigration), and so on. These attitudes, in one way or another, are held toward "the United States," as a government—as an official entity. There is little doubt that those attitudes are very negative, particularly among the adult populations of many of the world's societies. Poll after poll in recent times has shown that this is indeed the case.[10]

In other words, it is not difficult to see that there is something of a dichotomy in assessing attitudes toward ordinary people in other societies. That is, a distinction can be made between how people regard a particular country's *government* and *official policies* versus how they feel about the *inhabitants* of that country. For example, Americans and others have often had clearly negative attitudes toward a particular government, its leaders, and its actions—while, at the same time, having more sympathetic feelings about the ordinary people who live under that regime. To illustrate, currently Americans generally have negative assessments of the government of Cuba, North Korea, and Iran. In the case of Cuba, while most Americans may dislike Fidel Castro's (and now Raul Castro's) government and its repressive rule, they do not negatively assess or hate the everyday Cuban people. The same is true of people who live in North Korea or Iran. Similarly, few in the U.S. hated ordinary Iraqis who lived under the brutal government of Saddam Hussein. A logical question, then, is whether young people in other countries have positive feelings for ordinary Americans while entertaining negative views about the U.S. government, its leaders, and its official policies. The data to be presented will speak directly to that issue.

ASSESSING YOUTHFUL BELIEFS AND ATTITUDES

As has been explained, the overall objective of the *Learning to Hate* study of teenagers was to measure the beliefs and attitudes of a number of youths currently in high schools in twelve countries concerning *ordinary Americans and their lifestyles*. Specifically, the twelve countries were Saudi Arabia, Bahrain, South Korea, Lebanon, Mexico, China, Spain, Taiwan, Pakistan, Nigeria, Italy, and Argentina. Note that these include countries in distinct areas of the world—the Middle East, Asia, Africa, Europe, and Latin America.

This was a complex and difficult research undertaking. For one thing, there are a great many ways in which to go about measuring people's attitudes.[11] The measurement strategy used in the teenage project was the classic procedure originally developed in 1932 by psychologist Rensis Likert—with numerous modifications since that time. It is basically a simple procedure. The first step is to identify a clear "attitude object" (what the subjects have feelings about). In each country, as noted, the attitude object was "ordinary Americans" and not "the United States," its policies, its leaders, or its actions. The term "attitude" was defined in this project in a very basic way that lends itself to the Likert scale strategy of measurement. That is, an attitude can be considered as *a configuration of related evaluative beliefs about some specific object or situation.* An "evaluative belief" about something is one that implies acceptance or rejection—that is, a positive or negative assessment of the attitude object. (As opposed to some factual belief.)

An example of an evaluative belief (used in the project) was that "Americans are generally quite violent." Respondents were able to "strongly agree," "agree," be "neutral," "disagree," or "strongly disagree" with that statement. Half of the statements prepared for the attitude measure were positive (e.g., "Americans are a generous people") and the other half negative (e.g., "Many Americans engage in criminal activities"). The way in which the subject responds overall to the set of such statements (for example, by agreeing, being neutral, strongly disagreeing, etc.) provides an indicator of the person's attitude toward that object. For each subject, a numerical score is earned for each of the statements. These can be totaled across the statements to obtain an overall attitude score for the person. These individual scores can be averaged for particular country or for various categories of subjects.

The Likert procedure is simple, logical, intuitive, and easy for the subjects to use. The scores earned can easily be transformed mathematically to a quantitative continuum—as was done in this case. This ranged from –5 (expressing a very negative attitude) through to zero (for a neutral one) and then to +5 (for a subject with a very positive attitude). This transformation made it possible to represent the results in easy-to-understand graphic form (as in the charts that will be presented later in the chapter's section discussing the findings).

The Problem of Contacting Teenagers in Other Countries

Once the measurement procedure had been designed and pretested, the next step was to decide on what human subjects in what countries could be assessed. Gaining access to high school students to use as subjects for research in any country is difficult. In the United States, for example, gaining permission to have high school students respond in a classroom setting to a research questionnaire can be truly demanding. Approval must be obtained from administrators in charge of the school, from the teachers of the specific classes to be used, and, often, in writing from the parents of the students involved.

In the settings of nations unfriendly to the United States (as was the case with several in this project), obtaining official permissions would have been virtually impossible. It would have meant going through twelve different diplomatic channels in order to gain permission to access young people in their high schools. Then, constructing a random sample from a list of all students in each country would be the classic textbook procedure. Again, in a practical sense, virtually impossible. For that reason, such an approach was not even tried. The authors decided to use what can be called a "stealth sample." Like the military aircraft that enter a hostile country "under the radar screen," an approach to sampling was devised that bypassed local officials and bureaucrats. It relied instead on *personal ties* with educators in each of the countries studied.

To explain, the youthful subjects involved completed the questionnaire with the help of a network of friends and relatives of graduate students (from the countries involved) who were studying at a private university in the United States. These students served as a research team to help in completing the project. Each had either friends, fiances, spouses, and/or relatives who were teaching in or administering high schools in the specific countries from which they had come. Each member of the graduate student team identified and contacted by email or phone specific persons in their own countries who were doing such teaching. These individuals were asked if they would be willing to assist personally with data-gathering in their schools.

Initially, some of those contacted refused because of fears concerning possible retaliation if their attempt to assist Americans was revealed. In each case, pointed questions were raised by them about the purpose of the study and its sponsors. Some were suspicions about who was doing this and why. Was it the CIA conducting the study for some negative purpose? However, when the nature of the project—as a university research project involving graduate students from various countries and not spying by the CIA or some other agency of the U.S.—was clearly and fully explained, and as *total anonymity* was guaranteed for both the youthful subjects and those who assisted, virtually all of these individuals cooperated. In some cases, they did so with risks to themselves.

These same friends and relatives assisted with the translations of the overall questionnaire and the attitude scale within it into the various languages required (such as Spanish, Chinese, and Arabic). In some cases, professional translators assisted. The educators in the countries also made sure that in each case the wording was such that it would be readily understood by their students. The result was that all of the questionnaires were personally and effectively administered in classrooms by active teachers or high school administrators in each of the twelve different countries. The questionnaires were completed by the youths carefully and returned by those assisting promptly. Indeed, the level of cooperation exceeded the anticipations of all of the members of the research team.

Who Were the Teenagers Studied?

What were the characteristics of these subjects? What Americans think of as "high school" may be defined somewhat differently in other countries. However, this was not really a problem. To achieve comparability, those administering the questionnaires made sure that the respondents were in schools that were *beyond the primary level but not at the college level.* As noted, the total number of teenagers studied was 1,313. They were divided more or less evenly between the twelve countries. The median age of the subjects was just under seventeen years (that is, half were above that age and half below). Half were males (fifty-one percent) and half females (forty-nine percent). Only eleven percent had ever traveled to the United States, and those who had were primarily from Mexico and, in a few cases, the European societies. In social class terms, the subjects were from families that were neither rich nor poor. That is, almost all were in the middle level of their societies. Those who assisted with data-gathering were asked to make certain that the schools selected were neither humble ones attended by the very poor nor elite and expensive institutions attended by the children of the wealthy.

Is this a classic random and representative sample of all the youths in these twelve nations? Obviously not. As has been explained, in this multinational setting, obtaining such a truly random sample was simply not remotely possible. Even if a researcher had unlimited funds, it could not be done, given the political situation in some of areas. Simply stated, then, the results were obtained from 1,313 reasonably comparable teenagers from each of the twelve countries involved. Their responses provide a wealth of insights about how such youths in different parts of the globe feel about ordinary Americans. It seems likely that their views are at least reasonably representative of those of most of the young people in the middle levels in each of the countries studied. And there does not appear to have been any obvious or systematic biases used in their selection or in the patterns or responses that could have seriously skewed the results.

The Issue of Media Exposure

The questionnaire within which the attitude scale was embedded also probed *media usages.* The subjects were asked about seeing movies, watching television programming, and having interests in other forms of popular culture. Virtually all of the respondents in all of the countries attended their local cinemas, frequently with peers, and they often viewed entertainment programs on television sets at home or with friends. In almost all cases, the movies and TV content to which they were exposed had been produced in the U.S. While some of the Western nations have at least some production facilities for films and entertainment broadcasting, few of the others do. What their populations saw, then, was almost all imported or obtained via satellite or recorded sources.

Assessing the Influences of Depictions of Americans in Media Content

There are no simple answers as to the sources of anyone's beliefs and attitudes concerning any issue or object. Obviously, the sources of teenage views of ordinary Americans can be many. However, media entertainment content clearly appears in this case to have served as a significant one among those subjects. For one thing, like their American counterparts, the teenagers studied are heavy users of mass-communicated entertainment and popular culture. As noted, popular entertainment culture in the form of movies, radio, and television broadcasts or recorded content are almost universally available.

Although not many nonindustrialized countries have facilities to produce such media content, they all do have cinemas that show films, as well as radio and television systems in place that must obtain entertainment products to broadcast for their populations to enjoy. But even as indicated, they have to import such products; few governments rigidly censor all that is made available to their populations. To illustrate, on the evening in which the "shock and awe" bombing campaign began in Baghdad, initiating the U.S. involvement in Iraq in March of 2003, Saddam Hussein's Iraqi government-operated television system was broadcasting an American movie (*The Guilty*)—a film that contains a great deal of controversial violence and sexual content.

But even if a government does rigidly control what is disseminated via its media to its citizens, that does not mean that they have little or no access to entertainment produced in the U.S. Previously recorded movies, radio, and television programming are easily obtained. In some cases satellite broadcasts are directly received from across country borders. In addition, street vendors in all such countries rent or sell cheaply VCR tapes or DVDs with every form of media content imaginable. In some cases, audiences see pirated American movies before they are shown in U.S. theaters. From those sources, something of interest is always available to young people seeking media entertainment.

To assess the possible influence of American mass-communicated entertainment content on the beliefs of the youths studied concerning ordinary Americans, a *subscale* was derived from a selection of items in the Likert Scale. A subscale is simply a "measure within a measure." In this case, it was based on three of the evaluative statements that make up the overall scale. Specifically, these were the following:

1. "Americans are generally quite violent."
2. "Many Americans engage in criminal activities."
3. "Many American women are sexually immoral."

Why were these specific items chosen from the attitude scale to assess the influences of mass-communicated entertainment content on the beliefs of these youths about ordinary Americans? The reason is that the themes expressed in these three evaluative statements are very common ones that are used over and over by American producers of media entertainment and news to attract the largest possible audiences—both in the U.S. and elsewhere. That is, youthful audiences worldwide enjoy seeing fast action, and particularly *violence,* on their movie and TV screens.

Many young people are attracted to films and TV dramas that show *sexual activity.* These are particularly popular among teenagers in conservative countries where women are much more under the control of rigid codes of conduct than in Western societies. Finally, a very large number of movie plots and those of TV dramas include depictions of Americans engaging in *criminal activities.* Almost any movie, and many of the TV dramas that teen audiences in other countries see, therefore, will depict Americans engaging in at least some of these activities. It may not be clear to such audiences that those portrayed and their activities are just fictional entertainment that does not represent the ways of life and typical conduct of ordinary Americans. Therefore, the attitude scores of the subjects on these three items were averaged to obtain a *Media Influences Subscale.*

WHAT THE RESULTS REVEALED

The findings concerning the beliefs about and attitudes toward ordinary Americans held by the 1,313 teenagers studied are unequivocally clear: For the most part, the beliefs held by these young people are *flawed*; their attitudes are *negative*; and both have been shaped, at least in part, by attending to *mass communication content* depicting American people. In more specific terms, the overall attitudes of the teenagers averaged for each of the countries are shown below in Figure 2. Overwhelmingly, as the bar chart indicates, those overall attitudes were negative. Only two of the countries studied (Italy and Argentina) did not, on average, have negative attitudes toward Americans. The remaining ten, in one degree or another, did hold such orientations. Indeed, at least some were truly very negative.

Another way to understand what was found is to look at each of the items included in the attitude scale. These findings are shown below in Figure 3. Again, the results are mainly on the negative side. Only three of the items showed modest positive results.

More specific information about how these teenage high school students viewed Americans can be seen by looking at those scale items that express the three common themes

Country:	Very Negative	Generally Negative	Neutral	Generally Positive	Very Positive
	Negative			Positive	
1. Saudi Arabia		−2.13			
2. Bahrain		−1.86			
3. South Korea		−1.76			
4. Lebanon		−1.55			
5. Mexico		−1.50			
6. China		−1.06			
7. Spain		−0.89			
8. Taiwan		−0.79			
9. Pakistan		−0.46			
10. Nigeria		−0.05			
11. Italy			+0.03		
12. Argentina			+0.69		
OVERALL:		−0.83			

FIGURE 2 Overall Attitudes Toward Americans by Country

most used by the producers of American media content. These are the issues of personal *violence,* the degree to which ordinary Americans are likely to engage in *criminal activities,* and the belief that most American women are *sexually immoral.* As noted, it is these three themes that dominate in the plots of exported motion pictures and TV programming. It is also these three themes—violence, crime, and sexual improprieties—that are frequently reported in news concerning people in the United States.

Americans as a Violent People

While there are motion pictures produced and exported that do not emphasize violence, this is a theme that often dominates what Hollywood produces. Even the cartoon characters that appeal to children (such as the Roadrunner) are filled with violent activities. Fistfights and gun battles can be found any night on the TV programming shown in American communities. Even popular American sports show a considerable amount of violence (e.g., boxing

Scale Item:	Very Negative	Generally Negative	Neutral	Generally Positive	Very Positive
	Negative			Positive	
1. Americans are generally quite violent		−0.87			
2. Americans are a generous people		−0.24			
3. Many American women are sexually immoral		−1.18			
4. Americans respect people unlike themselves		−0.3			
5. Americans are very materialistic		−1.01			
6. Americans have strong religious values			+0.15		
7. Americans like to dominate other people		−1.43			
8. Americans are a peaceful people		−0.27			
9. Many Americans engage in criminal activities		−0.29			
10. Americans are very concerned about their poor			+0.29		
11. Americans have strong family values			+0.74		
12. There is little for which I admire Americans		−0.63			
OVERALL:		−0.83			

FIGURE 3 Overall Attitudes Toward Americans by Scale Item

Country:	Very Negative	Generally Negative	Neutral	Generally Positive	Very Positive
	−5 −4 −3	−2 −1	0 +1	+2 +3	+4 +5
		Negative		Positive	
1. Bahrain	−2.75				
2. Saudi Arabia	−2.18				
3. China	−1.78				
4. South Korea	−1.63				
5. Lebanon	−1.25				
6. Mexico	−1.18				
7. Nigeria	−1.18				
8. Pakistan	−0.93				
9. Spain	−0.55				
10. Argentina			+0.15		
11. Taiwan			0.73		
12. Italy			+1.45		
OVERALL:	−0.95				

FIGURE 4   Americans are Generally Quite Violent

matches and football). Figure 4 shows what the youths in the twelve counties believed concerning this issue as they responded to the statement that "Many Americans are generally quite violent."

If these results have validity, the majority of the youths studied held the belief that the people who live in the United States are generally quite violent in their daily behavior.

Americans as Criminals

As is discussed in Chapter 9 (the Magic Bullet Theory), the preoccupation of American news media with crime began with the earliest mass newspapers. Later, with the emergence of the "yellow press," that trend intensified. The same was true of the early motion pictures. Depictions of crime were seen as offensive by most of the movie-going public of the time. That fact eventually led to the imposition of the industry's *Motion Picture Producers Association's Code,* as discussed in Chapter 21. It was an industry-imposed code that screened motion pictures before they were allowed to be seen in theaters. This satisfied the public and made the films, as many parents saw it, more suitable for child audiences.

Obviously, however, all such efforts to make newspapers and films less focused on crime gradually came to an end as the industries found that profits could be larger if the limits were slowly exceeded. How that came about was discussed in Chapter 20 (the Creeping Cycle of Desensitization Theory). It should come as no surprise, then, that both the entertainment media products as well as the news reports presented by international news organizations—seen virtually worldwide—show that crime is a major factor in the lives of Americans. The data from the teenage study appear to show that (unintended) collateral instruction about this factor has helped to shape the interpretations of the youths studied as to the nature and behavior of the people who live in the United States. Figure 5 shows their pattern of response to the statement that "many Americans engage in criminal activities." As can be seen, once again, only a small number of those believed otherwise.

American Women as Sexually Immoral

The third theme that can be found in many of the entertainment products produced by the movie and television industries, which are then exported worldwide to be enjoyed by youthful audiences, depict Americans engaging in sexual behavior. As Figure 6 shows, the the results are quite clear. Once again, in all but two of the countries studied, this item was responded to by the youths studied in a negative way.

Country:	Very Negative	Generally Negative	Neutral	Generally Positive	Very Positive
	−5 −4 −3 −2 −1 0 +1 +2 +3 +4 +5				
	Negative			Positive	
1. Saudi Arabia	−2.45				
2. South Korea	−2.10				
3. Bahrain	−2.00				
4. Mexico	−1.68				
5. Lebanon	−1.60				
6. China	−1.30				
7. Spain	−0.98				
8. Taiwan	−0.90				
9. Pakistan	−0.43				
10. Nigeria	−0.43				
11. Italy				+0.10	
12. Argentina				+1.63	
OVERALL:	−1.03				

FIGURE 5 Many Americans Engage in Criminal Activities

It should be noted that this does not necessarily mean overt engagement in sexual intercourse—which is often shown in modern films and TV dramas. Activities that seem "sexually immoral" vary considerably from one society to another. For example, in some Muslim countries, a woman who dresses in a Western manner may be judged harshly as "immoral." Holding hands in public may be considered a serious violation of moral codes. Indeed in 2007, news reports seen in the U.S. showed a young Islamic woman being stoned to death at the insistence of her relatives. It was termed by those in the local culture as an "honor killing," inflicted by her family because of a display of inter-gender affection in public. Such killings are not rare. As noted, they can take place when a woman does not dress in the accepted code or when she commits an act in public that is locally defined as "improper" (such as kissing or even holding hands).

Generally, then, the 1,313 teenage high school students studied in the twelve countries noted held negative belief and attitudes concerning Americans. Only in few of those countries were their social constructions of reality concerning the conduct and characteristics of Americans on the positive side of the scale. In particular, when asked to provide their beliefs about Americans concerning three issues that are dominant in U.S.-produced media entertainment and news—violent

Country:	Very Negative	Generally Negative	Neutral	Generally Positive	Very Positive
	−5 −4 −3 −2 −1 0 +1 +2 +3 +4 +5				
	Negative			Positive	
1. Saudi Arabia	−3.23				
2. Bahrain	−2.83				
3. Taiwan	−2.30				
4. Mexico	−2.13				
5. Lebanon	−2.05				
6. South Korea	−1.68				
7. Nigeria	−1.63				
8. Spain	−1.48				
9. China	−1.20				
10. Pakistan	−1.13				
11. Argentina				+0.93	
12. Italy				+1.58	
OVERALL:	−1.43				

FIGURE 6 Many American Women are Sexually Immoral.

behavior, criminal activities, and immoral behavior by women—the majority of these young people indicated negative beliefs and attitudes.

In summary, the findings from the study of views concerning Americans appear to show that, on the whole, the teenagers who responded to the Likert Scale held *unrealistic beliefs* and *decidedly unfavorable attitudes* toward the ordinary people of the United States. Those attitudes were most unfavorable in Saudi Arabia and Bahrain. However, they were also negative in non-Muslim countries such as South Korea and Mexico, which have virtually no Muslim populations—and which are military allies of the U.S.

Most Americans would agree that the views held by these teenagers do not reflect reality. The fact is that people in the United States are no more aggressive toward each other than people who live in similar industrialized countries. Indeed, there are many societies in which acts of violence are by far more common than in the U.S. Most Americans do not have regular fistfights with each other or engage in gun battles in the street. There are those who engage in criminal activities, but these are neither condoned nor widely tolerated. Indeed, they usually wind up in jail. Moreover, American women who follow the general norms of their society are not seen widely in the U.S as behaving in an immoral manner. However, Americans behaving in such ways can frequently be seen in movies and TV dramas.

The beliefs held by the majority of the young people studied, then, are *social constructions of reality* derived from a process of communication. While this is mass communication, the principle is a modern version of Plato's description of the men in the cave who saw shadows on the wall and, through a process of communication, came to believe that they were reality. In the case of the youths in the twelve countries, their beliefs appear to have been influenced to at least some degree by the collateral instruction that is presented in the imported media products to which they attend and enjoy. Those lessons are learned incidentally while these young audiences are being entertained.

Generally, then, it seems clear that teenagers in the countries studied have flawed beliefs about ordinary Americans that result in negative attitudes toward them. It is also a reasonable conclusion, based on the patterns shown in the charts and on other statistical evidence obtained in the *Learning to Hate* study, that these views have been significantly influenced by the content of the entertainment media that their countries import from U.S. sources—particularly movies, television dramas, and other forms of popular culture (and possibly news accounts).

DEVELOPING THE FORMAL THEORY

The issues, concepts, and relationships discussed above can be brought together into seven formal statements that appear to offer at least a tentative explanation of what produced unrealistic beliefs about Americans among the majority of the young people studied. The set of propositions set forth below draws upon insights derived from ancient and modern scholars, including Plato, Lippmann, and Bandura—as well as from Schramm and his colleagues. In that sense, the theory represents a "programmatic" extension of earlier theories.

A Theory of Collateral Instruction, Incidental Learning, and Flawed Constructions of Reality

By incorporating the major concepts studied, then, as well as the empirical data that have been presented, the new theory linking the concepts into a related set of formal statements can be stated in the following terms:

1. The U.S. media and multinational media corporations producing news and entertainment products operate within a *capitalistic economic system* in which profits are essential.
2. To maximize those profits, their products are distributed worldwide to many countries that have *few or no facilities of their own to produce similar content* but in which their local media are used to provide such exported content for entertainment and information desired by their populations.
3. The themes, plots, and depictions that are most exciting, especially to youthful cohorts, stress *violence, crime, and explicit sex*, which are significantly emphasized in the globally distributed products.
4. Depictions of the characteristics and conduct of Americans are presented in news, movies, and TV programs, as well as in other media products distributed globally, but often showing or describing them in ways that *do not reflect* their actual characteristics of the majority.

5. Those portrayals provide *unintended collateral communication instruction* concerning the conduct and characteristics of ordinary Americans (and possibly other types of people) portrayed to audiences worldwide who attend to their local media.

6. By attending to such content, members of those audiences unwittingly experience *incidental learning* about the nature, behavior, and moral standards of those depicted.

7. **Therefore**, from this combination of unintended collateral instruction by exported media products and unwitting incidental learning by those who attend to such communications, audience members are likely to acquire unrealistic beliefs—that is, *flawed social constructions of reality*—about the people who are depicted.

A Note of Caution

While the above theory appears to be able to explain the results of the research, it cannot be concluded that the *only* source that teenagers in other countries have for developing beliefs about the nature of ordinary Americans is mass communication. It was noted that a few of the respondents (eleven percent) had traveled to the U.S. and that these were from Western societies (mainly from Mexico and a few from Europe). Generally, however, the research showed that almost none of the youths in most of the countries studied had any significant personal contact whatsoever with any American from which to learn of their ways. No formal instruction in schools or elsewhere could be identified that systematically disclosed realistically the actual lifestyles, values, and conduct of typical Americans. At the same time, virtually all had daily experiences with media content portraying Americans. The depictions of Americans and their lifestyles in these presentations, therefore, appear to have been a major source available for forming their views.

DISCUSSION

Given the combination of old and new concepts, relationships, and other factors in the theory (and if the present findings have validity), it is unlikely that audiences in many countries—and especially the young, who frequently see Americans depicted in unrealistic ways—will in the near future undergo any significant changes of a more positive nature in what they believe to be their typical conduct and national characteristics.

Obviously, the formal theory above is not restricted to unrealistic collateral instruction about Americans. As stated, it can be applied to any set of ideas, depictions, or portrayals of people, issues, or situations that are presented in mass communication where profit drives what is produced and distributed. The key, then, is whether producers are subject to economic requirements for profits from large audiences. Indeed, because competition among media producers is intense, and earning maximum profits is such a powerful goal, it is likely that in the depiction of Americans in movies and TV dramas, as well as in typical news stories, producers will continue to strive to develop their products in more and more exciting ways—that is, in a *creeping cycle of desensitization* (see Chapter 20). As this takes place in the future, the result will bring more and more unflattering misrepresentations of Americans, or of other people depicted, and their lifestyles.

This issue has implications beyond the process of mass communication. The question of how people in other countries regard Americans has become critically significant in an era of terrorism. Therefore, it is important to understand the process by which flawed constructions of reality about people who live in the United States are acquired as a byproduct of being entertained and informed by television, movies, and news stories distributed throughout the world.

Notes and References

1. Madeline A. Dalton, et. al., "Effect of Smoking in Movies on Adolescent Smoking Imitation: A Cohort Study." *Lancet*, 361, 9273, June 2003. (This was a cooperative study conducted by eight colleagues. This citation is the online version.)

2. R. M. Entman, *The Black Image in the White Mind: Media and Race in America.* (Chicago: The University of Chicago Press, 2001), pp. 81–82.

3. W. Schramm, J. Lyle, and E. B. Parker, *Television in the Lives of Our Children.* (Stanford, CA: Stanford University Press, 1961), p. 75.

4. *Ibid.*

5. A. L. Bandura, *Social Learning Theory* (New York: General Learning Press, 1971).

6. W. Lippmann, *Public Opinion* (New York: Harcourt, Brace and Company, 1922), p. 358.

7. M. L. DeFleur, "Where Have All the Milestones Gone? The Decline of Significant Research on the Process and Effects of Mass Communication," *Mass Communication & Society* 1, 1998, pp. 85–98.

8. M. L. DeFleur and M. H. DeFleur, *Learning to Hate Americans: How the U.S. Media Shape Attitudes of Teenagers in Twelve Countries.* (Spokane: Marquette Books, 2002), pp. 55–67.

9. A. E. Kramer, "50% Good News is Bad News in Russian Radio," *The New York Times,* April 22, 2007, p. 1.

10. An organization that periodically conducts such polls is the Pew Research Center for the People and the Press, located in Washington, D.C. It assess adult beliefs and attitudes toward the "United States" in many countries, as well as the opinions of local populations concerning many issues that may be influenced by U.S. policies and actions. Its website (http://people-press.org/) is simple and easy to use.

11. Melvin DeFleur, and Frank Westie, "Attitude as a Scientific Concept," *Social Forces,* 42, 1, (1963) pp. 17–31. See also Melvin L. DeFleur and William R. Catton, "The Limits of Determinancy in Attitude Measurement," *Social Forces,* 25, (1957) pp. 295–300, and Melvin L. DeFleur and Frank R. Westie, "Verbal Attitudes and Overt Acts: An Experiment with the Salience of Attitudes," *American Sociological Review,* 23, 6 (1958).

CHAPTER **24**

Other Formulations and Concepts

A number of additional theoretical essays, concepts, interpretative writings, and explanatory formulations were developed by mass communication scholars during the last half of the twentieth century. In each case, these formulations represented efforts to describe, understand, and explain either a narrow and specific process, an effect of the constantly changing system of mass communication, or a broad intellectual perspective for viewing the media. In many ways, this body of writings continues to offer valuable insights as to the nature of the mass media, how their operations and functions were shaped within their societies at various points in time, and the consequences that they appeared to be having on the populations that they were serving. The value of such insights is that they help in understanding how the political, economic, and cultural features of a society often shape the nature of some specific influence of mass communication content or the media that develop within them.

The reason why they are grouped together in this one chapter is that, for the most part, this category of scholarly efforts does not lend itself easily to either rigorous empirical verification or, in some cases, the more formal format that has been used in previous chapters. In any case, in this chapter, each of the concepts or perspectives discussed (in the sections that follow) has been summarized briefly so as to present its central ideas.

Providing the ideas of these writers in summary form in a single chapter does not mean that they are of minor importance. Indeed, several received wide attention in their time and have provided lasting perspectives that have been used to guide the beliefs of the public as well as the thinking of scholars about the role and influences of mass communication in society. At least some have been found useful in designing empirical studies of various aspects of the processes and consequences of mass communication. In other cases, these formulations have been focused very broadly as expository discourses on the nature of the press or other media. Others are much more narrowly focused on a very specific situation, a special kind of influence on a particular category of people in an audience. But whatever their nature or scope, each has played a part in the accumulation of ideas about the processes and nature of mass communication.

In the sections that follow, then, several such formulations are reviewed. The earliest, published in the mid-1950s, presents an analysis of four different ways in which the press can be viewed as it has delivered news to populations at different times within distinct political and economic systems. In their work *Four Theories of the Press,* media scholars Fred Seibert, Theodore Peterson, and Wilbur Schramm explained how these different versions of the press (mainly print media but also others of their time) were shaped by the political and economic systems prevailing within the societies during the historical period in which they developed.[1] Although they label their discussions "theories" of the press, they do not provide cleat-cut guides to empirical research for purposes of verification. Instead, they are broad *descriptions of the nature of the press* as it functioned during different periods in various political-economic systems.

In the 1960s, English professor Marshall McLuhan published *Understanding Media: The Extension of Man.*[2] It quickly became a popular work among the educated segment of the public. In this work, McLuhan introduced a number of catchy and colorful phrases into his discussions (e.g, "hot" and "cool" media, "the medium is the message"). While the American media have undergone many technological changes since his time, his writings remain as interesting interpretation of the nature, functioning, and consequences of mass communications.

McLuhan's explanation of the media and their influences was never intended to serve as a guide to empirical research. It was written in a complex literary style—as an expository essay sprinkled liberally with references to, and examples from, poems, classic works, and the creative products of various artists, musicians, and writers. Many found it both interesting and enlightening. While it makes for fascinating reading for those who enjoy high culture, it is difficult to classify McLuhan's work in terms of a particular type of theory. Nevertheless, because it is so widely known, it has become a part of the accumulated writings of scholars who have tried to understand and explain the complexities and consequences of mass communication.

Another well-known formulation was developed by media scholar George Gerbner during the 1970s and 1980s. In 1971, as was discussed earlier, President Lyndon B. Johnson appointed a group of media researchers and others as the *Violence Commission.* Funds were provided by Congress to conduct research and evaluate the influence of violent media content on American life. He did this because many citizens were concerned that increasing amounts of such content in the media and especially on television (see Chapter 20, on the Creeping Cycle of Desensitization). That trend seemed to be causing a rise in violence and crime, especially among the nation's youth. Over a twenty-year period, George Gerbner conducted a variety of empirical studies of media influences and advanced a formulation he termed *cultivation analysis.* His theoretical perspective was published in a series of journal articles during the 1970s and early 1980s and in a reprinted selective collection of those works by Nancy Signorelli and Michael Morgan.[3]

Essentially, Gerbner maintained that the content that people attended to in the media—particularly by viewing television—"cultivated" their beliefs. That is, he maintained that viewing television content brought people to believe in certain (flawed) conceptions about the world in which they lived. Gerbner's central focus was on televised violence. His studies indicated that media content often leads citizens to conclude that situations in reality—such as their personal risks from crime—are of a similar nature to what they had seen on TV.[4] In other words, television is seen as an "active" agent, penetrating the mind of the viewer—like a "magic bullet"—and altering the person's cognitive structure. This idea was, in many ways, a modern version of the "social construction or reality" theory, which was founded in the writings of Plato. It is also similar in some ways to the new theory presented in the previous chapter. Walter Lippmann had advanced a similar idea when he wrote that the function of the (news) media was to create "pictures in our heads of the world outside" (see Chapter 8). Additionally, Wilbur Schramm's concept of (unwitting and unintended) "incidental learning" speaks to much the same issue (see Chapter 23).

The fourth formulation to be considered was published as a book in 1984. Elisabeth Noelle-Neumann titled it *The Spiral of Silence: Public Opinion—Our Social Skin.*[5] Based on German data from several elections, it explained that, when one segment of voters with a particular point of view spoke out especially strongly, gaining the attention of the press, those with different views tended not to do so. The result was that the political positions of those who were very vocal in the press came to be seen as those of the majority. For many, this influence has long been well understood. Traditionally, it has been called a "bandwagon effect." Learning that one candidate seems to be winning attracts an increasing number of less committed voters to what they interpret as the majority position. Noelle-Neumann labeled this process a "spiral of silence," in which those with contrary views made fewer and fewer efforts to make their ideas public—effectively silencing media attention to their views. Ultimately, this author claimed, the resulting process shaped the results of the elections.

The phenomenon of "new wine in old bottles" occurs frequently in the scholarly world, as researchers and writers rediscover a relationship that they believe has not previously been identified and then give it a new creative label. This rediscovery phenomenon is by no means confined to studies of the media. Pitrim Sorokin, a well-known social scientist, has called those who were such rediscoverers "new Colombuses."[6] However, that does not suggest that they should not do such activity. Any discovery of a consistent relationship has merit, even if someone has already discovered it and given it a different name.

Finally, two additional conceptualizations merit consideration. One is the concept of "framing." It represents an adaptation of classical psychological theories of perception first advanced in the nineteenth century.[7] It has long been commonly understood that what people experience internally may differ in many ways from the objective situation that is "out there." Applied to mass communication, it refers to the way in which a member of an audience puts together a subjective interpretation, within his or her mind, of a news story or some other depiction of actions or events encountered in the media. Social scientists have for more than a century addressed this process—starting in the late 1880s, with the "brass instrument" experiments of Heinrich Helmholtz, and continuing with the experiments of the *Gestalt* theorists in the 1920s, who studied the subjective interpretive patterns that people imposed on stimili that they perceived. Thus, it was established early that the ways in which people "understand" something that they perceive may be different from the nature of the actual event.

Another concept to be discussed is termed the "third person effect." It is essentially a very simple and narrowly focused idea. A person who attends to mass communications may feel that he or she is not influenced by exposure to some form of media content, but he or she does believe that other "more susceptible" people usually are.

In the sections that follow, then, each of these formulations and concepts will be discussed briefly. As noted, each has been an influence on the ways in which contemporary scholars think about the media. In a least some cases, they have shaped research interests by providing a general way of viewing the media. For the reasons explained, however, most do not lend themselves as readily to a *deductive* form in which their major propositions can be set forth as a limited set of interrelated statements. This has in some cases limited their role in providing well-focused logical predictions that have served as guides to specific empirical investigations that have been designed to test specific hypotheses. Nevertheless, each of those discussed below has been a part of the accumulation of scholarly knowledge about the process and effects of mass communication.

FOUR "THEORIES" OF THE PRESS

An early and important formulation, published in 1956 by three distinguished media scholars, was titled *Four Theories of the Press*. As indicated, these were not "theories" in the sense discussed in Chapter 2. However, they were "theoretical" in a broad sense in that each was a complex explanatory essay describing how the news media were shaped and organized—and how they operated—at various times in four different kinds of societal and political contexts. Specifically, each essay was embedded in detailed discussions of philosophical, political, and sociological analysis as these applied to the press in different types of societies and cultures at various periods in history.

Essentially, then, these four essays were historical accounts. That is, the major purpose of the authors was to show how the press (news media in general) in each of these historical contexts had been shaped by the prevailing social orders within which they were developed and functioned. To accomplish this, they set forth their interpretations of how the press in these contexts were influenced by the nature of the formal relationships between individual people in a society, the nature of the state, its controlling leaders, and major societal institutions. They termed these four contexts the *authoritarian, libertarian, social responsibility,* and *Soviet Communist* "theories." Each, they explained, gave rise to a distinct conception of the nature of the press, the way it was controlled in those environments, and what it disseminated as content.

Its authors were, as they themselves noted, particularly concerned with *printed* media—as opposed to broadcast or film. Their reasons for this were that the print news media came first and set the basic nature of those that came later. In addition, over the centuries they generated far more in the way of debates and discussions as to their role in society.

Within this focus, then, this important book offered what perhaps could be thought of as four distinctive "models" against which press systems—at different periods of history in different countries—could be compared. As such, it offered valuable insights for understanding how the communication systems in contrasting political and economic settings came into existence, were organized, were controlled, and were used for the delivery of news and other information to their audiences. The authors put this overall goal in their introduction to the book in this way:

> In the simplest terms, the question behind this book is, why is the press as it is? Why does it apparently serve different purposes and appear in widely different forms in different countries? Why, for example, is the press of the Soviet Union so different from our own, and the press of Argentina so different from that of Great Britain?[8]

Authoritarian Theory

The guiding principle used by the authors in their analysis of each of the four types of press systems discussed in the book is this:

> Since the press . . . was introduced into an already organized society, its relation to that society was naturally determined by the basic assumptions or postulates which were then furnishing the foundation for social controls. Since most of the governments of western Europe were then operating on authoritarian principles when the popular press emerged, those same principles became the basis for a system of press control.[9]

The authors explain that these assumptions concerning *the nature of government*, on which controls over the press were first founded, were of ancient origins and extended back in time to the writings of Plato, Machiavelli, Hobbes, and many others. In more modern times, they took newer forms within the authoritarian systems established by Mussolini and Hitler. Essentially, these assumptions concerned the (1) nature of human beings, (2) the characteristics of society and the state, (3) the relationship between individuals and the state, and (4) finally, the nature of knowledge and truth.

In all such systems, the individual is of much less significance than the society as a whole. Moreover, the *state*, as an organized system of regulations and controls, provides for orderly life within society and is therefore assumed to be of the highest level of importance. It is only within that stable and controlled environment, according to this form of thinking, that the human being can achieve his or her highest potential.

> The individual's dependence on the state for achieving an advanced civilization appears to be a common ingredient in all authoritarian systems. In and through the State, man achieves his ends; without the State, man remains a primitive being.[10]

Given these observations, then, their first essay explains how, in a period of monarchies and not long after the process of printing was invented, the early newspapers that were produced and distributed *had to be controlled*. The kings and emperors of the time distrusted the press and saw it as a probable source of mischief that could threaten the stability of the state, the orderly life it provided, and (especially) their own power. Consequently, they imposed rigid requirements on publishers of all kinds. Those who operated printing enterprises did so only with the permission of the monarch. All information to be published had first to be reviewed by the monarch's representatives. Only after approval was gained could it be "published by authority." For understandable reasons, then, the authors label their analysis of this early system as the *authoritarian theory of the press*.

In the twentieth century, other types of rigid authoritarian systems were established by the fascist governments that developed—particularly in Germany and Italy. In these forms of government, the authority of the state was supreme. Even "truth" was subject to the goals of those controlling the state. Both Hitler and Mussolini made elaborate use of propaganda, disseminated as "truth" by a totally controlled system of mass media.

In some ways, these authoritarian systems for controlling the flow of information from their center of political authority to those that were ruled are similar to the communication model used by the Church of the Middle Ages. For centuries the Church also exercised authoritarian controls over people's beliefs and opinions. That is, it was the pope and his hierarchy in Rome that decided the nature of "truth," how it was to be disseminated to the population, and for what purposes. Any "truth" contrary to the teachings of the Church was (by definition) false and heretical. This got Galileo into serious trouble when he found (observed empirically), with his newly invented telescope, that the planets did indeed revolve around the sun and not the earth. It was contrary to the "truths" maintained by the Church, and when he made his findings public, he was arrested and confined to his home.

Generally, then, the authoritarian model of the press required that all information that is received by members of the society via media be first screened and authorized by those in control before being disseminated. If not, there was the danger that those who receive unauthorized information would form unwanted opinions and beliefs that could erode the power of those in charge. For that reason, in an authoritarian system, media that disseminate news and other forms of information to the public were allowed to do so only under rigid rules designed and implemented by those in positions of power. Thus, as literacy expanded, it became increasingly necessary under this system to prevent printers of pamphlets, newspapers, and even books to prepare and disseminate any content that was deemed threatening to those in power. This was done by making it *a crime* to print and distribute by any means any writings that were not first cleared by agents of the monarch.

Commonly, then, the monarch had agents who routinely reviewed, prior to publication, all forms of printed material that would be distributed to the population. In the American colonies, printers had to have everything reviewed by special representatives of the Crown. Whatever came off their presses, after passing that review, was "published by authority." In more modern times, by extension, during the Fascist period in Europe, this system was used for other media, such as radio and film.

Those who have enforced the authoritarian model have always maintained that they were justified in doing so. Their reasons offered for their actions were essentially these: It is obvious that maintaining a stable and predictable social order is essential to the well-being of its citizens. It is also obvious that if peace and order is not preserved, the resulting turmoil can have negative consequences for those citizens. Therefore, the claim goes, those in charge have an obligation to restrain those who would bring social disruption by publishing information that will foster discontent and conflict.

Today, the Soviet Union no longer exists. Nevertheless, for the reasons noted above, the authoritarian "Soviet Communist" model of press control is alive and well—even though the label is no longer correct. One need only to look at such nations as Cuba, North Korea, or Iran. In such settings, the press is rigidly controlled by those who hold power. There is no opposition press in Cuba, that openly criticized the actions of Fidel Castro, (or Raul Castro more recently) or one in North Korea denouncing the policies of Kim Jong Il. If someone were to try to start such an opposition press in those settings, he or she would be summarily jailed—or possibly dealt with more drastically. The same is true in the case of all governments where power is centralized in a similar manner. Again, the justification for enforcing such a system is that disruption and conflict fostered by a critical press cannot be tolerated and the public must be protected against such social instability. The authoritarian model of press control, therefore, is not just a system that is of historical interest. Such systems continue to exist, to disseminate "truth" and "knowledge" in the form of controlled versions of the news designed to shape the beliefs and opinions of populations.

Libertarian Theory

As the history of the American colonies shows, many people of the time chafed under the authoritarian system of press control imposed by the Crown. Increasingly, during the colonial period, a number of prominent individuals demanded more freedom to speak out against government—to have greater *liberty* to publish materials that may not have pleased those in power. During the time, the concept of political democracy was emerging. This idea represented a refocusing of the source of political power—which had for centuries been from *the top down*. Ever since political systems came into existence, some leaders claimed that their power had been granted by a supernatural source. The emerging new concept of government was that power was obtained from *the bottom up*. That is, rulers governed only with the consent of the people.

As systems of democracy were being shaped in France and the fledgling United States, the concept of *personal liberty* became a central one shaping the new political order. This concept of liberty included not only the right to play a personal part in choosing those who would exercise power at the ballot box but also the freedom to speak out—to criticize those in charge when that seemed called for. That meant not only in public meetings and speeches but also in print.

The system of publishing "by authority" continued in the colonies, even after it had largely been abandoned in Britain. In the 1730s, in the New York colony, a landmark trial of Peter Zenger, a newspaper publisher who printed articles criticizing Crown policy, was a major factor in shaping thinking about freedom of the press. He was charged with "seditious libel" (the crime of publishing untruths in an effort to undermine government). He was found "not guilty" by a jury of his peers, on the grounds that what he had published was *true*. The result of the Zenger trial was an awareness of the importance of a free press. This idea became a central issue in the intellectual foundations of the American Revolution. Eventually, these ideas about liberty, freedom of speech, and freedom of the press were incorporated into the Constitution of the United States, as a part of the set of ten amendments adopted as the Bill of Rights. For this reason, the authors use the term *libertarian theory of the press* to describe the type of newspapers that were developed within this social and political context.

Social Responsibility Theory

As the press matured, new technologies of printing and distribution were increasingly developed, and newspapers (and later other media) brought ever larger numbers into their audiences. As explained previously, Horace Mann had persuaded the legislature of Massachusetts to establish free and mandatary public education in order to increase literacy among the population. That innovation quickly spread to other states, expanding the numbers of people who could read. As subscriptions rose across the nation, with more and more people receiving information from newspapers, thoughtful journalists began to see the press in a new light. It was not, they began to believe, just a set of business enterprises operated by owners in any manner they wanted just to make a profit or so that they could speak out. It seemed clear that the press had significant influences on many people's beliefs, ideas, and behaviors about many kinds of important issues and events.

Based on this understanding, a conception was developed by both the public and those managing newspapers that, because of its influence, the press had *social responsibilities*. A newspaper, or other medium, should not be just a mouthpiece for those with special interests or political agendas. It had to serve many needs of a great variety of people by presenting news accurately in an unbiased manner—providing the population with a truthful, comprehensive, and intelligent account of each day's events. This way of thinking about the maturing press was referred to by the authors in their book as the *responsibility theory of the press.*

Early in the twentieth century, the period of "yellow journalism" came to dominate at least some newspapers—mainly in urban settings. Their content emphasized sensational reports of crime, corruption, and deviance, plus stories with emotional content and human interest. It was entertaining, and the goal was to increase circulations. It was remarkably successful in doing so. However, when the public tired of sensationalism, a more objective form of journalism came into existence. It had an obligation to be as accurate as possible, to separate fact from opinion, and to serve the public by full and unbiased reporting of the news.

Following World War II, a *Commission on the Freedom of the Press* examined the practices and characteristics of American newspapers and the broadcast media that existed at the time.[11] In many ways, it was a landmark development that brought the Social Responsibility Theory into greater visibility. While not all newspapers followed the principles that were outlined in the Commission's report, many did. Siebert and his colleagues summed up the functions of the press under this new conception in terms of six basic tasks:

(1) Servicing the political system by providing information, discussion, and debate on public affairs; (2) enlightening the public so as to make it capable of self-government; (3) safeguarding the rights of the individual by serving as a watchdog against government; (4) servicing the economic system, primarily by bringing together the buyers and sellers of goods and services through the medium of advertising; (5) providing entertainment; (6) maintaining its own financial self-sufficiency so as to be free from the pressures of special interests.[12]

Although one might question number five as not an important function of the press, these six responsibilities form a far more positive view of its nature and functions than any that had previously existed. It brought dignity and *gravitas* (a sense of seriousness and importance) to the craft of journalism as well as to the newspapers themselves.

Adding to their conception of their own importance in society, journalists invented a new basic "right" for citizens, to add to those that had already been specified in the U.S. Constitution. The public, they declared, had a *right to know*—which, of course, gave journalists the right to publish whatever they defined as something that the public should be able to learn about. In the beginning that meant *serious matters of public concern.* Today, it has also come to mean lurid details of the private lives and affairs of prominent people. The fact that this conflicts with a *right to privacy* does not trouble today's press. (Neither of these "rights" is stated in the Constitution.) Thus, from news reports, we learn the sordid details of many people's intimate activities, which they do not want made public. This is hardly consistent with points (1), (2), and (3) in the quotation above. Nevertheless, the social responsibility theory of the press was a great step forward from either the authoritarian model or the libertarian model. It was a very large step indeed from the earlier "partisan" newspapers that were supported and published to promote and support the goals of a particular special interest.

Today, the socially responsible press is alive and well—at least in principle. Not all newspapers today follow the mandates of the *Commission on the Freedom of the Press* as set forth in the 1940s, but the majority more or less tend to do so. Thus, in many ways, it is this conception of the nature and functions of the press that characterize most newspapers and other news media of the twenty-first century in the United States.

Soviet Communist Theory

One of the major concerns at the time the book was published was what was taking place regarding the press in the Soviet Union. World War II had only recently ended when the book was being developed. The Cold War was beginning, and the Soviet Union was being recognized as a potential source of danger. The manner in which Soviet leaders were using their news media as agents of social control had become a matter of considerable concern. It had been clear, before and during World War II, that in highly controlled societies, such as those of fascist Germany and Italy, the press was an extension of government. It was a highly controlled instrument used to shape public beliefs, interpretations, and opinions favoring those in power. That was also clearly the case in the Soviet Union.

The Soviet Union had been an ally of the U.S. and Britain in the defeat of the Nazis. Moreover, it was based on the political theories of Marx (who had himself been a journalist) and of Lenin (who applied Marxian theory to the development of the Soviet state). Basically, Marxism claimed that power was vested in the people. But the press system that had developed within Stalin's Soviet Union did not seem embedded in that concept. It appeared to be much more like those used in fascist societies as a means of gaining and retaining control over the population. While this became increasingly obvious, the exact nature of the Soviet press was not entirely clear. The explanations set forth in *Four Theories of the Press* provided important insights into its workings. It was made clear that it operated within a system of *state ownership*, exercising *heavy censorship*, and making *deliberate use of propaganda.* They used the term the "Soviet Communist theory of the press" to describe this system. Although the Russian society has changed greatly in recent times, in many respects, the model described by Wilbur Schramm, who prepared that section of the book, is still valuable in trying to understand the nature and role of the press in tightly controlled and centrally dominated societies today. Its principles can be summarized in the following terms:[13]

1. Mass communications are used instrumentally—that is, as an instrument of the state and the Party.
2. They are closely integrated with other instruments of state power and Party influence.
3. They are used as instruments of unity within the state and Party.
4. They are used as instruments of state and Party "revelations."
5. They are used almost exclusively as instrument of propaganda and agitation. They are characterized by a strictly enforced responsibility.

What made the Soviet Communist theory of the press so fascinating at the time of the Cold War was how greatly different it was from the Social Responsibility Theory that prevailed in the

United States. In many ways, however, there are many parallels between the Soviet system and the older authoritarian theory that characterized both Europe and the American colonies in the eighteenth century. Today, of course, the Soviet Union is now history, and the press in Russia has undergone at least some changes. However, as noted, versions of the Soviet Communist theory of the press still prevail in countries with Marxian political systems.

Overall, the important lesson from this work on *Four Theories of the Press* lies not in the details of the several models of the press that were closely examined. Indeed, while each version can be found to one degree or another today in various countries, the main point is that these scholars described and explained the direct and causal relationship between the type of government that provides stability in a society and the nature of the press that emerges and functions within it. That relationship will determine whether the press is, or is not, controlled by those in power; what content will be supplied to the public; and the nature of the "truths" that will be disseminated for what purpose.

THE INTERPRETATIONS OF MARSHALL MCLUHAN

In many respects, Marshall McLuhan is one of the most controversial scholars who has ever attempted to write about the nature and consequences of mass communication. His explanations, set forth in the mid-1960s, of the ways in which the modern media are an influence on individual and social life are often cryptic, contradictory, and generally difficult to understand.[14] Nevertheless, those ideas at one time became very popular among the more educated segment of the public. They were also very popular among those who owned and controlled the mass media.

McLuhan was not a social scientist or in any sense a media researcher or communications scholar. He was a Canadian English professor who undertook to develop a discourse on how the new media—specifically the mass media that came after print—were changing the ways in which individual people experience the world and also the nature of the social order itself. Radio and television, he believed, would open remarkable vistas for ordinary people, and that would change their ways of life.

The Global Village

One of the changes that McLuhan predicted was the disappearance of conflicts and tensions between different categories of people and societies worldwide. With the ability to exchange messages freely and instantaneously, he declared, conflicts could be resolved and people on the planet would come to be *one large community.* It would appear to many today that this state of affairs never materialized. Recent wars, social upheavals, genocides, and continuing acts of terrorism indicate that conflicts clearly remain, even though our ability to communicate with new technologies has increased dramatically.

McLuhan claimed that his ideas about the consequences of increased communication between peoples were original. In some ways, however, he was also a "New Columbus." For example, he made no mention of the work of sociologist Charles Horton Cooley, who, as the 1900s began, maintained that new communications media (of his time) would bring great changes in human life. Cooley saw the mass newspaper delivered to one's door, the new telegraph, and the telephone "enlarging" in dramatic ways the manner by which human beings could contact one another and "animating" them to be more involved in public affairs. He understood clearly that such an expansion was going to have profound influences on the human condition, and he tried to anticipate what those might be. One consequence, he explained, would be to *reduce conflicts and tensions* between people around the world, opening an era—a "global village"—of greater peace and stability. Cooley, therefore, was an earlier scholar who tried to analyze the forthcoming consequences of the new media by which human beings were able more swiftly to exchange messages. It would, he wrote, open a "whole new epoch in human existence."[15]

McLuhan maintained basically the same thing with respect to the new media of his time. But in spite of his failure to recognize earlier scholars, it was an intriguing idea. The new media would bring people together all over the world. Radio and (the then new) television were bringing information to people in ways that had never been the case before. Those ways involved not only the human senses (seeing and hearing) so as to influence the life of the individual but also the ways in which human beings would relate to each other. Again, ignoring earlier scholars who had maintained essentially the same idea, he used the term "global village" to forecast a time when barriers to communication between human groups would be so fully open that conflict would subside.[16]

Unfortunately, there are grounds today to see that such increased contact has had opposite results. In the preceding chapter, a major international study was discussed. It showed that teenagers in twelve countries in various parts of the world develop negative beliefs and attitudes toward the ordinary people who live in the United States when they view entertainment products that are exported to their countries. As was explained, television programs, movies, and other forms of popular culture routinely depict Americans as deserving punishment because they are violent and criminally inclined and also because women in the U.S. are sexually immoral.

The Medium Is the Message

The idea that a new communications technology can make major transformation in the human condition is not difficult to understand. McLuhan was well aware that, when a society changes from verbal-only mode of communication to one where reading and writing is common, that change can have profound results. For example, the development of their system of writing by the ancient Greeks greatly expanded knowledge and brought many changes in their society. Similarly, the development of printing and subsequent increases in literacy, as a result of Gutenberg's press, resulted in a great expansion of Western culture. In that sense, each new medium is a "message" that brings new meanings to the human condition.

To explain this idea, McLuhan embedded his discussion within a complex web of citations and references to modern and classical poets, philosophers, and writers. More specifically, he offered an analogy to explain what he meant by the phrase "the medium is the message." Using the example of "automation," he explained the idea in these terms:

> This is merely to say that the personal and social consequences of any medium—that is of any extension of ourselves—result from the new scale that is introduced into our affairs by each extension of ourselves or by any new technology. Thus, with automation, for example, the new patterns of human association tend to eliminate jobs, it is true. That is the negative result. Positively, automation creates roles for people, which is to say any depth of involvement in their work and human association that our preceding technology had destroyed.[17]

Although an interesting analogy, that passage does not seem to many to spell out in precise terms what McLuhan was saying about the media. Essentially, and however cryptically, he seemed to be making the point that changes in the ways people communicate—with new media technologies—bring about major changes in their personal behavior, their culture, and their social order.

That is a valid, but hardly new, observation. Major changes in communication have occurred many times in human history, and a host of scholars, before McLuhan, have discussed their profound influences on the nature of the human condition, culture, and society. These changes include the development of the ability to speak and use languages (about 45,000 years ago), the emergence of writing (about 5,000 years back), printing (in 1455), the development of a practical telegraph (in 1844), the telephone (in 1876), radio (in 1896), motion pictures (in 1900), and television (in 1922). Each of these technologies took awhile to develop, spread, and become widely used by the public through the process of the adoption of innovation (see Chapter 18). But that same point can be made by any change in a major technology. As we have often noted, an example is the steam engine. It brought the Industrial Revolution. Another example is the airplane. It has greatly increased people's ability to travel on this planet and to contact people in different places and societies. Essentially, then, McLuhan's discussion of the changes that followed the emergence of contemporary media adds nothing particularly new. Students of social and cultural change have discussed the role of technology in altering the human condition for a very long time.

Media Hot and Cold

McLuhan developed a simple classification scheme for the various media in human use. This definition was based on the amount of data that the medium presented in a given message to those who received it. A "hot" medium, in this system of classification, is one that provides the receiver with a large amount of data. A "cool" one provides less. McLuhan explained the distinction in the following terms:

> There is a basic principle that distinguishes a hot medium like radio from a cool one like the telephone, or a hot medium like the movie from a cool one like TV. A hot medium is one that extends one single sense in 'high definition.' High definition is the state of being well filled with data. A photograph is, visually, 'high definition.' A cartoon is 'low definition' because very little visual information is provided.[18]

Using these definitions, McLuhan went on to explain that both speech and the telephone are cool media on the grounds that both supply limited information to the recipient. The receiver has to be an active participant and must "fill in" a considerable amount of information in order to understand the message. In contrast, he maintained, a hot medium supplies far more, and the receiver does not have to participate as fully in the process of communication.

This distinction has confused many scholars. For example, he proclaimed print to be a "hot" medium. His explanation was not based on the amount of data that was provided on a printed page (as in the above quotation) but on the fact that print had resulted in profound changes in society. Beyond that, he predicted (as many others have) that the age of print would soon come to an end. The new medium of televison would replace it. This delighted the television industry but did not make sense to many scholars. As Baran and Davis note:

> His mantra became broadcast industry gospel: so what if children spend most of their time in front of television sets and become functionally illiterate? Eventually we will all live in a global village where literacy is as unnecessary as it was in preliterate tribal villages. Why worry about the negative consequences of television when it is obviously so much better than the hot old media that it is replacing?[19]

McLuhan's Legacy

Generally, then, McLuhan's ideas were proclaimed at the time as very insightful and important by many members of the public. However, media researchers and scholars found it difficult to understand what he was trying to say. As it turned out, when they examined his analyses closely, they were less than impressed. His works were complex, convoluted, and often contradictory. His ideas were embedded in long references to works from literature and the arts in his attempt to make them understood. Moreover, in his writings, he set forth a number of conclusions that had been expressed earlier in one way or another by many previous scholars. He made a number of predictions that have failed to come about (e.g., the emergence of a "global village" and the disappearance of print).

In terms of his contributions to research, these have been minimal at best. His theories do not lend themselves to the logical generation of hypotheses that can be studied and tested with empirical observations. Those investigators who have tried to design studies to test his ideas have found them too vague, contradictory, and abstract. As a consequence, no body of research findings has accumulated to either verify or reject the conclusions McLuhan reached concerning modern media or their influences on individual or social life. Nevertheless, it would be a mistake to assume that his ideas have no merit. They still have a following among some segments of the public. They make fascinating (if difficult) reading, and it may be that at some point in the future his insights and explanations will be seen as of greater significance to researchers and scholars.

CULTIVATION ANALYSIS

As has been explained, the introduction of television into the media mix in the United States began just after World War II. During the 1950s, the adoption of innovation process was proceeding rapidly. It was a dramatic new form of mass communication, even in its earliest black-and-white and small screen days. It caught on quickly, and within a decade almost all American households had a receiver.

Television had many of the features of motion pictures—movement, sound, and visual representations, just like films—but it went far beyond that medium. It also brought news, children's cartoons, documentaries, distance-learning lessons, police dramas, political campaigns, and many other kinds of content—all packaged into one remarkable box right there in the living room. Little wonder that media scholars didn't know quite what to make of it. Above all, it provided cheap and easily available entertainment for American families who did not even have to leave their homes.

As TV viewing increased dramatically, it did not take long for scholars to come to realize that its content was possibly having a profound influence on the lives of many Americans—and especially their children.[20] At the time, there had been increases in the levels of crime and violence in many cities in the U.S. Since TV had arrived, and as its use had climbed dramatically during that same period, it seemed obvious the one was causing the other (*post hoc, ergo propter hoc*). Indeed, many people were shocked to learn that the first "television generation" (those born after the introduction of the medium) were spending more time, on average, watching television than they spent in school. It is not surprising, then, that TV was proclaimed to be a new and powerful teacher:

> Television has become our nation's (and increasingly the world's) most common and constant learning environment. It both (selectively) mirrors and leads society. Television is first and foremost, however, a storyteller—it tells most of the stories to most of the people most of the time. As such, television is the wholesale distributor of images and forms the mainstream of our popular culture. For the first time in human history, a centralized commercial institution rather than parents, the church or the school tells most of the stories.[21]

Given this interpretation of the nature and functions of television, which was shared by many people at the time, it is little wonder that it was a matter of concern to parents, educators, and others in the society. Many, including the Parents and Teachers Association, the American Medical Association, and other professional groups spoke out, denouncing television for the harmful content that it was producing and disseminating.

The Scientific Advisory Committee on Television and Social Behavior

That widespread public concern was clearly perceived by members of the U.S. Congress. Its members constantly worried about being re-elected and were therefore always alert to issues on the policy agenda that disturbed voters. With street violence on the rise and with recent assassinations of Martin Luther King and Bobby Kennedy—adding further evidence about increasing violence—*something had to be done*. The solution, devised by the legislative branch, was to fund a large-scale research effort to investigate the role and influences of television. In 1969, a million dollars was provided to the surgeon general to establish a Scientific Advisory Committee on Television and Social Behavior. That committee included a number of prominent media scholars and researchers.

Earlier, during the late 1960s, George Gerbner had begun his Cultural Indicators project, a program of research aimed specifically at studying the content of primetime and weekend daytime TV network programming. He was able to gain financial support from the Surgeon General's Advisory Committee for an expanded program of investigations. Basically, his idea was to assess and document ways in which the content of network (broadcast) television influenced viewers' conceptions of reality. Although he did not portray it as such, in this sense, it was an extension of the "social construction of reality theory," and Walter Lippmann's discussion of the "pictures in our heads (see Chapters 3 and 8). Although he did not use those terms, the influences he discussed were based on the processes of "collateral instruction" and "incidental learning" (see Chapters 5 and 23) associated with what people saw on television. The term Gerbner chose to describe his research focus was "cultivation analysis."

Shaping Shared Beliefs

The basic idea of cultivation analysis, as it applies specifically to television as a mass medium, can be stated in the following way:

> In its simplest form, cultivation analysis attempts to determine the extent to which people who watch greater amounts of television (generally referred to as *heavy viewers*) hold different conceptions of social reality from those who watch less, other factors held constant.[22]

One of the problems that came to be associated with the term "cultivation" is that it implies that the medium, like a living thing, or a "magic bullet," has the power to reach out and actively shape the thinking and beliefs of human beings. Grammarians refer to such a claim as *anthropomorphism*—the attribution of human characteristics and abilities to a nonhuman entity. It is a mistake to assume that something that is not a living human being can act like one. In the case of mass media, it is—as previous chapters have shown—the people in the audience who themselves select, respond to, and create meanings for what they see when they view television.

Morgan and Signorelli made an attempt to dismiss this error. They explained that the term "cultivation" does not imply that the medium can act in the ways implied. They suggest that it meant only that "the generation (in some) and maintenance (in others) of some sets of outlooks or beliefs can be traced to steady, cumulative exposure to the world of television."[23] However, their interpretation that TV can "generate" and "maintain" outlooks and beliefs also looks suspiciously like anthropomorphism. Again, the medium is said to have "magic bullet" powers not ordinarily attributed to a non-human entity. It is, after all, the people in the audience who attend, perceive, experience, and then form their outlooks and beliefs—perhaps using information that they gained while viewing television—or perhaps not. There is nothing unique about TV in this respect. They could do the same with information gained from a newspaper, movie, radio program, magazine, billboard ad, the Bible, or even their neighbors. Presumably, they too should be included with TV as media that can "cultivate" peoples' conceptions of social reality.

Another of Gerbner's central concepts that appears to have problems in this description and explanation of the role of television in the American society is "mainstreaming." The basic idea here is that many people view television extensively, and since it is said to serve as *the great teacher*, its content becomes a major source from which the diverse population of the United States must surely acquire *common and shared understandings* of the American culture. This idea draws on the older concept of "mass society." Presumably, watching television makes people more and more alike because, as they view TV, their differences are presumably reduced in the sense that they share similar opinions, beliefs, and attitudes:

> *Mainstreaming* means that heavy viewing may absorb or override differences in perspectives and behavior that ordinarily stem from other factors and influences. In other words, differences found in the responses of different groups of viewers, differences that are usually associated with the varied cultural, social, and political characteristics of these groups, are diminished or even absent from the responses of heavy viewers in these groups.[24]

A problem with this interpretation of the functions of television is that it ignores the processes described in the Selective and Limited Influences Theory (Chapter 10). If there is one thing that can be said about television with confidence, it is that *it offers something for everyone*. Its content is not uniform, and even though two people may both be "heavy viewers," that does not mean that they are both watching the same programs. One may be a news junkie, another a soap opera fan, still another a spectator sports enthusiast, and so on. Moreover, adding to the selective feature of media exposure is the fact that Americans have a great variety of sources other than television from which to derive ideas and orientations. Finally, even if everyone did indeed all watch the same programs, there are few grounds to assume "uniform interpretations." As Cognitive Processing Theory (Chapter 5) explains, people develop interpretations of what they experience in their environment on the basis of their existing beliefs, opinions, values, attitudes, prior experience, and other personality factors, along with their memberships in distinct social categories, such as race, ethnicity, social class, and others. Because those factors can be very different indeed from one person to another, it is not clear that, even if everyone was a heavy viewer of exactly the same TV content, it would uniformly reduce whatever differences individuals may have from one another and "mainstream" them all into a uniform culture.

Therefore, while television can show the central features of the American culture, that does not mean that viewers either adopt them or ignore other sources that emphasize cultural differences. The latter include ethnic associations, neighborhoods of similar people, regional and occupational subcultures, parents, friends, neighbors, radio programs, newspapers, magazines, movies, and all other forms of media and interpersonal communication. Thus, in many ways, the assumption underlying the mainstreaming interpretation is one of *uniform exposure, uniform interpretations, and uniform effects*. In some ways, it is also similar to the imaginary experiment of

Plato, in which men had been chained in place since childhood and were unable to view anything other than shadows on the wall. The shadows on the screen may be an important source for audiences to learn about the general American culture, but that does not mean that they attend or learn uniformly, or that what they view displaces other sources, or that viewers representing various subcultures drop their distinctive characteristics.

The Violence Profiles

In spite of these questions, one of the most impressive features of Gerbner's formulation is the amount of empirical research that it generated in efforts to understand the effects and influences that the (then) new medium of television was having on the American population. Within his project, the amount of violence shown on network television was assessed for a number of years. These were termed the Violence Profiles.[25] In addition to research conducted by Gerbner and his associates, dozens of additional studies were undertaken by others to try and determine if the claims made by the cultivation analysis perspective had merit.

Important among these was the study of what people *believed* about their social environment. One of the major theses of cultivation analysis was that "heavy" television viewers came to believe that the world of reality in which they lived was *very similar to that which was portrayed on television* (an example of "cultivation"). Since violence was a central focus of the Cultural Indicator's project, Gerbner and his colleagues reached the conclusion that heavy viewers would see a great deal of violence on TV and that this would lead them to entertain *unrealistic beliefs* about their own neighborhoods—beliefs that they lived in a dangerous world. That specific idea came to be studied by researchers who were also seeking to understand the influences of television.

Empirical Challenges

One such study stands out in that it found results *contrary* to what cultivation analysis predicted. Media researcher Paul Hirsch investigated the degree to which heavy viewers of television actually did entertain unrealistic social constructions of reality in their beliefs concerning the *level of danger* from crime and violence that actually characterized their own neighborhoods. Simply put, his findings did not support the claims made by cultivation analysis.[26] He found that heavy viewers and light viewers made similar (and realistic) estimates as to the level of crime and violence in their neighborhoods and the degree to which they were at risk. There was no evidence that heavy television viewing had influenced their beliefs about this issue. Because the Hirsch study was so centrally focused on the main violence issue under study by Gerbner and others devoted to cultivation analysis, his work touched off a vigorous debate about the entire formulation.

Today, the concept of cultivation analysis still has many enthusiasts. However, its central focus on television and violence is now obviously dated. That does not mean that there is no longer violence depicted on TV. Quite the contrary. There is probably even more now (see Chapter 20, the Creeping Cycle of Desensitization Theory). However, during the 1970s, when the surgeon general established the Scientific Advisory Committee on Television and Social Behavior, there were no cable or satellite systems. No one had a VCR player in their home. There was no Internet from which people could get alternative media entertainment or other content. Television programs were broadcast over the air by a small number of networks that completely dominated what people saw on their screens. In many ways, then, TV was "the only game in town," in the sense that it was readily available to the public seeking cheap and available movie-like entertainment at home.

It is true that during this period of television's history there was a considerable focus on violence in the programming. The reasons for that have not changed much since then. The same forces were prevailing for the networks at that time as those shaping the content of other entertainment media (e.g., movies) with which they were competing. Television's focus on violence can be understood within the perspective offered by the Creeping Cycle of Desensitization Theory (Chapter 20). It provides an explanation of why the content that the networks offered to the public was designed the way it was. Violent content was seen as a way to attract the largest audience possible so as to generate the largest possible profits from TV commercials. That relationship has not changed since that time.

Even though terms like "cultivation" and "mainstreaming" may have overstated the influences of television as it existed then (and certainly now), Gerbner's formulation was an important milestone in the development of our understanding of the process and effects of mass communication. It provoked a great deal of interest in the consequences of television viewing, not only among children, but also among other segments of the population. The controversies that his claims generated have helped refine what we know today about the influences of television entertainment content. While the cultivation analysis formulation generated claims that were not uniformly supported, they also led researchers to seek alternative answers. That form of truth seeking, after all, represents the essence of science. Cultivation analysis, and the subsequent controversies, then, left an important legacy for those who are still trying to sort out the nature and consequences of mass communications.

THE SPIRAL OF SILENCE THEORY

After observing the events and results of the German national elections in 1965, political scientist Elisabeth Noelle-Neumann began to develop what she termed the "hypothesis of silence." This hypothesis is based on a political phenomenon that has long been termed the "bandwagon effect." That is, if one candidate in an election appears to the public to be significantly in the lead, voters whose initial preferences have been for his or her opponent—who is now seen as probably losing—will often "jump on the bandwagon." That is, they want to be on the winning side, so they abandon their initial selection and switch their vote to the one they believe will be victorious. Thus, the Spiral of Silence Theory is based on a time-honored pattern known as the "bandwagon effect" to students of politics.

For this reason, one of the problems posed by periodic polling in advance of an election is that, if the results that are made public and seem to indicate that one particular candidate is clearly ahead, that may produce such a bandwagon effect. That, of course, increases the prospects for the one who is leading in the polls and consequently decreases the chances to win that other candidates may have. Because of that consequence, critics of such periodic polls suggest that, when their results are made public, the resulting bandwagon effect significantly erodes the democratic process.

The Hypothesis of Silence

As noted, and although she never used that concept, Noelle-Neumann's "hypothesis of silence" is based squarely on the concept of the bandwagon effect. During the national elections in Germany in 1965, just such a state of affairs seems to have occurred. There were several parties in contention. However, one of the major parties, the Christian Democrats, had been more or less even with the other major party that was competing in the election, as shown by polls of voter intentions. However, during the last phase of the campaigns, the Christian Democrats suddenly surged ahead:

> What had occurred had been recognized and named centuries earlier, but was still not understood: the power of public opinion. Under its pressure, hundreds of thousands—no, actually millions of voters—had taken part in what was later called a 'last minute swing.' At the last minute they had gone along with the crowd, swelling the Christian Democratic ranks from a position of equality with the other major party to what official election returns recorded as a lead of more than 8 percent.[27]

While the idea of a bandwagon effect had been around for a very long time, no one understood the underlying process fully and just how it came about. What were people thinking? Why did they make this last-minute change to the Christian Democrats? What was going on to bring about such a result? In the next election, in 1971, Noelle-Neumann saw exactly that same pattern. The two major parties were neck and neck, as far as the polls concerning voting intentions could determine. Then, right at the end, when it was announced that the Christian Democrats were expected to win, there was another last-minute swing as voters "jumped on the bandwagon."

What Noelle-Neumann finally figured out was that the result of the election in cases where such a late change took place was that "the climate of opinion depends on who talks and who keeps quiet."[28] What that refers to is that those who are confident of victory "speak out," and the media carry their message. Then, those whose candidate is not seen as a winner command less media attention that reaches fewer potential voters. According to the spiral of silence perspective, this factor can be potent in the final shaping of public opinion, and that can significantly influence the outcome of the election.

Fear of Isolation

A classical experiment in social psychology appeared to Noelle-Neumann to offer at least a part of the explanation of what was taking place in the context of the elections. The experiment was this: In the 1950s, social psychologist Solomon Asch confronted student subjects with a "line-judging" task. That is, he showed each subject three lines drawn on a sheet of paper. Each line was of a different length. He then showed the subject another line and asked the person to make a judgment as to which of the earlier three lines (still visible) was of the same length. Only one of the three comparison lines was actually (and obviously) of the same length as the one about which the subject was to make a judgment.

If each subject had been asked to make this judgment in a setting where no other people were present, he or she would have had no problem. There was a clear and obvious answer. However, Asch rigged the experiment. He had ten "confederates," who seemed to be just other similar subjects. They were present in each trial and all made and indicated their judgments *before* the actual subject made his or hers. In making their responses first, all of the confederates uniformly chose one of the lines that *clearly was not the same in length* as the comparison one. The question, then, was this: Would the "naive" subject (who was not a confederate) go along with the majority and select the line that they uniformly indicated? Or would he or she act independently and select the one that his or her senses indicated was actually correct? The answer was that, overwhelmingly, the naive subjects selected the line that had been indicated by the majority.

To Noelle-Neumann this experiment appeared to offer a tentative explanation of the bandwagon last-minute swing in the election results. There is, she believed, a *fear of isolation* among human beings. They want to belong—to be like others in the group and to be accepted. Therefore, they "go along."

The Nature and Spread of Public Opinion

In an analogous sense, the uniform judgments of the confederates in the line-judging experiment represent "public opinion" concerning the task. When those naive subjects saw that the majority held an opinion that was contrary to their own—even though their senses told them that it was incorrect—they felt under pressure to go along with the majority. In this sense, then, the communication to the naive subject that the majority was in consensus about the line length made it difficult for the naive subject to become a "deviant" and express a judgment that ran counter to that shared opinion.

Another way of looking at the situation (not used by Noelle-Neumann) was that the opinions expressed by the confederates was seen as a "norm" by the naive subjects—a socially supported rule that a member of a group is expected to follow. Thus, every human group has such norms, and one deviates from them at his or her own risk.

If public opinion can be seen as an expression of a norm (concerning the candidate that will be likely to win the election), the question, then, is not whether people will conform to the norm but how they learn what it is. The answer in the election context is that the mass media provide the information (social definitions of reality) from which people learn of the prevailing norm of public opinion. If news reports of polls showing that one candidate (or party, in this case) appears to have taken the lead, that serves the same function as did the expressed judgments of the confederates in the Asch experiments. The role of the media, then, is to make public the norm to which people ought to comply.

But beyond that, when the news media and spokespersons make it known which candidate seems to be leading, then those who might have spoken out on behalf of an apparently losing contender are likely to make less of an effort to make their views known. What this means is that the media tend to reduce their interest in probable losers. When this happens, the public hears less and less about them. In a kind of spiral, then, more media attention is given to the candidate that is expected to be the winner, and less and less is devoted to the losers. As that spiral builds, more and more voters want to "jump on the bandwagon," further enhancing the prospects of the assumed winner who is receiving increasing media attention.

The Spiral of Silence Theory is an intriguing one that can be readily assessed with empirical observations of polls and vote counts. Simply stated, what it emphasizes is that, in the context of election campaigns, the content of reports circulated by news media concerning "who is ahead" can have a significant effect on the outcome. At the same time, however, it must be recognized that the focus of the theory is *very narrow*. That is, it is not applicable to other forms of media content, such as entertainment, popular culture, general news, and so on, or how such content may influence human ideas and activities. Its focus is solely on elections and especially on what happens when very specific kinds of information about polling concerning vote intentions is made public. It serves well in that context and has made an important contribution. But it has limited application in a broader sense to questions concerning the process and effects of mass communication.

DEPENDENCY THEORY

Using the analytical sociological perspective of "social system," DeFleur described the relationship among the *mass media*, their *audiences*, and the *society as a whole* as one characterized by "mutual dependency."[29] That is, the media could not exist without the other two components. Modern societies are dependent on their media, due to the part they play in their economic, political, and other institutions. Audiences are also in a situation of dependency insofar as the media supply their members with amusements and gratifications as well as with useful information that would be difficult to obtain from other sources. In this broad system, cognitive and emotional effects take place among audience members as a result of being exposed to mass-communicated messages.

While all of that is essentially correct, Dependency Theory does not provide a detailed explanation of any specific effects of any particular form of media content, as is the case in such theories as Agenda-Setting (Chapter 12), Modeling Theory (Chapter 16), or Adoption of Innovation (Chapter 18), among others. Thus, while Dependency Theory does identify significant relationships between major "parts" of a complex social system, it has not played an important role in generating empirical studies of media processes and effects that can be used to assess its validity. In that sense, it does not meet the criteria set forth for explanatory theories established in Chapter 2. Nevertheless, in a broad way, it does help in "making sense" out of the entire set of relationships that exist in contemporary societies among the media, those who attend to them, and the society in which these parts of the "social system" exist.

ADDITIONAL PERSPECTIVES

In recent years a number of additional concepts and relationships concerning the functions and influences of mass communications have come under study. In some cases, it is too early to assess the lasting importance of these newer formulations. Some show considerable promise as explanations of particular kinds of influences among certain categories of people. However, for the most part, it is not clear whether they will survive as a body of research accumulates to assess their contributions to understanding the processes and effects of mass communications.

Specifically, three relatively recent concepts have been added to the attempts of media scholars to understand and explain various features of the process and effects of mass communication. One of the most interesting and most recent of these advances is what can be termed the "looking-glass theory of media influences." Essentially, it is a process by which people in audiences learn about *themselves* from viewing depictions of people who are *like them* in mass media content and how other people, who are also depicted in the content, treat them.

A second relatively new concept is "frame" analysis—an attempt to understand the meanings that people subjectively apply when they attend to and perceive various aspects of reality depicted in media content. The central issue is whether the meanings that they impose on what they encounter correspond accurately to the realities that are being depicted. In other words, are the "pictures in their heads of the world outside" that they experience when attending to news or entertainment content distorted, or do they reasonably correspond to the realities portrayed?

Finally, it has been noted that at least some people in audiences are convinced that they are immune to any negative effects that might result from exposure to mass communications. At the same time, however, they believe that many other people are influenced negatively by that content. Termed the "third-person effect," this interesting phenomenon has now come under study by media scholars.

The Looking Glass Theory of Media Influences

A recent theory of the role of how mass communication content depicts certain categories of people is the Looking Glass Theory of Media Influences. It is an adaptation of the classic social psychological theory of Charles Horton Cooley, an American scholar who wrote extensively about the nature of human nature in the late nineteenth and early twentieth centuries.[30] Cooley noted that each of us develops an understanding of what we are like as a person—by observing the ways in which others see and respond to us. (In his time, a common mirror was called a "looking glass.")

For example, if we enter a room where there is an ongoing party of friends, and, upon seeing us, those present roll their eyes, look the other way, and offer no friendly greeting, that sends a clear message about what they think we are like. However, if we enter that same room, and the others rush up with warm greetings and smiles, indicating how nice it is to see us, that sends a very different message. It is from such interpersonal encounters in real life, noted Cooley, that we obtain information needed to develop a conception of ourselves—a self-image—as a human being. Obviously, neither television nor movies existed in Cooley's time, but today they offer their audiences information from which they can develop an understanding of themselves—a *mediated* "looking glass" that can contribute to a viewer's self-image.

Grable adapted this feature of Cooley's writings to help explain how a person's self-image can be developed by viewing mass communication content.[31] The basic idea here is that people in audiences see others *who are like themselves* in dramas or other depictions of human beings in the media. For example, African Americans see other black people portrayed in various kinds of dramas and entertainment. They can also observe other actors in the dramas—such as white people—as they react to the depicted black people. Are their portrayed reactions accepting, rejecting, friendly, hostile, or what? In a similar way, old people, fat people, or those who are excessively tall or short, or even those who are ugly or bald, can see their counterparts in media content and the way others respond to them.

The central question, then, is this: How are those portrayed people *treated by others* in the content? Do others in the portrayals and dramas accept them and provide positive responses? Or are there clear signs that those others in the plays and dramas reject them or regard them as inferior or unwanted? Those depictions can send not-so-subtle messages to viewers with information about themselves—messages defining how other people regard them. Thus, in that sense, television, the movies, or other media offer a kind of "social mirror" in which people with their similar personal characteristics are reflected.

Grable studied young, educated black women who were active television viewers. She found that they were very conscious indeed as to how black people were being portrayed on TV and were sensitive to how they saw others (particularly whites) responding to them. This provided subtle, but clear, indications to them as to their own status in society. In that sense, such media depictions appeared to play a part in the development of their "looking-glass self." The tentative theory's seven basic propositions are:

1. In their news and entertainment content, the mass media transmit to audiences *definitions of the social heritage*—including depictions of culturally shared beliefs about, and appropriate behaviors toward, various categories of people identified by age, race, ethnicity, gender, bodily features, and other significant factors.

2. The meanings of signs and cues depicted in media portrayals regarding such categories do not come from the way reality is actually structured but *reflect content-producers' views* of the manner in which beliefs, attitudes, and norms for behavior have been traditionally defined in *dominant majority perspectives.*

3. Through such transmissions, mass communications display unintended *incidental lessons* that can lead to or reinforce unwitting social constructions of reality on the part of audiences concerning the nature and worth of the members of various categories of people in the American society who are depicted in media content.

4. Insofar as the lessons and definitions provided in media content reflect *general cultural norms*—that is, portray dominant majority beliefs about, and appropriate behaviors toward, various categories in the society—such interpretations serve to provide guidelines for all citizens within the society.

5. In this manner, for all members of audiences, media content signifies and defines the rules of *social placement, desirability, and general level of acceptance* of individuals who are demographically located within the society's various categories (i.e., age, race, ethnicity, gender, and bodily appearance).

6. As individual members of audiences see and interpret how people with their own personal characteristics, that define their own category memberships, are portrayed and treated in media content, they acquire understandings about *their own personal or self-worth* by attending to the depictions of the norms of interpretation of the general and dominant culture of their society.

7. **Therefore,** mass media content, depicting the nature and worth of members of various categories, provides a *"looking glass"*—a social mirror—reflecting to individual audience members the manner in which the society defines them in positive or negative ways and, consequently, providing them with standards for defining themselves.

This, as noted, is a theory that was only recently developed (2005). Research is needed to determine how broadly it can apply, not only to blacks, but also to people of various other characteristics as they see persons like themselves (and the responses of others) depicted in media content.

Frame Analyses

An important issue that has come into the analysis of people's responses to media depictions of the "real world" is the ancient question as to whether or not the mental images that a person constructs "in his or her head" while attending to some feature of reality (such as a media portrayal) is a totally accurate representation of that reality—or some sort of illusion. In 387 B.C. precisely that question was addressed by Plato in the *Republic,* in his allegory of the cave (discussed in Chapter 3).[32] In contemporary times, the term "frame" and "frame analysis" has come into use to refer to the study of this issue.[33]

In its original meaning within the film industry, the term "frame" and "framing" referred to the view seen through the lens of the motion picture camera. It might be a close-up or a distance shot. Or what the camera "sees" might include a number of physical objects and background features that added meaning to what was being photographed. In media studies, the term is being used to refer to an analogous counterpart—to what elements in a situation a person "sees." That is, when viewing a situation in reality, what is it that he or she interprets through his or her senses? The focus, then, is on the conscious meanings that are brought to mind when the senses detect some feature or combination of features of reality *as depicted in media.* Thus, the contemporary use of "frame" in the study on the effects of mass communication implies that a person apprehends with his or her senses some depicted feature or features of reality in media content and experiences personal and subjective meanings for what is being apprehended.

For students of human behavior, this is a very important concept. A number of psychologists and sociologists, over the years, have addressed the issue of the relationship between what is actually taking place in reality, what that person *believes* is going on, and how those beliefs influence the individual's behavior.

For example, a tradition has developed among sociologists around the concept of a person's "definition of the situation." This is an important issue in understanding how people respond in social situations. For example, in 1917, sociologist W. I. Thomas maintained that it is the person's *subjective interpretation of reality* that guides his or her social conduct and not the objective nature of that reality. That is, if a person perceives a social situation as "real," then that person will act toward it as though it were real.[34]

An example that was cited earlier (Chapter 5) to illustrate selective perception can also illustrate the principle that if persons define a situation as real, they will act as though it is real. The example is Hastorf and Cantril's report of what happened at a football game between Princeton and Dartmouth—two football rivals.[35] The majority of the fans in the stadium who were watching the game were from one or the other of the two schools. It was a bitterly fought game, with many rule infractions on both sides. Those from Dartmouth "saw" that the referees were totally biased against their school's team and that they frequently made calls that were unfounded. Fans from Princeton saw the same thing—except they were convinced that the referees were biased against *their* school's team. The fans of the school that lost bitterly protested the outcome. However, movies that had carefully recorded each of the plays showed objectively that the referees had done a very good job, with no bias toward either team. Nevertheless, the protesting fans had defined the situation as real in their own way, and they acted as though that were real.

Over the years, the issue of the correspondence between the internal subjective meanings we construct in consciousness for some aspect of reality we apprehend with our senses, or from depictions presented by mass communications, has come under scrutiny—particularly in the fields of psychology and sociology. For example, Lang and Lang studied how a television presentation of an event brings to an audience a different set of meanings for a situation viewed than if those same persons experienced exactly that same event firsthand.[36] In 1953, when television was still a new technology and had started to become widely adopted, these scholars conducted a unique quasi-experiment. An important public event was scheduled to take place in their city (Chicago). It was a lengthy and complex event that was to be covered fully from beginning to end by television news. The research question was whether those who saw it only via television would have the same internal experience (of constructing meaning for the event) as those who actually went to see it in reality.

The event took place in Chicago. It was was McArthur Day, which included a parade through Chicago's downtown "Loop" in the general's honor, followed by a speech by dignitaries in which he was to be given the "keys to the city." General Douglas McArthur was being honored as the hero of Corregidor and for his additional military leadership in the recently concluded World War II. (He commanded the U.S. forces that recaptured the Philippines from the Japanese occupation.) Professors Lang arranged to have two sets of people observe the event. One set saw it as it was orchestrated on television. The other people actually went to the parade route, and, from various points along the way, they observed the parade firsthand. Others were at the site of the welcoming speech. Reports were received from 41 points of observation along the way.

The bottom line here was that there was *very little correspondence* between what these two sets of subjects experienced. The television crews "framed" (as we would now say) what they thought would be of interest to their audiences. Thus, they focused on areas along the way where many people were gathered—people who behaved in an exciting manner when the general was driven by. Moreover, the behavior of people who realized that the cameras were pointing at them was very different than when no cameras were present. They cheered and gestured enthusiastically when they saw the cameras.

In "framing" the event, the news personnel also focused their cameras on the general, with many close-up views—and on Mrs. McArthur, who was also in the open car. Few along the parade route could even see her. The camera operators ignored long areas of the same streets where there were few or no people or where observers simply looked on in a bored way, with no display of excitement. The Lang observers, stationed at various points along the parade path to observe the event firsthand, saw the general only fleetingly as his car quickly passed by them. For them it was a momentary and essentially boring event.

Those who viewed it on TV saw a very different reality—cheering crowds, a "seething mass of humanity," along the route. They saw frequent close-ups of the general and wife. They could see and hear the speech made by the dignitaries as they welcomed the general. These were very different "realities." As the authors put it:

> It has been claimed for television that it brings the truth directly into the home: the 'camera does not lie.' Analysis of the above events shows that this assumed reportorial accuracy is far from automatic. Every camera selects, and thereby leaves the unseen part of the subject open to suggestion and inference. The gaps are usually filled by a commentator. In addition, the process directs action and attention to itself.

Although those scholars in the early days of television did not use the term "framing," their study illustrates the basic idea very well. Every mass medium—print, broadcast, or digital—that presents some depiction of reality in order to attract an audience does so using its own particular techniques and manners of selection. Those who produce such media content clearly do so with the audience in mind. What will excite them? What will hold their attention? (And, basically, how can this enhance the profit line? (See Chapter 2.)

Underlying this phenomenon of how audiences interpret an event differently by either observing reality directly or by attending to a depiction of it via a medium is the basic process and the principles of *perception*. As was explained in some detail in Chapter 5, the key terms here are "sensation" and conscious "meaning." That is, as we apprehend an object or situation with our senses (sight, hearing, smell, taste, or touch), sensory impulses are sent to our brain. Calling upon prior personal experiences stored in memory, subjective meanings are aroused within the brain and assigned to those incoming sensations. Thus, a person's conscious understanding of whatever aspect of reality is being seen, heard, etc. (either directly or via a mediated version), is a complex product of sensory apprehension of the stimulus field plus the automatic assignment of personal and subjective meanings to whatever that field contains.

During the late 1800s, psychologists had undertaken research to clarify how such perception takes place. By the 1920s, the Gestalt psychologists had accumulated an impressive body of experimental evidence that provided many answers.[37] Other philosophers and psychologists continued to explore the process (and in some cases "rediscover" it). Philosophers and early students of mass communication, such as Walter Lippmann, were well aware of this process and applied it to the interpretation of mass communications. Lippmann discussed how news reports (of events in reality) often arouse inaccurate and distorted "pictures in our heads of the world outside"— that is, perceptions of whatever aspect of reality that the news accounts describe for their readers create a "pseudo environment" that may not correspond to what actually took place (Chapter 8).

It is in this sense that the term "frame analysis" is both an ancient and recent one. Based on the principles of perception, plus the audience-attracting techniques used by media content producers, it can help in understanding the assignment-of-meaning process as people attend to depictions and presentations provided by mass communications.

The Third-Person Effect

An interesting form of thinking about the media has been noted among some members of audiences for mass communications. Termed the "third-person effect," it is the tendency of some individuals to believe that they personally are *immune* to any negative influences of television programs (or what they may encounter in other media). But, at the same time, they believe that other people who see that same content are not immune and are influenced by it.[38] Some media scholars explain this phenomenon by the fact that there is a general norm among the public that it is not "smart" to be seen as easily influenced by what one encounters via mass communications. Thus, many audience members view themselves as "smarter" than others—especially those who are similar in other ways to themselves or those of lesser status. Thus, they imagine that those other people are "weaker" and more vulnerable to potential negative influences from a medium such as television than themselves.[39]

This is a very narrowly focused concept and one that has only relatively recently become an object of empirical research. It is an interesting idea, but whether it is of importance in understanding the process and effects of mass communication in larger perspective appears to be limited and remains to be seen.

Overall, the theories, perspectives, and concepts discussed in the present chapter appear to provide additional formulations that help in understanding the nature and effects of mass communication. In some cases, these ideas are new. In others, they are new wine in old bottles— representing the rediscovery of well-known principles by "new Columbuses." In still others, they are new adaptations of well-established principles of behavior to the task of understanding the process and effects of mass communications. The main point is that, as empirical research accumulates on these issues, it will be possible to evaluate the merits of each more fully. At present, however, these interpretations—new or old—provide potentially useful guides to the broader task of mapping the processes and influences of the ever-changing media in modern societies.

Notes and References

1. Fred S. Siebert, Theodore B. Peterson, and Wilbur L. Schramm, *Four Theories of the Press* 2nd ed. (Urbana, IL: University of Illinois Press, 1978), p. 1.
2. Marshall McLuhan, *Understanding Media: The Extension of Man* (New York: Mc-Graw Hill Book Company, 1964).
3. Nancy Signorelli and Michael Morgan, *Cultivation Analysis: New Directions in Media Effects Research* (Newbury Park, CA: Sage Publications, 1990).
4. An excellent summary of the central ideas developed by George Gerbner can be found in Stanley J. Baran and Dennis K. Davis, *Mass Communication Theory: Foundations, Ferment and Future* (Belmont, CA: Wadsworth/Thomson Learning, 2003), pp. 322–325.
5. Elisabeth Noelle-Neumann, *The Spiral of Silence: Public Opinion— Our Social Skin* (Chicago: University of Chicago Press, 1984).
6. A term he used to discuss the issue in an address at the annual meeting of the American Sociological Society in Chicago in 1963.
7. For a detailed explanation of the process of perception and how it can often result in "wrong conclusions as to what is out there," see John P. Houston, Helen Bee, and David C. Rimm, *Invitation to Psychology* (New York: Academic Press, 1983), pp. 115–130.

8. Fred S. Siebert, Theodore B. Peterson, and Wilbur L. Schramm, *Op. Cit.*, p. 1.

9. *Ibid.* p. 10.

10. *Ibid.* p. 11.

11. See *Commission on Freedom of the Press: A Free and Responsible Press* (Chicago: University of Chicago Press, 1947).

12. Fred S. Siebert, Theodore B. Peterson, and Wilbur L. Schramm, *Op. Cit.* p. 74.

13. *Ibid.* p. 121.

14. Stanley J. Baran and Dennis K. Davis, *op. cit.*, pp. 299–300.

15. Charles Horton Cooley, *Social Organization: A Study of the Larger Mind* (New York: Charles Scribner' Sons, 1909), p. 80.

16. See, for example, Louis Mumford, *Findings and Keepings: Analects for an Autobiography* (New York: Harcourt, Brace Jovanovich, 1979).

17. Marshall McLuhan, *Op. Cit.*, p. 7.

18. *Ibid.* p. 10.

19. Stanley J. Baran and Dennis K. Davis, *op. cit.*, pp. 300–301.

20. Signorelli and Morgan, *op. cit.*, pp. 13–14.

21. *Ibid.* p. 9.

22. Michael Morgan and Nancy Signorelli, "Cultivation Analysis: Conceptualization and Methodology," in Signorelli and Morgan, *ibid.* p. 18.

23. *Ibid.* p. 22.

24. *Ibid.* p. 24.

25. For example, see George Gerbner and Larry Gross, "Living with Television: The Violence Profile," *Journal of Communication*, 26, Spring, 1976, pp. 173–199.

26. See Paul M. Hirsch, "On Not Learning from One's Own Mistakes: A reanalysis of Gerbner et al.'s Findings on Cultivation Analysis, Part II," *Communication Research* 8, 1981, pp. 3–37.

27. Elisabeth Noelle-Neumann, *The Spiral of Silence: Public Opinion—Our Social Skin* (Chicago: University of Chicago Press, 1984), p. 2. (First published in German in 1980.)

28. *Ibid.* p. 4.

29. See the following: Melvin L. DeFleur, "Mass Media as Social Systems," in Otto N. Larsen, ed., *Violence and the Mass Media* (New York: Harper, 1968), pp. 24–29. Also, Melvin L. DeFleur and Sandra Ball-Rokeach, "A Dependency Theory of Audience-Media-Society Relationships," in *Theories of Mass Communication,* 3rd ed. (New York: Longman, 1975), pp. 261–275.

30. See Charles Horton Cooley, "Chapter 5, The Definition of the Social Self," in *Human Nature and the Social Order* (New York: Shocken Books, 1964), pp. 168–210. (First published in 1902.)

31. Bettye Grable, "African American Women's Reception, Influence and Utility of Television Content: An Exploratory Content Analysis" Ph.D. Dissertation, The Manship School of Mass Communication, Louisiana State University, 2005.

32. *The Republic of Plato,* trans. Francis MacDonald Cornfield (New York: Oxford University Press, 1958), pp. 227–235. Plato's work was written in 387 B.C.

33. For a detailed discussion of the concept, see Erving Goffman, *Frame Analysis* (New York: Harper and Row, Publishers, 1974).

34. See W. I. Thomas and Florian F. Znaniecki, *The Polish Peasant in Europe and, America* (New York: Knopf, 1927), p. 128.

35. Albert H. Hastorf and Hadley Cantril, "They Saw a Game: A Case Study," *Journal of Abnormal and Social Psychology*, 49, 1954, pp. 129–234.

36. Kurt and Gladys Lang, "The Unique Perspective of Television and Its Effect: A Pilot Study," *American Sociological Review*, 18, 1, February, 1953, pp. 3–12.

37. See Kurth Koffka, *The Growth of the Mind*, trans. R. M. Ogden (New York: Harcourt, Brace, Jovanovich, 1925).

38. Robert Petroff, "The Third Person Effect: A Critical Review and Synthesis," *Media Psychology*, 1, pp. 353–379.

39. Michael Salwen and Michael Dupagne, "The Third-Person Effect: Perceptions of the Media's Influence and Immoral Consequences," *Communication Research*, 1999, 26, 5, pp. 523–550.

INDEX